AHEAD OF THE PACK

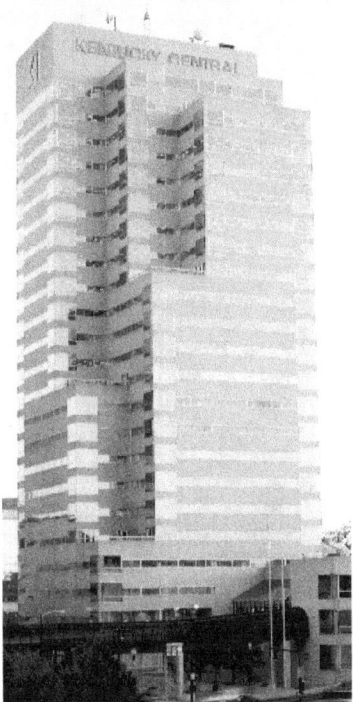

Kincaid Tower

Garvice Delmar Kincaid was an iconic visionary, a man ahead of his time, indeed Ahead of the Pack. This is the story of a Lexington, Kentucky Businessman who turned $1,500 into a $500 million empire over a 40-year period.

At his death, his five hundred-million-dollar empire was comprised of over one hundred and seventy-five organizations consisting of radio and television stations, banks, hotels, resorts, consumer finance companies, life insurance companies and real estate holdings. This is the true story of Kincaid's historic rise and the catastrophic fall of his organization after his death.

AHEAD OF THE PACK

Garvice Kincaid and His Empire

A Southern Saga

Robert A. Mucci

Rabbit House Press

RABBIT HOUSE PRESS

Versailles, KY 40383

Published in the United States in December of 2025 by Rabbit House Press
Copyright © 2025 by Robert A. Mucci - All right reserved.

This book is a work of creative nonfiction based on the author's recollection of actual events, experiences, and conversations. The events and any conversations herein that were not audio recorded have been portrayed to the best of the author's memory. All interviews have been edited for clarity and brevity. Parts of newspaper and magazine articles and other written information have been formatted to provide better context for the subject without changing the nature of the written documents.

All opinions, assumptions, and conclusions, along with any interpretation of events, expressed in this book, are the author's personal opinions and thoughts and are not meant to be taken as fact with regard to any person or place.

American Pie
Words and Music by Don McLean
Copyright © 1971, 1972 BENNY BIRD CO., INC.
Copyright Renewed
All Rights Controlled and Administered by SONGS OF UNIVERSAL, INC.
All Rights Reserved Used by Permission
Reprinted by Permission of Hal Leonard LLC

For inquiries about author appearances and/or volume orders contact us at rabbithousepress.com.

ISBN: 979-8-9929838-4-5

Edited by Elizabeth Seif
Interior and cover design by Brooke Lee & Daphne Vorel

This book is dedicated to my uncle and aunt, Emmett and Nonie Crump, who introduced me to Kentucky Central Life Insurance Company and the many aspects of Mr. Kincaid's life and empire. In addition, it is dedicated to the many people who worked for Mr. Kincaid's various businesses and enterprises. Mr. Kincaid was a brilliant, razor-focused businessman, and I think he would agree that he could not have accomplished so much without the dedication and efforts of so many.

Emmett "Boss" Crump
Aka "Mr. Kentucky Central"

Uncle Emmett & Aunt Nonie Crump
Celebrating Emmett's Orman Beach
Florida, 1995 Man of the Year Award

*They copied all they could copy, But they couldn't copy my mind; And I left them sweatin' and stealin', A year and a half behind.**

– Rudyard Kipling

*Appreciation and credit to Clifton H. Forbush, Jr., former vice president and chief investment officer for Kentucky Central Life Insurance Company and my cherished friend and boss.

Contents

Forward

by Ben Chandler

Albert Benjamin "Happy" Chandler is a former U. S. Senator, Kentucky Governor, and second ever Commissioner of Baseball. Garvice Kincaid was a great admirer and became friends with Chandler in 1928 when Chandler ran and was elected to the state senate. Some credit Chandler with mentoring Kincaid on how to navigate the complex world of politics, which Kincaid later used to his advantage. Their relationship involved Kincaid acquiring the WVLK radio station from Happy Chandler in 1949. Their friendship continued until Kincaid's death in 1975.

Albert Benjamin "Ben" Chandler III is the grandson of Governor A.B. Chandler. Ben is a Versailles, Kentucky native and two-time UK graduate who has spent most of his career in public service. He served four years as Kentucky's state auditor, eight years as Kentucky's attorney general, and nearly a decade as a member of Congress. Happy Chandler acquired The Woodford Sun Newspaper in 1942, and the Chandler family has owned and operated it for the last 82 years. In 2022, Ben assumed the position of publisher of the newspaper.

"Robert Mucci's, Ahead of the Pack fills an informational void in Kentucky history. Until now, no book has been written about Garvice Kincaid, a transformational figure of his day, who influenced the quality and direction of life in Lexington and the state of Kentucky. During the 1930s and up until his death in 1975, Kincaid built a business dynasty that gave him an unprecedented platform of influence. A man who was believed could make or break politicians, he was never modest about expressing strong opinions about important issues and expected others to listen.

Kincaid had an unrelenting work ethic some people didn't understand, which frustrated the local Lexington establishment as he built his empire. When Garvis Kincaid wanted to join the blue-blooded Idle Hour Country Club, the old boy's club rejected him. He will always be remembered for his gruff personality, but Kincaid was a complicated man. Mucci refers to this as a southern saga and indeed it is. It is a saga that educates the reader on how industry and business operated in the Twentieth Century.

Garvice Kincaid will be dead 50 years in 2025, and Ahead of the Pack is a great celebration of his life and accomplishments. Bravo Robert, thank you for telling the story of a powerful Kentuckian whose philanthropy and generosity toward Lexington and Eastern Kentucky cannot be ignored.

Introduction

The story of Garvice Delmar Kincaid is a story about a man who turned $1,500 into a $500 million empire over a forty-year period. It is a story of a young man who had an incredible need to be respected and appreciated but who also tended to intimidate and offend those around him with his brisk remarks and a talent for knowing as much, if not more, about their business affairs as they did. Mr. Kincaid died in November 1975 at age 63. It has been reported that at his death, his estate comprised over 175 organizations and business entities, including nineteen banks, consumer finance companies, a life insurance company, several radio stations, a television station, numerous hotels, a Florida resort, and multiple real estate holdings.

This is the story of the historic rise of Mr. Kincaid's empire and the catastrophic fall of one of Kentucky's premier business dynasties after his death. Mr. Kincaid was a true visionary and a man who was ahead of his time. He saw the importance of the media in its early years and appreciated how it had the ability to influence our perceptions and desires. He was smart and understood—before a guy named Michael Milken was ever born—that distressed debt and real estate could provide enormous returns. Finally, he understood, before Warren Buffet, that acquiring good businesses and holding them for the long term truly was the path to great riches. Mr. Kincaid was born in 1912, more than fifteen years before Mr. Buffet, who was born in 1930.

I initially learned of Mr. Kincaid and about some of his businesses in my youth during the 1960s and '70s. Emmett Crump, a favorite uncle in Lexington, was a Kentucky Central Life Insurance Company district manager who was hired by Mr. Kincaid. He often would travel around the state to visit his agents, and he sometimes stopped in Paris, Kentucky, to see our family. During these visits he would also usually surprise me with some type of company-branded item. In addition, during the summers I would sometimes stay with Aunt Nonie and him in Lexington. Those visits were fun, and he usually took me to his Lexington district office and to Kentucky Central's home office in the old Lafayette Hotel. Emmett loved to introduce me to his Kentucky Central Life colleagues and drive around Lexington pointing to various Kincaid properties and enterprises. By the time I was probably 10 years old, I already knew, when we listened to Caywood Ledford call a University of Kentucky basketball game on WVLK radio or watched the Cats on WKYT, that both these important media companies were owned by Mr. Kincaid.

Garvice Kincaid learned the importance of being competitive in business during his youth. He grew up in Richmond, Kentucky, and worked in his father's grocery store after school and on the weekends. He also delivered the local Richmond newspaper. He received great accolades from the owner of the newspaper for being able to sell and deliver a large quantity of newspapers. He was so proud of his efforts in selling and delivering newspapers that in 1965, Mr. Kincaid set up a scholarship for Kentucky youth delivering newspapers. He was inducted into the national "Newspaper-boy Hall of Fame." Working in his father's store, "D Kincaid" Grocery, he soon learned the importance of constant promotion and the need to be the best in your business. Kincaid's father, Douglas, was a master promoter who was constantly placing large ads in the Richmond newspaper promoting the store and suggesting that it had the best selection of produce and canned goods, at very competitive prices. Mr. Kincaid was born about five years earlier than Sam Walton, and like Walton, Garvice understood early in his life that promotion and meeting customers' needs was a formula for success.

Mr. Kincaid had a huge thirst for information and learning. This attribute, along with his work ethic, were important elements of his future success. He was an attorney by vocation and this training provided him with the skills necessary to navigate complicated business issues. He could evaluate the risks associated with them and then act quickly if he so chose. Making decisions and moving forward quickly were fundamental to how he operated during his life. I started my research expecting to finally understand how Mr. Kincaid created his business strategy. He certainly was progressive in some of his thinking, but what I found was that he worked hard and made himself known to as many people as possible, which allowed him to be very opportunistic in his business affairs. From his perspective, he was always risking only his own money, so his inclination to act quickly on opportunities was a significant strength. By the time Garvice was thirty years of age, he was a known commodity. People understood that he was open to looking at most any opportunity, and if he thought it had merit, he had the resources to act quickly.

Finally, Mr. Kincaid tried to surround himself with the best people he could find and afford for his particular needs and then worked to instill in them enduring loyalty to him. From the various interviews I've done and the stories I've heard over the years from his empire's many former employees and associates, this theme resonated over and over. While some people say he managed his staff through fear and intimidation, others expressed that his gruff persona was a byproduct of his work ethic and the amount of time and effort he exerted on building and growing his empire.

One also finds that the magnitude of Mr. Kincaid's business and the number of transactions he participated in required that he build a large staff of accountants and attorneys. They were initially a loose collection of people who either were recommended to him, worked in offices near his office, or were associated with certain political and economic groups. In the early years, he didn't know how much professional help he would need, but by 1950, his empire had developed the beginnings of an organizational staffing infrastructure. This infrastructure would grow and evolve as Mr. Kincaid's business interests did, and some of his early staffing would change as his needs did. As his empire moved from the minor leagues to the business equivalent of baseball's major leagues, so did the quality and depth of his staffing.

Kincaid enjoyed the adventure of buying, building, and growing his business interests, and he had a natural energy when it came to working. He was like a spring in a watch, and his empire was a machine that used his energy to keep moving forward. All machines need a source of energy to work, including clocks. The energy in clocks is stored in a spring. When the clock is wound up, energy is transferred into the spring, and then the energy is released into the clock as the spring unwinds. The energy released from the spring makes a gear turn, which makes the gears connected to it in turn rotate, and so on, throughout the timepiece's mechanism. Kincaid's empire operated similarly: his energy, his brilliance, and his work ethic were the forces that propelled his empire forward in the directions he chose.

Some people have described Mr. Kincaid as a mean, one-dimensional money-grubber. I don't believe this description captures the real Garvice Kincaid. He certainly was a driven and focused businessman, but the many charitable endeavors he started and maintained demonstrate a different kind of man, one who was either very concerned about his historical legacy or not totally one-dimensional in his thinking. For instance, Mr. Kincaid acquired Kentucky Central Life Insurance Company (Kentucky Central Life or Kentucky Central) in mid-1959 and in 1960 gave its 700 employees and employee-agents each one share of stock. He apparently understood the need for employees to feel they had ownership in the company. Of course, no matter how many good things he did during his lifetime, his personal legacy will probably always be that of a "disagreeable curmudgeon who took pleasure in the discomfort of others."[1] WVLK's Ted Grizzard probably said it best, though: "I wished I had

---

1   *Lexington Herald-Leader*, November 27, 1977.

worked for him my whole life. When he said "thank you," you could put that in the bank." I guess what Mr. Kincaid lacked in people skills, he made up for with how he rewarded people.

The story of Mr. Kincaid is also a story about the people who worked with and for him and the people who would most impact his empire after his death. It is a version of the '70s TV miniseries *Rich Man, Poor Man* where many in his circle respected his wealth but detested the man and where personal loyalties dissolved as greed and hubris overshadowed right and wrong. Mr. Kincaid created his wealth, and he allowed his associates to participate in his financial growth. He wanted and demanded loyalty; and this attribute may have been second only to the ability to do the job. He created competition between his business associates, and this sometimes bred jealousy and mistrust as business colleagues worked to gain his favor. He was the old family patriarch, and they were his children, all striving to gain the affection of their father. In the end, just as in many family dynasties, the children think they are smarter than their father and end up destroying the empire.

In the mid-1950s and 1960s, Mr. Kincaid suffered two heart attacks, and I believe this mortality scare motivated his long estate-planning process. He essentially created an estate trust made up of three separate accounts or funds: Fund A was for the benefit of his wife, Nelle; Fund B was for the benefit of his daughters, Jane and Joan Kincaid; and Fund C was to hold the interest of all his businesses and was for the benefit of all living beneficiaries and their future descendants. This is called a multigenerational trust, and it was projected to last about 100 years. His trust was administered by his bank, Central Bank & Trust, and was overseen by a three-person Advisory Committee, with three alternates also being named. He personally selected these six individuals to oversee his vast empire. The people on the committee were trusted lieutenants, people Mr. Kincaid had worked with for many years and with whom he had comfort. He believed they would be able to work together and manage and grow his empire as he had done. What he didn't count on was that:

> "Sometimes, it seems that everything goes wrong, despite our
> best efforts to make things right. We can do everything in our power
> to make something work, but life might have different plans."[2]

In Mr. Kincaid's case, he didn't factor in arrogance and greed. I can't answer all the questions a reader might have about some of the things that created the collapse of Mr. Kincaid's great empire. Some answers were taken to people's graves, and in a few cases, people aren't talking. What I hope I can do

---

2   Unknown.

is provide the reader with enough information on the most important questions to allow them to form their own conclusions. Mr. Kincaid died in 1975 and the journey to the collapse of his empire didn't begin immediately; it started in the early 1980s. I worked in the investment department of Kentucky Central Life Insurance Company from 1981 until 1995. I witnessed various aspects of this journey and researched other parts of it. The collapse of Kentucky Central Life and its impact on the rest of Mr. Kincaid's empire cost his estate trust hundreds of millions of dollars. In addition, it impacted thousands of families, not just in Lexington but around the country—probably millions when you include the company's employees, agents, policyholders, and shareholders.

I did not start out intending to write a book. I retired as the chief investment officer of a life insurance company in January 2020 after a forty-year career in the insurance industry, and just before the COVID-19 pandemic and its associated lockdowns. With lots of time on my hands, I undertook the project of digitizing my pictures and all the Kentucky Central Life information I had accumulated over the years. During this process, as I would see something that I thought my Kentucky Central Life colleagues might appreciate, and I would email it to them. These emails tended to get us talking about the old days and sharing stories. I guess one dear friend, Clyde Honaker, probably needs to take responsibility for this book above everyone else. Clyde began working for Kentucky Central Life in 1964, just after the company moved to Lexington from Anchorage, Kentucky. Clyde worked for Kentucky Central Life until it was sold to Jefferson-Pilot in 1995 and then worked at Jefferson-Pilot's Lexington office for the next five years and then in its Greensboro, North Carolina, corporate headquarters for another five years. I don't think most of us appreciated how much we loved Kentucky Central Life until it was gone, and Clyde has done as much as anyone possibly could to keep many of us connected. Clyde wasn't the only one who said I needed to write a book about Mr. Kincaid and Kentucky Central Life, given my long history and knowledge, but he certainly was the most vocal.

I am a trained investment professional, a Chartered Financial Analyst, and I have written many reports during my career. I know how to do research analysis and, usually, what questions I need to find answers to. In 2022, Clyde started talking to people about allowing me to interview them, so after a while the momentum of my digitization project became a research project for this book. To understand Mr. Kincaid and the history of his empire, I've reviewed thousands of pages of newspaper articles, company publications, court proceedings, probate orders, and other types of written material, and

I've conducted interviews of people with firsthand or secondhand knowledge of him and his empire. I've also included as many stories as possible about Mr. Kincaid, his business interests, and the people who were in his orbit so the reader can more thoroughly understand the man and the operation of his empire.

One thing a reader must appreciate is that Mr. Kincaid worked on many parts of his empire at the same time. I've tried to organize this book in sections that relate to the most important aspects of his timeline, while incorporating the general progression of his life. In addition, where I felt it would be helpful, I've included a brief history of the industry or business being discussed. I apologize if this work seems to ramble at times, but the story of Mr. Kincaid incorporates about fifty years of his life, and he acquired, created, and grew many of his business interests in various overlapping periods of his life. At one point I experimented with creating a timeline flow chart of important moments in his life and after he died, but soon found that this simple project was too confusing. Where time frames overlap, I've tried to focus on the clarity of the individual topic and not incorporate other things he may have been involved in at the same time.

Mr. Kincaid was a remarkable person who really did juggle a lot each day. He relied on his people to execute his business plans, but his mind apparently never rested. Today, we have so much information at our fingertips, it is easy to forget how limited this same information would have been during Mr. Kincaid's life. Everyone I interviewed described him the same way. His meetings and phone calls were short. He was quick to make a decision, and he didn't wait for his lieutenants to come to him with a problem because he was usually aware of it already and asking his lieutenants about it during his late-evening phone calls to their homes.

Finally, Mr. Kincaid didn't make time for fun and relaxation. he was "Mr. Business" twenty-four hours a day; his bedroom contained three telephones and his house was set up with a long-distance "WATS line." This long-distance service was introduced in 1961 by AT&T, and Mr. Kincaid and his organizations were active participants by 1963.

I refer to this work as a southern saga because it covers five decades of Mr. Kincaid's life, how he and his businesses affected the lives of many people, and how the management of his empire was a *Peyton Place*–style drama after his death. Mr. Kincaid built an empire where most of his's businesses were operated to support the economic business interests of all his businesses. If one entity needed capital to acquire something, funds were usually found in one of Kincaid's many other business entities, even if selling stock or borrowing money was required. In addition, his business entities leveraged their associations with other parts of his empire. They could borrow human talent when they needed to or direct business to his other entities; for example, advertise on his broadcast networks. Another example is Kentucky Finance Company, which used Kentucky Central Life's mainframe computer to process its business at the end of each day. The interrelationships of the people and his businesses are a true southern saga—one that spans almost a century.

Mr. Kincaid will have been gone fifty years in November 2025, and I hope this book honors his memory and achievements. He built an extremely large, successful organization, and over his lifetime created tens of thousands of jobs around the country. He was instrumental in the urban renewal of Lexington and in saving the Appalachian Regional Health Care System. In addition, throughout his career, he provided millions of dollars in educational scholarships and support to nonprofit organizations. Finally, in 1960, at the age of 48, Mr. Kincaid became the first Kentuckian and one of the youngest people to win the Horacio Alger Award. This award is bestowed upon "outstanding Americans who exemplify dedication, purpose, and perseverance in their personal and professional lives. Recipients have often achieved success in the face of adversity."

I hope this book becomes the most comprehensive narrative of his life and readers appreciate how important Mr. Kincaid was to Kentucky during his lifetime. Much of Mr. Kincaid's empire is gone, merged into other, larger organizations, and the man himself has become just a footnote in Kentucky's history.

In 1940, Belle Brezing, Lexington's nationally known madam, died at the age of 80. Brezing's brothel was known as the "most orderly of disorderly houses," and Belle is believed to have been the model for Belle Watling in Margaret Mitchell's *Gone with the Wind*. Mitchell allegedly heard about Brezing from her husband, who had lived in Lexington. Since her death, more than a half a dozen books and television documentaries have been written and produced about Brezing's life, while Garvice Kincaid's life has neither.

I hope this book captures the importance of Mr. Kincaid to Kentucky and especially to Lexington and provides some clues to why his great empire collapsed twenty years after his death.

PART I: No Problem!

It was Tuesday, February 9, 1993, in Lexington, Kentucky. The city had been enjoying a mild winter so far, with average daily temperatures in the low 50s. Over the last twenty years, downtown Lexington had experienced an economic revival, with many new commercial projects built: offices and hotels, apartments, condominiums, restaurants, and other entertainment venues. Working downtown was fun and enjoyable again. This revitalization took time, but an urban renew effort begun in the late 1970s had finally taken hold, and a vibrant downtown Lexington had returned. Yes, most people working in downtown offices still lived in the suburbs and shopped at suburban malls and shopping centers, but Lexington's downtown had reinvented itself, with thousands of people now working and, in some cases, living in the downtown metro area. The mildness of the winter encouraged folks to get out and enjoy the many restaurants that had opened over the last several years and, if a UK basketball game was at Rupp Arena, to come downtown early to party and eat.

On this particular day, though, storm clouds were gathering over Kincaid Towers. Kincaid Towers housed the many business interests of its patriarch, Garvice D. Kincaid, and a small museum on the first floor dedicated to him (a monument to his life that Mr. Kincaid never saw). Kincaid Towers was also the home office and corporate headquarters of Mr. Kincaid's largest and most important business, Kentucky Central Life Insurance Company. On this morning, the company's chairman, president, and CEO, W.E. "Bud" Burnett, Jr., had just stepped off the tower's low-rise elevator and was heading past the security desk on the first floor toward the high-rise elevators that would take him to his office on the twenty-first floor. Burnett had just spent the last thirty minutes being interviewed by Jack Pattie, a local radio celebrity, in the offices of WVLK. The station was the number one radio station in the market and had been acquired by Mr. Kincaid in 1951. On this day, Bud Burnett was on the air explaining that while Kentucky Central had certainly been stressed by the national commercial real estate recession, the company had "No Problem" in paying its contractual policyholder benefits. He went further:

> We at Kentucky Central have been here a long time. And we've experienced the Great Depression and world wars, and we have

survived, and we have grown. And that I think forms a good basis
for the future. It gives our agents and our home-office people a sense
of pride to know that they are dealing with quality products. And
creates an incentive for them to provide the best quality service that
can be provided.

What Burnett failed to acknowledge was that the Great Depression and
World Wars I and II occurred while the company was under the control of the
founders of Kentucky Central Life in Anchorage, Kentucky. In March 1992,
Kentucky Central Life had also produced a video interview with Burnett in
which he'd made these same remarks and others and suggested how financially
sound the company was.

The last twelve months had been difficult for the embattled CEO and his
company. The commercial real estate markets had been in a serious decline
beginning around 1990. The 1982 tax cuts had included provisions that had
allowed for generous depreciation allowances and tax shelters for real estate
investors. Also, during the 1980s, the deregulation of the savings and loan
industry had allowed these institutions to expand their investments to include
commercial mortgages. The tax laws had been changed again in 1986 to remove
many of the earlier incentives for real estate investment. The combination of a
general atmosphere of economic recovery, an increasing appetite for real estate
investment from institutional capital, and the introduction of the S&Ls as new
and often inexperienced lenders for commercial real estate had resulted in a
massive oversupply of commercial office and retail space in many markets.

In 1991, commercial mortgage loans and real estate were Kentucky Central
Life's largest asset class, so the company had come under siege by rating
agencies, regulators, and the press for its large exposure to this deteriorating
asset class. The pressure became so great that in late 1991, the CEO and his
senior management staff brought in a boutique investment banking firm,
Lang Capital Associates, and began work on a plan to bring in an additional
$100 million of outside capital to shore up the company's balance sheet. A
preliminary deal was even reported by Burnett in December 1992, but on this
day, the company had just announced that the negotiations for the additional
capital had ended and that the company would instead focus on selling non-
core business assets. Burnett had spent the last thirty minutes trying to assuage
doubt about the viability of the company. Now he needed to return to his office
and begin the difficult task of convincing various state regulators, who had
been threatening to shut the company down, to refrain from acting.

Burnett, or "Bud" as he preferred to be called, was a pudgy, quiet man who
was known to greet people with "Howdy" or "How you doing?" He had a degree

in accounting from the University of Louisville and was hired by Mr. Kincaid in 1959 after Mr. Kincaid acquired control of his first life insurance company. The Cardinal Life Insurance Company was a very small, Louisville-based, life insurance company that was organized in 1955 by the outgoing insurance commissioner of Kentucky, Syl Goebel, and some local businessmen. The company was struggling when Garvice was approached about an investment. Garvice didn't know much about the life insurance business but thought the company just needed more capital to grow. In December 1958, he initially invested $700,000 into the company, which gave him a one-third ownership. At the time of his investment, the company reported it had one thousand shareholders.

Garvice soon learned that he needed to be more hands-on with this investment. The company was in an industry that had unique accounting requirements and produced products that were actuarially developed based on assumptions that might or might not come true. In other words, the life insurance business was far more complicated than finance companies and banks, which earned an interest spread on assets. In addition, in 1959 some founding family members of Kentucky Central Life had approached Mr. Kincaid about acquiring their shares of the company. Kentucky Central Life had been around since 1902 and was much larger and more complicated than little Cardinal Life. Kincaid was interested, but only if he could obtain a controlling interest. Garvice also knew he needed some help. He was soon introduced to Paul Carr and W. E. "Bud" Burnett.

Paul Carr was a smart, Louisville-based, independent life-insurance consulting actuary. Paul would become instrumental in helping Garvice rapidly grow his life insurance empire over the next five years by acquiring other insurance companies and blocks of business. Bud Burnett was initially important to Garvice because he handled the accounting and coordinating the transition of the assumed business to Kentucky Central Life's Anchorage office.

History should identify Bud Burnett as Garvice's most consequential management addition. William Earl "Bud" Burnett came to Kentucky Central Life with little insurance experience in May 1959. Burnett had briefly served in WWII and had graduated from the University of Louisville in 1949 with a degree in accounting at the age of twenty-two. Burnett's first job out of college was working for an insurance agency in Louisville, Kentucky, but he soon joined a small property and casualty company, Louisville Fire & Marine Company (LFM), in 1953. In 1955, LFM became insolvent due to hurricane losses. That same year, Burnett moved to Inland Empire Insurance, in Louisville, after that company acquired the business of the insolvent LFM. Inland Empire Insurance was also struggling, and by February 1956, it had failed and was under the control of the Kentucky Department of Insurance. Both Inland Empire's and LFM's businesses were now in runoff, and the Department encouraged Burnett to stay on and continue to work with the Insurance Department in winding down these companies' business affairs.

In 1958, Garvice Kincaid was very involved in Kentucky's political landscape, and one can imagine that Burnett might have been introduced to him by Syl Goebel, the former insurance commissioner, who had helped start Cardinal Life Insurance Company in 1955. As insurance commissioner, Goebel was responsible for administering the runoff of Inland Empire's business, and he and his department would have been relying heavily on Burnett to do the administrative work. In addition, fifty-two-year-old Earl S. Wilson, who had been an assistant attorney general in 1940 and a special legal aid to Governor Earle Clements in 1950, had been working with Commissioner Goebel and investors in Inland Empire on a plan to acquire the insolvent LFM. Wilson had been a law school classmate of Garvice's and was now a partner at the prestigious Louisville law firm Bullitt, Dawson & Tarrant.

William Marshall Bullitt began his collegiate career at Princeton University, earning a bachelor's degree in 1894, and received his law degree from the University of Louisville in 1895. Bullitt then practiced law in his hometown of Louisville from 1895 until his death in 1957. He established himself as a senior member of his firm, Bullitt, Dawson & Tarrant. Bullitt was an avid Republican and was appointed solicitor general of the United States by President Taft in 1912. In 1958, the Bullitt law firm hired a young, Harvard-educated attorney named Edwin Frank Schaeffer Jr.

Ed Schaeffer was born in the Bronx in New York City in November 1930. He was the son of Edwin Frank and Rachel Townsend (Bouchier) Schaeffer. Schaeffer senior had worked for Western Union in New York since 1918 but was transferred to Louisville around 1940 and made superintendent of the Louisville Western Union office. He was active in the Rotary Club of Louisville and a member of Louisville's prestigious Pendennis Club, a club steeped in tradition and sophistication and a sanctuary for the city's most influential men.

The 1940s were a challenging time for Western Union, and the elder Edwin Schaeffer was directly in the line of fire. The problem involved illegal horse betting using AT&T telephone services and Western Union's news ticker service. Schaeffer was called to testify several times over the years, and at one point was charged with "maintaining a nuisance" by allowing the activities of the illegal betting shops to operate. The charges were eventually dropped after testimony failed to show he personally had information that tickers owned by his company were being used by bookies to collect information on the results of horse races. Schaeffer retired after a forty-five-year career in 1963.

After graduating from Louisville's Male High School in June 1948, Ed Schaeffer Jr. enrolled in Washington & Lee University in Lexington, Virginia. He graduated in 1952 with a bachelor of arts degree in economics and was awarded the prestigious honor of membership in the Phi Beta Kappa Society. Schaeffer was also part of the W & L young Republicans, acting as chairman of their mock Republican convention in 1952. Ed must have appreciated his years at Washington & Lee, since in 1988 he established the "Edwin Claybrook Griffith Scholarship" in honor of Emeritus Professor of Economics Edwin Claybrook Griffith. The scholarship is awarded annually to an economics major who demonstrates academic excellence and leadership in student activities.

After he graduated, Ed went to Harvard Law School. He graduated in 1955 and passed the Kentucky bar exam in July of that year. He enlisted and served with the Army's Judge Advocate General Corps from 1955 to 1957. He was initially stationed at Fort Walla Walla, just outside of Seattle, Washington. There he met his future wife, Joan Cameron Sherwood. Joan was the daughter of Cameron Sherwood, who was a respected Seattle attorney and who also served in the National Guard at the Fort Walla Walla JAG unit.

Private Schaeffer was soon transferred to the JAG office in Mannheim, Germany. Joan Sherwood soon followed Ed and they were married at the Mannheim Chapel in April 1956. They remained in Germany until his service was completed in 1957. Upon returning to Louisville, the twenty-eight-year-old Schaeffer joined the highly respected Bullitt, Dawson & Tarrant law firm in 1958. The couple purchased an 1,800-square-foot colonial ranch home at 311 Lotis Way in Louisville and joined the Louisville Country Club. In December 1958, their first child, Edwin Frank Schaeffer III, was born. They lived on Lotis Way until they relocated to Lexington in 1963, where they purchased a home in the Glendover neighborhood (790 Glendover Road).

In 1963, Garvice Kincaid brought Earl Wilson to Lexington to establish his personal law firm, and Wilson brought his protégé, Edwin Schaeffer Jr., with him. In 1975, Earl Wilson, Bud Burnett, and Ed Schaeffer would become important participants in this southern saga, assuming control of Kincaid's large and complicated empire after his death.

Whoever made the introduction, thirty-one-year-old Bud Burnett joined Kincaid in March of 1959, at Cardinal Life Insurance Company as the company's treasurer. Paul Carr was its executive vice president. Cardinal was still struggling, and Burnett worked to stabilize its operation. In July 1959, with both men's help, Garvice acquired 85 percent of Kentucky Central Life Insurance for $9.7 million. Garvice was now in the life insurance business! The company's press release described Burnett, in part, in this way: "W.E. Burnett, who has been a Louisville insurance executive for several years." This description of Burnett's early professional career would remain unquestioned for the rest of his life. But I don't believe most people would describe someone whose career involved managing the runoff business of two defunct property and casualty insurance companies, over a five-year period, as an "insurance executive." In fact, it wasn't until I started doing the research for this book that I knew the truth about his early career in insurance.

After Mr. Kincaid acquired Kentucky Central Life in 1959, he soon installed Burnett, at age 32, as its treasurer. Burnett would soon become Mr. Kincaid's right-hand man, straightening out both insurance companies, merging them, and working to complete six acquisitions over the next four years. Burnett, an accountant, understood insurance company accounting, which is complicated, and one can imagine that this was a significant benefit to Mr. Kincaid, who knew little about running an insurance company or its regulatory hurdles but had the capital to maintain and grow one.

By February 1960, Garvice Kincaid had already begun formalizing the roles of his management team. He maintained the foundation of the old Kentucky Central Life by integrating some of its existing management personnel with a spattering of new people. In addition, the company now was considered a multiline insurer with the addition of Kincaid's other new 1959 acquisition, "Kentucky Central Insurance Company," a property & casualty insurer.

Before the purchase of Kentucky Central Life, history indicates that Kincaid had never owned and controlled a publicly traded company. He had ownership interests in banks and other investments with partners, but according to interviews, he liked having control so he could make decisions quickly. When he acquired 85 percent control of Kentucky Central Life, it had 100,000 shares outstanding. It was publicly traded, but on a very limited basis, which is why the founding shareholders had contacted him. After over fifty years in business, they needed liquidity to address the financial needs of its many family-member shareholders.

Garvice Kincaid was truly a man ahead of his time. Shortly after acquiring 85 percent of Kentucky Central Life and thus control, he strategically changed the company to maintain this control, while also raising additional capital. In December 1959, Mr. Kincaid dramatically altered the capital structure of the company by instituting a 10-for-1 stock split. Overnight he increased the shares outstanding from 100,000 to 1 million, which translated into reducing the par value of Kentucky Central Life's stock from $10 to $1 per share. This change would reduce the market price and increase the shares available for trading, potentially making the stock more attractive to investors, but the most important change Mr. Kincaid made was to designate the newly issued 900,000 shares a new class of nonvoting stock. Since Mr. Kincaid owned 85 percent of the voting shares, he could control what the company did without much interference from others and still issue new nonvoting shares to pay for his future acquisitions.

Dual classes of common stock date back to at least 1923. Back then, many banks were started by wealthy individuals, and these founders wanted to have publicly traded companies, but they also wanted to maintain control of their organizations. To that end, the concept of nonvoting stock was developed. Since Mr. Kincaid had a strong knowledge of banking, he understood how to use this concept to his advantage. Another result of this change was that in the future, anyone responsible for his estate would have this same unbridled control of Kentucky Central Life.

In February 1993, Bud Burnett was witnessing, firsthand, how this unrestrained control over the last ten years had pushed Kentucky Central Life to a financial precipice:

> There are moments in life when it is all turned inside out—what is real becomes unreal, what is unreal becomes tangible, and all your levelheaded efforts to keep a tight ontological control are rendered silly and indulgent.
>
> – Aleksandar Hemon, The Lazarus Project

PART II: Heritage

A people without the knowledge of their past history, origin and culture is like a tree without roots.

— Marcus Garvey

Chapter One: The Railroad Comes to Appalachia

Douglas Kincaid was born in Lee County, Kentucky, in 1878. He was the son of a farmer, Socrates Kincaid Sr., and Cynthia Ann Trimble Kincaid. Little is known about his parents. Socrates's father came through the Cumberland Gap from Virginia in the early 1800s and was reported to be prominent in the public affairs of his county and in Virginia. We know Socrates was one of twelve children, he married Elizabeth Lutes in 1848, and she died in 1852 at age thirty. They had no children. In 1855, Socrates then age thirty, married twenty-year-old Cynthia Ann Trimble, and they had twelve children, of which Douglas was the eleventh. The 1880 and 1900 U.S. censuses list Socrates's profession as "farmer" and Douglas as a "farm laborer." Socrates died in 1910 at the age of eighty-five, the same year that Douglas married Minnie Johnson. Douglas was thirty-two and Minnie was twenty-five.

Douglas Kincaid's ancestors can be traced back to his great, great grandfather Jesse Bowling on his mother's side of the family tree. Jesse Bowling was of English descent and was born in Virginia in 1758. He migrated to Perryville, Kentucky, after the Revolutionary War. According to records of the U.S. Sons of the American Revolutionary War, Jesse was a private and served under George Washington at Valley Forge and the campaign against Yorktown, Virginia. In addition, he served under Lt. Samuel Cobbs and fought in the battle of Cowpens in South Carolina. Jesse sustained a chest wound at Yorktown, which would bother him the rest of his life. In 1776, Jesse married Mary Polly Green, who died young. In 1785, he married Mary Pennington, and they had Elija Bowling, who moved to Breathitt County, Kentucky, in the early 1800s. Later descendants all remained in and around Breathitt County until Douglas and Minnie moved to Richmond in 1915.

Beattyville is the seat of Lee County, and it was incorporated just a few years before Douglas was born. Beattyville marks the beginning of the Kentucky River, which traverses the state for 256 miles before meeting up with the Ohio River in Carrollton, Kentucky. The Three Forks area, as it became known, is made up of the North, Middle, and South Fork Rivers and is about three miles upstream from the city.

In the 1900s, the Three Forks area became an important location for transporting the area's resources of timber, coal, and oil down the Kentucky

River. In the early 1900s an "oil boom" occurred, and many families signed leases with the oil companies for the mineral rights to their land. These leases still exist today, and the countryside is dotted with oil wells in fields, backyards, and along roadsides.

Lee County is part of Appalachia and lies within the Eastern Kentucky Coal Field region. About half the county is in the Daniel Boone National Forest. The terrain is mountainous and very rugged, and limestone cliffs are abundant everywhere you look. Extracting its valuable commodities took a toll on the health of the land and its people while lining the pockets of the absentee industrialists. Many loggers lost their lives or were seriously maimed in accidents while felling the massive hardwoods or on the treacherous runs escorting the timber downriver to market. Generations of miners were killed or disabled by the dangerous methods used to extract "black gold" from the coal seams running deep within the mountains. In the words of Appalachian historian Harry Caudill in *Night Comes to the Cumberlands: A Biography of a Depressed Area*:

> Coal has always cursed the land in which it lies. When men begin to wrest it from the earth it leaves a legacy of foul streams, hideous slag heaps and polluted air. It peoples this transformed land with blind and crippled men and with widows and orphans. It is an extractive industry which takes all away and restores nothing. It mars but never beautifies. It corrupts but never purifies.[1]

Union College students, in *A Look into Appalachia* in 1988, vividly describe how Appalachia changed during this period:

> After the Civil War, agents from eastern corporations streamed into the mountains to secure extraction rights for the virgin hardwood forests and later for the vast beds of bituminous coal beneath them. Often, these eastern companies bought only the "dominant" timber or mineral rights—not the "subordinate" land rights—and so in many cases it was the local landowner who paid the property taxes, while the coal and timber companies waited for the railroads to finally infiltrate the isolated hollows and cart away their vast wealth. By 1910, a majority of the land in the Cumberland Plateau was owned outright by non-residents; non-residents also owned about three-fourths of the timber rights and 85 percent of the mineral rights.
>
> Appalachia's population at the turn of the century was still thinly spread out over the mountains and hollows. The coal companies often needed to build entire towns and infrastructure from scratch

---

1   Harry M. Caudill, *Night Comes to the Cumberlands: A Biography of a Depressed Area* (1963).

in order to support their businesses. They constructed hospitals, commissaries, schools, and government buildings, as well as houses for the miners and their families and nicer homes for the executives.

With the demand for coal during the First World War, the coal industry boomed. By the early 1920s, it was operating at peak production, employing more than 700,000 miners and extracting more than 40 million tons of coal annually. Thousands of people from all over the world flocked to the region to share in the wealth, and for the first time, many miners and their families could afford luxuries such as factory-made clothes, appliances, and even automobiles. However, a miner was dependent on his company for all of his needs; they "clothed his back, filled his belly, sheltered and lighted his household, and provided his family with medical treatment, fuel and water," according to historian Caudill. When the industry crash finally came in 1927, the miners had no insulation against the shock; the entire economic system of these communities collapsed.

Railway construction first started in the Appalachia's [*sic*] during the 1870s, when the commercial interest in eastern Kentucky's coalfields was growing. Earlier coal barons were tired of shipping coal out of the mountains on barges and they realized that railroads would be a faster, more economical method of transportation. At the time, some coal speculators expanded their interests to include railways, while others used their influence to encourage the construction of rails.

The early railroads brought big changes to the urban system of the eastern states. Because of brittle and fast-wearing iron track, small-scale rolling stock, and non-standardized railroad gauges, the first railroads were just short lines built between river ports and their immobile hinterlands to move farm commodities, minerals, and timber stock short distances.

During 1870-1920, a period of growth known as the Steel-Rail era was started by a revolutionary process that reduced the amount of carbon and silica in hot pig iron, producing high strength steel. Also, Henry Bessemer's discovery that high-pressure air would remove impurities from smelted iron in a bulk process helped the iron industry to produce large amounts of steel at cheap prices. It was during this era that rail lines were extended into the central Appalachian coalfields. As demand for coal increased, industrial companies from Europe bought rights to millions of acres in eastern Kentucky and southern Virginia. Tracks were laid in the most accessible areas, and towns were built by the companies to house the men they planned to employ as miners. Hundreds of Kentucky,

Virginia, and West Virginia towns, which had not existed in 1870, had at least five hundred people within a few months after the railroad arrived.

The railroads were built by small groups of contractors who worked on stretches of land two to five miles long. The work progressed fast considering the difficult terrain and the primitive methods used "Section" cars followed the workmen and were parked on the side of tracks for the laborers, their wives, and other "camp women."

Each county experienced growth when the railroad arrived in the 1880s and 1890s. For example, lumber mills or tanning companies were established, or sufficient local capital was collected to start a furniture factory or a textile mill. The railroad did not arrive in many counties until as late as 1900 to 1910, but it still preceded hard-surface roads by a decade.

The growing network of railroads in Appalachia from 1870 to 1920 started a shift in economic leverage away from that enjoyed by the large, coastal or gateway cities toward inland sites where agriculture and industrial production were being established. An example of this change would be in southern Appalachia where, at the eve of the Civil War, there were no towns that were larger than 10,000 people. By 1910 though, the population of Atlanta and Birmingham each exceeded 100,000. The influence of long-established small towns that were located at a mountain gap site or a river crossing point was assured when the railroad was built through them, and although their urban growth was fifty years behind the rest of the country, towns like Greenville and Knoxville became focal points for the southern Appalachian urban system.[2]

Growing up in Lee County during this period, Douglas Kincaid witnessed the economic impact of the railroad industry. It must have been exciting to watch all the new people, looking for work, coming into Lee County, so it isn't surprising that in 1903, at the age of 22, this son of a farmer struck out on his own and went to work as a "bridge carpenter" for the JB Carson Company. Up to this time, Douglas had been living and working on the family farm, and even though he now had a new job, he continued to live at home.

JB Carson was a small regional railroad construction company that did railroad bridge construction and repair projects. The Lexington & Eastern Railroad (L&E) ran from Lexington, Kentucky, to Jackson, Kentucky. The ninety-two-mile-long railroad track was constructed between 1886 and 1892. In 1910, the Louisville & Nashville Railroad acquired ownership of the L&E.

---

2   Patty Mills, "The Railroad Comes to Appalachia," in *A Look into Appalachia*, a collection Union College student essays.

A portion of this short-line track ran between Winchester, Kentucky, and the unincorporated town of Tallega, Kentucky, where Douglas would later reside. Railroad construction jobs required travel and being away from home for extended periods of time. These jobs were also considered more dangerous, so they paid a higher wage than many other jobs Douglas might qualify for.

Douglas probably enjoyed growing up in this rural area of Kentucky. We know he liked to hunt rabbits and quail, and since he had ready access to the Kentucky River, he probably also fished. These were both natural and necessary hobbies if one lived in the Appalachian regions of the country, and as a bonus, his employer, J. B. Carson, also enjoyed some of these activities. It was reported in the local paper that Douglas, at the age of 25, was hunting with Carson and some others and it was a successful day, in that the hunting party shot thirteen quail and two rabbits.[3] Douglas worked for Carson for fifteen years and was promoted to construction engineer before he resigned in 1917 to purchase a grocery store in Richmond, Kentucky.

In November 1910, Douglas married Minnie Johnson. Minnie was from Wolfe County, Kentucky, and was twenty-five when they got married. Douglas was thirty-two. Minnie's father, Thomas Crittendon Johnson, was one of the largest landowners in Lee County and also a commonwealth attorney and a founder and president of the Peoples Exchange Bank of Beattyville, which was started in 1912. Douglas's father, Socrates, had died that January, and Douglas's mother's and father's siblings were by this time either deceased or not living in Kentucky. One can only guess that the family farm was sold shortly after Socrates's death, since the newlyweds moved to Tallega, Kentucky, in 1910. Tallega was an unincorporated community located about ten miles east of Beattyville. It was a less expensive place for the family to live and was also where Minnie's father and mother, Mr. and Mrs. T. C. Johnson, lived. They owned a large farm on the Middle Fork. T. C. Johnson would die of a stroke in 1921 at the age of 72, and his wife, Eliza Jane Bowling Johnson, would pass away in 1943 at the age of 87.

By 1915, Douglas's bridge-work travels were taking him to Richmond, Kentucky. In 1987, the Madison County Historical Society published *Madison County Rediscovered* by Lavinia Kubiak which describes the area during this time.

> Richmond and Berea Kentucky experienced tremendous growth in the 1900's due to their accessibility by rail. Warehouses were built along the tracks, and Richmond and Berea both constructed freight depots. Two railroads intersected in Richmond in 1900, the

---

3   *Breathitt County News* (Jackson, Kentucky), January 1, 1904.

Louisville and Atlantic line and the Louisville and Nashville line, each with its own passenger depot. Mule-drawn street cars, buggies, or wagons carried travelers from either of the two depots to any one of a number of hotels. By the 1920's many miles of first-class track penetrated a large area of the county. Railroads flourished until the Great Depression of the 1930's, when automobiles and trucks began to supplant them.

In 1911, the Kincaid couple's boy and girl twins died during childbirth. In 1912, their third child, Garvice Delmar Kincaid, was born, and in 1914, their fourth child, Mildred Irene Kincaid, was born. Douglas's mother, Anne, was in her eighties and not in the best of health. She would die in 1919. Since Douglas's work was taking him to Richmond, the couple decided to make Richmond their home; they moved there in 1915. Richmond offered better educational opportunities for their children and was the center of Douglas's construction work. The couple soon became active in the community, with Douglas becoming a deacon in the First Christian Church of Richmond. Minnie also became pregnant with their fifth and last child, Beulah Grace Kincaid, who was born in 1917.

The year 1917 brought other changes to the Kincaid family. In April, after living in Richmond for two years, Douglas decides to make a career change. He bought the local Kennedy & Warford grocery store located on Second Street. The local newspaper, *The Richmond Climax*, reporting on the purchase, described Douglas as "Mr. Kincaid, a retired railroad man, who is pleasant and courteous, and someone who has resided in the city for the last two years, and . . . has made many friends." Douglas immediately changed the name of the store to "D Kincaid" and began aggressively promoting it in the local paper with language such as "leading grocers" and "[t]he best of everything kept in a modern and up-to-date grocery. Garden and field seeds for sale. Reasonable prices and courteous treatment. Your patronage will be greatly appreciated."

Douglas was a master promoter and understood how important it was to advertise. He was one of the most prolific newspaper advertisers around and promoted his store as offering the best products and the lowest prices. He endeavored to motivate people to do business with him. He offered customers services such as "deliveries to suit customers" and "warehouse-type" discount opportunities; for instance, they could bring their wagons to a railcar loaded with seed he had purchased to get a better price. He also introduced coupons as a way to create loyalty. Finally, as early as 1919, he encouraged customers to open a credit account with him. Douglas understood how to relate to his customers and build loyalty, and young Garvice was right there observing how his father did it.

The Kincaid family would probably not be considered wealthy by today's standards, but in all likelihood they were financially better off than most people in Richmond. Garvice, in a 1968 *Courier Journal* article, suggested that his mother, Minnie, ran a small post office inside the store. In 1922, the Richmond newspaper announced that Douglas and Minnie took ten-year-old Garvice to the State Fair in Louisville, and when he was in high school, it was reported that the Kincaids bought Garvice a saxophone so he could play in the school band.

How Douglas paid for the Kennedy & Warford grocery store is not publicly available information. We know his father-in-law was president of a bank and that Douglas had probably accumulated some savings by living at home with his parents while working for JB Carson. One can assume that at the age of thirty-nine, it probably wasn't too difficult for him to purchase the business. The sellers may have even provided him with some seller financing.

Garvice was only three years old when the Kincaids moved to Richmond and five when Douglas switched careers and became a local merchant. We know he spent a lot of time in his father's store, working there as a teenager after school and on weekends. As an adult, Garvice would become a master promoter of his businesses, and one can suppose that he learned a lot watching his father do business and listening to him at the dinner table at night.

At an early age, Garvice demonstrated a strong work ethic and a thirst for competition. He sold and delivered the local newspaper before school and received accolades from the owner of the newspaper for selling and delivering a large quantity of papers. In fact, the editor offered to make him circulation manager after he graduated from high school. He was so proud of these successes that later in life, in 1965, he set up a scholarship for Kentucky youth who delivered newspapers and was inducted into the national Newspaper Boy Hall of Fame.

Garvice's strong work ethic and intelligence were evident in his early academic years. He attended Richmond public schools and at age seven, made the honor roll in Miss Walker's first-grade class. In his senior year of high school, he was voted the most likely to succeed. By his own account, he was just an average student in high school. He honed his competitiveness by joining the high school debate team, which he would also do in college. As an attorney, these skills would prove valuable to him.

In 1927, Garvice witnessed something else that helped him in his adult years. This was the year that Minnie, his mother, acquired a home in Richmond through a commissioner's sale. The home had been built in 1924 and belonged to Robert L. Garrett. It was large—three-thousand square feet—and Minnie acquired it for $6,355. It was in her name only, which is surprising. One can probably assume that Minnie had learned about commissioner's sales from her father. As the president of a bank and also a commonwealth's attorney, he probably had been involved in foreclosures and understood the potential for a cheaper price in a commissioner's sale. He had died six years earlier. Perhaps he left Minnie some money for a home but specified that the deed be in her sole name. We know from the 1930 census that Douglas and the family were living there. Garvice was only fifteen at the time, but commissioner's sales would become important to him as an adult.

On June 1, 1930, Garvice graduated with fifty other seniors from Madison High School. The school had a week's worth of events leading up to the big day, including a banquet and a senior-produced play. This was impressive considering that the country had already entered the era of the Great Depression (1929–1939).

The Great Depression was a broad economic collapse and contagion that impacted most countries across the world. Historians usually consider the catalyst for the Great Depression to be the sudden, devastating collapse of the U.S. stock market beginning on October 24, 1929. Some dispute this conclusion, seeing the stock crash less as a cause of the Depression and more as a symptom of the rising nervousness of investors. The economy had boomed after World War I, causing an overproduction of goods as supply raced to catch up with demand. In addition, new industrial production techniques accelerated the ability of factories to produce goods. The world was rebalancing, and Europe, which had been a significant export partner, was still suffering from the war's devastation. The Great Depression was the longest, deepest, and most widespread depression of the twentieth century, with the U.S. unemployment rate rising to 23 percent.

The Depression had both an economic and emotional impact on the nation. Never before had so much destruction faced America's families, and this led to a large-scale distrust of government and financial institutions that would last for decades. More than one million families lost their farms between 1930 and 1934, and the life savings of millions of Americans were wiped out by bank failures.

In all, 9,000 banks failed, destroying more than $7 billion in depositors' assets. In the 1930s there was no such thing as deposit insurance, which was a New Deal reform. When a bank failed, the depositors were simply left without a penny. President Roosevelt didn't sign legislation authorizing the creation of the Federal Deposit Insurance Corporation until June 1933, and it would be many years before the public regained its trust in banks.

Not much is known about how this period affected Douglas and his family's business. We know that Minnie's father's People's Exchange Bank of Beattyville survived—today, it is recognized as the oldest operating business in Lee County. Garvice in his adult years would tell the story of how his father had put $5,000 in the Hargis Bank in Jackson County to send him to Harvard Law School, but the bank failed in March 1930, derailing those plans.

After high school, Garvice attended Eastern Kentucky State University (now known as Eastern Kentucky University (EKU) for three years.

Garvice and the Law

Well, I don't know as I want a lawyer to tell me what I cannot do. I hire him to tell how to do what I want to do.

– J. P. Morgan

Garvice in his later years said he enjoyed his college days. He played saxophone in the band, was president of the debating team, and started the Young Democrats Club. He attended EKU for three years, transferred to the University of Kentucky for his last year, and received an AB degree in 1934. The *Courier Journal* captured his memories of those days in a March 24, 1968, article[4]:

> Some people—many, in fact—insist that Kincaid's whole life has been a tense drive for recognition by a country boy with deep feelings of personal insecurity, but his college years give little hint of inner fires or the goad of inferiority. After high school he attended Eastern Kentucky for three years and enjoyed it.
>
> "I had a good time at Eastern," he recalls. "We did a lot of campus politicking. We had a band, and that was quite a deal, and I was associate editor of the paper. It was a small school then, and relaxed."
>
> After three years, he enrolled at the University of Kentucky, where he got an AB and entered law school, the Jackson bank in which his $5,000 nest egg was deposited having failed.
>
> "From the time I was boy, I meant to go to Harvard and be a lawyer," he says. "I was disappointed about Harvard, but it didn't make any big dent in my life."
>
> At UK, he was hardly a campus wheel, but his life was busy and pleasant. Among his classmates were such men as Bert Combs, later governor, and Robert Hensley who would remain a friend and business associate, and with whom Kincaid plunged into politics.

---

4   "Garvis Kincaid: Lexington's Maverick Millionaire," *Courier-Journal Sunday Magazine*, March 24, 1968.

Happy Chandler was exciting young Kentuckians and in his first race for governor, and Hensley and Kincaid rushed to help. Together, they organized the Young Democrats on campus. Kincaid went home to Richmond, won a precinct committee office and helped carry the county for Chandler over Thomas Rhea.

Even then, Kincaid was developing a curious reputation. Though active, he seemed to have few friends. Social life didn't seem to interest him, though he was not exactly a loner. One classmate remembers him like this:

> He was a strange fellow. Shy in some ways, but always trying to make a big impression. Had an abrasive sort of personality. He was sharp, but he wasn't really a good student; I don't think any of us thought he would be a great lawyer. He didn't really seem to have his heart in it. He was ambitious but he seemed to be trying to deny it. Dressed with no taste, had no social graces at all. Bull sessions bored him. So did dances. There was one girl, I remember, that I think he really liked, but nothing ever came of it, and she married another young lawyer. Maybe he was too busy. He started buying up real estate, even before he was out of law school. That was what interested him.

A sale of small houses for delinquent taxes marked the first turning point in Kincaid's life. "That was in May 1937," he says. "The last two weeks of law school. I was taking exams, and I read in the paper where they were selling these houses for taxes. I went down to the auction and bought this house, a little one out in a poor section of town, you know, for $12 or $14 hundred dollars. Only had $200, but my father signed my note. He thought I had gone crazy; he was a conservative fellow, always had been, but I didn't think that was too unconservative. Within a week I sold that house and made three, four hundred dollars on it. Within 10 days, with exams still going on, I bought four more for a total of $5,000. Well, my father was sure I'd lost my mind then, but helped me, within a couple of weeks I sold three of the four for a profit of $2,500. That was enough to pay for law school. I said to myself, "Lord, how long has this been going on?"

He (Garvice) was off.

The *Lexington Herald-Leader* recorded Kincaid's first real estate purchase in its May 12, 1937, edition: "Flora Luigart Dennison and Fred R. Dennison to G. D. Kincaid, property fronting 38 feet on east Seventh Street."

Kincaid passed the Kentucky bar exam in June 1936, one of 142 students who did. He took the attorney's oath of office on Saturday, September 25,

1937, at the Fayette County Circuit Court. It was administered by Judge King Swope.

Kentucky allows a student to sit for the bar exam if they have completed all work required for a JD degree but have not officially had a J.D. conferred on them. This is primarily for students who complete their J.D. work but won't officially graduate before the bar examination. Garvice graduated from UK Law School on June 4, 1937. At his commencement, someone he greatly admired, Governor Albert B. ("Happy") Chandler, received an honorary doctorate of laws. They would become lifelong friends.

In 1937, the United States was finally growing and moving past the effects of the Great Depression. Garvice had spent much of the Great Depression in college, and now his graduation from law school was happening after a year of solid economic growth. It took a long time for the economy to get its legs, but things were looking better. The memories of World War I were still vivid, and it would be two full years before people would begin to see the events leading up to World War II. And it wasn't until 1941, with the bombing of Pearl Harbor, that the United States would declare war on Japan. Now young Garvice, with an education and a vocation, could begin to think and plan his future

Chapter Two: Success Is the Sum of Small Efforts

Initially, Garvice considered setting up a law practice in Richmond. His family's home was there, and people in the community knew him. This idea didn't last very long, though, because his real estate dealings in Lexington kept him running back and forth between the two communities. In September 1937, he and E. L. Hutchison established a law office in a one-room suite in the Security Trust building. Garvice in later years indicated that two other lawyers were also included. Little did twenty-five-year-old Garvice realize how the relationships he would develop in the Security Trust Bank would change his life.

Garvice didn't immediately move to Lexington. He chose to live at home with his parents. But the *Lexington Herald Leader* reported, in August 1938, that he rented an apartment at 453½ West Third Street and that his phone number was #7228.

Garvice didn't stay in the Security Trust Building very long. He apparently decided to strike out on his own. By August 1938, he had relocated to the Citizen's Bank building located at the corner of Short and Upper Streets.

Interestingly, state banking officials appointed Garvice as a special deputy banking commissioner for the defunct Hargis Bank and Trust of Jackson. This is the same bank where Garvice's father deposited $5,000 earmarked as Harvard Law School tuition. The bank failed in 1930, and Garvice's role was to maintain its books and records and respond to enquiries. It's reported that depositors received about thirty cents on the dollar. Garvice must have been actively following the bank's situation, wanting to make sure he got everything coming to him. It's just too much of a coincidence otherwise.

After moving to Lexington, Garvice quickly became active in community affairs. He began volunteering for the Community Chest, the predecessor to the United Way of the Bluegrass, and joined the Lexington Co-operator Service Club, in which he was appointed to the entertainment committee. In addition, he became a member of the Junior Chamber of Commerce and was appointed its secretary in 1938. He was also active in the Fayette County Junior Bar Association. He was reported to be a member of Central Christian Church, the Lexington Country Club, the Pyramid Club, and the Elks Lodge. Finally, in

1939, he was selected as the chairman of the Sixth Congressional District for Young Democrats. His interest in politics would continue for his whole life.

By 1939, Garvice was well known in Lexington. His name was listed in the newspaper almost weekly as his real estate transactions were reported, and he had become quite active in the community. In December 1939, his largest real estate transaction to date was reported in the *Lexington Herald-Leader*. In 1938, Garvice had purchased a collection of delinquent county tax bills for almost $5,000, and by December 1939, a similar purchase is listed at a price of over $9,000. In less than two years, he had transformed those few initial real estate transactions into a full-scale business.

Garvice's real estate transactions, while lucrative, had one small problem: they tended to use up most of his liquidity. Garvice wasn't borrowing money from a bank; he was using his own money. He was always reinvesting his sales proceeds into new real estate transactions, and so at times his personal liquidity was limited. R. J. Colbert was a local attorney who had been appointed the master commissioner for the Fayette County Clerk since 1910. He was respected, and in 1929 was elected as the president of the Fayette County Bar Association. A master commissioner is in charge of auctioning off assets as directed by the court. Real estate assets are the most common assets auctioned. Before any auction, the commissioner needs to have the title researched to verify that the sale is legal. In those days, the commissioner would usually hire an attorney to do a title search and complete the paperwork so the auction could proceed. In June 1938, Garvice decided that he could make some extra income doing Colbert's title work. In addition, since he was purchasing properties from commissioner's sales, he probably hoped to get some early knowledge about possible bargains. Garvice did title searches for Colbert off and on during this time. Garvice, in an article, said he charged fifty cents an hour for his title work.

R. J. Colbert wasn't the only attorney for whom Garvice did title work. Samuel P. Strother was another attorney who had his office in the Citizens Bank and Trust building. Strother did work for Prudential Insurance Company's mortgage loan division and employed Garvice to do title work for him. This was convenient because both men's offices were in the Citizens Bank building.

In 1938, Eva Nelle Wilson was a twenty-three-year-old secretary for Mr. Strother. Nelle grew up in Lexington, in the North Broadway/Loudon Avenue area. Her father, Jesse Wilson, worked in road construction and at this time was foreman for the Lexington Quarry Company. Her mother, Jennie, was a stenographer for a local attorney. Nelle graduated from Henry Clay High School and then attended Lexington's Transylvania University. At Transylvania, she was a member of Chi Delta Phi sorority, the Women's Athletic Association, the Y.W.C.A., and the Women's Lampas Honors Society.

In 1940, Garvice still resided in his apartment at 453½ West Third Street, but things would soon be changing. In 1938, while doing title work for Mr. Strother, Garvice encountered Nelle Wilson. The two courted for almost two years and married on October 4, 1940. According to his 1940 draft card, Garvice was a striking, brown-haired, blue-eyed, young man. He was five feet and eleven inches tall and weighed 180 pounds. According to a 1968 article, Garvice said that he had purchased 300 to 400 pieces of real estate by 1940 and had made over $100,000. Kincaid said, "I took two big steps in 1940. Took my first drink and got married. I was twenty-eight." The couple were married, in the company of their immediate families, that Friday at 3:00 in the afternoon, at Lexington's Central Christion Church. Their wedding announcement said they "left for a short wedding trip and after October 12, they will be at home, at the Howard apartments, 453 ½ West Third Street."

Upon returning to Lexington, Garvice and Nelle immediately started working together to build their real estate empire. Before marrying, Garvice had always worked alone. He researched the properties he might want to acquire, attended commissioner's sale auctions, posted the properties he acquired for sale, prepared the ownership deeds, etc. Now, Garvice had a partner, someone he could trust and depend on and who he knew trusted him. Over the next two years, Nelle would help him by preparing deeds, attending commissioner's sale auctions, and bidding for properties. Nelle made it possible for them to accelerate the growth of their investment portfolio, and that is exactly what they did. Over the next two years, the couple would continue to buy many more properties, and they were now able to buy much larger properties because their net worth had grown. The *Lexington Herald-Leader* provides details about much of their real estate activity in its daily property transfer section. From 1940 to 1945, the newspaper lists hundreds of the couple's purchase and sale transactions. The Kincaid name appears almost every week, with some transactions being in both their names and many being in only Garvice's or only Nelle's name. They were very busy.

As the country entered 1941, war was looming on the horizon and Garvice faced the prospect that he would be called away from his growing business. In addition, Garvice lost his father, Douglas, in May 1941. According to Garvice, "[h]e had had one heart attack and one evening he was sitting on the side of the bed and just fell over." It's reported that his death was a deep blow to Garvice.

As for the war, in 1940, Garvice was registered for the draft, but he and his friend Robert B. Hensley, who was a local attorney and active in the local

Young Democrats Organization, tried to improve their positions. Kincaid said,

> Bob Hensley and I went to Washington to try to get a commission in the Army Air Corps, but they told us to go to St. Louis. I said to heck with it and figured I'd just get drafted. Later I went to Cincinnati and tried for a Navy commission, but one of my eyes wasn't good enough. I came home, folded up, sold the law office, and moved into a little office about ten feet square feet to wait for the draft. Sat there more than three years.[1]

The 1940s would bring many milestones for Kincaid and his family. His wealth and empire would grow at an extraordinary rate, and his family life would change with the birth of his twin daughters, Jane and Joan, on December 10, 1941.

---

1   "Garvis Kincaid: Lexington's Maverick Millionaire," *Courier-Journal Sunday Magazine*, March 24, 1968.

Chapter Three: Credit Where Credit Is Due!

America in the decade of the 1940s was changing. It had survived World War I and the Great Depression, but change was accelerating. The 1940s were defined by the United States entering World War II, the Holocaust, the atomic bomb, and the beginning of the Cold War, which was a period of geopolitical tension between the United States and the Soviet Union and their respective allies. The trend toward manufacturing and urbanism that had begun in the 1920s was accelerating. Women entered the workforce to replace the men who had been sent into war, and upon their return, the GI Bill entitled these soldiers to a college education. America's standard of living increased, and along with it its citizens' desire for better things. New inventions such as the television and the washing machine were expensive, but they made life better and were desired by the masses.

What helped to bring all these industrial and technological marvels within the reach of many consumers was the expanded use of installment credit. The breakthrough came in 1919 when General Motors took the initial step of creating a financing arm, the General Motors Acceptance Corporation, to provide financing for their customers. General Motors became the first to make financing available to middle-income car buyers. Instead of having to come up with the entire purchase price, prospective car buyers needed only a down payment and an income that was big enough to cover the monthly payments over the life of the loan. Soon, manufacturers of other big-ticket items began to adopt the practice, and if a consumer was hesitant to go into debt, they were flooded with advertisements in mass media outlets, newspapers, magazines, and radio to help him overcome his inhibitions.

Between 1910 and 1940, household finances were transformed by a revolution in consumer credit. A credit system that had been disorganized, disreputable, and poorly capitalized was replaced by a new corporate system that was regulated by the states, widely promoted, and in such demand that living on credit became part of the American way of life. In those early years, consumer credit companies were considered the "poor man's bank" because they lent money to those without a bank account and those who could not get credit at a bank.

Finance companies used various types of advertisements in newspapers, magazines, and radio to help households overcome their Depression-era inhibitions about borrowing. Credit for consumption is as old as the act of trading and bartering for goods. In the new economy of the 1900s, workers earned wages, and workers' salaries were so low that the slightest upsets—from illness, injury, layoffs, or firings—left households in need of borrowed money. Before the credit revolution of the 1900s, borrowers obtained credit from a market that was highly stratified based on one's social class. For instance, someone who had some wealth could get a loan from their local banker, but for the rest of society, it was friends, relatives, local retailers, and small-loan lenders who had to fill this need.

Pawnbrokers and small-loan lenders served the needs of the poorest and lent money to wage earners on security, usually liens on personal possessions or wage assignments. In the late 1800s, the first professional small-loan lenders were little more than dressed-up loan sharks, with one- or two-person offices, set up in dense, urban areas around the country. By the early 1900s, as America's need for credit increased, these loan offices were operating nationwide. Urban reformers launched campaigns against the "evil loan sharks," targeting these cash lenders that charged up to 500 percent annual interest for their small loans to working-class borrowers. In 1907, the Russell Sage Foundation championed "remedial" lending by semi-philanthropic private societies. The foundation raised capital from wealthy investors to meet the needs of the working-class borrower. In exchange, the foundation paid its investors a small, fixed dividend on their investment contributions.

Anne Fleming, an associate professor of law at Georgetown University Law Center, describes it like this:

> To address the "loan shark problem," the foundation did not want to exterminate the small-sum lending business, which offered a valued service to low-wage workers. Rather, beginning in the 1910s, it sought to devise a new scheme of regulation that would drive out those lenders who charged excessively high rates, while encouraging "honest capital" to enter the business. The foundation worked with the lenders' association to draft a mutually-acceptable model law that would include both limits on how much lenders could charge and rules for how they must disclose their charges to borrowers. The law, which became known as the Uniform Small Loan Law, could then be introduced and enacted in state legislatures across the country.[1]

---

1   Anne Fleming, The Long History of "Truth in Lending," *Journal of Policy History* 30, no. 2 (2018): 236–271, 239–240.

Lawmakers initially rejected the idea of allowing lenders to charge rates as high as 3.5 percent per month. The foundation defended its position by explaining that lower borrowing rates capped at 6 or 7 percent per year would simply drive the small-loan lending business underground. Lower rates would not cause the small loan business to cease or lessen the demand for these loans. Higher interest rates were required to compensate firms for the risks and work associated with these types of loans.

The foundation's position was that the shortfall between workers' wages and their cost of living, along with "enforced idleness, unexpected illness and similar emergencies," made borrowing a necessity. These conditions "cannot be eliminated without the entire remodeling of our whole social and economic system," it explained. Unwilling to scrap capitalism, early-twentieth-century reformers seized on regulated competition as the next best option. And thanks to the Russell Sage Foundation's campaign, the Uniform Small Loan Law was widely adopted over the course of the 1920s. By 1930, at least twenty-five states had the law, or a similar measure, on their books.

State regulation of the small-loan industry was inconsistent until about the mid-1930s, when state regulation became more standardized. Kentucky was one of the last industrial states to adopt a version of the Russell Sage Foundation Uniform Small Loan Law. Duke University's B. J. Lehman, in his 1954 report *Progress in Consumer Credit in Kentucky*, described it thus:

> As such, Kentucky represented one of the last bastions of boodle for nefarious loan sharks. The grasp of loan sharks upon Kentucky wage earners with each succeeding year pushed up personal bankruptcies until Kentucky became known as the Bankruptcy State and Louisville as the Bankruptcy Capital of America.
>
> The sixteenth biennial report of the Kentucky Department of labor covering the period from July 1, 1932, to June 30, 1934, shows the growth of wage earner bankruptcies in considerable detail. A chart therein illustrated that in 1930, in the United States, ninety-six out of one-hundred thousand wage earners sought bank relief, whereas in Kentucky there were three-hundred and twenty, and in Louisville, eight hundred, per one-hundred thousand. The report further states: "The disparity is directly traceable to the loan shark evil growing out of a lack of protective laws for the wage earners." In actual truth, when a victim became enmeshed in the loan shark toils, his only recourse for relief was "Bankruptcy or Death."
>
> Like rats in a corner, the sharks fought viciously to keep Kentucky as one of the fields of exploitation. Through crude but still clever devices—such as dual note forms, agency and brokerage

operations, phony merchandise purchases, forced insurance sales, and other equally deceitful methods—the loan sharks carried on their operations boldly throughout the entire Commonwealth. They placed their offices in prominent business locations in all the larger towns throughout the state.

By 1940, the modern personal finance company specialized in cash loans, and regulations usually limited the maximum loan to $300. Repayment of these loans was made in equal installments, generally extended over a period of five to twenty months or, in later years, up to thirty months. These businesses were now regulated and operated by permission of the thirty-nine states where laws resembling the Russell Sage Foundation model law was passed.

In most states these businesses charged borrowers monthly interest rates ranging from 2 percent to 3.5 percent. Interest charges were usually graduated based upon the amount of the loan. In Kentucky, businesses charged 3.5 percent on the first $150 and 2.5 percent on the remainder of the loan.

Lending companies need capital. In 1940, most state regulations required the business to have at least $25,000 in capital and a surety performance bond. In a business's early stage, practically all capital consisted of the investments of individual entrepreneurs. Then, over time, reinvestment of the business's earnings played an important and dominant role in growing its capital and ability to lend. If the business grew rapidly and additional capital was needed, the owners would sometimes offer investment securities, both stocks and bonds, to investors to raise capital. The bonds would usually have a higher coupon rate of 6 percent and sometimes provided profit-sharing provisions, and stock could be common or dividend-paying preferred stock. The smaller loan companies would usually find local people as investors, but if the business grew large enough, the offering of securities was marketed by established investment banking houses, and the commercial-paper facilities of the short-term money markets could be increasingly used if the business was one of the larger companies in the industry.

In July 1919, J. E. Richmire and J. F. Peck of Louisville, representing the Remedial System of Loaning, filed articles of incorporation in Lexington. In their announcement, reported in the *Lexington Herald-Leader*, the organizers said that the company already had operations in New Orleans, Memphis, St. Louis, Indianapolis, and Louisville; described Remedial Systems as "the poor man's bank"; and said it was "an organization similar to the Provident Loan Society of New York, which is headed by the Vanderbilts and Morgans," was established in 1893, and "has as its the purpose the financing of the poor man." The company's initial office was in the Hernando building, the same building that Garvice Kincaid would establish his law office in during the late 1930s. The principals involved in Remedial's organization were Samuel S. Yantis (president), John Gund (vice president), Edward T, Houlihan Jr. (secretary), and John T. Downing (treasurer). Two of these men would be important to Garvice in the future.

Nine years later, in October 1928, the Provident Loan Association of Louisville would set up a Lexington office. The company's announcement reported in the *Lexington Herald-Leader* was as follows:

> The Provident Loan Association of Louisville has opened a branch office in Lexington and will offer a loan service on the same plan in which it has operated in Louisville for 20 years. The local headquarters of the company are on the seventh floor of the Guaranty Bank building. The company also has offices in Louisville, Ashland and Paducah.
>
> R. M. Rutherford is president and Richard T. Benton, who has had wide experience in the industrial loan business, will be in charge of the Lexington office. The company makes loans on household furniture and other personal security.

Making small loans to the working class and the poor was a very profitable business. They needed the money and were willing to pay interest rates as high as 38 percent to borrow one hundred dollars for a year. The Provident Loan Society of New York was created during the financial panic of 1893. The United States was experiencing an uncertain economic environment, with a growing number of foreclosures and bank failures. The public gravitated to unregulated loan sharks and pawnbrokers for their cash needs. As a result, a group of powerful New York bankers and financiers pooled money, pledging $35,000 each to establish a not-for-profit organization to provide short-term loans at a lower rate than the loan sharks. The contributors included Solomon Loeb, Alfred B. Mason, J. P. Morgan, Gustav Schwab, Jacob H. Schiff, James Speyer, Seth Low, and Cornelius Vanderbilt II.

These prominent, wealthy New York businessmen, many already associated with the banking industry, the railroad industry, and Wall Street, created the Provident Loan Association of New York, a-not-for-profit organization, to make small loans to the poor. The organization was modeled after European organizations that served the poor. These men saw the need and understood that existing banking behaviors could not fill it. In addition, the men saw the potential for a pot of riches—being able to borrow at 6 percent and lend at 30 percent was the equivalent of a gold mine. The good news is that by the early 1900s, these same wealthy businesspeople focused much of their philanthropy and this organization's large accumulated profits on New York's poor. They built large hospitals and started other organizations to meet the needs of the poor. The Provident model soon expanded across the country as others saw its benefits, but these were now profit-driven entities, and the profits would accrue to the benefit of their owners.

During the 1920s, the Provident Loan Association and the Remedial System loan offices were the largest small loan lenders in Kentucky. Both were reported to be associated with the Russell Sage Foundation and were promoted as alternatives to the "evil loan sharks." There were a handful of other small loan lenders, but these two entities were well established and highly promoted by their owners and managers. Each lending office was established as an individual corporate entity, with one or two managers processing its loans and finding investors for additional capital if and when it was needed. This strategy also limited liability for failure to each office. The business was very profitable in the 1920s, but during the early years of the Great Depression this quickly changed as more and more customers defaulted on their loans and access to additional capital dried up. In addition, small loan regulatory and oversight changes, promoted by the Russell Sage Foundation, were being adopted by more states, and by 1940 there was an increasing risk of a second world war. The small loan, or industrial loan lending business as it was also known, was changing.

Kincaid and the Lexington Finance Company

In March 1927, Arie Quint Gillespie and some investors, including a Chicago retailer, started the Local Loan Company in Lexington. The company's office was located on North Limestone Street. A. Q. Gillespie, as he preferred to be called, was its manager. A. Q. was a local attorney who had always wanted to get into politics. He was a Fayette County magistrate and a Fayette County election commissioner, and in later years sold insurance. He was active in the Free Masons and Knights of Pythias and was a registered Republican. In the 1920s, he gained local recognition for his legal work with the area's railroad mechanics union. His legal background and his association with unions and knowledge of the local community made him a good choice for running the office. In addition, he had operated a small "chattel loan" business in the early 1920s but in 1925 had joined a local real estate firm.

A chattel loan business was essentially an unregulated loan business through which one would lend money upon the security of a "chattel mortgage" covering the borrower's furniture and/or household effects. These possessions, collateral for the loan, remained with the borrower unless they defaulted. They could also provide loans secured only by an assignment of the borrower's wages or salary. Some small loan businesses specialized in either chattel mortgages or wage assignments and some handled both types of contracts. A. Q. appears to mainly have focused on providing loans to local farmers and homeowners, based on the legal foreclosure notices published in the *Lexington Herald-Leader.*

A. Q. Gillespie never really settled into any one career and was always looking for that perfect job. He was a great example of "a Jack of all trades and a master of none." His real strength appears to be that people just liked him. Though he started the Local Loan Company in March 1927, by September he was also registering to run for the office of the commissioner of public works in Lexington, an election he soundly lost in November. In 1929, he was still manager of the Local Loan Company, but that fall he made a run for a seat in the Kentucky House of Representatives representing Lexington. He lost to John Y. Brown Sr., who would later become a member of the U.S. House of Representatives and governor of Kentucky.

In January 1929, another important change affected the Lexington small-loan lending industry: a small group of local men recapitalized the Remedial System loan company and changed its name to Lexington Finance Company. The men were Samuel Stuart Yantis, J. E. Kittrell, Dolph Wile, Charles R. Lauer, and Edward T. Houlihan Jr. Yantis and Houlihan were part of the original group that had started the Lexington office of Remedial Systems in 1919.

Samuel Yantis was a judge and master commissioner in Lexington. He was a graduate of the Kentucky Wesleyan College and Princeton University and had a law degree from Harvard. Ed Houlihan was designated the secretary and treasurer for the Lexington Finance Company and also listed as the company's general manager. Houlihan was the senior member of the Houlihan Insurance agency in Lexington and married to Mary Bernice ("Maysie") Hillenmeyer. The Hillenmeyer family and its nursery business, Hillenmeyer Nurseries, is one of Kentucky's biggest and oldest horticultural families, dating back to the family's arrival in the United States in the 1835 and settlement in Lexington, Kentucky, in 1844.

Ed Houlihan was very active in the Lexington community. His ties to the Hillenmeyer family pretty much ensured his status in the community, and his partnership with Judge Yantis also opened many doors for him. He was a member and president of the Lexington Junior Chamber of Commerce and a member of the Knights of Columbus and the Lexington Credit Managers Club. He also was a member of the Democratic party and worked on John Y. Brown

Sr.'s campaign for Governor. In 1930, Yantis, Houlihan, and R. M. Gaulding started the United Service Company to provide Uniroyal Tires and other automotive services for motorists throughout the state of Kentucky. By 1935, Houlihan would give up his responsibilities in the insurance agency and United Service to devote all his time to Lexington Finance. In the announcement in the *Lexington Herald-Leader*, he reported that his son, Edward T. Houlihan III, would be joining him.

In April that same year, Glover Randolph joined Houlihan at Lexington Finance. The announcement stated that he was a well-known "Lexington loan man" and had "a long experience in the loan field having been connected with the Employees' Loan Company here for nine years. He is a native of Lexington and well known in business circles." In addition, the company was promoted as "Lexington's Oldest Small Loan Company." This comment and the fact of local ownership would stay with the company for the next fifty years. In May of 1937, Edward Houlihan died at the age of fifty-one, but his son, Edward T. Houlihan III, stayed on with Lexington Finance and took over his father's role as its secretary and treasurer at the age of twenty-four.

Around 1936, banks, small loan companies, and retail stores selling on credit started the Lexington Credit Managers Club. The club held monthly dinner meetings, which provided a forum for local credit managers to socialize and learn more about all elements of their business. A typical meeting might have forty to fifty attendees and would include speakers who discussed such topics as social security, unemployment, the Workmen's Compensation Act, taxes, life insurance, education, etc. Some meetings also included some light entertainment. A. Q. was quite active in the organization and by 1937 was elected president of the club. In April of the same year, his Local Loan Company was acquired by Lawrence Flynn. Flynn, who also dabbled in real estate, owned a thoroughbred horse farm off Iron Works Pike and was "quitting farming to devote more time to other business." He was friends with T. C. Quisenberry and his family. Thacker Colby "T. C." Quisenberry would become an important player in the Kincaid story and maybe Garvice's most devoted friend during their professional lives. In 1940, life dealt Lawrence Flynn a bad hand and he died of an embolism at the age of forty-eight, but his decisions in 1937 probably were responsible for pushing A. Q. into Garvice Kincaid's orbit.

A. Q. Gillespie, probably knew Flynn's loan company was for sale at the end of 1936, and as one who was never known to be out of a job, he moved to Lexington's Provident Loan office in February 1937. By 1937, the Provident office had moved to the Citizen's Bank building—the building that housed Garvice Kincaid's law office.

The early 1940s was an emotional and pivotal time in America. Europe was already on the verge of World War II, and the United States would soon be pulled into it with the bombing of Pearl Harbor on December 7, 1941. Family life and normal commerce would change overnight, and the war's effects on everything would be felt over the next twenty years. Most Americans remembered World War I and the Great Depression that followed, so one can imagine the general fear that followed the bombing of Pearl Harbor. The bombing of a U.S. military base sparked a national outcry and support for the United States entering the war, which would change the economy and family household economics forever. Garvice Kincaid was mentally prepared to be called up for service in 1941, but that call never came.

In July 1940, Garvice Kincaid acquired probably the most important part of his empire. Nothing is recorded about how Garvice acquired Lexington Finance or why Judge Yantis and young Houlihan decided to sell the company. Garvice knew Houlihan's father from his work with the Junior Chamber of Commerce and John Y. Brown's Sr.'s campaign for governor and, as an attorney, he probably came in contact with Judge Yantis quite often. One can speculate that by 1940, both men were concerned about the prospect of war and its potential negative impact on their business. History had already demonstrated the large increase in bankruptcies due to the first world war and the Great Depression, and they may have felt compelled to cut their losses. In 1940, no one knew about the advancements made in nuclear arms, and most historians would agree that the bombing of Hiroshima changed how we would evaluate wars forever. Whatever their reasons, in 1940, after controlling their updated Lexington Finance Company for just a few years, Yantis and Houlihan decided to sell the business to Kincaid for what Garvice reported to be $100,000—the equivalent of $2,100,000 in today's money. After 1940, neither Yantis nor Houlihan is mentioned in connection with the Lexington Finance Company.

Kentucky Finance Company: Kincaid's Crown Jewel

By 1940, Garvice Kincaid was a known commodity. People knew he was smart and able to consider complex transactions, that his word was good, and that he had the wherewithal to complete larger investments. Robert E. Curtin was the first Kentucky Finance top officer to become associated with Garvice. A native of Washington, D.C., and a tax accountant, Curtin in 1947 went into business for himself in Lexington. He soon met Kincaid and began working for him on a fee basis. Before long, Curtin was spending all his time working on behalf of Garvice's financial interests, so he became a full-time employee and joined the Kincaid empire and Kentucky Finance in 1948.

Curtin gives this insight into Kincaid's shrewdness:

> I hadn't known Mr. Kincaid too long when a man came to see him to borrow money. The man wanted to start a rabbit farm in Clark County. Mr. Kincaid listened patiently while the man explained all the advantages of raising rabbits. Rabbits were good to eat, the fur could be used for coats, the feet made attractive good-luck charms, and so forth. After about fifteen minutes, Mr. Kincaid politely suggested to the man that he try to borrow the money in Clark County. After the man left, I asked Mr. Kincaid why he took time to talk to the man when he knew from the start he wasn't interested. Mr. Kincaid said, "Bob, one hundred people might come to me with different projects; ninety-eight may have wild ideas like this one, but I want to see those two with good ideas. That's why I talk to anybody who wants to see me."

I think a side note that is missing from the Lexington Finance Company story is that Garvice was probably more knowledgeable about the hows and whos of commissioner's sales than anyone in Fayette County. He knew all the lienholders because he was a local expert. He had been dealing with commissioner's sales for over five years, and his knowledge of the potential for losses was invaluable. One can guess that in 1940, his connections to Yantis, Houlihan, and Gillespie, in combination with his knowledge of commissioner's sales in Lexington, had provided him with a lot of comfort. In recorded interviews and historical articles about Kincaid's life there is no mention of why he purchased Lexington Finance Company, but most believe this transaction would later become Kincaid's entry into his most valuable business. That's understandable—borrowing at 6 percent and lending at 20-plus percent creates a lot of profit, and when your ultimate borrower is happy about getting the needed credit, it could be described as heaven.

In July 1940, after the death of Edward T. Houlihan Sr. the previous year, Garvice acquired the one-office Lexington Finance Company for $100,000. He retained Samuel Yantis and Edward Houlihan Jr. as officers, recognizing that both men were the influential backbone of the company. He also retained R. J. Fogg, Yantis's sister's husband, as vice president. Fogg would commit suicide two years later at the age of forty-eight. Garvice understood that he also needed his own loyal lieutenant to run the business. Fortunately, his office building housed a competitor and someone he was familiar with: A. Q.

Gillespie. In July 1940, Kincaid announced that A. Q. Gillespie had joined the Lexington Finance Company as its general manager. This demonstrates one aspect of how Garvice believed he needed experienced people to manage his companies, something he did throughout his life. Kincaid believed he should hire the most experienced and best people he could afford and let them run the business, with his oversight. Decades later, Kincaid's family and other business connections would criticize his hand-selected "Committee" for ignoring this most important Kincaid tenant. Before Garvice was thirty years old, he recognized the need to provide oversight and direction for his businesses *and* the need to rely on experienced people to implement his strategies and manage business operations.

Thacker Colby "T. C." Quisenberry's family were some of America's earliest settlers. Thomas Quisenberry immigrated from Kent, England, to Virginia in 1624. His ancestors didn't eventually migrate to Kentucky and Fayette County until the 1780s. While most of T. C.'s early ancestors were farmers, in 1920, his father listed his occupation as "bookkeeper" on the federal census. T. C. was born in May 1903, and the 1921 *Lexington City Directory* lists his profession as "real estate." By 1930, the federal census indicates he had become associated with small loan lending as a "collection agent."

In 1941, the thirty-eight-year-old T. C. registered for the World War II draft and joined the navy. He didn't return to Lexington until 1945. Beginning around August 1945, in large ads for Lexington Finance, his service in the United States Navy was acknowledged and it was announced that he had been named manager of Lexington Finance: "Mr. Quisenberry has had 25 years loan experience and is competent to advise with you when you are in need of financial assistance." Apparently around 1920, T. C. was employed by a small loan lender, and while no records indicate which organization this was, 1920 was the year that the Remedial Loan Company was started in Lexington.

The Great Financial Crisis of 2008 to 2010 demonstrated that lenders made riskier loans if they had no skin in the game. One can imagine that the small-loan industry faced similar risks, since most company office managers were employees, not owners. Garvice Kincaid had witnessed and profited from the mistakes that other lenders had made, and by 1945 he was probably looking for someone who was smart, experienced, dependable, and loyal to him and his business. T. C. Quisenberry checked all those boxes.

In April 1946, A. Q. Gillespie opened New Finance Company in the Central Bank building. A. Q. Gillespie would die in 1952 at the age of sixty-one, and T. C. Quisenberry would be a pallbearer at his funeral. The

New Finance Company was the brainchild of Garvice and M. C. Haddix, a prominent local businessman. After owning Lexington Finance for the last five years, Garvice wanted to expand and grow the business without sharing his profits with Lexington Finance's minority shareholders. In addition, he wanted to set up the organization so it could encompass multiple finance companies around the state. M. C. Haddix had the financial resources to help him finance this expansion, and they had worked together before.

Michael Cornelius "M. C." Haddix was born in Breathitt County, Kentucky, in 1897. He was the son of a farmer and in the 1920s tried working at a steel mill, operating a hotel, and starting a taxicab company. In 1931, he became a salesman for Brown and Forman Distillery, covering a thirty-five-county territory. Then he decided to enter the wholesale whisky business by organizing Distillers Products Company in 1933. This was the predecessor to his most successful company, which he started in 1938, the Lexington Distributing Company, which would become one of the state's largest wholesale liquor distributors. In later years his interest would turn to thoroughbred horses, and he had a farm bordered by both Iron Works and Newtown Pike. M. C. Haddix would die in February of 1950 at the young age of fifty-two. He had an estate worth over five hundred thousand dollars.

In July 1942, M. C. Haddix and Garvice formed a partnership with J. Howard King, a wealthy title company executive and thoroughbred owner, to acquire Lexington's Joyland Park for $54,000. The partnership didn't last long; in February 1943, Kincaid bought out his partners. In later years, Garvice made a point of saying that he didn't mind having partners as long as he maintained control. The 1942 Joyland partnership with Haddix may have been one of the reasons that after he acquired the Central Exchange Bank (aka Central Bank and Trust) in 1945, he installed Haddix as its chairman, with himself as president, and when he organized the New Finance Company in 1946, he brought in Haddix as a partner.

In later years, Kincaid would be known to incentivize his lieutenants and employees by allowing them to participate with him in the ownership of a business. One can imagine that he may have begun this practice with T. C. Quisenberry in 1945. Garvice understood that managers and employees with an ownership interest would act more responsibly in their business dealings. In 1975, after Garvice's death, his family and business connections would witness how Bud Burnett's and his other Committee members' poor business decisions and irrational loans helped to destroy his legacy.

In 1945, Lexington Finance was still a one-office business. The Second World War had ended with the Allies' success against Germany and Japan. Most

Americans initially viewed their place in the postwar world with optimism and confidence, but within about two years of the end of the war, new challenges and perceived threats had arisen to erode that confidence. By 1948, a new form of international anxiety had emerged: the Cold War and its tension between the United States and our allies and the Soviet Union and its allies. Over the next thirty years, the Cold War would create many tensions between the two superpowers as the fear of Communism and a potential nuclear war preyed on people's minds.

Americans became more affluent in the postwar years. Things were better than most Americans could have ever imagined. Government policies, such as the GI Bill of Rights, provided money for veterans to attend college, purchase homes, and buy farms. The overall impact of these policies significantly helped returning veterans and their families improve their lives. Forming families and having children in unprecedented numbers created the baby boom generation, which would become one of the greatest social and economic changes in a century.

Not all Americans benefited equally after 1945. America was still a divided nation in which African Americans, Hispanic Americans, and all women were largely excluded from achieving the American dream. It would take years and a generation of strife, aggression, and political battles for the full liberties of civil rights to be granted to these groups. During these years, the small-loan lending industry continued to play a significant role in helping these groups improve their economic situations.

In 1942, Garvice made his first significant change to Lexington Finance Company. In May of that year, he amended the company's articles of incorporation such that the company had twenty thousand shares of preferred stock and thirty thousand shares of common stock. Garvice could now sell preferred stock, paying a 6 percent dividend to outside investors, to help expand and grow his company.

In 1952, Garvice and T. C. Quisenberry made their second significant change to Lexington Finance Company. After years of being on the second floor of the Hernando building, they moved the company to a new, first-floor location on Short Street. In later years, it would be recognized that Garvice always wanted all his businesses to be visible in the community. This location, one block from the courthouse, fit that criterion.

The Lexington Finance Company was important to Garvice because it gave him an immediate investment in the local small-loan market and provided him with the people and infrastructure to grow the market, but it was the evolution of New Finance Company that really changed the nature of his wealth. In January 1946, Kincaid opened the first New Finance Company office and located it in Lexington's Central Bank building. By December 1948, Garvice had opened six more offices in other cities in Kentucky and had loan offices in Lexington, Louisville, Harlan, Henderson, Corbin, Maysville, and Frankfort. Their combined operations had assets of $750,000. This meant that each office had at least $100,000 of capital available for lending. The location of the finance company's first office is significant because in June 1945, Kincaid, with the help of a handful of other investors, had acquired the Central Exchange Bank. He then changed its name to Central Bank and Trust—a name that most of Lexington still knows. Thirty-six-year-old Garvice Kincaid was rapidly expanding his financial empire.

The next five years would see Kincaid work to grow New Finance Company's loan offices swiftly. He would also continue his management tenet of adding people he trusted to run the offices and be directors of his companies. Kincaid provided the strategy, financial resources, and oversight, and loyal lieutenants would manage his finance operations. This Kincaid management principle served him well all his life, and over the years, he would publicly credit his employees for helping to make his organizations a success. While early management consulting firms taught leaders to focus on strategy, organizational structure, and having the appropriate skill sets, it wasn't until the 1970s that these same firms began to evolve and acknowledged the importance of having a qualified staff with shared values and leaders that can communicate and motivate employees. Most of Kincaid's staff always feared his temper, but he demonstrated, by some of the things he said and did, that he recognized that he needed and valued his employees. In Garvice's own words, "[n]o one person is responsible for our success. A leader is only as good as his followers, and—in this regard—I consider myself fortunate to be blessed with so many talented and hardworking associates."

According to Robert Curtin,

> In 1948, Kincaid had New Finance offices in Lexington, Harlan, Corbin and Maysville and he merged the four offices and formed New Finance Company, Inc. Kincaid realized that a larger, consolidated corporation would be in a better position to raise investment capital. He became a master at putting deals together with borrowed money.
>
> I remember accompanying Mr. Kincaid to New York City in 1950. He wanted to establish a line of credit with several of the large banks there. We were just country boys out of the hills, I guess, but we were successful in getting a loan of $250,000 from The Chase Manhattan Bank, a sizeable sum at the time. Once the New York

bankers learned that Mr. Kincaid was a man of his word, we had little difficulty in securing loans in the future.[2]

February 1950 was a personally difficult time for Garvice. One of his earliest friends and partners, M. C. Haddix, died suddenly at the age of fifty-two of a cerebral hemorrhage. M. C. was one of the first people Garvice partnered with and someone he trusted. He had partnered with him on the purchase of Joyland Park and brought him in as president of New Finance Company. In addition, in 1945, Garvice made him chairman of Central Bank after he and a small group acquired it. Garvice Kincaid was always viewed as a private person, and by his mid-thirties he still had only a handful of close confidants and associates; M. C. Haddix was one of them. One can speculate that M. C. and Garvice could relate to each other because of their modest backgrounds and self-made wealth. Both men were considered knowledgeable entrepreneurs in their fields and both began making their fortunes at a young age, Kincaid in real estate and finance and Haddix in wholesale liquor distribution.

With the death of Haddix, Kincaid and another partner, La Marquis Deal (L.D.) Nickels, purchased M. C. Haddix's Central Bank stock from his estate that March. They paid $72,875 for his 2,653 shares. The stock was appraised at $25 per share, but they paid $27.50 per share to acquire it. M. C. Haddix owned 27 percent of the bank at his death.

Thirty-nine-year-old L. D. Nickels had been a branch manager for Lexington's Universal Credit Corporation ("C.I.T.") in 1930. In 1942, he entered the navy, and after his service, in 1945, he joined Central Bank as a vice president. In 1950, Kincaid promoted him to executive vice president of the bank, and in 1957, Nickels was made its president. However, Nickels was not president for very long. He died in March 1959 after a two-month illness. Kincaid and T. C. Quisenberry were pallbearers at his funeral.

In the 1930s and 1940s, Kentucky contained a handful of state credit associations. Most were made up of people in their region, similar to Lexington's Credit Managers Association. In the 1930s, a group of states formed the National Consumer Finance Association. Over time, states began to consolidate their multiple credit associations and create state consumer finance associations. Kentucky appears to have formed its state association around 1933, which would coincide with Kentucky's initial adoption of some of the Russel Sage Foundation regulations. By 1950, Kincaid was reaching his stride, and in November 1950, he was named president of Kentucky's Consumer

---

2   Interview of Robert Curtin, Kentucky Finance vice president, secretary, and treasurer, by Kentucky Central Life public relations staff in Kincaid Towers grand opening booklet created by the company and distributed beginning September 1980

Finance Association. Garvice had become a recognized and influential leader in Kentucky's consumer finance marketplace.

Kincaid and Robert M. Bartella – Moving It Forward

Garvice had a growing organization. In January 1950, he changed the name of New Finance Company to Kentucky Finance Company. The company had grown to eighteen offices in sixteen cities by this time and had over $2 million in assets. The thirty-eight-year-old Kincaid was now ready to take the company to the next level, and in August 1951, he recruited thirty-five-year-old Robert M. Bartella to join him in running Kentucky Finance as its director of operations. Bartella would become an important addition to Kincaid's management team.

Robert M. Bartella was born in Michigan in 1916. He was the son of John and Meta Bartella, both of whose parents had immigrated to America from Germany in the late 1800s. His father was a credit manager for a local department store; his mother, a homemaker. Robert graduated from Lawrence University in Appleton, Wisconsin. After college he moved to Milwaukee, Wisconsin, and began working for Household Finance Corp., which was considered the largest consumer finance company in the United States. In July 1943, he enlisted in the Army. He served in World War II and was discharged in April 1946. After the war, Bartella moved to Lima, Ohio, and began working at the corporate headquarters for Colonial Finance Company.

Colonial Finance had been started in the early 1920s in Lima and had expanded over the years. In 1940 it had more than fifty offices in eight states. Colonial was doing what Kincaid wanted to do, so he recruited someone he thought could help him do it. Managing a multistate consumer loan company wasn't a simple task. Each state had its own lending regulations and foreclosure procedures. Kentucky Finance would need to grow its corporate staff and structure the organization to be able to manage the new out-of-state offices that Kincaid wanted to open. Kincaid needed someone with experience, and Bartella brought it.

Kincaid took advantage of his position in the finance association by having Robert Bartella serve as the conference moderator at its 1951 annual conference, with Kincaid himself giving the keynote address to the attendees. In addition, he recruited Mrs. Robert (Polly) Layman, the wife of his vice president at Central Bank & Trust, to represent women and their perspectives. Robert Layman had also recently joined the bank (in November). Throughout his life, Garvice never missed an opportunity to showcase all his enterprises. His father's lessons regarding marketing and promotion clearly stayed with him.

Robert Bartella said this about Kincaid after his death: "Mr. Kincaid never stood still. He visualized expansion of the marketing area as the way to build, so we started opening new offices and buying existing ones." Bartella also said that when he started at Kentucky Finance in 1951, he was supervising 15 offices, and that at Garvice's death in 1975, he was now responsible for 152.

In addition, long-time business associate and friend T. C. Quisenberry described his relationship with Garvice and Garvice's marketing prowess in a publication[3] about the opening of Kincaid Towers in 1980:

> T. C. Quisenberry, his first business partner and close friend, recalls . . . "He never forgot his beginnings, he was tremendously sensitive to people, he had faith in them, and he enjoyed doing things for them."
>
> "In the early 50's when cars were still hard to get," Quisenberry recalls, "he (Garvice) phoned me and asked me to take him to Dixie McKinley's to pick up a Cadillac. On the way over he said 'T. C., would you like to have a Cadillac?' and I said 'yes, wouldn't anybody?' We got there and he told McKinley 'T. C. here wants a car and I'll take the next one you get.' And when I went to pay for it, I found out Kincaid had already paid."
>
> "I worked for him longer than anybody," Quisenberry continues, "and I never had a contract, just a handshake. I went with him in (managing) the Lexington Finance Co. operation, and when we had reached an agreement, he said for me to come back in a couple of hours, and he'd have a contract drawn up. I told him I'd watched my daddy in a grocery store at Camargo trust people for half a year and they'd always come in and paid him. I said if my word wasn't worth anything and his wasn't worth anything, they wouldn't be worth any more if they were written on a piece of paper. We shook hands, and that was the contract we had in force the day he died."
>
> Kincaid (also) had plenty of sales and marketing talent to go along with his financial ability. On this, Quisenberry comments, "Garvice never opened an office in any town that he didn't want it to be the best-looking. From the very beginning, he did a lot of remodeling. He knew that an attractive location helped business, and that was a plus for the community."

History portrays Garvice Kincaid as an impatient man. This appears to be true, just from some of the articles I found about tickets he had received. He

---

3   *Kincaid Towers Grand Opening Magazine*, 1980.

received tickets for speeding, failing to stop at a stop sign, and something to do with parking tied to Joyland Park, but I believe the best example is the one mentioned in the June 1951, *Lexington Herald-Leader*:

Charge of Horn-Tooting Against Kincaid Void

Police Judge Thomas J. Ready said last night he had voided a charge of unnecessarily blowing an auto horn filed earlier in the day against Garvice Kincaid, the bank and loan-company executive.

Kincaid was cited to police court at 9:40 a.m. on West Short Street by Patrolman Howard Lowery, who reported that as he and a fellow officer was attempting to unravel a traffic jam, Kincaid sounded air horns on his car.

Judge Ready said he did not docket the charge against Kincaid because "it was just a mix-up down there on Short Street; he was just blowing his horn too much."

The jurist added that he did not know the details of the case but said the arresting officer made no objection to voiding the warrant.

In January 1963, the *Andy Griffith Show* ran an episode that I have seen reruns of many times. The title of it is "A Man in a Hurry," and every time I see it, I think of Garvice Kincaid. The story line is about a high-powered businessman who is driving through when his car breaks down in low-powered Mayberry. The inpatient businessman, Malcolm Tucker (Robert Emhardt), becomes irritated when he tries to get his car fixed on a Sunday and discovers that Wally, the mechanic, doesn't work on Sundays. Little by little, he is forced to enjoy life in the slow lane and remember his small-town roots. In the end, his car gets fixed, and he can't believe Gomer isn't going to charge him for his work because he (Mr. Tucker) was forced to delay his trip. In the end, Tucker pretends his car is still broken down and he needs to stay another day until Wally can look at it. One can just imagine Garvice stuck in a similar situation: his car won't start, he has a meeting in another state that he must get to, and he finds out that two old ladies have tied up the town's phone lines talking about their feet falling asleep, so he can't make a call.

Garvice and His Early Lieutenants

Garvice commonly used people in more than one of his organizations. For instance, Robert Layman would become president of Central Bank while he was vice president of Kentucky Finance. Kincaid regularly had directors of his organization on multiple boards, and in many cases included various employee-officers as directors. Excluding the Committee members, over the years, Kincaid came to rely on his bank and finance people to help him manage and grow his various business interests—people like Robert Bartella, Robert Layman, Kenneth Davis, Robert E. Curtin, T. C. Quisenberry, D. I. Boyle, and L. D. Nickles. These men were considered a core part of Garvice's bank and finance company businesses during the 1950s and 1960s, and as Kincaid would expand his business into other industries, his circle of important people would also gradually expand and influence some of his decisions.

Dages (D. I.) Boyle is an example of someone who was a Kincaid associate and on the boards of Lexington Finance, Kentucky Finance, and Central Bank but not a Kincaid employee. He was a local real estate developer and owned a securities brokerage company in Lexington. His office was in Kincaid's Central Bank Building, and he would have been someone who helped Kincaid raise capital for his finance companies. In 1954, Garvice would even buy Boyle's sister's expensive Miami waterfront estate home. It appears the business side of their relationship faded away in the 1960s as Garvice expanded his empire, but in 1974 D. I. still referred to Garvice as his good friend and compatriot.

Several years after Kincaid's death, in 1983, Boyle sued Garvice's wife Nelle Kincaid to recover eight paintings worth several million dollars. D. I. claimed he had loaned Garvice the paintings for his home and offices in the early 1950s. Nelle claimed they were part of Boyle's sister's Miami property, which Garvice had purchased. According to testimony, D. I. had moved the paintings from his home in Pittsburgh in 1949 to his home in Lexington, where he had kept them. In 1954, he sent them to Lexington artist Tony Zappone for restoration and they were then delivered to Kincaid's home, at Boyle's direction, to be held there until Boyle wanted them back. Garvice paid the $750 restoration bill. Boyle claimed that Kincaid moved them from Zappone's studio to his home but never paid Boyle for them.

Boyle said that after a few years he asked Garvice to return the paintings, but that "Garvice kept putting him off." June Rollings, a former local television personality, gave the most influential testimony. She testified that she saw the Titian painting titled "Diana and the Hunter" twice while she was with Kincaid—once in Kincaid's office and once hanging in the bar at the Campbell House Motel. She said Kincaid asked her to look at the painting because "he was thinking of buying it for $2.5 million." Titian, born between 1480 and 1490, is considered the greatest Venetian painter of his era. The courts sided with Boyle and the paintings were returned to him.

Another example is T. C. Quisenberry. Quisenberry was the president and the face of Kincaid's Lexington Finance Company. He was well known in the community and someone Kincaid trusted as well as his friend. Garvice would even hire his cousin, J. W. Quisenberry, to operate the local Kentucky Finance office, and in 1964, when Garvice formed the Kincaid Foundation, Quisenberry was one of the original incorporators. In 1963, when Garvice's daughter Jane Kincaid was getting married, Quisenberry's wife and the wife of tobacco warehouse owner John Kingsley held a dinner at the Lexington Country Club in honor of the bride-elect and groom-elect. Also, in 1966, T. C. Quisenberry and Frank Trimble, a partner at Kincaid's law firm, opened Lexington Air Taxi Inc. at Lexington's Blue Grass Field (now Blue Grass Airport). They operated a charter service, hanger rental, and flight school. According to John McGarvey, an anchor at WKYT during this time, Kincaid instructed the WKYT staff to use the service when they could. McGarvey also said that twenty-five-year-old Joan Kincaid worked in the company's office for a time.

While Garvice was a private person, T. C. was outgoing and enjoyed socializing. He owned thoroughbred racehorses and had a well-placed box at Keeneland. In the early 1960s, he would be appointed by the mayor to the municipal board of the Lexington Housing Commission and serve two four-year terms. Garvice must have appreciated T. C.'s friendship, because in March 1963, he and Quisenberry formed a partnership and purchased Winganeek Stables, located off of Richmond Road. The *Lexington Herald-Leader* reported[4]:

Quisenberry, Kincaid Form Wiganeek Stable, Will Race at Keeneland

Keeneland fans will see a powerful new racing establishment come into action when the meeting opens on April 6, when the Winganeek Stable arrives from Oaklawn. Winganeek is owned in partnership by Garvice D. Kincaid and T.C. Quisenberry of Lexington. Winganeek has engaged the services of Vester R. (Tennessee) Wright to condition its thoroughbreds.

Winganeek at present owns 11 thoroughbreds but plans eventually to race an evenly balanced stable of 15 to 20 runners. It intends to secure the best racing material the market offers, including the yearlings on auction each July at Keeneland.

The stable at present is headed by Bold Sequence, by Bold Ruler-Sequence, by count Fleet, who sold at Keeneland as a yearling last July for $79,000. Bold Sequence is a half-sister to the stake's winners Noorsagga and Hermod.

Tennessee Wright, one of America's greatest trainers, probably has saddled more winners at Keeneland than any other conditioner.

---

4   "Kincaid Quisenberry Horse Racing," *Lexington Herald-Leader*, March 29, 1963.

Wright led the nation's trainers in winners in 1956, 1957, 1959, and 1961.

Investing in racehorses and a thoroughbred racing operation seems very unlike Garvice Kincaid. His purchase of the Bold Ruler mare in March 1963 would be the equivalent of spending $800,000 today on a horse. He was a man who liked numbers and certainty, and thoroughbred racing, while it is called the sport of kings, is as much about chance as anything else. In interviews with Garvice in his later years, he never mentions this diversion. He must have realized quickly that money doesn't guarantee success in thoroughbred racing. While Quisenberry would remain connected to the thoroughbred industry for many years, Garvice was pretty much done with it after three years. Quisenberry enjoyed the sport and in the mid-1960s would sometimes charter a plane to fly his friends and business connections to tracks where he and Kincaid had horses running.

No one I have spoken with about Mr. Kincaid remembered him ever owning any thoroughbred horses. In fact, what I heard from more than one person was that "that just doesn't sound like Kincaid." My personal opinion is that by 1963 Garvice was looking for a way to better connect with the Lexington establishment, and while he had proven he was smart and could make money, he just was not part of it. He was both an innovator and also unorthodox, and the Lexington establishment never appreciated his appetite for business and his passion for winning. In later interviews, it's obvious it hurt him to be considered an outsider in a city he truly loved. He wasn't allowed to join the Rotary Club of Lexington, and his application for membership in the "old money" Idle Hour Country Club was rejected. I think he and Quisenberry may have anticipated that getting into thoroughbred racing might help him be more accepted by the Lexington establishment or, as Kincaid referred to it, "the Power Structure of Lexington."

In 1924, William Wright traveled to Lexington from Chicago. Wright owned the successful Calumet Baking Powder Company and wanted to start a harness racing stable. After William Wright died in 1932, his son Warren Wright, Sr. took over the business and began converting it to thoroughbred breeding and training. Under Warren Wright, Sr. and his wife Lucille Parker Wright, who inherited the property on his death in 1950, Calumet was the top money-earning farm in racing for twelve years. Garvice had witnessed this wealthy Chicago business owner and his family being accepted and respected by "old money" Lexington, and one can see how he and Quisenberry might have thought involvement with thoroughbred racing could work for him.

The other reason I think Garvice had this three-year diversion in his life was that he had made a lot of money over the last twenty years and probably was looking forward to enjoying it a little more. He had many loyal lieutenants in place to oversee his interests and had already suffered the first of three heart attacks, a severe one in May 1953 at the age of forty. For ten days he was unconscious, and was bedridden for almost three months. In 1964, at the age of fifty-two, he would experience a second heart attack while on a trip to Florida. In an interview he said, "I guess you could call it an attack. They had to carry me out of the hotel one night in Florida, and I was laid up for a few days." One can see how the second heart attack might have affected his interest in thoroughbred racing and his interest in trying to gain the respect of "old money" Lexington. In addition, in 1959, he had acquired Kentucky Central Life Insurance Company in Anchorage, Kentucky, and he was now moving its operation to the renovated Lafayette Hotel (the Kentucky Central Building) in downtown Lexington. The needs of his empire were calling.

The culture was different in the 1960s, and business practices that are criticized today were considered normal or accepted. Some of Kentucky Finance Company's 1963 employment ads provide a glimpse into how different the world was.

GOOD AT FIGURES?

We are seeking a young lady, high school grad, 18 years or over, to work with our acct./Bkpng. Department. Must type 40 WPM.

Modern downtown offices, very pleasant people and working conditions. Excellent fringe benefits. Good starting salary, top opportunity.

No Experience necessary—we will train you to fill any of several positions that are always in demand.

Contact Mr. Bohan
Kentucky Central Building
200 E. Main St. 4ᵗʰ Floor
Lexington, Ky

SHANGRI-LA FOR
TOP
SECRETARY

Young lady under 30. If you are searching for a plush setting where efficiency is required, but also appreciated.... You've found it! Must be strong on shorthand, typing, and use the Dictaphone... Salary is commensurate with experience. Exceptional surrounding, pleasant people—You'll like it here! Apply in person to Mr. Bohan, Kentucky Finance Co., 5th floor, Kentucky Central Building.

~~~~~~~~~~~~~~~~~~~~~~~~

Male Help Wanted

EXPERIENCED, sober painters. Year-round work. Apply Luther Jackson, second floor Kentucky Central Life Insurance Bld./ between 7:30 a.m. and 8 a.m. ONLY.

~~~~~~~~~~~~~~~~~~~~~~~~

Cultural attitudes and perceptions were beginning to change as the nation entered the 1970s, but change was slow. In the 1970s, women's groups worked to create a more open and equitable society. To achieve this, they demanded and won access to male-dominated businesses and universities. Woman also made inroads into politics at the local, state, and national levels. They were having professional careers outside of teaching and nursing, becoming doctors, lawyers, stockbrokers, scientists, pilots, and reporters. Things were happening slowly, but women were breaking down employment barriers and expanding their opportunities, and these changes would transform the character of the American family and cultural norms. Lexington has always cherished its long history and southern culture, and even today you will hear somebody call someone "honey" or "sweetheart," but an old, popular Kentucky saying probably illustrates how much Lexington's culture would need to change as it entered the 1970s" "We're Kentucky and we love our fast horses, beautiful women, and smooth Bourbon"—and not necessarily with the adjectives in that order.

The Rise and Fall of Ken Davis

In 1960, Garvice realized that the growing small loan company needed a better organizational structure. Purchasing Personal Industrial Bankers Inc. (PIB) in July 1961 and consolidating its operations with Kentucky Finance would require a more formalized management structure and an increase in professional talent. One area that Kincaid saw he needed more support in was handling state regulation and loan defaults. He wanted to recruit a good general counsel, one who had experience in the consumer credit industry and understood the various states regulations. Thirty-seven-year-old Kenneth C. Davis was considered a consumer finance expert by his peers and had been a member of various state consumer finance associations for many years.

Kenneth Davis was born in 1923, was a native of Kent, Ohio, and had graduated from Kent State University. In 1943, he enlisted in the army at age nineteen and served in World War II. He was discharged in 1946, the same year he met his wife, Ella, at the Fort Knox Army base, where she was serving in the Women's Army Corp. Ella was born in 1920 and thus was three years older than Ken. After the military, Ken attended Kent State University, using his veteran benefits, and in 1953 he graduated from the University of Louisville College of Law. He briefly practiced law in Louisville but soon joined the Time Finance Company in Louisville as its corporate secretary. Ken's wife became a homemaker, taking care of their two children.

Garvice knew about Ken Davis from his work with the Kentucky Consumer Finance Association, of which Davis was a member. In May of 1960, Kincaid hired Davis as senior vice president and general counsel for Kentucky Finance and, in 1961, as president of PIB. Ken was smart and well connected and represented Kincaid and Kentucky Finance Company very well over the years until a personal crisis ended his career with the company in 1982.

In November 1960, the year he joined Kentucky Finance, Ken Davis and his wife Ella purchased a three-quarter-acre lot in the new Lansdowne development, just off Tates Creek Road. They constructed a three-thousand-plus-square-foot home at 704 Burkshire Drive and moved into it in 1961 with their two small children. Their home was described as a "lavish south Lexington home," and their neighbors described them as a lovely couple and said that Ella "kept the property in tip-top shape" and that "it looks like something out of Hollywood—she was great with landscaping and flowers." Another neighbor said of Ken, "He worked so hard on the house—he loved his home, and she did too." "He put in molding and built shelves downstairs and upstairs and she helped him." They were a team.

In July 1961, Kincaid added to his finance company holdings with the purchase of a controlling interest in PIB. PIB had thirty-nine offices located in six eastern and southeastern states—Pennsylvania, Maryland, Virginia, Kansas, Florida, and South Carolina—and had assets of $12 million. These were geographic areas of the country where Kentucky Finance did not operate. Kentucky Finance had twenty million in assets and operated sixty-two offices in six states. This was a great acquisition for Garvice, but it didn't start out that way!

Ken Davis relayed this story about the deal and how Kincaid dealt with problems:

> Kincaid kept tabs on his companies mainly by reading reports
> and financial statements, and he was a wizard at analyzing them.

Subordinates quickly learned that they had better put down the bare straight facts. He could see through anything else.

It wasn't all onward and upward for Kincaid, however. In 1961, he attempted to expand his consumer finance holding with a major acquisition, which nearly backfired. He purchased fifty-five percent of Personal Industrial Bankers, Inc., of Washington, D.C., which had $12 million in assets, with thirty offices in six states.

Without going into detail, PIB started out as one of Garvice's rare unattractive deals. The possibility of voiding the sale because of audit discrepancies and other factors was discussed, but Garvice chose to keep the company, risking the loss of several million dollars. His reputation meant more to him than the money.

We kept the company as a separate company until 1966, when it was strong enough to be merged with Kentucky Finance.[5]

Robert Bartella gave a little different color on the acquisition:

Late one night after hours of discussion whether or not to buy PIB, Garvice said, "This is a democracy, let's take a vote." There were seven men present, and the vote was six to one not to buy. You know who the one in favor was and you know he bought it.[6]

Davis closed the story by saying,

One of the Kincaid's greatest attributes was that he always did what he said he would do. If Garvice had told me before he died that he would meet me at 42nd and Broadway in New York City at midnight on October 1, 1980, I'd probably be there, thinking he would find a way to make it.[7]

Ken Davis hit the ground running for Garvice. He was overseeing the operations of PIB as its president, addressing Kentucky Finance's regulatory and litigation needs, and promoting Kentucky Finance nationally through his work with the National Association of Consumer Finance Companies and participating on the boards of directors of various state credit organizations. Ken was soon recognized as an industry leader and expert by his peers. He was a talented speaker and also had a personality that easily endeared him to people. Ken was just a smart, enjoyable person to be around and a dapper dresser to boot, with a fondness for bow ties.

In November 1971, the forty-eight-year-old Davis was having a drink at the Imperial House Lounge on Waller Avenue. The lounge was part of the Imperial House Hotel, a full-service hotel and restaurant managed by the

---

5   Kincaid Towers grand opening booklet created by the company and distributed beginning September 1980.

6   Ibid.

7   Ibid.

famous Lexington restaurateur Stanley Demos. The hotel included meeting rooms, a fine-dining restaurant, and a bar and lounge that would feature entertainment. Many Lexington groups and clubs used its facilities over the years for lunches and dinners. The Imperial House was also a popular place with people who were in town for equestrian-related activities and events.

That afternoon, Ken was having a drink with another Lexington attorney, Harold Slone, when he met Sloan's new girlfriend, Callie M. Hundley. Callie, or Millie as she was usually called, was twenty-nine years old and a recently divorced mother of two. She grew up around Danville, Kentucky, and her father worked as an ammunition handler at the Avon ordinance depot in Richmond. Millie was a strikingly beautiful young lady with black, shoulder-length hair that included soft, bouncy curls, and she had a penchant for wearing short skirts and dresses. Millie had been working as a cocktail waitress at the Imperial since her recent divorce and this is where she met and began dating Harold Slone.

In 1983 Sloan would plead guilty to federal income tax violations and mail fraud, and his law partner, Andrew Carter Thornton II, would die at age forty in Knoxville, Tennessee, upon landing on a driveway with several million dollars' worth of cocaine strapped to his waist and a failed parachute strapped to his back. Thornton would also be one of the main characters in Sally Denton's book *The Bluegrass Conspiracy*.

Millie married her high school sweetheart, Lynn R. Hundley, in 1963. Lynn had joined the Navy, at the age of nineteen, before finishing his senior year of high school in 1961. He was stationed in the South Pacific on the carrier the *U.S.S. Hornet*, an anti–submarine warfare support ship. The local Danville paper frequently reported on his service. In June 1963, Lynn was on leave and was able to visit Millie and his family. The visit had an unexpected consequence, though, and the twenty-year-old Millie traveled to Los Angeles, where she and twenty-one-year-old Lynn were married on July 28, 1963. Their son Roger was born the following April.

Lynn and Millie had one more son, Kelvin, in 1967. Lynn and Millie's marriage lasted only ten years, and in November 1971 their divorce was granted. Millie had been her high school sweetheart's child bride and a mother by the age of twenty-one. Working in and hopefully moving to Lexington, the big city, probably seemed exciting to Millie in 1971. The now mature, twenty-nine-year-old woman could be more than just a mother and wife. Lexington certainly had more interesting possibilities for a young woman, who enjoyed music and had been trying her hand at writing songs.

Millie and Harold Slone's romance didn't last long, and by February 1972 they were no longer dating. This is when Ken Davis called her and asked her out. She met him for a drink at the Continental Inn. This was the beginning of their long affair, which lasted over ten years. Ken Davis, twenty years her senior, was truly infatuated and intoxicated with Millie. According to Millie, she attempted to end their relationship twice over the next three years. Once she moved back to Danville, and another time, she moved to Dayton, Ohio. Each time, she said, Ken would come after her.

After a few years, Ken officially had a mistress, but even after contracting herpes, he denied he was seeing another woman and Ella believed him. Millie continued to work as a cocktail waitress, but Ken was now helping to pay the rent on her apartment. After a while, his friends knew of the affair and accepted the lie he lived. Things dramatically changed in 1977 after Millie became pregnant. Millie quit her job as a cocktail waitress and was totally supported by Ken. She continued to work on her music and songwriting and in later years claimed that while she hadn't worked for six years, she was a self-employed, "published" songwriter. Ken soon moved her to the Kirklevington South apartments only a mile from his home. Ken's lie persisted, but he just couldn't forsake his wife or end his long-standing extramarital relationship with Millie Hundley.

It's impossible to understand everything that was going on in Ken Davis's mind in 1977. Garvice Kincaid had died in November of 1975, and it's hard to imagine how the loss of Kincaid and the installment of his committee was affecting his businesses and their staff. In 1977, Nelle and the Kincaid daughters had already filed lawsuits against Kincaid's Committee over decisions they were making. In addition, Nelle Kincaid and the Kincaid daughters had been encouraging American General Life Insurance Company to make a run at acquiring Kentucky Central Life, which American General did in 1978. Kentucky Central Life owned the stock of Kentucky Finance Company. During those early years after Garvice's death, if you were an employee in Kincaid's empire, you couldn't assume things would ever be the same—there would of course be changes, but Bud Burnett was always fond of saying "no problem."

In December 1977, Ken discovered he was having a baby with his mistress of five years, but before this news and even though he had a good job with Kentucky Finance, he did something else to complicate his life. In October of 1977, he filed articles of incorporation with Kentucky's Secretary of State's office to incorporate World Wide Gallery Ltd., listing the incorporator as his twenty-two-year son, Gregory Davis. World Wide Gallery would do business as World Wide Gifts, an "exclusive new home accessory store."[8] The store opened in Fayette Mall in September 1977. It is logical to assume that Ken Davis was acting as his son's bank for this new enterprise and that he was responsible for the company's liabilities. This new enterprise had to add to the pressure he was already under. In September 1979, the store was renamed The Davis Collection, and by the fall of 1980, wholesalers began to file lawsuits for money his son owed for merchandise. Ken kept his son in business for the next couple of years, but the store was forced to close around May 1982. In April 1984, twenty-nine-year-old Gregory Davis was indicted on drug charges for possessing twenty-five thousand quaaludes he had acquired from South America with the intent to sell. He was sentenced to five years in prison. Ken's effort to help his son had failed.

Misty Dawn Davis was born in September 1978. Millie said Ken held her hand as the baby was born. Millie also said that Ken never denied the child was his, but in September 1981, she filed a paternity suit. In that litigation, Davis admitted he was the father of the child. By 1980 the stress was really building for Ken, and his wife would say that around 1978, she first noticed changes in him. She said, "He would wake up at three or four in the morning and begin pacing the floor. He would say he was all mixed up, that things were all wrong." She said she couldn't pin him down; he just said, "It's the pressure, the pressure, the pressure."[9]

In early 1978, Ken added to his stress when that spring he decided to build a $15,000 in-ground pool at his house. Work was taking place in June of that year when he was notified that they were uncovering bones at the site. He was summoned from his office and the discovery was explained to him. It marked the beginning of nearly two days of discussions and mediation for Davis. The bones appeared to be animal bones, and there were pieces of pottery said to date to maybe the twelfth or thirteenth century—before any European contact by several hundred years. The site was believed to be a trash or fire pit used by the Fort Ancient culture, which may have been ancestors of the Shawnee Indians. They speculated that this was probably the oldest site ever discovered in Fayette County.

The University of Kentucky archaeologist wanted to dig into the site and sift the earth around the Indian pit, but Ken was worried that they would damage the pool since its wall had been poured. Ken wanted to know if the bones and pottery might be valuable, but the archaeologist couldn't give him

---

8   E.g., *Lexington Herald-Leader*, December 1, 1977.
9   *Lexington Herald-Leader*, September 1, 1982.

a value. He said he figured if the value was high enough it would cover any potential damage to the pool. In the end, Ken did not permit them to explore the site, and the pool was completed, probably destroying much of any future archaeological value. The *Lexington Herald-Leader* carried a full-page story, with pictures, about Ken and his pool in June 1978: "Swimming Pool Prevails Over Indian Artifacts."

While many people knew about Ken and Millie, it wasn't until 1980 that Ella learned the full truth. Ella Davis answered the door one day in the spring of 1980 and a workman was there to apply for a job to work on the house that Ken was building for Millie and their daughter. According to Millie, Ken had tried to build a home off Tates Creek Road and incurred a $26,000 debt, and that had led to a lawsuit by the builder, and on another occasion they were going to build a house on the Kentucky River. These revolutions forced Ken Davis to come clean about his double life. He was forced to tell his wife about his thirty-seven-year-old mistress he had been having an affair with for the last eight years and his two-year-old daughter with her. With this news, the Davis marriage soon became the equivalent of the movie *The War of the Roses*.

According to various accounts, Ella Davis started tracking her husband's every move. His secretary would say that Ella might call the office ten times a day. She recalled one occasion when Ken had gone to the bank and Mrs. Davis didn't believe her: "He's not with that woman, is he? Because if he is, I'll Kill him."[10] Another friend of Ken's said Ella told him that she "beat the hell out of him (Davis) in a hotel lobby"[11] in San Diego. According to Carroll Horton, a longtime friend of Ken Davis, Ella overhead Ken speaking with Millie on the telephone, and she grabbed the receiver and used it to beat her husband in the head.

Apparently, there were constant incidents of violence and threats of violence, including a time when a policeman reported that Ella pulled up behind her husband's Cadillac at a stop sign and fired a bullet into the trunk. Ella said Ken owned more than a dozen guns and this one just happened to be on the floor of the car she was driving because it had slid from under the seat. Ken had been driving over to Millie's apartment at the time of the shooting.

In January of 1982, the marriage of thirty-eight years was ending. Ken moved out of the house and for three weeks lived at a friend's home in Frankfort before moving in with Millie at the Kirklevington South apartment. On February 8, 1982, Ella filed for divorce, claiming her husband physically abused her throughout their marriage, threatened her life on at least one

---

10   Ibid.
11   Ibid.

occasion, and caused others to threaten her life. In Ken Davis's response to the petition, he alleged that his wife had hit him with several objects, including a telephone and a marble cigarette lighter; had threatened to kill him; and had fired a pistol at him on one occasion. This same month, Ken would leave his position at Kentucky Finance. Initially it was reported that he retired early, but later accounts reported that he was terminated.

Each also accused the other of maliciously manipulating family finances. Ella said Ken had withdrawn all the money from their bank accounts, leaving her with no income or means of support. He, in turn, said she had been selling family assets without his knowledge or consent. The judge issued a court order providing that they were not to come in contact with each other, but friends said there were multiple occasions where they came into close contact.

In May 1982, everything came to a head when Ella Davis shot and killed Ken Davis at their Burkshire Drive home. Ken had arrived at the house a little after 1:00 p.m. to, Ella said, "drop off some utility bills"[12] that had been delivered to his law office. She said they briefly talked in the kitchen and Ken said, "While I am here, I am going to get something." Ella said she followed him upstairs, and after talking for a while in the bedroom, she watched as Davis went down the hall and into a large hall closet. Ella thought Ken was looking for a gun and she knew there was a pistol and shotgun in the hall closet. She said she tried to go down the hallway, but Ken saw her so she grabbed the .38 Special revolver from the hall closet, and he pinned her against the closet door and doorknob with his back. Ella said she pleaded with him to let her go but he refused. The gun was jammed into his back, and as she pushed against him, it went off accidentally.

The three-day trial began on August 31, 1982, and featured some of Lexington's most prominent citizens as witnesses, jurors, and spectators heard the riveting testimony about Kenneth Davis's extramarital affair with Millie Hundley, a cocktail waitress he'd met at a local lounge, and the daughter he shared with Hundley. The one issue that Ella could not explain was how she shot Ken three times in the back. The medical examiner described the shots as "well-spaced across his back." Ella said she remembered when the gun first went off but had no recollection of firing the second and third shots. The Fayette Circuit Court jury took only four hours to return a verdict of second-degree manslaughter against Ella Davis and recommended a seven-year sentence, which Judge George Barker agreed with at sentencing. Assistant Commonwealth Attorney Bennie Hicks termed the shooting "the final

---

12   Ibid.

desperate act of a scorned woman who had decided that if she couldn't have him, no one else would."

Ella's attorney, Mike Maloney, tried to get a mistrial and to have the verdict set aside, but to no avail. Ella was sent to the Kentucky Correctional Institution for Women at Pee Wee Valley and would be eligible for parole in seventeen months.

As with most Southern sagas, there was a Paul Harvey–like "rest of the story." The Davis saga doesn't end with Ella going to prison. First, her attorney was somewhat successful in his appeal and was able to get Ella released from prison on parole after only serving two months. His appeal focused on the trial judge allowing unproved and alleged statements by Ella in the Commonwealth's opening statement and as evidence:

> The court erred in overruling the motion of the defendant to prohibit the commonwealth in its opening statement and in its proof from discussing and introducing evidence regarding alleged or actual prior incidents of violence on the part of the defendant directed toward the victim. The court further erred in admitting as evidence statement allegedly made by the defendant.[13]

After entering prison, Ella's attorney wrote a letter to the parole board requesting an early parole hearing for Ella. A hearing was granted, and she was released after serving only two months. The head of the parole board indicated that early parole releases such as Ella's happen only maybe once a year. The reason for the hearing and early release was that "she was considered a good parole risk"[14] and they didn't think further incarceration would be in the best interest of society. Ella's son Gregory also would receive an early release from prison after serving only four months. After leaving prison, Ella Davis moved in with her sister, who lived in Prestonsburg, and began working as a retail salesclerk.

Her conviction for second-degree murder would stand. This would mean that Ella, even though she was released, could never profit from killing her husband and she had forfeited any interest she had in his estate or life insurance.

Not much is known about Ella's life after she was released. She died at her residence in Lexington in February 2007 at age eighty-seven after being in hospice. She is buried in the Lexington Cemetery next to her husband Kenneth.

Things didn't quite go as planned for Millie Hundley and her daughter Misty Dawn either. In January of 1982, Ken made a new will bequeathing $100,000 each to Millie and Misty. That will could not be probated, though,

---

13   *Lexington Herald-Leader*, September 10, 1982.
14   *Lexington Herald-Leader*, January 24, 1985.

because apparently it was executed incorrectly. Instead, the court probated a will dated April 29, 1970, and of course neither Millie nor Misty was provided for in that will. Since Ella Davis wasn't entitled to any of the estate due to killing her husband, the estate was to be divided equally between the three Davis children, Ken Davis's two sons and Misty Dawn.

There were various court proceedings about the Davis estate. The house and possessions were auctioned off first, in 1985, by Thompson & Riley Ltd. After the mortgage was paid off and commissions and expenses were paid, Misty received $21,000. The next battle involved Ken's life insurance and other employee benefits. In 1983, the estate of Ken Davis filed three lawsuits against three life insurance companies and Kentucky Finance seeking a total of $4,400,000. Davis held life insurance policies with Harford Accident and Indemnity Co., Kentucky Central Life Insurance Co., and Manhattan Life Insurance, and all refused to pay. Kentucky Finance was named because it held the group policies through the insurance companies. Kentucky Finance was eventually released from the suit.

Kentucky Finance's attorneys told the estate's executor, Marshall Woodson, that Davis resigned on February 8, 1982, more than three months before his death. However, the suit maintained that Davis continued to work for the company with the understanding that his job would officially end on August 6, 1982. During this time, the company continued to deduct the group life insurance premiums from his salary. The cases went on until late in 1984, when a Fayette Circuit Court jury determined that Kenneth Davis was still covered at the time of his death under two of the group life insurance policies. Apparently, Davis was really terminated, and as part of his severance agreement, he was to receive six months of salary and benefits. In addition, the jury agreed that his death was accidental, and the estate was entitled to double the benefits based on a provision in the policy. In the end, the estate collected $1,600,000 from Manhattan Life's $500,000 policy. The face amount of the benefit was doubled, and the company had to pay interest of $600,000 due to the delay in payment. Kentucky Central Life's policy was changed to an employee life insurance policy from an officer's life insurance policy, since Davis was no longer an officer of Kentucky Finance. Kentucky Central paid $12,000, plus interest. An undisclosed amount was paid in a settlement reached with Hartford Life.

The final chapter of this saga happened in March 1985 when Millie was removed as the legal guardian for the financial estate of her daughter Misty Dawn. Her former attorney petitioned the court to appoint an independent corporate guardian to oversee the financial affairs of Misty Dawn. That attorney was concerned that because Millie was not entitled to any portion of Ken Davis's estate and had no income other than the social security payment she received for Misty Dawn's care and upkeep, Millie was too conflicted and Misty needed independent professional management of her inheritance. He said that "Ms. Hundley is inexperienced at managing large sums of money."[15] The judge agreed. Misty Dawn would soon receive over $500,000 as her portion of her father's estate, and the judge would appoint Danville attorney Richard Campbell, who had been a temporary guardian several months before, as the new guardian for Misty. Richard Campbell said he would work with a Danville bank to manage Misty's estate. Millie would have little access to her daughter's assets.

In June 1962, Kentucky Finance formalized the management structure that Kincaid and Bartella had been working on in an announcement:

Kentucky Finance Creates Several New Exec Positions

Rapid expansion has made it necessary for the directors of Kentucky Finance Co. Inc. to create several new executive posts, R. M. Bartella, vice president of operations for the company announced. The decision was made at a recent directors' meeting held at the company's home offices here. [A detailed write-up of the promotions and new positions followed.]

By September 1962, Kincaid's Kentucky Finance Company had greatly expanded with the help of Robert M. Bartella. The company had grown from its eighteen offices located in sixteen Kentucky cities when Bartella joined the company to eighty offices in eight states. Kincaid recognized the work of Robert that year and promoted him to executive vice president of the company. He was still in charge of operations, but the forty-six-year-old Bartella was now responsible for a sizable staff and organization and would soon be consolidating the operations of PIB with Kentucky Finance's operations. Kincaid took the first step in October of 1964 and moved PIB's corporate headquarters from Washington, D.C., to the partially renovated Lafayette Hotel Building (aka the Kentucky Central Life Building) in Lexington.

In 1964 Kincaid held an open house in Kentucky Finance's new corporate headquarters in the Kentucky Central Life Building. Garvice invited bank presidents and other representatives from banks throughout the eastern half of the United States. He was eager to show off his "aggressively growing Kentucky based companies."[16] The company that year would have eighty-five

---

15 *Lexington Herald-Leader*, March 20, 1985.
16 *Lexington Herald-Leader*, October 4, 1964.

offices in eight states and assets exceeding $35 million dollars. In addition, PIB would have a total of fifty-four total offices operating in six states and assets of $14 million dollars. Garvice was like a proud father; he wanted to show how well his finance company offspring had done by the young age of eighteen.

In the decade before Kincaid's death in 1975, Kentucky Finance concentrated on phasing out offices located in areas that were not promising in terms of growth or that demonstrated signs of potential economic problems. Thirty-seven offices were sold or closed and an additional thirty-six were purchased or opened, resulting in 138 offices in operation on December 1, 1975.

In 1971, Garvice celebrated Bartella's twentieth year with the company and congratulated him for his many successes. When Garvice Kincaid died in November 1975, the finance company he had started from scratch in 1946 had grown to 147 offices, in thirteen states and had over $94 million in assets. Robert Bartella continued Kincaid's work for eight more years and retired in January 1984. In preparation for Bartella's retirement, the Committee brought in Luther Spence as president of Kentucky Finance. Spence had a thirty-year career in consumer finance and came from C.I.T. Financial Services, where he was a vice president. Spence would continue to lead the company until it was sold by the Committee in May 1991. The Committee hoped the sale would shore up Kentucky Central Life's financial strength by boosting its capital.

Associates Corporation of North America purchased Kentucky Finance in 1991. Associates Corporation was a subsidiary of Ford Motor Credit. At the time of the sale, Kentucky Finance had assets of $290 million, 159 offices, and nine hundred employees spread over ten states. The sale price was $145 million. While this helped to replenish Kentucky Central Life's capital, it only delayed the company's complete collapse.

In May 1991, things were so bad at Kentucky Central Life Insurance Company that Bud Burnett and the Committee were forced to sell Kincaid's crown jewel, Kentucky Finance, for $145 million ($65 million over its book value of $80 million). In addition, that June, they sold Kentucky Central Life's very profitable career insurance division for $39 million to Liberty Life Insurance Company. The Committee was raising $195 million through sales, for an additional $104 million ($65 million plus $39 million) of capital, to cover Kentucky Central Life's mortgage loan and real estate losses. In addition, by selling these operations, they had removed over $25 million of annual earnings from a company that had reported only $35 million of total annual earnings in 1989 and 1990 (before mortgage loan and real estate write-offs). This was a perfect example of the saying of Hippocrates, the famous Greek physician, "desperate times call for desperate measures." This extreme action may have worked if the Committee and specifically Bud Burnett had avoided any further investments in commercial mortgage loans and real estate, but they didn't; business and personal relationships appeared to be controlling the decisions they were making.

Chapter Four: Kincaid Moves into Banking

In the early 1930s the United States was still struggling with the effects of the 1929 depression. Bank failures and the attitude of those bankers who had survived continued to restrain the economy. Government legislation enacted in the 1930s was designed to protect banks from competing with one another too aggressively, and this also restricted bank behavior. For instance, the Banking Act of 1933 prohibited the payment of interest by member banks on demand deposits. It also authorized the Federal Reserve Board to set a ceiling on time deposit rates offered by member banks to prevent potentially damaging competition among banks. In addition, it ordered the separation of investment banking from commercial banking.

The Banking Act of 1935 similarly incorporated provisions designed to limit bank behavior. The legislation expanded the supervisory powers of the Federal Deposit Insurance Corporation (FDIC) and set more rigorous standards for admission to receive this valuable insurance. Economic conditions improved from their low point reached in 1933. Unemployment declined significantly, and real GNP increased at an average annual compound growth rate of 9.5 percent between 1933 and 1937, and price increases moderated. A recession in 1937–1938 interrupted the nation's economic expansion, but conditions improved once again as real GNP rose and unemployment abated. These 1930s bank regulatory improvements were credited with reducing the severity of this recession.

Most banks in America are state-chartered banks. It's the same today as it was in the 1930s and 1940s. What has changed today is that the majority of all bank deposits are held in banks with national charters. The banks are federally regulated by the Office of the Controller of Currency. State-chartered banks are considered easier to start and are regulated by local state agencies, in conjunction with the FDIC. This has historically meant that local relationships and local politics can cushion the impact of any regulatory oversight. In Kentucky, state-chartered banks have traditionally been started by local community leaders, and Kentucky has historically had a great many state-charted banks. Acquiring or starting a state-charted bank is a relatively simple method of entering the world of banking.

One limiting factor, though, in Kentucky's early years was that banks were prohibited from operating outside their county. In addition, multi-branch bank holding companies were prohibited. These restrictions would not change until 1984, when the Kentucky legislature would pass House Bill 67, which allowed holding companies to acquire banks in more than one county. Still in existence are restrictions that limit a bank from having more than 20 percent of the deposits in a county. An additional restriction for Garvice Kincaid was that Kentucky's regulations prohibited individuals from controlling more than one bank in the state. Kincaid pieced together his bank holdings despite the state law against an individual having more than 50 percent ownership of more than one bank. Kincaid once explained it this way: "Your wife can own 10 percent and you can own 50 percent."[1] Kentucky state banking laws wouldn't be changed until 1984, and even then, the path to the legislation was marred in scandal and corruption, including an FBI investigation and the nephew of Governor Wallace Wilkinson and others being fined and/or going to jail for bribery and violating the state's ethic and corruption statutes.

Stan Galbraith, a former vice president at Kincaid's National Bank of Paris, explained it this way.

> The Kentucky Banking Statutes back in the 60s and the 70s prohibited Kincaid from owning more than 50% of the stock of more than one bank, so Kincaid would own 35% and then put some of that stock in his wife's name and sometimes also in Jane and Joan's name. After Al Florence became involved, he would put some in Al's name and others depending on the situation. So that way, he still controlled all of these banks and there were probably 15 or 16 banks in Kentucky he controlled in the 1970s at any one time. Plus, he had the two or three banks he owned in Florida.[2]

While some third-party investors might legitimately own up to maybe 25 percent of a Kincaid bank, Kincaid's close business associates who had ownership interests in his banks were given stock by Kincaid if they signed a loan agreement and also executed an option agreement that allowed Kincaid to reacquire their shares at any time. After his death, the *Herald-Leader* reported that the option price was usually set at 75 percent of the bank's book value. Kincaid may have structured the option price this way so that options were always "in the money." It was a live option and had monetary value. The collateral or security for the loans was the bank's share certificates, which prevented someone from doing anything with their shares, and the options

---

1   *Louisville Courier Journal*, July 25, 1971.
2   Interview of Stan Galbraith by the author.

gave Kincaid the ability to make sure the nominee-owners always voted according to Garvice's wishes. He was just a brilliant guy!

After his death, Kincaid's daughters would file a lawsuit against the Committee and Central Bank. They owned shares in four Kentucky Banks—Danville, Manchester, Winchester, and Carlisle—and also the Marathon Bank in Florida. The Committee was trying to exercise Kincaid's options to acquire these shares, and the daughters contended that only their father could exercise them. A similar suit involved the stock of Lexington Finance Company, which owned 10 percent of the shares of Central Bank & Trust. The courts ruled that the trust could exercise the options on the bank stocks but that the option on the shares of Lexington Finance Company was not structured correctly. This verdict led to his daughters owning 10 percent of the shares of Central Bank & Trust. The case began in 1977 and continued to 1981. The Kincaid daughters wanted to appeal their bank verdict to the U.S. Supreme Court but waited until the last day they could file to submit their papers. In the rush, a $50 filing fee was omitted, and the court rejected their filing.

A couple of 1970 and 1971 bank purchases are good examples of how Garvice acquired his banks:

Peoples Bank and Trust Co., of Berea. The Berea Bank and Capital Trust Co. closed on October 9, 1970, having been declared insolvent. Kincaid and Al Florence purchased the fixed assets of the defunct bank for an undisclosed sum during the next week. On October 19, a new bank was incorporated, Peoples Bank and trust Co., of Berea by Kincaid and his group. The Commissioner of Banking, E. G. Adams, had approved its articles of incorporation for this bank on the same day. The organization was capitalized at $200,000, with 20,000 shares of stock, par value $10.00 each, being authorized for sale. Subscribers to the stock in the new bank included the following: "Donald Pennington—150 shares; Howard Jennings—1,500 shares; Hirshel Jones—1,250 shares; J. Lee Young—1,250 shares; Robert Long—250 shares; C. Sergeant—50 shares—All of Berea; Garvice D. Kincaid—5,317 shares; Al Florence—5,667 shares; and Earl S. Wilson—5,316 shares—Lexington."[3]

Kincaid and his group of buyers owned 16,300 shares or 78.55% of the bank and the other shareholders owned 4,450 shares or 21.45% of the bank. Apparently, Kincaid also amended the articles of incorporation and increased the shares to 20,750 shares. It appears the Berea shareholder group needed 750 more shares than Kincaid initially planned to issue. Kincaid directly owns 25.6% of the bank and Al Florence is the bank's largest shareholder, by one share of stock.

---

3   *Lexington Herald-Leader*, October 21, 1970.

Citizens National Bank of Somerset, Ky. On Monday, September 27, 1971, Garvice Kincaid and Al Florence purchased 650 shares of the 1,000 outstanding shares of the bank for $1,592,500. The stock was sold at an administrator's sale, at Pulaski County Courthouse, to settle the estate of J.J.B. Williams, who was president and board chairman of the bank. He had died in November.

Kincaid and Florence acquired 65% of the bank shares and together could now control the bank. One can probably correctly assume that each of them was the registered owner of 325 shares.[4]

These factors were relevant because they restricted how Kincaid could own and control his banking businesses. In addition, and more importantly, these restrictions would affect how Kincaid's Committee could handle these assets after his death. Those banking assets would be held in his estate trust, at Central Bank, and just as the Purcell estate was forced to sell Central Exchange Bank, the Kincaid trust would be required to dispose of most of Garvice's banks.

Bank managements learned to avoid some of these bank restrictions by forming "chain or group banks." A chain bank is a collection of banks owned by an individual or a group of individuals. A "group bank," which is the historical term used for a bank holding company, is a collection of banks owned by a holding company or a trust. A bank holding company could operate branches in multiple states. These branches would be considered independent banks and therefore in compliance with the law. As Garvice acquired control of more banks, they all were operated independently until around 1970, when he developed the operational umbrella The Kentucky Group Banks. They were still independent corporations, but their systems and management structures were synchronized and coordinated as a single organization.

Kincaid and Central Exchange Bank

In March 1938, things had improved, so it wasn't surprising to see some enterprising men organizing a new bank in Lexington. The men were Harry W. Moores, John S. Yellman, James H. Alexander, W. David Thompson, and William S. Branaman. Harry Moores had been associated with banking in Lexington for many years and had recently served as an executive officer for the old Fayette Bank until it became affiliated with the First National Bank and Trust Company. John Yellman was also a local banker and was a vice president at the First National Bank and Trust Company. James Alexander was a local businessman and farmer who owned two farms in Woodford County. David

---

Thompson was a 1934 University of Kentucky graduate who had worked in Goodyear Tire and Rubber Company's accounting department in Akron, Ohio. He had resigned his position in Akron to become associated with the bank. William Branaman was a native of Lexington and a University of Kentucky graduate. He had recently worked for the FDIC covering five states. Branaman would be a vice president working in the bank.

The September 1938 announcement noted:

> The bank is headed by officers well known in the banking circles and is in a position to render a valuable service to those seeking funds to finance or refinance real estate, automobiles or any sort of saleable chattel. The bank also makes co-maker loans. . . and should be in a position to make F.H.A. loans within 30 days and at the present time offer loans on real estate at interest rates as low as 4 ¾ percent.

In April, the company had amended its articles of incorporation to specify that the name under which it would be conducting and "contracting" business would be "Central Exchange Bank." Jefferson Davis (J.D.) Purcell isn't mentioned, but he and Harry W. Moores were the controlling shareholders of the bank. J.D. Purcell was a prominent, wealthy, local retailer with various real estate and business interests. His J.D. Purcell Company was the forerunner to the modern five and dime stores. He came to Lexington after working in New York as a jobber and in Virginia, where he opened a retail store. After he met his wife, Ida Campbell Plumber, he moved to Lexington and opened a store, which he eventually sold to American Department Stores in 1927. In 1933, during the height of the Great Depression, he regained control of his former business. J.D. Purcell Company would remain an important retailer on Lexington's Main Street for decades.

In 1938, the Central Exchange Bank was initially capitalized with $70,000 of capital, and by June of the following year, the bank had grown to two $245,000 in assets. It wasn't until July 1941 that the bank was granted certification by the FDIC and had its depositors' individual accounts insured up to $5,000. In December 1940, Central Exchange Bank had total assets of over $300,000, and by June 1944 the bank had total assets of almost $550,000. The bank, while still quite small, had grown by over 500 percent in five years. In its FDIC insurance announcement, J.D. Purcell is listed as a director of the bank.

J. D. Purcell died in June 1943 at age eighty-three. He had been seventy-eight years old in 1938 when he agreed to help Harry Moores start the bank. J.D. Purcell loved Lexington and the Bluegrass. In a letter to the *Lexington Herald* published on January 7, 1940, he wrote:

About fifty-three years ago I came to Lexington, and at that early date the possibilities for progress were outstanding—I immediately decided to locate my new store in this thriving community—My judgement of the then small village proved accurate, as the years rolled by—I watched Lexington grow, saw one improvement after another take place. My pride increased constantly from year to year in my adopted home, until now I would feel honored at being considered a native.

···   Nowhere can a community be found where a person is so interlocking to his fellowman as in this locality—We thrive as our community thrives—We depend on one another here for everything we possess. Where else could be found such magnificent farms—such gorgeous colonial mansion—so many historic buildings—so many fine institutions of learning—and literally hundreds of other fine features that few, if any, communities can boast.

J.D. Purcell and his impact on Lexington would be remembered for many decades after his death. Purcell's daughter was appointed executrix and was required to post a $452,000 bond. His estate had an estimated value of over $8,000,000 in today's money.

In 1945, Bill Courtney was president of First National Bank & Trust in Lexington. First National was considered Lexington's oldest bank. Bill had been associated with the bank since 1913. According to Kincaid in a March 24, 1968, *Louisville Courier Journal* story, Bill Courtney contacted him in June 1945 about acquiring Central Exchange Bank. The bank was in the Purcell estate, and First National controlled the estate. First National needed to raise money to pay Purcell's estate taxes, and it also faced a regulatory issue of owning a controlling interest in a third-party bank through its trust department.

Garvice had never considered owning a bank, and he said the idea shook him. "I thought Courtney was kidding, I didn't know anything about banks. The bank had $400,000 in assets and our costs (purchase price) were about $100,000. There were six banks in town then. I said sure." Garvice and four other investors acquired Central Exchange Bank from the Purcell estate and also Harry Moores' stock on June 23, 1945. Garvice was of course the majority shareholder. The four other investors were A.G. Evans, R. Mack Oldham, Eldon S. Dummit, and William S. Snyder. Kincaid was named president; A.G. Evans, executive vice president, and Mrs. Patton, cashier.

Garvice's 1968 description of the purchase may have been a little off, because the bank's June 30, 1945, financial statement shows the bank had total assets of almost $700,000 and capital of over $125,000. This might suggest that Garvice paid $100,000 for his interest in the bank and brought in investors for the additional twenty-five thousand. It was reported in June 30, 1945, that

Garvice had also brought in M.C. Haddix, whom he had partnered with in 1942 on the purchase of Joyland Park. He had also made Haddix a director for Kentucky Finance Company, replacing Dummit and Snyder. This probably means that M.C. Haddix was an early investor in Kentucky Finance. With Kincaid's 1945 purchase of Central Exchange Bank, he had started on a path to becoming a major force in banking and the financial community. In 1950, M. C. Haddix died and Garvice and L.D. Nickles acquire his 26 percent of the bank for almost $73,000.

Central Exchange had its office on the corner of Short Street and Upper Street in what would become known as the "old" Central Bank building. The advertised address was 159 West Short Street, and in its beginning it shared its first floor with a Curry's Drug store. The seven-story building still exists today and is the home of Traditional Bank.

The building was erected by Byron McClelland in 1896 as a five-story building, and two years later was increased in height by two stories. It is regarded as Lexington's first skyscraper. The building was known as the McClelland Building until January 1946, when Kincaid acquired it. He purchased it from Mrs. T.B. "Nettie" Satterwhite for $150,000, and that April changed its name to the "Central Bank Building." On the ground floor, in addition to the bank and the Curry's Drug store, it contained the Kentucky Female Orphan School and the law office of Kincaid and M.H. Harris. In the other six stories there were approximately one hundred offices.

In 1946, Kincaid had been in business for almost ten years. He had made a small fortune buying and selling real estate, he owned and managed Lexington's Joyland Amusement Park, and he had plans to rapidly grow his consumer finance businesses, Lexington Finance and Kentucky Finance Company. Garvice was already a very busy person when he received the call from Bill Courtney, president of First National Bank & Trust, about purchasing the bank. Much of Kincaid's history suggests that he tended to be an opportunistic investor. In other words, he would see something or be approached about something and, if interested, move quickly. As he would say in later years about his empire, he was always risking only his own money. During the first twenty years of Garvice's business career, he wasn't using loans to finance his acquisitions. If necessary, he might bring in some minority partners or possibly have one of his businesses issue common or preferred stock to give him some extra capital. Kincaid wasn't crippling his businesses with debt or his new acquisitions with debt, and this gave him a tremendous amount of flexibility. Kincaid also didn't have to answer to anyone but himself, and the way he financed them made his investments safer and more self-sustaining.

In later years, as Kincaid's empire moved into radio and television broadcasting, with those industries' high, embedded, fixed costs, Garvice might have one of his banks or his insurance company issue a mortgage loan on the facilities, but it was a loan he would control. In the 1940s and through most of the1960s, most lenders, borrowers, and households retained some memory of the Great Depression. The shadow of that period, though, would begin to rapidly fade in the 1970s, and by the 1980s, Wall Street's leverage buyout boom would begin and a man named Michael Milken, at a firm called Drexel Burnham, would create a whole new class of investments called "junk bonds" or "high-yield debt." These instruments would revolutionize how business acquisitions would transpire and cause acquisition prices to dramatically increase.

One can only imagine what Kincaid would have thought of this phenomenon. In future years, Kincaid's Committee would fail to respect Garvice's conservative financial wisdom and prudent investment principles, and much of his empire would disappear. Most of what this one man built, so meticulously and prudently, would be massively mismanaged and financially destroyed by the very men he trusted.

Garvice and the Joyland Amusement Park

Joyland was Fayette County's largest amusement park for nearly forty years. The park sat on twenty-five acres of land and contained a kiddie railroad, a midway with arcade games, Lexington's first public swimming pool, the Club Joy Dance and Casino, and the park's most popular attraction, the Wildcat roller coaster, which was built in the late 1920s. During the roaring '20s, Joyland was Lexington's place to be during the summer.

Kentucky author Kurt Robinson did a nice job describing Joyland in his "Explore Kentucky History" piece:

> The park officially opened on May 30, 1923 along Paris Pike on the northside of Lexington. Early on it was owned and operated by Frank Brandt and brothers John W. Sauer and F. Keller Sauer. The Sauer brothers ran the park while Brandt managed everything else. Another partner, A.M. James, ran the Club Joy Dance and Casino. The parking lot was big enough to hold nearly 5,000 cars and admission during the week was free but, the rides, food, and games cost money to enjoy. However, the owners would let the orphans of Lexington come and play games and ride rides for free several times a year. White children could also take free swimming lessons at the pool.

Club Joy Dance and Casino cost 50 cents during the week and 75 cents on the weekend. They hosted many parties that included dancing, which were held Tuesday-Saturday. The Club also hosted the Miss Kentucky Beauty Contest throughout the 1930s. But what made Club Joy stand was the many celebrity acts, singers, and bands, that they hosted. Throughout the '30s and '40s, the club hosted acts like The Bluegrass Troubadours, Smoke Richardson and his Orchestra, and even Duke Ellington and Arte Shaw. Many of the acts were broadcasted live through the radio with the call letters WLEX beginning in 1933. Those call letters were licensed as an official radio station in 1946.

Despite the word casino in its title, Club Joy did not actually have gambling games or machines in the casino area. Although there were reports of illegal gambling behind the scenes, but it was never confirmed, and no one was ever charged.

The Joyland Amusement Park also had a playground for kids to spend time on when attractions got too crowded or parents could not afford to pay for the other rides. There were also baseball and softball fields on the grounds where they hosted many different league games and teams from other communities came to play games and tournaments. There was also a miniature zoo that featured many animals including a bear, monkey, wolf, alligator, and an anteater.

Joyland remained a segregated entertainment venue throughout its era of operation. Black families were welcomed to the park only on "special" reserved days. Black children were not allowed at the Joyland Pool. The Lexington Leader provided free swimming lessons for white children at Joyland's pool and for Black children at the Douglass Park pool. Though host to many Black entertainers, the casino and Club Joy were segregated as well.

Throughout the 50s, after Joyland had changed owners, the park slowly began to close sections down as people began to lose interest. As more amusement parks, particularly bigger ones, and movies became much more popular, people slowly stopped coming to the park. It wasn't until August of 1963 when the park shut down fully as loss of business finally struck its final blow.

After the shutdown, Club Joy caught on fire in 1964 and was damaged beyond repair so it was torn down. . . .[5]

After the 1964 fire, Kincaid formed Kentucky Colonial Farms Inc. to hold Joyland and had the park rezoned for development in 1965. The rezoned land would become the home of the Joyland subdivision, several apartment buildings, a shopping center, and Mary Todd Elementary School. Garvice

---

5   Kurt Robinson, "Joyland Park," ExploreKYHistory, accessed May 9, 2023, https://explorekyhistory.ky.gov/items/show/870.

acquired Joyland for $54,000 in 1942 and in 1965, with the rezoning, turned the twenty-five-acre park into a multimillion-dollar residential and mixed-use development.

Garvice's history with Joyland Park is important because of how he developed and used his relationships. Many of the relationships he developed and depended on over the years were with people that he just gotten to know. In the early years, many important relationships and employees were people he went to law school with or local attorneys whom he had come to respect. Sometimes it would be people who had offices in buildings where he kept his law office. His chief accountant for Central Bank was a local man named H.A. Smith, who had a small public accounting office in the Central Bank building.

Hardes Avery "Bud" Smith became a loyal and dedicated Kincaid employee and worked at the bank for thirty-five years. He joined Kincaid and Central Bank as assistant cashier and became cashier shortly thereafter. Bud Smith was a well-known vice president who became a loan officer, a director in the trust department, and a financial advisor, and who was a member of the bank's board of directors. Smith retired from the bank in 1981.

Smith had worked as an accountant for Lexington's National Biscuit Company (Nabisco Brands) and Sylvania Electric from 1942 to 1945 and only had his accounting practice open for about a year when the thirty-year-old was recruited to the bank. Garvice was known to be always looking for talented people who could help him, and in 1946 he found Bud Smith.

John Irving—It's for You!

Joyland Park also brought Garvice in contact with another young person whom he would later hire in March 1975 before his death in November 1975. That person was John G. Irvin. In 1946, about nine months after Kincaid acquired Central Exchange Bank and admitted that he didn't know anything about banking, he did something that was pure Kincaid: he purchased 75 percent of the stock in First National Bank of Carlisle from Mrs. Harry S. King of Carlisle and Mr. and Mrs. Leer Buckley of Lexington. Garvice again brought in partners: Dr. William S. Snyder Jr., a Frankfort surgeon, and Edward Jones of Lexington, who had been in banking for eighteen years with Security Trust Company before entering the military.

Garvice and the other men became directors, and the bank's president for the last twenty-five years, Harry T. Letton, was retained in that position. First National Bank of Carlisle had $50,000 of capital and $2,000.000 in deposits. This acquisition would have cost the men around $38,000, and one can assume that Kincaid maintained majority control by owning at least 51 percent of the bank and that his investment would have been a little over $25,000.

One may wonder how a bank in Carlisle has anything has to do with Joyland Park, and this is where a person can begin to appreciate how Kincaid's circle of relationships developed. Dr. Walter Granville Irvin was a Carlisle veterinarian who was one of the local shareholders of the First National Bank of Carlisle. Dr. Irvin left private practice after several years and went to work for the U.S. Department of Agriculture, where he spent thirty years. In addition to eventually becoming president of the Carlisle bank, he was president of the Ratliff Brothers Lumber Company in Carlisle and also an extensive landowner. He died in 1963 at the age of seventy-seven.

Garvice Kincaid got to know Dr. Irvin through his ownership in the Carlisle bank and probably appreciated his accomplishments and status in the community. He eventually appointed Dr. Irvin president of the bank, a position he held until he died in 1963. His son, John Irvin, explained his first experience with Kincaid and how important Kincaid's Joyland Amusement Park was to the Central Kentucky community in a 2004 *Lexington Herald* article written by Don Edwards.

> "Garvice Kincaid was nothing if not a risk-taker." Irvin was looking at a circa-1946 photo of Harry James, husband of movie star Betty Grable. James was playing his trumpet to an entranced crowd at the Joyland Casino at the old Joyland Amusement Park, which once stood next to Paris Road just outside of town. Admission was $2.50.
>
> Garvice Kincaid was the owner. "What you can't see in the picture, is that there's no roof on the place. Kincaid took a chance that it wouldn't rain. If it had rained, he's have lost a lot of money on that one." No wonder Joyland used to advertise "dancing under the stars."
>
> "When I was a twelve-year old kid, I can remember my older sister being excited about going on a date to Joyland to hear Vaughn Monroe and his orchestra. Monroe was going to sing his hits that we had heard on the radio, such as "Racing with the Moon" and "Ghost Riders in the Sky."
>
> "Six years later, I was a teenager going to Joyland to hear rock 'n' roll acts. The Big Band era had ended abruptly when the popular music of young people had taken a whole new direction. I couldn't believe how quickly it was over. When I was working at Joyland booking bands after World War II, I had no idea it would be over in the next decade."
>
> "There were two venues, actually. The casino was a big dance

floor, and the smaller bar was called the Club Joy. There was a popular cocktail in the 1950's called a zombie, made with three kinds of rum, one which was 151 proof. I can remember a sign behind a Joyland bar: "If You Can Drink Three of Our Zombies and Walk to the Bar, You Get the Fourth One Free."

Irwin, a Carlisle native whose father was a veterinarian, grew up in several counties in Central Kentucky and knew the territory. He was a music fan and had played the clarinet. "My parents asked my clarinet teacher if I had any talent. He said: 'Your son holds the clarinet exactly like Benny Goodman. Unfortunately, that's as far as it goes.'"

John Irvin had gotten the Joyland job when his father told Kincaid that Irvin was taking only one course in summer school at the University of Kentucky and needed more to do (circa 1946, age twenty-two). Kincaid gave him a job selling hotdogs in July at the amusement park. On his first day, Irvin saw a man working hard for twelve hours, heaving a case of soft drinks in each hand and was astonished to find out the man was Kincaid. Irvin, hot and tired and discouraged, told Kincaid he wasn't cut out to sell hotdogs.

Kincaid had recently made a mistake booking a band. He had thought he was booking Fletcher Henderson, famed in the 1940's for his "rolling saxophone sounds." Instead, the booker was sending someone he'd never heard of: Lyle "Skitch" Henderson (later to be famous as the director of "The Tonight Show" band).

Irvin says he spread advertising material about Skitch Henderson within a thirty-five-mile radius of Lexington (even in restrooms) and handed out some free passes. When Henderson played, he drew a huge crowd, and Irvin got the job as Joyland's band booker.

"I knew Henderson was good. Once we were somewhere in Lexington and Henderson got a phone call from Frank Sinatra wanting to hire him. People here thought the call was a joke, but it wasn't."

Right away, Irvin was offered a bribe to book Jimmy Dorsey's band. Dorsey's alcohol abuse had hurt his career, and national agents were desperately seeking venues for him. "I don't think I'd better do that," Irvin told the agent.

Louis Armstrong, Duke Ellington, Count Basie, Lionel Hampton, Les Brown, Ray Eberly, Sonny Durham—they all played at Joyland, and Irvin got to meet his musical heroes. He remembers a crowded disc-jockeys' interview in a downtown basement studio with Stan Kenton. "He invited everybody over to the Golden Horseshoe. I had about $1.25 in my pocket and wondered how I was going to pay for all this. Fortunately, Kenton picked up the check.

Once, Irvin recalled, Sammy Kaye brought his "swing-and-sway" sound to town and did a live national radio broadcast from Joyland with a contest called, "So you want to be a bandleader." Irvin's friend Fred Luigar won the regional contest and went on to win the national competition in New York.

Irvin looked again at the old photo of Harry James standing under the Japanese lanterns, sending out romantic sounds from his trumpet. "The better the band, the less people danced. They just stood by the bandstand and listened."

Garvice Kincaid would remember that young John Irvin for the rest of his life. He would follow his career, make investments with him, and encourage the use of John's firm for public financing projects. The phrase "never met a stranger" was the essence of John Irvin, and Garvice could see that the young man would be successful in whatever future endeavors he chose. In addition, Kincaid's love of big band music would continue for the rest of his life, and in later years, when he would sponsor his famous Christmas parties for his employees and friends, he would always have a big band and dance floor for everyone to enjoy. From 1967 to 1992, the local Lexington Men of Note band would play at all of his and his empire's Christmas parties.

This relationship, one that started from Garvice's investment in Joyland Park and then an investment in a Carlisle bank, may sound unusual, but for Garvice Kincaid, it wasn't. He was always looking for quality talent and tended to build his universe of trusted employees from various parts of his life. Attorneys he went to law school with would be his partners, and one would be put on his estate trust Committee. People who had offices in buildings where he had his law practice would become business partners and empire employees. Friends and children of friends might catch his eye and in the future be considered for a position in one of the financier's businesses. His memberships and work in the Junior Chamber of Commerce and the Young Democrats organization were all important avenues to his universe. He was interested in intelligence, work ethic, and loyalty, and he was pretty good at recognizing these attributes.

Kincaid announced he had hired John Irvin as senior vice president, business development-marketing for Central Bank on March 1, 1975. John's career and ties to the Lexington community made him a perfect fit for the job. After graduating high school, John briefly attended the University of Kentucky but was soon drafted into the army, at the beginning of 1943, at age eighteen. After Private, First Class Irvin finished his basic training, he served most of his service in the South Pacific, serving almost one year in Hawaii and several months in Osaka, Japan. The military soon recognized his promotional capabilities and appointed him "public relations unit correspondent" with the Eighth Army.

Twenty-two-year-old Irving was discharged in February 1946, just after the passing of his mother. As he told the story, that summer, he was readmitted to the University of Kentucky and was taking one summer school course when his history with Garvice begins, and he became the promotional director for Joyland. John always liked history, and during the summer of 1946 he wrote and published *This History of the 389th Infantry Regiment in World War II*. It was published by Hobson Book Press that September.

John always enjoyed being around people and doing just about anything if it got a laugh, and this would continue throughout his life. At UK, he was a proud member of the Kappa Alpha fraternity, and in 1949, he would start the Central Kentucky Kappa Alpha Alumni Association and become its first president. In 1949, probably with some prompting from Kincaid, he restarted the Nicholas County chapter of the Young Democrats. In 1948, John graduated from UK with a degree in "arts & sciences."

Irvin continued to work for Kincaid at Joyland after college, and on December 2, 1948, he made the front page of the *Lexington Herald-Leader*. Garvice had sent him to Chicago for the National Association of Amusement Parks, Pools, and Beaches' annual convention. In John Irvin style, he poured water on his head to emphasize his opening remarks in an address titled "Pouring on Promotion," in which he outlined details of the Kentucky Press Association Crippled Children's Day promotion held at Joyland the previous summer. He had a photographer standing by to capture the moment, and that picture and story made the front page of the *Lexington Herald-Leader*.

Kincaid's interest in entertainment venues increased briefly in 1948, when he and Haddix purchased Gentry's Old Mill on Athens-Boonesboro Road. This was a restaurant and entertainment venue with a pool and beach. The original building was built in 1805 and sat on four acres. It had been refurbished and expanded a few years before Garvice's investment, and the facility could now seat one thousand people. It also housed a casino. Garvice's interest in Gentry's Old Mill quickly faded, and in 1949, he had the property auctioned off. This happened around the same time that Kincaid was indicted for assault and battery and Joyland Park was indicted for having gambling machines.

While the charges sounded severe, the assault charges were dropped two months later and Joyland was cleared of the gambling charges about a month after that. Garvice wasn't happy about the bad publicity, though. The assault charges were the result of a scuffle with two UK law students who were intoxicated, and the gambling charge came from a grand jury foreman who didn't like kids playing with the casino machines. Kincaid said publicly that since he had acquired Joyland, no gambling machines had ever been on the site. One can see how this may have caused Kincaid to lose interest in Gentry's Old Mill. Garvice still had an interest in the hospitality industry, and in later years would own or control all the major hotels in Lexington at one time or another.

John Irvin worked for Garvice until 1949, when he was recruited to be an account executive with the local Merrill Lynch office. Merrill Lynch would provide John with the tools he needed to understand investments and help people manage their money, but it was depending on John's strong personal skills and ability to form relationships to grow his client list. John was successful, and in early 1952, Merrill Lynch sent John and his wife to Norfolk, Virginia, to open a Merrill Lynch office there. This was a nice honor for the twenty-eight-year-old Irvin. After a year, though, John and his wife, Helen, grew homesick and relocated back to Lexington, where he became top salesman for the Kentucky Ignition Company, a wholesaler of automobile parts.

John did well and was promoted to sales promotion manager and secretary for the company. In 1959, he was honored by the Automotive Service Association at its New York convention. At the convention, Irvin read his essay "The Man in MANagement: His Responsibilities and Opportunities." The association represented three hundred and fifty manufacturers and four thousand five hundred wholesale distributors. John's natural abilities and strong understanding of sales and marketing continued to serve him well.

In 1961, John was recruited back to Lexington's Merrill Lynch office as an account executive. He would remain with the firm and also do some business with Kincaid over the next decade. In March 1975, Garvice recruited the fifty-one-year-old Irvin to a position with Central Bank & Trust. Garvice brought John in as senior vice president-business development and marketing for the bank. John would remain with the bank until he retired in 1995. After he retired, he was appointed curator of the Central Bank Art Gallery. In 2010, after his death, the gallery would be renamed the John G. Irvin Gallery at Central Bank.

Garvice hired John eight months before his death. He was looking for someone who was locally known and who would effectively represent his bank and be very active in the community. Garvice knew this would also garner more business for his bank. Throughout Kincaid's business career, he demonstrated a belief in marketing and promotion, and bringing in John Irvin supported this strategy. John was a known commodity. He had worked for and with Kincaid over the years. John was famous for his humor and jokes, but it was his love of people, the arts, and Lexington that had made him a Lexington celebrity.

Even before joining the bank, John was making his mark in Lexington. He had served four years on the University of Kentucky Alumni Association board of directors, two as its chairman. He had been a member of the board of Transylvania University's Alumni Association and was chairman of the National Alumni Fund in 1971. He was a former member of the President's Council of the Greater Lexington Area Chamber of Commerce and had served on an advisory commission to Governor Ned Breathitt. He was a member of the Lexington Kiwanis Club, a past president of the Lexington Country Club, and a member of the Civil War Roundtable. Finally, John Irvin loved the arts and devoted a considerable amount of time to the arts community and the Lexington Philharmonic.

Much has been said and written about John Irvin's sense of humor and love of practical jokes.

Lexington Herald-Leader columnist Don Edwards, in a June 5, 1983 article, called him:

> "The inveterate prankster of downtown Lexington." "He's the one who's always planting money on the street and then startling innocent victims by pretending that he just found the cash right under their noses. He's the one who pulls a telephone receiver out of his jacket pocket and, with a deadpan expression, hands it to someone and says, 'It's for you.'"
>
> In his college days, Irvin was president of a jolly organization called the Friday Afternoon Club, that met at the old Canary Cottage Restaurant. Back then, Irvin, who roomed in town, was always driving his elderly landlady crazy by doing things like sneaking out at dawn and nailing her morning newspaper to the front porch. Finally, she had enough. Irvin, with a long face, agreed to leave. He went upstairs, packed his suitcase, came down and went out the door. A few minutes later, he came down the stairs again—same suitcase, same long face—and went out the door. Later, he came down the stairs again... A true prankster can never resist one final gag. Irvin was going outside each time, climbing a tree, and getting back in the house through an upstairs window.

In 1985, Bob Babbage recalled the time when he was on the Lexington Fayette Urban County Council and was making his rounds at all the local civic clubs.

> He was telling each group the same funny, fictional story that had Central Bank executive John Irvin as the butt of the joke. [He] might

have known that Irvin—one of Lexington's renowned practical joke players—would get even. Sure enough, when Babbage spoke at the Bluegrass Kiwanis Club at Levas' Restaurant, Irvin was there. Just before the speech, Babbage decided to clear his throat by taking a big drink from the water glass in front of him. He choked, sputtered, coughed, wheezed, and had an instant sensation of gastric discomfort. The reason was, like water, perfectly clear. Irvin had filled his glass with vodka.[6]

There is no question that by 1945, Garvice's name was well known in Lexington and also in the Kentucky Democratic party. His name was probably in the local papers at least once a week. This was the 1940s, when the local papers were people's primary source of news and the radio was more about listening to music or a baseball game. One can only speculate how Kincaid knew the Carlisle bank was for sale, but it's an example of how many of his transactions would take place. Kincaid also understood by 1945 that growing a business organically was a slow process. He was doing this very thing with Kentucky Finance—growing by opening new offices one at a time. Undertaking the Carlisle bank purchase so quickly after acquiring Central Bank indicates his recognition that building a business through multiple acquisitions is more efficient and certainly faster than planting a garden and watching it grow during the summer.

Making the Central Bank Building in His Image

Kincaid started making changes with Central Bank almost immediately. Besides the name change, the bank had a great location, and while the 1896 building had great bones, it had deteriorated cosmetically. In addition, his bank had to share its first-floor space with a drugstore. In January 1946, Kincaid announced his plans to make "extensive improvements and repairs"[7] to the building. They would include the installation of a vault and safety-deposit boxes for the bank. He said all offices would be renovated and that he might install a new elevator. In addition, he announced that he had struck a deal with the C.W. Curry Drug Store and it would vacate the building.

The renovations were completed by October 1947 and Kincaid had a formal grand opening of the bank's new headquarters. The *Lexington Herald* reported that

> [t]he entire first floor of the newly named Central Bank Building, Short and Upper streets, has been remodeled for the occupancy of the bank, approximately tripling its area.

---

6   *Lexington Herald-Leader*, April 1985.
7   *Lexington Herald-Leader*, January 31, 1946.

> Improvements include installation of a solid glass exterior with storm door section. A terrazzo floor was laid in the lobby section which also has indirect lighting and a spun-glass acoustical and insulated ceiling. A new heating and air-conditioning unit also were installed. The new bank counter, consisting of five tellers' cages, several check counters and the executive offices are finished in golden oak with aluminum trim. As soon as possible, bank officials plan to install a large vault with several hundred safety deposit boxes available.[8]

In November 1948, the *Lexington Herald* reported on the installation of Kincaid's vault and included a large picture of the workmen installing it.

> Workmen are shown moving a 32,000-pound vault door through the wall of the Central Bank building, Short and Upper streets. To install the huge door, it was necessary to shore up the floor of the building with heavy timbers. The vault itself is constructed of 18 inches of steel and reinforced concrete, while the foundation, 20 feet down, rests on solid rock. The vault will hold 600 safety deposit boxes.[9]

The vault was completed in December, and beginning the first week of January in 1949, the bank began advertising its new vault: "Safety Deposit Boxes Available in Our New Vault!"[10]

In a 2021 piece published by the bank in celebration of its seventy-five-year history, the bank proudly proclaimed that

> Central Bank was the first bank in Central Kentucky to install a vault (1951), offer Saturday morning hours (1956), and provide drive-through banking facilities (1962) and online ATMs (1978). Today we remain committed to offering the latest digital conveniences to our customers through our online, mobile and phone banking services.

Kincaid was proud of his bank and corporate headquarters, and even though he dreamed of one day having a new, grander Lexington landmark to hold his businesses, he continued to maintain and make the Central Bank building a significant downtown building. In 1962 he announced that he had acquired the building behind the bank building and would demolish it and build a new, connected, three-story addition to house all the modern-day electronic tools that banks were using. He also would be doing another major remodel of

---

8   *Lexington Herald-Leader*, "Central Bank Formal Opening Is Scheduled on Monday Night," October 12, 1947.

9   *Lexington Herald-Leader*, "Vault Door Weighs 16 Tons," November 23, 1948.

10   *E.g., Lexington Herald-Leader*, January 16, 1949.

the bank's lobby, expanding it and creating more office and employee space; adding another structure near the building for drive-up banking that would be connected to the main bank by pneumonic tubes; and adding a new parking lot on Short Street. No estimated costs were announced. Garvice completed the remodel in May 1963 and held another grand open house, just sixteen years after the last one.

History indicates that Garvice was always a fastidious person. He liked things neat and tidy and preferred to be in updated surroundings. The remodeling of the Central Bank building is a great example of this. The before and after pictures of the Central Bank building are impressive. There are no reports on how much Kincaid spent to rehabilitate the tired old building, but we know he paid $150,000 for the building and held it in a single-purpose corporation whose articles state that its maximum indebtedness would be $500,000. One can only guess what Garvice spent to remodel the building, but a case can be made that considering his cost and the maximum indebtedness article, he may have expected the renovations to cost up to $300,000. This would leave him a $50,000 contingency buffer.

Mr. Kincaid Liked a Clean and Neat Office Environment & "I Was Here . . ."

A few years after I started working for Kentucky Central Life in 1981, and more people were getting to know me, my boss, Cliff Forbush, and the head of public relations, Charlie Thomas, were in my office. Both men knew my uncle Emmett very well, and Charlie liked talking about the markets, so occasionally these discussions would lead to "story sessions." I think I had just received a promotion and Mr. Thomas wanted to take me to lunch to celebrate—he joked that he knew "Cliff was too tight to do it." As I was getting up to go with Mr. Thomas and stopped to put on my blue sport coat, Mr. Forbush looked at me and said, "Charlie, Garvice would have fired him for wearing that outfit. Remember, you couldn't work for one of his organizations if you didn't wear a suit." Mr. Thomas said, "Cliff is correct, but then Garvice didn't like young folks like you, so you would have gotten fired anyway or not have been hired." Both men just laughed and then went on to tell me about Mr. Kincaid's clean-desk requirement and how the company used to write all-employee memos about it. Apparently, each day when it was time to go home, everything on your desk had to be put away. The company even had special desks so typewriters could be—and were required to be—lowered into the body of the desk. When I worked in the old Kentucky Central Life building, I recalled how people used to do this in the late 1970s. It was still a requirement in those early years after Mr. Kincaid's death.

The reason this information is important is that one day, in the late 1960s, Mr. Kincaid stopped by Charlie Thomas's office late one evening. Charlie was head of public relations, and in all the time I knew him, his desk was always covered in papers and folders. Charlie did public relations work for all of Mr. Kincaid's companies, including the banks, and I can imagine this kept him quite busy. Well, that evening Mr. Kincaid walked into Charlie's office and, seeing his desk was covered in stuff, pushed everything off the desk and onto the floor. He left Charlie a note: "I was here, where were you – G.D. Kincaid."[11]

The next day, when Charlie got to his office, he saw the mess on the floor and the note. What did Charlie do but pick up the phone and call Mr. Kincaid. Before he could say anything, Mr. Kincaid said that he had paid Charlie a visit the evening before and he wasn't there. Charlie then asked, "Mr. Kincaid are you the one that threw everything on my desk onto the floor." Mr. Kincaid said, "Well yes I am—I wanted to encourage you to clean up your desk." Charlie said it was a wonder Mr. Kincaid didn't fire him, because he pushed back, saying that all that mess was for projects that Mr. Kincaid had him working on and that Mr. Kincaid's "encouragement" would now delay those projects getting done because it would take him time to get things put back in order. He said Mr. Kincaid just grunted and hung up on him.

The Central Bank building was Garvice's first corporate headquarters, one that he owned and knew people would consider to be associated with his image, and his corporate image was important to him. Here was a self-made millionaire from eastern Kentucky who was still being treated as an outsider in Lexington. In 1945, he had lived and worked in Lexington for over ten years, but he still felt like an outsider. One can imagine that owning "Lexington's first skyscraper" was important to him. In addition, his history shows he preferred to house his various businesses in one location or, if one location wasn't large enough, then within a block or two of each other. Garvice didn't want to do the day-to-day management, but he did want to meet with his various lieutenants and get progress reports. In later years, Kincaid would tell Cliff Forbush that he didn't like to invest in things he couldn't drive to. The phrase "out of sight, out of mind" would never be associated with Garvice Kincaid.

Garvice Kincaid wanted his properties to represent his image. He preferred a fresh, modern look, and most of his properties were built to reflect this or renovated and adapted to respect this desire. As Garvice added banks to his empire, he would in many cases build new branches that were nicer than the main bank or in some cases relocate the main bank to a newly built building. Their look was important to him and, he assumed, to his customers. Perception

---

11   Personal communication.

was everything. In December 1968, the Kentucky Society of Architects would give Central Bank & Trust a "distinguished achievement in architectural design" citation for its three new branch banks. The judges said, "The image achieved by the design of the banks is one of solidarity, elegance, and strength."[12] It could be argued that Kincaid owned some properties that were not always beautiful, and this is true, but I think the difference is that Garvice viewed investment properties in a different light than his business-occupied properties. In addition, the properties he used for his finance-company offices were intended to not intimidate its lower-income customer base.

Stan Galbraith, a former vice president of the National Bank in Paris, Kentucky, relayed this story[13] about Kincaid and how he wanted his properties to look:

> Then another story I think about is when my ex-wife Marilyn was working there at the old Central Bank Building on the corner of Short and Upper, and the way those windows were. There were a kind of ledge out above each one of those windows as you went up. I think the building was five or six stories. Anyway, Kincaid was always worried about icicles coming off the building, and he was always worried about icicles falling off and stabbing someone. You know they were like daggers and people were always walking down the street and things.
>
> Marilyn also used to tell a story about Kincaid working late at night and the young guys would also be in the building working in their offices, or particularly down in the lobby of the bank, where anybody that came in could see their desk and if you didn't leave your desk almost clear or neatly stacked, Kincaid would come in and just take his arm and shove everything onto the floor . . . and you knew when you came in the next morning and all your stuff was on the floor that that didn't need to happen again.

After this story I had to tell Stan about Charlie Thomas and Kincaid and his desk. Stan then continued:

> That made me think of another funny story. Ron Burton, before he came over to run the Paris bank, he worked at a couple of Central Bank branches in Lexington. I think he was working at the North Park branch on the north end of town when this happened. Anyway, he said one morning the phone rang, and he said it was Kincaid on the phone. Well Kincaid used to get out and drive around Lexington in the 70s, when the bank had three or four branches, and he could look around and see things...look for things out of place. So, Ron says, he picked up and said "Yes Sir" . . . and he says, Mr. Kincaid

12   *Lexington Herald-Leader*, December 8, 1968.
13   Interview of Stan Galbraith by author.

says, "Mr. Burton, would you do me a favor? Would you go outside and tell me what you see? Ron says "Yes, sir." So, Ron puts the phone on hold and he says he goes outside. If you remember, Robert, most of those branches at the time, they had like, indoor outdoor carpet or something, you know, that fake outside carpet. So, Ron says he looks around out there and all he could see were just a few little pebbles that were on the carpet. So, Ron kicks the stones off the carpet and comes back to his desk and he says, "Well, Mr. Kincaid, the only thing I saw was some gravel on the carpet." Kincaid says "That's correct, Mr. Burton and I will tell you what you do. Why don't you roller skate and go out there, roller skate and Bust Your Ass" and then the phone went click and that was it. Ron said I was never so nervous and all my life. Kincaid was out there just driving through the parking lot and I can see him stopping to just look at the building, to see if it all looked good and things. You know they bought all of those branches from, I think, Congleton and White. That was the company that put up all of those pre-cast concrete and steel buildings. He put those up during the 1960's and 1970's, all over town.

After Stan's story, I had to tell him about what they did in the lobby of the old Lafayette Hotel building after Kentucky Central life relocated there in 1964. I had just started working my summer job for the company in 1977 when a couple of the building maintenance men told me this story. They also knew my uncle, Emmett Crump, and told me to ask him if it wasn't true.

People Communicated Around Mr. Kincaid to Help Everyone

When I first started working part-time for Kentucky Central Life during college, the job brought me in contact with the building maintenance staff. Most of the guys had worked for Kentucky Central Life for several years and they also reported to the same department head of the mail/supply room. Mr. Kincaid had only been dead a couple of years when I started, so his aura and culture still permeated the company, and people would talk about little things that they used to do to keep him happy. Apparently having a clean and ostentatious look at his companies was important to Mr. Kincaid. The maintenance guys said that someone over at Mr. Kincaid's office or at WKYT would contact the company and let them know when he was coming over. They said there was then a rush to make sure the lobby was clean, the brass shiny, and the red carpet was rolled out. Literally, the company had a red carpet that they rolled out from the old Lafayette Hotel front doors over to the elevators. They didn't keep it out all the time because it would get dirty, and it also interfered with cleaning the marble floors, which made up most of the lobby area. When Mr. Kincaid would leave the building, someone at Kentucky Central Life would then call his office or WKYT and let them know he had left the building. Stan responded to this story:

> Wow, you know the same thing would happen at the bank in Paris. We'd get a phone call or something like that…and they say "Garvice is going to Danville," so the bank in Danville would, you know, get everything picked up and put up, because you know, Garvice is coming. You knew everything needed to be picked up and look great! It was all hands-on deck.

While these stories are entertaining, I think they also demonstrate the importance that Garvice placed on how his properties looked. Kincaid never served in the military, but his eye for this type of detail reminds me of the president & CEO of the company I worked for in Madison, Wisconsin. He was an attorney and accountant by education but also a brigadier general in the Wisconsin National Guard. He had served in the Jag Corps in Okinawa, Japan, and had a forty-year career in the military, and when it came to how our home office and its grounds looked, he was a stickler for details. If the flag wasn't hanging correctly out front, the flower beds didn't look pristine, or cigarette butts were on the apron around the building, he was on the phone to the head of building and grounds and to me in later years, when it was part of my responsibility. My point is, he viewed our home office as a reflection of him, and I think one can see where Kincaid also felt the same about all his properties.

Cliff Forbush told me that Garvice really liked the image that IBM's employees reflected—dark suits, crisp white shirts, and conservative ties—and he expected his management employees to reflect a similar image. Sometime in the early 1970s, Garvice was in Central Bank's lobby and spotted a young employee in a sport coat and tie. Well, Garvice made a beeline over to the young man and said, "You must go home." The young man was startled and started to say something, and Garvice immediately turned around and left him. The guy was shocked and went to his boss and said, "I think Mr. Kincaid just fired me." His boss asked him what happened, and the employee explained what Garvice did, and the manager said, "Mr. Kincaid expects everyone to wear a suit and you are wearing a sport coat." He told the guy to hurry home and put on a suit. Mr. Forbush didn't witness this, but he learned about it later from one of the bank officers.

A similar thing happened in the late 1960s or early 1970s. This story was relayed to me by two different people; Clyde Honaker was one, and I can't recall the second person. It also involves an employee at the bank. Garvice expected his male employees to wear a clean, crisp, white shirt, and one morning he was in the bank and spotted an employee in either a striped shirt or colored shirt. Kincaid marched over to the employee and loudly told him that he had ten minutes to get over to Graves Cox and purchase a white shirt, get it on, and get back. The guy was shocked, and Garvice apparently just stared at him for a few seconds. The employee then turned and ran out of the bank. According to Clyde, the guy probably didn't make it back in ten minutes, but he had a white shirt on when he returned.

The Central Bank building already housed some of his finance company operations and his bank. Mr. Kincaid's real estate operation and his law practice were still in the Citizens Bank building, but would move to the Central Bank building by 1950. WVLK radio remained at the Phoenix Hotel until Kincaid Towers was built. All of Kincaid's empire wasn't under one roof, but it was within a block of him. As for Kincaid's personal life, he and Nelle and the twin girls, Jane and Joan, had moved to a home next to Lexington Country Club on Paris Pike in 1943. They would stay in this two-story home until 1953, when Kincaid would suffer his first heart attack at age forty.

After acquiring Central Exchange Bank in 1945 and changing its name to Central Bank, Garvice did what a master marketer always does with a business: he promoted the heck out of it. In his first month of ownership, he started referring to it in ads as "Central Kentucky's youngest and fastest growing banking institution" and listing all the services the bank offered. In later years, it would be recognized that Kincaid's broadcasting network was the "voice of the Kentucky Wildcats," but in September 1945, even without a broadcasting company, Garvice immediately began sponsoring the UK football games on WLAP radio. His Central Bank ads were "loud and proud," as the saying goes. The initial ads were for Central Exchange Bank, since Garvice hadn't changed the name of the bank yet.

By 1949, the ads would be built around phrases like these:

Large enough to serve you—Small enough to know you

The Fastest Growing Bank
in the
Blue Grass

We Attribute This Unusual Growth to the Many Exclusive
Services Offered by Our Bank to This Community:

- We Pay the Highest Rate of Interest on Savings
  in this Trade Area.

- For your convenience we stay open until 4 p.m.
  Daily, Except Saturday.

- There is no charge on Checking Accounts
  where minimum balanced is maintained.

By 1949, Garvice was also displaying the growth of the bank since 1945, saying that "deposits increased from $500,000 to $4,000,000." He also provided a summary comparative balance sheet for two stated years showing the bank's assets and liabilities and, more importantly, that the bank's capital account had increased from $20,000 to $60,000 and that accumulated undivided profits totaled over $130,000 versus just over $8,000 in 1945. Finally, he would showcase pictures of the new vault and remodeled offices and the fact that the bank had six hundred new safety deposit boxes to offer customers.

Garvice and his partners continued to purchase banks over the next few years, and by December 1947 he owned a total of five: Central Bank & Trust—Lexington, the First National Bank of Carlisle, the Commercial Deposit Bank of Winchester, the First State Bank of LaGrange, and the First National Bank of Midway. M.C. Haddix and Dr. W.S. Snyder of Frankfort were his normal bank partners for several years. Garvice would usually own 51 to 75 percent of the bank, his partners would own 15 to 25 percent of the bank, and in many cases, the existing management would own stock. Garvice had control, he had associates who were also directors of his banks, and the management-stockholders were in charge of the day-to-day operations. His model was designed to be a win-win for everyone. They all had skin in the business, and if there were problems, Kincaid had the controlling interest.

Kincaid was a shrewd businessman, and he was known to have his partners provide him an option to buy their shares at a price probably tied to a formula or price such as the bank's book value. There are no reports of his doing this with his bank stocks, but it would make sense given how many private partner-shareholders he was involved with. In addition, he had recently had the experience of dealing with the M.C. Haddix estate to acquire its Central Bank shares after his death. If he did this, and he needed to own less than 50 percent of a bank, he had his option agreement to influence his control.

Over the next fifteen years, Garvice acquired control of more banks, and he would occasionally merge one or two together, dispose of a few, or start a bank from scratch. In September 1962, he acquired his sixteenth bank, the Clark County National Bank in Winchester. Kincaid now owned thirteen banks in Kentucky and three in Florida, and their assets totaled $150,000,000. His first bank acquisition and flagship bank, Central Bank & Trust Company, would make up $125,000,000 of those assets. Garvice had worked his magic and increased the assets of his first bank by one hundred and 78 percent.

The Loan Man and His Law Firm

Owning a portfolio of banks and consumer finance companies wasn't without its issues. While a lender normally doesn't lend money to someone expecting them to default, it happens, and as Kincaid's lending empire of banks and loan companies expanded, so did the legal work that was necessary to foreclose on any secured assets or to collect from any personal guarantees. In addition, he was a perpetual incorporator, meaning he was always setting up corporations to start new businesses or to hold particular assets. Fortunately for Garvice, he had a small personal army of attorneys and a staff of accountants to assist him in this process. Initially, early in Kincaid's legal career, he and Frank Trimble Jr. shared a law office in the Citizen's Bank building. The men probably knew each other from the University of Kentucky Law School. Garvice had graduated from the school in 1937, and Trimble had graduated in 1939. Both men were also active in Kentucky politics, Kincaid working for the Young Democrats and Trimble for the Young Republican Club. Trimble was its treasurer from 1937 to 1939, and by 1948 he would be named chairman of the Fayette County GOP.

Frank Trimble Jr. was born in Mt. Sterling, Kentucky, on January 23, 1915. He was the son of Frank and Emma Trimble. His family moved to Lexington in 1923, when Frank was eight years of age. Frank graduated from Henry Clay High School in 1933 and graduated from UK's College of Arts and Sciences in 1937 and UK's College of Law in 1939. He started practicing law in the McClelland Building after law school but soon, in March 1949, entered the Navy and World War II. He served eighteen months in Naval Intelligence and two years in the Pacific area as a lieutenant and assistant communications officer on Admiral Gerald F. Bogan's staff on the USS Lexington, which was awarded a Presidential Unit Citation. He was also on the Bunker Hill and Essex, both of which earned presidential citations, and was awarded the Navy Commendation Ribbon by Admiral Halsey.

In February 1944, when Frank was on leave, he married Frances in Cincinnati, and in October 1945 he was released from the Navy. Trimble soon resumed his law practice and joined Charles A. Thornton in an office on Lexington's Cheapside, but by 1947 he had moved to the fifth floor of the Central Bank building. The practice was now called Thornton, Carroll, and Trimble. James S. Carroll had joined the men in November 1946. Trimble was still active in politics, and in 1947, he was selected as Fayette County's chairman for Eldon S. Dummit's campaign. Dummit was seeking the Republican nomination for governor. By 1949, Frank joined Kincaid on the fourth floor of the Central Bank building. In March 1950, Garvice added Trimble to the board of Central Bank & Trust. Kincaid must have considered Trimble as much a friend as a business associate, because in 1951, when Garvice's mother Minnie died, Trimble was listed as an honorary pallbearer at her funeral. Other notable Kincaid business associates listed were L. D. Nickles, T. C. Quisenberry, H. A. Smith, Robert Layman, and Carmine Johnson (Kincaid's Joyland Park manager).

Frank Trimble had many roles in the Kincaid empire. He initially worked on bank and finance company loan litigation, incorporating Kincaid's many businesses, and handling Garvice's many real estate transactions. Later he became instrumental in arranging and originating loans for borrowers at Central Bank and Kentucky Central Life.

Bart A. Brown and the Beginning of the Firm

Bart A. Brown is a former law firm associate attorney who worked for Garvice from 1963 to 1966. Even though Bart is ninety-one years young today, he has a memory of those times that's extraordinary. Bart not only worked for Kincaid, he was the attorney who drafted Garvice's will and trust agreement. Kincaid must have been impressed by his work and his strong professional demeanor, because in February 1964, when he signed it, he selected him as the first Committee member alternate. He ranked ahead of Ed Schaeffer in the beginning but was behind the initial Committee members, T. C. Quisenberry, Frank Trimble, Earl Wilson, and Ralph Worster. Bart had this to say[14] about his days at the law firm and Frank Trimble's and others' roles in the Kincaid empire:

> I grew up in Louisville, Kentucky, and went to the University of Louisville, law school, and undergraduate school. I majored in accounting in college and graduated from law school in 1955. I was particularly interested in tax law and took all the tax classes and intended to attempt to practice in the tax area. When I got out of law school, I immediately went into the Army for two years. After the Army chased me off, I then went to work for the Chief Counsel's Office of the Internal Revenue Department on July 1, 1957. This was the legal branch of the Internal Revenue Department. Their offices were in the Internal Revenue building in New York and Washington, D.C. They had branch offices in various districts throughout the country, and the branch office that I was in was the Cincinnati office, and it covered the states of Virginia, West Virginia, Kentucky, and Ohio.

---

14   Interview of Bart A. Brown by author.

Our basic responsibility was to try tax cases on behalf of the Internal Revenue Service before the Tax Court of the United States . . . headquartered in Washington D.C. They had their own building in Washington D.C. and had about twenty judges that would basically travel to all the major cities in the United States and hear tax cases. They would lump them so that, you know, they'd have twenty to twenty-five cases on the docket, and then they would try all those cases in a week or two, then come home, write their opinions, etc.

In our Cincinnati region, we had the Tax Court that would travel to Cleveland, Cincinnati, and Columbus, Ohio. In Kentucky they would just go to Louisville, and in West Virginia, they would only go to Charleston. In Virginia, they went to Richmond, and then some of the Richmond cases were also tried in Washington, D.C. So that's what I did for five years; I was a traveling trial attorney for the Internal Revenue Service and represented the Internal Revenue Service in those cases. We [would] try a case or write the brief and attempt to settle as many cases as we could. In 1962, they asked me to take over the head of the Tennessee office of Chief Counsel's Office, and there were four lawyers and myself in that office. I went down there for a year. And they really didn't have enough work for my lawyers, and I told them so. You know, part of the reason that I was with Internal Revenue was to get some experience from a tax viewpoint. The Chief Counsel's Office was a breeding ground for tax lawyers in private practice throughout the United States.

Okay, so anyway, about early 1962, I decided it was time for me to explore going into private practice, and I wanted to get with a firm of some kind or another. My father at the time was the head of a trust department at the largest bank in Kentucky. It was a bank by the name of Fidelity and Columbia Trust Company. As I've heard the story, Garvice Kincaid was in the bank one day and stopped by to see my daddy and talk with him. Garvice told my daddy that he was having terrible tax problems, and that Internal Revenue Service agents had been examining all the companies within his empire, as you refer to it. For simplicity, you and I will refer to it as his empire, which is all the companies who were being audited. Garvice said he didn't really have any good tax people within his organization, and Daddy suggested that he talk with me. So, Daddy then called me and said, you need to call Garvice Kincaid. He told me a little bit about him, and so I called him. He offered me a job, and so on April 1, as I recall, in 1963, I started to work for him.

I did a telephone call with him (Garvice) first and then I went up to meet him in his office in Lexington, and at that time, he made me an offer and I accepted it.

I will tell you this, throughout his organization, Garvice Kincaid called all the shots. He had people working in various areas, but he called the shots, absolutely, positively. Every decision, every important decision, not the day-to-day details, but every important decision was made by Garvice Kincaid.

Author: The way I've termed it is he set the strategy and the people he hired, what I call his lieutenants, were to implement the strategy and manage the day-to-day affairs.

Right, they manage the day-to-day details. Well, let me just tell you, when I got there, I was the only tax guy, and so basically, I had the responsibility of dealing with several [IRS] agents working on the audit of Garvice's companies as well as the personal tax returns of Garvice and his wife. You know, all of a sudden, I had the responsibility of all those many, many tax audits and dealing with the auditors doing the audit. I even remember the names of two of the principal agents in it, guys by the name of McCubbin and Robinson. Those were the two guys that I basically dealt with for the entire three-year period that I was with Garvice. They were just two agents, out of the Lexington office, that had the responsibility for the audits of all of Garvice's companies, as well as his personal returns.

Now, when you talk about Garvice's empire, I found when I got there, first you had Kentucky Central Life Insurance Company. That was a big, important company at that time, and I remember the name that was, I guess, the president of Kentucky Central, Paul Carr. Paul Carr was the person that I knew that was running the day-to-day activities of the insurance company.

Author: Paul Carr was a Louisville actuarial consultant that Kincaid used. Carr basically helped to get Garvice into the life insurance business by first helping him acquire Cardinal Life Insurance Company and then Kentucky Central Life. He lasted until Garvice moved the company to the Lafayette Hotel, and then Carr left and David Brain was made executive vice president, and from then on, Kincaid was president and David Brain stayed with Kentucky Central Life until the beginning of 1976, shortly after Kincaid died. He left because Bud Burnett, who had been secretary-treasurer of the company, was put on Kincaid's Committee. Here is David Brain, who Kincaid had made president in January of the year he died, 1975, and who was now going to be reporting to him. In short, when Kincaid died, Bud Burnett was on the Committee and David Brain wasn't, and from everything I've been told over the years, these two guys really didn't get along. I've been told this so many times. David Brain would go around trying to figure out what Bud Burnett was doing for Garvice, and Burnett was going around trying to figure out what David Brain was doing for Garvice. There was animosity, as much as a competitive nature between the two. After Kincaid's death, it would have been a difficult work environment.

When Paul Carr left around the end of 1964 or the beginning of 1965, Garvice gave him a three-year salary contract, with a noncompete clause, and the Committee did the same for David Brain when he resigned. Both Garvice and the Committee were concerned that either man might do something to negatively impact Kentucky Central's business. Both Paul Carr and David Brain had three years to figure out the next chapters in their lives. Paul Carr took it easy for a while, and David Brain moved forward and started a successful health insurance enterprise.

Well, in any event, I remember most of my dealings were mostly with Burnett. I do remember dealing with Paul Carr early on. I don't remember dealing with David Brain at all, during my period, but one of the things that was on my plate was that Kentucky Central had acquired an insurance company that was headquartered in Houston, Texas, and they had a very substantial tax case. I took care of working with the agents that worked on that particular tax case, and because it was a financial matter, my interface at the company was Burnett. So, any dealings that I had with that case [were] through Burnett.

Mucci: *That would make sense. He basically was the chief financial officer for the company at that time.*

Exactly. So, then you had Kentucky Finance Company, and they had a fella by the name of Bob Curtin. You know, nobody among the lawyers [at the law firm], or the people at Central Bank's office, where Garvice hung out, had much day-to-day dealings with either the insurance company or the finance company. Both of those were handled over in the Kentucky Central building, and periodically, either Burnett or Brain or Carr or Curtin would come over to [the] Central Bank offices and talk with Garvice about whatever needed to be talked about. Or sometimes they would come over and talk with a fella by the name of Ralph Wooster.

Wooster was kind of a general guy, and he took care of a company—or kind of oversaw a company—called Cardinal Life or something or another. It wasn't an insurance company. I don't know what it was. It started out as an investment company or a service company, and Wooster and Hart Hagan were the interfaces in connection with it. They [Wooster and Hagan] were the Bob Curtin [Kentucky Finance] and David Brain [Kentucky Central] of Cardinal Life. And then there were all the various real estate investments. Then in addition to that, you had the Kentucky banks. As I recall, there were about twenty of those Kentucky banks, and they were overseen by Al Florence. Al Florence kind of talked with Wooster and Hart Hagan in connection with, you know, whatever big issues arose with respect to those banks. He also reported directly to Garvice.

Then kind of off to the side was T. C. Quisenberry. I never really dealt with him at all. He ran the business operations of Lexington Finance. Quisenberry would have reported up to Wooster and Hart Hagan in connection with Lexington Finance, and so you had those four groups. You had Kentucky Central. You had Kentucky Finance. You had all the real estate that Garvice owned, or the several [holding] companies that owned it. You had the Cardinal Life, and Lexington Finance, and then in addition to that, you had another group of finance companies. And I don't remember the name of this one. It was kind of operated in Pennsylvania or Delaware. PDI?

Mucci: PIB. Personal Industrial Bankers.

Right. Okay, and those guys reported to a guy by the name Ken Davis. Ken Davis kind of reported to or worked for Kentucky Finance and worked with Bob Curtin. I never understood the division between the two of them, but I do know that PIB was basically Ken Davis's responsibility.

Mucci: I told Bart the story of Garvice purchasing PIB and the democratic vote and six-against-one vote and brought up Robert Bartella.

You and I can agree, Garvice called all the shots. I can imagine six to one. And he had the one. And that's what they did.

Well, I mean, I do know that Kentucky Finance was Curtain, Bartella, and Ken Davis. And PIB would have been in that same category, that their day-to-day operations would have been Curtain, Bartella, and Ken Davis.

Let me tell you about the law firm. So, I joined the law firm. I became a lawyer for Garvice Kincaid on April 1 [1963]. At that time, there was no law firm. At least, I didn't recognize it as being at a law firm. There was Frank Trimble, Montjoy Trimble [Frank's younger brother], Fred Copelin, and Bill Van Inwegen. And as I saw it, the four of them basically did real estate work, particularly Coplin and Van Inwegen for the banks. Frank kind of oversaw them, along with Montjoy, and also, they papered [created] the loan agreements for the various banks, particularly Central Bank, which was the main bank there of the twenty-plus Kentucky banks.

Oh, one other thing I'd forgotten about was Garvice also owned two banks in Florida.

Mucci: Dania and Marathon.

Dania was one and I don't remember the other one ever. Both of them were under audit by Internal Revenue when I got there. So, I made trips to the Miami area where Dania was and worked with the [IRS] agents that were working on those audits on numerous occasions during 1963 and 1964. I believe that we concluded those audits sometime in 1964. Overseeing those two banks also were Wooster and Hart Hagan.

Mucci: I didn't realize Hart Hagan was involved in the banks that much.

You know, he wasn't involved in connection with the banks, but, you know, he was the Burnett [Kentucky Central] of all the miscellaneous investments of one kind or another.

Al Florence kind of reported to him and Wooster in connection with those miscellaneous banks. The only bank of any real substance among those banks was Central Bank. All the rest of them were little, you know, country banks, maybe $30 or $40 million in deposits or something along that line. They weren't big, but they were enough that Garvice was interested in what they were doing.

Mucci: I think Garvice could see the writing on the wall of being able to do a bank holding company with cross-border banking. It didn't happen as soon as he thought it would happen, but he was ahead of his time in his thinking. Also, his Florida banks were larger banks.

Right. I don't think there's any question about that. And I mean, you know, those banks were small. The one bank that I remember was a bank in Middlesboro. It was a nice little bank down there, and then, of course, Central Bank was the third-largest bank in Lexington at the time and meaningful in size.

The lawyers [who] operated in Central Bank's headquarters were really the real estate attorneys, doing what I'll call the real estate bank papering in connection with loans, and then me, I am kind of a separate guy, and I didn't talk to any of them really, except occasionally to Hart Hagan and Bob Curtin, and to Burnett and to Garvice. And, I mean, I would say hello to Montjoy and Fred and Van Inwegen, but other than that, I had no day-to-day working relationship with any of them.

Now, Garvice had a business lawyer he had worked with for several years, but at that time, and just prior to my arrival, or shortly after I got there on April 1 in 1963, he died. He died in Nashville, Tennessee, at a motel he was staying at in connection was something that he was working on. The lawyer was in Nashville doing some work for another client down in Nashville, and he had a heart attack during the nighttime and died in a motel room down there. His name was Tommy Dawson, and some years prior to the early 1960s, he was with the Bullitt, Dawson and Tarrant law firm.

In the early '60s, he had set up his own law firm. He had with him a young lawyer by the name of Richard Eiler. It was just the two of them, and his principal client was Kincaid, but it was his own law firm, not affiliated with one of the big law firms in town. When I came to join Garvice, he [Kincaid] told me at the time that they were in the process of making arrangements with Tommy Dawson and Eiler to close their firm in Louisville and to move to Lexington sometime over the late summer. They'd be moving [to] Lexington and setting up a law firm with the Trimbles, Van Inwegen, Coplin, and me, and Garvice, etc., to handle all his business, but then, of course, Dawson died before that happened. When he died, Garvice reached out to Earl Wilson, and Earl Wilson agreed to come and bring Schaeffer with him.

Garvice said immediately after that, he needed to find somebody else to fill that role. And, and that's when he got in touch with Earl Wilson, and I understood that Earl Wilson and Garvice went to law school together at the University of Kentucky. Earl Wilson was a partner in Bullitt, Dawson and Tarrant, in Louisville, and Ed Schaeffer Jr. worked with him. Garvice talked Earl Wilson into coming—moving to Lexington—and Garvice and Earl Wilson forming a law firm to handle all of Garvice's work, across all his entire empire. I don't recall whether that law firm was formed at the end of 1963 or early 1964, but it was around the end of the year 1963, early 1964, that the law firm of Kincaid, Wilson and Trimble was formed.

Six months after I came to Garvice's office, I wasn't a part of any law firm or anything. I was just there, and I reported to no one but Garvice.

Author: Well, you can't go any higher up than that, as they say. The notice in the paper says October 1963. I am just telling you because you are in the picture as an associate. Also, for some reason in 1967, Hembree, Coplin, and Van Inwegen left and set up their own firm for a short period of time. Now, by the time I joined Kentucky Central, they were all back working at the law firm. So Garvice brought them back or allowed them to return. I don't know what happened though.

Well, that's okay. I'm three months early. I have no idea what happened. You know, I was long gone by that time. So, I don't know what happened. Let me ask you this. Are all those people dead now?

Author: Everybody is dead except for Ed Schaeffer. Rusty Hembree died in 2022. I wrote Schaeffer a letter hoping to interview him about those early years, but I never had any reply. I was a young kid, in my early twenties, in 1981, when I joined the company, and by the time I left Kentucky Central in 1995, I was in my mid-'30s. I knew Mr. Schaeffer well enough to say hello, and he liked my old boss, Cliff Forbush, and I thought he might talk to me about the old days, but I imagine being front and center in all of the litigation tied to the collapse of Kentucky Central brings back too many bad memories. I just wished we could have discussed Garvice in those early years. He was there. You know, the collapse of Kentucky Central ruined many lives, and so it's understandable that folks who have put this episode in their life behind them would have no interest in discussing it.

I just sent you Frank Trimble's obituary.

You know, Central Bank and Kentucky Central kind of had a reputation in Lexington and the Bluegrass area as being the lender of last resort, and Frank Trimble was the guy that handled that. He had a nickname, "the loan arranger," because he handled all of the tough-to-do-loans and the larger loans for the two companies—primarily the bank, but some for Kentucky Central. They were high-rate loans, so the terms were tougher. They made loans to real estate developers and used-car companies and automobile dealerships, and things like that, that were traditionally high-rate payers, high-rate interest payers, in connection with their activities. So anyway, that's what he did, and he did loans on behalf of Central Bank principally and to a lesser extent Kentucky Central.

There are some other things you should know. You focus a lot of attention on the Committee, and the will and the trust, etc. I wrote Kincaid's will and trust.

Author: *Wow, you did really well. Congratulations! You know, I have a book called Wild Ride. It's the story of the Calumet thoroughbred farm and the collapse of it. I had that book for many years, and well, I retired, January 4, 2020, right in time for the pandemic. So, of course, I had a lot of time on my hands and decided to pull that book off my bookshelf and read it. I never got a chance to read the book before, and so I'm reading about their multigenerational trust and everything that happened, and I'm like, this is Garvice Kincaid's story, only with different names. You know, because of what happened to them and then Kincaid, it just shows you that no matter how well you plan, things don't always work out. I just had to tell you this, because to hear you say you wrote Kincaid's will and trust, and to realize Wright was doing his will and estate planning around the same time, I find it amazing.*

Well, and, you know, the only interface that I had with anybody in connection with that will and trust was with Garvice. He and I would meet and talk every two or three days, as I was writing it.

Author: *How long? How long did it take you to write it from when you started?*

Oh, I'm going to say six weeks.

Author: *Okay, that's sooner than I would have thought. I didn't know, I thought it would be one of those things where he would need to think about it for a long time.*

Garvice didn't think for very long about anything. You know, you give him six questions and he would give you six answers back, in less than ten minutes. He made decisions and made them quickly.

Mucci: *Why do you think he had your version of it, the first version of the trust, have the Committee divided into family versus non-family? Did he talk about that with you—the concept of what he was trying to do?*

I mean, he wanted the Committee to *be* Garvice Kincaid, to run everything exactly the way he had been running it. You know, when the trust became operational, he was dead, and so the Committee, as he envisioned it, would step into issues and be responsible for making all the decisions for all the companies.

Mucci: *Well, that's true. I was trying to tie the family versus non-family because in the latter two versions, he removed them [family] completely. It looks like he wasn't sure if what he did in the original version was going to work. When I told you he removed them in the 1967 amendment, did this surprise you?*

The truth of the matter is I never saw anything like that, because I was gone in June of 1966. I am not surprised by anything he did.

He made decisions based on what he believed at a particular time. And sometimes you could anticipate the decisions he would make and sometimes—frequently—you could not anticipate what Garvice would decide to do.

Author: *Garvice had his first coronary attack at age forty in 1953, and he would suffer a second one in 1964 at age fifty-two on a trip to Florida. Do you think his health had anything to do with the estate planning he had you working on in 1963, that he signed in February 1964?*

Not that I recall. You know, he carried a lot of weight around, but he never talked about that [his health], as I recall, or talked about death or anything. You know, he just recognized that it was a prudent thing for somebody that had accumulated a substantial wealth to have a will and trust and what have you. I was more of a business lawyer than any of the other lawyers—Frank Trimble, Montjoy, or any of the rest of them. I had done work like that previously, and so he asked me to do it.

Author: Do you think the people that he listed in his estate plan, in the version you created, knew, or understood their role when it—when he adopted it, or did he and you just keep that close to the vest?

I don't think anybody knew at the time. Well, Frank Trimble might have known. But I don't know that one way or another. I never talked with Frank Trimble about it. I suspect that Garvice and I were the only ones that knew what was in that will and trust.

Author: This is a legal question, and I am just curious—to do a trust like this, do you have to bring your wife into the planning process? I mean, when you are disposing of marital assets, I thought the wife might have had to participate. As I have thought about it, did he discuss it with Nelle and tell her this is what my plan is, and this is what we're doing and then they sign up to do it, but in 1967, he just does what he wants and changes it completely.

No. I have no idea whether he talked to his wife or not. I don't know one way or another.

Author: One of the things I have no color on is what Garvice's office was like. Can you paint me a picture of his office—what you remember about working there for him?

Well, his office, I'm going to say, was thirty feet long and fifteen to eighteen feet wide. Right in the middle of the thirty feet was his desk. He had a number of chairs around it, and it was a very nicely decorated room. Outside his office was another long room, where Frank Trimble's secretary, or assistant, sat. She sat down at the far end away from Garvice's office, and close to Garvice's office his secretary sat, and then across from the two ladies, there were four or five or six seats. And I can remember when Garvice called you and you went there, you never went in immediately. You had to sit and wait. Then, all of a sudden, you'd hear [a] voice from inside his office say "Next!" That was the summons for whoever was next in line to go in and meet with him. It was repeated frequently that it was like waiting in a barber shop for a meeting with Garvice.

Mucci: I heard he had three phones in his office, and some of the people and articles I have read suggest he was always on the phone. I know he actually had a WATS line installed at his home on Richmond Road and that really surprised me.

I don't recall that.

Mucci: This may seem like an odd question, but I think he really never went anywhere for lunch and just ate at his desk. Jim Host also wrote about a meeting in his office where he was eating at this desk. Do you think I have the right impression?

That's my recollection. He would have his secretary pick up a sandwich or something, and this happened virtually five days a week or six days a week.

Mucci: I have heard many times from various folks at Kentucky Central, and in later years Kilbern Cormney, who ran the Campbell House, confirmed it, that Garvice had four or five restaurants in town where he liked to have dinner, and he had a certain table at each place that was "his" table. The owners, managers, or maître d' at each place would then get on the phone and call the other restaurants to let them know Garvice was there so they could release "his" table. Mr. Cormney called it "The Eagle has landed."

Let me ask you this. You mentioned Al Florence and you mentioned T. C. Quisenberry. As I told you in one of my written questions, Al Florence is kind of an enigma to me. I have a history of him—just a black-and-white history of some things he's done—but he never seems to fit the mold of the other people I see Kincaid working with. I'm just trying to get a little better understanding of him. Can you give me some?

I don't have any recollection of T. C. Quisenberry at all. I'm sure I met him, and I was introduced to him, but I don't recall any business that I had with him anytime during the three years.

Author: My old boss, when he would mention his name—and frankly his name didn't mean anything to me at the time—but he always classified him as a real gentleman. When I look at his history and some of the different things I found, his comment kind of made sense. What about our Al Florence? Some people I worked with referred to him as Garvice's henchman or bagman when it came to handling some of Kincaid's politician friends. He would handle things behind the scenes, when Garvice needed something.

Al Florence's background—as I recall, he was a Kentucky bank examiner for a number of years. At the time that I met him he would have been probably forty years old or thereabout. Garvice had brought him in to be an overseer, a day-to-day overseer, of all the various banks in Kentucky and the two banks in Florida. He would be on the road virtually from Monday morning until Friday afternoon at one or two or three of the banks, you know, doing whatever he did. But everybody understood at the banks that Al Florence had Garvice Kincaid's ear, and you better listen to what he had to say.

Mucci: Let me ask you this, and this this may sound unfair since I never met him [and don't] really know anything about him. To me, I get the impression that he wasn't well polished, and he was probably a little bit rough around the edges. Is that fair?

Let me say it's probably overall fair, but he certainly knew his business.

I can tell you have some misgivings about the role that Al Florence played, and maybe I didn't emphasize this, but he dealt with all the banks and oversaw all of the banks in Kentucky, as well as the two banks in Florida. And Garvice had a lot of respect for him. He definitely had Garvice's ear in connection with the banks, both Florida and Kentucky. Garvice listened to him.

I don't know his educational background, but I do know that before he joined up with Garvice, he was a Kentucky bank examiner. He was held in high regard in the ranks of the Kentucky bank examiners, and apparently that's the reason that Garvice reached out to him to oversee the banks, because nobody was overseeing the banks in general. He had confidence that Al Florence had the capability to do that on his behalf.

I didn't mention this yesterday, and you mentioned it and I had forgotten about that. The TV [and radio] stations that Garvice owned, again, they reported through Wooster and Hart Hagan. Wooster and Hart Hagan oversaw the stations, and what have you, and kind of managed them on behalf of Garvice. Garvice took a lot of interest, though, and the television stations particularly because of their capability of reaching out to a broad audience and reputational-wise, he was interested in all that.

You know, one of the things he did shortly after I came on board—he wanted to up the profile of Central Bank and the investment activities of Kentucky Central. So, Garvice brought on board, I'm going to say within six months after I got there, he brought in a guy by the name [of] Jim Lewis as trust officer for the Central Bank. He also did some trust work, to some degree, for Kentucky Central. In addition to that, he brought in a relatively young fella, but a very smart guy, as an investment officer in stocks and bonds for the portfolios of Kentucky Central and Central Bank. His name is Bill Engel. He was a very smart guy, and very good in stocks and bonds and portfolio investments, along that line. All of that was a direct competitive effort against First National Bank and Security Trust Bank.

You know, those were the banks where all the wealthy people in Lexington and the Bluegrass area banked, and Garvice wanted to be somewhat competitive with them. He was always going to be at a disadvantage, being competitive with them, but he brought on two very high-profile guys, and very smart guys, in order to compete, in bringing in Lewis and Engel, to compete with those two banks.

Author: Garvice saw the value in having a trust company.

Exactly, and he had nothing. I mean, it was a trust company, but he had no people to manage it, the trust side of the business, until Jim Lewis and Bill Engel came along.

Author: *My old boss, Cliff Forbush, talked to me a little bit about Engel. He met him some years later, after he joined Kentucky Central and of course after he was gone, and I got the impression— and it's an impression and not a fact—that Bill didn't like the pressure cooker of Kincaid, and that was why he left. I mean, it wasn't anything other than, you know, sometimes people just emotionally can't handle working for somebody that they're always intimidated by.*

I did a decent amount of work with Engel, particularly, and in fact, one of the things that happened, probably in 1964, was Garvice sent Bill Engle, Jim Lewis, and me on a tour of all the banks within his portfolio in Kentucky, and we gave a seminar at each of those banks. We spoke to their principal clients about estate planning, tax considerations in connection with estate planning, and how a bank administers trust assets and how they invest your assets, with Bill Engel providing the experience in connection with managing a portfolio of stocks and bonds for wealthy investors that were customers of those outlying banks.

Mucci: *Yes, one of the articles that I sent you yesterday, or a couple of days ago; it's from 1964 and it's where you and Engel and Bob Layman spoke to the life underwriters association, and it discusses what you are going to talk about. I can see Kincaid had you all doing road shows, and not for just his banks and their customers. I thought you might enjoy reading about that.*

I don't remember that particular article, but I am sure Jim Lewis would have been mentioned, because he was always a mainstay, along with the rest of us, in any of those seminars.

As I told you yesterday, taxation for an insurance company was very unusual, not anything like other corporations. And they had [a] phase one tax base, a phase two tax, and a phase three tax. The Houston/Dallas company [Professional and Business Men's Insurance Company] that Garvice acquired, which we discussed, had big losses for a number of years in connection with phase three tax, and then all of a sudden, in [a] later year, they had a substantial tax liability. And there were no tax-loss carryforwards and carrybacks under the existing legislation to allow losses in one year to offset profits in other years. So, I contacted the Treasury Department and the Ways and Means Committee people in Congress and said, hey, this is totally and completely unfair, that we're being taxed on profits in one year when we had big losses in other years. And they said, when we wrote that legislation, we were assured there were no companies that had that situation. And I said, I'm telling you that we've got that situation in spades for this company down in Dallas, and they asked me to write correcting legislation. I then worked out the language with the Treasury Department and I testified before Congress in connection with that situation. And they amended the tax laws to provide that there would be carryforwards and carrybacks, in connection with that legislation, to take care of our problem because they said we never intended for that to happen, and we're surprised that there is a company out there where it has happened. Well, and that was one of the very big issues in connection with the tax case for the Houston company.

In Kincaid's original estate trust agreement, which he signed on February 26, 1964, Frank Trimble was on the Committee, and not as an alternate. In later years, when Kincaid amended his trust agreement, Frank lost this place of honor to Ed Schaeffer.

By 1963, Garvice had grown and expanded his law practice, and in October that year, he joined his firm with a former law associate Frank Trimble's firm and formed Kincaid, Wilson, Trimble. The name was changed over the years as new partners were added and others left, and before it was disbanded in 1993, its final name was Wilson, Schaeffer, Trimble, Hembree & Kinser P.S.C. Charles "Rusty" Hembree joined the firm as an associate counsel the year it was formed in 1963.

Rusty Hembree would also be the last person installed on Kincaid's Committee in 1989, replacing Hart Hagan, who resigned due to an internal dispute. Hagan's relationship with the other two Committee members apparently began deteriorating around 1986. The problems actually began in 1983, after Leslie Combs II and his son Brownell Combs II sold stock in the renowned Spendthrift Farm near Lexington. It was the first breeding farm ever listed on a stock exchange.

Iowa State University's Department of Accounting, in May 1, 2019, issued a report described what the horse racing industry faced in the 1980s. Author Mia Vettese wrote this:

> The Tax Reform Act of 1986 played an important role in the equine industry in the United States. The tax act impacted all areas of the equine industry, specifically for the owners of race horses, competition horses, breeding and work horses, and recreation horses. The changes of the tax act created the most impact on the race horse industry. The Tax Reform Act of 1986 created changes to depreciation and class lives of horses. The Tax Reform Act of 1986 created a negative impact on the equine industry in the United States by causing an increase in number of unwanted horses. The changes

to the tax laws created by the act caused a decrease in the number of horse races and an increase in number of horses slaughtered in the United States, reduced the attractiveness of owning thoroughbred horses, and precipitated a dramatic drop in the price of thoroughbred horses and breeding rights.

The Combses ignored this problem and continue to spend lavishly. In addition, they underplayed the tax issue in their prospectus and financial statements. This saga led to six lawsuits seeking over $70 million and accusations of fraud against not only the Combses but also anyone who worked on the transaction, including the Kincaid law firm and attorney Rusty Hembree. Hembree was a close friend of Leslie Combs II and an expert tax attorney. By 1986, Spendthrift had to file for bankruptcy. In general, the lawsuits alleged that the defendants engaged in a scheme to induce investors to buy Spendthrift stock and concealed relevant information.

In July 1986, Earl Wilson Sr., who was age eighty, wanted to retire from Central Bank's board of directors and relinquish his position as chairman. Rusty Hembree was nominated by one of the other Committee members, and three directors dissented—Joan Kincaid, David Brain, and H. Hart Hagan. The three felt that Central Bank could not afford a "cloud of impropriety in its chairman or on its board of directors." Joan Kincaid specifically requested that Hembree resign from the board until the situation was cleared up. Hembree was elected chairman of the bank in a 5-to-3 vote. The depth of the rift among the directors was so strong that Hagan, at age 62, resigned from the Central Bank board while retaining his other Kincaid positions. Earl Wilson remained on the board as chairman emeritus.

This appears to be the beginning of a parting of the ways between Hagan and the other two Committee members, Burnett and Schaeffer. One Central Bank director remarked, "It's amazing that one of the trustees [of Kincaid's estate] would resign from one of the assets of the Kincaid trust." Hagan only said, "I resigned for business reasons that I don't care to discuss at this time." The lawsuits against the law firm and Rusty Hembree were dismissed on April 26, 1989. The judge ruled there was no evidence that Hembree or the law firm intended to commit fraud or knew of any alleged fraudulent scheme. The judge allowed most of the counts to continue against Brownell Combs II and his financier, Garth Guy. Leslie Combs had already turned over his assets and remaining stock in the farm to the plaintiffs. The ruling came during the eighth week of the trial.

On December 31, 1989, H. Hart Hagan retired from all his Kincaid positions, including the Committee. He had had enough. He could already see how some of the mortgage loans to the various Webb-related entities and others were negatively impacting Kentucky Central Life's financials. One can only assume that he felt his input was no longer appreciated or wanted. As was previously noted, in May 1991, things were so bad for Kentucky Central Life that Burnett and the Committee were forced to sell Kincaid's crown jewel, Kentucky Finance, for $145 million, and in June, they sold Kentucky Central Life's very profitable career insurance division for $50 million to Liberty Life Insurance Company. The Committee was forced to raise $195 million to cover Kentucky Central Life's mortgage loan and real estate losses. One must assume that in 1989, Hart Hagan, as a smart accountant and CPA, intuitively knew things were bad in the house of Kincaid.

The Kincaid Wilson law firm was dissolved in March 1993 following the February collapse of Kentucky Central Life Insurance Company. It was just thirty years after it was formed by Garvice. The firm had seven partners and thirty-four associate counsel and staff when it was closed. By far the firm's largest customers were Kincaid's companies, but other clients included The Associated Press, First National Bank of Georgetown, Taco Tico of Lexington, Mason & Hanger, Silas Mason Co., Inc., East Kentucky Power Cooperative, National Tour Association, and Liberty National Leasing.

Garvice Kincaid and his companies were important to Lexington, and they tended to associate with other important Lexington businesses and people. Mason & Hanger was a large client that was established before the Civil War in 1827. The company is considered the longest operating American architectural and engineering firm in the country and has partnered with the United States Government for nearly two centuries. Mason & Hanger is a trusted partner of the U.S. Department of Defense (Army, Navy, Air Force, Marines, National Guard), Department of Defense Reserves, Department of Homeland Security, Department of State, Department of Energy, and the intelligence community, among other government agencies critical to the U.S. National Security Mission.

In 1921, Mason & Hanger constructed the Lafayette Hotel, which Kincaid acquired in 1960, and transformed it into the home office for Kentucky Central Life Insurance Company. It was Lexington's second-tallest skyscraper at the time. Mason & Hanger also represented the Committee and Kentucky Central Life Insurance Company in 1976 when Kincaid Towers was constructed, and in 1999, Mason & Hangers moved its offices there. When Kincaid Towers was constructed in 1977, it was the tallest building in Lexington.

The importance of professional talent wasn't lost on Garvice Kincaid. As his empire grew, so did his need for accountants and attorneys. In November 1968, Kincaid addressed a group of University of Kentucky law students, and according to a *Herald-Leader* article dated November 5, 1968, he had this to say:

> Local businessman, financier, and banker Garvice Kincaid, Monday told a group of University of Kentucky law students to get good backgrounds in "current tax structure and accounting."
>
> Speaking in a question-and-answer format at the UK Law Forum series, Mr. Kincaid told the students that more than "half of you will not practice law as such except corporation law . . . and no matter what you do, companies always need top tax counsel, real estate men and accounting specialists.
>
> He added that a good knowledge of dealing with governmental agencies was important since most corporations do "more than 50 per cent of their work through these agencies."
>
> The problem with agencies, especially the Internal Revenue Service, he said, is that taxes run "10 or 12 years behind . . . and businesses can't run like that."
>
> Mr. Kincaid also chided the newspapers and the power structure here, and said that he had "no power at all" since power is held through politics or newspapers, and he held a position in neither. . . . On the newspaper situation here, he said there should be a competitive newspaper and reminded the audience that Fred B. Wachs did not own the paper, but that it was held in a trust by the First Security National Bank and Trust Co. . . . He added that there should also be a competitive bank on an equal basis with First Security.

Kincaid Goes to Court

In 1949, Garvice appeared in court as a witness for Central Bank and the First National Bank of Carlisle against a local food distributor, The Brown Brothers Wholesale Distribution Company.[15] The banks were suing Paul L. Brown and the company for $24.833. Kincaid testified that "the company was in bad shape financially and giving a lot of trouble" although the company and one of its officials had received "25 to 30 loans" in a three-year period. The Brown Brothers' distributors countersued the banks for $8,561 due for their merchandise in an attempt to get their claims ahead of the banks'. The trial ran for four weeks and (at the time) was reported to be one of the longest civil trials in the history of the court.

Kincaid testified that the "note and mortgage (originally for $29,833.11 of which $4,000 later was repaid) represented a total of several notes, two of them personally guaranteed by Brown, on which payment had defaulted. The

---

15   *Lexington Herald-Leader*, December 9, 1949.

wholesale company, at that time, was in bad shape financially, and Brown's personal signature was for added security."

Brown claimed that the note was made November 10, 1948, by the company and that a week later he was forced by bank officials to add his personal signature to the papers. He declared that he signed only after "Garvice D. Kincaid, president, and L.D. Nickles, executive vice president, drew guns on him and M.C. Haddix, chairman of the board, grabbed him and pounded his head against the wall."

A Fayette Circuit Court jury, on December 10, 1949, deliberated ten minutes before returning a verdict for the amount of the banks' claim (a total $43,034.68) on a note and mortgage made in November 1948. Paul Brown appealed and lost and then requested a new trial in September 1950, claiming to have new evidence. Brown said that "an unidentified person mailed him the originals of the two notes, and he found two deposit slips after the trial. He said they were material evidence in the case." In January 1951, a commissioner's sale was set in the case to raise $43,034.68, and Kincaid's lieutenant, Frank Trimble, was appointed as trustee.

Garvice Kincaid understood the value of distressed assets, and many of the properties he acquired in the 1960s and 1970s were because of defaulted or distressed bank loans. The loans or foreclosed assets were held by his banks, and he would in turn remove the problem asset. Kincaid understood these types of issues, and he had a significant advantage over the traditional small bank owners. Kincaid was wealthy and could rehabilitate a bank overnight by either removing/purchasing the loan/asset personally or adding capital to the bank. He was what Wall Street would later, in the 1990s, term a "vulture investor," someone who can make a living by seeking out troubled companies and assets. These investors are able to deal with the complexities and contentiousness of bankruptcy or out-of-court workouts and manage those assets for their long-term economic potential.

Garvice was a genius at recognizing the value of assets. His wealth was initially created by buying and selling real estate assets at Fayette County commissioner's sales in the 1930s and 1940s. Acquiring real estate properties through the acquisition of banks was also a no-brainer for him. A bank would lend up to 80 percent of the value of a property. It might also require a personal guarantee from the borrower or additional security, depending on the type of property the mortgage was on. The borrower might become distressed, or economic challenges might negatively impact the business, and the loan would become past due. Garvice could acquire the loan, foreclose on the property, and rehabilitate the situation or bring in another partner to manage it.

I was told many years ago by an old boss, "No one makes a bad loan; they go bad after you make it." Kincaid understood the game and had the wealth to rehabilitate a bad situation, and he could do things personally that a regulated bank might struggle to accomplish or be prohibited from doing.

Mr. Kincaid Goes to Florida

Sometime during the 1950s, Garvice became fascinated with the state of Florida, especially the areas of Fort Lauderdale, Miami/Palm Beach, and the Florida Keys. Some of his interest may have come from his friend and associate D.I. Boyle. Boyle had a sister who lived in the Miami Beach area, and the Kincaids and the Boyles are reported to have vacationed in the area, together, several times over the years. In June 1954, D.I. Boyle's sister and her husband, Trixie and Lt. Colonel James McKeldin, sold their two-story waterfront mansion, 4580 N. Bay Road, in Palm Beach to the Kincaids. Garvice had experienced his first heart attack the previous year and had been confined to bed for three months. The purchase of the McKeldins' home was his initial attempt at slowing down.

The McKeldins' 5,865-square-foot home was built in 1932 and contained eight bedrooms, five baths. In addition, it had an upstairs maid's room plus an office or an apartment with dining room, kitchen, and bath. This showcase home also had patios leading to three boat docks, all on the Chattahoochee River and the north bay. The dock area also contained a chickee hut with huge ceiling paddle fans. The McKeldins were downsizing, so some of their furnishings were included with the sale of the home. It was reported that Garvice paid $125,000 for the property.

In Garvice Kincaid fashion, he immediately updated it to suit his needs and partially furnished it to his and his wife's tastes. He also installed an elevator and a full-house air conditioning system. Finally, to complete his personal waterfront resort home, Garvice purchased a yacht and christened it "The Colonel". The renovations were completed quickly, and on July 30, 1954, the *Lexington Herald-Leader* reported the following and included a nice picture:

Kincaid Buys Florida Home

This 20-room mansion on North Bay Road in Miami Beach, Florida, has been bought by Mr. and Mrs. Garvice Kincaid of Lexington for a price reported to be about $125,000. The home, which the Kincaids plan to use as a vacation home, was purchased from Colonel James R. McKeldin and his wife. Mrs. McKeldin is sister of Dages I. Boyle of Lexington, president of Bankers Securities Corp.

The house is constructed of brick and stucco underlaid by steel. The patio in the picture faces the ocean, and there are three docks. On top of the porch is a solarium. The house is air-conditioned and has an elevator. Kincaid also has bought a yacht. He and Mrs. Kincaid and their daughters, Jane and Joan, have just returned from Miami Beach; they plan to go back to Florida for another stay before school starts here.

Garvice always liked to make a big impression and be the topic of conversation, and he usually knew how to do it. The *Miami Herald*'s gossip columnist, Gwen Harrison, in her column "Conversation Piece," featured several "notes" about the Kincaids over the next year, and Garvice gave her plenty to gossip about.

In December of 1955, Kincaid decided to host a buffet and dinner dance at his Miami mansion. This grand soirée was planned with the assistance of James McKeldin's mother, Mrs. John George (Bessie) Simmons, who also hosted the occasion. The event was scheduled for Friday, February 18, 1955, and the *Miami Herald*'s "Conversation Piece" column reported that invitations would be mailed in late January and said to "Watch the Letterbox." After the party, the newspaper did almost a full-page story on the event, with pictures of the mansion, the outdoor dance patio, and Garvice in his white tuxedo dinner jacket and black pants and Nelle in a lovely white dress. Kincaid, to further impress his guests and also pay homage to his roots, "had tons of Kentucky ham and beaten biscuit flown in from their home in Lexington for the party. There was enough champagne flowing to float their handsome yacht, 'The Colonel,' docked at their waterfront home. Mrs. Lino Sertel and Mrs. Julio Sanchez received guests with the hosts and Mrs. Simmons."

Since the George Washington's birthday (Presidents Day) celebration was to be on the following Tuesday, February 22, Garvice decided to give his event a patriotic flair. He brought in cherry trees, with cherries on them, and the lady hosts wore dresses that were also patriotic, with Mrs. Sanchez in red, Mrs. Sertel in blue and Nelle Kincaid in white.

By May of 1955, Kincaid had changed his mind about taking it easy and decided to sell his fabulous resort home. The furnishings they wanted to keep were boxed and shipped to their Richmond Road home in Lexington, but a large portion of the house's contents would be sold with the home. Before the announcement in the *Miami Herald*'s gossip column, Garvice, Nelle, and their twin girls left Lexington for a two-week vacation at their Miami Beach home. Dages Boyle and his wife vacationed with them on the trip. One can only guess why Kincaid changed his mind so quickly, but his business affairs probably had something to do with it. Kincaid listed the home with a real estate agent, and the *Miami Herald* ran the following ad over the next six months. It does make one wonder what was on his mind:

Colonial Bayfront

4580 N. Bay Road
Open For Inspection
125' Frontage – air-conditioned, heated – 5 bedrooms,
5 baths, 3 staff rooms, elevator, expensively furnished.
Owner anxious for quick sale.
SEE IT! And Make Offer
Brokers protected – Photographic Brochure available.
M. D. Futch Realtor
Better Class Homes Since 1923
420 Lincoln Rd. Phone JE 8-1843

The *Miami Herald* gossip column reported that Kincaid sold the home to Maude Daoud, a wealthy widow from Atlantic City, New Jersey, in July 1956. "Ms. Doud had been coming to the area for a few seasons and renting winter homes." It further said, "Kincaid was in town quietly, closing the long-rumored deal." The price wasn't disclosed, but the Miami Dade County property records indicate that Garvice probably sold it for his purchase price plus the cost of improvements, so maybe $135,000. The first reported sale of the property, after the period in question, is for $169,000 in 1976. The 1932 home was later acquired in 1984 for $620,000, and the house was razed to make way for a new structure. In 2003, the property value is listed at $2,650,000, and in 2021, the property sold for $32,150,000. Garvice had a great eye for value, and the location of his one-time resort home proved it.

In 1981, a long-time Kincaid employee and broadcasting lieutenant, Ted Grizzard, wrote a book about his own career, *#1 is Chicken*. In theory it's an autobiography, but as the *Lexington Herold-Leader*'s Don Edwards described it, it's really a 359-page "stand-up routine of vintage Grizzard." It's also a history of his life and the people and companies that were a part of it, including Garvice Kincaid. In it, he discusses Kincaid's Miami mansion:

> Somewhere in these years Garvice bought a mansion in Miami Beach. Everybody in the organization had heard about it. It was one of the show places the tourists see on the boat of tours of "millionaire's [sic] row" around Biscayne Bay. This could have been late 1953 'cause we had a 1952 Cadillac.

> Carlouise and I are going to Florida in January for a change. We had been going in March to see the "Reds" [Cincinnati Reds] in spring baseball training. As usual, I told Garvice I'd be away and

in Florida and gave him the dates. This time, too, bless him—he checks his calendar and says, "Why don't you and Carlouise stay at that house I bought down there. Nell [*sic*] (Mrs. Kincaid), and I are coming down next week-end, but you'll have the place a week all to yourselves."

I was afraid to thank him too much—remembering the Fontainebleau—but I did tell him we'd like it very much. He gave me a letter to "Eddie" the house boy who would take care of us— and we're off to the mansion on Biscayne Bay!

I think the entrance was off Alton Road (something like that) and this beautiful place faced Biscayne Bay. It was in an area where the police would stop and check you if you looked like you didn't belong around there. I never knew how you were supposed "not to look" but Carlouise and I and the '52 Cadillac seemed to meet the requirements of "proper looks."

A big Spanish-style gate—wooden—opened on a driveway to the house and on the right of the drive were several guest cottages. These were kinda tired-looking and they adjoined what could have been servant's [*sic*] housing—since the latter were smaller and next to several garages. Anyway, there were enough bedrooms in the place to handle a small convention so I doubt that they needed the guest cottages at any time. The two-story red brick (that was rare too) home, with big attic, had a curved front with four big white columns and the front and back of the house were exactly alike in looks and design.

You see, I've never been around this sort of place so I remember. The entrance was through a tremendous reception hall and this went—or was open—right on through to the other front or back of the house that overlooked a terrace, a huge garden and the bay, with a colored tile stairway that graduated downward toward the boat dock.

Strangely, there was no pool. When you entered that big reception hall coming from the bay side you faced two curved stairways to the second floor but at the top of one there was a beautiful iron grillwork door which the previous owner had kept locked at night so no one could get in that side of the upstairs. Beautiful but kinda spooky. Of course, Garvice didn't keep it locked even though his master bedroom was on that side.

In the first-floor drawing room—directly under his second-floor bed room—Garvice had installed an elevator. This was not too long after his heart attack and stair-climbing was out.

In that drawing room, near the elevator there was—of all things—a Steinway grand piano. Not a "baby grand." But the big job—almost as big as a concert grand—was the Grand Steinway. I think there is a concert grand—the 16-wheel, four door job, but I'm not sure. But wait a minute. This was no ordinary Steinway grand. No Steinway grand is ordinary. This Steinway was especially out of the ordinary because it was an "electric" player Steinway grand piano!

The previous owner had bought that little tidbit too—after opening I don't know how many Cracker Jack boxes and having no luck at all. I wonder how many Steinway electric player pianos there were in the whole world? I could have been looking at the only one—but on the other hand (and I forget which hand) such pianos could have been in Sear's [*sic*] catalogue for 1948. To me it was something just a bit out of the ordinary anyway. I wanted to give concerts to help pay for our trip but Garvice wouldn't let me.

The mansion had been built, I was told, in the late '20s and presented as a wedding gift to the lady who sold it to Garvice. The story was that she had not seen it 'til she came to Miami Beach. Tied around the entire house was a big ribbon (hell, it had to be big, didn't it?) to denote gift wrapping. The color of the ribbon I wasn't told and this disappointed me—I like details. Red, surely. And, naturally, my next thought—was the bride the type of lady who "saves ribbons"?

When Carlouise and I arrived at the house rather late in the afternoon, Eddie, the house man, was expecting us. Garvice had sent to him a copy of the letter given to me.

Eddie was "colored" but medium light skin. On the slim side and with touches of gray in his hair. He had come with the house, I think, and Garvice didn't care much for him. Garvice kept a car there—a Cadillac—but he didn't leave the keys with Eddie so when Eddie went shopping, he had to get a cab or a bus. Eddie didn't like this. He told me.

Our car was dirty from the trip and Eddie noticed this when he was unloading our luggage. Evidently, he liked cars and especially Cadillacs. He said he was going to put us in the Chinese room which he thought was the nicest guest room because of the view of the bay, the breeze and the bath was bigger too. I learned there were four or more bedrooms and baths—in addition to the master bedroom—on the second floor.

The Chinese room was just that. Lamps, bed covers, pictures, color schemes—the whole theme. Exotic and beautiful. I tried to squint my eyes just a little to feel more at home but had very little luck and quit that after running into a couple of chairs. What a place!

A big palm tree whose fronds reached almost into the bedroom window would rustle a lovely lullaby in the breeze and sleeping was grand. We had eaten a big and late lunch and didn't want dinner—which Eddie had offered to prepare for us. We just wanted to shower,

relax and look the place over. Eddie said—in that case—and with
my permission he'd like to take the night off and go to town, but
he'd be back by 11:00.

Before he left, he asked what time we'd like breakfast, and we
told him about 10:30 would be fine. The next morning at 9:30 Eddie
knocked at our door to ask about eggs—how many, how we liked
them—whether ham, bacon or sausage—juice, milk or coffee—the
works. We told him. He said, "It's a beautiful morning and I'll serve
you on the patio at 10:30."

At about 10:30 on a beautiful and warm morning in January in
Miami Beach, Carlouise and I go out on the patio to a breakfast I'll
never forget. At a white table under a multi-colored umbrella, we
were overlooking Biscayne Bay. The fresh table linen and bright
China and silver and cold orange juice—along with the morning
paper.

In a minute or two out comes Eddie in his starched white coat
and he brings the coffee. At just the right interval later he's back with
the bacon, eggs and toast and marmalade—under shiny, aluminum
covers to keep warm. I could have hugged the guy. I had seen
such things—but only in movies. In January this was happening to
Carlouise and me. A warm breeze rustled those palm trees and here
we were. Do you wonder that I didn't mind working real hard for
Garvice Kincaid?

Then—all of a sudden, I thought—there are people who live
like this all the time! More power to 'em and bless 'em! Don't talk
to me about share—everybody having the same and being equal and
that crap. To hell with that stuff. I'll never make it to this point of
daily living—never. But if I ever did—don't try to take it away from
me just because somebody else is stupid or lazy or, for any other
reason, hasn't done as well as I have.

After breakfast I walked to the other side of the house—through
that beautiful reception hall and there was our car. Spotless and
shiny. I don't know what time Eddie got up but it was early enough
for him to have washed the car. Maybe Garvice didn't like Eddie—
but I did! I wanna finish with Eddie now.

That afternoon Carlouise and I went over to Miami for awhile
and then came home. We loafed and dozed in the sun on the patio
and I don't know what Eddie fixed for dinner but we ate at the
"mansion." The next day Eddie asked me if I liked to fish. I told him
no. But he had several fishing rods and in a kidding way urged me
to come on down to the boat dock and fish in the bay. Okay. So, I
let him take the car to go to a market and get shrimp pieces for bait.
Now here it comes. While Carlouise is knitting—Eddie and I go to
the boat dock of the mansion to fish.

You've forgotten—and I wanna talk to you about your memory in connection with these important things—but I said that Kincaid's "mansion" is one of those they show to tourists on the boat tour of the bay around "millionaire's [*sic*] row."

On this day I'm sitting on the railing around the boat dock—Garvice keeps his boat at a marina place somewhere else. I'm wearing sneakers and slacks and have a sweater tied around my shoulders and I'm fishing—I think—in the bay. Standing beside me is a colored man of most dignified appearance—in his white coat. As I pull in my line and hook, my "servant" in the white coat, rebaits the hook and I cast again, hoping for better luck—I think.

All this takes place as the tourist boats go by and the travelers are taking pictures of Eddie and me—and maybe some home movies too. "Home" movies? I don't think Paramount or Fox came that day! They're getting good shots—the tourists—see that beautiful-white columned mansion in the background too. My home!

Now to add a little action to the scene—the spielers (you know, the guys on the boats who point out the homes and make up some name as to the owner) would—without the tourists seeing the gesture—wave to Eddie and me in a friendly greeting.

And, Eddie and I, being the friendly sort of wealthy people—certainly not snobs as are so many of the rich—would wave back toward the spieler and the boat. This would cue a frenzy of hand-waving and picture-taking from the travelers and no doubt did much good for the Miami Beach Chamber of Commerce. We repeated that little scene—being aware of what the spieler was doing—any number of times during the afternoon.

I gave some thought to a commercial deal with the boat tour people. After all, being waved to by a genuine millionaire and his servant—and Eddie and I had the white coat and white-columned mansion to prove our position—added a lot to the tour for these travelers. 'Cause when they got back to Idaho or Kansas (or anywhere but around Lexington) they could show their snapshots and their movies of Eddie and me waving to 'em—then direct attention to the mansion and say—see, even the millionaires and their servants are friendly down there.

Then they could add— "Now, Uncle Waldo, when you sell the farm or give up cattle rustlin' (they were never quite sure how Uncle Waldo made a buck but were afraid to say anything for fear he'd cut 'em off the list) you should retire to Miami Beach!"

I often wondered what their thoughts would have been had they known their friendly millionaire was a "free-loading announcer" at his boss's home. Likely they wouldn't have cared. They would have lied to Uncle Waldo just the same. Oh, by the way—I caught several good-sized fish. Eddie and a houseman buddy of his from next door ate the fish for their dinner that night.

Carlouise and I went over to Miami for dinner. I remember the evening well because at the restaurant a nice-looking family—mama, pappa and three children, none of whom could speak English—sat at a table next to ours. Their waitress didn't speak Spanish but she soon found a waiter who did and everything went smoothly, I think.

The next day Carlouise and I went shopping and looking and when we knew we'd be late getting home we agreed we'd not have the heart to ask Eddie to fix dinner for us. We had eaten a late lunch—and too much at that. I knew that when Garvice wasn't there, Eddie had at least two nights off each week and often, after dinner, he would take another evening off.

On this night Eddie fixed drinks for us and served them on the patio. Man, that's living. He offered salads or snacks and these we refused and then he asked if we were staying home and we told him we were. He's back again before long and this time all dressed up. He tells me the story again about Mr. Kincaid's not letting him use the car, but he doesn't know why. He drives it when Mr. Kincaid is there and never had any trouble.

Now—he says he has a really important date that night and wonders if he could use my car if he's home by 10:30? I told him I'd be glad for him to use it but there is just one problem. I doubt my insurance would be worth anything to me, him or anybody else if anything happened while he was driving the car. I didn't know. He assured me he would be extra careful and I told him the keys were on the table in the reception hall.

At 10:30 I had a phone call from Eddie and it scared the hell out of me. He was most apologetic and the first thing he said was "The car is alright." Then, would it be alright if he got back a little after 12:00. I don't know what time he got home but nothing happed to the car or Eddie. Two more days before Garvice and Mrs. "K" came down and Eddie didn't ask for the car again. I liked the guy.

I don't know—of course—what became of him. I heard he left Garvice's employ shortly before Garvice sold the house. Eddie was a hell of a good man for the job. Appearance good—tactful—he could cook—knew how to serve—chauffeur and the house was always spotless. I'm sure he found a job.

I don't think Mrs. Kincaid was ever too impressed with the "mansion." But then, she was accustomed to nice things. While she didn't especially care for the house—in my opinion—she did like some of the things in it and had Carlouise and me bring back two of the pictures from the Chinese room. I liked those too.

. . .

Years later, when Carlouise and I were in Florida, we took the boat tour of "millionaire's [*sic*] row" hoping to see the Kincaids' house where we had stayed. It was gone. I can't imagine destroying it, but it was old when we were there. We didn't know enough about the area to spot the site where it might have been. Later we drove on Alton Road—but even that side was changed—the big, wooden Spanish gate was gone. I don't think Garvice kept the place very long after our visit, but I wish we could have gone back. It was wonderful—really, another world to "the man on the street."

After losing Eddie and finding that the "mansion" has been torn down, I come across this note. We had been enjoying a new kind of world for a week and had more pleasure to come when Garvice, Nell [*sic*] and D. I. Boyle came down on the weekend. Nell brought a big country ham—already baked, bless her heart—and we loved that.

Of course, I had learned a long time ago not to ask Garvice any questions about anything other than something pertaining to WVLK business. In that way, I learned quite a lot about other projects of his. But if you asked—he sure as hell wouldn't tell you.

There was an exception—I didn't ask about this and he didn't tell me—but in some fashion, the purchase of the "mansion" included a membership in the exclusive Surf Club at Surfside—Miami Beach—and Garvice took us to lunch there one day. In fact, the only day he stayed in town.

Now this was about the time that some fellow named Wolfson (Louis, I think) had created a sensation in the financial world. He was buying and selling traction companies and railroads or whatever. Reportedly, he had made quick millions and had, they said, just recently bought a home not far from the place Garvice had.

[Note from the author to explain Kincaid's interest in Wolfson: Louis E. Wolfson was a self-made industrialist and financier whose 1966 legal troubles were central to the resignation of a Supreme Court justice. Wolfson was born in St. Louis on January 28, 1912, and attended the University of Georgia. His immigrant father was a scrap-metal dealer in Florida, and this permitted Louis to obtain $10,000 of borrowed capital and use it to trade in war surplus materials. From this modest beginning, Wolfson ultimately created a diverse group of industrial and commercial holdings, controlling total assets estimated at $250 million.

In 1955, he drew national attention for his unsuccessful attempt to acquire Montgomery Ward Company in a hostile takeover. At the time, it was the country's second-largest mail-order house. His career in high finance effectively ended in the mid-1960s when he became involved in a scandal involving the sale of unregistered company stock. The case wound its way to the Supreme Court and led to the resignation of Justice Abe Fortas in 1969 after it as discovered that Wolfson's foundation was paying him a $20,000 annual retainer for unspecified work. Mr. Wolfson spent nine months at a federal minimum-security prison in Florida for securities violations.

In the 1960s, Wolfson established Harbor View thoroughbred farm near Ocala, Florida. He operated the farm for years breeding and raising thoroughbred racehorses. In 1978, he achieved a cliff-hanging sweep of the 1978 Triple Crown with his Harbor View–bred Affirmed. Affirmed was only the eleventh horse to win the Triple Crown. Wolfson died at his Bal Harbour, Miami Beach, home in 2008, at the age of 95.

By the mid to late 1950s, Garvice would have been reading about Louis Wolfson in most of the national financial publications he read. We know Kincaid like to read the *Wall Street Journal* and *New York Times,* and he also subscribed to several business publications: *Forbes, Fortune Magazine,* and *Business Week.* Louis Wolfson would have been well covered, especially after he tried to acquire the Montgomery Ward Company.]

> On the way to the Surf Club to lunch that day Garvice kept driving around trying to find the place Wolfson had bought. It amused me. He was like a little boy wanting to see whether another little boy had a better bicycle. Frankly, I don't think he really gave a damn. We never found Wolfson's place but Kincaid still ate a big lunch and so did I.
>
> The beautiful home on the Bay was gone but later Garvice bought a small hotel on the beach—Collins Avenue—along with some other properties in Miami Beach. This one was kinda tired-looking. It was near the Americana Hotel and named the Crillon. Not the Carillon. An apartment hotel and it was kept full of Kincaid's employees and friends and politicians. We went a couple of times.
>
> We were down there once when I saw the lady who was the assistant manager and she had just finished talking long distance with Garvice. He had been giving her hell 'cause the place wasn't making any money. She said, "Mr. L, how can it make money?" I agreed with her. About the only people I had seen there were those like myself— "free-loaders."
>
> Ralph Worster [Kincaid's main real estate accountant] was handling a lot of things for Kincaid at the time and he was the one who (supposedly) passed along much of the free-loading stuff for Garvice to okay. Anything I enjoyed came directly from Kincaid but one day I happened to think of Herman [Ted's brother who worked at a Nashville radio station]. God bless him—I don't think that in all his life he had anything given to him. I went to Ralph. Was he the

one to okay a couple of weeks at the Crillon—as a favor to me—for Herman and his wife—or should I go to Garvice?

I didn't want to "go over" Ralph's head if he was handling all of that kind of thing. He said, no use going to Garvice, he'd be glad to take care of it for me. He did take care of it and Herman and Reta had a wonderful two weeks down there. They both loved Florida and could never have afforded Miami Beach at any spot. Thanks again, Ralph. I still appreciate it.[16]

In a May 20, 1962, interview reported in the *Miami News*, Kincaid says this about his North Bay home and how it was tied to his interest in Florida banks and his vetting process:

He's a Big Bank Buyer

Anyone with a bank for sale in Dade—and there are 36, with four more on the way—doesn't have far to look. Garvice Kincaid's in town . . . he's got the money . . . and he's in a buying mood.

Kincaid, of course has some pretty snappy assistants on his management team, like Robert E. Layman, president of the Central Bank & Trust Company of Lexington. He's been in Miami and Fort Lauderdale for weeks, a sort of advance man for Kincaid's force.

But the final decision, the final word, is up to him. It's usually a split-second decision . . . but certainly from the cool sharp mind of one who knows where he's going, what he's doing.

Although many of his deals are made over the telephone, Kincaid sends in a staff of sharp-eyed investigators to make certain that what he's bought has a solid ring to it.

That's how he bought Curtiss National from Harry Playford— over the phone. And also, Everglades Bank in Fort Lauderdale from James Sottile, which he since sold.

Kincaid said, "I don't remember how I found out Playford wanted to sell, but I called him up and asked if he was interested in a deal. He was, and here I am," said Kincaid.

The Dania Bank? "When I decided to get into Florida in a big way, a real estate salesman started to show me a home in Lauderdale. But he told me I had to buy a bank, first," he laughed. "I bought the bank, but I haven't bought the home yet."

Actually, Kincaid's move into Florida—in the beginning—was more necessity than anything else.

In 1953 he suffered a severe coronary, was ordered to lose at least 50 pounds, move to the Sunshine State and quit work. He

---

16   Ted Grizzard, *#1 Is Chicken*, 317–25 (Jim Host and Associates, 1981).

bought a home on North Bay Road, Miami Beach, which he's since sold.

"But while I was here, I saw the tremendous possibilities for growth in Florida. I'm convinced the state has a tremendous future, and that's why I'm here."

When Garvice did this interview, it was shortly after his $1.5 purchase of Curtiss National Bank. Curtiss National was Kincaid's fourth purchase in Dade and Broward counties in three years. He's kept three. Eating up banks like they were candy bars is Kincaid's pleasure. He wants more.

"Sure, we're looking," drawled the soft-spoken Kentucky multimillionaire, fresh from his latest purchase, Curtiss National of Miami Springs, for a reported $1.5 million.

We want to fill in the gaps in our South Florida operation. But that doesn't mean we'll buy just anything. We've looked at about 10 here, but you don't buy one in every 20 to 25 that you see."

Altogether, the chunky 40-year-old Lexington banker controls 15 banks in Florida and Kentucky, three hotels, a life insurance company four radio stations, huge chunks of real estate, office buildings and a finance company with 129 offices in 14 states.

A reporter, after listening to a discourse on all of Kincaid's enterprises, asked if an accurate estimate of his holding might be $100 million.

"$300 million" was his rapid reply.

There was no boast in his tone, only pride. And he confides, "I'm long past the money-making stage. I guess you might call it fun. Running all these things. I get a great deal of fun watching them go."

Kincaid may seem unorthodox to some . . . but his operations make money. And he knows how to draw a crowd. At the opening of the Everglades Bank, 14,000 showed up—a Wild West promotion, in all its grandeur, was doing the trick.

What does he expect from Curtiss, which has in the neighborhood of $18 million in assets? "We'll double it in three years," answered Kincaid, and there was plenty of positiveness in his voice.

One can also guess that Garvice's habit of reading four or five newspapers a day, along with various weekly and monthly business publications, may have created or increased his interest. Florida's population in the 1950s and 1960s was growing faster than practically any other states. California-based Walt Disney wouldn't begin looking to develop Florida's Walt Disney World until 1963, and he wouldn't announce the creation of the theme park until 1964. In the early 1960s both Kincaid and Disney saw the potential of Florida.

Edward Fernald, state geographer of Florida and associate vice president for academic affairs, director of the Institute of Science and Public Affairs, and professor of geography at Florida State University, in his 1981 work about the Florida economy, describes the historical factors creating Florida's economic growth over the years:

FLORIDA'S POPULATION IN THE MID 1980's: LOOKING BACK AND AHEAD"

Florida has always been a growth state. Since the first census of the territory in 1830, population increases of less than 30 percent have occurred in only two decades, 1910–1920 and 1930–1940. The 1950s showed the largest percentage increase, 78 percent, although the largest numerical increase occurred in the 1970's. Following the 1970 census, demographers nationally were surprised that a state which started with a base of 5 million people in 1960 had grown at the rate of 34.7 percent.

During the 1950s growth came from economic stability. Social Security, union movements in the north, assured retirement programs, early retirement and (increased) disposable income for vacations all contributed to Florida's growth. In the 1960s, the space program and the associated expansion of electronics industries fueled much of Florida's growth. Interestingly enough, both economic booms and busts in the national economy have motivated people to move to Florida. Over the years, improvements in transportation and in technology, such as air conditioning, as well as publicity campaigns, have had positive impacts on growth. Finally, the low cost of a high quality of life in Florida has attracted people who also wish to benefit economically from homestead exemptions, no income or inheritance taxes, and the relatively low total tax burden.

During the 1960s, Kincaid acquired five Florida banks, some of which had issues in their commercial loan portfolios. The Dania Bank, with more than $35.6 million in deposits, was Kincaid's flagship bank of the Florida group. In July 1969, Kincaid and a small group of investors paid two Chicago businessmen $6 million for their interest in the bank. Garvice retained 55 percent of the ownership of the bank, with two Fort Lauderdale residents, R. H. Gore Sr. and K. T. Keller, retaining 45 percent. In addition, the seller allowed Kincaid to pay for the bank in four equal installments over two years. Dania was Garvice's initial Florida bank purchase, and his total initial investment was $3 million. Over time, Kincaid acquired more stock from other shareholders and owned 82 percent of the bank. At Kincaid's death, the stock was being held by Kentucky Central Life Insurance Company.

In 1969, Kincaid and his lieutenants started slowly adding assets to Kentucky Central Life. They wanted to make publicly traded Kentucky Central Life a larger company, and in the 1960s, companies that had a diverse mix of businesses had become popular. Garvice was hoping to capitalize on this fact and create further interest in the company's stock.

The following appeared in Kentucky Central's 1969 annual report published in April 1970:

Diversification

Diversification of holdings, in the interest of increasing Kentucky Central Life's future overall profitability, is being achieved through the company's subsidiary holding company.

Major subsidiary holdings at this time include:

Dania Bank, located in the greater Miami area, one of the oldest state banks in Florida.

Television station WKYT-TV, located in Lexington, Kentucky. This is the highest rated and most powerful station in Central Kentucky and its new facilities are among the finest in the Mid-South.

Indies Inn and Yacht Club, located in the Florida Keys, one of Florida's most beautiful resort hotels.

Kentucky Central Insurance Company, a weekly-premium fire insurance company founded in 1960.

In the end he and his appointed Committee were successful in moving most of his broadcasting, finance, and real estate investments into Kentucky Central Life. These were mainly held in an investment subsidiary called Mid-Central Investments Co. His banks were the problem—regulations prohibited a corporation from doing what Garvice could do personally. Central Bank remained held under his trust, but the Dania Bank, which was moved to Kentucky Central in 1969, soon became a problem for the Committee. In April 1978, the Committee sold its stake in the bank for almost $11 million. Banking laws had changed, and the Committee needed to sell the bank stock.

The Bank Holding Company Act of 1956

The Bank Holding Company Act of 1956 is a United States Act of Congress that regulates the actions of bank holding companies. According to the Federal Reserve's Website, the original law (subsequently amended), specified that the Federal Reserve Board of Governors must approve the establishment of a bank holding company and that bank holding companies headquartered in one state are banned from acquiring a bank in another state. The law was implemented, in part, to regulate and control banks that had formed bank holding companies to own both banking and non-banking businesses. The law generally prohibited a bank holding company from engaging in most non-banking activities or acquiring voting securities of certain companies that are not banks, but there were loopholes that created confusion and opportunities to operate outside the intent of the law. The Bank Holding Company Act Amendments of 1970, in general, tried to fix those loopholes and require a bank holding company (generally any company controlling a bank) to divest either its banking or nonbanking properties on or before December 31, 1980.[17]

In the footnotes to Kentucky Central's 1976 annual report (released in April 1977), the following is reported:

> A subsidiary company's investment in the capital stock of the Dania Bank represents an ownership interest of 82.32%, as of December 31, 1975 and 1974 and is shown in the consolidated balance sheet at the net assets of the bank.

> The board of Directors (The Committee) has resolved that the Company will cease to be a bank holding company, as that term is defined in the Bank Holding Company Act, by divesting itself by January 1, 1981, of the investment in the bank.

Kentucky Central's 1977 annual report provided the following footnote:

> On December 14, 1977, a subsidiary company entered into an agreement to sell its investment in the Dania Bank. Closing of the agreement is contingent upon receiving approval from a bank regulatory agency. Under the agreement the purchase price will be one-and-one half times the book value of each share of the bank's stock, as of the month end preceding the month in which the transaction is approved by such agency.

> Total assets of the bank were $128.4 million and $110.4 million as December 31, 1977, and 1976, respectively, and net income was $975,000 and $553,000 for 1977 and 1976, respectively. Shareholders' equity of the bank at December 31, 1977 was $8,615,000.

In April 1978, the company released this announcement to the press:

> THE SALE OF THE 82 percent of the Dania Bank by Kentucky Central Life Insurance Co. was "close to" $11 million cash, the Kentucky firm's chairman, Earl S. Wilson Sr., said. The buyers were J.J. Gonzalez Corrondona Jr., a Venezuelan banker, and George L. Childs Jr., New York investment banker.

---

17   "Introduction to the BHC [Bank Holding Company] Nonbanking and FHC [Financial Holding Companies] activities—Section 3000," in *BHC Supervision Manual* (July 2012).

Garvice's initial $3 million investment had done very well since 1969! In nine years, it had increased by over 300 percent, adjusting for the additional shares he had acquired.

A June 22, 1987, story in the *Miami Herald*[18] celebrated the history of the Dania Bank:

The Dania Bank was started in 1912 by a Georgia financier, sensing potential in this Florida frontier farming town; tomato growers needed cash for seeds and labor until their harvest are sold. The banker was W.S. Witham of Atlanta. He erected a stark, white building at the town's only crossroads and brought in 23-year-old I.T. Parker, a promising young cashier, as the bank's sole employee.

Over the next 40 years, I.T. Parker and his brother William S. Parker, who joined I.T. in 1918 would steer their small, but solid bank safely through two killer hurricanes, a real estate boom and its following panic, and the ravages of the Great Depression and World War II. According to the bank's Clark Walden, the bank's attorney since 1955, the bank did ok until the real estate bust in the mid-1920s, that's when four men persuaded the state banking authorities to allow them to affiliate with the Bank of Key Biscayne in Miami and be liquidators of the old bank. Within a month they were back in business as the Dania Bank and within a few years had repaid most of the deposits people had lost.

In 1953, with most of the principal owners/managers in their 80s and 90s, the bank was sold to a Philadelphia grocery chain magnate and four others. Later, in 1960, Garvice Kincaid acquired the bank. All during this period, William stayed with the bank as a bank officer, approving loans and banging out financial forms on an old black typewriter that he hammered with two fingers. Walden would come to tell how long-time customers would walk right past the young loan officers to wait in line to see William.

In the early 1970s, with William in his 80s, he continued to work, until Garvice Kincaid felt obliged, around 1975, to nudge him into retirement. Kincaid told William he was being relieved of most of his duties, including making loans, but was welcome to report to work daily, keep his secretary and draw his full salary for as long as he wished.

Walden said, "I think he threw his pen down and walked over here . . . and he said, Mr. Walden, after 58 years, they fired me."

Kincaid may have been a cunning businessman, but this story also shows he was a man of compassion and didn't put money above a loyal employee's dignity.

---

18   Colleen Gallagher, *Miami Herald*, "Customers Fondly Remember Bankers Who Bank on Trust," June 22, 1987.

Garvice liked banking. It was considered a more respectable type of lending than the consumer loan business. In addition, banks made loans secured by real estate and sometimes those borrowers defaulted, and Kincaid understood that just because a loan becomes distressed, that doesn't mean the collateral value isn't there to support the loan.

Garvice Kincaid had a history of dealing in distressed real estate. Typically, the situation would involve a mortgage loan—a loan secured by real estate. He may have made the initial loan, he may have acquired a bank that had made the loan, or he may have sold a piece of foreclosed or defaulted loan property to someone and made a loan to them. One can believe he enjoyed the challenge of turning one person's mistake into a profitable situation for himself.

The Dania Bank in Miami and the Everglades Bank both brought important investment properties into the Kincaid empire—and also a banker by the name of Clyde W. Mauldin, who would become important to Garvice.

Garvice Kincaid and Miami's Famous Fontainebleau Hotel

When I joined Kentucky Central Life and Cliff Forbush in January 1981, I soon heard about Garvice Kincaid and the Fontainebleau Hotel. As with most legends, some of the supposed truths are more mythical than factual. The stories about the Fontainebleau Hotel revolved around Garvice foreclosing on the hotel three times. Each time he supposedly would sell it to someone else and make them a loan, only to go through the foreclosure process again. It wasn't until I started doing the research for this book that I finally understood the real story.

The Fontainebleau Hotel opened in 1954. It was reported to be the largest and most expensive hotel in Miami. It was named after France's Chateau Fontainebleau, once a palace of French kings. The hotel was constructed in three phases over twenty years. The site was the former winter estate home of Harvey S. Firestone. Ben Novack, a Miami Beach hotelman who resembled the American comedian and actor Jerry Stiller, purchased the property from Firestone's heirs in 1952 for a reported $2.3 million and constructed the fourteen-story, 554-room hotel in 1954 for a reported $14 million (equal to $154.5 million today).[19] When the three-building hotel complex was finally

---

19   Information about Ben Novack Sr. and the building of the Fontainebleau Hotel comes from the following sources: John Glatt, *The Prince of Paradise: The True Story of a Hotel Heir, His Seductive Wife, and a Ruthless Murder* (St. Martin's 2013); Steven Gaines, *Fool's Paradise: Players, Poseurs, and the Culture of Excess in South Beach* (Crown 2009); "Fontainebleau: Hotel Masterpiece," *The Miami Herald*, February 21, 1954; more than twenty articles about the hotel and Ben

completed in 1970, it contained 1,250 rooms, 265 cabanas, two swimming pools, seven tennis courts, two gyms, five bowling lanes, and an ice-skating rink.

The luxurious Fontainebleau Hotel was located in South Miami Beach, and after it was built it soon became a vacation paradise for the likes of Frank Sinatra, Esther Williams, and Marilyn Monroe but also many U.S. presidents and foreign dignitaries. The hotel also soon became a favorite destination of Garvice Kincaid. After Kincaid moved out of his Miami home in 1956, he still made many trips to Florida. Some of the trips involved his banking and radio broadcasting interests and some were for pleasure, and his two favorite places to stay were the Fontainebleau Hotel and Duck Key's Indies Inn and Yacht Club.

Garvice was a celebrity in his own right, and he also owned the Dania Bank, which was one of the Florida banks that Novack and the Fontainebleau Hotel did business with, so it's not surprising that sometime in the mid-1960s, Kincaid decided to keep a personal suite, for himself and his guests to use, at the hotel. In fact, in the fall of 1972, when my old boss, Cliff Forbush, interviewed with Kincaid and Garvice found out that Cliff was going on vacation the following week, he insisted that Cliff bring his family down to Miami and stay in his suite at the hotel. Luckily their plans involved a family beach house and they were able to adjust their destination to the Fontainebleau. Garvice was a difficult person to say no to.

One can see how it was easy for Ben Novack and Kincaid to become business associates. Both men were successful, with Garvice being a wealthy business financier and Novack owning a resort that catered to celebrities and high-powered politicians and businessmen.

In the book *Fool's Paradise*, author Steven Gaines paints a vivid portrait of the Novack family.

Ben (Novack) Sr.'s first major foray in the hotel business, the Sans Souci, came at the beginning of his courtship to (his wife) Bernice, a beautiful model whom he had met at the La Martinique nightclub. He pursued her relentlessly, hoping she, still married to a soldier, would say yes to dinner just once. Rebuffed numerous times, he was finally able to get her attention in a way that only a rich man can.

Bernice flew to Cuba for a photo shoot, Gaines wrote, only to discover that it had been an elaborate ruse. There was no photo shoot. Though they were

---

Novack Sr. in *The Miami Herald* dating from December 1971 to November 1986; these also include information about Kincaid's loans, the ultimate foreclosure and sale of the property, and what happened to Novack Sr. over the next several years.

both married at the time, they eventually were able to marry each other: Ben got a divorce, and her prior marriage was annulled. They were married in front of a judge in New York. Bernice and Ben moved into the upscale confines of the Sans Souci hotel.

In 1952, the plans for the Fontainebleau were announced—backed by a host of investors, some in the liquor distribution business, another running a taxi and limo service. Despite a period of contention between the architect, Morris Lapidus, and the elder Novack, the Fontainebleau was ultimately a huge success after it opened on December 20, 1954. The behemoth sprawled over 85,000 square feet, boasting seven restaurants that could churn out over 2,000 meals a day. The pool itself was a massive attraction—and over the years, served as the backdrop in movies like *Scarface* and *A Hole in the Head*, featuring Frank Sinatra at the height of his rat-pack fame.

When it appeared in the 1950s, the hotel, a sprawling, 1,504-room property, upped the stakes in the high-end resort game. Its signature facade has since been featured in numerous movies, including the James Bond film, *Goldfinger*, cementing it in pop culture memory. Its unique design, including an elaborate two-story grand staircase, earned it a place in the U.S. National Register of Historic Places.[20]

The success of the Fontainebleau launched the Novack family into high society. His wife, Bernice, a beautiful and poised ex-model would meet and greet foreign dignitaries, celebrities, and powerful politicians in the family's penthouse suite.

Novack Sr. was a compact but charismatic man who came to Miami Beach from New York. After several failed ventures in real estate, he finally hit it big with a small hotel in South Miami Beach during World War II, setting him on the path to the Fontainebleau.

From the *Miami Herald*'s April 7, 1985, obituary for Ben Novack:

> The Fontainebleau Hotel was one of the world's most pretentious luxury hotels. Governors stayed there, kings, William Randolph Hearst, Joe DiMaggio, Liberace, even Frank Sinatra, who got a suite named after him. Ed Sullivan broadcast TV shows from the hotel. Carl Wallenda walked a tightrope stretched between the Fontainebleau and the Eden Roc [hotel].
>
> The Fontainebleau, the Beach's largest hotel, became known the world over. Its distinctive shape and broad beach marked post cards selling Miami's sand and surf. It was a museum of sorts, where people paid $5 just for a glimpse of the papier mâché mannequins, bronze and marble sculptures and gaudy furniture.

---

20   Tricia Romano, "The Glamorous Life and Grisly Death of Ben Novack Jr.," TruTV.com.

At the hotel's forefront was Mr. Novack, a fast talker who loved gold and diamond jewelry, and particularly fancied a charm with a tiny gold reproduction of the Fontainebleau Hotel hanging from a heavy gold chain.

. . . Son of the owner of a resort in the Catskill mountains of New York state, Mr. Novack was a Brooklyn native who mispronounced words but was terrific with numbers—perhaps the reason why, 20 years after moving to Miami Beach in 1940 with $1,800, Ben Novack was worth $20 million. He started by operating hotels, the Monroe Towers, the Cornell, the Atlantis, and the San Souci.

Then he decided to build his masterpiece. He did it in one year, 1954, on the former estate of the tire magnate Harvey Firestone.

To build the hotel in 1954, Ben Novack needed investors, just like Garvice did in building and growing some of his empire's businesses. Over time, Novack, who wanted full ownership, was able to purchase some of the stock back. In November 1971, Kincaid, through Dania Bank and Kentucky Central Life, helped Novack purchase the remaining shares of stock. Dania Bank loaned him $900,000 and Kentucky Central Life loaned him $3,750,000. The loans were structured as second mortgages on the hotel and carried an interest rate of 14%. Connecticut General Life Insurance already had a $13,250,000 first mortgage on the hotel. In addition, Novack pledged two-thirds of his shares in the hotel as additional collateral. From Kincaid's perspective, he either had a high-interest-rate loan with a return equivalent to an equity investment, or he had an option to acquire a Miami Beach flagship property. In addition, he liked staying at the property and allowed others in his universe to stay there.

In *#2 Is Chicken*, a book by Kincaid's long-time employee and broadcasting lieutenant Ted Grizzard, Grizzard gives a vivid description of his relationship with Kincaid and, in his vintage Grizzard style, includes various memories about the radio and television station and its people. Ted Grizzard liked and respected Garvice Kincaid. He didn't totally understand him, but he appreciated how hard Garvice worked and his desire to be number one in anything he did. Ted Grizzard's writings are an important first-person account of those early broadcasting years. They also provide important insight into Garvice Kincaid and some of the people in his empire. I have included several of his stories about those years in the pages that follow. The following passages are about Kincaid and the Fontainebleau Hotel:

I never pushed or pursued my association with Garvice. For years—and until his death, I suppose—he maintained a beautiful apartment at the Fontainebleau in Miami Beach. Not a room or a suite of rooms but an apartment. I had heard of that many of his friends and business associates were allowed to use the apartment when he wasn't there.

Carlouise and I were going to Miami on vacation, and I phoned Garvice to tell him that I'd be away from the station for a while and where I was going. He wanted to know the dates we would be in Miami, looked at this schedule and said, "Why don't you use my apartment at the Fontainebleau? I won't be there until the following week."

I thanked him profusely—and he didn't like that at all. Almost brusquely, he said, "I said you could use it, didn't I? I'll give you a letter to the Fontainebleau, so they'll let you in the apartment. I'm busy, goodbye." We went and it was marvelous.

One big thing I'll always remember about the stay as Kincaid's guest at the Fontainebleau. His letter of introduction did the job. We were hardly in the apartment when the phone rings and there's an assistant manager on the line. He wants to know if the apartment is in order—do we need anything—can he, personally, be of any service to make our visit more pleasant.

He added, "As Mr. Kincaid's guest you are most welcome at the Fontainebleau, and we want to make sure everything is as you want it. If you need anything, please don't call the bell captain but call my office direct."

Al Florence, who then helped handle Mr. Kincaid's banks, came the next day. Florence had been there many times. He said—when I told him about the assistant manager's call— "If you think they jump when Garvice shows up around Central Bank—I can tell you they jump when Garvice shows up around the Fontainebleau, too."

The apartment had two big bedrooms, a beautiful living room and dining room and a big kitchen. The kitchen was stocked with everything in the food line. Even a variety of cookies. I don't remember the apartment number, D-17 or something like that, but it was in a wing of the hotel and to get to the apartment you walked through a beautiful corridor to special elevators for the VIPs who lived in these apartments.

It seemed that many of the regular hotel guests and tourists like sitting in this corridor just to see who went to those special elevators. The big-time entertainers and other big shots. They got to see Carlouise and me several times. And once they had a big thrill when they saw me carrying a bag of groceries I had bought to replenish Mr. Kincaid's pantry.

From our balcony I had seen a cabana area near one of the pools but when we got over there a sign said $3.00 admission. I told Al Florence about this, and he said Garvice had a cabana over there. At the area gate just say "D-17"—or whatever that number was. We went over and I said the magic number. The young man on the gate almost jerked it off the hinges opening it.

On cold winter days after that, when I'd see Garvice in Lexington, I'd think about that apartment and the cabana. He could have been there—running things by telephone.

And he never even had to bother with luggage. At the apartment in the Fontainebleau there were closets filled with suits, shirts, everything—the bathroom (there were two of these, of course) with all the shaving materials. Just get on the plane in Lexington—or anywhere—and then get a cab in Miami.

I suppose I was like most any poor guy when he's surrounded by such luxury—but "the man on the street" was duly impressed. Don't try to understand Garvice Kincaid. I knew darned well he liked to do nice things for people, and I know he wanted them to appreciate 'em. I never understood his reaction to "thank you." But just the same—I always thanked him anyway. Lots of times I'd stop by his office—lean in the door and preface a "thank you" with— "Now before you can say anything smart, I wanna thank you" for whatever he had just done for me—then I'd shut the door and run.

When I started working in the investment department at Kentucky Central Life, Cliff Forbush and Charlie Thomas both told similar stories about Kincaid's Fontainebleau residence. Mr. Forbush always referred to it as a very large suite, but I think Ted Grizzard's descriptions are the more accurate. Garvice enjoyed being appreciated for his wealth, and the management of the Fontainebleau went out of its way to roll out the red carpet for him and his visiting guests.

There's an old investment saying about lending on hotels: "The person who makes the real money on a hotel is the person who purchases it during its third bankruptcy." The rationale is that (1) people overspend when they build hotels, (2) the hotel business is very cyclical and economic downturns tend to destroy the weaker owners, and (3) usually each person acquiring the hotel during a bankruptcy process is acquiring it for less than what the previous owner had invested in it. Certainly not every hotel goes through bankruptcy, but there are enough that do, that there lies some truth in this old adage.

As Kincaid's history has shown, he loved hotel and entertainment properties, so providing financing, even a second mortgage, was not a difficult decision for him. One problem with many hotel properties is that the owners fail to reinvest their profits back into the hotel or fail to keep sufficient rainy-day funds. Ben Novack had operated the Fontainebleau Hotel for seventeen years in 1971. The economy had just started coming out of a mild recession, so he never considered that the U.S. would be back in a much longer and harsher one by 1974 that would not end until 1976. In addition, he had focused so much of his resources on buying back stock and on completing the final phase of the hotel in 1970 that he hadn't been updating the hotel and its appearance had become neglected. In fact, in 1975, he announced a two-year program, a plan to spend $2.6 million refreshing the rooms and carpeting. It takes a lot of money to replace twelve acres of carpeting. Garvice Kincaid died in November 1975, so his Committee would now be Novack's lender.

In February 1976, Novack started falling behind on his debts and soon had lenders and creditors wanting to foreclose on his hotel. By January 1977, Novack even owed the city $322,000 in old tax bills, water bills, and resort taxes. The number would have been much larger but for Connecticut General purchasing the oldest tax bills for $560,000 to forestall a foreclosure sale. In addition, the Committee was in the process of selling the Dania Bank in 1977 and had moved the bank's hotel loan to Kentucky Central Life. Now Kentucky Central had a $4.3 million second mortgage on the hotel.

The two main lenders, Connecticut General and Kentucky Central, worked with Novack for almost a year trying to allow him enough time to find investors, but by November 1977, both lenders and many of the other 325 creditors wanted the hotel sold at auction to satisfy its liabilities totaling $25.8 million. In early 1978, a court approved the sale of the property for approximately $27 million. This covered all secured lienholders. Kentucky Central Life's loan had increased, due to accrued interest, to $5.4 million by the time the property was sold.

The new owner, Hotelerama Associates, then obtained new financing to extensively renovate and update the hotel. It borrowed $35 million from Equitable Life Assurance Society in a first mortgage, and Kentucky Central Life provided $10 million in a second mortgage. The new loans more than doubled the highest levels of indebtedness ever encumbering the hotel complex. Payments on Kentucky Central Life's loan were interest-only for three years. By 1979, Steven Muss, the primary principal in Hotelerama Associates, borrowed against his stock in the hotel and increased total borrowings related to the hotel to $57 million. Steve Muss's loan was with Chase Manhattan Bank. In conjunction with the 1979 Chase loan, Equitable Life Assurance increased the interest rate on its loan to a minimum of 12 percent or 3 percent over prime, and in addition would participate in the profits of the hotel when annual occupancy exceeded 60 percent.

In 1976, Kincaid's Committee had its hands full. Kincaid had died in November 1975, and by 1977 the Committee was in a legal dispute with his immediate family. In addition, in December 1976, Al Florence resigned from the Committee due to too many disagreements with the other two members. Finally, add to the situation that they needed to settle Kincaid's estate and address his more than two hundred business interests and one can see that dealing with the Fontainebleau Hotel was probably not very high on their list. In the end, they probably placed their trust in the due diligence of Equitable Life and the knowledge that Stephen Muss was part of a wealthy fourth-generation New York real estate development family.

In 1978, Stephen Muss rescued the aging Fontainebleau Hotel. Muss had moved to Miami in 1950 and during his years there, he saw the birth and long-term neglect of this historic hotel. In all, it is reported that Muss invested an additional $100 million into the hotel for improvements and expansion. He also hired the Hilton company to manage it. In 2005, it's reported that the Muss organization sold the Fontainebleau to Donald Soffer's Turnberry Associates for $165 million. Just like Garvice Kincaid, Stephen Muss could recognize an important real estate diamond and knew how to get the most out of it. In addition, just like Kincaid, he had the financial wherewithal to make it happen.

One has to wonder how Kincaid would have handled his investment in the hotel. He was certainly enamored with this Miami-based signature property, and he had known Ben Novack for several years. He easily could have taken over Connecticut General's $13.2 million loan and probably could have worked a deal with Novack that gave him a controlling interest in the property. One can only guess, but I believe he would have played his hand much differently than his Committee did.

As for Ben Novack, he claims to have lost everything when he lost the Fontainebleau Hotel. Initially it was suggested that he would be retained to manage the hotel, but that may have been Novack trying to save face or maybe even Stephen Muss just needing a short-term onsite manager until Hilton's management could take over. The hotel never closed, and Ben Novack left his penthouse suite during 1978. In interviews, he claims to have never returned to his "mistress and obsession for twenty-five years," and for years he claimed he was cheated by his creditors. He even found investors willing to finance litigation for a piece of any recouped compensation and damages. In the end, though, he failed in those endeavors and in a 1980 article is found living with his sister and her husband on Normandy Isles, a North Beach neighborhood of Miami Beach.

In January 1981, he was invited to be a minority owner/operator of the Racquet Club, a boutique ninety-room hotel in the North Bay village. This club used to be a hangout for Miami's wealthy but had fallen on hard times and was now run-down and out of favor. In 1979, a Washington, D.C., attorney and some Ohio businessmen purchased the property for $1.3 million. It was a choice location, and if Novack couldn't resuscitate it, they planned on turning it into condominiums. After a year or two, he was no longer involved in the project.

In November 1983, Novack held an auction for a large collection of Fontainebleau Hotel furniture, fixtures, art, and jewelry. He had held them in storage since he left the hotel. For six years he claimed he was penniless, but the auction raised a few doubts about that. Ben Novack died in April 1985 at the age of 78. His estate was valued at $1 million.

Of course, any southern saga doesn't just end with the death of someone, and there's still one more sad chapter to the Novack story. Ben's son, Ben Novack Jr., had an unusual childhood.[21] He spent his whole youth living in the penthouse suite of the Fontainebleau Hotel, where celebrities and the wealthy were a major part of his environment. Add to this the fact that his mother was a former model for Coca-Cola and Salvador Dali and his father the famed owner of the Fontainebleau Hotel. Ben Jr. was born in 1956, shortly after his father opened the Fontainebleau Hotel, and at age twenty-one, he watched as his father lost everything.

When Ben Novack Sr. died in 1985, the relationship between the father and son had become strained. Having very little left of his fortune, Ben's relationship with his son deteriorated so badly that Ben Jr. tried to have his father declared mentally incompetent.

As an adult, Ben Jr. used the connections he had made at the hotel to start a successful event-planning business, Convention Concepts Unlimited, which he ran from his house in Fort Lauderdale. He concentrated mostly on one

---

21   All information about Ben Novack Jr. and his life is from the following sources: John Glatt, *The Prince of Paradise: The True Story of a Hotel Heir, His Seductive Wife, and a Ruthless Murder* (St. Martin's 2013); Steven Gaines, *Fool's Paradise: Players, Poseurs, and the Culture of Excess in South Beach* (Crown 2009); Annette Witheridge, "EXCLUSIVE: Ex-stripper Murdered Millionaire Playboy Husband Who Was Friend of Sinatra 'and Funneled $10m of His Cash Through Rabbi She Was Having Affair With,' New Book Reveals," *The Daily Mail*, April 20, 2013, https://www.dailymail.co.uk/news/article-2309654/EXCLUSIVE-Ex-stripper-murdered-playboy-husband-friend-Sinatra-funneled-10m-cash-rabbi-having-passionate-affair-new-book-reveals.html; Julie Brown, "Homeless Drifter Turns Out to Be Heir to Novack Fortune," *Palm Beach Post* (January 31, 2010); Tricia Romano, "The Glamorous Life and Grisly Death of Ben Novack Jr.," *TruTV.com*, https://www.crimelibrary.org/notorious_murders/family/ben-novack-jr/just-there-on-business.html; Leslie V. Marenco, "Daughter of Fontainebleau Heir's Killer—Wife Can Inherit?!" *TrustCounsel* (February 4, 2016).

client, Amway. He planned major conventions for the company and traveled around the country to oversee the events. In later years, it was said that his clients ran $50 million of convention business through his firm annually.

Ben Novack Jr.'s first wife was a beautiful Las Vegas showgirl in her late twenties named Jill Campion. They married in June 1979 and received wedding gifts from Frank Sinatra and Ann-Margret. Their marriage was short, though, and they divorced in 1981. It's reported that Sinatra became a close family friend and was like an uncle to Ben as he grew up. He had his own suite at the hotel and even flew the family on his private jet to President Kennedy's inauguration in 1960.

It has been suggested that in Ben Jr.'s later years he was a playboy and always juggling girlfriends, but he also became famous for a more eccentric reason: he was considered a world-renowned collector of Batman memorabilia estimated to be worth over $2 million. A prized collectible was an original Batmobile from the television show. Later, in his thirties, Ben Novack Jr. did what many rich, idle men in resort areas do: he married a former Hialeah stripper, Narcisa (Narcy) Véliz Pacheco.[22]

Narcy Pacheco was born poor in Ecuador in 1956 and as an adult moved to America to make her fortune. She met Ben at the strip club where she worked and soon moved in with him. As soon as they were married, their relationship became volatile, with Ben once calling the police and accusing Narcy of pistol-whipping him and holding him hostage for twenty-eight hours and Narcy showing the police her husband's sick photo collection of naked amputees. She claimed his fetishes were becoming dangerous and that she had once gone under anesthesia to fix a broken nose and woken up with enormous breast implants. The marriage was always explosive, and toward the end it had become downright dangerous; they both slept with loaded guns under their pillows.

It was a strange, tumultuous marriage that lasted nearly twenty years until Ben Jr.'s death in 2009, three months after the death of his mother, Bernice Novack. While Ben's death was listed as murder, Bernice's death was considered an accident, and it would take two years and the dogged

---

22   Information about Narcy Novack comes from the following sources: "Narcy Novack," *Murderpedia* (compiled by Juan Ignacio Blanco); Julie Knipe Brown, "'48 Hours': How a Reporter Uncovered the Murder of Miami Matriarch Bernice Novack," *CBS News* (July 13, 2013); Julie K. Brown "Tale of a Married Life: Sex, Limbs, and Duck Tape," *Miami Herald* (March 3, 2012); "Bound for Murder," *American Greed: Deadly Rich* (2018), https://www.directv.com/guide/EPISODE/American-Greed-Deadly-Rich-Bound-for-Murder-84dc7aef-356b-8a95-4645-8b06f8f8d85e.

determination of a reporter for the *Miami Herald*, Julie Knipe Brown, before the police would consider a more perverse reason for what would ultimately be determined to be two murder-for-hire killings at the behest of Ben's wife, Narcy. Ben, age 53, had been found bludgeoned and suffocated to death in the penthouse suite at the Hilton Hotel in Rye Brook, New York. He was bound with duct tape and his eyes were gouged out.

On July 10, 2009, Ben Novack Jr. flew to Newark International Airport from his home in Fort Lauderdale. He brought his wife, Narcy Novack, and her daughter, May Abad, to the 455-room Hilton for yet another Amway conference. The conference was a big one, with over a thousand guests. On Sunday, July 12, according to Narcy Novack's police statements, Ben worked through the night, staying up till 6:30 a.m., before finally coming to bed. Around 7:15 a.m., Narcy told police, she left the room to get breakfast. Hotel security videos show her leaving the room. She told police she returned to the room about forty-five minutes later and found the gruesome scene.

In the months leading up to his death, Ben had fallen for heavily tattooed ex-hooker Rebecca Bliss, who was known by her porn star name, Mona Love. He wanted a divorce and Narcy was becoming desperate. She was in her mid-fifties, had lost her once-beautiful looks, and, prosecutors said, feared losing access to the family's multimillion-dollar fortune, due to a prenuptial agreement, if Ben divorced her. According to prosecutors, Narcy orchestrated the brutal killing of Ben Novack Jr. and his mother Bernice Novack. Narcy hoped to inherit the family estate.

Narcy conspired with her brother Cristobal Veliz to kill Ben and his mother, Bernice. Veliz recruited a Miami car wash owner, Alejandro Garcia, who executed Bernice Novack for a couple thousand dollars. Garcia then enlisted an employee at the car wash, Joel Gonzales, to help him murder Ben Novack at the Rye Town Hilton. Prosecutors said Narcy and Veliz were motivated by "jealousy, retribution and greed" when they hired the thugs who carried out the killings.

Prosecutors alleged that Narcy and her brother told the hit men to kill Bernice Novack because she mistreated her daughter-in-law, encouraged Ben to beat his wife, and once drugged her daughter-in-law. In addition, Veliz also told one of the killers that Ben had a business involving artificial limbs that he used to lure amputees or their relatives into having sex with him in exchange for free limbs. He was engaging in "sick sexual habits."

Prosecutors also said that in 2008, a year before the murders, Narcy told the FBI that her husband was arranging sham marriages and that one of the sham brides in the scheme was Bliss, with whom he had been having an affair. That same year Narcy also told a Mexican customs official that her husband had illegally smuggled $10,000 into Mexico. When the FBI failed to take action against her husband, prosecutors said, Narcy began to plot her husband's murder in earnest.

Narcy, age 56, and her brother, age 59, were convicted of arranging the murders after the hit men gave evidence against the siblings. Both Narcy and her brother are serving life sentences.

According to the hit men's testimony and court records provided on the website Murderpedia, the encyclopedia of murderers,

> The bloodshed began on April 5, 2009, they drove to Bernice Novack's home in Fort Lauderdale. One of the hit men, Alejandro Garcia, said he hid next to Bernice Novack's garage and as it grew dark, Bernice Novack, clad in a nightgown, came out of her house and pulled her car into the garage. Garcia followed her inside, and as she began to step out of her vehicle, he clubbed her on the head with a monkey wrench. As she screamed, he continued to beat her in the face.
>
> "The plan was to hit her in the teeth and give her a good beating," Garcia testified during trial.
>
> Garcia then fled, leaving the Novack matriarch sprawled in the front seat of her car. She managed to pull herself out of the vehicle and get inside her house, where she tried to clean up the blood. But she collapsed and died in the laundry room. Her son, Ben, found her body the next morning, drenched in blood with blood smeared in her car, the garage and throughout the house.
>
> An autopsy showed that her teeth were broken, along with a finger, and that her skull was cracked. Fort Lauderdale police and the Broward medical examiner, however, ruled the death an accident, theorizing that she died from a fall.
>
> Believing that they had gotten away with one murder, Narcy and her brother then focused on getting her husband out of the way. In addition to his $10 million estate, they intended to take control of his company, Convention Concepts Unlimited.
>
> On July 12, Garcia and another hired accomplice, Joel Gonzalez, were driven to Rye Brook, N.Y., a wealthy Westchester County suburb, where Ben Novack was organizing a convention at the Hilton Rye Town hotel for his largest client, Amway International. That morning, after working most of the night, Ben Novack climbed into bed at about 6:30 a.m., to get a few hours of rest. About 7 a.m., Narcy Novack opened the door to their suite, and Garcia and Gonzalez entered.
>
> She motioned toward the bedroom where her husband was sleeping, and the two thugs began pounding him with hand weights,

as he screamed and tried to fight back. Narcy Novack became alarmed by her husband's cries and gave the killers a pillow to muffle his shouting. They then bound his arms and legs with duct tape and wrapped his mouth so tightly with the tape that he choked on his own vomit.

Garcia said that Novack then told him to finish the job by gouging out her husband's eyes with a utility knife, purportedly the last act of a wife who had endured years of her husband's sexual perversions and infidelities.

Then she calmly went downstairs for breakfast before returning to the room and raising the alarm. She maintained her innocence from the start, even claiming that her grown-up daughter, May Abad, from a previous relationship was responsible.

Ben's lover, Rebecca Bliss, a onetime porn star, claimed in court that she had met Novack on a website and that at the time of his murder, the two had fallen in love and that she believed he was going to leave his wife. Ben Novack had set her up in a comfortable apartment in Fort Lauderdale, bought her furniture and sound equipment, and paid for her to have lavish spa treatments. He also bought her a puppy.

Narcy Novack discovered the affair, and, in January 2009, she tracked Bliss down and offered her $10,000 to stop seeing her husband, saying that if "she couldn't have him, no other woman was going to have him." When she refused, Narcy Novack called Bliss's landlady and informed her that Bliss' rent would no longer be paid by Ben Novack because he was dead. The landlady didn't buy the story.

Her husband continued the affair and Novack enlisted her brother to plan the murders.

After her husband's death, she cleaned out his safe deposit boxes and began to liquidate some of their assets. During her initial interrogation by police, she flunked a polygraph test.

The investigation soon led New York detectives to Garcia and Gonzalez, who lived in Miami. Garcia was paid $600 to beat Bernice Novack and $15,000 to kill Ben Novack Jr. Gonzalez received $3,500. Both men confessed and testified against the siblings during trial.

Prosecutors detailed for jurors a long trail of bank and credit card receipts, cellphone records, wire transfers and a damaging video from an ATM showing Veliz withdrawing cash in route to New York with the killers following him.

According to John Glatt's book *The Prince of Paradise* and his interview with the *Daily Mail*'s Annette Witheridge, after Ben's death, Narcy had her own affair with a rabbi who helped her fence some of Ben's stuff for $10,000 in cash. The ex-stripper murdered her millionaire playboy husband.

Prosecutors said she feared losing access to the family's multi-million-dollar estate if Ben divorced her. But the rabbi's role was never revealed during the three-month trial.

. . .

"I was told by numerous sources that Narcy, once a self-proclaimed voodoo priestess, had become involved with a very well-connected rabbi after her husband's death," Glatt told MailOnline.

"She openly boasted about their relationship. I was also told she had funneled large amounts of cash from the estate and valuable Batman comics through him.

"Ben had the second largest Batman memorabilia collection in the world, including an original Batmobile he bought just months before his murder.

"Much of the stuff went missing but detectives followed the trail through to the rabbi and his network of orthodox associates.

A detective who investigated the murders told MailOnline that he had confronted the Brooklyn, New York, born rabbi about the affair.

"He denied it—and acted like he was very offended—but ultimately he led us to some of the memorabilia," the officer said.

"We will probably never see the money. Ben dealt only in cash and Narcy was the same. We found $390,000 in cash in the Florida house and they kept safe deposit boxes everywhere.

"Narcy walked out of one bank vault with a duffel bag of stuff—we will probably never know how much cash was in there.

"She was a cold, calculating woman. She had previously been into Santeria—South American black magic—and in every storage facility we went to we found rabbits feet and voodoo things. Yet, she converted to Judaism when it suited her purposes."

. . . "Yet, despite playing the hard-done-by spurned wife, Narcy herself quickly embarked on a relationship with the married rabbi. They were spotted together in numerous restaurants and even after her arrest he was driving around in her Mercedes sports car."

With Narcy serving a life sentence in prison, the estate was expected to go to Narcy's daughter (Ben's stepdaughter) and May Abad and her two adult sons until reporter Julie Knipe Brown discovered that Ben Novack Sr. had a long-forgotten adopted son, Ronnie Novack, who was homeless, having lived on the street most of his life.

A March 31, 2012, *Palm Beach Post* article about Ronnie gives the following information:

> It was a curious rags to riches story: the long lost 62-year-old man who spent most of his adult life living in the woods could now eat a handsome meal and sleep in his own bed. A little more than a year ago, a homeless drifter named Ronald Marc Novack surfaced to claim a $100,000 inheritance from the estate of his late mother, Bella Novack.
>
> What wasn't known at the time was that his mother's estate wasn't worth $100,000; it was worth millions—and he was the sole heir.
>
> He also carried a secret: He was the adopted son of Bella and the late Ben Novack Sr., who built and ran a number of hotels in Miami Beach, including the storied Fontainebleau resort.
>
> His father and mother went through a bitter divorce. Ben Novack Sr. was having an affair with a model, Bernice, whom he later married, and together, had a son, Ben Novack Jr., in 1959.
>
> Ben Novack Sr. had very little to do with his adopted son after the divorce. And when he died in 1985, he left the bulk of his estate to his biological son and, in a codicil, willed Ronald Novack just $1.
>
> The step-brothers would live very different lives—one would fall into mental illness and eventually wander the streets, panhandling; the other enjoyed all the spoils of rich and famous parents: private schools, elaborate parties, exotic vacations, chauffeur-driven limousines.
>
> Until last July, when tragedy befell part of the Novack family. Novack Jr. turned up dead in a New York hotel room leaving police to sort out the murder and family members to fight over his multi-million-dollar estate.
>
> In the meantime, Novack's disowned son surfaced to collect his mother's inheritance—eight years after her death.
>
> And in a twist of fate, Ronald Novack would end up with something from his father that was far more valuable than the $1 he had left him.

Ben's cousins, Meredith and Lisa Fiel, believed that Narcy could still indirectly benefit from Ben's fortune, in contravention of the policy behind the slayer statute, which prohibited her from inheriting his estate. In 2016, they argued in court that Narcy's daughter and grandkids could simply deposit money inherited from Ben into Narcy's prison inmate account. Based on the potential indirect benefit to Narcy, the Fiels sought to convince a Florida trial court that the slayer statute also barred Narcy's daughter and grandkids from inheriting under Ben's will. It appears that after several attempts they failed in these efforts.

The old adage that no one can predict the future is very true, and one can only imagine how the Novack story would have changed if Ben Novack Sr. hadn't lost everything. If Kincaid had lived longer, would he have become a partner with Novack in the Fontainebleau Hotel, and if so, would Ben Novack Jr. later been put in charge of the hotel, and if so, would his provocative and sexual nature have destroyed the hotel in another way? One can only imagine that if Garvice Kincaid was told today how the story of the Fontainebleau Hotel and the Novack family turned out, he wouldn't believe it.

As to the misunderstanding about Kincaid foreclosing on the hotel multiple times, I believe it can be traced back to two facts: (1) Garvice had at least three different Florida properties in which he had a lender's interest and (2) one property, the Duck Key Resort & Indies Inn, was involved in multiple loan foreclosures and restructurings.

Garvice Kincaid and the Duck Key Resort & Indies Inn

Most good stories start off with an unusual beginning, and the story of the Duck Key Resort is no different. Duck Key is a 350-acre island that sits ninety-five miles south of Miami. Duck Key was an uninhabited island before the 1950s. In its earlier years there was a salt-mining operation in the lowlands area.

Bryan Newkirk is said to have purchased the island during a golf game, sight unseen, in 1951 for a reported $47,000. According to the website The Keys, Newkirk agreed to the transaction because the Florida judge he was playing with was badgering him to buy the small island and all Newkirk wanted was a peaceful round of golf. Even though the property was just a mixture of swamp and mangrove trees, Newkirk soon envisioned an island resort community that would become the "Mecca of the Americas." Just his simple description of the project can make one understand why Garvice Kincaid might one day have an interest.

The Keys website provides this background on Newkirk and what soon became his life's passion:

> Bryan Newkirk purchased Duck Key—sight unseen—during a golf game in 1951.
>
> According to Newkirk, he agreed to the transaction because the Florida Judge who he was playing with was badgering him to buy the small island. All Newkirk wanted was a peaceful round of golf.

"So, I bought it about the ninth hole so I could enjoy the remainder of the golf game."

By the end of 1957, the Miami News reported that Newkirk had spent over 4 million dollars on his 326-acre island and had yet to sell the first lot.

A commonality among Florida Keys developers was their colorful backgrounds. Bryan W. Newkirk was on top of this vibrant list.

Newkirk came from an aristocratic North Carolina family. His first employment was as an automotive industry writer for an Atlanta newspaper. He next surfaced as the owner of a "Hupmobile" automobile dealership in Jacksonville, Florida. When the Florida Land Boom exploded, in the early 1920's, Newkirk was recruited by Admiral Telfair Knight to manage sales for George Merrick's "Coral Gables" development. Bryan Newkirk brilliantly managed Merrick's sales force.

"It was a crazy time, I had 4,000 salesmen working for me at once—and we were moving real estate . . . ."

Newkirk had a falling out with Merrick over the incorporation of Coral Gables. He left Florida just before the 1926 hurricane brought the Land Boom to a screeching halt.

Newkirk recalled "I had sold one of our salesmen a Lincoln automobile and he had not paid me. When I left Miami, I went to New York and this fellow calls me and says he'll pay me if I come to Montreal."

"I went, the next day, this fellow and I are partners . . . and I've been in business (in Canada) ever since."

Newkirk built a Canadian mining empire, first in gold, and later in Uranium. It was his world market dominance of this fine mustard-yellow powder that defined him. Whether it was to be peacefully refined for rods in nuclear reactors or used for atomic annihilation, in the 1950's, Uranium was the world's most sinisterly sought resource.

In the early days of Newkirk's Duck Key, the island was frequented by some extremely controversial characters.

It is probably no coincidence that Jacob M. Alkow, who would soon be disgraced and suspended by the Securities and Exchange Commission, arranged for the financing of Duck Key with Israeli Investors. Alkow, who was also an esteemed archeologist, was a leader of the Zionist Organization of America. Israel vowed "We shall never again be led like lambs to the slaughter." Much to the displeasure of both President Eisenhower and President Kennedy— The Israelis were developing an atomic weapon program which required, of course, Uranium.

Roy Cohn was both a board member of the Florida Southern Land Corporation (Newkirk's development company) and an early resident of Duck Key. Newkirk had gifted a home to Cohn—his New York "fixer."

Cohn had been the ruthless chief counsel of Joseph McCarthy in both the "red" and "lavender" scares.

He later defended Fred and Donald Trump in New York. He was young Donald's "Studio 54" mentor. Much of Trump's pit bull instinct, as well as his penchant for litigation, was acquired from Roy Cohn.

In the mid-80's Cohn was diagnosed with AIDS. When Trump found out about Roy's diagnosis and homosexuality, he turned his back on his longstanding friend—refusing to take his calls. When Cohn was asked how it felt to be abandoned by his associate, he commented—"Donald, $#%# he pisses ice water."

Newkirk was also host to the European royalty and Persian princes. A Who's Who of Canada was always on hand. U.S. military brass such as General Omar Bradley and General Richard Sutherland were winter guests.

Bryan Newkirk was 70 by the time he opened his grand hotel—"the Indies House," in January of 1960. With this luxury hotel, Newkirk was following the "tried and true" Florida Land Development Business Plan established by Henry Flagler, George Merrick and Carl Fisher.

That same fall Hurricane Donna delivered a devastating direct hit to the Middle Keys. Coupled with the personal loss of his only adult son to bulbar polio, the destruction was too much for Newkirk. He lost interest in the Island.

Duck Key would sit, semi-abandoned, for nearly a decade.

No one knows exactly how many millions Newkirk spent creating his "Mecca of the Americas." We know he put over $3 million into the island. He pumped in 2 million cubic feet of fill, dug four miles of canals, installed over forty miles of freshwater lines, and built ten-and-a-half miles of paved roads. He also built himself a thirty-room private home and constructed a quarter-million-dollar nursery. In 1952, he had a wooden bridge constructed to connect Duck Key to the mainland, and that's when the major dredging and filling actually began. In various newspaper reports involving creditor litigation, the estimates range from $5 to $10 million, with $5 million the most common.

Bryan Winslow Newkirk II was born in Wilmington, North Carolina, on December 18, 1888. One newspaper article stated, "Bryan W. Newkirk, the financial colossus of Canada, is the son of an aristocratic North Carolina family with a tradition more of gentility than big business." He was known as a super-salesman but made his fortune but made his fortune in a Canadian mining business by the age of forty. He also invested in oil wells in the Middle East and diamond mines in Africa and was truly a world industrialist and visionary. In the late 1950s, his fortune was estimated to be worth more than $100 million.

While Bryan Newkirk II loved business, his other great passions were his family and sailing. His son Bryan Newkirk III was probably the most important person in his life, and when the Duck Key development project was started, Newkirk III would oversee most of the actual work. This large project was the perfect endeavor and would provide his son with the experience necessary to carry on the family legacy, given that the Duck Key development project was one of the largest undertakings ever attempted in the Florida Keys by a single private developer.

In 1954, as details about the development were made public, the Newkirks estimated that when completed, the project would have cost $25 million. The project would include a 100-room hotel and yacht club, a nine-hole golf course, tennis courts, two swimming pools, 485 home sites, and a shopping center.

In 1955, tragedy struck Bryan Newkirk II when his son died due to complications from polio. His son was thirty-seven years old. As one can understand, the father soon lost interest in the Duck Key project. As the family genealogy website states, "He had no one to give his keys to the Kingdom that he had built. He never retired and passed away from a heart attack while doing business in Cornwall, England in 1966" at the age of seventy-eight.

In 1955, Bryan had already invested a reported $1.7 million in the Duck Key project, and as a practical businessman he needed to finish it. With his son no longer involved, Newkirk no longer saw the need to personally finance the development, so he decided to take the project public. In 1956, Florida-Southern Land Corp. was created, and in March 1957, the public was offered the opportunity to acquire 17.5% of the project for $3 million. In 1959, Newkirk needed additional capital for the project, so Florida-Southern Land Corp. issued an additional two million shares of stock, raising $4 million.

From the company's SEC filings:

FLORIDA-SOUTHERN LAND PROPOSES OFFERING

March 12, 1957

Florida-Southern Land Corp., Tom's Harbor, Monroe County, Fla., filed a registration statement (File 2-13151) with the SEC on March 11, 1957, seeking registration of 600,000 shares of its 10¢

par Common Stock, to be offered for public sale at $5 per share. The offering is to be made on a "best efforts" basis by Keystone Securities Company, Inc., of Philadelphia, for which a 75¢ per share selling commission is to be paid. In addition, for each 100,000 of the first 300,000 shares sold, the underwriter will be entitled to purchase 8,000 common shares from the company at 10¢ per share. Thereafter, the underwriter will be entitled to receive from Bryan W. Newkirk, of Toronto, the company's founder and president, 8,000 shares of Mr. Newkirk's personally-owned stock for each remaining 100,000 shares which it sells to the public. Thus, if all the 600,000 shares are sold, the underwriter will receive a total of 43,000 shares for a cash payment of $2,400. The company also has agreed to reimburse the underwriter for its actual expenses in an amount not to exceed $30,000, at the rate of 5¢ per share sold.

Florida-Southern was organized under Florida law on July 31, 1956, to engage in the business of buying, selling, developing and operating real properties. Its present business consists of the ownership and development of a tract of over 300 acres of property, known as Duck Key, which is located on the Atlantic Ocean in the Florida Keys. Duck Key, according to the prospectus, is being developed as a luxury-type, island resort community. Duck Key and the structures, furnishings and equipment thereon were acquired from two companies controlled by Newkirk, for which 2,750,000 shares of stock were issued by Florida-Southern. Newkirk has agreed to deliver 24,000 shares to the underwriter; and he has sold 80,000 shares to officers and directors at $2 per share. The company has sold 46,500 shares to three other persons for $186,000. The prospectus further indicates that, assuming the public sale of the 600,000 shares, the purchasers thereof will have acquired approximately 17½% of the then outstanding stock for an investment of $3,000,000 while Newkirk and his associates will own 2,726,000 shares or slightly over 79% of the stock issued for property with respect to which aggregate cash of $1,731,362 had been spent prior to the transfer. The three purchasers of the 46,500 shares, Thomas J. Day, A. B. Wkitelaw, and J. W. Metelnick, all of Toronto, will own approximately 1½% of the stock for a cash investment of $186,000; and the underwriter will hold about 1½% of the stock received by it for services and the payment of $2,400 cash.

Net proceeds of the public offering, assuming all shares are sold, are estimated at $2,490,000. Of these funds, $793,000 are to be used for the construction of a 50-unit hotel-motel (at a cost of $405,000) and various other and related buildings and improvements; $161,000 for furniture and equipment; and the balance of $1,136,000 to be added to general funds, to be used for either the construction of lease accommodations on Duck Key or the acquisition of additional land sites in other areas.

FLORIDA-SOUTHERN LAND PROPOSES OFFERING

April 14, 1959

Florida-Southern Land Corp., Tom's Harbor, Monroe County, Fla., filed a registration statement (File 2-14918) with the SEC on April 13, 1959, seeking registration of 2,000,000 shares of common stock. The stock is to be offered for public sale at $2 per share. The offering is to be made on a best-efforts basis by Alkow & Co., Inc., for which it will receive a 36¢ per share selling commission. The underwriter also will receive an expense allowance of $50,000, payable at the rate of 5¢ per share on each of the first 1,000,000 shares sold; and it will be entitled to purchase, at one cent each, 200,000 four-year warrants to purchase a like number of common shares at prices ranging from $2 to $3 per share. A finder's fee of $15,000 also is payable to Roy Garcia of New York in the event 150,000 shares are sold in this offering.

The issuer was organized in 1956 to engage in the business of buying, selling, developing and operating real properties. Its present business consists of the ownership and development of a 300-acre tract known as Duck Key, located on the Atlantic Ocean in the Florida Keys. It proposes to develop Duck Key as a luxury-type, island resort community. The Duck Key properties were acquired in 1956 from Florida corporations controlled by Bryan W. Newkirk, president of the issuer. In consideration thereof, the company issued 2,150,000 common shares to Newkirk Realty Corp. Newkirk Realty, which is said to have expended $1,131,362 on the properties, has been liquidated; and of the 2,750.000 shares. 2,529,000 were distributed to Lorita Trading Corp., a Liberian company owned by Mr. Newkirk and 138,000 shares to Newkirk personally. The company now has outstanding 2,801,655 common shares, of which 220,888 shares owned by Newkirk are to be donated back to the company.

The company first proposes to expend some $770,000 for the construction of 50 motel units and other facilities on Indies Island, one of its island properties, plus $153,000 for furnishings and equipment. $400,000 will be reserved for working capital, $125,093 will be used to repay advances by Newkirk, and $1,136,901 added to general funds to be used for either the construction of lease accommodations on Duck Key or the acquisition of additional land sites in other areas.

While Bryan Newkirk may have been worth $100 million, one can begin so see that he had no desire to further increase his personal investment in Duck Key, and by 1960, the project was in need of additional capital. The Indies Inn had opened in the spring, and work was still being completed on the golf course, swimming pools, and tennis courts. Garvice Kincaid had purchased the Dania Bank in April that year, and Newkirk and the Duck Key development were one of his customers. Up until 1960, the project had always been financed by equity capital from Newkirk and his shareholders, but now they wanted to borrow against the project. In the summer of 1960, Garvice and the Dania Bank loaned Florida-Southern Land Corp. $1.1 million dollars in a first-lien mortgage loan. The interest rate was 15%. Garvice again was playing the odds; he might end up owning the famous resort or, worst case, earn an equity-type return on a secured first-mortgage loan.

Kincaid understood numbers and could see how much money had been invested in the property. On the one hand, he knew the sponsor of the property, Newkirk, was a multimillionaire and this was his signature project, and on the other hand, he probably recognized that converting the project into a publicly traded, shareholder-owned enterprise was Newkirk demonstrating that he was stepping back from the project. In 1960, Bryan Newkirk was seventy-two years old and had been experiencing some health issues.

The $1.1 million still was not enough money to complete the development and cover the operating expenses of the Indies Inn, so in late 1960, Florida-Southern Land Corp. approached Guy W. York, a wealthy Houston, Texas, oilman, for a $600,000 second mortgage and the Bank Germann & Co., Basel, Switzerland, for a $442,394 in a third mortgage. By May 1961, the company was further behind on its debt payments and also had a growing list of other creditors who hadn't been paid. In May 1961, the owners petitioned the courts for a reorganization.

By January 1963, the creditors petitioned the court to order the sale of the development to satisfy debt. Their petition pointed out that the corporation had in excess of $3 million in debts, which included their $2.2 million in first, second, and third mortgages. The shareholders of Florida-Southern Land Corp. fought the forced sale. In court they complained that the interest rate on a $1.1 million loan for a development worth $10 million was not made in good faith. In a July 10, 1962, *Fort Lauderdale News* article, Kincaid rebutted their estimated value: "Kincaid termed one $10 million appraisal of the Duck Key development as 'silly.' He estimated the value of the development, including the luxurious Indies House Hotel at $1.8 million. He said he made the first mortgage commitment on this appraisal."

According to the article:

- Joseph Taravella, of Ft. Lauderdale, executive vice-president of Coral Ridge Properties, Inc., testified he believes the development, including the hotel, was worth $1.6 million.

- Telfair Knight, a Dade County real estate broker, had placed the $10 million value estimate on the property.

- E. A. Stevens, of Irvington, Va., who leased the hotel from November 1961 until April 1962, said the development was worth "not more than $900,000."

- "The location is horrible, he testified. "The utilities costs are higher than I have ever experienced."

- Stevens, who paid an annual rental of more than $100,000, said he would not consider leasing the hotel again if rent was more than $6,000 a month [$72,000 annually].

E. A. Stevens bought the hotel alone from the company for $2.25 million on a lease-purchase deal, which would make it his property in fifteen years. The Stevenses were long-time Ft. Lauderdale winter residents on their yacht Miss Ann.

The hotel's total liabilities were listed at $2.7 million in July 1962.

In August 1963, U.S. District Judge Emett Choate approved the sale of the Indies House development on Ducky Key for $2,208,234. Four businessmen comprising "Duck Key Inc. offered $80,000 cash to buy the property from the Florida-Southern Land Corp. The group included William Bradley, a Marathon real estate man; Gilmore Nunn, a Lexington, Kentucky, broadcasting executive; G.D. Kincaid of the Cardinal Corp., Lexington, and W.D. York, Houston, Texas, financier."

Garvice had brokered a deal with the second mortgage lienholder, York, to acquire the property. He only had to buy Bank Germann's $442,394 third-lien mortgage and then convert the mortgages into Duck Key Inc. equity. They probably paid the $80,000 to Florida-Southern Land Corp. to cover the company's bankruptcy costs. Garvice Kincaid now owned and controlled the luxurious Indies Inn and Yacht Club Resort, and the first thing he would do was rezone and divide the property in a way he felt would create the most value. Before this change, everything on the development was one large parcel, and Kincaid believed the sum of the parts was worth more than the whole. In addition, shortly after the acquisition of the property, Garvice began work on the hotel so it could be ready to open by January 1.

By September 1964, Kincaid had worked another deal. He sold Duck Key Inc., which owned the resort hotel and properties, to Canaveral International Corp. for $2.2 million and made the company a mortgage to cover its acquisition cost. Canaveral was a Miami-based land development and shipping firm. After

1963, W. D. York is no longer mentioned, and one must assume that Kincaid also purchased its interest and that when he sold it to Canaveral, he controlled 100% of the property. We don't know the interest rate on the mortgage, but one should expect it was probably 15 percent or more. Canaveral was also going to lease the hotel to E. A. Stevens for an undisclosed amount. Canaveral's main interest was in selling the eight hundred single-family home lots located on the island and the opportunity to build apartments and shopping and restaurant facilities. Home lots were originally expected to sale for $50,000 each but were replated and listed for $11,000. Only five private residences were ever built on the island. One was Bryan Newkirk's and another was Roy Cohn's.

By 1966, Kincaid had reacquired Duck Key Inc., which owned the resort property. Apparently, Canaveral was unsuccessful in its endeavors and Garvice took back the property again. Here is a *Miami Herald* article dated December 6, 1966:

Indies to Be Restored

A $300,000 renovation is being planned for the Indies Hotel on Duck Key to restore the once plush resort as the grand hotel it used to be.

If a legal tangle can be straightened out in Circuit Court here, the 100-room facility could reopen its doors next month, a Lexington, Ky., millionaire who helped finance the original development of the area said Friday.

Garvice Kincaid said Duck Key Inc.—owners of the hotel— plan to buy $100,000 in new furniture, replace the air-conditioning system, modernize the kitchen and erect a $70,000 boat marina.

And that's just for openers. Kincaid said an addition may be built onto the Indies Hotel sometime next year.

A new roof at a cost of $20,000 has already been affixed to the resort.

But before any of the improvements can be enjoyed by prospective customers, a suit brought by Duck Key Inc. to cancel the lease on the hotel held by Marathon Motel Corp. and Fallon Smith must be settled.

Fallon Smith, a Colorado corporation name, bought stock in the Marathon Motel Corp. in June.

The hotel—now in receivership—recently had its electricity shut off by the Florida Keys Electric cooperative because the Marathon Motel Corp. and Smith didn't pay a $6,175 bill.

Kincaid said the hotel owner Duck Key Inc. is suing the Marathon Motel Corp. and Smith to cancel the lease because of a number of bills [that] piled up over the years and [were] not paid by the corporation.

He said the unpaid bills are the responsibility of the Marathon Motel Corp. and Smith, not the hotel owner Duck Key Inc.

Duck Key Inc. is headed by a Lexington accountant named Ralph Worcester [*sic*]. Kincaid said the electric co-op will turn the power back on at the hotel next week.

Kincaid said a new $200,000 water system is also in the works for the residential plots on the island which will provide outlets for 1,000 homes.

The Duck Key Inc. suit to cancel the lease with the Marathon Motel Corp. maintains the corporation failed to pay bills and insurance and sold furniture out of the hotel.

December 1966 was just two years after Garvice Kincaid's second heart attack, which took place in Florida, and less than two months before the second update to his estate plan. By January 1967, Garvice was involved in another tax case, this time involving the property taxes on Duck Key. Apparently, the Duck Key tax authority took Kincaid's recent reacquisition of the property as an opportunity to reassess the unsold home plots. The following is from reports[23] about Kincaid's lawsuit against the municipality:

The suit said the controversial land on Duck key was reassessed by Hunnicutt tax assessor, Joe Allen, at $5,136,300. The January 1, 1966 "fair market value" of the property, it said, was $2,180,964.

The corporation—headed by millionaire Kentuckian Garvice Kincaid—refused to pay the taxes on the new assessment and mailed off a payment to Willson (tax collector) of $32,485.

Based on its $5.1 million assessment, taxes on the plots total up to $78,365.

The outcome of Kincaid's lawsuit was never reported, but other property owners in the area also objected to the increase in assessments. One has to assume that the municipality and Kincaid negotiated a settlement and the case was dismissed.

In December 1970, Kincaid would begin recognizing the value in one of the parts of the Duck Key Resort when he sold the 450 choice lots to a Marathon, Florida, developer and builder, Herb Cameron, who had been doing most of the recent building on Duck Key. The sale price for the purchase of the lots was $1.03 million. Kincaid retained only the Indies Inn and Pub, the Duck Key Marina, the golf course, and the shopping center properties.

---

23   *The Miami Herald*, January 7, 1967.

Part of the additional attraction of the parcel that Cameron purchased was that in subdividing and rezoning the property, he had gotten approval to build high-rise condominiums on the property. This added value to the parcel Garvice had acquired.

The Committee disposed of the rest of the Duck Key property, the Indies Inn and Pub, the Duck Key Marina, the golf course, and the shopping center properties shortly after Kincaid died in 1975. It appears the Committee sold Ducky Key Inc., which owned the property, to Herb Cameron in early 1976, because it is reported that in June of 1976, Cameron was expanding the hotel by adding sixty units. Cameron continued to own the property until June 1983, when he sold it to a "trio of venturesome South Floridians"[24] for $10.3 million. Their plans were to spend $5 million for improvements to the property. Kentucky Central reported no details on the sale.

In 1976, Mid-Central Investments, a subsidiary of Kentucky Central Life, acquired all the stock in Bluegrass Broadcasting from Kincaid's trust for $2.9 million. It spent $2.7 million in cash and issued his trust a note for $68,338 from Mid-Central. Duck Key Inc. was held in Mid-Central, and after working in the investment department of Kentucky Central Life for thirteen years, it's my opinion, and a pretty fair guess, that they sold Duck Key Inc. to Cameron for $2.7 million. If this is correct, then Kincaid's $2.2 million investment in Duck Key in 1966 had returned $3.73 million (both sales), an increase of $1.53 million or a 70 percent increase, in just ten years. This excludes any positive or negative cash flow created by the property.

Garvice wasn't around to see the value he envisioned realized, but it was there! Herb Cameron was the biggest benefactor of Duck Key. He acquired the property and began selling home sites and building homes. He sold everything roughly ten years later for an incredible $10.3 million. I don't know how much Cameron invested in the total project, but my guess is that he didn't have $5 million in total in it.

Garvice liked to use his businesses to support each other, and Duck Key was no different. In February 1966, Kincaid hosted a nine-hundred-person cocktail party and reception at the Indies House on Duck Key. The party was sponsored by his Marathon State Bank. It's reported that bank directors and guests spilled all over Duck Key. In addition, Kentucky Central Life held some sales conventions at the resort. Garvice was always the grand host, and I'm sure he enjoyed telling everyone that this was a Kentucky Central Life property.

In November 1971, Kentucky Governor-elect Wendell Ford held a planning session at the resort for his incoming staff and their spouses. The

---

24   *The Miami Herald*, June 27, 1983.

entire staff made the trip. Nothing about the gathering was supposed to be made public, but of course it came out. Also, at the resort during the three days of meetings was who else but Kincaid himself. Garvice was quoted as saying he just happened to be at the Duck Key on banking business while the Ford group was there. He left the island about the same time the Democratic Conference ended. Kincaid refused to comment on his relationship with the Indies Inn. Thomas Preston, Ford's communications chief, said he "knew of no participation by Kincaid, whatsoever." Preston also said the cost of the Duck Key meeting was being paid by the Democratic Party and by participants themselves.

Apparently, Earl Wilson wanted one last trip to Duck Key before it was sold. In July of 1976, he took a group of people to the resort for a fishing excursion. It was reported in Kentucky Central Life's internal company magazine publication, *The Keynoter*, with a great picture of the group and this caption:

Champion Fisherman

Joe Hall is a champion fisherman along with being coach of the national basketball champion Kentucky Wildcats. Coach Hall went fishing off Fort Pierce, Florida, in May with Earl S. Wilson, Sr., Chairman of the Board of Kentucky Central, and two other Kentuckians. The party caught seven African pompano, and several other fish, weighing approximately 200 pounds. From left, are Clemont Bolton, Somerset, Kentucky; Coach Hall; Don McCormick, an assistant to Kentucky Governor Julian Carroll, and Mr. Wilson. The following day, Coach Hall and Mr. Wilson caught five tarpon off Duck Key, Florida, weighing about 500 pounds.

[Note: Clemont Bolton was county co-chairman for Julian Carroll's campaign.]

In October 1966, Kincaid had to take over another hotel and golf club in Florida, the Plantation Hotel south of Crystal River. Kentucky Central Life held the mortgage on the property and was forced to take it over. Kincaid dispatched Len Shouse III to Tampa to run the hotel property for him. Garvice knew Len's father from the Lafayette Hotel in Lexington. Len had managed the Lafayette Hotel. The Plantation Hotel property was also in need of a little rehabilitation, and Kincaid soon made plans to renovate and reopen the property in January 1967. The plans included a new sprinkler system for the golf course, additional villas at the hotel, and the repaving of the driveways in the hotel.

The Paradise Plantation and Country Club was built in 1962 along the banks of the pristine Crystal River. It was developed by A. D. Griffith of

Orangeburg, South Carolina, and associates. It was a grand hotel of colonial design and established with one hundred guest rooms. It had a convention hall, swimming pool, and boat dock, along with shops. The initial phase of the hotel was built for $1 million. After its construction in the early sixties, it is said that the Plantation Hotel on Crystal River stood alone along Florida's "Nature Coast" as a testament to elegance, southern hospitality, and natural splendor. The Florida Nature Coast website describes it as "an area of almost a million acres where it is easy to discover the 'real Florida' . . . dense forests, prairies, and blackwater rivers."

Kentucky Central owned the property until 1967, when it was sold to the Alabama Life Insurance Company.

Kentucky Central Life and Brevard Groves

If one looks at any annual report of Kentucky Central Life Insurance from about 1980 on, one will see a business description, many times including colorful photographs, of Brevard Groves. My understanding from Cliff Forbush is that one of Kincaid's banks had a loan on the property and had to take possession. Garvice in turn moved it in to a subsidiary of Kentucky Central Life, Mid-Central Investments.

According to the company's annual reports, Brevard Grove Inc. was organized in 1970. The groves are made up of 1,800 acres of land located in the Indian River region section of East-Central Florida, midway between Melbourne and Vero Beach. The groves are named after the county where they are located. Ed Schaeffer is listed as the incorporator of the company.

Little financial information on the company is reported until around 1980, and then it's sporadic. In 1971, it is reported that W. E. Burnett failed to pay the taxes on the property and the certificates were sold at auction. The bills amounted to $2,900 to the county and $16,100 to the Drainage District. In September of that year, the San Sebastian Drainage District asked Brevard County Circuit Court for permission to seize a square mile of the citrus grove for nonpayment of drainage district taxes and maintenance and assessments. The suit contended that the company had failed to pay some $62,266 in taxes and assessments for the year 1970. The suit noted that the grove was encumbered by a $1 million mortgage issued by Kentucky Central Life Insurance.

It appears that Kentucky Central purchased the bank's loan, foreclosed on the property, contributed it to Mid-Central Investments and, in exchange, issued a $1 million mortgage to Kentucky Central Life. One of the important capacities Kincaid had was the ability to remove a distressed asset from his regulated banks and place it somewhere else. Mid-Central Investments Co. was an unregulated downstream subsidiary that held Kentucky Central's non-life-insurance-company businesses. Moving the groves to Mid-Central made sense. Holding them for a long period of time is a different question.

Brevard Groves produced oranges for Tropicana Juice, and in any given year the groves could produce anywhere from 150,000 to 400,000 ninety-pound boxes of oranges. The problem with its business was that it couldn't control the weather, and if it turned cold before the fruit was ready to be picked, the fruit was damaged. If the weather turned really cold, then it probably would kill a lot of fruit trees. In 1987, the grove had to reset over 22,000 trees. Resetting is the removal of dead trees and the planting of young ones in their place. It takes four to five years for the trees to mature enough for fruit to be harvested. Orange groves also must battle various bacteria which can destroy the trees. To aid in the management of the orange grove, Brevard Groves had its own nursery which could hold 2,500 plants.

The price of oranges changes based upon the quality and size of the local harvest, but on average one can expect to earn anywhere from $2.00 to $4.00 a box. When the local harvest is down, prices are higher, and if it's a boom year, prices are lower.

The first financial information on the groves was published in the Kentucky Central Life 1978 annual report. In 1977 the groves lost $649,000 in net income, and in 1978 they lost $650,000. The assets listed for the company are $2.3 million in 1977 and $2.2 million in 1978. So, in two years the company lost the equivalent of 56 percent of its assets.

By 1982 the company lost $147,000, and in 1983 it lost $107,000, but it finally turned a profit of $921,000 in 1984. The operation had increased in size by 1988, and the company produced a profit of $1,564,000 on revenues of $3.3 million and now showed assets of $6.4 million. It made $617,000 the next year and lost $1,226,000 in 1990. In 1990 the company's assets had increased to $5.5 million. In addition, in 1984, Kentucky Central funded the purchase of 1,340 acres of land near the groves to launch a tree-farming operation. In 1984, 77,000 pine trees were planted, and 250,000 were scheduled to be planted in 1985. It was expected to take fifteen years for the trees to mature.

The point of all this information is why would a company with almost $2 billion in assets and over $30 million of net income hold on to a tiny orange grove business? If it made a million dollars every five years but lost half of it every two or three years, it was doing nothing for the overall results of the organization.

Part of the answer to the question is *who* was running Brevard Groves. The person in charge of Brevard Groves was John A. Burnett, the youngest son of W. E. "Bud" Burnett. When I started at Kentucky Central after high school in the summer of 1977, I worked with John. He was a supervisor in the company's supply department. John was a nice person but probably not the most ambitious or industrious person I ever worked with. When I found out who he was related to, I wondered if this was some type of career path that his father had laid out for him.

John was born May 1, 1955, and was only four years older than me. As I recall, he had been working at the company for a couple of years, so I assume he didn't go to college after graduating from Lafayette High School. John got married in February 1977, at age 21, to Diane D. Degonia. Diane was the 19-year-old daughter of Kentucky Central's switchboard operator, Alberta Degonia. Everybody knew Alberta because she was in charge of the company's long-distance WATS lines and was quite a character unto herself. John and Diane were divorced in March 1978.

In the fall of 1977, I started at Transylvania University and continued to work off and on for Kentucky Central part-time as my schedule would permit. In June 1978, when I returned to the supply/mail room, John was no longer there. I don't recall knowing that John had gone to work at Brevard Groves. I found that out after I started working full-time in the company's investment department in January 1981.

When you are young and just out of college, you don't have the historical business experience to fully understand the details of everything you see. In those early years, I never questioned why we had orange groves and didn't think too much about Bud's son overseeing them. As I gained more professional experience and had more practice doing financial analysis, I did start to wonder about it, though. I recall one time that Kentucky Central reported a bad fourth quarter. Its earnings had fallen significantly that quarter, and my old boss, Cliff Forbush, saw Wendell Gunn, the company's CFO, and questioned him about "what the hell had happened." Apparently, the property & casualty insurance subsidiaries had lost about $3 million, and that Brevard Groves had lost $200,000 was part of the answer. I think that's when I began to appreciate that the company's profitability was subject to things other than just the spread that Cliff and I could earn on our fixed-income investments.

John managed the orange groves until they were sold by the insurance department in May 1995. The state sold them to Wheeler Farms Inc., in Lake Placid, Florida, for $3.8 million. I never saw any financials on the groves after Kentucky Central Life was taken over by the state Insurance Department in

February 1993. The last annual report ever produced by the company was for 1991. Assuming nothing major happened after 1991, when it was sold, Brevard Groves should have had a book value of around $5 million. The price is understandable though, given the volatility of its business—make one million one year and lose $250,000 the next two years.

John Burnett still lives in Palm Bay, Florida, and appears to have retired from work in 1995, after the state sold the groves. I could find no businesses or incorporations tied to him or his home address in later years.

American Resources Insurance Company

This wasn't the only time Bud Burnett would take care of friends and family. In 1980, an old friend, William K. (Ken) Bennett, contacted him. Bennett had worked with Burnett in Louisville at one of the bankrupted property and casualty (P&C) insurance companies Burnett had worked for. I believe the company was Inland Empire Insurance Company, based upon the story Stephen Pate relayed to me. Pate joined Bennett at American Resources Insurance Company (ARIC) in 1981 as its secretary and treasurer and chief accounting officer. In 1980, Bennett called Burnett because he wanted to start a specialty P&C insurance company in Alabama but needed $2 million.

In 1986, The Southeastern Claims Executives Association held a conference in Bal Harbor, Florida, and William Ken Bennett was a speaker. His topic was "Loss Reserves and the Games People Play" and the conference program had this to say:

> A discussion of the reserving aspect of insurance company liabilities in light of the various areas of company management. Particular interest will be paid to the results of reserving practices and the need for input as it reflects the end results and the "true" financial picture of the company as a whole.

About Our Speaker
Biographical Data

W.K. (Ken) Bennett

> Ken Bennett has over 39 years of insurance experience. Mr. Bennett began his career in 1945 in Louisville, Kentucky. He was involved with the first application of computer machine accounting, the forerunner of today's computer. In 1956 he assumed the position of Executive Vice President of Stonewall Insurance Company. Stonewall was formed in 1866 to provide coverage for the trade goods going up the Alabama River systems and the cotton from the Delta plantations. Mr. Bennett remained with Stonewall until 1962.

At this time, he formed Morrison Assurance Company, a wholly owned subsidiary of Morrison Cafeterias, and served as C.E.O. During the period of 1977 through 1979, Morrison Assurance company was the most profitable division of Morrison, Inc.

In 1981, Mr. Bennett formed American Resources Insurance Company. American Resources was the first domestic company formed in Alabama since 1971. As a full line property and casualty insurance carrier, American Resources is heavily involved with the surface mining industry. As President of American Resources Company and with his many years of experience in the industry, Mr. Bennett has been able to keep abreast of the many changes in our industry and its effects on the day-to-day operations of the company.

I reviewed the last reported financial statement of Stonewall Insurance Company, and as of July 1962, Ken Bennett's title was secretary of the company, and its president was listed as F. E. Patrick. In his biographical data above, he claims to have been executive vice president. Stonewall was a tiny $2.7 million asset company when it was sold. As for Morrison Assurance, the Mobile, Alabama–based company, I reviewed the April 1963 incorporation notice and Bennett is not included in the list of six incorporators. When he left the company in 1979, it had assets of $18 million, and he was listed as vice president and general manager. It was acquired by First Southern Financial Corp of Tampa in 1984. It had assets of $40 million.

In an interesting coincidence, when Kincaid Towers was built in 1979 and employees moved into it in 1980, Morrison's Cafeteria had been chosen to run the building's cafeteria. Of course, Morrison Assurance was a subsidiary of Morrison's Cafeteria. Bennett's relationship with Morrison's Cafeteria wasn't known at that time.

Stephen Pate explained the beginning of ARIC like this when I interviewed him:

> Bennett and Burnett were friends. The way Ken Bennett explained it, he and Burnett worked together years ago at some P&C company and had built a personal relationship through that.
>
> *Author: Can I ask you this: Did Bennett ever work in Louisville?*
>
> Not to my knowledge. I don't know. Like I said, I'm telling you what I know. They were personal friends due to a relationship where they worked for the same company, a company that apparently went into receivership or something. They were managing it or something because I remember a story from Bill about Bud talking to Bill about "let's capitalize the wallpaper." [Note: refers to the fact that the wallpaper had more value than anything else in the company.]

Which later on, with my experience of Bud Burnett, makes perfect sense. What a big crook, he [Burnett] and Robert Preston were. I can't believe he [Preston] was a former insurance commissioner, and that he did some of the things he did, but anyway, they were friends. Ken wanted to start the company, but he had to take out a loan and they [the banks] needed a guarantee. He went to Bud. Bud guaranteed it through Kentucky Central in exchange for, I think, [Kentucky Central Life taking] a seventy-five percent ownership [in the company]. And that's how American Resources came to be part of the Kentucky Central umbrella of companies.

Author: But it was started from scratch? Right, in 1980?

It was started in 1981. April of '81 on a $2 million loan.

. . . We had a bond program. I think we were the only one in Kentucky at the time, except for somebody, Jimmy Godfrey, I believe or somebody else. . . . But we did have a surety business. We did a coal surface coal program. But that evolved over the years. We evolved out of that and went into something more mainstream, rural market business.

But that's how it [ARIC] came to be, all the way up to, I guess it was about 1990. We had a suitor. They wanted to purchase it, ARIC. They [ARIC] had some problems with the pricing. I remember that's when I found out what a shyster Bob Preston was.

He [Preston] came down and did a thorough review of our reserves and decided there was about a $1.8 million adjustment that needed to be made. And when we got the claims people involved, none of the adjustments were made, because they were not appropriate. He was in there shaving $10,000 off an $800,000 reserve: "Oh, I don't think we need this extra medical."

Well, let's just go ahead and fabricate our numbers so we can get a sale, but needless to say the sale did not go through. Then in 1994, after they [Kentucky Central Life] started having their issues, that's when a group, consisting of a couple of people within ARIC, some of our agents, some of our attorneys, got together and purchased it from Kentucky Central Life.

Author: Okay, you know, I'm an investment guy, I understand financials and have been in the insurance business for forty years and I'm not sure, listening to you describe it, that I understand what Preston was doing? You kind of lost me the way you described it.

He [Preston] was an officer up there. I don't know what his position was.

Author: He was a senior vice president, corporate development.

Yeah, he was a former insurance commissioner, senior vice president of an insurance company. They go to sell the company. We had a suitor for ARIC. There was some disagreement on the amount of the reserves and whether they needed an adjustment or not. They [the buyer] wanted more [increase reserves] put up on bonds or something like that. So, Bob Preston came down and did a thorough review of all our claims and recommended that we lower our reserves by $1.7 million. Because basically that was this amount of money that they [Kentucky Central Life] were not going to get. In the end, the guy didn't want to pay. And so our claims person, our vice president of claims, got up and said no. He said "I can't do that. I can't justify any of these [numbers]. Maybe, you know, yeah, I could maybe do maybe a grand here or something there on a few of them, but it's not going to be near a million-seven, Bob." And so, none of the reserve adjustments were ever made and the sale never did go through.

But that's when I've learned what a crook that shyster, [Preston], was.

Author: I gotcha, now.

I thought, How the hell do you come down here and do something like that, being a former insurance commissioner? Jesus Christ.

Author: Well, what Preston was doing in our primary P&C companies was that Bruce [Bud's son] was writing surety bond business. . . . Bruce was out writing surety bond business and things like that, and on some of it, he was withholding the premium and not submitting the application until there was a claim. This went on for quite a long time. And this was reported in the papers during his criminal trial. But, you know, when people heard about that, during Kentucky Central Life's rehabilitation, everyone just about threw up. They couldn't believe that one of the company's senior officers was allowing this type of thing to happen; you know, it was just nuts, and both he and Bud Burnett were involved in the cover-up.

He and Bud were in constant cahoots, it seems, about all of it. When I think of Bud Burnett, and I never thought he was the nicest or most honest of men, but I would have thought an insurance commissioner would have been so far above that, but he was just as down and dirty a pig as any of them up there. Sorry, I hope he is not a personal friend of yours, but I have absolutely no respect for the man.

Author: No, he isn't a personal friend, and I also think he was dishonest. I really do. I think it's also a shame. He was directly involved in Bruce Burnett's scam. He didn't take the money, but he helped to cover it up.

Bud and Preston, and there was another one. I think the only honest people up there were Bob Mattscheck, the VP of finance, and I think, oh my god, Enoch Roberts was a good guy. Good guy. But Bob Preston and Bud Burnett. They all should have gone down real hard. As I recall, Bud died before anything could happen to him. I don't know what they [the regulators] ever did with Preston . . . and I remember meeting him [Burnett] in presentations. He was not a nice man.

American Resources was another one of Bud's deals that most people at Kentucky Central Life didn't understand. Here was this tiny P&C company in Alabama, that wrote specialty insurance—workers' compensation insurance for mining companies, and general liability, surety, and reclamation bonds for that industry. Many people at the company thought it was set up to support Bruce Burnett's business, but after speaking with Stephen Pate, I think it was just set up so Bud could do a favor with a friend. In addition to Ken Bennett running the company, Bennett's wife, Linda M. Bennett, was also drawing a salary as an officer of the company.

A person can understand why Kentucky Central might have a property and casualty subsidiary writing home and auto insurance. That's what large multiline insurers like Allstate and State Farm have done for years. Kentucky Central Life focused on insurance for the "family unit," so supporting the needs of the family made sense, but starting an insurance company focused on the mining industry is another story.

ARIC was so small that its results from operations were never broken out in Kentucky Central Life's annual report. The only information that was disclosed occasionally was ARIC's annual premium. It would usually come in between $13 million to $40 million. The problem was that ARIC lost money more often than it made it. Also, this Alabama division would prepare its own financials and send the reports to Lexington, where the Lexington financial reporting staff would incorporate ARIC's results into Kentucky Central's. The investment department managed the investment portfolios for the life company and our two property casualty insurance companies, but we never managed anything for ARIC. We did maintain its mandatory state deposit. This was a trust account. We usually purchased a ten-year treasury bond or some other high-quality security and deposited it in the account. The trust account was also in a bank located in the state of domicile, in ARIC's case, Alabama. ARIC never made much money and so the investment department never had excess cash to invest. ARIC was just another "FOB" situation—friends of Bud. From Kentucky Central's 1991 annual report:

> Property and casualty insurance subsidiaries are subject to off-balance sheet risk in the normal course of business as a result of land reclamation and surety bonds issued. As of December 31, 1991, and 1990 such companies issued reclamation and surety bonds with face amounts approximating $93.9 million and $105.6 million respectively.

When one considers the risks associated with the mining industry and the long-tail nature of these risks, one has to wonder why Burnett ever thought this friend, Ken Bennett, could make money in it. This was a specialty line of insurance, and it required specialty knowledge, and an Alabama start-up company probably isn't going to have it. The reason ARIC could sell $30 million in premium was because other larger, more experienced companies had either raised their prices significantly or exited the market. There are companies in the United States that may need to transport nuclear waste, but that doesn't mean a person with a truck should consider applying for the job.

Banking and Kincaid in the 1970s

Garvice always enjoyed bending the rules and finding and using the gray areas in the rules and regulations. He also liked the public visibility that banks provided him. The industry was considered more upscale and professional than his consumer finance business and far more visible to the public than owning a life insurance company. While his broadcasting companies were visible and important to him, they didn't provide the status that owning banks did.

Kincaid also delighted in being involved with the influential and wealthy, and his banks provided him with the visibility he craved and the avenue to encounter these individuals in business. By 1970, the Kentucky financier had a financial empire large enough to handle most enquiries, if he was interested. Garvice Kincaid wasn't interested in making others famous, but he was interested in how others' endeavors might benefit him. Garvice made his fortune by investing his own money. He understood the risk of debt. In articles written in the late 1960s and early 1970s, he would criticize others for always looking for ways to get someone else to finance their grand schemes because they had little money of their own. His Committee failed to listen to these comments and in later years would be criticized for the risky and ridiculous lending they did.

While Garvice held on to most of the banks he acquired, he would sell one occasionally. To some it might appear he was almost playing checkers with them, sacrificing one piece for the option of making another piece a king. For instance, in May 1960, he purchased a controlling interest in the Everglades Bank from the investment company Harvard Industries Inc. after its president was indicted by a federal grand jury on two counts of misapplying $300,000 in bank funds. It's reported that Kincaid acquired over thirty thousand shares of the bank in the transaction.

Garvice never disclosed how much he spent acquiring the bank, but the bank's December 31, 1959, balance sheet shows it had 57,000 shares outstanding and had a book value of $1.2 million, or $21 per share. Everglades Bank's stock wasn't listed on an exchange, but its shares were quoted in the paper on a semi-regular basis. In early May the stock was quoted around $23 per share. Given these two pieces of information, one can probably correctly assume he spent around $650,000 acquiring his 52 percent ownership in the bank.

On March 8, 1963, the *Fort Lauderdale News* reported that Kincaid sold his position to the Robert O. Law Foundation for $33 per share, or about $1 million. In about two years, Garvice had made $350,000 or 50 percent, on this bank investment.

Garvice also wasn't a long-term owner of the American National Bank of Ft. Lauderdale. He acquired 80 of the bank for $1.245 million in September 1960. He soon sold this bank in December 1961 for $1.463 million. The *Fort Lauderdale News* on December 12, 1961, reported that Garvice paid $40 per share for the bank and sold it for $48 per share—a 20 percent increase.

In August 1963, Kincaid acquired 80 percent of the stock of the Marathon Bank of the Florida Keys from the Hialeah publisher John Morton for $600,000.

Boulevard National was a fifteen-year-old bank whose controlling interest had been acquired by the lieutenant governor of Alabama, James B. Allen, and three others in 1965. Control was later purchased by the holding company Teleposit Inc. On August 26, 1971, Garvice purchased control of the Boulevard National Bank of Miami for $1.83 million from Teleposit.

Banking rules and regulations prevented Garvice from combining his banks, and Kincaid wanted to gain the efficiencies of a larger organization. In mid-1972, Garvice and Al Florence created The Kentucky Group Banks (KGB). KGB was an umbrella organization for his Kentucky banks where they could combine advertising and coordinate services for their banks' customers. An example of their strategy is found in a large August 27, 1972, ad where they advertised 4 percent automobile loans.

You'll be sitting pretty with a 4% new auto loan.

The Kentucky Group of banks is stripping down automobile loans to the essentials. Now, at any one of the 36 banking offices of the Kentucky Group, you can finance that new 1973 automobile for the incredibly low cost of only 4 percent annual interest. That's just $40 for each $1,000 you borrow—the greatest loan value in Kentucky banking history. No other banks in Kentucky have ever dared to offer so much.

Visit your nearby Kentucky Group banking office today and make arrangements for the outstanding 4 percent new automobile loan. You'll be sitting pretty.

Available at all Kentucky Group banks

The ad included a list of KGB's eighteen member banks and their twenty-one city locations.

KGB banks were independent banks controlled by Kincaid and his bank lieutenant, Al Florence, but they were promoted as members of an affiliated group. In fact, while Central Bank was the flagship bank of the group, Kincaid and Florence were quick to point out the overall size of the affiliated group of banks and their locations around the state. It was a strategy ahead of its time, and it skirted the issue of control and banking across county lines.

Kincaid and Florence liked the concept so much that in July 1974, the duo started advertising a similar concept in Florida, as Star Banks. Kincaid controlled his Florida flagship bank Dania Bank and also the Marathon Bank and Boulevard National Bank. He had sold his other Florida bank holdings. These three banks made up the Star Bank group of banks, which covered the east coast of Florida from Fort Lauders to Miami to the Florida Keys. They would advertise this way until he died in November 1975, and after that, all but the Dania Bank would be quickly sold by Kincaid's Committee.

When Garvice died in November 1975, he controlled eighteen banks in Kentucky and three banks in Florida. These twenty-one banks had assets/deposits in excess of $500 million. In December 1976, KGB added the North Middleton Bank to the group. Kincaid had apparently negotiated the purchase of the bank before his death and the Committee just completed the transaction. Another possibility is that Al Florence went ahead and acquired the bank without the knowledge of Wilson or Burnett. The announcement was not as professionally written as previous purchase announcements, and the Committee already knew they would have to liquidate much of Kincaid's banking interest in KGB. In addition, Al Florence already wanted to buy all the KGB banks.

Al Florence

Alvin (Al) Florence was born in Bueno Vista, Kentucky, on April 20, 1926. Bueno Vista is an unincorporated town in Garrard County. His parents, Ora and Frances "Fanny" Upton Florence, were married in 1909 and lived in Garrard County thirty-four years before moving to Lexington in 1943. In Garrard County, his parents lived on a farm and raised tobacco. The Florences had seven children and fourteen grandchildren. In Lexington, the family lived in a small, bungalow-style home on Waller Avenue, just off Nicholasville Road.

Al Florence attended Lafayette High School but entered the U.S. Navy in February 1944 before graduation. In the Navy, he achieved the rank of WT3C (Watertender third class). A watertender maintains the fires and boilers on a steam-powered ship. He was discharged from the Navy in May 1946 and returned home to Lexington, where he completed his studies and participated in a special graduation ceremony for fifty-six returning GIs. He briefly attended the University of Kentucky but soon went on to sell life insurance. He was a licensed agent for the Life Insurance Company of Georgia and Ohio State Life Insurance Company. The 1952 Lexington City Directory indicates that in addition to selling life insurance, he was a salesman for the Transylvania Printing Company.

In late 1948, he met the love of his life, twenty-six-year-old Arline Dillon, and they were married in June 1949. Arline had been a secretary for an office of the Prudential Insurance Company. In 1950, Al Florence began a new career working for a division of the National Cash Register Company (NCR). Initially he was responsible for selling and servicing NCR's traditional cash registers. The dates may sound contradictory, but one can probably assume he was a salesman who wore many hats. With the help of a GI loan, Al and Arline were able to purchase a small, newly built home on Meadow Park Road, just off Brian Station Road.

Computerization Comes to Banking and ERMA— Electronic Recording Machine—Accounting

In a 1993 article by Harvard law student Amy Weaver Fisher and Harvard Business School's Professor James L. McKenney,[25] they describe banking in the early 1950s:

---

25   Amy Weaver Fisher and James L. McKenney, "The Development of the ERMA Banking System: Lessons from History," *IEEE Annals of the History of Computing* 15, no. 1 (1993): 44-57.

In the early 1950s, the banking industry was on the brink of a crisis. Between 1943 and 1952, check use in the United States had doubled from four billion to eight billion checks written every year. Bankers projected by 1955 the number of checks would be increasing by approximately one billion per year, and, by 1960, 14 billion checks would be written each year. This dramatic increase in checking . . . led to a substantial, twofold problem for the industry: The paperwork was staggering and banks were unable to retain bookkeeping staff. This situation had banks at a standstill; they were neither able to expand, nor, in some cases, even to keep pace with the increasing flow of paper.

The overwhelming growth of paperwork at the banks was created by the check-clearing process. Each of the 28 million checks written every business day passed through approximately two and one-third banks, taking more than two days to be processed. This led to a staggering 69 million checks in process throughout the United States banking system on an average day. Unless a check was deposited at the bank where both accounts were located, the check had to be sorted by hand and individually rung up on a machine a minimum of six times during the clearing process.

In a 40-person branch, at least seven people were employed as full-time clerical workers. Most were young female bookkeepers between the ages of 18 and 24. Their monotonous work mainly consisted of sorting pieces of paper, running an adding machine, and bundling checks. Not surprisingly, considering the drudgery of the position and the age of the women, who traditionally left the banks upon marrying, the turnover rate was exceedingly high—in some areas reaching 100 percent turnover each year.

Once a check was deposited at a bank, two things needed to be accomplished quickly: proofing and bookkeeping. Proofing was done to identify the originating bank or branch and verify the amount on the check. Checks, identified only by signature, were received in batches by the tellers and given in batches to proof-machine operators. The operator keyed in the number of the issuing bank and the amount for each check. The proof machine then fed the check into one of as many as 32 pockets associated with the number of the bank. An adding machine attached to each pocket printed the amount of the check, the total for each pocket, and a running grand total on a paper tape. One of the pockets was reserved for "on us" checks—those written by customers whose accounts were with the bank. It was necessary to finish proofing early to catch stop payments or overdrafts on accounts.

At the end of each day, the checks in each pocket (excepting the "on us" checks) were removed, packaged with the adding tape from the pocket, and forwarded to the Federal Reserve system for distribution to the issuing banks. At each routing step the checks again passed through proof machines and were accumulated into new batches with control tapes. Once the checks were distributed by the Federal Reserve, the receiving bank added these to its "on us" checks and processed them accordingly. In general, the proofing system was manual, subject both to operator mistakes and to machine errors even when the operator performance was perfect.

Bookkeeping consisted of manually keeping a customer's account balance up to date daily according to deposits and withdrawals. Each afternoon, "on us" checks were sorted to accounts on the basis of signature and taken to a conventional ledger-card accounting machine, where the amount of the check was subtracted from the balance and a new balance noted and posted to the account's ledger by an operator. A copy of the ledger card and the checks were mailed to the depositor as the monthly statement, and a ledger card with the new balance was saved for the next month's cycle. Timing was very important in this process. Each morning the banks received checks processed by the Federal Reserve that had to be debited from the check writer's account. In the afternoon, banks exchanged all except the "on us" pile of checks with other banks in the same city. Most banks were forced to shut their doors to business at 3:00 p.m. each day to handle the daily bookkeeping and proofing needs.

The processing of bank transactions needed to change, and large banks such as Bank of America were investing in computer research to find an electronic solution to this paper madness. In February 1953, NCR acquired Computer Research Corporation (CRC). CRC had created a specialized electronics division, and in 1956, NCR introduced its first electronic device, the Class 29 Post-Tronic, a bank machine using magnetic stripe technology. Also in the 1950s, NCR introduced magnetic ink character recognition and the NCR 3100 accounting machines. Both the Burroughs Corporation and NCR would become important early providers of electronic equipment and software for the banking industry.

In 1953, a new opportunity was developing at NCR. In recent years, the company had begun developing systems to help banks process their work, and Al Florence was offered a position in Houston, Texas. His job was to learn about these new systems and then travel around Kentucky, Tennessee, and Kansas and sell the systems, oversee their installation, and train the bank's staff. These systems offered NCR a continuing stream of revenue tied to its annual maintenance agreements for NRC's revolutionary systems.

Al Florence must have enjoyed the work, because he and Arline remained in Texas for the next six years. Something finally brought the Florences back to Kentucky in 1959. In June 1959, they purchased a new home in the Stonewall Estates area of Lexington and Al began a job with the state in the office of the Controller of Currency as a bank examiner. This was a natural job for him to assume since his work at NCR had provided him with so much knowledge about the operations of banks. There isn't anything written about his new job, but attorney Bart Brown distinctly remembers that when Florence joined Garvice, he had been a bank examiner and Kincaid certainly would have encountered the people examining his banks. Another Kincaid milestone in 1959 was that Garvice acquired Kentucky Central Life Insurance in Anchorage, Kentucky.

However it happened, Kincaid and Florence formed an unusual partnership, and Florence joined Garvice in 1962. A February 29, 1976, *Louisville Courier* article, after Kincaid's death, describes Florence and his background:

> With Wilson on the Committee is Al Florence who, more than any of the others, resembles Kincaid in appearance, manner, and passion for banking. Tall, heavy-set with a jowly face, and saggy brows, he has much of Kincaid's gruff, level-eyed way of speaking, and is a firm believer in the Kincaid way of doing business. As head of 21 banks, he gets plenty of practice.

> Born in 1926 in the small Garrard County town of Buena Vista, Florence attended UK, The University of Houston and did graduate work at the University of Dayton. In 1949, he married Arline Dillon of Paint Lick, Kentucky, and a few months later went to work for the National Cash Register Company as a bank Consultant, traveling through Kentucky, Ohio, Oklahoma and Texas. When Kincaid offered him a job in 1962, he grabbed it. He has never regretted it.

> "Mr. Kincaid never demanded anything of me," he says. "He gave you a job and you did it. If you kept pace with him, you worked hard. And you learned, for he was a brilliant businessman. I guess if you didn't want to learn, you didn't stay."

> Florence stayed and gradually took over the direction of the Group Banks. When he began [in 1962] there were 12 of them, with assets of $75 million; today there are 21, with assets of $800 million. Banking is his job and his hobby. "My recreation is my work," he says, "and I have big time doing it. A man shouldn't do what he's not happy at." [Note: in 1962, Central Bank was over $25 million of the $75 million number.]

> If Wilson is the elder statesman, Florence is the strong man of the Committee, considered by his associates as "sort of a diamond in the rough, tough but smart, and a driver. He makes up his mind very carefully, but when it's made up, it's made up.

Stan Galbraith said this when I interviewed him:

> Garvice was trying to grow the banks. His philosophy was that, well, if I'm going to buy these things, and I got to pay for these things, then why would we want to stand still and not try to grow, you know. So, he worked to grow his assets and things like that. And again, that's what kind of call it put Garvice on the map. Even though he died, right around Thanksgiving in 1975.
>
> My memory of Al Florence was, I would say he was a spitting image, physically of Garvice, short, rotund and, you know, kind of balding and things like that. So, probably when Garvice looked at him, he thought, "Hell that's me, that looks like me over there."

Author: I think there's some truth in that. I think that if Garvice thought you had a skill or a talent, you know, Garvice would use you. And one of the things that I think that Al brought to the table was, he could go into a bank and represent Garvice and get there and make the people, I hate to say this, to intimidate them, but . . .

> No, you're exactly right, Robert, because when you walked in and you saw Al you thought, oh hell. Here comes the pit bull. He was like the guy that ran Lexington Insurance agency . . . Carl. What's his name? Carl Ratliff.
>
> Carl ran Lexington Insurance Agency, I call it, back in the day. Okay. And like, and Lexington Insurance Agency was in the building when I first got to know Carl and things back in the '70s. The Lexington Insurance Agency was in the building where they were, where Central Bank was, on the corner [of] Short and Upper. There was a parking lot there and it kind of circled around the building on Short and Upper, and his office was in the building right on the other side of that parking lot on the same side of the street. Anyway, Carl was the same way as Florence. If Carl liked you, you were in, but if Carl didn't like you . . . And that's kind of what the impression I got of Al . . . was that, you know, he was always gruff, but if he liked you, he talked to you, but if he didn't like you or something, he didn't give you the time of day.

Author: I can believe that, you know, Kincaid was odd about the banks. When I look at everything else and how he managed those businesses, I can understand the process, but the banks were different and a little harder to understand. You know, he brought Clyde Mauldin in from Florida to run Central Bank and Clyde was actually on the Committee in the second draft of Kincaid's will and trust agreement in 1967. It was Wilson, Mauldin, and Ed Schaeffer on the Committee and not as alternates. Bud Burnett was an alternate. Kincaid had the original version drafted and signed in 1964. There is an update to that agreement in February 1967. Then the final version created in January 1972. Well, in the 1967 version, Clyde is on the Committee, and this made sense to me. I could understand why, but I was surprised, after everything I learned, to see the 1972 version that put Al Florence on the Committee. Al Florence never fit the profile of the type of people Kincaid included on the Committee. He wasn't professional like the others.

Yes, because didn't the Committee end up being basically Bud Burnett and then part was the law firm—Kincaid, Shaeffer, Hembree, and all the group?

Author: *The Committee was Wilson, Burnett, and Al Florence and then three alternates. And the way it was set up was that if anything happened to Wilson, then Schaeffer got on immediately. Al Florence got off within twelve months of being put on it because he got into a pissing match with everybody else. He wanted to buy the nineteen Kentucky Group Banks. And now I'm giving you what I think is correct information, based on other people agreeing with what I've suggested, that Al Florence didn't really have any money. He may have had some wealth because he had some small personal ownerships in some of the banks (outside what Kincaid provided him via loans and option agreements with Kincaid), and when I say he didn't have any money, I mean he didn't have the cash to buy the banks unless someone loaned it to him.*

That's right, Al wouldn't have had cash.

Author: *And so, he wanted to buy the Kentucky Group Banks. Well, I think what he wanted was for the Committee to finance him, so he could buy them. . . . And they wouldn't do it. . . . And so, what they ended up doing was working a deal. I imagine Wilson and Burnett also didn't like working with Florence and this was probably also part of it.*

In this November 27, 1977, Lexington Herald article about Al Florence resigning from the Committee, one paragraph pretty much says it all, "Officially, according to Burnett, Florence resigned 'to pursue his own business interests.'" However, a report published at the time quoted an unnamed source as saying there had been many two-to-one votes on the Advisory Committee and that Florence's "position within the Committee was not favorable to his interests." I think the other Committee members (Burnett and Scheaffer) just worked a deal with Al to get rid of him. Schaeffer had replaced Earl Wilson in April 1977, when Wilson reached the mandatory resignation age of 70. It looks like the estate had an interest in—I think there were twenty banks or close to twenty banks in the Kentucky Group.

Somewhere around that number, it was either in the teens or around twenty or something like that.

Author: Garvice would buy, sell, and merge banks and do stuff, so it's a little bit hard sometimes to know the exact number at a certain date. The way I look at it, it was no more than twenty and no less than fifteen . . . and no more than twenty has kind of been number I have been thinking, based upon ads for the Kentucky Group. Also, there may have been, say, nineteen banks, but twenty-five or more locations (main bank and branches), and this sometimes distorts how his holdings are described.

Robert, I think fifteen is closer to the number.

Author: Anyway, I figure Al Florence probably had ownership in most of the banks, but not every one of the banks. Kincaid liked giving stock to his lieutenants as an incentive and so giving Al Florence 5 percent or maybe even 10 percent was something Kincaid probably did with some of the banks. Kincaid already owned a bunch of banks prior to Florence arriving and so Florence may have only personally participated in the last eight or nine Kentucky banks Kincaid acquired. I think Wilson, Schaeffer, and Burnett worked a deal to consolidate some of his equity stakes into a handful of the banks. One thing that makes me suspicious about how they structured the sale of the banks to him is that a purchase price is never disclosed. That means they had a lot of latitude in the price Florence, and any of his investors, paid for the banks.

Also, certainly by the time Florence entered the picture, Kincaid had already purchased his Florida banks. Robert Layman really was Kincaid's bank man in the 1950s and early 1960s and, in the late 1950s, the president of Central Bank.

It's always been my impression too—and I don't want to interrupt your thinking—but it's always been my impression that state law, the statutes, I guess, on the books back in the 1960s and some of those in the '70s and things like that, when Kincaid was back, you know, buying banks; the regulations in fact read something like that if you own 50 percent or more stock in any one bank, you can't own controlling interest in any other bank. So, Kincaid would own, say, 35 percent and then need to put some of that stock in his wife's name, and then he put it in Jane's and Joan's names, and he might put some of it in Al's name, and then he would put it in, who knows [whose] name and that kind of stuff . . . so that way, he could still control them all.

Author: And, you know, he was a brilliant guy and had anyone that wasn't family—he had them sign a loan to count as consideration, with the stock as collateral, and then everyone signed an option contract that allowed him to buy them back. There is one article which indicates he generally did everything at 75 percent

*of book value. That way the options were always in the money. I
assume that was important for appearance reasons.*

He only did that with people he could trust. He did deals like
that with people that were kind of close to Garvice, not everybody.
They were really close to Garvice. I mean, he had a lot of confidence
in this group and his family and people that work for him. So that's
kind of how he circumvented those regulations. . . . And then
sometime in the late '70s or early '80s, the state changed that law.
But that was how I was told Kincaid always got around it—the
banking statutes. I guess at that time, in the state of Kentucky, that's
when he decided to set up the Kentucky Group Banks.

*Author: That's why . . . Kincaid could do some things that the
Committee couldn't do. Kincaid as an individual could end up owning
all these different banks. But his trust couldn't own and control all
these different banks. Because of that, the Committee didn't have a
choice but [to] get out of the banks after he died. The last bank they
ended up owning was his flagship bank in Florida, called Dania
Bank. And Dania was in a holding company subsidiary of Kentucky
Central Life. The law change happened in the early 1980s, when
Wilkinson was governor, but by 1980 or 1981, the Committee had
sold Dania Bank. If they hadn't sold the bank in two years, Kentucky
Central Life was going to be subject to banking regulations. Garvice
Kincaid was about ten years ahead of his time. He wanted to create
a large, diversified financial institution with banks, with life and
P&C insurance, and consumer loans—a financial conglomerate—
ten years before regulations and other industry leaders started
lobbying for the necessary changes so they could do it. Citigroup's
Sanford I. Weill was one of the first, and he didn't get his financial
conglomerate established until the mid-1980s. Garvice was twenty-
two years older than Weill and a good ten years ahead of him.*

I don't remember Bob Layman.

I remember, I think Jean Karrick was there after Garvice died,
and somebody that worked at Central Bank for a number of years,
and when Mauldin ended up being president of Bank of Lexington
and Trust, they left Central Bank and went down there and worked
with Clyde Mauldin until he retired.

[Note: In 1975, Mrs. Karrick was the first woman to become a vice president
at Central Bank. She was an active member of the National Association of
Banking Women.]

Several people at the bank followed Mauldin to the Bank of
Lexington, some of them Central Bank executives. They jumped
ship to join Mauldin, and it was an instant shot in the arm for the

Bank of Lexington. According to this article, Jim Rose, who bought the Bank of Lexington in 1983, . . . said Mauldin's strengths included his ability to assemble an outstanding staff. Yeah . . . and Jim Rose is the guy that bought three or four of the banks from the Kentucky Group, when the Committee was liquidating them.

Author: In the what's crazy category? See, in 1967 Mauldin is on the Committee. When I say he was on the Committee, he wasn't an alternate, he would have been an initial member.

Yeah.

Author: Of course, he leaves in whatever year [December 1971 the article says]. They tell you he leaves, and Kincaid updates his will in January 1972, and of course he is no longer on the Committee. Yeah, and that's when Al Florence gets put on it. Well, kind of what's crazy is Kincaid starts out with the president of Central Bank, Bob Layman, initially in 1964. He was an alternate, but the Committee was made up of seven members—three family and four nonfamily—and Layman was an alternate nonfamily member.

I just don't remember Bob Layman.

Author: He was someone that everybody liked and respected, but I don't think he could handle the pressure. At one point in the 1950s, he left Kincaid and went to Oak Bank in Tennessee for a little bit, but Garvice brought him back within a year and a half, and he worked for Kincaid for a couple of years, and then he left again. Kincaid liked his abilities so much he moved him to Kentucky Central Life as a senior vice president, from being president at Central Bank. In fairness to him, he lost his wife Polly in 1968, at age 46, and that devastated him. She must have been seriously ill, because she had been in Central Baptist Hospital for fifteen days. Everyone I have spoken to about Bob Layman had nothing but good things to say about him, and some say they both were totally devoted to each other. Anyway, when Bob Layman went to Kentucky Central Life—and that's when Garvice brings Clyde Mauldin up from Florida to be president of Central Bank—Layman remained a director of Central Bank and a vice president of Kentucky Finance.

Once Al Florence entered the Kincaid empire, he soon demonstrated his value to Garvice. Florence began his career chauffeuring Kincaid around to all his banks, but Garvice knew he needed a boots-on-the-ground lieutenant overseeing his banks. These institutions needed to grow and become more efficient, and their loan activity needed to be monitored. In addition, he wanted the banks to make larger loans, which would then need to be spread (participated) among his banks, so he would also need a process put in place to make this possible. Finally, when Florence joined him, Garvice owned twelve banks in Kentucky, and he wanted to acquire control of more. After several years of Florence watching, learning, and working with Garvice and his banks, Kincaid gave him more responsibility.

Al Florence was intimidating and enjoyed mimicking how Kincaid dealt with people. He would spend days on the road, traveling the state of Kentucky and overseeing the management of Kincaid's banks and also looking for opportunities to acquire new banks. He was Garvice's dedicated resource to grow and manage his banks. As Kincaid bank empire grew, the need to formalize the management process also grew, and in 1966, Florence incorporated Bank Management Associates, Inc. (BMA), a bank services provider. From 1967 through 1969, Al Florence worked to cement his position with the various bank managements and continue to gain Kincaid's trust and respect. He visited the banks frequently and reported to Kincaid on what was happening, and he also called upon non-owned banks hoping to discover new banks Garvice might acquire. Florence also supervised the building and remodeling of the banks and new branches, and when Berea Bank & Capital Trust was taken over by the FDIC, Kincaid worked through Al Florence to negotiate with the FDIC the purchase of the bank's assets and the chartering of a new Berea bank. By 1969, Al Florence had become what others eventually referred to as "Kincaid's right-hand bank man," but Garvice didn't let him mess with Central Bank. He wasn't an officer, only a director of the bank, in later years.

By 1960, Florence began hiring some key employees at BMA. In 1970, he hired Charles Watkins, formerly vice president of the First National Bank of Carlisle. Charlie would consult with banks and coordinate their operations and integrate the banks with a new central computer system that was installed at BMA in October of that year. In 1971, Florence brought in Edward Hall from Kincaid's Winchester bank as an auditor and Harry Lee Smith as director of marketing. Hall was also a former bank examiner, and Smith had been working at Citizens Fidelity Bank in Louisville. These employees would deal with the day-to-day work and provide assistance in the areas of marketing, credit analysis, auditing operations, and management of bank assets.

According to Stan Galbraith, Al Florence and BMA provided many services and functions for the banks. One of the most important functions was providing an electronic platform for the banks to operate, and since Florence had spent almost ten years with NCR, one can imagine that it was the NCR platform that he chose to provide this service. In addition, BMA provided most of the supplies the banks used and would review larger loans and decide how the larger loans should be divided/participated among the Kincaid banks.

Charlie Watkins, when he was at First National Bank of Carlisle, is who talked with Stan about going into banking. Here is what Stan recalls about Charlie Watkins and his role at BMA:

> Okay, that kind [of] ties back in, because I want to say by, well, 1971, or around that time, I told you about a guy named Charlie Watkins. Charlie was kind of like a vice president or something at the First National Bank, Carlisle. Well, it was somewhere around that time, Kincaid was buying banks and putting them under his KGB umbrella, [and] that's when Al started heading up Bank Management Associates, and he brought on Charlie Watkins to be in charge of the operations side of it. BMA had different people doing different things, or with different responsibilities. Charlie Watkins at one time was also with the Bank of North Middletown, and Ed Hall, who also worked at BMA, was in charge of auditing all of the banks.
>
> Charlie ended up there and then he was president for a while, and then worked at the North Middletown Deposit Bank, which got in trouble on loans and things like that. And that's when I guess Kincaid bought the bank and brought it under KGB. And then it wasn't long after, he came to the Deposit Bank of North Middletown. He came on board, and they [the Committee] ended up selling the deposit bank to Bourbon Agriculture Bank or Kentucky Bank.

Many people over the years have referred to Al Florence as "Kincaid's fixer." The connotations of this term are endless, but generally I think people knew Florence didn't have an issue handling sensitive things—things that some might find borderline illegal or unethical. For instance, it's reported that when Kincaid wanted approval for some banking proposal, it was Florence who carried the torch to Frankfort. When I joined Kentucky Central, Cliff Forbush referred to Al Florence as "Kincaid's bagman," and in Jim Host's book *Changing the Game*, Host relays a story in which both Garvice and Florence are significant participants. Host was interested in entering politics, and Louie Nunn was the sitting governor and would dictate who the Republican candidate for governor would be against Wendell Ford. Initially, Host thought he would be at the top of the ticket. He had been a popular commissioner of public information and also the commissioner of the Department of Parks under Nunn, but Nunn didn't think he could control him and selected Tom Emberton for the top of the ticket. Since both positions, governor and lieutenant governor, were elected, it was possible to have a split-party outcome.

> I was thirty-three years old at the time, and the Democrats attacked my youth and inexperience. I tried to spin this to my advantage and argued that I had fought the corruption of career politicians. Ford effectively used the [Nunn] tax increase against

us, even though he knew the state desperately needed the revenue it produced. He incessantly criticized "Nunn's nickel" and accused Republicans of raising taxes on hardworking people. It was a brilliant strategy because we spent much of the campaign on the defensive. Ford attacked us, knowing that, if elected governor, he would benefit from the additional funds.

The entire campaign felt like uphill sledding. The Republican party brought in St. Louis campaign consultant Roy Pfautch, who tried to find some way to promote Tom Emberton. Since the governor and lieutenant governor were elected separately, we cooperated but communicated less than we should have. This became apparent when I walked in Pfautch's office and sitting on his desk was an Emberton-Carroll bumper sticker. Julian Carroll was the Democratic candidate for lieutenant governor, and Pfautch (with Governor Nunn's support) had tried to cut a deal with Carroll's campaign to support Tom for governor. I cannot prove this, but I believe Watson and Murphy pushed to divide the ticket so that I had no chance of winning.

Despite these deals, some people still thought I could win, and various moneyed interests were eager to try to buy my allegiance. For example, Garvice Kincaid invited me to his office during the campaign. When I arrived, Clyde Mauldin and Al Florence (Kincaid's personal moneyman) were in the room. Garvice said, "My people tell me you are going to win because you are working harder than anyone they have ever seen. They say you are to run the governor's office. Is that true?" I said, "I don't think so." He said, "Well, that is what my people say." Garvice proceeded to lift a sack full of cash onto his desk. He said, "I know you don't have any money. I want you to take this. I don't want anything in return other than when you win, I just want to be able to call you from time to time." He reminded me that he had given me my first break on the Kentucky Central Network and asked whether I would be in my current position if not for him. I said, "I suspect I would not." Then he said, "Well, I want you to take this bag in appreciation." When I refused, he snorted and said, "Do you know how many people have been in this office and have graciously received money like this?" I just said, "I'm sorry. I am not like other people." He concluded, "No you are not. This meeting is over!" I was escorted out of his office.

Jim Host lost the election for lieutenant governor, and Democrat Wendell Ford won the governor's race. Clyde Mauldin might have brought Kincaid the bag of money, but I always suspected that Al Florence was his man for silently accumulating cash for his payoffs. He could pull a little money out of each of Kincaid's banks, and no one would be the wiser. Kentucky politics has always been known to contain a fair amount of backroom agreements and handshakes, and during the Kincaid era I am sure he used this to his benefit.

John Rampulla, the former vice president of mortgage loans for Kentucky Central Life, has a little different version of a similar story. John went to the University of Kentucky College of Law with Steve Wilson, Earl Wilson's son. In 1969, he had just returned to Lexington after a thirteen-month tour of duty as an Army captain in Korea.

Initially John joined James E. Keller and Henry E. Hughes's law firm, but he soon realized that starting a law practice from scratch was difficult. Steve Wilson knew that Mr. Kincaid was looking for a man to run his mortgage loan department at Kentucky Central Life, and Steve recommended John to him. Garvice was interested and had Steve bring John over to his home on Richmond Road during one of his summer pool parties for his friends and business associates. John says he and Steve walked over to Garvice, John put out his hand to introduce himself to Kincaid, and Garvice didn't shake and turned and looked to his side and said, "So you want to work in the mortgage department," and then abruptly just walks off. John was a little shocked and thought, *What have I got myself into*. Things worked out, and in 1971, he joined Kentucky Central Life as assistant vice president, mortgage loans, and began working with Mr. Kincaid. Garvice must has liked him because in May 1973, he was promoted to vice president, mortgage loans.

John acknowledges that Kincaid was extremely active in influencing Kentucky's political structure and gave me this example:

> During a governor's race, Mr. Kincaid would set up a meeting with each candidate running for governor. He would space the meetings about three hours apart and hold them in his office on the fifth floor of the Central Bank building. He never did them alone and almost always had two other people with him, and usually Al Florence was one of those people. At the appointed time, and probably after making the person wait a while, Mr. Kincaid would have them come in. They would sit and chat about things for maybe thirty minutes to an hour, and when they were standing up to leave, Garvice would reach down behind his desk and hand them a briefcase. Nothing was really said, and they always knew to take the briefcase, and they left. A couple of hours later, the next candidate would arrive and the process would repeat.

As for Jim Host's version, John suggested that maybe Mr. Kincaid didn't believe the lieutenant governor position deserved the briefcase.

Ray Hornback, U.K.'s marketing and alumni vice president, provided a little more color on Garvice's political influence when I interviewed him:

> There was a rumor that Governor Ford was going to add Garvice to the UK board of trustees, and neither Singletary nor I wanted him on the board because Kincaid always wanted to control everything.

We make an appointment with the governor and President Singletary and I drive over to Frankfort to meet with Governor Ford.

We go in and try to say something cute about what they wanted, and he says, "I guess you heard the rumor that I am going to put Garvice Kincaid on the board of trustees, and we just look at him. Then he says, "You have to understand that Garvice gave me $50,000 for my campaign, and when he did, I told him, "Mr. Kincaid, that's a lot of money and I can't imagine someone donating that much money to a campaign without wanting something." He said Garvice told him the only thing he wanted was to be put on the UK board of trustees and [he] told him [he] would.

Governor Ford then says, "After telling him that, I can't back out now, can I? If I did, my word wouldn't be worth anything." He also told them he understood Kincaid could be difficult to deal with but that he felt like there were some other strong board members on the board of trustees that could stand their ground with him. Then he mentioned William "Bill" Sturgill and some others.

Former WKYT Frankfort reporter Barry Peel also wasn't surprised that Garvice used his wealth to purchase political influence. He had this to say when I interviewed him:

And I'm glad you told me that story because Jim Host—and I'll say this for the public record and I think I've said it before—when UK interviewed me for three years for their oral history project, I guess they were desperate [with a laugh]. They interviewed me, and I said on the record, and I will not deny it, I think Jim Host was one of the finest public servants I ever covered. I'm not at all surprised that he turned down the money, because I know of a couple of cases of people who didn't.

I heard his story, and again I can't prove it, and if there are lawyers out there, please don't sue me, because I said in advance, I can't prove it. I just heard it, so I am just passing along a rumor. But the story I heard is that when Louis Nunn ran for governor the second time, Wallace Wilkinson raised a bunch of cash for him. And he supposedly—and again I can't prove it, but I did hear it— Wallace took the cash to a hotel room in a briefcase. He goes in the room and throws the briefcase on the bed and opens it up and says, "Here, Louis, here's $100,000." I can't prove it; it's just a rumor. I wasn't there, so I don't know if it's true. Louise Nunn is dead and so is Wallace Wilkinson, but I heard it. So, I'm sure that there were many people that came to Kincaid's office and took the money.

Jesse Unruh used to be the speaker of the California House legislature, and he famously said, "Money is the mother's milk of politics," and it is, and today the milk has soured, and that's why our political system is so soured. The public interest is no longer the interest that comes out of the legislature, it's the 1% that buys public policy. I don't think there can be any question about that.

But again, I'm not at all surprised to hear that Jim Host didn't take the money, because he's one of the finest public servants we have ever had—the hardest working and the most honest person that I have ever covered, and it's a shame he couldn't have been a congressman or, God forbid, our governor. The first time I encountered Jim Host, he was in fact the candidate for lieutenant governor with Tom Emberton. Well, that was in 1971. That's when Wendell Ford won. That's when I first met Jim, and I'm not at all surprised that Jim didn't take the money. But again, let me just say for the record now again, I don't know who would have done it, but I'm not at all surprised that Garvice said several other people did.

John Rampulla also confirmed that Frank Trimble was Garvice's "loan originator" and sought out all the tougher, higher-interest-rate loans. In addition to automobile dealerships and such, John says Trimble really loved doing subdivision loans. He said developers would approach him about a loan and he would discuss what they probably could do and take it to Mr. Kincaid. Usually, the loan terms were acceptable to Mr. Kincaid, and he would tell Trimble to proceed. Frank would then contact the developer and tell them, "I almost have your loan approved through the loan committee, but it probably would help if you would throw in a couple [house] lots." The lots weren't for Mr. Kincaid or the bank, but for Frank Trimble. John said that Mr. Kincaid knew what Frank was doing and didn't say anything and just let Frank think he was getting away with something.

John also said Frank was a "heavy smoker, hard drinker and liked the women," and he was told that when Frank Trimble died in 1972, he had just had sex with his new wife, Ann McIntyre Cushman Trimble. They were still almost newlyweds, having married in April 1970. Frank married his first wife, Frances, in 1944, while he was in the Navy. In the 1950s and 1960s Frances was very active in the Lexington Junior League, which raises money for local charities. Their largest fundraiser is the Lexington Junior League Horse Show and its associated social events.

Ann McIntyre Cushman was the daughter of a Bourbon County man, Luther T. McIntire, a well-known breeder, horse trainer, and showman of world champion American Saddlebred horses. Ann in her own right, while not a professional, was considered a significant horsewoman herself and was well-known locally and on the national saddlebred horse show circuit. Ann's husband, Robert S. Cushman, was a local home builder. He constructed homes in most of Lexington's better subdivisions during the late 1950s and 1960s. It's understandable that Frank Trimble and Ann's husband Robert probably crossed paths over the years on loans. In addition, Ann's name appears in many of the articles about the Lexington Junior League Horse Show, in which Frances Trimble was involved in putting on. One can assume these two couples interacted socially many times over the years.

In 1966, the Vietnam War was escalating, inflation was rampant, interest rates were surging, and concerns over a global recession pounded stocks. Stocks suffered a bear market in 1966, with the S&P 500 falling about 22% from peak to trough. It's easy to see how this would have affected Robert's construction business, and by late 1967, he had creditors demanding payments on his past-due loans. Every marriage has problems, but a situation like this can destroy one quickly, and by late 1968, Ann had found affection for Frank Trimble and the two began an affair, which would lead both of them to filing for divorce in 1969. In March 1970, fifty-five-year-old Frank Trimble married forty-one-year-old Ann McIntire Cushman.

When Frank and Frances split, they were living at 141 South Hanover Avenue in Lexington. It was a massive 5,640-square-foot home with four bedrooms and five bathrooms. In 2022, this home was sold for $1.8 million. When Frank died, he and Ann were living at 3997 Toronto Court, just off Nicholasville Road. This was a small, 1,140-square-foot newly built home that had sat empty and unsold for over two years. The property was always listed for sale, so one can assume Frank was just renting it. This dramatic change in lifestyle had to be traumatic for Frank Trimble, a former city commissioner, someone who had helped manage Republican campaigns for governor, a vice president and director of Central Bank, and Kincaid's "loan man."

John Rampulla said that according to Trimble's wife Ann, Trimble got up from bed and had just taken a hot shower, and as he walked out of the bathroom, he dropped dead. He had collapsed after a massive heart attack. Frank Trimble was fifty-seven years old. He was one of Kincaid's earliest lieutenants, having shared an office with Garvice in his early years of practicing law. In ten years, Frank Trimble had become an important player in the Kincaid saga. He had been an incorporator of many of Kincaid's businesses and, many times, also a director, and he was Kincaid's "loan man." Trimble was listed as an initial Committee member in Kincaid's 1964 estate plan but was removed in the February 1967 update and replace with Earl Wilson. Apparently, by the mid-1960s, Frank's importance to Garvice was waning just as Al Florence's importance was beginning to increase.

John Rampulla and I were discussing how much money Mr. Kincaid donated to various charities, schools, universities, and other organizations and to just people in need. He gave away far more money than he ever gets credit for, and most of it was dedicated to health and human service–related issues and needs. You didn't find Garvice Kincaid donating money to get his name on a building, like so many wealthy people do today. He did it because he believed that people with resources should help those who are in need. John told me the following story, which he witnessed in the early 1970s, and which I thought demonstrates a person who understood how tragedy affects people.

> Mr. Kincaid was in the lobby of Central Bank one morning and learned that an employee had just lost his wife the night before. The employee was a Black man and probably worked in maintenance or the supply and mail room areas of the bank. When Garvice heard this, he immediately walked over to one of the teller windows and told the teller to put $200 in the man's account and then walked off. Mr. Kincaid knew the man had limited resources and would need some extra money to get through his crisis. Kincaid putting $200 in the man's account might not sound like much money today, but at the time in question, a person making minimum wage was making only around $65 a week, and after taxes, insurance, and social security, they were probably bringing home only $38 to $40 a week.

After hearing this story, I told John about a Kincaid story I had read in the company's home office magazine. I assume it happened in the late 1960s at either the law firm, Central Bank, or possibly Kentucky Central Life, because after IBM introduced its Selectric line of typewriters, Kincaid's companies became fast adopters. In fact, in July 1964, when IBM introduced a magnetic tape system for storing characters (the Magnetic Tape/Selectric Typewriter), Paul Carr was pictured in the *Lexington Herald-Leader* signing a purchase order for the first machine to roll off IBM's assembly line in Lexington. This machine was the world's first word-processor device. So, in the 1960s, Kincaid's companies were replacing a lot of typewriters. Here is the story:

> Though presumably out of touch with the problems of everyday living, he could be approached by a secretary who wanted to buy her daughter an office typewriter when trade-in time came around and convincingly answer, "I don't know about such things," and then remember at Christmas to buy a new typewriter for the girl and have it delivered as a surprise.

After Kincaid died, the political backroom deals continued and so did the questions about ethics in Kentucky politics, and by 1987 and the era of Wallace Wilkinson (1987–1991), political corruption in the state would reach its pinnacle. The FBI would begin Operation Boptrot, an investigation into corruption among the Kentucky General Assembly and the commonwealth's legislature. The operation was highly successful, with the investigation culminating in several indictments in 1992, leading to the conviction of more than a dozen legislators between 1992 and 1995. The investigation also led to reform legislation being passed in 1993. Bruce Wilkinson, the nephew of then-Governor Wallace Wilkinson, was serving as the governor's appointments secretary; he was convicted of conspiracy to commit extortion and sentenced to three years' imprisonment and fined $20,000, the amount of the bribe he was convicted of taking. Governor Wilkinson was investigated but not charged, but left the state in disgrace and moved to Florida.

When I was at Kentucky Central Life in the late 1980s, it was said by some of the company's senior management that Wallace Wilkinson had the best briefcase collection in the state, apparently alluding to all the people who would stop by his office carrying a briefcase but fail to walk out of there with it. After the FBI's Boptrot investigation, I always assumed there was more truth to this rumor than not.

When Kentucky Central Life was eventually taken over by the Kentucky Insurance Department in February 1993, many accusations were made regarding Governor Wilkinson's involvement in protecting Burnett and the company. Some criticism involved his appointed insurance commissioner, Elizabeth Wright, who at best neglected her duties in relation to regulating Kentucky Central Life. The general assumption was that she had received direction from her boss, Governor Wilkinson. In published newspaper articles, it was reported that she had received a $350,000 loan from Central Bank in 1990, which later her husband explained was tied to his practice. She wasn't regulating the bank, so there was no direct conflict of interest, but given that the bank was under the control of the same Committee that controlled Kentucky Central Life, she probably should have voluntarily disclosed it.

In addition, in 1990, Kentucky Central was under an intense state audit, and the state auditors were so surprised by the number of problem mortgage loans and real estate they found that they brought in Deloitte & Touche, the company's auditors, to do a special review of these areas. In the end, Deloitte recommended a $76 million increase in reserves, but the Insurance Department required the company to increase its loss reserves by only $30 million. When questioned about where the $30 million came from in a deposition related to the many lawsuits that followed the company's collapse, Wright responded that she believed Bud Burnett suggested/negotiated it. Apparently, the audit staff had recommended a $40 million increase and Burnett had pushed back against even that amount. The audit wasn't completed until September 1991.

Finally, during the exam, it was reported that the values for the properties that Kentucky Central Life used were based on extremely optimistic leasing and cash-flow assumptions. The cash flows were reported to have been produced by the Webbs. The assumptions, while extremely unrealistic, were not questioned by the Insurance Department. In other words, a large project with negative cash flow would miraculously be leased and fully cash flowing in twelve to eighteen months. When questioned in court about those projections and who analyzed them, the company's former secretary, treasurer, and CFO, Wendell Gunn, indicated that the Webbs had produced the cash flows and that he never questioned them. During the state examination, Deloitte & Touche also indicated that Kentucky Central did not maintain any spreadsheets on the cash-flow loan properties. The examiners claimed the company didn't even track how much income it should be receiving from these loans. This is something else the Insurance Department found out during the examination and failed to react to.

How much of a role politics played in the relationship between Kentucky Central Life and the Kentucky Insurance Department will never be known, but the company had a long history of having a cozy relationship with the Kentucky Insurance Department. When I joined Kentucky Central's investment department in 1981, my boss, Cliff Forbush, told me that Burnett and Preston authored Kentucky's investment regulations for insurance companies. I looked up Preston's history and learned he was the state's insurance commissioner from 1967 to the end of 1971. This is when Kincaid brought him into the company as vice president, corporate development. It appears many insurance regulations were updated in 1970, so I assume this was when the investment regulations for insurance companies were also updated.

The reason this is important is that Kentucky's insurance regulations and statutory accounting rules included a provision called the "basket clause." Cliff said the basket clause wasn't an uncommon provision, but the way it was written provided a basket amount that was too large and too ill-defined or liberal in its wording. The basket clause regulation allows an insurance company to own assets that would normally be non-admitted on its balance sheet. It typically includes a limit related to a company's surplus and dictates how the limit is to be calculated and administered. For instance, a typical limit may be up to 10 percent of the company's assets but further limited so that no one investment can exceed 2 percent of total assets, and the basket is limited so it may not exceed 50 percent of a company's statutory surplus. The intent of the provision is to recognize that insurance companies may invest in long-term assets for which market values are not easily known. For instance, if a company has an investment in several office buildings and apartments, the only way to a market value can be found is to get an appraisal. This would be complicated and expensive, so the basket clause provides that the amortized, depreciated, or adjusted cost of the asset will be used for valuation purposes.

The problem with the Kentucky statute was that it was too liberal in just stating that a company could have a basket amount of up to 10 percent of its assets, with no other limits. This meant that in 1990, Kentucky Central Life could designate up to $132 million of assets under the state's basket clause though it had only about $50 million of statutory surplus (the equivalent of shareholder's equity for insurance companies). Now consider that Kentucky Central Life, according to the 1990 Insurance Department examination/audit, was expected to experience at least $40 million of additional losses on its mortgage loans and real estate investments, and at the same time, the rating agency Standard & Poors and the State of California Insurance Department were projecting $80 million to over $100 million of additional losses. Kentucky Central Life was literally projected to be insolvent in the near future, barring an infusion of new capital or a massive sale of assets.

When Garvice Kincaid died, Kentucky Central Life had a strong 12 percent surplus position, but Burnett and the Committee began to take on so many policyholder liabilities (adding new business) and experiencing so many problem mortgage loans and real estate that the company's surplus was eventually reduced to 5 percent. A life insurance company will normally have a surplus position of eight percent to 12 percent of assets, depending on its product lines. Most state insurance department regulations require a company "remediation plan" if its surplus drops to 5 percent. By 1991, when the Insurance Department had completed its examination, it should have already stepped in to oversee the management of the company.

Did Bud Burnett use whatever remaining political influence the company had to keep the regulators at bay in 1990? I think that Burnett thought he was smarter and more powerful than Garvice Kincaid. He spent years working for Mr. Kincaid and never recognized that Mr. Kincaid used his political influence only in very limited ways. He wanted the political establishment to work with him and not for him, and he never wanted to be in a situation where he owed anyone. Garvice Kincaid was entitled to display his ego because he created everything he had, while Burnett was just someone who carried his bags. Burnett wasn't as smart as Mr. Kincaid, and while Garvice Kincaid risked only his own money, Bud Burnett had none of his own money to risk. By 1991, Kentucky's political establishment had to recognize that Bud Burnett had lost control of the company, and while they probably hoped for a miracle solution, I believe they also closed the political influence door on him. The politicians had seen that the emperor had no clothes, and while they weren't laughing, they knew he would soon be dethroned. Did politics play a role?

Columnist Robert T. Garrett, in a *Courier Journal* article on February 21, 1993, asked the same question:

As regulators slept, Kincaid empire foundered.

To the dismay of Lexingtonians, the business empire of the late Garvice D. Kincaid is collapsing. Most of Kincaid's companies—banks, loan companies, a Lexington-based broadcasting chain that has made a fortune as the official voice of the Big Blue Religion here—grew and prospered long after his death in 1975.

But the Kentucky Central Life Insurance Co., after making a lot of ill-fated real estate loans in the 1980s couldn't woo new investors in recent months. Earlier this month, after regulators elsewhere said it was too shaky to keep selling policies, Kentucky Central became a ward of the state.

Burnett, the company's top executive, is gone. Would-be buyers are salivating over the broadcasting properties in Lexington and Hazard, which are for sale. Policyholders and annuitants, such as 27,000 public sector workers in Kentucky who have a big chunk of their retirement savings invested in Kentucky Central [products,] are nervous.

The three-member advisory committee in whose hands Kincaid left control of his empire faces seemingly unending litigation brought by his own twin daughters, who were angry over both his will and its execution. And many Lexingtonians fret about what will happen to their city, especially its downtown, when the anticipated axe falls on Kentucky Central's bad real estate loans.

Who will get hurt? How did this happen? Who will be held accountable?

It will be months before the full story unfolds. But by its conclusion, I'll bet that the Kentucky Department of Insurance will have egg on its face. And Kentuckians will be confronted with yet another example of how regulation of businesses in this state is often an absurd mismatch between a weak public sector and the few sizable corporations domiciled here. Our history teaches our regulators to be timid and our corporation executives to be bold, if not brazen.

Look at Garvice Kincaid. An outsider who was blackballed by Lexington genteel, mostly Republican business establishment, he financed Democratic candidates at both the local and statewide level. He was a real power politically. And Kincaid collected: He had a reputation as someone who virtually named state banking commissioners. Often, it was someone who'd worked for one of his 19 banks in Central and Eastern Kentucky.

His influence was likewise felt at the insurance department. Governor Louie Nunn's Insurance Commissioner? Kentucky Central's Robert Preston. Although Harold McGuffey had titular control of the department under Governor Wendell Ford and Julian Carroll, many people will tell you that Preston, though back at Kentucky Central, still called many of the shots. Preston's protegees wielded considerable influence at the department during the Collins and Wilkinson administrations.

The 1981 indictment of Sonny Hunt, Carroll's patronage boss, certainly suggested a Kentucky Central knack for pleasing governors. Burnett's son, Bruce, co-owned an insurance agency that got $16,000 of state insurance commissions controlled by Hunt. It then kicked $8,000 back to Hunt's son Allen, who in 1976 had received an insurance agent's license after signing a blank exam answer sheet and letting Preston walk it through the department.

Perhaps the best example of Kentucky Central's "getting right" with a governor, though, came in 1987. Bud Burnett did not back longshot Wallace Wilkinson in the primary, which disappointed Wilkinson. (He had been allied with Burnett against the Lexington business establishment in a 1981 mayoral race and reportedly had high hopes of getting his support.)

So, it was not surprising that Kentucky Central gathered a massive bundle of contributions—at least $61,250, as last calculated by my colleague Tom Loftus for subsequent Wilkinson political causes. But the kicker came only the day before Wilkinson took office [December 1987], when Kentucky Central took Frankfort's Capital Plaza Hotel off Wilkinson's hands, for a sum never disclosed. Why would Kentucky Central buy a hotel that had never turned a profit?

A year later, Wilkinson put Burnett on the University of Kentucky Board of Trustees. Was that why Burnett's company bought Wilkinson's Hotel? Nah, no way.
Two years thereafter, Bruce Burnett was part of a Lexington joint venture that won a controversial state contract to build and lease a new dormitory to Northern Kentucky University. Was that why? Huh? Nah?
But throughout the Wilkinson years, as Kentucky Central watched the loans to the Webb brothers [entities] of Lexington, and other real estate developers go sour, state regulators slept. Could that be why? Nah, it couldn't happen here in Kentucky.

Al Florence carried out many duties for Garvice. He initially helped to build and grow his collection of Kentucky banks, which eventually led to the creation of Kentucky Group Banks. He and his staff at BMA also provided the management oversight and the business support that Kincaid's collection of small banks needed. Finally, he was Kincaid's strongman and bagman, someone who could deliver a private forceful message or provide a "bag of political influence" when needed.

The problem Al Florence had was that he wasn't the polished professional that Kincaid preferred as the face of his organizations. Al Florence was never in line to be the president of Central Bank, and until January 1975, he was just a director. Garvice did elevate him to vice-chairman that year, along with making nineteen other Central Bank promotions.

At the end of 1971, Kincaid lost a valuable lieutenant, Clyde Mauldin. Mauldin began working for Kincaid in October 1960 at the Everglades Bank in Fort Lauderdale, Florida. Kincaid acquired the bank in May 1960. Mauldin had been in banking since 1951, and Kincaid brought him to Everglades to be in charge of the bank's commercial lending operations. Garvice didn't get comfortable with people quickly, but Clyde was a seasoned commercial loan officer, and Kincaid soon made him president of the bank. In 1965, Garvice moved Mauldin to Lexington to be president of Central Bank. Mauldin had made a big impression on Kincaid in five years.

In Lexington, Clyde was a respected banking professional, someone who made connections easily and who was also active in the community. When Kincaid updated his will and trust agreement in February 1964, he removed any mention of family members being part of the Committee and reduced its size from seven participants to three. He also made Clyde Mauldin one of the initial three members. The other two were Earl Wilson and Ed Schaeffer.

Clyde Mauldin worked for Garvice until end of 1971, when he resigned as president of Central Bank. In an April 1989 *Lexington Herald-Leader* article, when he discussed his retirement from banking, he also discussed his reasons for leaving Central Bank and Kincaid:

Mauldin cashes in bank posts for retirement

Clyde W. Mauldin resigned as president of Central Bank and Trust Co. in January 1972 to join a bank in his home state of Florida.

Before he left town, however, Mauldin made a fateful stop at the upstart Bank of Lexington and Trust Co.

"I think I primarily did that because my family didn't want to leave Lexington," he said recently. . . . Mauldin solved their problems when he became president and chief executive officer of the 6-year-old Bank of Lexington—a position he has held until today, when he officially retires after 17 years as the bank's top executive. . . .

Central Bank was Kincaid's Kentucky flagship [bank], and Mauldin had been the bank's president since coming to the Bluegrass in 1965.

"The pressure was intense. Kincaid was a hard man to work for.

"He made life difficult," Mauldin remembered. "He wanted it that way."

Kincaid would test his executives to get information or simply to find out "what people were doing."

A favorite tactic was the late-night phone call.

"Oftentimes he (Kincaid) would call you at night and ask you something, and he knew that it was only a rumor or that it wasn't true," said Mauldin, "but you had to spend 15 minutes denying something that wasn't there."

Finally, Mauldin had enough. He decided to leave Central Bank and accepted a position with a bank in Miami.

Meanwhile, Forrest E. Hansen, who had been president and chief executive officer of the Bank of Lexington since it opened in 1966, announced that he was selling his stock and resigning, effective Jan. 1, 1972.

Mauldin decided to meet with the Bank of Lexington executives before going to Florida. He decided that he liked the upstart bank and the challenge it offered, and he agreed to succeed Hansen. . . .

One of Mauldin's first objectives was to patch up his differences with Kincaid, who was simply too powerful to be ignored.

"He (Kincaid) was kind of upset with me, but after a short period of time—I would say six months—we became very close, and very good friends again," Mauldin said, "He didn't hold a grudge too long."

But Kincaid, he added, was "something else to work for, I've never seen anyone else like him."

On January 5, 1972, Garvice Kincaid made his final update to his trust and estate plan, defining the Committee members who would ultimately oversee his empire at his death. Clyde Mauldin had to be replaced immediately since he was no longer a part of his empire. In his place he added Al Florence, who was overseeing his other banks, and W.E. "Bud" Burnett, who was the secretary and treasurer of Kentucky Central Life Insurance Company.

Garvice was more than a little surprised that Mauldin decided to leave. He had come to rely on him, and because he added him to his committee in 1967, it's obvious that he thought he had the professional capabilities to work with the other members to manage his empire after his death. He was the president of his flagship bank and had demonstrated in Florida and in Lexington his leadership capabilities. In addition, Robert Layman, who moved over to Kentucky Central Life, had worked with him and supported his advancement to president of Central Bank.

After Mauldin resigned, Garvice took over the position of president at Central Bank. He had Richard Jordan as his executive vice president, and he handled most of the new-business and public-relations-type work at the bank and Robert Powers, a senior vice president at the bank, oversaw operations. Things remained this way for the next four years, until the spring of 1975, when Jordan resigned and took a position at a bank in Florida. In retrospect, I believe Jordan left because he wasn't being considered for president at the bank. Garvice wanted a president who had worked at a larger organization, someone who could strategically see what the bank needed to do to grow and succeed. Jordan had only worked at Kincaid's Georgetown and Corbin banks before coming to Central Bank. His career didn't meet Garvice's résumé requirement.

The changes above are important because Garvice also never considered Al Florence for the president position. In fact, Florence never had an officer position at the bank and was only a director until January 1975, when Kincaid made him vice-chairman of the board. Al Florence was Kincaid's bank sergeant, and Kincaid knew he wasn't a strategic thinker—Al Florence knew how to take orders and execute them. In January 1975, one can assume that Kincaid already had a professional recruiter looking for the bank's next president and that both Jordan and Al Florence knew it. Richard Jordan appears to have resigned in March, and in January, when Kincaid made Al Florence vice-chairman of Central Bank, Florence was probably also involved in the executive search.

In May, Garvice hired Harold A. Yates to be Central Bank's next president. In addition, he brought in Wayne L. Smith as executive vice president. Wayne would replace Richard Jordan. Both men were from banks with over $1 billion in assets. Yates was a thirty-year banking professional who had been at Merchants National Bank in Indianapolis, and Smith had been a senior vice president at Cleveland, Ohio–based Commerce Bank, overseeing its commercial loan operation. Garvice wanted Central Bank to be more than a small community bank and thought he needed to bring in leadership who could understand his vision and develop strategies and people to make it happen.

I believe that if Kincaid had lived just a little bit longer, he would have amended his trust and estate plan again in early 1976. We know that he told

David Brain in January 1975 when he promoted him to president of Kentucky Central Life that he would add him to the Committee, and I suspect he wasn't happy having Florence as a primary Committee member. Al Florence was not a strategic-thinking career professional. In 1967, his estate amendment had been a reaction to Mauldin leaving, and now five years later, he knew it probably needed to be changed. In addition, one might assume that Earl Wilson suggested that Florence wasn't a good fit. Finally, in 1975, Kincaid was focused on urban renewal in Lexington, and I believe he expected Bud Burnett to continue his vision.

I believe Garvice still wanted someone on the Committee representing Central Bank, and he possibly thought Earl Wilson could provide strategic oversight for the bank after he brought in Harold Yates. If he had added David Brain as he said he would, Brain could have represented Kentucky Central Life, and this would have allowed Bud Burnett to devote his time to Lexington's urban renewal. In 1975, both Kincaid and Earl Wilson would have known that his estate would be unable to hold on to the other banks and that they would need to dispose of most of them. Al Florence was superfluous and didn't need to be on the Committee because the banks would be gone. Central Bank was Garvice's flagship bank, and it was this bank that needed to thrive and grow.

After Kincaid updated his estate plan in January 1972, something changed in him, because from mid-1972 until his death in November 1975, Garvice started adding a significant number of experienced professional staff to his companies and also began strengthening the companies' management structures. At Central Bank, he brought in senior management from larger out-of-state banks and, in January 1975, promoted seventeen employees to management positions. At Kentucky Central Life, he brought in new senior leadership personnel in Investments, Tax, Operations & Administration, Actuarial, Marketing, and Pensions. These individuals came to the company, with fifteen to twenty years of experience, from large insurance companies such as Connecticut Mutual, Aetna, and Bankers National Life Insurance.

Not all of Kincaid's new hires worked out, and by May 1975, Harold Yates had resigned as the president of Central Bank. According to a *Lexington Herald* article about Wayne Smith dated December 30, 1985, this is what happened.

> In May 1975, Harold Yates, a college friend [of Wayne Smith] who had been named president of Central Bank, hired Smith as executive vice president. Yates had philosophical differences with Kincaid, however, and stayed just a few weeks. Kincaid died in November 1975, and Robert L. Epling was named president of the bank in February 1976. Epling lasted less than nine months.

> Finally, Smith, who had run the bank between Yates and Epling, was promoted to president. "I waited them out," Smith said. "I won by default."

We can never know what issues drove both Yates and Epling from their Central Bank positions. Certainly, Harold Yates may have had issues with Kincaid, but Epling had been president of Dania Bank, so Wilson, Burnett, and Florence would have been familiar with him and he with them. One might suspect Al Florence played a part in their leaving, though. In January 1975, Kincaid had made him vice-chairman of Central Bank, which may have gone to his head. Remember, Al Florence has been described as "intimidating and enjoyed mimicking how Kincaid dealt with people." In addition, one might assume that after Kincaid's death, Florence considered himself the rightful heir to direct what was happening at the bank. Finally, Florence resigned from the Committee in November 1976, which is less than a month after Epling resigned and moved back to Florida. It doesn't take much imagination to envision how being on Kincaid's Committee magnified Florence's personality and made him even more difficult to work with.

Regarding dealing with Garvice, Stan Galbraith told me this story about him and what was affectionately called "Black Sunday":

> My only recollection of being around Garvice much was when, after my third or fourth year at the bank, I got to go up to Lexington with a group for what we called "Black Sunday." Black Sunday happened once a year, and I think it was usually in December. All the affiliate banks had to go up. Each one of the affiliated banks had a time frame to show up and go to Kincaid's office on the corner of Short and Upper [the old Central Bank building].
>
> You would go up to his office and tell him what had happened the previous year, and what was going to happen going forward and what were the outcomes of this and that and the other. But during that period of time, Kincaid was calling people like J.M. Alverson [owner/editor of the *Paris Daily Enterprise*] and others. He would call people like him and others around town to find out what was going on in Paris. He would want to know what this is or what that is and so on.
>
> So when, let's take Mr. Perkins. . . . [I]t was usually, I think, Mr. Perkins [president of the bank], Ron Burton, after he got there and then for a couple of years before he became president, and then myself. We all three went representing the bank. And then after we went in and told our story, Garvice would look at Perkins, and he'd say, "Now Perk, you know that's not true." You know, because, in theory, Mr. Perkins was trying to put a positive spin on something,

but Kincaid had already heard from somebody on "Well, this is going on, and that's going on, you know, this is happening." Well, he would hear a whole other version of the story.

Author: Can you think what kind of issue would drive a discussion like that? Was it just the business environment in general, or what?

Just business in general and I don't have any real specifics, but you know, what the prospects are. What do you see the future of being in Paris and that kind of stuff. Also, what the competition was doing.

Kincaid basically had everyone take a turn and tell their story, and then at the end of the day, Al Florence and all of the bank management people, and I don't remember who all was there, but we'd all go out to Campbell House and have dinner. Everybody would be standing around, and of course we would have drinks and everything else, and it would go on at the end of the day.

Author: Was Central Bank represented there also?

Oh yes, of course, all the banks were represented. But it happened only once a year and we called it "Black Sunday."

Garvice Kincaid was his own loan committee at Central Bank and Kentucky Central Life. He didn't review every small loan, but the loans that were significant he did review. At the other Kentucky Group Banks banks and his three Florida banks, Al Florence and BMA provided the general oversight of loans and bank operations.

In May 1966 when Al Florence incorporated BMA, Kincaid isn't mentioned. In fact, throughout its existence, BMA was owned and controlled by Al Florence. In addition to providing various services to Garvice's bank, the other link to Kincaid was that most of BMA's employees came from various Kincaid banks. Florence had been with Garvice since 1962, so he and Kincaid were familiar with these people and understood their capabilities.

In 1962, Kincaid owned controlling interests in sixteen banks, thirteen in Kentucky and three in Florida. Before Florence's arrival, Garvice had relied on Bob Layman as his primary bank support. Layman had been instrumental in doing due diligence on potential bank acquisitions and had superb leadership skills. He was a smart, polished professional and also someone Garvice trusted. He had been president of Central Bank and moved to Kentucky Central Life after Paul Carr left. In addition, he had been initially put on Kincaid's Committee as an alternate. When Bob Layman left the Kincaid empire in 1966, he left a void, and to fill this void BMA was created. BMA would provide the economies of scale of a bank holding company (which wasn't allowed) and the needed management oversight that Kincaid required.

Al Florence's main job in the beginning, in 1962 was getting in a car and visiting all of Kincaid's banks and reporting back to Garvice on what he was finding. This also meant providing competitive intelligence to Garvice on other banks in the area and any rumors about possible acquisition targets. On some of these trips, he would bring Kincaid and act as his driver and keep notes about observations and comments Garvice made about each bank, its personnel, and the community. Garvice always provided oversight and direction and expected Florence, in conjunction with each bank's management, to handle the day-to-day business. After Florence arrived, Florence soon realized the issue with having a bunch of small banks is their expense structure. Each bank duplicated what every other bank did. While Kincaid was focused on their loan portfolios and the potential for credit-related losses, Al Florence saw the need to provide some common services.

In the beginning, Florence worked to consolidate and control some of the simple banking tasks, such as managing printing and supplies, asset management, and loan coordination. Kincaid wanted his banks known in their communities for being able to make larger loans than their size would normally suggest. To do this, he needed to have several of his banks participating in the same loan. One of the first people Florence recruited for help was Maurice Knight.

Maurice had worked for Beneficial Finance Company in the 1950s before taking a job at Central Bank around 1965. He was a good credit underwriter and by 1968 was managing Central Bank's new Eastland branch, but by 1969, Florence had recruited him to BMA, where he focused on assisting the Kincaid banks in their underwriting, loan placement, and handling of any problem loans. He kept track of each bank's capital structure and knew the average-size loan amount they could take. One bank might take $300,000 of a $1 million loan, while another seven banks might take only $100,000 each.

Around the same time Florence brought on Knight, he also recruited Edward Hall to be in charge of bank auditing. This would eliminate the need for each bank to have its own internal audit personnel. Hall was a former bank examiner and had been an operations manager at Garvice's Winchester Bank. With the changes Al Florence was planning, Hall's position in the Winchester would become redundant.

In 1969, Florence started planning the addition of a central computer system at BMA. Installing this would allow BMA to centralize all of Kincaid's twelve Kentucky banks' processing in one location. This would allow the Kentucky banks to operate as if they were a part of a bank holding company structure.

Al's NCR experience gave him the knowledge that this was possible. In 1970, Florence recruited Charlie Watkins from Kincaid's First National Bank of Carlisle. Charlie handled the bank's operational functions and joined Florence as BMA's director of operations and was in charge of BMA's computer system. He was in charge of coordinating the operations at Kincaid's twelve Kentucky banks.

Florence also wanted to coordinate the marketing for Kincaid's banks and in March 1971 brought in Harry Lee Smith at BMA as its director of marketing. Smith had been at the Citizens Fidelity Bank in Louisville in its public relations department. With the addition of Harry, Al could be the advertising department for each bank.

BMA had grown into a real company offering important services to Kincaid's banks, and in November 1971, Kincaid and Florence took their creation to the next level and introduced the doing-business-as concept for the Kentucky Group Banks in a Christmas Club Account announcement. The Kentucky Group now included fourteen banks, and over the next four years, Garvice and Florence would sell some and acquire others.

The Kentucky Group Banks in November 1971

Central Bank and Trust Co. – Lexington
First National Bank and Trust Co. – Georgetown
Peoples Commercial Bank – Winchester
Citizens National Bank – Somerset
Corbin Deposit Bank – Corbin
Bank of Williamsburg – Williamsburg
First National Bank and Trust Co. – Nicholasville
Bank of Danville – Danville
Powell County Bank – Stanton
First National Bank – Carlisle
National Bank and Trust Co. – Paris
Peoples Bank and Trust Co. – Berea
First Farmers Bank and Trust Co. – Owenton

When Florence began working with Garvice in 1962, Kincaid controlled nine banks in Kentucky and three banks in Florida, and now in 1971, his stable of Kentucky banks had increased by five, but Garvice believed Kentucky would one day in the near future allow banks to operate under a bank holding company and thus allow one bank to operate throughout the state.

Kincaid wanted to increase his Kentucky bank footprint, and now that Florence had the support of the well-staffed BMA organization, he could devote more time to calling on potential banks to acquire. Garvice was selective about the banks he acquired a controlling interest in. He wanted to understand not only the underlying assets they held but also the prospects for the community they were in, the quality of their management, and the bank's competitive position. Over the next four years, Al Florence would work to grow the Kentucky Group Bank's footprint to nineteen banks, with the last bank being under contract during the month of Kincaid's death and closing that December. The Kentucky Group Banks controlled assets in excess of $500 million dollars, and Lexington-based Central Bank accounted for almost one-third ($175 million) of the group's assets.

While Florence helped Kincaid supervise his three Florida banks, BMA didn't provide the same level of services to his Florida banks. The distance and state regulation made this too much of an issue. Al did visit the banks frequently and reported back to Garvice on what he found, but Kincaid limited his involvement. He was happy with each bank's management team, and there had been few issues with their lending practices. Also, Kincaid understood his audience and knew that Florence was better suited for handling Kentucky rural banks than his more urban Florida banks. I believe this is why he never offered Al Florence an officer position at his flagship Kentucky bank, Central Bank. He understood Florence's limitations, and while he was happy to include him on the bank's board of directors, he didn't want him swimming in the pool. Kincaid was always a master at reading people and understanding their nature and how they could help him or hurt him.

BMA had become a real business, and Florence owned 100 percent of it. In the beginning, Kincaid probably had Central Bank loan him the money to set up the business. Al needed to lease space and purchase furniture and equipment. In addition, Florence needed to set up a computer operations center with electronic connections, including more equipment at Kincaid's fourteen Kentucky banks. These banks would pay BMA lease payments and consulting fees for the various services that BMA provided them. Garvice Kincaid would benefit by having the banks operate more efficiently, and Al Florence would benefit from the revenue the banks paid BMA. His overhead was such that the revenue from providing services to Kincaid's fourteen banks, with their $500 million of assets, worked well, but in 1977 things would change.

I asked Stan Galbraith if there were ever any questions about how much BMA was charging the banks. In other words, were the charges reasonable. Stan answered this way:

> No, I don't remember any of that. You got the BMA's invoice and you paid it. Yeah, but nobody ever felt like they were getting out of line. Because, again, you're in a business; you know what

payment systems cost and that those companies need to make a profit. In addition, you know that BMA is shouldering the costs of running the whole computer side of things, so I think people thought they were fair.

Kincaid had no interest in managing the bank's operations. He was strictly, "That's your job, so you run it," and it probably was maybe a little better deal for everyone.

The point is that Al Florence didn't appear to be trying to take advantage of Kincaid or the banks, which was good.

Things were good for Al Florence until Garvice died in November 1975, and while he was immediately part of Kincaid's three-man Committee, his representation wasn't fully appreciated by the other two members, Earl Wilson and Bud Burnett. First, they understood that banking and trust regulations were going to require the estate to liquidate most of Kincaid's bank holdings. Garvice could hold and control things individually that his estate and trust could not. They were going to be forced to liquidate the banks. Second, there were personality differences. Florence viewed his position as being in charge of Central Bank, and Wilson and Burnett disagreed. For instance, in early 1976, Florence started making public announcements about Kincaid's new corporate headquarters. Instead of there being a coordinated announcement, Al Florence was taking a lead role. Also, in February, the Committee brought in Robert Epling from the Dania Bank to run the bank, and by October, Florence had run him off. Third, and last, Florence wanted to acquire all the banks in the Kentucky Group and felt the Committee should help him by providing financial support. Florence didn't appreciate that any insider deals would be scrutinized by Nelle Kincaid and her daughters and their advisors.

In the end, Wilson and Burnett bought Florence off by selling him and some outside investors nine of the nineteen Kentucky Group Banks in December 1976. The price was never publicly disclosed, and they were the smallest of the banks, with total assets of only about $150 million. Florence also never disclosed who his investors were, but in April of 1977, he and Wallace Wilkinson partnered to purchase the Spectrum building at the intersection of Vine and Main in Lexington, so one probably can assume that Wilkinson played a role in purchasing the nine banks from the Kincaid trust. If the Committee sold them to Florence and his investors at book value, the total transaction might have been $7.5 million, but since Florence already owned some shares in many of the Kentucky Group Banks, I suspect that Wilson and Burnett may have negotiated a deal that released him from the loans backing his bank holdings and swapped his equity interest in banks that were not sold for the estate's interest in the ones that were. Al Florence had limited financial resources at the time, and the two men wanted to get shed of him, so accommodations were probably made. For instance, they may have sold him the smaller banks at a discount on their book value, because, as an example, "What is a little bank in North Middletown worth?" Wilson and Burnett could have rationalized how the transaction was put together in many ways.

Al Florence and his undisclosed investors purchased the following banks:

Peoples Commercial Bank – Winchester

First National Bank and Trust Co. – Nicholasville

Bank of Danville – Danville

Peoples Bank – Berea

The London Bank & Trust – London

Powell County Bank – Stanton

First National Bank – Carlisle

First State Bank – Manchester

North Middletown Deposit Bank – North Middletown

Al Florence didn't own his nine banks very long. It appears that by early 1978, the Kentucky Group Bank concept was history and various members of his BMA staff had left the organization. We also know that in 1977, Florence began focusing on investing in real estate, and by 1978, it was taking a majority of his time and he had acquired the Big Ben Farm at Boone's Trace and begun investing in racehorses and boarding up to 250 horses.

When exactly Florence disposed of his nine bank stocks isn't publicized, but we know that he sold four banks to James L. Rose and three banks to Elmer Whitaker. It appears the sales happened around 1978 and 1979. In 1984 after Kentucky passed the state's bank holding company legislation, James Rose would create United Bancorp of Kentucky and also acquire the Bank of Lexington and Elmer Whitaker would create the Whitaker Bancorp. The other two banks were probably sold to local managements around the same time.

BMA began being scaled down, and it was primarily providing technology and operational services to these banks after they were acquired. It is listed as an inactive corporation in 1981.

After leaving the Committee, Al and Arline Florence built a large home at Boone's Trace and created residential lots and roads for an additional twelve homes. They also owned and managed the Boone Square shopping center in Berea. Arline worked as a transcriptionist for thirty-seven years at the Lexington Clinic and after retiring in the early 1980s became very active in charitable organizations and endeavors. Al Florence died in March 1998 and Arline died in May 2019. At Al Florence's death, his estate or his portion of their marital assets was valued at $2.7 million. Al Florence probably didn't have much wealth when he started with Garvice, but he worked hard and did well, and after he left the Kincaid empire, he took what he learned from Garvice about real estate and invested it well. Al began his career selling insurance, transitioned into selling cash registers, transferred out of state to learn about electronic banking processes, and then applied what he had learned from Garvice Kincaid ten years later. In the end, his hard work paid off and he and Arline had a net worth of over $5 million, and while he devoted a significant portion of his life to the banking industry, at his death, his probate records show he held only a four hundred–share interest in the Madison Bank in Richmond, Kentucky. It was valued at $10,000.

As for the Kincaid estate's remaining ten Kentucky banks and three Florida banks, the Committee began selling the Kentucky banks in 1977 to local managements and small investor groups, but by late 1977, the Kincaid daughters began a lawsuit to prevent the sale of the banks. The daughters held shares in some of the banks personally, but the estate also had options to acquire them. These suits slowed the disposition of some of the banks. Most of the Kentucky banks stocks in the suit involved banks that were sold to Al Florence, and it's reported that Florence had acquired options directly from the daughters to purchase their shares. The Committee never reported any sales in the press, and one might assume this was because of the Kincaid lawsuit.

The Committee also began selling Kincaid's three Florida banks in 1977. The Boulevard Bank was sold in January 1977 to Joseph Kanter, a Cincinnati banker and real estate developer. Mr. Kantor also acquired an option to purchase the Marathon Bank, and it appears from the Florida Secretary of State's website that he exercised that option in 1978. Only the purchase information was reported to the press by Mr. Kanter, and the purchase price was never disclosed. The Dania Bank was sold in April 1978 to a Venezuelan businessman. End here

Teddy J. Mims

By 1981, the Committee was escalating its efforts to sell the remaining Kentucky banks, and it appears that it wanted to consolidate the last three into the hands of a friendly acquirer. In 1981, Burnett found a solution, and it's this story that provides the background for the later years of this southern saga. That year, a Lexington man named Teddy Mims and three other investors purchased two banks from the Kincaid estate—the Richmond Bank and the Waco Deposit Bank. The Richmond Bank had assets of about $19 million, and the Waco Deposit Bank had assets of about $11 million. Capital requirements in 1981 were 5 percent and both banks should have been sold for around their book value, so one can assume that the total purchase price for both banks would have been about $1.5 million ($950,000 and $550,000). The Committee structured the sale such that the Kincaid estate provided the owner with financing for a portion of the purchase price. It accepted $500,000 in preferred stock in the banks. The investors had obtained a loan for $1 million ($600,000 and $400,000) and put up their stock in the banks as collateral. No details about the $1 million loan were ever reported.

The same year, the Committee also quietly sold a controlling interest in the First Farmers Bank–Owenton, to a local attorney, Danny R. Branstetter. Branstetter just happened to be the attorney who represented the investors in their purchase of the Richmond and Waco banks. This isn't important to the story now, but in a November 1985 article in the *Louisville Courier Journal*, Teddy Mims was quoted as saying he purchased control of the First Farmers Bank–Owenton in 1981 and owned 92% of the stock. Apparently Branstetter was a straw man purchaser for Mims.

George Hampton, Teddy's old high school football teammate, remembers Teddy talking about getting a loan from a Cincinnati bank, but interest rates were high—the prime rate was 21 percent—so he needed to pay off the loan quickly. Teddy got Hampton and others to buy stock in the Richmond and Waco banks to get the loan paid off. George recalled that he and one of his salesmen invested about $180,000, and he thought the president of the bank, Jay Congleton; John Sword, a Richmond attorney; William S. Stewart, and Danny Branstetter were investors. In addition, some individuals, such as William Green, Robert Prewitt, and Gary Allgeirer, may have been involved. Some had to borrow the money, including George and his salesman, and others may have had the cash. Everyone thought the bank would be worth a lot more when the Kentucky legislature passed the proposed bank holding company legislation that was being discussed.

One can also probably safely assume that the Owenton bank may have provided a loan to anyone needing it. That bank had around $20 million in assets, and the loan would have been collateralized by their shares.

The rest of the story is remarkable and well documented in an April 15, 1993, article by David Heath in the *Louisville Courier Journal*. The story was obtained from court documents in the lawsuits brought by the Kincaid daughters against the Committee and interviews with Teddy Mims, who is the central character of the story. What follows are portions of the story that was part of a series of reports titled "Under Siege," along with some clarification comments by me:

Wins, Losses and Ties

Dealings offer a view of insurer's loan practices.

Teddy J. Mims quit coaching high school football and baseball 20 years ago to make more money.

After stints as a Xerox salesman and also being an agent selling insurance, he struck gold when he bought a Lexington Insurance agency with high school acquaintance Bruce Burnett, whose father ran Kentucky Central Life Insurance Co.

A review of court records shows that Mims eventually developed a reputation as a man with money. Not his own, but money he borrowed from Kentucky Central. . . . Over [ten] years, Mims borrowed a total of $80 million from Kentucky Central and built a small empire of restaurants, banks, horse farms, condominiums, office buildings, shopping centers and a hotel. But he was using new loans to pay off old debts, and the empire collapsed in 1989 when Kentucky Central stopped lending and repossessed most of Mims' property. . . .

Evidence from the Kincaid lawsuit provides a rare inside view of how Kentucky Central handled real estate loans. "Kentucky Central was a liberal lender to people they had trust in," Mims said in interviews with The Courier Journal.

The company sometimes loaned him more money than his collateral was worth, Mims acknowledged. He used the extra money to pay debts on projects gone sour, a pattern Mims described in testimony as "leveraging properties to pay for mistakes in the past."

Whenever Mims couldn't pay his debt, he would move on to a bigger project, borrowing enough to consolidate or pay part of old debt. . . . Mims denied in interviews that he received special treatment. He acknowledges doing personal favors for Bruce Burnett, but he traces his close ties to Kentucky Central to his efforts to save a failing bank in which the Kincaid estate had invested $500,000.

Yet it was Mims' partnership with Bruce Burnett that introduced him to Kentucky Central. After attending Lafayette High School with Burnett, in 1964, Mims moved to Tampa, Florida, returning to Lexington in 1976.

Once back, Mims hooked up with Burnett, who had a fledgling insurance agency and wanted a partner to help him buy an established agency. To finance the deal, they borrowed $178,000 from Central

Bank, part of the Kincaid estate. Burnett's father was a Central Bank director.

Mims said in an interview that the insurance agency was profitable, but disagreements broke up the venture within a few years. Mims testified that he sold Burnett his share of the business for what he considered a bargain price: $50,000.

Helping Bruce Burnett

By that time, Mims had several real estate loans from Kentucky Central Life and had bought the Saratoga Restaurant with a Central Bank loan. His lending ties [to the company] by 1982 were so close that builder James Bird offered him an interest in the Park Hills Shopping Center if Mims could get Bird a loan from Kentucky Central, according to court records.

Mims had a counterproposal. If Bird and his partner, Tony Satterly, would buy an office building from Bruce Burnett, Mims would get them the loan.

According to court documents and Mims' testimony, Burnett owed [Kentucky Central Life] $750,000 on the office building across from the Red Mile race track and was charging rent to business partners James Dale Creech and Lloyd Stafford. But the agency couldn't keep up with the debt; [Bruce] Burnett was near bankruptcy. Bud Burnett asked Mims to help his son dissolve the business.

Mims, who owned two financially shaky small banks [Richmond and Waco] by then, loaned money to Bruce Burnett, Creech and Stafford. He then agreed to assume the loan [Bruce Burnett's loan] on the [1051 Red Mile Rd.] office building, which he immediately assigned to Bird for $825,000. Mims said he gave [all] of the money, including the $75,000 profit to [Bruce] Burnett. [Kentucky Central still retained the loan on the property, so Bird paid Mims $75,000 in cash and assumed the $750,000 loan with Kentucky Central. One can assume the $75,000 was Bird's money.]

Bird knew it was a bad deal, and he eventually lost his investment [$75,000]. But he testified, "We rationalized that this was the cost of doing business [to get] financing." [Kentucky Central eventually took the building back from Bird in lieu of foreclosure.]

Soon after the deal, Kentucky Central loaned Bird and Satterly $3.6 million to build Park Hills Shopping Center.

Troubled bank

At the same time Mims was helping out friends, his banks [Richmond and Waco] were in serious trouble. . . . Within a month [after buying the banks] the group learned that the Federal Deposit Insurance Corp. was threatening to take over the Richmond Bank & Trust Co. and Waco Deposit Bank. Within the next 18 months, the Richmond bank would lose $1 million in capital.

"I foolishly never looked at the loan portfolio" before investing, Mims testified. "At the time I went into banking I was an ex-football coach and restauranteur. The only experience I had in banking was on the other side of the desk."

Soon the other investors walked away from the $1.5 million loan they used to buy the banks, but Mims testified that he felt obligated to save the institutions.

[One should assume the $1.5 million loan refers to $1 million in bank loans and $500,000 in preferred stock. Two million dollars for these two banks in 1981 doesn't appear to make financial sense.]

The Kincaid estate still had $500,000 worth of preferred stock in the banks, so Mims went to the advisory committee, made up of Bud Burnett, Hart Hagan and lawyer Edward Schaeffer. Each man was also a director of Kentucky Central.

Mims considered this meeting the key to his relationship with Kentucky Central. He said he told the committee that he would come up with a plan to save the banks if they would support him.

"I left the room; they came back, and they said, "We're going to stay with you. We're going to help you, Mims recalled during an interview.

Seventeen days after Mims bailed out Bruce Burnett on the Red Mile building, Kentucky Central loaned Mims $1.5 million to save his banks, using the Richmond bank building as collateral. The plan included merging the banks. Mims testified, however, that the building probably wasn't worth $500,000. The loan's initial interest rate was 9 percent, even though the prime rates in April 1983 were 10.5 percent.

Eventually, Mims sold the bank. He lost at least $2 million but preserved the Kincaid estate's $500,000 investment. How was he able to absorb the loss? By buying a horse farm with a loan from Kentucky Central.

Buying a horse farm

In July 1985, Mims and thirty partners bought the Castleview Equine Center in Woodford County for less than $1 million. Kentucky Central loaned him $1.6 million, based on an appraisal of $2.1 million, which took into account plans to add a swimming pool and other improvements. In time Mims bought more land, but he said the horse farm was never profitable.

[The fifteen-acre equine facility was initially developed by Bob Zielke, a local realtor, and some other investors. It opened in 1979 and cost $500,000. Kentucky Central provided the financing for the project, but it was failing when Mims was brought in. Mims had no experience with horses or horse training, but he brought in a local veterinarian, Gary Priest, to assist him. Mims soon made plans to add an equine hospital and training track and renamed Castleview Farm and Equine Center the Bay Harbor Farm. He also leased the newly built hospital to a group of veterinarians. Kentucky Central rewrote Mims's farm loan twice and increased the loan amount to $2.65 million and then foreclosed on the property in 1989.

Mims continued to borrow money from Kentucky Central, and between 1987 and 1989, he and some other partners borrowed $32.5 million on two projects in Lexington: The French Quarter Square on Richmond Road and Chevy Chase Plaza and Condominium.]

Perhaps Mims' biggest failure was the Chevy Chase Plaza, a shopping center-condominium project on which he owed almost $14 million when Kentucky Central cut off his loans.

Without more loans, Mims' business ventures couldn't sustain themselves. Mims agreed to turn over most of his property to Kentucky Central to stave off bankruptcy. . . .

In retrospect, Mims says he believes Kentucky Central mismanaged its dealings with him. But he doesn't agree that any of his deals were bad ideas and doesn't consider himself central to the company's failure.

"Ted Mims was just a borrower at Kentucky Central," he said. "We had quite a long relationship with them and did some very good projects. . . . I earned my stripes, so to speak, over there."

Teddy Mims was the poster boy for the old saying "a legend in his own mind." He grew up on Lexington's south side and was the son of Wilburn and Elizabeth Mims. His father was an appliance salesman who worked for the old Purcell's Department Store and Pieratt's, and his mother was a waitress and manager of the restaurant in the Downtowner Motel. Teddy went to Lafayette High School and was a typical high school jock who played football and baseball. According to a high school friend of Teddy's, his personality made him very popular, and he was even the class president in his senior year. In 1966, he won a scholarship to Tampa University, where he met his wife, Sandra Onis. The couple married in May of 1969, and in June, Teddy graduated with a degree in physical education. Sandra graduated with the same degree the following December. Both soon found teaching jobs in the Tampa Bay area, with Teddy also coaching football at Chamberland and then East Bay High School.

Sandra grew up in Tampa, Florida, and was the daughter of Manuel "Curly" Diaz and Zoraida Onis Diaz. Manuel played major league baseball for twelve years and retired with a disability from the Tampa Fire Department. Zoraida taught elementary school for twenty-six years and during World War II and worked as an interpreter for the State Department. After her retirement in the late 1970s, she enjoyed her nephew Denis Diaz's interest in thoroughbred races and learned to handicap races, and she even partnered with Diaz and Sandra in owning a handful of horses. After Teddy and Sandra moved to Lexington, Zoraida made many trips to the bluegrass state and considered Lexington her second home.

Teddy and Sandra worked as teachers for four years, and then around 1975, Teddy decided he wanted to do something else. He took a position with Xerox and briefly sold copiers, and then he moved on to selling insurance. Sandra had a cousin, Denis Diaz, who owned a successful insurance agency and real estate business. Diaz had purchased his agency in 1965 with the financial help of his father and had worked the long hours necessary to build it into a 245-person business that included insurance, real estate, and construction interests. He had become a millionaire, and Teddy was impressed.

Dennis Diaz's grandfather, Sacramento, emigrated to Florida from Spain in 1910 at the age of fifteen. He earned enough to eventually start a dairy farm outside Tampa. Diaz's father, Sacramento Jr., grew up working on the farm, as did his sons, Dennis and Lesley. Dennis developed his work ethic from the long hours he worked on the farm. He eventually left the dairy farm for college but dropped out after two years. He then sold insurance and, later, fertilizer products. Dennis worked hard, often from 4 a.m. to midnight. He never experienced the stardom of high school sports—he didn't have time for sports. The wealth that Teddy Mims now witnessed didn't reveal the sacrifices Diaz had made over the last ten years.

Teddy was convinced he could also do this, and the place he had the most connections was back in Lexington. He had friends and contacts of his father and mother and a network of friends he went to high school with—Bruce Burnett, George Hampton, and Fred Burns. Teddy's best friend in high school was George Hampton, who was his best man when he and Sandra got married. George was also good friends with Bruce Burnett, who was a year younger than Teddy and George. When Teddy Mims was thinking about going into business on his own, it was George Hampton who encouraged him to come back home to Lexington. In February 1977, thirty-year-old Teddy and twenty-nine-year-old Sandra Mims arrived in Lexington and purchased a new split-foyer home at 4100 Solberg Road in the Plantation neighborhood for $52,950.

Teddy was already licensed to sell insurance in Florida, but he needed to get licensed to sell insurance in the state of Kentucky, which he did that April. By September, the Mimses made their second real estate investment when they purchased a small home on Holly Hill Drive in the Southland neighborhood for $39,000. Teddy was going to flip houses. He and Diaz had partnered on a home flip in Florida, so he felt he knew what to do. The Mimses moved into the Holly Hill home and in March 1978 sold the Solberg home for $62,000. They made almost $11,000. In April 1978, they purchased a two-thousand-square-foot home with an in-ground pool at 749 Glendover Drive for $93,000. They sold the Holly Hill home in May 1978 for $48,250, making almost $9,000. In fairness, their actual profits were probably less, since no real estate commissions or the costs of any property improvements are accounted for. The Mimses remained at their Glendover home until they sold it in July 1988 for $175,000.

Teddy's most consequential Lexington business contact would be Bruce Burnett. Bruce became licensed to sell insurance in 1972 and worked in the beginning for Kentucky Central Life and then the Lexington Insurance Agency, which was owned by Garvice Kincaid. Shortly after Kincaid's death, Bruce joined the Jack Fife Insurance Agency, where he could control more of his business and income. He brought his high school friend, Teddy Mims, into the partnership in 1977. Jack Fife still owned the agency but since 1965 had devoted most of his time to real estate development, similar to what Dennis Diaz had done. Bruce was also interested in getting into real estate, and he had his father's connections at Central Bank and Kentucky Central Life, which would make things easier for him and his friends, such as Teddy Mims and George Hampton.

Bud Burnett and Ed Schaeffer actually started working with Teddy Mims shortly after he joined Bruce Burnett's insurance agency. In July 1977, Committee member Ed Schaeffer incorporated "Richmond Properties, Inc.," with its principal officers being S. Jay Congleton, Teddy J. Mims, and John Sword. S. Jay Congleton, age thirty-four, was the president, director, and trust officer of the First Farmers Bank and Trust company, Owenton, and John Sword was a forty-two-year-old Richmond attorney. In September 1977, the Committee sold two tracts of land in Richmond to the new corporation for $1 million. There isn't an exact description of the properties, but my guess is that one of the properties is the Richmond Bank building, which Kincaid had owned personally. I find it odd that Ed Schaeffer, a Committee member, created the new corporation for this transaction though Sword, one of its officers, is an attorney. Another thing that seems odd is how did Teddy Mims, a physical education teacher, just back from Florida, arrives in Lexington in February and is now involved in a $1 million transaction with a new corporate entity and two new business partners.

By 1979, Teddy was searching for a business to invest in even though he had minimal financial resources. In January 1978, Mims incorporated a company called "Easy Money Inc." Its primary purpose was listed as follows:

> To Acquire by purchase or otherwise, and to own, hold, buy, sell, design, construct, build, convey, lease, mortgage or encumber buildings, real estate or other property, to survey, subdivide, plat, improve, and develop lands for the purpose of sale or otherwise, and to do and perform all things needful and lawful or the design, construction, erection, development and improvement of buildings and real estate for residence, trade and business purposes; and in general to do all things necessary or incidental to the conduct of said business, both within and without the State of Kentucky.

Easy Money Inc.'s directors and officers included Teddy J. Mims, George E. Hampton, William H. Green, and Robert C. Prewitt III. Hampton was a local businessman who specialized in the production of business forms and, as mentioned, a high school friend of Teddy. Prewitt was a pharmaceutical sales representative, and Green was a local attorney and real estate investor. In 1978, the group must have decided their business name was a little problematic, because they amended their articles of incorporation and changed the name to "South Lexington Enterprises Inc." Their first and only acquisition was an old, four-unit apartment building off Versailles Road on Hill Rise Drive, for $23,000, in June 1978. This is the only transaction listed for the company, and in May 1984, the group sold the company and its one asset to a local accountant, R. Douglas Anderson.

In addition to starting Easy Money Inc., Teddy quickly began partnering with Bruce Burnett on real estate projects. In November 1978, Teddy and Sandra purchased a one-third interest in a small apartment building on Lyndhurst Drive from Bruce for $10,000. In addition, in January 1979, Teddy incorporated The Saratoga Restaurant Inc., and in March, he and Sandra, along with his parents, purchased a small retail/restaurant building in Chevy Chase for $98,189. It housed the Saratoga Restaurant and Bar. The Saratoga was located at 856 East High Street and was a Chevy Chase landmark best known for its unusual clientele of bookies, college professors, socialites, and city hall types. (Thomas Morgan "Totsy" Rose, an early developer of Chevy Chase, had opened the restaurant in 1951, naming it after New York's famous Saratoga Race Course. Ed Whitlock purchased it from Rose in 1953 and ran it for twenty-four years.) Teddy's mother had managed the Downtowner Motel Restaurant for eighteen years and would now co-manage the restaurant with Teddy's wife, Sandra.

The Mims family ran the Saratoga Restaurant until 1989, when Teddy's real estate business collapsed under a massive amount of debt. Teddy's father, Wilburn Mims, had died in 1984 at the age 61, and his mother, Elizabeth, now age 65, had worked in the restaurant industry for over fifty years. Teddy's parents made the Saratoga work. His mother was well known for her cooking, and the restaurant's location was a Lexington landmark. Teddy also began to dabble with opening a second Saratoga Restaurant in Richmond, and he purchased the Little Inn restaurant on Winchester Road in 1985 and moved it to a Chevy Chase location in 1987. He partnered with Jim Foley, another former Lafayette High School and University of Kentucky star football player. Jim Foley was the son of a local developer and was looking for something to do. Teddy wasn't a passionate restaurateur, just a man with easy access to loans.

That easy access to money meant that Teddy and his wife could be open to new opportunities no matter how much they lacked specific knowledge, and this included their new interest in thoroughbred horses and owning a horse farm. To be fair, their interest probably began with her cousin in Tampa, Dennis Diaz. In 1980, Dennis, age thirty-eight, was burned out from working so hard, and he sold everything and retired. Diaz had always enjoyed the horse races. He knew how to read a racing form and over the years had become friends with Elliott Fuentes, who had bred horses for thirty-seven years. With time on his hands, he started fishing, playing the stock market, and going to the racetrack.

Diaz and the Mimses had stayed in touch since Mims return to Lexington in 1977. Diaz hadn't yet purchased his fifty-acre Tampa horse farm or his first horse, a filly named Heated Rush, for $9,000 from Fuentes, but they both discussed how Mims's return to Lexington, the "Horse Capital of the World" and the center of the thoroughbred breeding universe, might be beneficial to him. Teddy had sold insurance, flipped houses, invested in small four-plex apartments, and owned a restaurant, so doing something with horses was (he somehow apparently thought) just a natural progression. He certainly knew people who had horse connections, and Diaz was willing to participate.

In April 1978, a group of local realtors, equine veterinarians, and third-party investors announced the proposed construction of an equine rehabilitation center just off Versailles Road and across from the famous Kentucky "castle." The facility, known as the Equine Therapeutic Clinic, would be on seventeen acres and contain a special swimming pool to provide hydrotherapy to horses recovering from surgery. The complex would include turnout paddocks and forty stalls. It would be the first equine center of its type in Kentucky and would open in May 1979.

Teddy Mims is never mentioned as an investor, and like many of the stories involving Teddy, an article in the November 11, 1985, *Lexington Herald-Leader* explained his later ownership in the venture this way:

> Castleview Equine Center opened in 1970, and by 1982 it included a 15-foot-deep swimming pool, jacuzzi, electro-biology equipment, 1/8-mile indoor jogging track and 41 stalls.
>
> Mims purchased the Castleview Farm, along with 30 partners, for $1.6 million in 1979. When that partnership dissolved in May [1985], Mims and his wife Sandra, took full control of the property, which gets its name from the fact it is across the highway from the "castle" under construction on the north side of U.S. 60 [Versailles Road].
>
> Mims credits his wife with much of the success to date of the equine center, which has a dozen employees and is expected to double that number with the expansion. A full-service veterinary hospital and half-mile outdoor training track are being added, at a cost of more than $750,000.
>
> Ms. Mims, a former director of women's sports at the University of Kentucky, began applying her knowledge of sports medicine to horses about four years ago.
>
> "Horses, like people, have hurts, but they can't tell you about them," said Mims, who played football at the Tampa University and has a degree in physical education from the Florida school.
>
> So, Ms. Mims began using an electrical stimulator to pinpoint the problem. The stimulator delivers currents of varying degrees via wires to rubber patches on the horses. By monitoring the muscle twitch reaction, Ms. Mims can determine the location of any soreness. Ultrasound therapy is often used, because it forces heat to penetrate deep into the muscle tissue.
>
> . . . Mims believes it will take a couple of years to get the Castleview complex on a truly profitable basis, after which he will be open to new challenges.
>
> . . . The Mimses also own Borderline Farm on Paris Pike, and plan to merge it with Castleview to offer a full-service care, breeding, training, and racing facility. They own several horses and had three winners in four starts at the fall Keeneland Meet, Mims said.
>
> His goal is to get all the businesses "self-sustaining," which he expects will occur in five years.

> After that Mims would like to "give back to Lexington" some
> of the benefits that have come the way of the Lafayette High School
> graduate.

Based upon the 1985 article and some property records, it appears that the 1978 equine center property had been part of a larger one-hundred-acre farm when it was originally developed. Property records suggest that in the 1980s, before the center was developed, the farm had been divided, with the remaining land parceled into a fifty-four-acre farm with a dwelling and thirty acres of land. The equine center was developed on twenty-seven acres. According to the 1985 article, Mims said that in 1979, he and thirty partners purchased both the Equine Center and the fifty-four-acre Castleview farm adjacent to the center for $1.6 million. The initial loan for the venture isn't reported on, but if thirty partners each put up $54,000, the financing would have been simple. In addition, Sandra's millionaire cousin, Dennis Diaz, may have been a significant investor. In 1982, Diaz had purchased his fifty-acre Tampa horse farm, Hunter Farm, and was racing and raising thoroughbred horses.

In 1981, with Burnett's and the Committee's assistance, Mims had controlling interests in three Kentucky banks, and while the Richmond and Waco banks would quickly have problems, the Owenton bank was okay. In fact, according to Teddy's high school friend George Hampton, in the early 1980s Teddy's banks were making loans to people purchasing thoroughbred horses, and it was these loans that created more problems for Teddy to solve.

Teddy had the Thoroughbred horse bug; he wanted to breed, raise, train, race, purchase, and sell Thoroughbred horses. His only problem was that he didn't have any experience—he knew he could learn the business. Most people trying to do what Mims was trying to do would work on a farm and become an apprentice trainer. In other words, learn the business first. Teddy, on the other hand, had easy access to money and knew people who knew people. One of those people was William S. Stuart.

Williiam Salem Stuart was born in Barbourville, Kentucky, on July 10, 1932. He was the son of a coal company manager and graduated from the old Kentucky Military Institute in Lyndon, Kentucky, and received a bachelor's degree in business from Davidson College in North Carolina. He worked in the family coal business for several years and then moved to Cynthiana, Kentucky, where he owned a hardware and farm supply store. In 1971, he became the president of the Farmers National Bank of Cynthiana, where he had been a director for several years. In 1981, he acquired an interest in three banks controlled by Teddy Mims and two Burger Queen restaurants, subsequently known as Druther's restaurants. He dabbled in real estate and opened Stewart Galleries in Lexington, which specialized in expensive antiques, and he owned a jewelry store and computer store in Cynthiana. Finally, Stuart was the cousin of Kentucky's famous state treasurer, Frances Jones Mills.

For almost a hundred years, the Kentucky Constitution didn't allow the holder of a statewide office to succeed themselves for a second consecutive term. As a result, a handful of Kentucky politicians became known as "musical chair" officeholders because they would run for one statewide office and then a different one repeatedly. Thelma Stovall, Drexell R. Davis, and Mills were some of the best known "musical chair" officeholders. The three often traded offices in given election years in the 1970s and 1980s. Kentucky politics always seems to have problems, and in 1984, Frances Jones Mills and six of her secretary of state employees were indicted for violating state ethics laws in relation to her election as state treasurer. Mills was acquitted after a two-year-long case. In the early 1990s, she was charged with violating the state's ethics laws and fined $11,000. She filed an appeal, and the case was still pending at the time of her death in 1995 at age 75.

William S. Stewart had everything that Teddy Mims could hope for, and Stewart gladly invested in Mims's Castleview Farm and Equestrian Center. He and Teddy were cut from the same cloth in that both were personable and enjoyed getting into new ventures. Stewart had money and connections, and Teddy had easy access to loans. In 1981, both men saw the promise of riches that the horse industry could provide, and they wanted to participate. Later Teddy would find out that Stewart wasn't the person he thought he was, and as for the Thoroughbred industry, it was near the end of its historic boom era.

A September 14, 2016, *Paulick Report*, "Back to the 80s: The Era of Easy Selling," described it this way:

> By all accounts, the Thoroughbred bloodstock market in the 1980s was a world of crazy extravagance and a relatively different one than today's auction environment. People remember the record-setting $13.1 million sale of Seattle Dancer at the 1985 Keeneland July sale, but the colt's shocking price tag was the end of one era and the start of another.
>
> The sales market at the July yearling sale had experienced incredible growth in the early part of the decade, and the 1985 auction was the turning point. Hundreds more yearlings were coming to the sales from around the country than had 15 years earlier and were commanding more than double the average price. For ten consecutive years, average and median sale prices had increased at the "select sessions" of the July auction, reaching $601,467 and $315,000 respectively in 1984.

Bill Landes, the right-hand man for Seattle Dancer's consignor Warner Jones at Hermitage Farm in the mid-1980s, recalled the July sale taking on its own social life. Hermitage was one of several farms that hosted parties where potential buyers could rub elbows. Consignor Tom Gentry once hosted a sit-down dinner for eight hundred potential buyers with entertainment from the likes of Ray Charles, Bob Hope, and Paul Anka. Guests were offered the chance to tour his farm via helicopter or ride on an elephant.

By the time the sales began, there were so many people present, many of them dressed to the nines, it was hard to move through Keeneland's sale pavilion. By the 1980s, Landes remembered, people had taken note of Robert Sangster's business model of buying expensive horses and turning a profit not on the track, but in syndication deals. Sangster attracted attention when he purchased The Minstrel, a $200,000 yearling who won three major European stakes before being syndicated for $9 million. Sheikh Mohammed bin Rashid Al Maktoum similarly found success with Shareef Dancer, a $3.3 million yearling purchase in 1981 who sold for $40 million as a stallion prospect two years later.

"Those were really heady days, just because of the people involved and the amount of money they were willing to spend," said Landes, who remembers the early success of Coolmore, led by Sangster. "They had little competition back then, so they were able to do it and then take the horses back to Ireland and stand them for a lot of money. But you know, it's like everything else—when people find out about it, they think they can do it and get involved also."

After all, when that model worked, it really worked. In 1982, Devil's Bag was a $325,000 yearling purchase at the July sale by Hickory Tree Stables and was syndicated the next year (while still running) for $36 million by a group led by Claiborne Farm. Conquistador Cielo was a $36.4 million syndication deal, and Halo was also $36 million. Whether any of the trio (except maybe Halo) justified their expense in the breeding shed remains up for debate.

There also may have been fewer analytics fueling the bloodstock world in the 1980s. Those were the days before the radiograph repository, Landes pointed out, and it was rare for a potential buyer to send a veterinarian to shoot x-rays before the sale. In fact, he doesn't remember a vet taking a look at Seattle Dancer before his record-setting sale.

"Most of the x-raying and scoping was done after the hammer fell, and that was always my complaint with the market in those days—at what juncture did the buyer own the horse and the seller could spend the money?" said Landes. "Now, that said, the repository has now taken a life of its own."

Although he remembers it being rare that horses were actually turned back to sellers because of x-ray or scope results, it only took a couple of cases to set sellers somewhat on edge.

In the background of Seattle Dancer's high-profile sale in 1985, there were signs that things were beginning to take a turn. Just minutes after he went through the ring for a record $13.1 million, a Northern Dancer colt out of Native Partner failed to attain his reserve at $7.4 million. Numbers for the select portion of the 1985 July auction were down (though overall numbers were up). By 1990, indicators had fallen. The highest price at the July sale that year was $2.9 million with just 11 horses selling at seven figures (the number in 1984 was 33 or 12 percent of those sold in the select sessions).

By 2003, the declining foal crop and economic downturn forced Keeneland to put the July sale on hiatus. Modern spending is characterized as more sensible than it was in the crazy 1980s. For most buyers, there seems to be a greater interest in getting good deals than making big headlines.

"I think the idea that at an auction there are eight or ten 'good' horses is ridiculous," said Cot Campbell, president and founder of Dogwood Stables. "It's a hell of a good time to buy underneath that. I've always been fond of saying that if you go in the paddock of a stakes race, they're not all million-dollar horses. I believe there's a lot of value to be found beneath those gaudy figures."

A September 15, 1993, *Paulick Report* described Robert Singer this way:

Robert Sangster's purchases, perhaps more than those of his predecessors or contemporary big spenders, revolutionized the Thoroughbred market forever.

Sangster got his fortune from his family's business, Vernon's Pools, a company managing betting pools on soccer games. After buying his first racehorse, Chalk Stream, as a wedding present for his fiancé in 1960, Sangster was hooked. He decided to invest in the empire which ultimately became Coolmore, together with Tim Vigors, Vincent O'Brien, Simon Fraser, and John Magnier in the mid-1970s. Together, the group came to the United States "to take racing by the neck." The plan was to buy high-dollar colts, focusing on descendants of Northern Dancer, and turn a profit when they were syndicated.

The plan worked. Among the group's first American purchases in 1975 was The Minstrel, a $200,000 yearling who won the English and Irish Derbies before being syndicated for $9 million. Sangster bought Alleged that year for $170,000, and the horse became a two-time winner of the Prix de l'Arc de Triomphe before being syndicated for between $13 and $16 million.

The profits from those first purchases fueled the group—often called "Sangster's gangsters"—to make more expensive purchases. Between 1975 and 1984, no one else could buy a horse once the group set their eyes on it. That didn't exactly thrill buyers, who accused the group of cornering the market to an unreasonable degree.

"It's ridiculous to say that we have taken over world bloodstock; no single man or group of men could possibly do that," Sangster told The Horseman's Journal in July 1982. "If I have one criticism of racing, it must be that it is a very jealous game. I'm not some silly woman flashing her money about in Harrods."

Following up the success of Alleged and The Minstrel were Irish One Thousand Guineas winners Lady Capulet (a $70,000 yearling) and Godetia ($60,000 yearling who also won the Irish Oaks), Irish Two Thousand Guineas winner Jaazeiro ($24,000 yearling), Arc winner Detroit (FR) (a private weanling purchase), and Epsom Derby winner Golden Fleece ($775,000 yearling). Storm Bird, a top-rated European 2-year-old, was also a Sangster syndicate success story after the $1 million colt retired undefeated in five starts and sold in 1981 for $28 million. Vincent O'Brien trained most of Sangster/Coolmore's horses.

The biggest Sangster purchase was world-record yearling Seattle Dancer, who brought $13.1 million in 1985 for a Sangster syndicate. The half-brother to Seattle Slew proved considerably less successful on and off the track than his predecessor and retired with two ungraded stakes wins in Ireland.

Sangster had about 200 broodmares by 1980 at his network of farms all over the globe, including Creekview farm in Paris and Walmac in Lexington. Sangster was among the first breeders to begin shuttling his stallions to the Southern Hemisphere for stud duty, further increasing his profits. In 1984, Coolmore purchased Ashford Stud for $9 million ($19,000/acre) and has filled its stallion barns ever since.

In 1981, Teddy, Sandra and William Stewart were caught in the wave of excitement of what would be considered one of the biggest investment bubbles in Kentucky's history. They, like many, didn't appreciate that the trees don't grow to the sky. Some people are lucky and some people are unlucky, and when it comes to the Thoroughbred industry, Woody Stephens, the American Thoroughbred horse racing Hall of Fame trainer, in his 1985 book *Guess I'm Lucky*, probably said it best. Stephens was elected to the National Museum of Racing and Hall of Fame in 1976, and in 1983, he won the Eclipse Award as the top trainer in the United States. While he is often remembered for wearing rumpled clothes, it was his earnings from racing, plus investments in successful breeding stock, that made him a very wealthy man, and the title of his autobiography reflected this. Stephens believed pedigree, hard work, and knowledge went only so far because he understood that too many factors were beyond his, the jockey's, or the horse's control, and these factors were probably an important influence on the success of a horse. Too bad Woody didn't write his book sooner—maybe Teddy could have read it.

In 1981, Teddy and Sandra were already managing the Castleview Equine Center in conjunction with some local equine veterinarians. He and Sandra also owned the adjacent fifty-four-acre Castleview Farm and had acquired the adjacent thirty acres of land next to their farm and had plans to expand their Thoroughbred business venture. They needed more land and soon found a forty-acre farm for sale on Paris Pike. Teddy's parents were running the Saratoga Restaurant, and he had worked on a deal with Bud Burnett and the Committee to acquire control of the Kincaid estate's remaining three Kentucky banks. Life was good, and he had found another business associate, with similar interests, in William S. Stewart.

In late 1981, Teddy got with Stewart, and they agreed to purchase the forty-acre Paris Pike farm from Juanita and Roger McCombs for $400,000. We don't know how it was financed, but since Teddy now controlled three banks, one could assume they may have initially provided the financing. The real estate purchase closed in February 1982. What's more interesting is that in October 1983, Mims and Stewart sold the Paris farm to Teddy and Sandra for $540,000, and this time Kentucky Central Life financed it, along with refinancing the 856 East High Street Saratoga Restaurant building (purchased for $98,189) and the 749 Glendover investment property (purchased for $93,000) for a total loan amount of $2.1 million.

What is important about the above transactions is that they occurred after Teddy worked with Bud Burnet to get Bruce out of his problematic Red Mile building with the help of James Bird and his extra $75,000 for his son, Bruce. In addition, this happened after the Committee loaned Mims $1.5 million for the Richmond Bank building, about which, in court records, he acknowledged that "the building probably wasn't worth $500,000." This building was in Kincaid's estate when he died. So, during 1983, in these two transactions alone, Bud Burnett and the Committee provided Teddy Mims with excess financing dollars of approximately $2.4 million ($1.4 million and $1 million). We know from Mims's testimony that he used a portion of it to backstop the Richmond and Waco banks, but what about the rest? Finally, in June 1984, Bud Burnett refinanced the Richmond Bank building again, for $1.74 million, increasing the loan amount by $240,000.

An April *Courier Journal* article said, "The company sometimes loaned him more money than his collateral was worth, Mims acknowledged." He used the extra money to pay debts on projects gone sour, a pattern Mims described in testimony as "leveraging properties to pay for mistakes in the past." This is what Bud Burnett continued to do with Mims and others throughout the 1980s. By 1988, when Mims's real estate ventures were collapsing, Kentucky Central Life had increased the loan on his farm and equine center to $2.65 million and the loan on his Saratoga Restaurant building, with the addition of a $240,000 North Limestone property, to $2.7 million. Kentucky Central Life restructured, refinanced, and increased loan amounts and property pools so many times over ten years that it's actually a research challenge to follow everything, but the impact of the general scheme that took place is quite evident.

Teddy and Sandra did have some Thoroughbred luck during the early 1980s. In 1984, they purchased a young filly named Slippin N. Slyding from breeder John Pierce and selected Cam Gambalati to take over the two-year-old's training. The filly won some stakes races and had about $150,000 in career earnings by the time they sold her at the end of 1986.

Teddy and Sandra also witnessed what happens to an industry when there's a major downturn. Their equine operation depended on customers boarding their equine investments with them and paying their clinic to keep them healthy. The problem was that the price of Thoroughbreds collapsed almost overnight, and immediately lending for both farms and equine livestock dried up. Lexington's storied Spendthrift Farm went public in 1984 and was in bankruptcy in 1986, and while Calumet survived longer, through the manipulation of Alydar breeding rights, it too was virtually insolvent by 1990. Since 1986, Calumet had taken out mortgages on the farm totaling $65 million, and in 1990 creditors filed suit asking for payment of $27 million in debts. By 1986, Teddy and Sandra's equine venture was suing boarders for past-due payments.

Horses are expensive to keep and maintain, and as the industry slid into a depression, equine owners looked for alternatives to writing checks. Horses have been slaughtered for years in the United States and Mexico. It's a practical solution to dealing with livestock but not something people like to think about. The old adage about sending a horse to the "glue factory" or "turning it into dog food" is a reality of life. The number of horses slaughtered in North America peaked in the 1980s, with as many as 350,000 horses per year being destroyed. The Mimses' equine venture depended on equine owners needing their services and writing checks, and by 1986, the winds of change were upon them. By 1987 their loans would be rewritten once again, and by

1988, Kentucky Central Life would repossess it all.

Sandra's cousin Dennis Diaz had a little better luck than Teddy and Sandra. Dennis began his Thoroughbred operation in 1982. Below is part of an article by Peter Early in the *Washington Post* that was published about him on June 30, 1985:

> So, in 1980, two years after his third marriage, at age 38, Diaz sold everything and retired. He went fishing, played the stock market and went to the race track.
>
> His interest in horses came easily. He had a pony as a youngster he named Dynamite. He liked the slower-paced, baronial life style of horse breeders. A horse farm would be good for him, he decided, and a great place for him and Linda to raise her daughter Jenifer.
>
> Diaz's second life seemed to be taking shape around the idea of horse breeding, but his business instincts told him to hold off awhile. "Everyone was getting into horse breeding at that time (1981–82) out of greed. They didn't have any love of the business or horses. They just wanted to make a lot of money and they thought if they bought a racehorse they would."
>
> Diaz waited for the slide. "That is when I like to get into any business, when it is hurting, when everyone else is getting out."
>
> He bought 50 acres of land in mid-1982, land his grandfather once had owned. It bordered a ranch owned by Elliott Fuentes, an acquaintance who had bred horses for 37 years. The men became friends and Diaz bought this first horse, a filly named Heated Rush, for $9,000 from Fuentes. In her first race, Heated Rush won $10,000. Diaz thought he had a magic touch. He was wrong. The horse didn't win another race for nearly two years.
>
> Just as he had done in his insurance business, Diaz mapped out a long-range strategy for horse breeding. He would breed mares, race one or two horses a year and slowly improve the bloodlines. Horse breeders follow a simple genetic philosophy: winners beget winners.
>
> Diaz decided it might take him 10 years to breed horses that could compete in the nation's big-stake races, but he'd get there. "I didn't set out in this business to lose money," he says.
>
> He began looking for stock and, in the spring of 1983, a distant relative (Teddy Mims) employed at a Kentucky bank called him about a horse sale: Harper Rowe had several good-quality yearlings and mares to sell, some cheap. Diaz studied their pedigrees.

Also, from the *Orlando Sentinel*:

> At the time, Harper, 40, was operating a modest racing operation out of his Irish Hill Farm near Owensboro, Ky. The luck

of the game had not gone his way, and Harper threw in the towel with a bankruptcy sale, unable even to wait for a scheduled sale that likely would have brought better prices for his stock. (Spend A Buck's half-brother already had sold for $120,000.)

"I asked around if anybody knew of someone who wanted to pick up some horses quick at rock-bottom prices," recalls Harper, a dapper man in his patchwork sport coat. "A friend (Teddy Mims) in Lexington turned out to be Diaz's cousin, and he knew Dennis was just getting into the horse business. It's one of those things. That's the racing business. If you stay around this business long enough, you're going to have a horse of this caliber — if you have enough cash flow to get through the low tides. It so happened that I couldn't weather that period without selling off my horses and farm."]

The following is from a June 30, 1985 article by Peter Earley in the *Washington Post* titled "Fast Ride to Riches":

One mare, Belle de Jour, interested him [Diaz]. The horse had been sired by Speak John, a son of Prince John, who had won $212,818 racing. Harper also had one of the mare's foals for sale, a colt sired by Buckaroo, son of Buckpasser, a $1.4 million race winner. The horse's blood wasn't blue, but it was darker than red.

Diaz liked what he saw when he examined Belle de Jour in March 1983, but found the foal disappointing, smaller than the other yearlings and awkward. Diaz wasn't sure the colt was worth buying. But then he noticed something unusual: Whenever Diaz approached, the colt fled and ducked behind a bigger yearling.

"He was using the bigger horse as a bodyguard," says Diaz. "I liked that. It proved that he was smart." Diaz bought both horses.

"I had at least five other yearlings that were better—stronger than that colt—for sale," says Harper of the yearling that became Spend a Buck. "He didn't look like he would have won a race."

Meanwhile, back at the farm, Diaz's luck was running bad. "I had bought a mare for $125,000 that was about to foal. She stepped in a hole, fractured her leg and delivered four weeks early," Diaz says. He raced the colt to the veterinarian's, nearly burning up the engine in his truck. "We got there, pulled the tailgate down and I lifted out the baby. The vets were coming with oxygen, but it just died in my arms."

Two weeks later, a promising filly worth $60,000 died of a virus. "We couldn't do a thing right for months," Diaz says. "We could have raced against cows and lost."

Fuentes told him to relax. "He said your luck always turns in horse breeding. This is a business of sheer joy and utter heartbreak where you get to experience low lows and high highs."

Diaz decided to improve his cash flow by selling the flighty colt he had bought from Harper. He notified the operators of the Ocala Select 2-year-old sale and set a price of $30,000 for Spend-a-Buck. When the horse wasn't accepted for the sale, Linda Diaz remembers her husband "kicking a stall" at the time and saying, "I'd sell that damn colt in a second if someone would take him."

At the time, the only bright spot at Diaz's stables was the arrival of Camillo Michael Gambolati as trainer. Diaz had met Gambolati when they happened to sit next to each other at a horse sale.

"I was impressed by his intelligence and his style. Too many trainers try to push horses instead of listening to them," Diaz said. "Horses don't lie to you. If you're smart enough to listen, they'll tell you what kind of condition they're in, what kind of ability they have. Cammy understands that."

Gambolati, 35, was not a hot prospect in the racing community. Since graduating from a Tampa-area college, he had done a number of things, from owning a laundromat to being statistician for the Tampa Bay Buccaneers. His passion, however, was horse racing.

At [Diaz's] Hunter Farm, Gambolati had fewer than 10 horses to work with including the ill-tempered Spend-a-Buck that stable hands called Harvey Wallbanger because he tried to knock them against the walls of his stall.

In August 1984, Gambolati declared the colt ready to compete. In his first race, Spend-a-Buck came in second behind a horse named Smile. Two weeks later, Spend-a-Buck won. He then took another first place in the Miller High Life Cradle race, winning by a whopping 15 lengths.

"We knew the horse was fast," says Diaz, "but we still didn't know how fast."

Diaz entered Spend a Buck in the $622,200 Arlington-Washington Futurity in Chicago, the horse's first race against top national talent. "A number of people told me I was nuts for taking him out of Florida," says Diaz. "They said he'd never make it."

A promising colt named Proudest Hour was favored to win the Chicago race, but he was put away early in the race. When the horses reached the top of the stretch, Spend-a-Buck surged, winning by a half-length.

Diaz began to dream. "I knew this horse was really special then," he said.

A few days after the race, a representative for jockey Angel Cordero Jr., a two-time Kentucky Derby winner, telephoned Diaz. "When I was first contacted by Angel's people, I said, 'No, absolutely not! I'm not interested in switching jockeys.' [Charles

Hussey], his jockey, had ridden Spend-a-Buck from obscurity to his Chicago win. "But then I decided that it was inevitable," Diaz said. "It would be easier now than later."

Diaz dumped Hussey and hired Cordero. It was the "hardest thing that I've ever done," Diaz says. "I love that guy." Diaz keeps a photo of Hussey in his office.

In his next race, the "Young America" at the Meadowlands, Spend-a-Buck led most of the way but lost at the wire. He then finished third in the Breeder's Cup held Nov. 10. Diaz was happy—his horse had run well, losing to strong contenders, Chief's Crown and Tank's Prospect, two horses that would be favored in the Kentucky Derby.

The day after the race, Diaz went to see Spend-a-Buck. "He came out lame. I couldn't believe it," Diaz says. "I thought I had blown it."

A bone in Spend a Buck's right front knee had been chipped during the race. Diaz called in a surgeon who specialized in the use of arthroscopic surgery on horses. The operation took 12 minutes. Three months later, Spend-a-Buck was galloping.

Diaz chose the Bay Shore, a seven-furlong race at Aqueduct, for Spend-a-Buck's return to racing. "We were pressed for time if we wanted to make the Derby, but we didn't want to hurt the horse." He told Cordero to give the colt a good workout, to win, if possible, but not to "do anything to hurt the horse."

Spend-a-Buck finished third and Diaz was exhilarated: "He was okay." Handicappers were less enthusiastic. They saw Spend-a-Buck as yesterday's news. Even Cordero began saying he might bypass the Kentucky Derby to ride another horse at another track on Derby Day.

Then Spend-a-Buck won spectacularly. In April, the horse won two races at Cherry Hill, N.J., and came within two seconds of breaking the world record set by the mighty Secretariat for a 1-mile race.

Spend-a-Buck had earned his spot at the Kentucky Derby, but he was clearly an underdog: some handicappers felt Diaz was bringing his horse back too soon after surgery; others said Spend-a-Buck liked to breakfast from the starting gate and would have trouble maintaining his speed against a field of horses considered the most competitive in recent Derby history. Some still maintained that Spend-a-Buck couldn't cut it against top competition.

Diaz was unflappable. "If Spend-a-Buck gets a good start," he predicted, "no one will catch him."

[Will] W.S. Farish, a wealthy Kentucky horse breeder, quickly put Diaz's faith to a test, asking the owner to sell him a 50 percent interest in Spend-a-Buck for a reported $4 million.

Diaz, Linda, Gambolati, and Peter Hall, Spend-a-Buck's veterinarian, held a meeting. If the horse won the Derby, his worth would increase by millions, but if he lost, they might not be able to equal Farish's offer. Diaz called for a vote: "Linda said sell, Cam said sell, and the vet said sell. I was the only one against selling the colt before the Derby.

"I'd promised to be democratic, but I'd retained the right to set the conditions of the sale." He made them so restrictive that Farish declined. "I had faith in that horse. I was going to stay with him."

Linda Diaz's favorite photograph from the Kentucky Derby shows her husband holding their adopted son, Elliott, in his arms while she holds the gold trophy aloft with daughter Jenifer beside her.

"We planned it that way," says Linda. "We wanted to make a statement to the Derby people and the world that this was our family and we had done it together—as a team."

In a May 1985 *Lexington Herald-Leader* article, Teddy and Sandra Mims said:

"It was a Derby to remember. The couple had a full house of guests from Florida—including Diaz's mother, Wanda Diaz of Tampa—and were part of a 23-person entourage that went to the race from Lexington. When Dennis Diaz made the decision to bring the horse to the Derby, the Mims household became part of the family's Derby headquarters. 'We had eight of them here, four stayed at the Campbell House, and Dennis and the rest were at the Executive West in Louisville,' Sandra said."

Dennis Diaz probably understands why Wood Stephens titled his autobiography *Guess I'm Lucky*!

Kentucky Central Life and many Lexington businesses had to deal with the financial fallout from the collapse of Kentucky's Thoroughbred industry, and the Mims equine ventures weren't the only farms that they had to foreclose on. Russell J. Michael's famous Lann-Mark Farm was next door to the forty-acre property that Teddy Mims purchased on Paris Pike. Russell knew everyone, and he was a customer of the Kincaid, Wilson law firm, Central Bank, and Kentucky Central Life. In 1981, Russell and his wife, Ann, began divorce proceedings and the Kincaid law firm represented Russell. The couple's farm, Russell suggested, was worth $10 million, but illiquid, when it came to dividing the couple's assets. When it was appraised in 1985, it was valued at $4.5 million.

Not all the financial details are known, but Kentucky Central Life made a $2.7 million loan on the Lann-Mark farm during 1982 or 1983, which appears to be tied to the divorce settlement. The Michaels' divorce was finalized in May of 1982. After the divorce, and also as a consequence of the downturn in the equine market, Michael began acting strangely and having other problems. In 1985, Russell's behavior had become somewhat erratic, and he was arrested for wanton endangerment after the police were called to the farm. Russell was accused of discharging a firearm dangerously. In 1986, a tenant's farmhouse was destroyed in a fire. Lann-Mark Farm was an expensive operation to run; according to Michael, the farm employed sixty people and had annual expenses of $1.8 million. By 1985, Russell had listed the farm for sale. Singer Diana Ross even had a viewing that year, but nothing came of it. Russell Michael had owned the 146-acre farm since 1967. In 1985, the sales information lists the farm at 106 acres. Given the location of Teddy Mims's forty-acre tract, one can probably assume that Teddy's Paris Pike parcel used to be a part of the original farm but was sold off for some reason before 1982.

By 1985 Michael began downsizing his stable of horses and looking for ways to reduce his overhead. The stress finally took its toll on him, and in 1988, he died after a short illness. He was fifty-four years old. His obituary lists Ed Shaeffer, Henry Kinser, and Charlie Burnett as his casket bearers— Schaeffer and Kinser from Kincaid's law firm and Charlie Burnett a local real estate investor and a close friend of Bud Burnett and Ed Schaeffer. Kentucky Central Life continued to work with his estate to sale the farm but was unable to. On January 22, 1990, the farm was sold at the courthouse in a master commissioner's sale and Kentucky Central Life acquired it for the amount of its mortgage loan. The property was appraised in 1990, as required by GAAP accounting rules, and was valued at $1.2 million versus Kentucky Central Life's $2.7 million mortgage loan. After a handful of property transactions, the farm was sold a few years ago for $7 million and is now part of Winterhaven Farm L.L.C., which is located in Barboursville, Virginia.

In 1981, after Teddy worked with Bud Burnett to acquire the Kincaid estate banks, he was ready to do something big. He owned the Saratoga restaurant and liked the neighborhood, and by 1980, the thirty-five-year-old Mims had become friends with twenty-eight-year-old William York Varney Jr., a local real estate agent who had acquired a few small rental properties. York also had limited resources, but the two wanted to work on something together. Their first project was converting Parke's Bestway Grocery store in Chevy Chase to a plaza of shops. The store was located at 836 Euclid and the Parkeses acquired the property in 1978 for $100,000. We don't know when Mims and

Varney purchased the property, but in 1979, the *Lexington Herald* showed Park's property taxes were several thousand dollars' delinquent. The newly named Chevy Chase Plaza by then contained three stores and a bar. One of the stores was Mims's good friend and business partner William Stewart's Stewart Galleries. In November 1981, the partners' remodeled Plaza project opened.

By 1983, the developer duo still hadn't found a large, interesting project to invest in, but by the fall of that year, they had submitted a proposal to Southern Railway to develop Lexington's historic railroad depot on South Broadway. They were one of three groups submitting proposals. The seventy-five-year-old depot had been abandoned for many years and had decayed significantly. Neither Mims nor Varney had any experience dealing with a property like this one, but they still thought they could handle it. The actual cost of the property would be cheap, but the remodeling estimates were in the range of $2.5 million. In addition, the South Broadway underpass next to the depot would need to be completed in the future and this would greatly impact any traffic to the redeveloped depot, not to mention the blasting and demolition work that would take place. In other words, they were looking to buy more than a fixer upper; they were also potentially purchasing something akin to being on a fault line. Luckily for them and probably Kentucky Central Life, their bid was not selected, and the actual project, while announced, never happened and the depot was destroyed by fire in 1992.

In March 1984, the dynamic duo developers unveiled their new vision for Chevy Chase. They wanted to reshape most of two city blocks in the Chevy Chase neighborhood and build two nine-story buildings. They said it would turn the area into a Lexington showcase. The development would involve raising at least twelve properties. In making their announcement the developers brought along the project's designer, Graves/Sherman/Carter Architects. "Graves" referred to Steven Graves, who would later become a partner in the Mims, Graves, Turner development company, or "MGT" as they preferred to call it. Their wide-ranging proposal involved spending $25 million and included two to three floors of retail shops, with office space on the lower levels and two hundred-plus condominiums above and a three hundred-plus parking garage sandwiched between. The second building would also include retail shops on the ground floor and eight floors of apartments.

I managed investments for forty years, for two insurance companies, and spent the last twenty-five years as the executive vice president, treasurer, and chief investment officer for a $5 billion company in Wisconsin. One thing I heard early on in Wisconsin from the president of the company and a mortgage loan officer from a large local bank is that developers falsely assume that if an institution loans them the money for a project, the institution considers it a good idea. This I know from experience is just wrong. Institutions lend money assuming they will get paid back, and they may or may not think a developer's project is a great idea. Sometimes the loan characteristics check the boxes of all the lender's loan requirements, sometimes the borrower is an existing customer and the lender wants to make concessions to please them, sometimes the lender is just depending on the track record of the borrower, and sometimes internal politics play a role. Just because a lender lends money to a developer, that doesn't mean the lender thinks the project makes sense or is a great idea.

I mention this because there is no doubt in my mind that Teddy Mims and William Varney had great opinions of themselves, and having a lender such as Kentucky Central Life and others back them on a project just encouraged them to believe their own BS. My old Wisconsin management team will tell you that I firmly believe an investment person needs to have confidence in what they believe, but they also need to retain a shadow of doubt that they could be wrong. Believing one's own BS is a dangerous trap, and I've seen many an investment professional caught in it. It's one reason our country experienced the Great Financial Crisis from 2008 to 2010. The Financial Crisis wasn't just an accident or totally based upon fraud; it was mainly driven by a bunch of Wall Street types believing in their own financial hype. The same thing happened in the mid-1980s after Mike Milken at Drexel Burnham created the junk bond market and high-yield bonds. In no time, Wall Street began creating investment products that held nothing but below-investment-grade junk bonds, but they were able to convince rating agencies to give these new products an investment grade rating of "A." In other words, if you owned one bond rated "BB," it was a junk bond, but if you held a unit trust and it held a hundred "BB" bonds, it was rated "A." Executive Life Insurance Company believed the hype and was eventually taken over by the California and New York Insurance Departments, when the junk bond market collapsed.

In 1984, Mims had already been able to acquire the Saratoga Restaurant and its building, three Kentucky banks, and a horse farm and equine center. The problem was that he was still unproven, just as getting a driver's license doesn't make one a great driver. For instance, in 1981, the developer duo had spent money and remodeled the Chevy Chase Plaza shops and now this was one of the buildings they wanted to demolish. Finally, in an April 1991 *Lexington Herald-Leader* article, it was reported that the duo had been acquiring parcels of land since 1983 for the proposed project, and by 1987 they had spent $1.6 million on just the land. In addition, after the project was eventually downsized and approved, the developers appear to have only allocated about 40 percent of the land cost to the building site from the land parcels they used. This meant the remaining undeveloped parcels had to bear this excess expense.

Mims and Varney's only research for the project was their own observations about Chevy Chase. They spoke with local businesses and residents after the neighborhood raised concerns about what they were proposing. The duo knew their vision was correct, and since current city zoning rules wouldn't permit the project, they would just work to get them changed. The mayor, Scotty Baesler, was good friends with Bud Burnett, which couldn't hurt. In a May 30, 1987, advertisement for the development, the developers described "Chevy Chase Plaza" as a collection of boutique shops like a person would find on "A Worth Avenue & Rodeo Drive." In addition, they mentioned its luxurious condominiums and reported that 80 percent of the retail space was leased. Finally, it had William Varney saying that "Lexington has a glut of office space, and the market is soft, but the demand for office space in the Chevy Chase Plaza is soaring."

The movie Field of Dreams wouldn't be on the big screen until 1989, but Mims and Varney had already found a use for the movie's famous line: "build it and they will come." Little in this ad foretold that in a little over twelve months, this project, along with most every venture Teddy Mims controlled, would be repossessed by Kentucky Central Life.

In December 1984, William Varney Jr. wasn't just optimistic about this venture, he was also excited about the NCAA Final Four coming to Lexington in March 1985. This is why the young entrepreneur decided to start a new business, Grand Hotel-Homes of Lexington, a company specializing in matching up visitors to Lexington for the NCAA tournament and other events, such as Keeneland and the local horse sales, with private residences. He claimed in an interview that he had over two hundred homes to offer, ranging from suburban tract homes, townhouses, and condos to prestigious horse farm properties. He indicated that he had already sent brochures to all the people who had established credit at the local horse sales and advertised in the Thoroughbred journals. He said homeowners could make anywhere from $37 to $200 a night, depending on the property. He claimed he had already booked five hundred guests, about sixty of whom had already come and gone, and that he had a waiting list of another five hundred, and yet he had incorporated the business only in late August. Finally, Varney described himself as a horse breeder and real estate developer whose other endeavors included the proposed Chevy Chase Plaza.

The reason the information on Grand Hotel-Homes is relevant to the Chevy Chase Plaza story is that the facts around both just don't match reality.

Widespread use of personal computers and the internet wasn't even a dream in 1984, so Varney having already served sixty guests and having a five-hundred-person waiting list isn't plausible, in my opinion. The reality was that in 1984, everything was tied to telephones and the U.S. mail. Even faxing someone a document wasn't mainstream yet. When one considers how he promoted this new business and then looks at the statements made in the May 1987 ad and in statements made during and after the construction of the project about tenants, the adage "take it with a grain of salt" has a lot of meaning. Developers often misrepresent or embellish their projects details and tend to see the positive in everything. While lenders should live by the motto "expect the worst and hope for the best," developers live by the motto "everything will fall into place; just be patient." If a sinkhole appears in an apartment project, a developer will look at it as a potential way to save money on a pool. It's the nature of the beast, and Mims and Varney both saw sunshine behind every dark cloud.

In December 1984, the developer duo unveiled a revised version of their project after objections by neighborhood groups and zoning problems became too big of an issue. They had already acquired most of the necessary land parcels needed to construct something. In addition, after six months of negotiations, they had changed architects to Donald Wallace and were now having a few neighborhood meetings to discuss their new concept. They hoped this new design would convince residents that Chevy Chase needed to polish its image.

Their new, revised project was still nine stories but with what they called a scaled setback, meaning that higher floors would be set back further from the street. This version was supposed to address people's concern about its height. The project was now estimated to cost $12–$15 million. They called the previous version a midrise and they called this version a pyramid-rise. They still ignored people's concern about traffic, and they hadn't completed a study or discussed it with the city. The neighborhood wasn't impressed. In addition, they wouldn't discuss what tenant rents for the retail and office space or the price of condominiums would be.

In the summer of 1986, the developer duo reached a compromise with the city and the neighborhood. The city passed a conditional-use amendment to its existing zoning ordinance that permitted Chevy Chase Plaza to be built. This amendment would also affect other areas of Lexington. The new Chevy Chase project was now only one tower and would be built on 1.5 acres of land, leaving the majority of the extra parcels they had purchased undeveloped. The mixed-use building would be only five stories tall, with set-backs beginning on the third floor. The first two floors would house retail shops and restaurants, offices would take up the third floor, and twenty-two condominium units would be located on the fourth and fifth floors. In addition, the site would include a 203-space enclosed parking garage at a cost of $1.3 million. In a March 9, 1987, *Lexington Herald-Leader* article, the developers estimated the cost of the project at $11 million. Finally, in March 1987, only Mims and Varney were mentioned, but in 1987, the duo would be joined by Steven Graves and Craig Turner.

In 1986, the Webb Companies had just opened The Mall at Lexington Green, a collection of boutique stores and restaurants. The Mall at Lexington Green was considered a "hybrid enclosed shopping mall" and outdoor lifestyle center. It was located adjacent to Target and Fayette Mall at the intersection of New Circle and Nicholasville Roads, the region's largest retail district. This development was direct competition to Mims and Varney's vision of Chevy Chase Plaza, and it had significant advantages over Chevy Chase. For one, a shopper didn't have to use a parking garage and could drive close to the shop they wanted to visit. In addition, it was close to other major shopping areas. Lexington Green was designed as a destination, and one of its main draws was the Joseph-Beth Booksellers and Café. Finally, it had a large water feature next to it and provided for restaurants to have patio access.

In August 1986, the developers had a well-publicized groundbreaking for the project. The mayor spoke and the developers gave away $5,000 in donations to five charities. The developers provided an initial list of tenants for the project and informed the public where the financing would come from. Money for the project would come from Commonwealth Life Insurance of Louisville (aka Capital Holding Corp.), First National Bank of Louisville, and Kinder Financial Services, a small, Ohio-based financial services firm. It was reported later in the press that Mims tried to get Kentucky Central Life to finance the project but Committee member Hart Hagen declined to vote for it. He reportedly persuaded Kentucky Central's board not to finance the complex, saying he thought the site costs were too high to recoup the money unless the building was at least twelve stories.

This was a very controversial project, and while some businesses in Chevy Chase welcomed the project, many businesses and area residents were against it. For instance, Doris Smith, a Chevy Chase resident, said that while such sentimental attachment to Chevy Chase was "wonderful," it is "not very practical. I still have my mother's old corset with its stays and laces, and I have a sentimental attachment to it, but that doesn't mean I'm going to wear it." William Farmer, a local business owner opposed to the project, thought the developers were going to "build another empty building. They're putting a

10-pound fish in a five-gallon tank," he said. Of course, Mims disagreed, but in the end, Bill Farmer understood the neighborhood better than Mims, and in a twist of fate, after the project was taken over by Kentucky Central Life, Bill Farmer was brought in to manage it.

Mims was able to arrange commitments from other lenders. Capital Holding Corp. promised to lend $6 million on the project on the first three floors if he could get a construction loan from another lender. Kentucky Central Life obliged Mims with a construction loan for the project, with the expectation that Capital Holding would take them out when the project was completed. The top two floors of the project were being financed by a $4 million loan from the Pikeville National Bank. However, the developers' project quickly developed soil, contractor, and roof problems. Additionally, Capital Holding pulled out of the project when its $6 million loan, which was held in a Central Bank escrow account, was invested in a risky futures contract. The investment lost $300,000, according to Mims. The bank covered the loss on the irregular investment, but the event gave Capital Holding an out. An insurance company's permanent financing commitment requires a project to be built to specifications with a minimum amount of required leasing. The insurance company could see the cost overruns and knew the project was already in trouble. Because of the cost overruns, Capital Holding could cancel its commitment. At that point, Kentucky Central agreed to support the project to save what it had invested in the project already. Hart Hagen said, "You get caught in a trap to save yourself." Kentucky Central Life also replaced the loan from Pikeville National Bank, which also now had reservations.

Kentucky Central Life now had $13.75 million invested in Chevy Chase Plaza and another $2 million invested in the other parcels of land that Mims and Varney had acquired. To put this in perspective, in 1985 there were fewer than twelve thousand households in the Chevy Chase neighborhood, so Teddy Mims had spent about $1,200 per household building this mixed-use project.

One question that's always bothered me is that Capital Holding was five to ten times as large as Kentucky Central Life, so why didn't it finance the whole $11 million project? Just the fact that Mims had to find three sources of money indicates that no one found the economics of his project attractive, and they all wanted to limit their financial risk of loss. As for why Pikeville National Bank was involved, I will always believe that Bud Burnett promised the president of the bank that he would take them out of their loan if the project had problems. This makes sense given that he did this on loans to his son Bruce that Pikeville National Bank had made. Bud Burnett used company assets to pay off those bank loans.

The main detail that a reader should appreciate just from looking at the Chevy Place Plaza loan information is that Bud Burnett didn't require Mims to contribute any equity to the project. If Bud Burnett was following insurance regulation guidelines and company policy, then Teddy Mims should have contributed over $2 million to the project, but he didn't. Bud Burnett was financing 100 percent of Chevy Chase Plaza, and Mims, like many other Kentucky Central Life borrowers, was not required to bring money to the table. Normally 20 percent equity is required for a mortgage loan. It's there to protect the lender if something goes wrong, and without it, the lender has nothing but the quasi-risk of a 100 percent equity holder, with no upside. The question is, why would Bud Burnett do this?

I explained earlier how Bud Burnett used Kentucky's 10 percent basket clause regulation to permit these noncompliant loans to be considered admitted assets. This regulation effectively allowed Burnett to take on a significant amount of unreasonable risk. Since Kentucky Central Life was under the control of Kincaid's Committee, there was no fiduciary oversight to protect the company, and with Ed Schaeffer always siding with Burnett, it was always two votes to one on any disagreement.

Insurance regulations require a company to have an MAI appraisal completed on the property for every mortgage loan. This is done to protect the company from overlending and to demonstrate that the loan is no more than 80 percent loan-to-value. Kentucky Central Life usually outsourced this work to one of three qualified Lexington appraisers: Robert W. Crabtree, Michael Dolan, or Charlie Murphy. Crabtree and Murphy were well-respected and distinguished local realtors and qualified appraisers, and Dolan had also worked as Lexington's property valuation administrator. In addition, Crabtree and Murphy were former business associates of Garvice Kincaid.

Kentucky Central Life's mortgage loan department would order the appraisal and provided the appraiser with a copy of the borrower's loan commitment. This wasn't unusual because commercial property loans can be complicated. The more important issue is that sometimes Bud Burnett would indicate to the department which appraiser to use. In retrospect, one can now probably assume that Bud Burnett may have provided some specific guidance to the appraiser. In other words, it was very common for loans to come in at 80 percent loan-to-value, even if Kentucky Central Life was providing 100% financing. One might wonder why and how the appraisers could do this, but from their perspective, they were following the direction of the company. For instance, if a property was only 50 percent leased and they were instructed to assume 100 percent leased or to use the projected rental rates from the developer, that's what they did. The simple reality is that if Bud Burnett wanted to provide a loan to a certain borrower, he controlled the levers to make it happen.

When the project failed in 1988 and Kentucky Central Life repossessed it, Teddy Mims was able to walk away cleanly. He had failed, but there would be no penalty. As for Varney, since he had little to nothing in the project, Mims took control of his equity before Kentucky Central Life took it over.

In a 1991 postmortem, the Lexington Herald-Leader described it as a project plagued with problems from the beginning. First the dynamic-duo developers acquired more land than they would be permitted to use, and they also paid too much for the thirty-plus parcels they acquired. Second, while the developers and even Hart Hagan knew the project needed to be taller—at least nine to twelve stories—to cover the cost of the land and parking garage, in the end it was only five stories, and its rentable density was reduced by its pyramid-rise setback. Third, the developers initially budgeted $10.5 million for the project, but quickly increased that estimate to $11 million and then to $12 million, and they had an actual cost of $13.75 million.

The construction cost increase changed the economics of the project. The developers had originally planned to charge $12 per square foot for retail space, but in the end were charging $21 per square foot, which was uneconomical since most of the tenants had been paying only $7 to $9 a square foot before the project was built. Shops couldn't afford the rent and quickly went out of business. In addition, the luxury condos were a flop, and while Mims claimed to have purchased two of them, they had been financed by the Pikeville Bank and in the end went back to Kentucky Central Life. The twenty-two luxurious condos were originally projected to be sold for $100,000 to $150,000 but were marketed for $155,000 to $385,000. At the end of 1988, Mims reported that he'd sold four of the twenty-two units, including the two he was purchasing. In the end, only one unit closed before the state took over Kentucky Central Life, leaving twenty-one units to be disposed of.

In 1984, the project was initially proposed to include a 302-space parking garage and to contain fifty luxurious condominiums. The developers stated in December 1984 that the project needed to be nine stories to cover the cost of the parking garage. Reducing the height of the project eliminated twenty-eight condominiums. In addition, the developers reduced the size of the parking garage by one-third, or by ninety-nine units. They stated in various articles that they spent $1.3 million on the garage, or $6,403 per parking space. This amount seems incredibly low. The Webb Companies built the Vine Center (Radisson Hotel) 493-space parking garage in 1981 for $5.5 million, or $11,156 per space. This aligns with the national average of $9,300 per space. This implies that the garage probably cost the developers $1.9 million and not $1.3 million.

After the state took over Kentucky Central Life in 1993, the state began disposing of this project along with over $300 million of commercial mortgage loans, commercial and residential real estate, and raw land. Mims and Varney's $13.75 million Chevy Chase project wasn't sold until July 2000; the purchase price: $3.7 million. This included Chevy Chase Plaza and its twenty unsold condominiums but not the extra land the developer duo acquired. The project was resold in February 2008 for $4.35 million and sold again in February 2009, during the Great Financial Crisis, for $3.2 million. As of 2023, the Lexington-Fayette County Property Valuation office had valued this project at $4 million.

The unsold condominiums were eventually sold by the bankruptcy investor as unfinished shells from about 2008 to 2010. The Lexington Property Value Administrator's website indicates they were collectively sold in their initial arm's-length transactions for about $4.4 million (an average of $200,000 per unit), and it appears most owners spent about $125,000 finishing out the shells. Today the owner-completed units are valued at $7.6 million—an average increase over their purchase price of $145,000 per unit. The developers spent $13.75 million on this project, and the condominium owners invested an additional $3.2 million to complete their units, for a total of $16.9 million. Today the total Chevy Chase Plaza and Condominium project is valued at $8.4 million by the PVA office.

In the beginning, Bud Burnett kept Teddy's borrowing limit to a very reasonable amount. Teddy bought a couple more small, single-family homes and flipped them, but then things changed in 1981. The estate was selling off Kincaid's Kentucky banks and still had three. In 1981, bank investors were optimistic that Governor John Y. Brown Jr. would get the bank holding company legislation passed so investors could control more than one bank. For some reason, the Committee found it desirable to sell the Owenton bank to an attorney associate of Teddy Mims, Danny Branstetter. The bank had assets of around $20 million, and its 5 percent equity capital meant the bank was worth around $1 million. It appears Branstetter was a strawman purchaser for Teddy Mims, because in a 1985 article, Mims was quoted as saying that he purchased the bank in 1981 and owned 92 percent of the bank. The question is, where did Teddy Mims get $1 million to buy the Owenton bank? A loan from a Cincinnati bank could have been an option, but with a 21 percent prime interest rate, no one could afford this type of loan for very long.

The answer may have come out in March 1993, after the Insurance Department took over Kentucky Central Life Insurance. A *Lexington Herald*

Leader article dated March 23 said that a local banker had recently approached the Insurance Department about purchasing Kentucky Central Life's interest in Owenton bank. Apparently, Bud Burnett and the Committee had made a Kentucky Central Life loan to Teddy Mims, and he had pledged his bank stock as collateral for the loan. In 1988, when Mims's real estate ventures were collapsing, Kentucky Central foreclosed on the overdue loan. There is no mention of when the Mims transaction was initially done, but given his lack of financial resources in 1981, one can speculate that Bud Burnett got Mims the loan through either Central Bank or one of the company's downstream subsidiaries, and as Teddy did larger real estate deals, the balance on the loan was rolled into a new loan.

An April 15, 1993, *Louisville Courier Journal* article shows that from 1977 to 1989, Kentucky Central Life made thirty-three separate loans to Teddy Mims and his various ventures and that sixteen of the loans were existing loans that were rewritten at increasingly higher loan amounts. In the end, Bud Burnett and Kentucky Central Life provided Mims and his ventures over $80 million in loans during those years. By the end—the end of 1993—over $47 million in loans to Mims ventures were either repossessed or foreclosed on. Much of the difference between $47 million and $80 million amounts to the accrued interest that was never paid. As the loan amounts grew larger, the annual unpaid accrued interest was almost $6 million.

Loaning in excess of $80 million to an inexperienced developer, a former physical education teacher and high school football coach, is just ridiculous; it demonstrates how Bud Burnett operated. Mims' Chevy Chase project, Ed Schaeffer was there as the second Committee member to enable Burnett's wishes.

When Earl Wilson and Bud Burnett negotiated Al Florence's resignation from the Committee in November 1977, Burnett knew that adding Hart Hagan on the Committee to replace Florence might be problematic, but Ed Schaeffer had just joined the Committee in April 1977 after Earl Wilson reached the mandatory removal age of 70. Ed Schaeffer was Bud Burnett's enabler, and as Hart Hagan found out, it would always be two votes to one in any disagreement.

What Bud Burnett did with Teddy Mims is how he managed most of Kentucky Central Life's lending in the 1980s and early 1990s. As Bud Burnett would say, "no problem," because he wouldn't allow problems to happen. Consider how he used Teddy Mims to bail out his son, Bruce, in 1982 and then continued the shell game of loans over the next six years, inflating the balloon of debt larger and larger until it popped.

Lending mistakes happen, but covering them up doesn't make them go away! In addition, the shell game that was played with the three banks that Teddy Mims purchased from the Committee makes one wonder what Burnett was really up to in selling Mims the banks. A physical education teacher was heading up three Kentucky banks within less than five years of arriving back in Lexington. Things like that happen only in the movies! In addition, consider that Teddy Mims had never worked for a developer of large commercial projects. All professions require people to earn their stripes; it's called apprenticing or working entry-level positions. Teddy Mims also liked to call himself a horse trainer, and yet he'd never apprenticed with a professional trainer. The Mimses purchased a horse farm and equine center and were novices. They just had easy access to money—or, as Teddy's first company was named, Easy Money Inc.!

As Paul Harvey would say, "And now for the rest of the story." After 1989, Teddy Mims lost his public face. He no longer owned the famous Saratoga Restaurant and didn't even own his home; he rented a condominium in Lexington. After a massive failure, what does a high school jock and physical education teacher do? In Teddy's case, he dusted off his insurance license and rejoined the Stafford and Creech insurance agency, which used to be Bruce Burnett's agency and where Sandra got her realtor's license. Teddy sold insurance for a few years, and then he got the political bug and ran for mayor of Lexington in 1993.

Mims had an interesting platform; he said his financial "lumps made him the best suited to be Lexington's mayor" and that "Lexington needs a mayor who has walked in the shoes of a small businessman." "I am the American dream," he said. "My mother was a waitress, and my dad was a disabled veteran. We had five children in my family, all of them have college educations. I was able to parlay nothing into a really nice financial nest egg."[26]

The timing of Teddy Mims's entry into politics is interesting. He filed his mayoral paperwork with the clerk's office on January 27, 1993, just fifteen days before the state Insurance Department would take over Kentucky Central Life Insurance. Teddy's two biggest ventures, financed by Kentucky Central Life, were the Chevy Chase Plaza (loan amount $14 million) and French Quarter Square hotel and shopping center (loan amount $24 million). In a May 16, 1993, the Lexington Herald article, Mims called Chevy Chase Plaza a mistake, but cited the French Quarter Square as "a successful development." What he meant by "successful development" might be debatable, because in October 1993, about one month before the election, the French Quarter Square Partnership reorganized under chapter 11 bankruptcy. I guess he forgot that in January 1992, this business venture was already over seventeen months' past

---

26   *Lexington Herald-Leader*, May 16, 1993.

due on loan payments to Kentucky Central Life and owed $3.35 million in back property taxes. Incumbent Pam Miller easily beat Teddy in the Lexington mayoral race that November.

Teddy never seemed to have a plan or strategy for anything he did. He seemed to grab any opportunity that someone would finance: flip homes; invest in small fourplexes; buy a restaurant; buy another restaurant (Little Inn); open a restaurant in Richmond Bank Building; buy three banks (Owenton, Richmond, Waco); buy into an insurance agency with Bruce; move the Little Inn to Chevy Chase; buy an equine center and farmland around it; buy a farm on Paris Pike; buy thirty acres of undeveloped land in Tampa, Florida; develop the $14 million Chevy Chase Plaza; and at the same time develop the $24 million French Quarter Square shopping center and own the hotel; which his development company will then partner with a two-year-old Tennessee hotel firm to privately run. Of course, maybe the name of his 1978 first venture, "Easy Money Inc.," was just a prediction of things to come.

I don't know if Teddy has attention deficit disorder, and certainly environmental factors drive and motivate people differently based upon their personal histories, but what Teddy Mims was doing from 1977 to 1988, when Kentucky Central Life cut him off, was more than over the top. It's easy to see that some of the transactions, scams, and schemes were to benefit Bruce Burnett and his father Bud, like the purchase of the Red Mile Road office building and the Angliana Avenue warehouse, but they weren't included in the list above. Teddy Mims had loans of over $80 million from Kentucky Central Life, and even when his business and real estate ventures were collapsing under the weight of this massive amount of debt, he bought the Little Inn Restaurant and more land on Shannon Run Road in 1987.

Failure is supposed to make a person humbler, but Teddy never seemed to learn that lesson, considering that he ran for the office of Lexington's mayor in 1993 on a platform of concern about Lexington's current debt load. Teddy Mims, a legend in his own mind. While Teddy may not have been a financial genius, he did have one quality that Bud Burnett relied and depended on: he kept his mouth shut. This was an important attribute and something that made him valuable to Bud Burnett, at least until his ventures collapsed in 1988.

Since this is a southern saga, there's always another unusual tale, and Teddy Mims's friend and partner, William S. Stewart, has his own. Stewart, a dapper man with a fondness for hats, always appeared well off. He entertained with lavish parties and traveled out of the country quite often. He claimed many of these trips were to find furniture and other items for his store, Stewart Galleries Ltd. In fact, in the mid-1970s, he began making regular trips to

Britain in search of antiques. He had banking relationships with several banks in Lexington and other parts of the state and invested some of his wealth in real estate.

Stewart was married twice. His first marriage, to Jean Ann Patterson, produced a daughter, Mary. He and his second wife, Valeri, often quarreled. She was employed as a sales agent in a local real estate agency, and to smooth things over, Stewart would send her expensive floral arrangements, as many as a half dozen in one day, at the office. On one occasion it's reported that he sent a Jaguar and a mink coat to his wife at the office. The car was delivered, and a mink coat, in a beautifully gift-wrapped box, had been placed in the trunk. The receipt was also in the box; Stewart wanted her to know how much he paid for it.

The problem for Stewart was that he was spending his money faster than he brought it in. According to one article on November 7, 1987, in London's *Daily Mirror*, "he financed his lavish lifestyle by running cocaine from Mexico to the United States for the Mafia."

Stewart liked to boast. He claimed he owned expensive homes in Kentucky, Florida, and Britain, said he was buying an apartment in New York City's lavish Trump Tower, and told people he didn't have time to take two free, round-the-world trips that TWA owed him under its frequent flyer program. In the end, Scotland Yard's Detective Chief Inspector Drummond Marvin said, "As near as we've been able to make out, it was all a load of rubbish."

By the end of 1984, Stewart wanted a new life. His creditors were starting to chase him, and he had separated from his wife, Valeri; a divorce would be messy given his financial circumstances. According to a Daily Telegraph article on November 7, 1985, in early 1985, Stewart contacted John Landrith, a private investigator in Lexington. He offered him $40,000 in cash to "murder, or arrange to murder" his second wife, Valeri. Landrith refused the offer, so Stewart asked him to draw up a plan to fake his disappearance. Landrith agreed and suggested he drive a car off the road into a lake near Inverness, Scotland, in the mountains.

Stewart had already begun quietly liquidating what assets he could and had also taken out personal loans at various Kentucky banks. He now had a plan, and on February 2, 1985, the 53-year-old Stewart arrived in Britain. He had about $40,000 in cash, plus documentation to reassure immigration officials at Heathrow Airport that he was a legitimate businessman and could support himself it he were allowed to take up residence in Britain.

In 1983, Stewart had a financial statement that showed he had $10 million in assets, mostly stock in banks and mineral rights in land in Kentucky and

West Virginia, but by 1985, all those assets appear to have disappeared, and he owed $750,000 to $1 million in Kentucky, with more debts in Britain.

Scotland Yard agreed that Stewart was trying to escape his past and his debts but was never sure if he was broke or had liquidated his assets and was trying to hide them. In his previous trips to London, Stewart had met a 45-year-old blonde divorcée, Carole Gadow, who became his lover. Ms. Gadow soon introduced Stewart to the whirl of London's social scene, where he bragged about his wealth at cocktail parties and in high-class wine bars. He put $7,000 down and moved with Ms. Gadow into a new house, then worth $500,000, in the suburb of Dulwich. The house was next door to the house Prime Minister Margaret Thatcher bought to live in after she retired from No. 10 Downing Street.

Ms. Gadow said the couple planned to marry and that Stewart gave her a diamond engagement ring insured for £15,000 ($18,000), and they planned to spend £300,000 ($360,000) on furnishing the home.

After arriving in Britain, Stewart soon began making trips to Switzerland and taking out large life insurance policies. He also had policies on his life from companies back in the states. One policy he had taken out was for £1 million ($1.23 million), naming John Keogh, a new British associate, as beneficiary. In fact, between June 10 and 12, three insurance policies were issued on the lives of Stewart and Keogh, the would-be business partners who hadn't done any real business together. Under the policy terms, if either man died in an accident, the other would receive $1.7 million. They paid the first $1,000 monthly premium with an overdraft from Oakbriton's corporate checking account.

On July 11, after Stewart's check for the second payment on the new house bounced, the builders went to court to evict him.

On the dry, clear afternoon of July 16, 1985, on a quiet road alongside Alpnachersee, a scenic lake in Switzerland, a farmer working his field heard a splash and went to investigate. He found Stewart's rented Ford Sierra upside down in sixty-five feet of icy water at the bottom of the mountain lake. The fifty-three-year-old Stewart was dead. The body was found with its head at a window, as if the driver were attempting to escape. Swiss police treated the death as a routine traffic accident and shipped the body back to London, England, for burial. A local pathologist said the cause of death was asphyxiation due to drowning. There was no sign of alcohol, drugs, or poison. But there were questions. For instance, was the dead man really William S. Stewart? In addition, Stewart's fiancée wanted to know what happened to the $1 million in cash and securities she claimed he had. She said he phoned her on the way home and told her he was bringing over £1 million ($1.23 million) of cash, securities, and jewels with him. Nothing was ever found or discovered to confirm he had anything.

Scotland Yard was interested and soon started a two-year investigation into his death. The Yard obtained a court order and exhumed Stewart's body and contacted the FBI to get help with obtaining Stewart's medical records. Stewart's initial identification was done based upon documents found in the car. Dr. John Baldwin, Stewart's former physician in Lexington, provided chest X-rays to the Yard. Dr. David Flanagan of Lexington provided Stewart's dental records. He had treated Stewart a few months before his death and had read about the case. The dental records proved the dead man was William S. Stewart.

Scotland Yard also began investigating Stuart's business associate, forty-two-year-old John Keogh, whom Stewart had met through Ms. Gladow. Keogh had entertained Stewart in his "private box and the Royal Enclosure" at the Ascot races and flew him to the Henley Regatta by helicopter. "But Keogh was a fraudsman," said Martin Challis, another Scotland Yard investigator on the case. "He traveled all over the world and did things you and I could only dream of, but never with his own money. He had the gift of blarney, and people fall for his schemes."[27]

Keogh had formed a property business, Oakbriton, but it had never made any property deals. He formed the company even though it was forbidden under his 1976 bankruptcy. He made Stewart chairman of the board.

Stewart had given his twenty-eight-year-old daughter power of attorney over his affairs, but it was no longer in effect once he died. She came to Switzerland to make the funeral arrangements and then disappeared. Relatives began looking for her in Switzerland, Britian, and America. This added more mystery to the case. Ms. Gadow testified that Stewart was stashing money and securities in numbered bank accounts and in safe-deposit boxes on his several trips to Switzerland.

Ms. Gadow traveled to Switzerland upon learning of his death and reported going to his hotel and discovering John Keogh and his associate, Peter Cracknell, making photocopies of credit cards belonging to Stewart. They told her she shouldn't keep asking questions and claimed that they had believed Stewart's life had been in danger and his death was a mafia hit. Ms. Keogh testified that Keogh tried to break a special code that Stewart used on many of his electronic documents.

Scotland Yard said they would probably never be able to explain his death—was it an accident, suicide, or murder? They were certain Stewart

---

27   *Lexington Herald-Leader*, September 6, 1987.

drove his car into the lake deliberately, but they didn't know what he intended. With his head stuck out the window, it was obvious that he wanted out of the car, and if he'd planned to escape, he didn't practice it; if he had, he would have understood how the childproof locks worked. Scotland Yard's Marvin said, "If Stewart had intended to climb out of the car and swim to shore and a new life, he made a tragic mistake in not checking the windows first. The body was found with the head at a window, as if the driver were attempting to escape. Child-proof locks, however, prevented the glass from being rolled down far enough for a person to slip through."[28] Finally, Marvin pointed out that if he was trying to fake his death, he would have needed the missing money to live on.

As for Stewart's associates, John Keogh and Peter Cracknell, they were arrested on insurance fraud charges. Keogh received a sentence of four years in prison; Cracknell, three. Martin Challis suggested that Keogh may have figured out that Stewart was full of blarney too, and he and Stewart may have seen each other as the answer to their financial straits.

Stewart's death is still listed as an open verdict and a mystery that will truly never be solved. It's just another story in a traditional southern saga.

Central Bank Under the Committee

The Committee in the late 1970s and during the 1980s didn't do much with Central Bank. Nelle was initially on its board after Garvice's death but resigned about a year after the lawsuits began. The bank had assets of about $175 million at his death, and in February 1993 had assets totaling $426 million. Bud and the Committee had restricted what they did at the bank during their reign because the Kincaid daughters had a presence on the board. They owned 10% of the bank's common stock and maintained at least two positions on the board. They could see information and ask questions. This extra oversight helped to protect the bank from the radical lending that Bud Burnett did at Kentucky Central Life, so when Kentucky Central Life was taken over, Central Bank & Trust was saved.

My old boss, Cliff Forbush, always said that Bud and the Committee treated the bank like a stepchild. They marketed and promoted it, but in a much more limited way than Garvice had. In addition, Kentucky Central Life financed transactions that would usually be the domain of banks. One of the reasons that Central Bank didn't collapse under the control of the Committee is that the bank had some fiduciary oversight from the Kincaid daughters and their representatives. In addition, they were able to better monitor what the bank

---

28   *Lexington Herald-Leader*, September 6, 1987.

was doing. The only way they could get answers about what was happening at Kentucky Central Life was through long, drawn-out litigation, and even then, if you didn't ask the right question, you wouldn't get the right answer. For instance, in the litigation, Teddy Mims discussed purchasing the three banks, but apparently no one asked him where he got the money, or where he learned about the banks, or anything about the 1977 Richmond property purchase of two parcels of land from the Kincaid Trust.

As of 2025, Central Bank & Trust has survived and thrived under the daughters' leadership. The bank today has almost $4 billion in assets and a capital base of 12%. It's the region's largest independent bank and a major sponsor of the Kentucky Wildcats, just as it was under their father!

Chapter Five: Kincaid's Communication Machine:
Radio and Television

Garvice Kincaid witnessed the importance of advertising early in his life. His father, Douglas, was a master of promotion and promoted his store and services frequently in the local Richmond paper. He taught Garvice that, as my uncle Emmett use to say, "if you don't toot your own horn, nobody else will!" Douglas wanted people to know that his store offered the best products and at a great value. Garvice remembered those lessons and understood how important providing information to and communication with the public was. He also found a way to take Douglas's lessons to a new level by owning and controlling local radio and television stations.

A steady stream of inventions pushed radio forward in the early 1900s, bringing it beyond a bunch of dashes and dots of the Morse code age. In 1907, an American inventor, Lee De Forest, introduced his patented Audion signal detector. It allowed radio frequency signals to be dramatically amplified. Another American inventor, Edwin Armstrong, developed the superheterodyne circuit in 1918, and in 1933 he discovered how FM broadcasts could be produced. FM provided a clearer broadcast signal than AM, but RCA's top executive, David Sarnoff, was pushing for the development of television, so Sarnoff withheld FM from the public for more than a decade.

Still, public demand for radio grew exponentially. Entertainment broadcasting began in about 1910 and included programs that De Forest aired from the Metropolitan Opera House in New York City. An entertainment broadcasting venture based in Wilkinsburg, Pennsylvania, became the first commercial radio station, KDKA, in 1920. WWJ, in Detroit, Michigan, began commercial broadcasting that same year. Among the early proponents of entertainment broadcasting was David Sarnoff, who used radio to create corporate empires at RCA and NBC.

The period between the late 1920s and early 1950s is considered the Golden Age of Radio. It was a time when comedies, dramas, variety shows, game shows, and popular music shows drew millions of listeners across America. But in the1950s, with the introduction of television, the Golden Age faded. Still, radio remained a pop-culture force. Developments like stereophonic broadcasting, which began in the 1960s, helped radio maintain its popularity.

Another important focus of radio was giving people up-to-date news during World War II. Throughout the 1930s, in spite of the Great Depression, radio was entering most US homes. By 1939, the industry reported,[1] the majority of housewives considered the radio to be more indispensable to their home than the clothes iron or the refrigerator. Most radio listening was still focused on music and entertainment, but the various radio networks soon developed news departments, and these new departments began to rival print media, if not in the extent of their coverage, certainly in its immediacy. CBS news and Edward R. Murrow became "On Air" news department fixtures, and on September 1, 1939, when Nazi forces invaded Poland, the entire CBS broadcast that day was dedicated to the invasion.

The press brought World War II into our homes. The battleground correspondent's job was to stay out of the way, so the soldiers could do their job, and then send reports back to the States. But it was difficult to stay objective when the people around them, whom they had come to care about, were fighting and dying. Translating the grueling reality of war into verbal mental pictures became a trademark of journalists such as Edward R. Murrow. The importance of radio to the American household was cemented, and while the introduction of television would reduce its intrinsic value, its importance would continue into the next century.

In the 1930s, Garvice was in college and attending law school. It's questionable just how important radio was to his life. It was an age of jukeboxes and pinball machines, and a young college man probably was more concerned with dating and athletic events than with this new electronic box. Remember, those first radios were monstrous boxes of tubes, wires, and speakers, and they wouldn't be introduced to the automobile until the 1930s as an expensive option, often adding 20 percent to the cost of a vehicle. It wasn't until the 1940s that radios became a mainstream addition to cars and America took its music and news on the road.

There are no reported stories about when Garvice decided he wanted to own a radio station, but we know that in March 1946, he withdrew an application to operate a station. Three applicants had sought a license to operate a 250-watt station on a frequency of 1340 kilocycles. In February, the FCC granted a license to the Kentucky Broadcasting Company to operate a station. Garvice Kincaid and his partners and a company controlled by J. S. Bell, The Central Kentucky Broadcasting Company, protested the new license. The American Broadcasting Company, operator of WLAP in Lexington, was also protesting

---

1   "World War II on the Radio," *OTRCAT.com*, https://www.otrcat.com/world-war-ii-on-the-radio.

the license, on the grounds that it had requested a 1300-kilocycle frequency twice and been denied. WLAP had been started in Louisville and was allowed to move to Lexington in 1934. What is interesting is that in 1946, the thirty-four-year-old financier had just acquired Lexington's Central Exchange Bank (aka Central Bank) the year before and was pursuing other bank and real estate opportunities. Garvice now had a plan, and it involved broadcasting.

In June 1945, J. Sneed Yager, Lampert U. Suppinger, and Roger Adams organized the Frankfort Broadcasting Company to license Frankfort radio station WFKY-AM. The station was on the air in early 1946. In April 1946, C. H. Fleming, Marshall L. Peace, and Robert B. Hensley incorporated Tri-City Broadcasting to seek a license to operate a radio station in Newport, Kentucky. On May 29, 1947, the FCC evaluated a license proposal from Tri-City Broadcasting and listed C. H. Fleming as the president, owning 26 percent of the stock of the applicant. Garvice Kincaid, Robert B. Hensley, and Aaron L. Ford each owned 21 percent, Marshall L. Peace owned 5 percent, and two individuals from Fort Thomas each owned 3 percent.

In addition, the Tri-City application describes C. H. Fleming as the owner of 26 percent of WFKY in Frankfort and lists him as its president and general manager. Apparently the three original Frankfort Broadcasting Company incorporators were investors and attorneys, and when WFKY opened in 1946, Fleming was its general manager and Peace was its commercial manager. By 1947, when the Tri-City application was filed, ownership and control of WFKY had changed. After Tri-City's application was approved, C. H. Fleming moved to Newport to run the new station and Marshall Peace took over as station manager of WFKY. Apparently because majority control didn't significantly change, the ownership changes weren't reported until the station's license was up for renewal.

In Francis M. Nash's 1995 *Towers Over Kentucky*, he described the Frankfort station's ownership evolution this way:

> Radio in the state capital came to life again on March 18, 1946, when WFKY began its history from the East Main Street studios. 1490-Frankfort is the oldest of the post-war stations still in service. Started by a group of local stockholders under Frankfort Broadcasting Co. Marshall Peace, was program director and later general manager. The station announced it would strive to bring news from state government and aligned itself with the Mutual Network.
>
> By 1948, Garvice Kincaid had purchased an interest and in 1952, Ken Hart became president of the stockholding group. In 1959, C. A. "Bud" McClain took over as station manager. William

Clay, R. J. Reynolds and William R. Reynolds, who also owned
WMST in Mount Sterling, purchased the station in 1962, with Bob
Doll becoming executive vice-president of both stations, and in
1964 taking over as general manager of WFKY.

Power was increased to 1,000 watts for the daytime station in
1963 and a companion FM [station] was built in 1967, at 104.9 with
3,000 watts. The FM station gave new life to the old Louisville call
letters, WKYW.

Kincaid understood that every public endeavor required some form of
advertising. Whether one operated a business or was pursuing a political career,
one needed to communicate with the public, and the vehicles that provided
these connections made a lot of money. Before radio, newspapers, magazines,
and billboard signage were the primary ways to advertise. Today, most people
would never consider a newspaper classified ad, but before about the year 2000,
newspapers were a bedrock for advertising. They contained the classified ad
section, the real estate section, and their famous Sunday advertising circulars,
with their coupons. Newspapers were the primary vehicle for people to read
about their favorite sports teams and major and minor events coming to the
area. Radio now offered a new way to reach the masses, and Garvice could
understand how important this new medium of communication would become.
Radio was passive entertainment; people had only to turn on the power, tune
in, and listen to their favorite broadcast and its commercials. Radio offered
important news faster, such as FDR's 1933 fireside chat, or news of the 1937
Hindenburg disaster, or Joe Lewis's 1938 Fight of the Century, or the 1941
attack on Pearl Harbor, or the United States' victory over Japan in 1945. By
the 1940s, radio had become an important medium of communication, and
Garvice wanted a slice of it.

Francis M. Nash in 1995 wrote what many Kentucky broadcasters view
as the bible of broadcasting in Kentucky. "It's a history written not only for
broadcasters to reflect and reminisce, but also so those new to the business
may know the past, and the general public may understand the building of the
radio and TV industry, in Kentucky."[2] Nash's 1995 *Towers Over Kentucky: A
History of Radio and Television in the Bluegrass State* vividly and succinctly
describes what Garvice was witnessing in the industry, how he participated,
and unfortunately how it ended:

In the 1930's, live sports reports continued to find a prominent
place on radio schedules, as local stations did college and high school
games. In 1934, WLAP broadcast three University of Kentucky
football games. By 1936 the station had an extensive schedule of UK

---

2   Francis M. Nash, *Towers Over Kentucky* (Host Communications, 1995).

coverage with Ed Ashford handling the play-by-play. On March 7, 1935, Ashford broadcast the first live description of a UK basketball game. He also re-created some UK away basketball games from the newswire copy in the 1934-35 basketball season. This practice was popular in all sports, for several decades, when travel to away games was not possible. The announcer used his creativity and imagination to "voice" the game when actually all he had of what took place were short descriptions from the Western Union wire.

WLAP carried the high school state tournament action in 1935 and assisting Ashford were Adolph Rupp and A. B. "Happy" Chandler. Ashford also broadcast races from Keeneland and sent the Bluegrass Stakes out over the Mutual Network to 103 stations in 1939. They carried reports from Keeneland regularly and soon were using the Morning Line and wire service to re-create racing from major tracks around the country. WLAP dubbed itself the "Thoroughbred Station of the Nation." [It's easy to see why Garvice wanted to participate in this growing business.]

In 1947, Baseball Commissioner A. B. "Happy" Chandler built a radio station for his hometown, Versailles. Chandler had also been governor and U.S. Senator from Kentucky. The studios were in Versailles, but the company also maintained offices in Lexington. The station went on the air November 26, with Chandler throwing the switch to start up the 1,000-watt transmitter operating at 590 kHz. The Bluegrass Broadcasting Company had been formed, with Chandler as president and W. S. Lukenbill, formerly of Louisville, as general manager. Paul Dunbar was chief engineer in building the station, beginning a career that would encompass many later improvements at the station for which he worked more than 40 years. The station identified itself with both cities with call letters, WVLK.

Only one year into his new project however, Chandler agreed to sell to Scripps-Howard of Cincinnati, which proposed to move the station to Ohio, replacing their WCPO facility with a new frequency and power. Scripps-Howard had at the same time been seeking the 630 channel that was being applied for by WLAP. Neither deal was consummated for WCPO, and controlling interest to WVLK would eventually be purchased by local real estate developer Garvice Kincaid in 1951. Kincaid moved the main studios from the library in Versailles to Lexington, first at the Lafayette and then to the Phoenix Hotel on Main Street. He began to assemble a staff that would impact broadcasting in central Kentucky for the next 20 years. Ted Grizzard, who had managed WLAP and WKLX in the city, became program director, and Don Horton was named general manager. Grizzard also had sports duties primarily with high schools and later helped to tutor such announcers as Jim Host, Van Vance and Tom Hammond, who all became great sports people in their own right.

Some might have thought he was starting them a little young when they heard 12-year-olds Richard Weaks and Lawrence Yates, Jr. doing a youth basketball game from Henry County in 1949. They had appealed to Grizzard at the old WKLX to do some games, and he agreed, but had them actually do the play-by-play!

Claude Sullivan became sports director and voice of Kentucky Wildcats football and basketball for WVLK during the 1950s and '60s. Sullivan had started in radio as a teenager in Ashland. He would later follow Waite Hoyt as the announcer for Cincinnati Reds baseball from 1963 until his death in '67.

Arty Kay was brought on board to wake up Lexington with his morning show, a chore he would have until 1972. Commercial manager George Webb began implementing the new trend in radio sales, rotating spot announcements instead of straight sponsorship of programs.

But the big change came when WVLK went rock 'n' roll, a decision made by Don Horton, but challenged by Grizzard, Kay and much of the Lexington religious community as well. Those protests aside, the station joined WAKY and others around the country turning to the new format, one that would spur advertising sales and listenership. Like the others, ratings quickly jumped for 590 radio and although Louisville's WAKY remained popular even in Lexington for years, WVLK eventually took the ratings honors. Ironically it was at WVLK that the legendary Bill Bailey, of WAKY fame, would end his career in 1994. He had been brought back with Johnny Randolph for a reunion program and was hired to work the afternoon shift. retiring after four years at age 63.

The AM format had become more adult contemporary over the years with ABC news as well as extensive local news, sports and public service efforts. Just as the shift to rock helped WVLK, a changeover at its sister station WVLK-FM took that station to the top of the ratings, when in August 1982 it became K-93 Country overnight and quickly doubled its audience.

WVLK-FM had been the city's easy listening music station. It went on the air in 1961 at 92.9 FM. The original 32 kilowatts were increased to 50 and then 100 kilowatts with the antenna located on the Channel 27's TV tower, more than 850 feet in the air.

The change to country from the beautiful music was not popular with everyone, as angry protest letters were filed with the station and local newspapers. K-93 began with an automated tape programming and rode the country popularity wave as the area's only FM country station. Later, the station made the transition to a compact disc/

live announcer studio combination, with Matt Austin as program director.

Earlier, Kincaid and Horton began expanding their radio interests in the late 1950s to other stations in Kentucky, Florida and Ohio as the Horton-Kincaid group. Many of these were sold, but Bluegrass Broadcasting Company under H. Hart Hagan would acquire others and purchase WKYT-TV. Bill Stakelin, who managed WVLK then WHOO in Orlando, became vice-president of the company and moved on to be chief executive officer of the Radio Advertising Bureau. Ray Holbrook, who had worked in sales at the station in its early days, was brought in from Danville to become general manager from 1968 to 1971. WVLK had been in danger of not having its license renewed when in 1968 the FCC raised what it called "serious questions" about certain billing practices and commercial time standards at the station. The FCC announced hearings on the matter and Holbrook was called on to work in satisfying the concerns of the Commission and get the station back on track with renewal, with the FCC finally voting to approve license retention.

Some 15 years later, the license would come under attack in a suit filed by African-American groups against WVLK and WLAP radio. The charges were investigated and resolved in WVLK's favor and the action dismissed.

Bluegrass Broadcasting came under the umbrella of Kincaid's Kentucky Central Life Insurance firm in 1976 and three years later moved into modern new studios and offices in the Kincaid Towers, downtown.

Ralph Hacker, who had worked at WVLK in sales and sports since 1965 and as color commentator on the UK Network with Cawood Ledford beginning in 1972, became the general manager of WVLK AM/FM in 1974, and has led the station since that time.

Some of the other WVLK notables with lots of airtime were Bill Cody, who went on to Nashville radio, and "Captain Tag" Veal, for years the helicopter traffic reporter. In the early days there was announcer and newsman Reynolds Large, whose stepson Jack "Catfish" Pattie later became the popular air personality from the late 1970s into the '90s. Large worked at several central Kentucky stations, while Pattie became one of Lexington's most enduring radio stars.

WVLK seemed to be blessed with sales people who stayed around awhile, including Connie Joiner, vice-president of sales, with the station since 1969, and Lee Harper, who began as an account executive in 1962. The sales staff put together a rather unusual package in 1983, when in a recessionary period it offered $10,000 worth of free advertising to any business that created 15 jobs or any existing business that added 30 jobs during the year.

Promotional stunts on billboards seemed to be popular in Lexington, as Robert Lindsay of WVLK vowed to live on one until Kentucky hired a basketball coach, they did—Rick Pitino! In 1994, "Roadkill" Kessler of WKQQ swore to camp on one until the Kentucky football team won another game—they didn't!

Since the purchase of Channel 27 by Bluegrass Broadcasting in 1967, the radio and TV have often worked together in not only UK sports, but in news and other coverage. The two "Ralphs"—Ralph Gabbard at WKYT and Ralph Hacker at WVLK—have often been seen as the most powerful people in Lexington media since the mid-1970s. They had actually known each other much longer, meeting for the first time in 1956 while grade schoolers in Madison County, and they have been close friends ever since.

The radio/TV staffs would be surprised with news in 1993 that their successful stations had been ordered sold by the state after the insurance commissioner was forced to take over the financially troubled Kentucky Central Life Insurance Company, the parent firm of WVLK and WKYT-TV. The stations would go to the highest bidder. General manager Ralph Hacker immediately put together a group of investors, including staff people, and formed HMH, Inc., to become the successful bidder at $11 million and announced that the station would continue to operate as normal with no major changes.

While only three commercial AMs and FMs were officially licensed to Lexington until the early 1990s, other stations in smaller towns nearby went on the air with AM stations beginning in the mid-1950s. These broadcasters would work to serve their local area and battle for audience in the shadow of the towers of Lexington. Paris to the northeast, Winchester to the east, Georgetown to the northwest and Nicholasville to the south all had their own stations and by the 1980s had built FMs that would become more valuable when operated as Lexington stations. In each case, the four FM stations of these towns started identifying with the bigger city with relaxation of ID rules in the 1980s.

. . . The state insurance commission takeover of Kentucky Central eventually led to the sale of the assets of the Lexington insurer. The liquidation meant WKYT and WYMT would go to the highest bidder. A Georgia firm, Gray Communications, with President John T. Williams, outbid Ralph Gabbard for the television stations by a small margin. A request by Gabbard to the state that would allow him to increase his bid was rejected and the sale was declared completed. The $38 million transaction was approved by the FCC and Gray took over operations in September 1994.

Gray, which owned stations in Georgia, Florida and Louisiana and two newspapers as well, made Gabbard the president of their television holdings. Wayne Martin became general manager of WKYT and the basic staff of both Lexington and Hazard remained intact. Gabbard said the new owner wanted the "best television possible"—the same philosophy he had followed in the past. Gray moved its headquarters to Lexington and Gabbard took on the task of building and expanding the company's television interests, a job he called "exciting."

The number of commercial stations in Lexington expanded in the mid-1980s to five with two independent stations signing-on, but only one surviving.

In 1945, Kincaid wanted to enter the broadcasting business, and his initial plans in 1940 had failed. He had petitioned the FCC for a license and fought to get his request approved but had failed. In a *Herald-Leader* article in January 1947, "Radio Stations in Blue Grass Grow at Unprecedented Rate," Elmer Sulzer described the "unparalleled mushrooming of radio stations in Central Kentucky during 1946" and the "prospect of having more radio stations than any community of equal population in the United States." The area already had "four standard broadcast stations and one frequency-modulated station and applications pending for two more stations of each type."

WLAP was Lexington's oldest station operating with a power of 250 watts and also Lexington's only network station associated with the American Broadcasting Company. It had an application pending to increase its power in 1946 to 5,000 watts. WLAP's "lone-wolf status, which it had enjoyed since 1933,"[3] was abruptly shattered that year when two other stations went on the air. The first of these was WKLX, with its one thousand watts of power, which went on the air in October 1946, and the second newcomer was WLEX-Radio, which went on the air in November 1946.

Outside Lexington, but still in the Bluegrass, was Frankfort's new station WFKY, which began operating in March 1946. Danville had two applications with the FCC for one license, and Versailles had one pending application. In addition, the University of Kentucky had a 500-watt educational station, WBKY-FM, which went on the air in 1945. The FCC was issuing licenses, but the demand for licenses was exceeding its ability to review applications in a reasonable period of time. In 1947, any application for a license was not expected to be approved or rejected for at least two years.

In the 1940s, the FCC was trying to manage the allocation of bandwidth, the dangers and abuse that could result from one organization owning a concentration of media interests, and the advancement of communication

---

3   Elmer Sulzer, "Radio Stations in Blue Grass Grow at Unprecedented Rate," *Lexington Herald-Leader*, January 1947.

technology that could create pockets of "radio congestion" in various geographic locations around the country. C. F. (Red) Fleming, who operated WFKY in Frankfort, described it this way in an August 4, 1946, *Courier Journal* article: "Red is convinced, the [FCC] applications are tossed into large piles in the office of the Federal Communications Commission, and it takes a world of hunting to find them and get them dug out of the dust-gathering stacks."

The FCC was created by the Communications Act of 1934. The Act granted the FCC the authority to regulate "communications by wire and radio so as to make available to all the people of the United States a rapid, efficient, nation-wide, and worldwide wire and radio communication service." By 1945, the agency had to face a landmark court case about the importance of the comparative hearing process in awarding a broadcast license when there are multiple applicants. This case made it all the way to the US Supreme Court, and its decision set the legal precedent that a publicly distributed license must be assigned through a process that does not exclude competition for the license. The FCC was instructed that its process should disfavor applicants who would gain a monopoly in a particular region. Media interests were not limited to broadcast media; rather, they could include newspapers or other media outlets. So, Kincaid's application in 1945 was made at a time when the FCC was in the process of updating its own rules.

In 1949, Garvice developed a new plan, one that involved his good friend A. B. "Happy" Chandler. Chandler was a former US Senator and Kentucky governor and also the commissioner of baseball and the unofficial leader of the Democratic party in the state. Chandler and Colvin Rouse had incorporated Bluegrass Broadcasting Company in October 1945 and in 1946 applied for a license.

In 1947, politically connected Chandler had been granted a license to operate a new station in Versailles, Kentucky. An advertisement in the November 23, 1947, Sunday *Herald-Leader* reflects the one-thousand-watt station WVLK 590's beginning. The station went on the air three days later, becoming Lexington's fourth local radio station, joining WLAP (1450), WLEX (1340), and WKLX (1300). The letters "WVLK" stood for "Versailles, Lexington, Kentucky." The main studios were in Versailles, in the two-story Logan Helm Memorial Library, and the station's radio tower was located off Leestown Pike in Lexington. The total cost to open the station was $100,000, and its twenty-five-person staff had a payroll of another $100,000. Chandler also owned the *Woodford Sun*, a weekly newspaper. When the station was granted FCC approval to move to Lexington, it began broadcasting from the Lafayette Hotel. Its executive offices remained in Versailles, providing program continuity, and its bookkeeping and traffic departments and news, promotion, and sales offices were in Lafayette Hotel. Broadcasting studios were maintained in both locations.

Little is reported about Kincaid acquiring the station from Chandler. The purchase price wasn't listed, nor was the reason Happy sold it. It was reported in June 1949 that the Hearst Corporation sued Bluegrass Broadcasting for $4,256 for nonpayment under a contract for News Wire Service. Apparently, Bluegrass Broadcasting had paid promptly until October 1948 but had made only a few sporadic payments since that time. In May 1951, it was announced that Garvice Kincaid was elected president of Bluegrass Broadcasting Company Inc. and that he, John E. Perkins, and Frank Trimble had acquired Chandler's and some other investors' stock in Bluegrass Broadcasting.

In a 1980 Kentucky Central Life publication written by Charlie Thomas, the head of public relations for the company, Thomas recorded Kincaid's history in radio and how his operations evolved over twenty-five years:

> Garvice Kincaid had always wanted to run a radio station. He talked about it as far back as 1944. But those were the war years, and nobody could get a license from the FCC. In 1947, he had bought a low wattage, hand-built army transmitter which proved to be unusable. That same year WVLK began broadcasting from Versailles on AM frequency 590.
>
> One of the principal figures involved with WVLK in Versailles was former governor A. B. (Happy) Chandler. The station, which played the so-called "good music," a mixture of conventional rhythms and melodies, was plagued by many difficulties, but the frequency, 590 KHZ, was a good one.
>
> When Kincaid gained controlling interest of WVLK on May 22, 1951, the station was financially broke. The first step by Kincaid was to get the FCC approval to move the station to Lexington. Studios were first located in cramped quarters in the Lafayette, then a short while later were moved to the Phoenix Hotel.

[Note: This may sound confusing since WVLK already operated an office/studio in the Lafayette Hotel. I think it can be explained this way: Kincaid moved anything that was in Versailles and combined it with the Lexington operations. In addition, he changed the station's primary address listed with the FCC to the Lafayette Hotel.]

> At the time Kincaid bought WVLK, rival WKLX was having problems with some questionable stock. The FCC finally allowed WKLX's owner to sell the station, but when the new owners took

over all they got was a shell of a station. The WKLX staff had been hired away, by Kincaid, for his soon to be rejuvenated WVLK.

Ted Grizzard, the genius behind WKLX, and a well-known radio celebrity, became the new station director for WVLK, and Arty Kay, WKLX's number one DJ, also traded stations. Claude Sullivan, the original "voice of the Kentucky Wildcats," also went to WVLK from WKLX, but the real impetus behind the new WVLK was an outsider named Don Horton.

With the best personnel and some new equipment purchased by Kincaid, WVLK began challenging all other rivals for a piece of the ratings.

Horton then made a decision that quickly propelled WVLK to the top. WVLK was going to play only rock and roll!

The idea met with bitter resistance from Station Director Grizzard, but General Manager Horton had the final word. The town's most popular radio announcer, Arty Kay, refused to play rock and roll, and promptly quit. Ministers and entire congregations of local churches petitioned the station to cease broadcasting the new music. Most of the listeners loved it, however. Advertisers were quick to realize the potential, and in a matter of weeks WVLK was dominating the air waves.

Ted Grizzard, a great innovator in his own right, remarks, "I think eventually we would have been on top anyway, but with rock and roll it happened overnight."

After Grizzard was converted and Arty was persuaded to return, the station with the best personnel now had the best programming.

The station continued to improve its sports cover and developed a unique sports format which is still being used today. On many occasions they ran two networks: "Pick of Dixie" (SEC) football and basketball, and University of Kentucky football and basketball, both the same day. This provided the serious sports fan with the opportunity to compare upcoming opponents with current competitors of the Kentucky Wildcat teams.

The new WVLK had an unorthodox and aggressive advertising approach spearheaded by salesman George Webb that helped give the station a competitive edge over its rivals. Webb, like all the other newcomers to WVLK, was an innovator. Through his efforts, advertisers in Lexington were shown the advantages of buying rotating spot advertising, rather than just sponsorship of one particular type of program. Many of the ideas instituted by Webb were incorporated and are still being used by radio stations across the country. In order to promote this new station, the management of WVLK introduced other new ideas to the broadcasting business, such as "media mix." This meant the station would use means other than just radio to advertise itself, including newspapers and magazines, a strategy unheard of in those days.

In November 1961, WVLK gave birth to the first commercial FM station in Lexington, WVLK-FM 93, which also was the first Lexington station to broadcast stereo. Its daily fare of eighteen hours of beautiful music was warmly received by culture lovers and intellectuals who were thrilled with the station solely programmed for serious listeners. The best AM station in Lexington now had an opportunity for potential listeners who preferred entertainment of a more cerebral nature.

Rodmau Sullivan, a professor at the University of Kentucky, summed up the sentiments of many people in the community with his short note to the WVLK management dated November 17, 1961: "Gentlemen, I've bought a new AM-FM for the kitchen. Best wishes for the new program."

WVLK-FM would later increase its power from the original 30,000 watts to 50,000 watts, and eventually to 100,000 watts at which it broadcasts today. The station's antenna is now 854 feet in the air on the Channel 27 television tower, which allows WVLK-FM 93 to be heard by the many thousands who live and work in the Central and Eastern Kentucky area. Many businesses throughout the state pipe the music of WVLK-FM through their offices and plants during working hours.

"WVLK has always been the leader in public service broadcasting. That was an integral part of Kincaid's policy," say Vice President and General Manager Ralph Hacker. "Whatever we could do for the betterment of the community, he had us do."

Hacker, who also is part of the University of Kentucky Sports Network, is typical of the managers now in the Bluegrass Broadcasting Group, having joined WVLK 14 years ago as a salesman and sports announcer before assuming his present position 5½ years ago. As H. Hart Hagan, Jr., president of Bluegrass Broadcasting, likes to say, "We grow our own executives."

One example of the consistent public service policy of WVLK is the "Todd Trease Teddy Bear Fund," a program that distributes thousands of Teddy bears year-round to young children in area hospitals. Involvement in charity promotions like the "Cardinal Hill Hospital Dance-a-thon" is part of the way of life for the station personnel who continually give their time with a smile.

The first Lexington area station to install weather radar in the broadcast studio was WVLK. This was an innovation that allowed disc jockeys to give immediate and accurate weather reports.

WVLK also was the first Kentucky station to have a mobile news unit for live, on-the-spot news broadcasts. While not the first station in Kentucky to provide live, in-the-air traffic reports, it is generally considered to have the most thorough and colorful coverage. This operation is headed up by the salty and outspoken "Captain" Tag Veal in his helicopter. Tag, a former musician, recently won a name recognition poll, beating all local radio and television personalities and a host of other community figures including Lexington mayor Jim Amato.

While there are many other colorful personalities at WVLK, the attitude at the station is one of "the sum is only equal to the total of the parts," with no one person ever trying to steal the show.

For a number of years now, "adult contemporary programming" has been the rule at WVLK. "Adult contemporary programming" is a term that substitutes for "Top 40" hits, but goes further and is inclusive of a wide range of music tastes—current hit songs, mostly from the rock and roll charts, plus jazz and country hits.

WVLK is under the umbrella of a subsidiary of Kentucky Central Life Insurance Company, Bluegrass Broadcasting Company, which is directed by Hart Hagan. Bluegrass Broadcasting manages a rather autonomous chain that includes: WHOO/AM & FM, Orlando, Florida; WVOC FM, Columbus, Georgia; WKYT/TV, Lexington, and most recently, radio stations WWSA/WCHY-FM in Savannah, Georgia. Of all the radio stations, Hagan seems to hold WVLK in the highest esteem.

"WVLK is that station everyone else in the chain aspires to be like, the model," says Hagan. "It is a good, solidly operated station with good personnel, good programming, and it holds number one ranking consistently."

Jim Jordan, vice president of operations and program director at WVLK, stresses that contemporary programming must be done professionally to maintain high standards at WVLK. The station also has a clearly defined policy for its announcers.

"We only have three rules for the DJ's," says Jordan. "We don't talk about sex or drugs on the air. We don't editorialize unless it is done as a station, and we always try to be positive. It's too easy to be negative these days so we do our best to always be positive on the air."

Immediately upon tuning-in to WVLK-AM 590, one is aware of the up-beat tempo. Traffic with Captain Tag, Paul Harvey, "Caywood Ledford's Comments," ABC News, "Pick of Dixie," football and basketball, Dick Clark, Fran Curci, Joe Hall. There's something for everyone, and all of it is supported by contemporary music.

A list of former employees who helped write the WVLK success story reads like a "Who's Who in Kentucky Broadcasting." David Dick, now a CBS correspondent, Van Vance, Reynolds Large, Ted Grizzard, Ray Holbrook, Arty Kay, Claude Sullivan, Earl Boardman, O. C. Halyard, Kenny Hart, Mimi Chandler, Mimi Host, Don Horton, Gig Henderson, Bill Stakelin, Denny Mitchell, Hal Rogers, and Dan Kelly.

The list could go on and on, but WVLK, while proud of its heritage, choses to live in the present and the future, secure in the knowledge that current personalities—people like Dave Murray, Lee Sherwood, Captain Tag, Neil Steel, Jim Jordan, Caywood Ledford and Ralph Hacker—are making their mark and will someday be placed among those on the honor roll.

WVLK is also blessed with a number of long-time, less well-known employees whose experience and talents are unmatched in the local broadcast industry. They included: Paul Dunbar, chief engineer, who helped construct WVLK's original facility in Versailles, and has built and supervised each installation since for 34 years; Lee Harper, George Pugh and Rick Shaw, sales representatives who joined the station in 1961, 1965 and 1968, respectively; Connie Joiner who joined the staff in 1971; Stella Merritt bookkeeper, who came to WVLK in 1967; Joe Catt, news director, who joined the staff in 1969; and Charles Damron, engineer with the station since 1967.

Charlie Thomas knew a lot about Garvice Kincaid and his endeavors; he had worked closely for Mr. Kincaid since 1961, and while Garvice didn't always appreciate Charlie's work habits, he did appreciate his professional abilities. Charlie handled public relations for Garvice personally and for all his business entities. Charlie was probably also one of the most respected public relations people in the state and the region during his life. He won numerous local, regional, and national awards for his work and after his retirement continued to be an active participant in the editorial pages of the *Lexington Herald-Leader*. Charlie was also a treasured personal friend, and I always appreciated how he treated me as a young fellow, just starting at the company, and his willingness to share stories about the company and Mr. Kincaid.

What's amazing about Kincaid investing in a radio station in 1951 isn't that he did it, but that he did it while continuing to build his consumer loan and banking businesses and of course also investing in real estate. In fact, he had already acquired the Joyland Amusement Park in February 1950 and was actively overseeing its operation. In addition, in January 1951, Garvice partnered with M. H. Holliday to start Holliday Publications. Holliday owned four weekly newspapers serving eastern Kentucky, and he and Kincaid would acquire another three. Holliday was president and general manager of the new corporation, and Garvice was chairman of the board of directors. The publications had a total circulation of 5,600.

In 1954, M. H. Holliday Jr. accepted a position with US Senator John Sherman Cooper, so Kincaid incorporated Eastern Kentucky Publishing Company, Inc. and purchased the assets of the Holliday Corporation, which consisted of the seven eastern Kentucky publications. By 1958, though, Garvice was winding down this publishing enterprise. He closed four of the newspapers and sold off the remaining two (one had been closed earlier). This Kincaid enterprise had stagnated and become a distraction, and Garvice wanted businesses he could build and grow. In fact, Garvice would say many times, "What's the reason for owning a business, if you are not going to grow it?"

When Kincaid acquired WVLK in 1951, the station employee roster contained one employee who Garvice would really depend on in those early years. His name was Donald J. Horton. Horton was born in Covington, Kentucky, on February 8, 1927, to Russell and Irene White. Russel White abandoned his family shortly after Donald's birth, and he and his mother soon moved in with her parents. While his mother would one day remarry, Donald's grandparents essentially raised him. He grew up in Estill County and graduated from Irvine High School and attended the University of Kentucky.

In 1943, sixteen-year-old Donald had his mother change his name from Donald John White to Donald John Horton. He had been known as Horton his whole life and now wanted his grandparents' last name. In 1945, at the age of eighteen, he enlisted in the Army. In 1947, he was discharged and living in Lexington and attending the University of Kentucky. At UK, Donald met his future wife, twenty-year-old Janet Elizabeth Sulzer of Lexington, and they were married on June 7, 1948. Elizabeth was from Lexington and was a graduate of Lafayette High School. At UK she was a member of the Kappa Alpha Theta Sorority and a cheerleader for two years. She had also been a cheerleader in high school. The couple set up house in an apartment in the Ashland neighborhood on 249 Irvine Drive, and on March 31, 1949, the couple welcomed their son, Donald John Horton Jr., to their family.

Janet Elizbeth Sulzer's father, Elmer G. Sulzer, was a professor at the University of Kentucky's Radio Arts Program. Sulzer established UK's Radio Arts Department, which began around 1929. He was recruited to the university to lead UK's marching band and orchestra but did much more. He also served as head of the UK Publicity Bureau. UK's campus radio productions were abundant during the 1930s. Multiple programs were produced at the university, and phone lines between Louisville and Lexington were leased to transmit the programming from UK's campus to WHAS.

A May 14, 1953, *Herald-Leader* article about UK's Radio Arts majors says:

> Although the department at UK is only seven years old, more than 300 persons have majored in radio arts. Each majoring student must take 21 hours of radio courses, such as announcing, script writing, production, advertising, and regulations. They also much participate in the radio programs and do 16 nights of radio engineering which involves handling tape recordings, control boards, and remotes . . . .
>
> Three people make up the faculty of the Radio Arts Department. They are Mrs. Camille Halyard, who is acting head of the department and director of the radio station; Stuart Hallock, teacher and production director; and Leonard Press, teacher and program supervisor. In addition, Dave Wright is employed as full-time engineer, and Miss Ruth Brophy as full-time secretary . . . .
>
> Stations and the UK Radio Arts Department graduates they employ are as follows: . . . WVLK (Lexington)—Reynolds Large, disc jockey; O.C. Halyard, program director; Donald J. Horton, manager.

Elmer Sulzer was instrumental in establishing UK's own WBKY-FM station in 1947. The University of Kentucky, through Professor Sulzer, offered classes in radio writing and radio acting, which also included laboratory work, where students could listen to recordings of their work. WBKY established itself at 91.3 in the country's new FM band in 1947, which made it the first FM college radio station in the United States. The broadcast facilities and transmitter were in McVey Hall on the University of Kentucky's main campus. The station was on the air nightly for three hours, five nights each week. According to the 1946 *Courier Journal* article, "There is a lot of interest in it at U.K. now, especially since so many people have gone from the informal classes held in the past to positions of importance in radio. Those names include a lot of big-timers with N.B.C., WLW, WLAP, WAVE and C.B.S. They are writers, directors, engineers, and announcers." Elmer Sulzer is also credited with pioneering a system of educational radio listening centers across Kentucky.

Donald and Elizabeth faced many changes beginning in 1948. Donald left the University of Kentucky and began a career with WVLK (where the couple's wedding announcement lists him as working). Elizabeth also left college but would one day finish her degree at Indiana University and earn a doctorate in philosophy. When Garvice acquired WVLK in 1951, twenty-four-year-old Donald had worked at the station for three years and was now the director of programming. In addition, he and Elizabeth were living in a home in Lexington's South Arcadia Park neighborhood.

In addition to Horton being listed in the 1953 *Herald-Leader* article about UK's radio arts major, his obituary says, "Horton, who started in the broadcasting business as a teenager . . . ." One can probably assume that his broadcasting career began during his time at the university and his involvement in Professor Sulzer's Radio Arts Program. This may be how he met Professor Sulzer's daughter, Elizabeth. In UK's 1948 yearbook, Horton is listed at a junior in the Art and Science section, but he isn't listed in UK's 1949 yearbook.

In 1947, when Chandler's WVLK began broadcasting, it was part of the Mutual Broadcasting System. It referred to itself as "The Burley Belt Station" and focused on a farm community audience. In 1947, when her father launched WVLK radio, twenty-one-year-old Mimi Chandler became the station's early morning disc jockey, hosting "Coffee Time" Monday–Saturday, starting at 7 a.m. "From the time the station opened, I was the first disc jockey that WVLK ever had," she told the *Lexington Herald-Leader* in 1986. "The only thing on the air earlier than my show was the farm report."

A family trip to California when she was fifteen years old had resulted in a screen test for Mimi. Paramount signed her to a seven-year contract, but she appeared in only two motion pictures, Henry Aldrich's *Swings It* (1943) and *And the Angels Sing* (1944). An article in the *Tampa Bay Times* on January 6, 1948, reports, "The daughter of baseball czar 'Happy' Chandler, will alternate between acting in movies and being a disk jockey on her father's station near Louisville, Kentucky." In 1949, a *Lexington Herald-Leader* article reported that Don Horton was WVLK's assistant station manager.

Kentucky Mountain Barn Dance and WVLK

The *Kentucky Mountain Barn Dance Song Book*'s foreword describes several aspects of the program. It was the inspiration of Don Horton, and it debuted on WVLK on September 10, 1949. The program explains:

> It has ever been our uppermost ambition to make the Barn Dance a home for everyone, with a spirit of brotherhood for all, and where the welcome mat is always on the door step and the latch string always on the outside, a place where our many friends can come and mingle in company with the entertainers so that both the audience and the entertainers may work together and enjoy themselves to the fullest.

In November 1949, Donald Horton, assistant manager at radio station WVLK, worked out a contract between the Clay-Gentry Stockyards Company, Inc., the Kentucky Barn Dancers Gang (cast), and WVLK. The contract stipulated that the entertainers would be paid $150 a week "with certain bonuses for radio broadcasting of their performances."

The barn that was used as the background for the show/program was part of the "oldest gathering places in the entire South, having been in constant operation as a livestock selling center for over fifty years. The arena was where the first livestock auction market in the United States was established."

The Eureka Flour Company of Beaver Dam, Kentucky, sponsored the show, which aired on Saturday night, and the Eureka Network that broadcast it included eighteen radio stations in five states. The show reached listening audiences in Kentucky, Indiana, Ohio, Tennessee, West Virginia, Virginia, North Carolina, and South Carolina.

The Barn Dance cast included the Foggy Mountain Boys, Lester Flatt, Earl Scruggs, Bennie Simms, Curley Seckler, and Cedric Rainwater.

In April 1950, WVLK discontinued broadcasting the show, which created a legal/contractual controversy for the show. The Clay-Gentry Stockyards Company, Inc. wanted to continue the show and asked the Fayette Circuit Court to "prevent the Foggy Mountain Boys and five of their entertainers from performing at any place except the Kentucky Mountain Barn Dance on Saturday nights."[4]

The entertainers were in doubt about whether they were still under contract and required to perform per the contract terms. An attorney for the stockyards, Robert Odear, claimed the actual dispute was between the Clay-Gentry Stockyards Company and WVLK radio station, which had the "Kentucky Mountain Barn Dance" under contract. The question was whether the "Kentucky Mountain Barn Dance" was the show at the arena or the radio broadcast. The issue arose from the fact that the Stockyards company had quit its broadcast but was continuing the barn dances, and the entertainers felt that when the broadcasts ended, that terminated their contract.

Clay-Gentry went to court and sought to "prevent the entertainers from performing at any other place between 7:00 and 11:00 p.m. on Saturdays until their contract with Clay-Gentry expires, six months after November 1949."[5]

A hearing on the matter was scheduled for Saturday, April 8, 1950. Fayette Circuit Judge Chester D. Adams ruled that

> Clay-Gentry Stockyards Company is the originator and owner

---

4   *Lexington Herald-Leader*, April 3, 1950.
5   Ibid.

of the Kentucky Mountain Barn Dance and . . . radio station WVLK cannot produce a similar show under the same name. Furthermore, the Foggy Mountain Boys, including Lester Flatt, Earl Scruggs, Bennie Simms, Curley Seckler and Cedrick Rainwater cannot perform on Saturday nights from now (April 12) until May 15 for anyone except Clay-Gentry.

Further details arose during the trial. Apparently, the Clay-Gentry Stockyards Company had decided to discontinue the broadcasts over radio station WVLK, which was owned and operated by the Blue Grass Broadcasting Company, Inc. It wanted to switch the broadcasts to another station, but WVLK made the decision to put on the Kentucky Mountain Barn Dance at the Woodland Auditorium as well as use the Foggy Mountain Boys on its program. Clay-Gentry then stepped up and claimed it had exclusive rights to the program and the Foggy Mountain Boys, along with others, under their remaining six-month contract. The performers thought they could continue to work for the radio station, though. But Judge Adams ruled that the Foggy Mountain Boys and others "would have to perform for Clay-Gentry on Saturday nights or not perform at all and said the radio station could not broadcast a Kentucky Mountain Barn Dance (or similar program)."[6]

By December 1950, the Barn Dance gang had given sixty-four performances in the Clay-Gentry Arena since the show began. But the Clay-Gentry Arena was struggling to have enough seats to accommodate the crowds. Beginning with the Saturday night show on December 16, 1950, the venue was changed to the Woodland Auditorium. Mickey Stewart was cited in a newspaper article[7] as informing fans, "Business as usual—but at a different stand." He emphasized that the show would be unchanged, with all the barn dance gang on hand to provide the entertainment. The show had been doing two shows a night at Clay-Gentry to reach a wider audience due to the 600-seat capacity limit. At the Woodland venue, there would be only one program at 7:30 p.m.

Woodland Auditorium, built about 1906, stood near the corner of East High Street and Kentucky Avenue. It was built at a cost of $20,000 and had a capacity of nearly 3,000. It was the area's largest venue for a while, and the University of Kentucky Wildcats played at the Woodland Auditorium between 1914 and 1916. It was condemned for public use in 1952 and was torn down sometime in the 1970s.

The last show appears to have been on Saturday, May 5, 1951, at the Woodland Auditorium. No further promotional ads appeared in 1951 or in 1952. May 1951 was the month Garvice acquired WVLK.

6   *Lexington Herald-Leader*, April 12, 1950.
7   *Lexington Herald-Leader*, December 17, 1950.

Kincaid and WVLK's Early Management Organization

Garvice and Donald Horton appeared to work well together in those early years. Kincaid probably appreciated Horton's Kentucky Mountain Barn Dance arrangement, since it had some relationship with Joyland Park's entertainment business.

By 1952, another local station, WKLX, was in financial trouble. Garvice had Horton and others at WVLK evaluate whether he should purchase it. It would take out competition and possibly increase WVLK's market share. In the end, Kincaid and Horton passed on the opportunity. They found that WKLX's broadcast signal wasn't superior to WVLK's. WKLX's most valuable asset was its staff, and Garvice immediately began recruiting them for WVLK. In September, he hired Ted Grizzard, WKLX's station manager. Grizzard was a well-known local celebrity and had been with the station fifteen years. He was named a director of Bluegrass Broadcasting and station manager, and Donald Horton was promoted to vice president and general manager of the station. Grizzard's *Man on the Street* daily broadcast was considered one of the most entertaining shows ever on local radio due to his sparkling and spontaneous humor.

Ted Grizzard was born May 30, 1904, in Nashville, Tennessee. As a young man, he tried his hand at several jobs, including selling burglar alarms in Nashville. In 1931, he got his big radio break and went to work for WLAC. WLAC, one of the nation's first radio stations, began broadcasting in November 1926. Created primarily as a promotional venture and publicity medium for the Life and Casualty Insurance Company, WLAC originally operated only part-time and on a noncommercial basis.

Grizzard made his way to Lexington after working for WHAS in Louisville and WBBM in Chicago, as well as for stations in Texas and Arkansas. Ted Grizzard joined WKLX in 1935 and progressed from staff announcer and through other responsibilities to general manager in 1939, but he is probably best remembered for his *Man on the Street* and *Quizzer and the Cop* programs. "He was considered a tremendous adlibber," according to Jim Jordan. "He was a "people's person, a Southern gentleman" who had an ability to "take any situation and just make it very humorous,"[8] Jordan said.

Ted Grizzard would work for WVLK for almost fifteen years and eventually transition to part-time in the 1960s and then join June Rollings at Kincaid's television station WKYT in the 1970s for a what became a popular television

---

8   *Lexington Herald-Leader*, March 22, 1985.

program called *Town Talk*. Rollings and Grizzard had wonderful chemistry, and people would refer to Ted as her father. On one occasion when she tried to set the record straight on the show, she said, "Ted, would you clear this up once and for all?" Ted replied, "I don't know why you're ashamed of me."[9]

At WVLK, Grizzard was the radio station's boss, but Donald Horton was Garvice's chief lieutenant. WLEX ended up acquiring the WKLX's assets in 1952. Kincaid, Horton, and Grizzard had recruited much of the staff by 1953, so essentially WLEX was getting WKLX's frequency and transmission facility, which was expected to boost its signal.

In 1952, Kincaid had Horton apply with the FCC for WVLK to get a new television license for UHF channel 33 for Lexington. The FCC then decided that channel 64 would be a better channel for the area, so they had to resubmit their application if they were interested. The other competitor for the channel was radio station WLEX. The competition between these two Lexington stations would go on for years.

In 1953, WLEX filed a $55,000 lawsuit against WVLK claiming that the station was issuing "fraudulent and misleading advertising." Apparently when Garvice was looking at acquiring WKLX, an independent research firm indicated that in the evening, WVLK's nighttime signal reached more households than WLEX's. After Kincaid passed on WKLX, he had Don Horton work with one of the station's engineers to put together a map demonstrating, from the information in the report, that WVLK had superior coverage.

C. E. Hooper, who did the research, didn't dispute what WVLK had produced but didn't endorse it either. Horton and the engineer had created advertising pieces with nonstandard language. For instance, instead of using the term "time segment," the pieces referenced other less-technical words like "daytime" and "nighttime." WLEX had a problem, in that it had technically used the wrong entity in filing the dispute and had ignored the recent acquisition of WKLS's frequency and transmission facility. Stanford Helt, the WVLK radio engineer who prepared the coverage maps, said in a deposition that he reportedly requested that his map not be used in any advertising because the contour lines were computed rather than measured.

The trial lasted seven days. Judge Joseph J. Bradley in the end refused to restrain WVLK's advertising practices. He gave his ruling in a brief oral opinion delivered from the bench on March 24, 1953, immediately after attorneys finished closing arguments. He explained that injunctive relief in such a case was an extraordinary measure and not employed unless there was urgent necessity. He also noted that equity courts did not employ injunctive

---

9   Ibid.

relief where the plaintiff complained of a completed act. "There must be a series of repetition or threat to commit further acts,"[10] he said. Donald Horn during the trial had already said he had dropped the advertising concept because it had been found not to be useful.

Judge Bradley indicated that he felt some of the brochure maps WVLK used in its advertising campaign since the previous May and August could have been better but that he felt WVLK was justified in relying on the figure in the Hooper rating report that was the basis of some of the advertising that WLEX objected to.

WVLK's attorney, James Park, in his closing argument told the judge that "there's more to this case than meets the eye. It's in evidence here that both stations have applications for television stations pending before the FCC." Park opined that WLEX brought its suit to attempt to discredit WVLK before the Federal Communication Commission in its effort to secure a television channel. Park said he had an idea of the effect of a station going before the FCC and saying of WVLK: "Their dishonest and dishonorable and were put under a court injunction for fraudulent advertising."[11]

Park may have been on to something with his suspicions, because it was reported in the *Lexington Herald-Leader* on March 18 that WLEX complained to the FCC that WVLK was guilty of unfair business practices. The complaint asked the commission to determine whether WVLK's license should be revoked.

An FCC spokesman said that the complaint was "unusual" because the two stations were involved in a lawsuit. He said the commission had no routine procedure for processing complaints but that the case would be considered eventually.[12]

While no FCC investigator had been sent to Lexington, "the commission had not yet decided to send one." He also said "the commission might very well wait for the outcome of the lawsuit because a decision in the suit could affect the commission decision on the complaint. All the commission can do is decide to take the [WVLK] license away", he said. Radio licenses are issued on a three-year basis and are renewable every three years. He said "WVLK's licenses would expire August 1, 1955." Something else important happened to Garvice around this time. In April 1953, he had his first of three heart attacks and was told to take it easy, lose fifty pounds, and move to Florida. While Kincaid did spend more time in Florida, he didn't slow down and mainly used

---

10   *Lexington Herald-Leader*, March 25, 1953.
11   Ibid.
12   *Lexington Herald-Leader*, March 18, 1953.

it as an opportunity to acquire more businesses.

One can imagine that the management of WLEX was pretty angry at Kincaid and Horton for raiding their staff and the opportunity to hit back was too hard to resist after Horton released his ads. The station waited several months after they were released to call foul in court, and WLEX did try to taint WVLK's radio license and its application for a television license with the FCC. Garvice won in the end, and in time, Bluegrass Broadcasting dominated Lexington's radio and television market for several decades.

1953 was a stressful year for Donald Horton. He was applying for a television license, dealing with the advertising lawsuit, and going through a divorce. On June 1, Donald and Janet were granted a divorce. They had been married only four years and had one child. Apparently, Donald had met someone else, because the next day, twenty-six-year-old Donald married thirty-five-year-old Wilda L. Campbell in Valdosta, Georgia. Wilda had been married before, at the age of eighteen, to a man nine years her senior. She divorced him in 1948 on grounds of abandonment. The newlyweds initially made their home in an apartment at 1204 Fontaine Road.

The battle for a television channel in Lexington appeared to be escalating by August 1953. The FCC was moving forward with its review, and Horton contacted it on behalf of WVLK and requested that it consider allowing four channels in Lexington and also requested that it consider allowing the relocation of a channel from another area. In November the FCC ruled that it would issue two new channels in Lexington, channels 18 and 70. Immediately a fight between WLEX and WVLK was on for channel 18. Horton, now listed as the president of Bluegrass Broadcasting, said, "WVLK will seek channel 18— obviously more desirable because of its lower frequency range and attendant wider signal range." WLAP, which was a part of the American Broadcasting Company, was now expected to get channel 27.

In mid-February 1954, Horton and WVLK announced they were recalling their FCC application for a UHF channel. This left WLEX as the sole bidder for channel 18. Horton said that WVLK would "sit on the sidelines" and "press the FCC for a VHF channel." Horton said they decided to drop their application after checking other markets and that they now "question[ed] the value of the service." Most television sets were equipped to receive only VHF channels. Households had to acquire a special converter to receive UHF channels, and he wasn't sure people would spend the money now when they could receive VHF broadcasts from Louisville and Cincinnati. He also said that five UHF stations had recently closed, with the most recent being in Kansas City. Horton said the station's focus and energies would be devoted to radio.[13]

The next day, radio station WLAP abandoned its plan to operate UHF channel 64 and stopped construction on its television transmitter facilities. Gilmore Nunn, president of the station, called it a losing proposition. He described the station's issue as "a general unacceptability of an areawide UHF system" and questioned the marketability to advertisers and the viewing public.[14]

The FCC launched UHF channels in 1952. By 1955, many of the initial broadcasters had folded. It wasn't just that twenty million households needed to purchase a $40 UHF converter box for their television sets, it was also that the UHF stations operated on a lower power that affected the quality of their reception. In addition, UHF stations always had a low share of an area's television advertising market. The FCC had overestimated the interest from local and national advertisers, and advertising dollars were needed for the stations to pay their bills.

By 1958, Donald Horton had been with Garvice and Bluegrass Broadcasting for ten years. After 1955, he focused on making WVLK a market leader. They had most of the local on-air talent that listeners preferred, so much of his work was dedicated to tweaking on-air programing and experimenting with different advertising formats. He had been married to his second wife for five years and nine months when they became the parents of boy-and-girl twins, Donald John Horton Jr. and Wilda Donna Horton. In addition, while it was unsuccessful in acquiring a television station, in July 1955, Bluegrass Broadcasting was able to acquire radio station WFKY-1490 AM in Frankfort, Kentucky. The purchase price wasn't disclosed.

In 1958, Kincaid still wanted to acquire a local television station. Since turning down the UHF channel three years before, he had waited patiently for something to change. In February 1958, that change happened, and he had an opportunity to purchase WKXP-TV, channel 27, from the Community Broadcasting Co., which also operated WLAP. The parties reached a tentative contract to acquire the station for $275,000, assuming the FCC approved it. The station would move to the Phoenix Hotel offices of WVLK. Horton said they also planned to invest another $125,000 to $150,000 to "put the station in top condition." The incorporators of the new WVLK-TV were Kincaid, Horton, and Frank Trimble.

Horton was said to be president and general manager of both stations when the deal was completed. Garvice indicated that the station would be affiliated

---

13   *Lexington Herald-Leader*, November 6, 1953.
14   *Lexington Herald-Leader*, February 19, 1954.

with a network. He said, "I can't say which network it will be, because it's a choice sometimes of which one you get the best deal with."[15] In 1958, the station was independent and had no network affiliation. Kincaid also indicated that the station would boost its power to 300,000 watts from 249,000 watts, reaching more households. WKXP-TV originally went on the air in September 1957. Two weeks after the Kincaid deal was announced, negotiations were suspended after Garvice proposed to acquire both WLAP and WKXP-TV for $650,000. Nothing can be found regarding why Community Broadcasting Co. wanted to sell that station less than a year after going live, but one can guess it was probably undercapitalized and they hadn't factored in all the capital and operating costs associated with the operation.

While Kincaid's Lexington TV deal floundered, an out-of-state buyer, Radio Cincinnati, Inc., expressed interest in WLAP and WKXP-TV. This company was under the control of Hulbert Taft. Taft's company also owned WKRC radio and television in Cincinnati. Taft quickly negotiated the purchase of the station, bringing WKXP-TV into a broadcast network that included radio and television operations in Ohio, Tennessee, and Alabama. The sale of WLAP and WKXP-TV was formally announced on March 17, 1958. Taft also announced plans to broadcast some of WKRC-TV's programs over WKXP-TV. In addition, while the deals were being negotiated, Community Broadcasting had secured a CBS affiliation contract for WKXP-TV.

After the sale was approved by the FCC and completed, in June, the Taft group changed the station's call letters to WKYT. The new ownership continued operating WKYT as a CBS affiliate and began an expansion of the station's studios. The various Taft broadcasting properties were then consolidated under a new corporate entity, Taft Broadcasting, in 1959.

In 1961, WKYT-TV switched network affiliations from CBS to ABC as part of a Taft Group affiliation agreement that also saw WKRC-TV and WBRC-TV in Birmingham, Alabama, convert to ABC. The Taft family cited their good relationship with the American Broadcasting Company network at its existing ABC affiliate, WTVN-TV in Columbus, Ohio.

It would take Garvice Kincaid almost ten years to eventually acquire WKYT from Taft, but his persistence paid off and he did. Kentucky Central Television, a subsidiary of the Kentucky Central Life Insurance Company, reached an agreement to acquire WKYT-TV in 1967 for $2.5 million. The deal was noteworthy because Kentucky Central Life had a pending application for what would have been Lexington's third station, channel 62. The application was withdrawn.

---

15   *Lexington Herald-Leader*, February 8, 1958.

After Garvice lost WKYT to Taft in 1958, he had Horton focus on boosting the power of WVLK from one thousand watts to five thousand watts. This increase was approved by the FCC in July 1958. Before that, Kincaid and Horton had also been acquiring other radio stations in Kentucky and Florida.

Garvice liked the economic growth prospects of Florida. In 1954, he had purchased a mansion in Miami after his first heart attack and had also begun exploring ways to do more business in the state. He and Horton soon acquired the radio stations WHOO-AM and -FM in Orlando, Florida, for $350,000.

Back in Kentucky, in July 1955, Garvice and Horton acquired control of WFKY-AM in Frankfort from James F. Cox, W. E. King, and Robert B. Hensley, and in October 1959, they acquired control of WCMI-AM in Ashland, Kentucky, and WOMP-AM in Bellaire, Ohio, for $163,000 and $170,000, respectively. Garvice was building his broadcasting business. Most of these radio station acquisitions are listed as transactions with Garvice, Horton, and others before eventually being acquired by Bluegrass Broadcasting. This probably had to do with the FCC change-of-control regulations.

Kincaid liked to move quickly, but the FCC rules and regulations didn't allow this. His initial radio station investments were minority stakes, and it wasn't until 1951 and his acquisition of Chandler's WVLK that he achieved control of a station. One can imagine that Garvice was frustrated with his progress. In December 1959, he controlled five stations: WVLK-AM (Lexington), WFKY-AM (Frankfort), WHOO-AM and -FM (Orlando), WOMP-AM and -FM (Bellaire, Ohio), and WCMI-AM and -FM (Ashland, Kentucky).

The FCC adopted a station ownership limit in November 1953. The rule known as 7-7-7 was adopted with the goal of assuring a broad diversity of ownership in the broadcasting industry. The rule limited an owner to seven AM-radio stations, seven FM-radio stations, and seven television stations. The rule remained in place until 1984, when it was replaced with a 12-12-12 rule. So, in 1959, under this rule, Garvice owned five AM stations and three FM stations. In addition, 1959 was the year that Garvice acquired Kentucky Central Life Insurance in Anchorage, Kentucky, which he quickly began growing through additional acquisitions.

By 1960, Kincaid was really focused on making WVLK Lexington's best radio station. In February 1960, he and Horton joined the CBS radio network. WVLK already had some of the best local programming in Lexington, and now Garvice was aligning the station with the network that was considered the strongest in national and international news reporting. In addition, Kincaid and Horton applied for an FM license for the station WVLK, which offered a sophisticated mix of music and information. The station obtained its WVLK-FM license on March 9, 1962. It was Lexington's "beautiful music station," playing fifteen-minute sweeps of mostly instrumental versions of popular songs. (In a controversial move in the 1980s, the station switched its format to country music, which was a major success for the station and its management.)

By 1961, Donald Horton was again struggling with personal challenges. In 1953 when he and Janet divorced, it was a local news story. Janet's request for a divorce was based upon the grounds of cruelty. Janet received full custody of their son, and while they had a proposed settlement agreement, the judge changed it in Janet's favor. After the divorce, Janet moved to Indiana to be near her parents.

Based upon various court appearances, in 1955 and beyond, Donald may have had issues with alcohol. On April 28, 1955, he was ticketed for "breach of the peace," on April 29, 1955, he got a ticket for running a stop sign, and in February 1956, the fire department was called to release his children, who were locked in a room. In April 1961, thirty-six-year-old Horton was jailed for being drunk and driving while under the influence of alcohol on a Saturday afternoon. He had been involved in a three-car crash at 166 St. Ann Drive in which three teenagers were injured. The patrolman indicated that the evidence showed that Horton was driving south on St. Ann Drive in the wrong traffic lane and that his car hit a northbound automobile and knocked it into a parked automobile own by the city. Horton was also identified as the driver of a car that struck and destroyed a concrete flowerpot, owned by Frisch's Drive-In Restaurant a short time before the accident. In that instance he left the scene before a report could be made.

In court Horton was represented by Kincaid's friend, Harry B. Miller Jr. He pleaded guilty and was fined, but Garvice had had enough of Horton's personal dramas and negative publicity and soon severed their business relationship.

Before Horton left in 1961, he made a controversial programming change at the station in the summer of 1958. He had WVLK adopt a rock 'n' roll format. This proved to be a very popular move. Eventually the station took over the top ratings spot from Louisville's WAKY, which was popular in Lexington. The move was challenged by Ted Grizzard and Arty Kay and by much of the Lexington's religious community. Letters to the editor were written, and some called it the "devil's music." *Lexington Herald-Leader* staff writer Joe Coyle used his column to criticize not just WVLK but society in general for this cultural change. Those protests aside, the station joined WAKY and others around the country turning to the new format, and it spurred advertising sales and listenership, just as it had done at other radio stations.

Kincaid and Horton weren't breaking new ground as much as acknowledging the significant attitudinal changes that were taking place in the country, and much of it involved America's youth. This new music was a soundtrack for rebellion, however mild, and when Bill Haley and His Comets kicked off the 1955 motion picture *Blackboard Jungle* with "Rock Around the Clock," teens in movie houses throughout the United States stomped on their seats. Radios were everywhere in the 1950s, and people took their music with them. If a radio station didn't adjust to changing listener tastes, then that station wouldn't remain number one for long. In 1958, the lasting power of rock 'n' roll was not known, but Kincaid and Horton took a chance. In 1957, they had already observed what happened at ABC affiliate WFIL-TV after it started broadcasting Dick Clark's *American Bandstand* to a national audience of teenage consumers. They were capitalizing on a national youth culture built around pop music records, and advertisers were clamoring for it.

In May 1960, before Horton's departure, Garvice received his first broadcasting award from the Kentucky Broadcasters Association, "The Kentucky Mike," given to him for his service to the radio industry.

In Ted Grizzard's book *#1 is Chicken*, he discussed Kincaid's purchase of WVLK and Donald Horton and others and described the work environment at the station during this period. In the quote below, I retained most of his folksy language and style and made only minor adjustments or added comments where I thought it would benefit the reader. Enjoy his significant insight into Garvice Kincaid and how WVLK operated in the 1950s and 1960s:

> . . . It was sometime in the spring of 1952 that WKLX was sold, and the good staff of that station began scattering. I don't know exactly how many were there but about eleven of the key people "scattered" to WVLK and almost overnight made it a radio station.
>
> . . . Garvice Kincaid must have heard the first announcement about the sale of WKLX because he began at once having his program director contact Sullivan and Arty Kay, offering them jobs at WVLK. Then Garvice phoned me. Not to offer me a job but to ask me what I planned to do. I didn't know. I knew WLEX didn't want me, and I wanted no part of them.
>
> I felt sure WLAP wouldn't want me back—but I wasn't sure positive about it. Kincaid said, "Well, they tell me I'd be foolish to make you manager of WVLK after you turned down the job, but I'll have a job for you if you want it. We will talk about it." I told him I'd probably need a job—thanked him. Then I remember Chicago and Hollywood—and my refusing the offer they made—just so I could stick with the "good people" at WKLX.

It was September of 1952 before I could leave but during that time I had sued and collected my $2500 [bonus they reneged on], minus the attorney's fee. I had talked with Kincaid and knew that Don Horton would be manager of WVLK, and I would be "station director"—whatever that meant. I know I was pleased to think that somebody else would do the worrying for a while. At least—I thought they would.

At WVLK I would continue the "man on the street" and [my sponsor] Honey Krust [Bread] had told me to let them know when I changed stations, and they would change with me. Garvice—after I told him my salary at WKLX—which was the same as it had been for five years—told me that at WVLK I would receive almost $50.00 a week more from him in addition to 10% of any profits. The 10% I always got [from Kincaid], by the way—and I never had to sue for it.

My "station director's" job had been in effect for about two weeks when there was an important meeting with Mutual in Chicago. Horton was to represent WVLK and that was a relief to me but—a few days before the meeting Garvice decided I should go with Horton. I declined the privilege and Kincaid said—"Let me make it a little more firm. It's in the interest of WVLK and I'm not sure Horton can handle it. You go with him." I went. Horton had asked Garvice to have me go. The first lines of this "station break" don't tell the reason for the item. But in thinking about the "subject" I remembered something extra. It's likely that not many people know that Jim Host—W. James Host of Jim Host & Associates—was a pretty good baseball pitcher. I've been told—and I believe—that Host was the recipient of the first baseball scholarship awarded by the University of Kentucky—and later he earned a contract with the Chicago White Sox organization and pitched for a season with one of the club's minor league teams. At the end of that season Host received a contract for a second year but like many other young players he didn't like the contract terms and returned it unsigned. He heard no more from the Chicago White Sox. I doubt that there were headlines on the sports pages about this matter, so unlike the horses and the sheep—you didn't read about it. But now you know that Jim Host was a baseball pitcher.

. . . Now here is the real reason I mention Jim Host and I like this part better. During the time Jim Host was going to UK and perhaps for some time after, he did play-by-play radio broadcasts for WVLK—both football and basketball. And I quickly add—he was darned good. Host would do our broadcasts when Claude Sullivan would be on the road with UK teams. Sullivan had designed a form consisting of lines and small squares and this greatly simplified the listing of lineups and keeping statistics. Next to the space for the players' names there were little boxes in which to insert the height, weight, age and whether the player was a second, third- or fourth-year student. This was shown by "2" for sophomore, etc. No freshmen were playing on varsity teams at that time.

Right here I'll add that Host had a good sense of humor but during play-by-play he was serious, and I never knew him to "break up" or laugh about anything. There was one outstanding exception. I had the pleasure of doing color and commercials on these games and at a timeout I could cover the lighter aspects of the broadcast.

Jim and I were doing the State High School Basketball Tournament at Freedom Hall in Louisville. A timeout was called and during this time out a substitute was put in. Host looked at the player's number and the chart describing the boy. Evidently the young man was a junior since the chart showed a "3" for his year in school. Jim gave the name, height and weight correctly but somehow—hurriedly he got the wrong square for the "age" and confused it with the boy's year in school. So, Host says, "Joe Smith is 6 feet tall, weighs 175 pounds and he's three years old!"

Just before "time-in" was called I said to Host, "Jim, the boy who just entered the game is real good but they don't let him shoot very often." Jim glanced at me, and I added, "You see, at three years old, every time he shoots his diaper comes off." By then Host knew what he had said and that did it. This time—a really big "break-up" and while he was laughing, he missed a couple of plays. Jim Host— another of the many play-by-play gentlemen with whom I enjoyed working.

One more touch of high school basketball. Hoot Combs was another of the capable play-by-play announcers who worked with me when Sullivan was out of town. Hoot and I were in Frankfort for a game and as usual we arrived at the gym in the late afternoon to set up equipment (our engineer did this), check our telephone line through to WVLK and then go to dinner. We always found the team manager too and he would give the announcer all the information about the team, the players and the team's win-loss record. On this visit a nice young fellow was talking with Hoot and in giving the team's record he mentioned another Frankfort school and added— "Y'know, they've UPSET us twice." Hoot paused a minute but managed to keep a straight face—and so did I. We looked—but there's nothing in the book that says how many "upsets" equal better play.

Don Horton was a hell of a nice young fellow. Like so many others I saw and knew during my association with Garvice—he was real strong with Garvice behind him. Without Kincaid's strength behind him he—and the others—were not much.

. . . Still about Garvice and money. I'm not likely to forget to include this but I want to get it in now—maybe several times too. Saying I had to sue WKLX to get my $2500 (bonus). And never had to sue Garvice for my 10%—Kincaid not only paid the 10%, I'm sure he had it figured on the "long" side many times. I don't know how much more than 10% he okayed, but I recall with great pleasure two beautiful checks for $15,000 each.

They came at the end of different years, but they came. More money than I'd ever had in one lump in my life. With the people, the programs and sports we brought from WKLX in 1952, WVLK started up. It may have been #2 for part of 1952 because it took people awhile to learn to change [the station]—but from 1953, WVLK was a solid #1 and stayed there. Is still there today—thanks to the hustling young people who run it.

I think back on this next part and make a comparison. When I took over WKLX I had a bankrupt station. I was resented and opposed by a staff of misfits and gravy-train riders who were determined that I couldn't make the place go. No money. Even the owners were sick of the radio business. When Garvice put Don Horton in charge of WVLK, Horton had been program director at the station and there was no manager there. Horton had been told to keep the place open so long as he could meet the payroll. When he couldn't—then sign it off and close up shop.

That's when Garvice bought it and when WKLX sold out and the WKLX staff moved in. Now—Horton had the financial backing he needed from an owner who liked owning the station and wanted it to succeed. He also had the top people in the radio business and radio accounts being moved to WVLK every day.

I've made reference to other happenings during sports broadcasts, but I'll never remember half of the things I'd like to tell you. However, here is one that is associated with Freedom Hall and high school basketball tournaments. We had the usual laughs over there, but it was hard work too—from Wednesday night through Saturday night.

One afternoon of our first high school tournament in Louisville I had—between afternoon and night sessions—hurried downtown to the hotel. I think it's Watterson Expressway that was the quicker and better route from the Hall to downtown. I had made it down okay but, on the way back I couldn't find an entrance to the expressway. I was way off in some neighborhood—lost. Time was running out on me and finally I drove into a filling station to ask directions. A big and not too bright-looking young fellow comes to the car. I tell him where I want to go and ask how I can get to the expressway. After a short pause this guy says—while pointing—"You go down here two blocks to the traffic light, then turn right and when you get to another light, you angle off to the left and" but here I interrupted him to repeat, for my own benefit, what he had just told me. I said, "Now I go down here two blocks to the traffic light, then turn right and at the next light." But that's as much as he would let me repeat. He frowned at me, so help me. And then said, "If you know so much about it you can just find it yourself!" With that, he turned, and I thought he stomped as he went back into the station office. I yelled and tried to tell him that I was just repeating his instructions but by then he couldn't hear me.

I found the expressway and sort of liked the idea of going back the next day and asking for more directions. I doubt that I could have found the station and from the way he had scowled at me—maybe I was smart not to try.

This is where I step aside and give all the credit—except for some guidance in policy—to Don Horton. Without Garvice he was not much. With Garvice he became a real "goer." 1953 was rock n' roll time. I hated it. Arty Kay disliked it so much he finally quit WVLK. Horton, with Kincaid to back him, went all the way with "rock."

No more popular or standard music. No more church programs. And that took guts. I cringed and would not have cried had the plan failed. It didn't fail. WVLK became an even stronger # 1. We created a news department and Horton bought a mobile unit.

That mobile unit was the first one in Lexington and cost $7000. When Horton first talked of a mobile unit, I was afraid the novelty of the thing would wear off and it would wind up sitting in a garage with nobody using it—and seven thousand bucks was too much to have that happen.

I did persuade him to do it right. Hire a news director to be responsible for keeping that Chevrolet van and all the equipment it carried in service. Garvice agreed and we hired guys to do nothing but gather news. And that first-in-town big, red, glass-windowed mobile unit was a fine ad for WVLK too. Here's more. Because when you have an owner to back you, and good people, you can roll.

Came time to buy a new and more modern news unit and Horton was going to trade or sell the big red one. I suggested we give it away. All a listener needed to do was send his [or her] name, address and phone number to WVLK to be eligible to own the vehicle.

We would draw the lucky name at half time at a high school football game to be played at Stoll Field—UK's football field. We got thousands of entries. I don't know who the hell won the thing, but it was a sensational promotion and worth far more than whatever we would have received for it in trade.

We simply painted out the WVLK letters on the unit—took out the equipment and somebody drove it home or to California or used it to haul whisky. They couldn't have hauled whisky though—it had big glass windows on both sides.

By the way—the news director we hired was Paul Warnecke. To my thinking one of the best, most intelligent news, radio and television man in these or other parts. He was program and news director with me at WVLK too, for I don't know how many years. And because of such outstanding qualifications he, of course, is not associated with commercial broadcasting now. Lexington broadcasting, or telecasting, if you choose, lacks the "class" that Warnecke could give it today and it's a shame somebody doesn't realize that.

It's easy to understand the attitude—the enthusiasm of the WKLX staff that came to WVLK. Pay increases were coming just before the big "sell out," but at WVLK everybody was paid more immediately. Horton was managing the station, but Garvice phoned me frequently to see "what's going on" and I had a chance to tell him about the kids who had worked for me.

We had new desks, new typewriters. The salesmen could take advertisers to lunch anytime they chose. It wasn't until I couldn't think of anything else we needed that Kincaid said, "Okay, how about getting the job done now?"

A few weeks after we all moved to WVLK and Garvice had dinner at the Campbell House for all of the staff and a fine evening it was. I had a chance to compare situations at WKLX and WVLK and those present could appreciate the comparison. But at the same time, I could tell him, and the staff knew, the spot he had put us on.

At most stations, like at WKLX, you could always say, "Well, if we only had this or that we could do a lot better." At WVLK no excuses were left open—we had everything a radio station could need. I wasn't sure I liked it that way. The only thing left was to make WVLK the best station in the market and that means it should make money too.

As long as I knew Garvice, that was his policy. Spend what you have to spend, but just be sure it returns more than you've spent. That wasn't quite all there was to it at that.

I don't know how to describe the top guys who couldn't stand the prosperity Kincaid made possible. Don Horton was one of them. From what I saw and heard Garvice never insisted on the highest moral standards for even his top people and yet—somewhere, he had a line drawn. Go beyond that and there was no return. Ever.

I never knew of a second chance for anybody—even the best ones or the highest-placed ones. Maybe it was allowed, and I just never heard of it. But when anybody crossed whatever "the line" was, in the belief that his case would be an exception, that was his last mistake as an employee of Garvice Kincaid.

That is not to imply that I understood Garvice. I did not. I didn't try. A few people who thought they had him "figured out" were left in a state of surprise and shock. Likely they were those who tried to put the "bite" on him for a half million bucks for some kooky plan.

I attended many meetings at which he presided and at which I cringed during his insults to and berating of others present. How they could take it I never understood. Though these tirades were not directed at me, I'd get a little nauseated and often find an excuse to leave the room.

Never once, in the years I worked for him, did he raise his voice to me. With a grin, he would toss in some sarcastic dig on occasion and then look to me for confirmation of what he had said. I got nothing "heavier" than the slightly sarcastic stuff which he had to manufacture—for the simple reason that I made whatever effort was needed to be positive. I did things the way he wanted 'em done!

I didn't understand Garvice. But he understood me. He knew I couldn't, let's say, be fussed at or "chewed out." I simply couldn't take it and I was always most grateful that he permitted me to continue in his employ by avoiding any of the harsh things toward me that he directed toward "the" others.

Don't get me wrong, please. Not that he would have given one tiny damn if I had walked out. He wouldn't. It was just another of his—I guess—ways of doing things. We had some pretty good arguments at times, and he let me win a few when I had real good facts to back me up. However, at times, even when I had the facts, he still won—because he was Kincaid.

And you know, I didn't mind that. There's no use being as smart as he was if you don't say "no" sometime just to be saying it. In those cases, I'd wrap it up by saying, "Okay, I think you're wrong, but it's your station and I'll do it your way." I remember two such instances when he phoned me after I got back to WVLK and said, "Okay—if you're so smart—you do it the way you want to." I liked him.

I've found a note that reminds me of the "brown bag days" at WVLK. These days were pretty close to our "hot tea" times. About the tea, we had a machine that made boiling hot water and this— the water—we used for instant coffee. Okay, I regret saying that in the staff we had a few hot tea drinkers, and a couple of these weird people converted a few of our coffee drinkers. Now—the usual digression—every time I write the word "weird" (if I haven't used it in a couple of days) I have to look up the spelling. And this time I discovered that "wieners" are "wie." So, if you should write anything about "weird wieners" there's the correct spelling. Incidentally, I was one of those converts—from coffee to hot tea. But just until I was sure I hated the stuff.

I tried that nauseous beverage for a few days, trying to believe it acceptable, then gave up. Should I ever hold office with the power needed, I would make it illegal to serve hot tea. Iced tea? I like it very much. Drinking hot tea for a few days made me wonder about the "happening at Boston"—that tea party at the harbor. I'm inclined to believe that dumping that tea in the water was not a tax protest. I think the dumpers were protesting hot tea.

Now the "brown bag days" at WVLK. Somebody had the idea of bringing lunch from home. Times were pretty good, and we all had lunch money for the restaurants but the "brown bag lunch from home" caught on and soon all the staff on duty at noon was opening their little or big brown bags—making instant coffee (or tea, yuck) and eating in the offices. The novelty wore off after a couple of weeks and we were back in the restaurants at noon. The "brown bag" prologue or preface was used (and I know you are pleased) as an introduction to the item I want to relate. Here it is. I said that times were good at that period, but we went all out on the conservative kick and were parking our Cadillacs and Lincolns and Buicks in a municipal lot on Harrison Avenue. This lot was a bit too far from our studios in the Phoenix Hotel, but we could park there all day for 25¢. Imagine that.

One day I had put my quarter in a meter and was walking— toting my brown bag—to the studios. On the Harrison Avenue viaduct, I was stopped by a panhandler—a bum. Not badly dressed— the bum, that is. This fellow asked for money to buy "something to eat." Instead of giving him a handout or refusing to give, I said, "Look, I'll tell you what we'll do. Let's search each other and the one who has the most money gets to keep it all." This bum took a step back from me—clamped a hand on his pants pocket and in a kind of frightened voice said, "Aw, naw." I said, "Okay, goodbye." After I had walked maybe 25 feet I looked back, and the guy was still standing there staring at me. I would guess he told the story at the next meeting of Professional Panhandlers.

So now I'm "Station Director" at WVLK—not manager. That means when or if anything goes wrong, shall we say, "the protocol" says Kincaid phones Horton, the manager.

I'm handling national business, doing "the man on the street," sports commercials and color and special stuff and sleeping nights and the world is lovely. But somewhere along here Garvice has a heart attack. He must stay at home and after a few months Don and

I go out to his home—at his request. We're to learn how much, if anything, we have coming on our 10% bonus deal.

An accountant, an attorney, and Garvice are there and after some figuring the accountant says, "Ted, it looks like you and Don have $400 each coming to you. I said, "Fine." Garvice said, "You won't have much of that after you pay taxes on it." I said, "It's more than I had when I came in here."

Garvice turned to the accountant and said, "That's not enough—double it anyway." We got $800 each. And I thought of the WKLX owners and wished I could have spent the five years doing for Kincaid what I had done for those awful people.

After the $800 we talked awhile about television. Neither Don nor I had a TV set. Garvice said, "You're in radio, but you ought to know what's going on in television and you can't know anything about it unless you can watch it. Both of you buy TV sets."

I started to say I can't afford it. Garvice said, "Charge them to the station and pay the station $50 a month." "I didn't want to, but he had just given me $800, so we said "okay." I bought a $450 Magnavox and paid $150 for an outside antenna. Six hundred bucks' worth. It's amazing how quickly I figure those things, isn't it?

I paid $50 a month on this $600 for six months ($300). How's that for more instant mathematics? We had another meeting and Garvice asked us if we were paying for our television sets. I said, "I am, I've paid $300 on mine." You see—there's that old maverick policy of staying clear of any "excuse" for fussing or chewing so I won't have to quit.

Don looked kind of silly and said he hadn't been able to pay anything on his—yet. Just six months. Garvice gave him hell and then said, "Ted, I guess you're not as smart as he is, though. Let's just forget the TV payments." Then he chewed Don out again and kidded me for being honest. Anyway, it cost me only $300. As business got better, the bonuses got better—two thousand, five, six, nine, ten, twelve and two consecutive years at $15,000.

The first time I got $15,000 I told Don I thought I'd phone Garvice and thank him. Ralph Worster had given me the check. Don said, "Okay, if you want to." I phoned Garvice and said, "That was a hell of a nice bonus and I wanted to thank you." He said, "Is that all you wanted?" I said, "Yes, sir." He hung up on me.

The next 15 grand, I didn't phone. I told Don, "Hell, if he hung up on me the first time—when I call now, he'll not only hang up but stop payment on the check." A few days later I was in Central Bank and felt a hand on my shoulder—then from behind me, a voice said, "That was a pretty nice bonus this time too, wasn't it?" It was

Garvice. Whoever said they understood the man was wrong. I know damned well I liked him, bonus or not—and I miss him.

If I find this in my scribbled notes later, I can skip it, but right here—every time I drive down High Street and see the beautiful building—Kincaid Towers—I wish devoutly (I think that could be the word) that he could be here to see it. And I sincerely thank the gentlemen who followed through and caused it to be built—surely, just as he wanted it. Aw hell, he would have found a hundred things wrong with it—but why not—it's his.

Whatever the year, it was before the Kentucky Group of banks was being promoted and Central Bank was being heavily advertised. I never liked their newspaper ads because to me they looked like special ads for a discount clothing store fire sale. Big black type stuff. I must have been wrong because the bank got bigger and bigger. At least I could change and, I thought, improve their radio copy.

The outcome was that I was doing about all of their radio copy and looking after the schedule on WVLK. At one point some copy ran too long and Garvice phoned me to change it. I changed some. He phoned again and said he had heard some of the old stuff. Change it all.

I spent an entire day rewriting and rescheduling all Central Bank's radio copy (ads) and then I phoned Garvice to tell him every bit of the Central Bank copy was new and rescheduled. But WVLK had just begun staying on the air all night and we had some Central Bank stuff in the all-night show to which I never listened.

One night or morning at about one o'clock, my phone rings at home. It's Garvice. "You told me Central Bank had all new copy." I said, "It has." He said, "I heard some of the old copy not five minutes ago—good night."

I had to laugh. Here's a guy with a thousand things, important things, to think about. (Like) what to do the next day with a few million dollars he has lying around, but he's phoning me at one in the morning about an old piece of radio copy that might have been heard by a few night watchmen, some cab drivers, and some drunks not eligible for loans.

I phoned the transmitter where the all-night disc jockey worked and asked him to skip any other Central Bank spots, bring in any copy he had, and please put it on my desk. He did. Even without the bonuses—working for Garvice Kincaid was a pleasure. An experience almost to be classified as an adventure.

. . . In those good days of martinis, bonuses and free living in Florida, Don and I shared a lot of it. I knew that Don's income had to be much greater than mine since he was spending at least five times what I spent. I never knew or cared what Horton was paid—and I mean that. That was up to Kincaid.

I was not accustomed to having a lot of money to spend and stayed on the conservative side. Don was not used to having money and went the opposite route. The fact that Garvice gave him hell about it now and then didn't retard him at all—he kept on rolling.

I was invited to share many of these spending expeditions—vacations at White Sulphur Springs and at Sea Island, Georgia. Trips to Florida. A vacation in Cuba. Parties in New York and Chicago were quite ordinary events. And finally skiing in Colorado.

[Claude] Sullivan and his wife shared many of these goodies, but they were a bit on the rushing side for Carlouise and me. Don's invitations were always sincere and made after he made reservations for the Grizzards. I repeat—he was spending Kincaid's money, but he was liberal as hell in doing so. Now I'll tag this with a note about the bonuses. One day Don came in my office, closed the door and almost whispered when he said, "About our bonuses—have you shown 'em on your income tax?"

Now bonuses were paid without any withholding tax. I told Don I had reported all of them. I hated to include them, but I was chicken and what I would have saved in taxes wouldn't be worth the risk. He looked at me in doubt for a minute and said, "Have you really?" I assured him I had reported every dollar and then asked him why he brought it up.

He told me he was being checked and a man from the IRS was in his office right then. They knew he hadn't reported the bonuses—had seen the company records that I had received the same amounts and asked Don whether I had reported mine. That did it. I said, "To hell with them. Have the so and so ask me. Not you."

Don said, "Oh no—please—don't make him mad. He wants to see your returns, too." I told Don I wouldn't show the guy anything unless he came to me and maybe not then. That really shook-up Horton. He said, "I'm already in a jam and you'll just make it worse. As a favor to me—if you really reported the bonuses (he still doubted it)—would you let him see copies of your returns?"

I felt sorry for Horton—no kidding. I said, "Okay—I'll bring them in tomorrow." I went across the hall and told the IRS guy he could see the returns in my office the next day. He said he'd like to see them at his office, and I told him nix. He could look all he wanted to but in my presence in my office. He agreed.

I did my own return in those day and I remember—every time I'd come to the $2,000, $3,000, $5,000 or whatever the bonus, I'd hate like hell to show it because I'd been checked only once in 25 years but boy, was I glad I didn't weaken.

After the guy checked my returns for about three years—I mean three separate returns (he didn't spend that much time on them) they must have been okay because I heard no more about it. I never asked Don what happened in his case. He didn't bring it up again and I forgot it too.

He amazed me at the way he could spend. But—as I have said—he was one of the most unselfish spenders I've ever known. For an Estill County boy, he really learned fast. One thing he never bought was a Cadillac. Lincolns yes. Seems there was—at the time—an unusual sort of feeling among the so-called executives in the Kincaid group about Cadillacs. They shied away from them. Garvice had a new four door Fleetwood sedan each year. The little story that follows might be a clue as to why the others had a—I thought—silly idea about owning Cadillacs.

Seems that some young fellow who managed one of the branch offices of Garvice's loan companies owned a Cadillac. They said the guy was real young and Garvice thought his youth and position as manager with the company just didn't "fit" Cadillac ownership.

Mr. Kincaid passed the word down that it would look better for the company if the lad got rid of the Cadillac and bought another, smaller kind of car. The boy didn't agree. The boy was fired immediately. That did it. I doubt that any other executive from then on would have even rented a Cadillac—[even] out of town!

Frank Trimble and Al Florence—two of Garvice's top and close associates at the time—sort of took "turnabout" in getting Kincaid's year-old Cadillac but that was it. I owned a Cadillac when I went to work for Garvice at WVLK and I'm sure he knew it because he saw me in it many times. I never changed and nothing was even hinted about my changing cars.

I have a feeling that if some of the other and older executives had wanted Cadillac, Garvice wouldn't have given the matter a second thought. I thought his judgment correct, however, in connection with the "youngster." Had I been the boy—I would have felt just as the boy did, I'm sure.

A new Cadillac dealer took over in Lexington and Garvice didn't get along with the new owner of the outfit. So, Mr. "K" began buying Cadillacs in Danville Kentucky, and persuaded at least sixteen others who had bought in Lexington to buy Cadillacs in Danville.

The Lexington dealer told me this—and the number. But by the time Garvice got word to me I had just signed an order in Lexington with the "enemy" dealer. Garvice wanted me to cancel the order. I had ordered some special things on the convertible and had no reason to cancel because they had been real nice to me. Kincaid was persistent.

He knew that Carlouise and I ate breakfast out every morning, so he invited us over to his house to have breakfast with him and Mrs. Kincaid and she, bless her heart, even fixed a country ham breakfast for us.

Garvice spoiled it because he spent the morning and the breakfast with a pen and paper showing me how much he could have saved for me if I'd cancel the order in Lexington and buy in Danville. I could not stop the order I had already signed.

Two years later and time for me to buy another Cadillac. Garvice's feud with the Lexington dealer still is on, and since I knew this time, I don't hesitate in going to Danville to buy. The Lexington dealer heard about it and phoned me to say, "Well Kincaid finally got you, too." I told him he almost got me last time but this time there was no question about where I'd buy although Garvice hadn't said a word.

The car dealer finally figured the squabble was costing him too much and Garvice won. Hell, I never even asked what it was about. But I understood that Garvice had wanted the dealer's business for Central Bank, but he had gone to another bank when he came to Lexington. He, at last, went to Central. I bought my next Cadillac in Lexington and I suppose 16 others did too. The "man on the street" got mixed up in a lot of things—listen to this.

As a result of [Claude] Sullivan's and my broadcasts of Clark County high school basketball we had a lot of friends in that area. One day Garvice phoned me to say he wanted me to go to Winchester with him that night to a meeting. Several people there were planning to build a radio station. Garvice had heard about it and the meeting on the radio project was at the Old South Inn.

He and I were to attend the meeting—uninvited—to advise the people that he and I were going to build a radio station in Winchester and would be in competition with them. He thought he should tell them before they invested in a losing proposition. I wanted no part of this thing, but he said, "You just go along and don't say a word. Your presence will confirm what I have to say to them." Oh man— they were friends of mine!

I went with him to Winchester. We walked in unannounced into the meeting of surprised business men—all of whom knew me quite well and considered me a friend. I wanted to get under the table in spite of their friendly greeting and welcome to me. Garvice, with a bold and yet quite casual manner, interrupted their meeting to tell them of his plans for a radio station in Winchester and we left.

They were dumbfounded (that word shows up here now and then) and I think I was too. On the way back to Lexington I told Garvice I didn't know what he really had in mind, but please, please don't build a station in Winchester. I have checked, but I think they have a couple of them now. I never asked Garvice about the dern thing again—I was afraid he would ask me to go over there on another visit. The people there always seemed glad to see me, so it worked out okay.

For the moment, and for this typing, reluctantly I'll forget Garvice Kincaid. But one thing is quite positive, "As long as I'm around I'll miss him. Lexington, Kentucky should!"

When Horton was at his peak of wheeling, dealing and imitating Garvice, he was—at Kincaid's suggestion I'm sure—aways looking for radio properties to buy. They bought WHOO in Orlando. This, I think, turned into a hell of a good deal eventually and had Don kept his head on straight, it would have been a good deal even sooner. Bill Stakelin is down there now and from all I hear, doing a fine job, bless the little rascal. I'm going to get back to WHOO even though I'm not sure I have notes on it for typing. But right now—this.

About the time Garvice bought WHOO (early 1950's) I had a favorite ballpoint pen! That's right. And what a thing to remember. I'm superstitious and I remember that pen because I'd used it to sign some really good accounts for national business and I hung on to it. The pen had some kind of advertising on it, but I don't know what that was. It finally split and I kept it together with scotch tape.

One afternoon I was patching the pen—for about the third time—with some new tape and across the hall I could hear Don on the phone. He was saying to somebody—"No, we offered them $500,000 for it once and they turned it down. Now we just don't want it. Not even at that."

When he finished the phone conversation I went across the hall to his office and said, "You know, this is a screwy outfit." He looked a little surprised and puzzled and said, "Whatta ya mean, Ted?" I said, "Well, in one office just across the hall there is a Vice President who is nursing and carefully Scotch-taping an old ballpoint pen. A pen with advertising on it, a pen that has split. All this to save a pen."

"But over here—the President is talking—casually—about half million-dollar deal!' Is that sort of thing a paradox?" Anyway, we both laughed about it. Timeout here—I'm going to watch a ball game.

After a long, long time of remembering and scribbling, and then typing and after that typing again and paragraphing, I've reached a genuine "flaky" stage of this ton of pure stuff. Right here I'll kill not two birds with one stone—I'll decimate an entire flock with a teeny pebble.

John Rutledge—one hell of a fine radio man. The Standard Oil Sports Network. First, the network. Standard Oil's [Kentucky] key people were in Lexington. They heard and liked Claude Sullivan (the voice of the Kentucky Wildcats) but they liked the 50,000 watts of WHAS which they were using for sports. Their agency man phoned me to ask whether I could organize a network of small stations which they could use instead of WHAS. They would do this in order to get [Claude] Sullivan.

Standard Oil wanted both football and basketball and that of course, meant daytime and nighttime. I found 17 radio stations, but it was a mess. Not all [were] on at night [and you had to deal with] rates, line charges, two schedules for travel, [and] school fees for broadcasting. At last, I had it finished and submitted to the finest example of a true Southern gentleman. A Mr. Burton Wyatt—the Standard Oil agency man in Atlanta. Hell—there are forty more pages to that but there's the story.

About Rutledge. His station in Owensboro was one of those on the Standard network. I think he was sales manager there. A year or two later the other Owensboro station (newspaper-owned) persuaded Standard to leave Rutledge's station and switch to them. Rutledge fought the deal with more effort, common sense, and sales ingenuity than I'd ever seen or heard of. A real battler even though he was going to be a loser. He impressed the hell out of me.

Garvice and Don were looking for a new manager at WHOO (in Orlando) right after they bought that property. They talked to several prospects and liked none of them and then I thought of Rutledge. I asked them to take a look at Rutledge. He came to Lexington, and he was [made] the new manager at WHOO.

From then on, I had no voice in anything that occurred, and I was sorry because after Don was gone, WHOO lost Rutledge to another Orlando station, and he was tough. Hard times came to WHOO, and in my opinion, it shouldn't have been that way. Hart Hagan, who now runs radio and television for the Kincaid estate, told me not long ago that Rutledge had just bought radio WINN in Louisville from him (Bluegrass Broadcasting). I still think Rutledge is a hell of a radio man.

Incidentally, the Standard Oil Network worked beautifully with Sullivan too. When Claude went with the Cincinnati Reds to do their games he formed Sullivan Enterprises, Inc. and took over the Standard network.

. . . Radio was work, but a hell of a lot of fun and good times too at WVLK in those days. Horton's departure meant my moving up but I'd ten times rather have kept things the way they were. He was a good boy. A hundred times I wished he could have accepted his position and money with better control, bless him.

In the "let's remember trips" section of WVLK I came across another. This one's not as glamourous as Russian tours but far more enjoyable insofar as I was concerned. There was to be a national convention of broadcasters—and this in Los Angeles. I never went to conventions of any kind. Being a genius, I didn't learn anything by attending and I had good food and drink at home.

But the Los Angeles deal—especially since it was in early May—appealed to me. Don, of course, attended all of them. I told him this was one I planned to attend, and he said, "Fine, Garvice and I are going too." I said, "I don't want to go with you and Garvice. I'm going to take Carlouise and drive to Los Angeles and really enjoy a few weeks off." That was great too.

Don said just let him know when I was leaving and planned to return so he could be around most of the time until he and Garvice flew to Los Angeles. This was 1958—I believe. I got a "Triple A" motel book and found what appeared to be a nice motel on Sunset Boulevard and telephoned them to make reservations for several days—I forget how many.

Sometime in April—a few days before we were to leave, I talked to Don and asked him how much [expense] money I should take. He said "Hell, take all you want!" I said, "Except for Los Angeles, we plan to keep moving and looking. I think $800 will do it. I have my credit cards for gas and oil. He couldn't believe me [and] insisted that I take more. Finally, I got $1,000 and told him. That wasn't enough—no kidding.

I went back to the bookkeeper and got another check for $250 and this [money] I put in my luggage and returned to the bookkeeper when we got home. I think I had about $100 of the $1,000 when we returned and this [money] I put aside to apply on my gasoline bills when they came.

Whatever else was said about Horton or the foolish things he did—he was completely without the one thing I dislike most in a person—"tightness" [and] "stinginess"! He spent Garvice's money—I repeat—but he didn't have to let others spend it. I know that the three weeks of the California trip were the most enjoyable Carlouise and I ever had.

Before we left Don asked me to phone him occasionally while we were on our way just in case, he needed help with anything I'd been handling. We left Lexington about 9:00 one morning and I phoned him from Versailles—which was a long-distance call then—about 9:15. When the operator told him long distance was calling and then he heard me on the phone from Versailles it perked up his day. Up to that time he seemed to be handling everything in fine fashion and I complimented him highly.

The next time I phoned Don, Carlouise and I were in Hollywood, and I was using a gold telephone in our beautiful room at the Sunset Sands Motor Hotel. I told Don I had phoned just to tell him we planned to stay there.

Before we left Lexington, he had told me he wasn't sure he and Garvice were coming to Los Angeles and asked me to register for them, get their convention material and show them as staying at the hotel where they had reservation. All of this I did. They never showed up.

I registered—but that was my only participation in the convention. From what I read later I didn't miss anything. I did get luncheon tickets for a special event at the Beverly Wilshire Hotel for the broadcasters' wives. This was a fashion show with a lot of movie and television stars as models. Carlouise and Betty Narz (Tom Kennedy's wife) used the tickets and loved seeing the stars and all the lovely clothes they modeled.

On the renewal application that Bluegrass Broadcasting submitted to the FCC on May 3, 1961, there is no mention of Horton. The major stockholders are listed as Ken Hart, Ralph Worster, Frank Trimble, Garvice Kincaid, Ted Grizzard, and George Webb. In addition, all news announcements about WVLK and Bluegrass Broadcasting were now communicated by Garvice. After Horton left, Garvice promoted Claude Sullivan to the post of executive vice president of Bluegrass Broadcasting. Sullivan had been at WVLK for eleven years serving in various capacities, most notably being the play-by-play announcer for the University of Kentucky Wildcats.

In December 1961, Donald Horton sold his interest in radio station WOMP in Wheeling, West Virginia, to Howard Weiss for $165,000. After 1961, he and his wife owned and operated WWKY in Winchester, Kentucky. Horton and Gerald Cashman, the station's general manager, had purchased it in 1960. Gerald Cashman had also worked at Bluegrass Broadcasting in the 1950s. Cashman left their partnership in May 1965 to pursue an advertising and marketing firm he had started.

Donald Horton died in October 1969, at the age of 47, after suffering several heart attacks. He had owned and operated WWKY in Winchester since leaving Bluegrass Broadcasting and had returned to the University of Kentucky at age 40 and earned a law degree. At his death he was also the assistant Clark County attorney. After his death, his widow, Wilda, took over as president of the company until 1984, when she sold the station to Bayard "Bud" Walters in 1984.

Sullivan–Grizzard Tag Team

In October 1962, Garvice continued to move forward with his broadcasting acquisitions and purchased the Louisville-based radio station WINN-AM for $500,000. He immediately relocated Claude Sullivan to the city where he began his broadcasting career and made him vice president and general manager of WINN. Sullivan also continued his role in announcing UK's football and basketball games. In October 1963, Kincaid and Sullivan added WINN-FM to the Louisville station. After Sullivan moved to Louisville, Ted Grizzard became WVLK's general manager and president of Bluegrass Broadcasting. Some former employees say Grizzard was always the boss. Grizzard would spend almost thirty years with Garvice and Bluegrass Broadcasting, rotating from WVLK to WKYT as needed. In addition, in 1967 he and June Rollings created Lexington's most watched morning talk show at WKYT, *Town Talk*. There was a natural affection for the show, since Grizzard had such a large fan base and Rollings was considered "Lexington's First Lady of Television." At a time when men dominated the airwaves, she was the first woman on Lexington's television and she and Grizzard had an addictive natural chemistry.

An August 10, 1944, ad for Louisville's WHAS radio in Murray State's *Princeton Leader* easily shows why Ted Grizzard was so popular:

HE "AIRS" THE DEPOT *daily*

[Photo: Ted Grizzard interviewing a lady at the bus station with about twenty people watching]

"...Interviews hot off the bus make homespun entertainment for WHAS radio listeners."

TED GRIZZARD . . . the casual conversationalist you hear at four-thirty every afternoon, finds a nugget of news and nonsense in every person he "interviews." The big Irishman claims people as his hobby and vocation . . . and, unlike Sinatra, his fans fall in all age groups. Rated high on listener charts by Hooper and Crossley, he has built up huge followings on southern air, ribbing the public and sponsors alike.

Giving out over a Lexington station for seven years on what is known as a "dead air" program . . . (one not pulling mail), the ether suddenly went editorial on Ted when he dropped a hint at his last broadcast that he was pushing on . . . probably to California, did not have a sponsor, and that only written recommendations carried any weight when applying for a job on radio. Over eight hundred letters poured in . . . representing every level of listener audience.

Ordinarily Grizzard says that the most ardent response comes from children, religious-minded folks and sports fans.

A big, red-haired Irishman with merry blue eyes, Ted takes his stand in the bus terminal at the same hour daily, approaches travel-ridden people from everywhere, engages them in conversation, and within a few moments brings up some item of interest to listeners. Significant example is the interview with a woman whose conversation failed to sparkle until he asked what unusual dishes she had cooked. "I once baked a cat," she answered, "when I was a child."

In demand by Rotary, Lions, Kiwanis, Exchange Club and The American Legion, Ted ad libs his way through unrehearsed programs nimbly leading his audience in a merry chase, at once exciting and informal. Giggle with Ted Grizzard as he "lays 'em in the aisles" of busses . . . just for fun.

Garvice Kincaid could spot talent, and bringing Grizzard to WVLK shortly after acquiring the station was a master stroke of genius. Grizzard had the respect of his peers and the public recognition necessary to attract listeners, and Kincaid had the wealth necessary to finance their employment. Garvice was playing the long game and viewed his expenditures for important employees as an investment and not an expense. It was a luxury he had, since he was always spending only his own money. Most of his partners were strawmen, and because he always had actual or contractual controlling interest, his decisions were "the" decisions! In addition, Kincaid understood he was a big fish in a little pond and so most of his interest was focused on Lexington and Kentucky, where his wealth could influence the fishbowl. For instance, Garvice understood the importance of UK sports and its impact on the community, and that he who controls the UK microphone has immediate access to most of the public. The "voice of the wildcats" was an advertising magnet.

His approach to building a management structure was something that many other business entities could not afford to do and it's one reason so many of the staff at his business interests had such long careers with them. As WVLK's Ted Grizzard said: "I wished I had worked for him my whole life, when he said, "Thank you," you could put that in the bank." What Mr. Kincaid lacked in personal skills he made up for in how he rewarded people.

This may sound odd or unusual, but employees at Kincaid's business organizations tended to bond together like a family. I witnessed it at Kentucky Central Life Insurance, and I think WVLK and WKYT and the other organizations also demonstrated a similar relationship. People like belonging to successful organizations, and Garvice's companies were successful. Kincaid wanted to be number #1 in whatever he did, and while most people agree Garvice was a difficult person to deal with, his desire for success brought a lot of pride to the employees of his businesses.

"Job satisfaction" is a consultant buzzword, and it has meant many things over the decades of its use. At Garvice's businesses, it wasn't as much about your paycheck as the feeling of success and overall job enjoyment a person had. Yes, people were usually under a lot of pressure to do better, and yes, Kincaid's demands could be unreasonable, but you didn't see people leaving in droves. Garvice's companies tended to have a lot of people who worked for them for twenty, thirty, and forty years. Kincaid's companies tended to pay a slightly above-average wage, so it wasn't the money. I personally believe a lot of loyalty was created because of the relationships people built, the success of the individual organizations, and finally how important and appreciated these businesses were to the Lexington community. Old money Lexington may not have appreciated Garvice Kincaid, but it certainly appreciated what his businesses and employees brought to Lexington.

I mention the above because Bluegrass Broadcasting had two sets of employees, the old guard at the radio station and the new up and comers at WKYT, which Kincaid acquired in 1967. While both employee groups were part of Bluegrass Broadcasting, they were housed in separate facilities and operated independently of each other, and yet, both entities had those same familiar employee relationship bonds. Everyone always struggled to make Garvice happy, but they did their work as a quasi-family. Garvice was like the high school or college football coach the players respected, but they hated to feel the pain of his disappointments.

Paul Dunbar is a great example of someone who found a home with a Kincaid organization. Paul was with WVLK when Kincaid acquired the station in 1951. He was the chief engineer for WVLK and is credited with being involved in building every station WVLK had for the next forty years. (As a side note, he isn't the person who a Lexington, Kentucky, high school was named after—that was African American poet Paul Laurence Dunbar (1872–1906), whose parents had been enslaved in Kentucky.)

Paul was born in Princeton, Kentucky, on December 3, 1921, and was the son of the late Leonard and Ada McGregor Dunbar. Paul was a 1940 graduate of Caldwell County High School, attended the University of Kentucky, and was a World War II US Navy veteran.

Paul began his radio career with WVLK in 1947 in the Versailles library and was instrumental in moving the studios to Lexington's Lafayette Hotel. He also designed, and oversaw the construction of, the studios when the station was moved to the Phoenix Hotel and to its present-day studios at Kincaid Towers. In addition, he designed and oversaw construction of the original WVLK transmitter building on Yarnallton Pike and later the construction of the replacement building to house the transmitter and auxiliary studios. That building today is appropriately called the Paul Dunbar Building.

In the early '60s, Paul built WVLK-FM, designing and installing one of the first automated systems ever used by a broadcast station. Later he designed and oversaw the increase in power to 100,000 kw and an increase in tower height to over 900 feet. He was also responsible for designing and building the first remote broadcasting studio in Kentucky when he built the WVLK mobile van. In the 1950s, when radio stations were being built in Frankfort, Richmond, Winchester, Danville, and other small towns around Central Kentucky, Paul was the man called upon to advise and assist in their completion.

Paul was also the field engineer for those early broadcasts of the legendary University of Kentucky play-by-play announcer Claude Sullivan. While Claude provided the description, reading reports from the teletype in a studio during the away games, it was Paul who provided the sound effects, with crowd noise, bands, and assorted sound effects to make the games sound as if Claude was there in person. Finally, he used his knowledge of the broadcasting industry to educate many future engineers, announcers, and managers over the years.

When Lester Flatt and Earl Scruggs traveled around the South doing weekly radio shows, it was Paul who was the engineer for their performance on WVLK. He also engineered a weekly program featuring the Davis Sisters, one of whom was Skeeter Davis. All are now in the Country Music Hall of Fame.

As you can see, while many people in Lexington have probably never heard of Paul Dunbar;[16] he was a very important person in Kincaid's broadcasting business and one who remained with the organization for forty years. With his knowledge and skills, Paul could have landed a position anywhere, but he was already working at the number one radio station in Lexington, and he liked what he was doing.

Claude Sullivan was one of the first voices of the University of Kentucky men's basketball program and became a nationally known sportscasting pioneer. His career followed Kentucky's rise to prominence as he announced the first four NCAA championship title games under Coach Adolph Rupp and

---

16   He wasn't the namesake of Paul Laurence Dunbar High School in Lexington.

covered scrimmages during the canceled 1952–1953 season. Claude's mentor was Ted Grizzard, and by 1963, Ted had long since moved the majority of his on-air time to non-sports programming. His *Man on the Street* show had already been a WVLK fan favorite for years.

Claude began his full-time UK broadcasting career in 1947, at WKLX, at the age of twenty-three. The 1940s witnessed a tremendous growth in sports broadcasting across the country, and Sullivan, as a seventeen-year-old from Winchester, Kentucky, had entered the field when it was still a novel occupation. He covered some early UK football teams under coach Paul "Bear" Bryant and UK basketball coach Adolph Rupp's first two NCAA championship teams. Some of the players on Rupp's famed "Fabulous Five" squad were older than Claude, but his career was taking off, and he enjoyed covering scrimmages during the canceled 1952–1953 season following the NCAA sanctions scandal.

Sullivan also revolutionized the coverage of the UK football program with the introduction of a coach's show with Bear Bryant—a national first that gained significant attention and later became a staple at other institutions. Sullivan's reputation in Kentucky eventually propelled him to Cincinnati, where he became the voice of the Reds, and even to the 1960 Summer Olympic Games in Rome.

During the height of his career, Sullivan was named Kentucky's Outstanding Broadcaster by the National Association of Sportscasters and Sportswriters for the eighth consecutive year. His success was tragically cut short in 1967, when he passed away from throat cancer at the young age of forty-two.

Ted Grizzard's last sports broadcast was in 1968, with Ralph Hacker. The duo broadcast Claude's son Alan Sullivan's last high school football game at Tates Creek, against Frank Lemaster and Doug Flynn's Bryan Station High team. Ted paid tribute to his career with Claude and also said hello and acknowledged the support of Alyce Sullivan during her husband's career as she left the stadium that evening. Ted Grizzard had officially retired from broadcasting altogether by the time WVLK celebrated its fiftieth anniversary in 1979, and he passed away in Lexington in the spring of 1985 at the age of eighty, after almost a half-century in broadcasting.

Kincaid: Managing Radio and Transitioning to Television

Another person important to Kincaid was Ray Holbrook, who joined WVLK in September 1949. He was already on the staff when Garvice acquired the company in 1951 but soon that year had to leave for the Air Force, in which he was a captain. Ray returned to WVLK in 1953 and remained there until Kincaid and Horton transferred him to Orlando, Florida, in 1959 to be the station manager for radio station WHOO-AM and FM. Kincaid had acquired the station in June 1958.

In 1960, thirty-one-year-old Holbrook was lured back to Kentucky and away from Kincaid and WHOO to be an owner and the president and general manager of Danville's new radio station, WHIR-AM. He did that job for about eight years and then returned to Bluegrass Broadcasting and Kincaid in January 1969. Garvice and Hart Hagan had recruited him back and made him executive vice president and general manager of WVLK. The next year, Kincaid put him in charge of WKYT, which he'd just acquired. Before Ray Holbrook returned to WVLK, and after Donald Horton had left, Kincaid had depended on Ted Grizzard and George Webb to keep things on track.

In 1964, Kincaid finished moving Kentucky Central Life Insurance from Anchorage, Kentucky, to its new home in the remodeled Lafayette Hotel building. This was a major endeavor because much of the Anchorage staff didn't want to relocate to Lexington. In addition, Garvice and his chief insurance lieutenant at the time, Paul Carr, had acquired several insurance companies and blocks of business. The extra business meant that Kentucky Central Life's total staff needed to almost double.

Before relocating Kentucky Central Life to its new headquarters, Garvice and Carr made a major upgrade to the company's data processing equipment. For a short time, Kentucky Central Life probably had the most technically sophisticated computer system in the state. Kincaid was proud of his computer system and used it to process both the insurance company's business and Kentucky Finance's business.

The presidential election was approaching in the fall of 1964, and Garvice had an idea that was marketing genius to promote his new computer system, Kentucky Central Life, and WVLK. He worked with Paul Carr, who was an actuary trained in statistics, to create a program that his organizations could use to predict the presidential winner in Fayette County and the state. Charlie Thomas, Kincaid's head of public relations, understood which precincts would be important to follow and set up a network of people to call in the vote totals as they were announced. Paul Carr would then have this information programmed into Kentucky Central's mainframe computer, and his program would compute an outcome based on this limited data.

On November 10, 1964, the following large ad was displayed in the *Lexington Herald-Leader*:

HISTORY WAS MADE ELECTION DAY 1964 AT 6:22½ P.M. ON WVLK

No other radio station, no television station, no network, no newspaper, no wire service so fast and so accurate in predicting the outcome of the Presidential race in Fayette County and Kentucky on last Tuesday, November 3, as Radio Station WVLK. Within 22 ½ minutes after the polls closed at 6:00 P.M., WVLK announced that President Johnson was certain to carry the county and the Commonwealth by a substantial margin.

As a public service, WVLK arranged with the electronic data processing staff at Kentucky Central Life Insurance Company's national headquarters in Lexington to forecast the election on the basis of returns from key precincts in Fayette County. Thus at 6:22 ½ P.M., we were able to predict that President Johnson would receive 56.4 percent of the vote in the County (we missed the actual count by nine-tenths of one percent!) and 62 percent of the vote in Kentucky (we erred by 2.2 percent in this instance). In terms of actual votes, our prediction in the county missed the mark by only 307 votes. In the state race, we scooped everyone by a matter of hours.

THAT WAS ELECTION NIGHT, 1964. BUT NIGHT OR DAY, YEAR AFTER YEAR, MORE PEOPLE LISTEN TO WVLK THAN TO ANY OTHER LEXINGTON STATION. WVLK IS DEEPLY GRATEFUL.

PULSE RADIO SURVEY
METROPOLITAN LEXINGTON – JULY 1964

[Table showing statistics]

Radio WVLK

590 ON YOUR DIAL

WVLK's history-making election night coverage was made possible by:

[Table showing list of eight sponsors, all independent of Kincaid]

Kincaid always wanted the public to know his business interests were the best, and the 1964 election-night ad promoted WVLK at the expense of all the area's other media outlets.

In 1969, Garvice recruited Holbrook from the Danville station to help him with a problem. Ray Holbrook was a well-known, popular, on-air talent and news announcer recognized for his booming voice. He had spent a short time at WLEX before joining WVLK, and in 1963, his position and star were rising with Garvice. Kincaid already knew that Grizzard, who was nearing age sixty, wanted to cut back his hours. He also appreciated Holbrook's serious personality and penchant for knowing the details, which mirrored Garvice's own personality. In 1959, when Kincaid allowed Horton to transfer Holbrook to Orlando, Florida, to be the WHOO-AM and FM station manager, he hadn't anticipated Horton's personal problems derailing his career.

Holbrook had worked in sales at WVLK in its early days, and in 1968 WVLK was in danger of not having its license renewed. The FCC had raised what it called "serious questions" about certain billing practices and commercial time standards at the station. The FCC had announced there would be hearings on the matter, and Holbrook was brought in to work on satisfying its concerns and getting the station back on track with its FCC license renewal. In 1967, the FCC began investing an alleged $35,000 in overcharges for advertising involving twelve of the company's advertisers.

When the hearings took place in August 1970, the *Lexington Herald-Leader* reported, on August 26, 1970, the following:

FCC Hearing of WVLK License Renewal Continues

The hearing opened yesterday and FCC hearing examiner Millar French heard testimony from H. Hart Hagan Jr. president of Bluegrass Broadcasting Co., which owns the station, and John Clines, secretary-treasurer.

Hagan said he was ordered in 1967 by Lexington financier Garvice D. Kincaid—who controls Blue Grass Broadcasting— to investigate "billing improprieties" concerning the station's advertising accounts.

He said former station manager George Webb had made inconsistent statements about the billing procedure used by WVLK.

Clines testified about programming at the station, rescheduling of advertising spots, program pre-emptions and conversations he had with station personnel.

The hearing is a probe of WVLK's:

- Alleged misrepresentation of the station's commercial airtime standards.
- Keeping of the station log and other records required by the FCC.
- Compliance in airing public service announcements.

And the FCC will determine if the station misrepresented facts in exchange of correspondence after the Federal agency's initial letter of inquiry about the station procedures.

The license was to have been renewed in 1967. Continuances in the case have delayed the renewal . . .

The FCC will determine if the station—which has a slogan of "radio in the public interest"—exercised responsibility in management.

The paper also pointed out importantly that "Kincaid also controls local television station WKYT and other radio stations in Kentucky," so this issue potentially might lead to more significant consequences for the rest of Bluegrass Broadcasting.

In the end, the FCC voted to approve the station's license renewal and Ray Holbrook, now Garvice's hero, was promoted to executive vice president overseeing all of Bluegrass Broadcasting, which included all the radio stations and WKYT television. Garvice even testified at the hearing, stating he had formed the radio station in 1952 to have "the best station around, based upon public acceptance of its programming." The FCC approved WVLK's license renewal for only one year to assess the remedies put in place by the station. The FCC called the station "derelict in its responsibilities" but commended it for addressing the issue, implementing new procedures, and providing "complete restitution to the advertisers who were overbilled." General manager George Webb appeared to get the worst of its remarks, in that he was criticized for "depending on his memory when completing paperwork," and the FCC said that "it's apparent that his memory is inadequate for the task." In August 1973, George Webb died, and his obituary reports that many of the station staffers were his pallbearers, but more importantly, four of his honorary pallbearers were Garvice Kincaid, T. C. Quisenberry, Ralph Worster, and H. Hart Hagan Jr.

Ray Holbrook managed WVLK and WKYT until 1976. At the age of fifty-three, he left Bluegrass Broadcasting to become vice president of the Radio Advertising Bureau, where he served an area that included Washington, D.C., Boston, and Buffalo, New York, for eight years. The year he left was shortly after Kincaid's death in November 1975 and the beginning of Kincaid's Committee's oversight. One has to wonder how much this significant oversight change had to do with Holbrook's decision to leave.

One accomplishment that Ray gets credit for is recruiting Leslie C. Veal to WVLK. Veal, also known as "Captain Tag," was a Lexington radio fixture in the 1970s and 1980s. Many in Lexington believe WVLK pioneered rush-hour traffic reports from the air, but actually WLAP started broadcasting air-traffic reports in June 1965. Pilot John Hunt of the civil air patrol flew the plane and officer Don Duckworth provided the report on WLAP.

Veal became part of the program in 1968, and then WLAP dropped the program in 1970 due to its costs. Veal's flying career had begun in 1940 at the former Cool Meadow Airport near the present day I-75 and Newtown Pike interchange. "I was in high school [at Henry Clay] and just got the idea that I would like to fly," Veal said in a March 30, 1973, *Courier Journal* article. "I started saving lunch money to fly Piper Cubs. Fly lessons were about $6 an hour then." He then, after messing up his Air Force physical, served in the Army for three years during World War II. After returning to Lexington, he began a career as an independent flight instructor.

Captain Tag originated his eye-in-the-sky reports at WVLK in November 1972 and became a Lexington legend. He started with Dave Murray and then became the on-air sidekick of Jack "Catfish" Pattie in 1975. The tag-team fit together like an old married couple. Tag could comment on Lexington's traffic conditions and suggest alternate routes for drivers and at the same time joke and tease Jack Pattie. He was famous for signing off his airtime with "See you on the flipside, Jack," alluding to how disc jockeys in the old days played music on two-sided 45s. Jim Jordan, WVLK's program director during those days, described the station's work this way: "We thought there was a definite need for this type of public service. There are a number of bogged-down spots in Lexington traffic, and we thought that if somebody could get a bird's eye view of these spots . . . he might be able to point them out and get people to work and home a little bit more safely."

Captain Tag retired from broadcasting and air-traffic reporting in May 1987. Letters to the editor described his retirement as the "end of an era" and described how people listened to his broadcast or would scan the sky for his "little red helicopter." While Kincaid and WVLK didn't originate Lexington's air-traffic reporting on the radio, most people give him and WVLK credit for making it a listener staple for so many years. It was also a commercial success for WVLK. It was so popular that the station always had a commercial sponsor for the broadcast.

Ray Holbrook eventually returned to Kentucky, in 1982. He had been working as general manager of WOND-AM/WMGM-FM in Atlantic City, New Jersey, and returned to run station WTKC-AM in Lexington. WTKC-AM was a country music station that would soon compete with WVLK-FM when the latter changed its easy-listening format to country music in 1982. It was a controversial move for Ralph Hacker, who had become the station manager in 1974, but soon rocketed the FM station to first place in the ratings. Holbrook's timing could have been better, because about a month after he took over WTKC-AM, WVLK-FM became K-93 Country, eroding WTKC's audience, as listeners became attracted to country music on their FM dial. The FM station made it too difficult for WTKC-AM to compete. The owners of WTKC-AM sold the station about three years later and it was converted to a talk-radio format.

Holbrook returned to WVLK-AM as a newscaster in 1997, and in November 2000, he was included in a four-person roundtable discussion about the "Historic Aspect of Election 2000." The panel included Holbrook, Jack Pattie, Sue Wylie, and David Kruser and was promoted as "well known and respected voices." Ray was seventy-one years old and by 2000 had already had a broadcasting career that spanned over half a century. In 2001, he left the station to become general manager for four Clear Channel Communications radio stations in Frankfort, Kentucky. At a farewell lunch of prime rib and barbecued ribs with his friends and colleagues at WVLK, he said, "Obviously the business is still in my blood. I hope it won't be over until I die."

Ray died in November 2014 at the age of eighty-five. Besides his broadcasting career, Ray became well known as a speaker and the voice of numerous venues and ad campaigns, including for Midway College, Citizens Commerce National Bank, Jack Kain Ford, and the public service announcements at the Blue Grass Airport (which he did free of charge).

After Claude Sullivan left, his successor at WVLK for his sports show, Wiedemann Sports Eye, was another young talent from Lexington, Tom Hammond. Tom had worked at WVLK while Claude Sullivan was there and knew of Claude's reputation at the station but had never worked directly with him. Tom was influenced equally by Sullivan and Caywood Ledford, having worked with Ledford and Mike Battaglia at Keeneland. Tom was let go at WVLK and soon moved on to television and Channel 18, Lexington's NBC affiliate. From there, he became involved with the first Breeders' Cup held at Keeneland in 1984 and worked as a contract employee for NBC. That catapulted him into a career with NBC that included the Barcelona Olympics four years later. Tom would go on to broadcast each of the summer and winter games until he retired in 2018. In an interview about Sullivan, Tom recalled, "Claude in his convertible with the 'whiplash' antenna on the trunk, driving down Reed Lane near Lafayette High School in his neighborhood . . . . It was a big deal to the players when Claude came to broadcast our high school games."

I have written previously that many people who were employees of Mr. Kincaid's businesses agree that there was a family-type spirit of camaraderie. In Ted Grizzard's book #1 is Chicken, he described some social interactions that support this thesis:

Christmas time at WVLK! That was something to see and to hear! All available time for the week preceding Christmas would be sold days in advance. Copy written—schedules made. The staff would have little to do but check in and then check out to go Christmas shopping.

The male members would begin imbibing. That last is a good word. The tree is up in the reception room. Names are drawn for the exchange of gifts which must be in the ridiculous category. The gifts, of course, although we had some unusual names [employees] on the payroll. Eggnog, whiskey, cookies and other goodies had been ordered and we [would] just spend the time waiting.

And mentioning "goodies." Did I mention this earlier? Sara Hensley, our bookkeeper, had done some shopping for George Webb. He gave her a check to pay for whatever she bought for him. On the face of the check on that line that is marked "for," Webb had written "goodies." Sara would not accept the check. She said the gossipy people at Central Bank would see and misinterpret that word "goodies" and there was enough talk about the WVLK staff already—she was not going to have them saying she had sold Webb her "goodies."

Little things but laughable things that made WVLK radio real nice. By the 20th of December the sales staff would have stopped even "courtesy" calls, and I can still see and hear [George] Webb, the sales manager, as he strolled the corridor, loaded with bourbon and mumbling, "C'mon Christmas."

We had an assistant bookkeeper. A young lady who was so shy she would almost blush if you even looked at her. She said she had a three-year-old daughter, and I figured the child must be adopted because I just couldn't imagine her—well, anyway—hell, she might have locked all that bashfulness in her desk when she went home at night.

Also—we had but one restroom on the floor with the [Phoenix Hotel] studios and offices. Boys and girls often hit head on at this tiny facility. Our Chief Engineer was (and still is) Paul Dunbar. One day [George] Webb and I were in the hall just outside of the restroom door and out comes the bashful bookkeeper. She blushed at our even being so near the door and almost fainted when Webb, in a most casual tone, asked her, "Is Dunbar in there?" She ran without answering.

There was a lumber company for which I did a lot of "personalized" commercials. I liked the owners—a young fellow and his dad—and the "pitch" for them must have been okay cause they stayed with us exclusively for a long time.

One day during the Christmas "relaxing" period, I came in the office and Webb invited me into his office to have a drink. Fine. We talked and had a few more from a quart of Old Fitzgerald. After a while I told Webb I had some work to do and started to leave.

As I stood up, Webb handed me the bottle of whiskey—what was left—and said, "By the way—your lumber company sponsor left this for you just before you came in." He had been treating me and himself to my Old Fitzgerald and he'd had a few before I arrived. They were good and enjoyable days at WVLK.

Several of us bought eggs from some country lady who lived near Versailles. Sara (our bookkeeper) lived over there and she would bring the eggs to us. Sara may have stopped in Kroger's and got the eggs and told us a lie about this old country lady because everybody had a racket going in those days.

Seriously, they were good, fresh country eggs. I was out of town when Sara brought my eggs on one delivery day, but I picked them up at the office the next day. Carlouise and I ate breakfast at home in that era and the ensuing event (how about that "ensuing") may have been one of the reasons we cut out that silly "home breakfast" stuff.

Anyway, I was shaving when Carlouise came in to show me the first bad egg—real dark brown. Then she's back with the third and fourth bad ones and she's almost in tears. It finally dawned on old stupid me. The whole damned dozen had been hardboiled—returned to the carton—taken back to the station where I got 'em.

That's a sample of the awe and respect which I, the Vice President and Station Director, commanded from my employees! They were awfully nice days, and nutty and nice employees. [George[Webb had a good beer account (a good account that had a beer distributorship would be better—I don't know about the beer), and the distributor wanted Webb to go with him to Cleveland to the brewery to get even more radio money for WVLK and the Lexington market.

That was fine with Don and me, we (also) wanted Webb to go. And I went to a friend of mine at Greyhound—an executive there. I got this friend to furnish me a roundtrip ticket for two —Lexington to Cleveland and return (of course). It was a beautiful job of about four yards of bus tickets. Properly stamped with bus depot changes in Cincinnati and the whole works.

The afternoon of the day before Webb was to take his client to Cleveland, he, Don and I met in Don's office. After some discussion Don presented Webb with his transportation. The round-trip bus tickets. I thought Webb was going to cry. We began selling Webb on the virtues of bus travel—time to talk with his client—the scenery—relaxation—"the fun of getting there." We did a whale of a selling job—almost to the point of getting Webb to accept the phony bus tickets. But not quite.

Then Don told him that he—Don—had already phoned the airline and had the reservations for the two of them. The shake-up we gave Webb almost made up for the whisky he took from me and the eggs he had hardboiled.

There's yet to be "much ado" about WVLK. But before I go astray—a big salute to the female members of the staff. Several of the super girls moved in from WKLX in 1952 and we were lucky as hell in adding good ones from then on.

I know we always had the most intelligent and efficient and nice to look at young women anywhere. Not only did they possess the attributes mentioned—they were a real pleasure as business associates. Oh, now and then we'd run into a clinker, but not for long. When I think of how little I have accomplished—how vast my ignorance—I'm consoled to a degree with the thought that I, somehow, was able to acquire the help of intelligent people.

Every now and then I hear from the good ones—those I thought above average—and it's nice to know that they recall with pleasure having been associated with me. Really nice. One of the "above average" of whom I was especially fond, wrote to me a few weeks ago.

She's now the editor of a weekly newspaper she and her family bought in a small town in Virginia—she sent a copy of the paper and a damned good one it is. She, her husband, mother, and children were in Lexington, and they took me to lunch. I enjoyed the hell out of the visit. The lunch was good too. Damn—they were all such smart kids.

The lady who is now the editor is the one who would come in my office every morning to discuss any traffic (radio logging) problems she might have. Quite often Webb would be in there just visiting and telling me his troubles. 'Most every day this young lady would hear Webb say he had not slept well the night before and had taken sleeping pills.

After hearing this story over and over, one day she said, "Mr. Webb, those things are habit-forming." Webb looked at her and in a most serious tone said, "Oh no, not as long as you keep taking 'em."

Webb too is the one who made [an] application for a job with a pharmaceutical firm for a sales job. He told them he had one year of pre-medicine at Transylvania College and spelled both medicine and Transylvania incorrectly. They didn't hire him and told him why.

A reminder that at WVLK, I'm "Station Director" and Horton is the "General Manager." Horton was involved in so many things he had little time for general managing, and I knew his social life was taking up much too much of his time. This was up to him and Garvice and WVLK, was actually left to me, but I did not want that "manager" title or official responsibility. WKLX had left some scars.

Horton came to me a couple of times and asked me to take over the station, but I refused. The day finally came, as I was afraid it would, when Horton's "affairs" would destroy him. By now there were several radio stations involved under the title of Horton-Kincaid Radio Stations and one day when Don was in my office I said, "Don, why don't you slow up, 'podnah' [partner] and save some money?" In an almost plaintive tone he said, "Hell, Ted, I wish I could, but I just can't."

I wondered. Don had seen the destruction of other executives in the Kincaid organization, but I suppose that, like the others, he thought Garvice would go that extra step with him. Maybe Garvice did.

One afternoon Horton came in my office, and I wasn't sure I was seeing things right. He was crying. He stood by my desk and said, "Would you run this place for a while?" There was something different in his asking this time. I said, "Sure."

We went to his office and Frank Trimble and Ralph Worster were there. Horton sat and then said, "Garvice has fired me. I'd appreciate it if you'd run WVLK for a while." I told him I'd be glad to and was sorry as hell if he were leaving. The three of them then left.

Kincaid came over to the station two days later and made it official. He had had enough of Don, his women, spending and his neglect of the business. I think Horton was already paying alimony to his first wife. He was married and had twins by his second and current wife. Naturally, I never knew the whole story but understood that Garvice gave one radio station to Don's second wife and the twins and another station to Don, which Don sold.

Horton went to law school and on his second try he passed the bar examination. I don't know what he was doing when he died. Heart attack. I think his second wife still benefits in some way or maybe still owns the radio station, but I never inquired. I saw Don a few times after he left WVLK and when he passed the bar exam, he came by home on Sunday to tell me about it. I know this, I had hoped Garvice would take him back, and I would have welcomed him anytime.

Seems like I would remember taking over a radio station, but I don't. I don't even know whether it was 1960 or 1961. [George] Webb and I were very close as working partners, both at WKLX and

WVLK, and when I moved in at WVLK, I asked Garvice if Webb might also have the 10% share of profits that I enjoyed. He said if I wanted it like that—okay—but he thought I was too damned generous. I felt Webb would earn it—and he did—but not for long.

. . . Now back to radio for a few minutes. When I first met Don [Horton] he was "program director" for the almost defunct (there's another good word) WVLK. Ed Willis was managing WLAP, and I was managing WKLX.

I don't know why the three of us met but it was for some reason that amounted to nothing. Don was the meek, say almost-nothing type of young fellow. With Garvice to back him he became what is known today as "tiger." WVLK made money, but today, with WVLK sales about four times what they were when I ran it, I would guess they're doing rather well. Inflation, sure—but still it's one hell of a job and I get a kick out of knowing the job the young people there are doing.

Now—the sorry part. And this I'll reduce to the minimum. About five years after Don left, that gave me a total of five years of the ordeal at WKLX and then five more of running WVLK. The WVLK part was fine—but in all those years I'd still been the man on the street, along with all the sports color, special events and commercial work and copywriting and I was tired. I asked Garvice to let me turn WVLK over to the Sales Manager. He didn't like the idea and wanted to think about it.

A few weeks later I asked Garvice again and told him I'd be right next door to the new manager, but I'd make no suggestions or offer help unless he asked for it. I'd do all my other chores but, at least, I hoped I wouldn't take the station home with me at night. He still didn't think it [was] a good move but okayed it. Typical of Kincaid there was no mention of my getting less money and my salary or bonus arrangement was not changed.

However, it hardly had time to because Garvice was right, and the change was the worst thing I'd ever done. Our excellent sales manager turned out to be just as wrong as a manager. A smoldering feud between him and the bookkeeper flared and she, with evidence of his mishandling of accounts, went directly to the FCC instead of to me, Garvice or Hart Hagan who had succeeded Ralph Worster. WVLK was in bad trouble and on a temporary license. More on this later.

[Note: Ted Grizzard discusses Kincaid's purchase of WKYT, and his move to television and then reflects back on what was happening at WVLK.]

The FCC mess at WVLK is getting worse and the manager has moved out and away from the station. Garvice told me to move in again—more as a figurehead than anything else, but he wanted somebody there. Hart Hagan really had the burden of straightening out the trouble.

I spent the afternoons telephoning advertisers I knew asking them if they would write a letter saying that WVLK had handled their accounts honestly and fairly. Everyone said they would. I also phoned those prominent citizens with whom I was acquainted, asking them for letters of recommendation for WVLK along the lines of public service. We needed all of this for the Washington attorneys.

So I'm at [Channel] "27" before 9 in the morning, at WVLK by 10:30, on the "street" at 12:15, and back at WVLK after lunch to do more telephoning for the rest of the day. The "man on the street" is pretty busy.

The slow battle with the FCC grinds on. Hagan has brought Holbrook in to manage WVLK and I'm not needed as that "figurehead" any more but am needed to go on making the phone calls and seeking help from advertisers and friends of WVLK. Holbrook had been with WVLK a long time ago as program director—he had been with the company at WHOO in Florida, and when Hagan hired him, he was managing WHIR in Danville. In my opinion—a good, honest and likeable fellow.

By now it's August 1969, and Holbrook comes in one day to tells me that WVLK had suggested to "Webber's Sausage" that a higher rate for the "street" program is in order. Webber's said no. Holbrook asked me whether I'd like for the station to try to sell the program to somebody else.

For a long time, the "street program" had been a bit of a battle, what with all the other things I'd had to do. It was an ideal time to quit. Forgetting the start in 1936—the time in Louisville too—I'd been doing the program for about 22 years since I came back to Lexington.

I'll wrap it up as briefly as possible with a few things that stand out. When "Honey Krust" bread, my first and longtime sponsor, sold out to "Rainbo," somebody asked me what that would do to the "street" program. I remember telling the person that the bakery sale was due to my program. I had such a tight contract they had to sell the "Honey Krust" bakery to get rid of the street program.

You may remember—if you're real, real, old—that at some time all bakery breads went to a different style or texture. I didn't like them. Still don't. "Rainbo" made a bread unlike the "Honey Krust" bread I liked, and I didn't want to recommend "Rainbo." I knew that. Then the "Rainbo" advertising agency man came to Lexington, and he started off by saying he wasn't sure whether "Rainbo" would keep the "man on the street" program. I let the young fellow get about halfway through his talk and interrupted him to advise that I was sure "Rainbo" would not keep the program. Because I had no intention of doing it for "Rainbo."

So help me, he then began selling me on doing the program for them. I never knew why he began the way he did. Maybe he thought he'd get a lower rate. He got a shock and no program. I forget the date of the talk with the "Rainbo" man, but WVLK phoned "Webber Sausage" that afternoon and they started with the "street" program the next day. Over that last span of 22 years there was no written copy for "Honey Krust" or for "Webber's Sausage." I'd been many times to see both products made and liked what I saw. That's all I needed.

I think we sold a lot of sausage and I doubt that any radio program sold as much and yet—I've never heard a word from the Webber people acknowledging what I thought was a pretty good job. That sort of disappointed me.

I do remember this. On the last "street" broadcast, Ed Ashford (WLAP's play-by-play sports announcer and sport editor for the Lexington Herald-Leader) came by to be on with me. A lot of others too, but Ed reminded me that he had been on my first broadcast in 1936 and wanted to be on the final one. I appreciated the hell out of that.

As for Garvice Kincaid, in the *Lexington Herald-Leader* on December 9, 1977, Ted is interviewed about his career. He had retired from radio and television broadcasting in 1973 and Garvice Kincaid had been dead since November 1975. In the article he says, "Garvice Kincaid was tough, mean, a smart aleck. . . . I wish I had worked for him all my life. When he said, "Thank You," you could put that in the bank. Ted Grizzard understood that Garvice lacked patience and didn't suffer fools gladly, but he appreciated talented people who could get the job done.

Around 1967 and in conjunction with the FCC license mess, Hart Hagan took more control of managing the radio and television stations. He brought in former employee Ray Holbrook as general manager in January 1969 to help resolve the FCC licensing issue. George Webb stayed with the station until he died in 1973, but Ray Holbrook was now executive vice president of Bluegrass Broadcasting and general manager of WVLK. Hart Hagan was now president of Bluegrass Broadcasting, with Kincaid as its chairman. Holbrook would stay with Bluegrass broadcasting until August 1976.

During the 1960s and 1970s, several other nationally and regionally recognized people were involved in the running of WVLK and Kincaid's other radio stations: William (Bill) Stakelin, Jim Jordan, and Ralph Hacker. All three worked together at WVLK, at one time or another, but each would have a different career path. Bill Stakelin was vice president and general manager in 1970 to mid-1974, but then he was transferred to Orlando, Florida, to help run WHOO. He was from Georgetown, Kentucky, and had started hanging around the local radio station, WAXU. Robert Johnson put WAXU on the air in 1957 at 1580-AM, with 250 watts of daytime broadcasting. Well-known Lexington television anchors Billy Thompson and Jim Stephens also got their start at the Georgetown station. By the early 1960s, this small-town neighborhood station was challenging some of the big-city towers for audience and doing well. Jack Webb, who was the program director, also became "Jumpin' Jack" on the air, and "Wild Willie," who was on in the afternoons, was news director Bill Stakelin.

William "Bill" Stakelin explained his path to and journey at WVLK when I interviewed him this way:

> *Author: Bill, thank you for giving me your time today to discuss your history with Mr. Kincaid and Bluegrass Broadcasting. I know your history dates back to when the radio station was located in the old Phoenix Hotel, and I am sure you observed some interesting things involving Mr. Kincaid and the management of the station. Certainly, with Ted Grizzard around it had to be exciting.*
>
> Well probably not as much as you might think. I actually was hired by George Webb, who took over as general manager from Ted Grizzard, and of course, Ted and George were a team for Garvice for years and years with the radio stations or whatever. And so, for most of my day, while I admired and knew Ted very, very well, I basically worked for George Webb, when I joined the company after college.
>
> *Author: Well, tell me tell me a little bit about how you got there.*
>
> Oh, how I got there? You know, sometimes I think like many people, that I'm one of the luckiest people in the world. I mean, I'm from pretty simple means, from a little town called Georgetown, just north of Lexington, and you know, our little town did not have a radio station. And finally, somebody got a license and put a little daytime radio station in Georgetown, Kentucky.
>
> I was always interested in music and this and that, and I just fell in love with it. I made a pest out of myself and hung around the station forever and ever in a day. And low and behold, that was when the rock and roll era had just come in. I like to tell everybody, Elvis and I started together. And so, one day, the manager of the station said, "Hey, you know, we got to play some of this 'race music' for the kids after school." He never referred to it as rock and roll in

those days. It was "race music." He said "It's not going to last, but I want to play an hour of this 'race music' after school. You want to come in, and do it?" Nobody else knows anything about it. I said hell yeah. So anyway, that started the whole thing. I was on at four to five in the afternoon, after school playing rock and roll. And it just grew from there into a 55-year career that was very good to me.

Author: *How old were you? Were you riding your bike to the station or were you able to drive when you started?*

Oh, I walked. I wasn't old enough to drive. I started when I was 14. Yeah, and I walked. As a matter of fact, the program director of that station taught me how to drive in his car, if I remember right, but anyway. And so, you know that that just kind of grew. One day, the guy that did the shift after my four to five show decided he didn't want to work anymore, so he didn't show up and the manager says "you do his shift too." So then instead of one hour, I was doing three a day and it just kept, kept growing. And then, you know, finally I got into sales because I saw those were the guys driving the big cars. And that worked out okay. And I'd had a couple of offers from the Kincaid group to come over to WVLK and Lexington, which of course was the premier station in all of Central Kentucky, but I didn't want to leave Georgetown until I graduated from college. But as soon as I graduated college, I accepted their offer and went over to WVLK, so that's how I got with the Kincaid organization.

Author: *Don Horton was gone by then, correct?*

Don Horton was gone, and I had no dealings with Don whatsoever. Of course he was famous, a famous legend good or bad, but no, I had no dealings with Don.

Author: *The reason I asked the question was that you mentioned rock and roll in Georgetown and that was the one thing that he gets a lot of credit for, switching the station to a rock-n-roll format, correct?*

Yes. No that preceded me, but yes that that's true story, he's the one that that did that, and it was the right move, at the right time and contributed greatly to WVLK's success. Although I don't think Mr. Kincaid ever really cared for that type of music. But then later on, it [the program format] was changed again. I'm sure you have heard of or know of Ralph Hacker. Ralph was my number one guy, and he became the voice of the Kentucky Wildcats following Claude Sullivan at WVLK. And then later on when everything [Kincaid's empire] blew up and after Mr. Kincaid was gone. He joined a group and bought the place [the station], so he wound up owning WVLK. He's quite a guy.

Author: *Do you remember, when you think about your early days there, and you are working for George Webb, how the station was managed? What kind of interpersonal relationships did you see. There are two things I would like to talk about, the interpersonal relationships, and how it was managed. Also, most of Mr. Kincaid's companies appear to have a lot of a family atmosphere, Mr. Kincaid's companies, not with Kincaid, but with the employees amongst themselves.*

Stakelin: Oh, absolutely!

Well, you know, Mr. Webb was 100% sales, and Ted Grizzard was 100% performance, and on air with "man on the street" and all the programs, so they were like water and oil, and they were always kind "at it," but that was all above my pay grade.

I continued to be very, very lucky, and they made me program director at a very early age. Then along came computerization for radio and television stations, and Mr. Kincaid decided that he wanted WKYT-TV and WVLK to be a couple of the first to computerize all their business processes and everything in broadcast, which was totally new to all radio television stations across the nation.

So, the consultant that did all that work to computerize our facilities came to town and I don't know why, because I'm not that bright, but I just had a real interest. I just stayed around and watched and paid attention and listened, day and night, and once the computerization got done and whatever, I was one of maybe two people that knew anything about how to work it or whatever. And that kind of put me in a pretty good spot. And then on top of that, there had been a blow-up between our business manager and Mr. Webb, a serious one. She had called the Federal Communications Commission in Washington to report irregularities and she thought they should come to Lexington to look into them. And they did.

Author: *And the famous license issue over advertising.*

Well, it was back, you know, back before computerization, Mr. Webb couldn't say no to [advertising business], you know. If you brought in more commercials than we could air in a day, he would keep a list and he would honestly think he could make up all these [advertising obligations], you know, nobody would get cheated or get less than they bought or whatever, but of course, you couldn't control it, and so you lost control. And that's what that issue was all about. We had a long fight and almost lost our license over that issue, but we didn't.

Author: *That's when Hart Hagan brought in Ray Holbrook, right?*

No, that's not true, when that issue first blew up, and whatever, and I'm standing there, one of the only people that upstands computerization and is now running the place. They made me the youngest manager of any major radio station in the state of Kentucky. Holbrook came along later, to my surprise, but I think it was because of Hart [Hagan] and I loved Hart. I worked directly for Hart for years, and he was the only guy on the Kincaid team that really gave a damn about any of the broadcast businesses. I mean, Kincaid loved the television and radio stations. He loved WVLK. As far as all the other lieutenants [people on the Committee], they were either lawyers, accountants, or financiers, and they could have cared less about this little piece of the Kincaid pie, that was called broadcast.

I think Hart thought because Ray Holbrook had been president of the Kentucky Broadcasters Association and had a great reputation . . . I think Hart thought it would look good if he hired Ray Holbrook and put him in charge. So, I got demoted without even trying. But I still had a great job and so it was fine. Ray and I got along great, but I don't remember a lot. I was probably the manager for about a year.

Author: Is that when you went to WHOO in Florida?

No, that's one of the great stories. Has anybody told you that story? Not about us. Not about me, but about WHOO?

Author: I have a lot of newspaper articles about it, and I can tell you this and you may not know this. In 1958, Kincaid and Horton purchase WHOO. They paid $350,000 for the AM and FM stations. In 1987, when the Committee was raising money to put capital into Kentucky Central Life, in one of the first phases of raising capital, they sold those two stations for $13.5 million.

I know, you want to know that story?

Author: Sure.

Okay, then, Kincaid's daughter, Jane, decided to get married to a guy that was working at the radio station.

Author: Nickell?

Yes, I was trying not to use names, but yes, Ron Nickell. Well Ron was full of himself from the get-go, and he used to come in to the radio station and he'd say, "You son of a bitches better behave yourself because I'm going to own this place, one day. I'm going to get Kincaid's daughter pregnant, and you guys are all going to work for me." Well, damn, if that's not what happened. So, after that happened, Kincaid called Ron in, and again, Ron has always been very full of himself, and he [Kincaid] says, son you have an interest in this broadcast business, so I tell you what I've done, I've called the Harvard Business School, and I bought a house right off campus. You and Jane can go up there and have the baby and you can get a business education, so you will know what's going on, because I know you're going to take over the broadcast business one day. That's your only interest.

Well, the intelligent Mr. Nickell looked right at Kincaid and said, "I'm not going to no damn Harvard. I know everything there is to know about the broadcast business and I don't need to go up there." Well, that was the beginning of the end of Ron.

There were other things that entered and also played a part, like when Jane would travel, Ron would find it very hard to stay faithful. He would even go to the length of taking ladies into Jane's bedroom, instead of somewhere else.

I mean, yeah, and more than once Mr. Kincaid would come into my office, and he'd say, I got a tape I got to listen to, put it on in a production room and then get out. I'd say, "Yes, sir." Well, what had happened was, Mr. Kincaid had hired detectives because he knew what was going on, and he had it all on tape or whatever. And so finally, he called Ron in and said, "Here's the deal. I'm going to give you x, you're not to see my daughter, or my grandchildren ever again, or to speak to them, or the financial deal is off, and I don't want to ever see you again. And that's how all that ended. But that's how it came about.

So, let me get back to WHOO, because that's an interesting part of the story. So, Kincaid sent Ron or Ron sent himself, I don't know, down to WHOO in Orlando, to run the station. Well, he did, he ran it right into the ground, in a shorter time than probably anybody else could. I mean, he was selling assets, like furniture and putting it under "sales" to make people think something good was going on at the radio station.

Well Mr. Kincaid called a meeting one day, and I was a little surprised because I was still low on the totem pole. I didn't get called to many private meetings in his office. Well, when we get there, one of the topics was and he says, "Henry Appell, at Susquehanna Broadcasting has offered me a million dollars for WHOO and I'm going to sell it to him. Ron has ruined it. And so I'm going to take the million dollars and I wanted you all to know that in case you've got anything you want to say about it.

Well, the little hillbilly from Georgetown has always talked too much, so I raised my hand and I said, "Sir, you can't do that" and he says, "Well, why can't I Sweetheart?" Sarcasm was one of his favorite things to use. "I own it, and I can do anything I want to with it."

I said, "Yes sir, you can, but here's why you can't do it—Orlando, Florida, because of Disney coming to town, is now one of the hottest, fastest growing business areas in the United States of America and we can make the station work, and if we go down and do that, it's going to be worth a lot more money than a million dollars. And if you sell it for a million dollars, people are going to wonder what the hell you were drinking that night. We cannot sell that station."

Mr. Kincaid says, "Well, Sweetheart, who do we send to Florida and make that work?" Well, that's when I said, I'll go sir, I'll go myself. I can make it work. So, we went down, and we turned it completely around in less than a year. And instead of the million dollars, as you say, later on, it was worth $13.5 million. And that was another thing that kind of boosted my image and value, I guess at Bluegrass.

Author: I knew the cold hard facts of some of it. Yes, but I didn't know the color and that's perfect. That's exactly what kind of information I'm looking for. I was going to say, when you brought up Ron, that I believe he had shoved him off to Virginia Beach or someplace like that for a while, also.

Yeah, that's right, that's when he [Kincaid] got most of his tape recordings from the detectives and whatever else he had.

You said something in your notes about Jim Jordan going to Orlando. Jim Jordan was never in Orlando at WHOO.

Author: Yes, he was; I have some newspaper articles about it.

Was that after I left the company?

Author: Yes. It was after you left. What happened was this: He was sent there by Hart Hagan and probably the Committee. You know, people say that Kincaid was a tough bastard and things like that you know, or similar words like that, but he had some fairness to him. If you did a good job, he paid you well and things like that. So, you know, he was both a blessing and a curse, I guess is what one might say.

The Committee always did everything in secret. In Jordan's situation, when you read between the lines, you can see they had a different plan, other than just fixing the station. I worked in Kentucky Central's investment department, and I witnessed some of the way they worked, like only giving you enough information to do your job, and never letting you see the whole picture. The Committee transferred Jordan and his family down there in 1985, with the idea of fixing the station, but I suspect they already knew they planned on selling it.

Yeah, okay, I was already in New York then. That's interesting because Jordan had never managed or run anything.

Author: Now they put him down there in 1985. The station was down to a 2.5% market share, and the manager down there was looking at doing a major program format change from pop to something else. I don't remember exactly what it was, it wasn't that big a deal to me. Anyway, it was written up in the papers several times. So, Jordan comes in, he puts everything on hold, evaluates everything for several months and this is kind of interesting, they make the change.

About the same month or a few months later, the Committee negotiates to have the station sold for $13.5 million dollars. So, what happens then, they sell the station in June, and in September, Jordan is brought back to WVLK in Lexington. I suspect, based upon reading in between the lines, and given how long he was gone, that he was kind of being shuffled into a place at WVLK, without a real job. You know, he was at the station, but the job and the position he left probably isn't what he came back to. And so, he is at the station for less than 12 months and he leaves to start his advertising company with another gentleman from WLAP.

I remember the WLAP guy. Well, the story that I told you about Ron Nickell happened in and around 1974, which is when I went to Orlando, and that story I told you, that's the period of time, when I was there until I decided to leave the company and not manage the station. Hart Hagan had made me president of the "Radio Group" and when I was in Orlando, I ran the "Radio Group" from Orlando, but when I left, he promoted a guy out of Louisville, Max Ryan, as the general manager there and he did a great job. He was a good radio guy. So, all that [Jordan story] followed Max Ryan. I had no knowledge of that and I'm surprised Ralph Hacker didn't tell me all about it.

Author: Well, you know, if you think about that period of time. You know, Ray Holbrook left. Kincaid had died in November 1975, and Ray Holbrook was out of Bluegrass Broadcasting by June 1976.

Right.

Author: And again, reading between the lines, and also because I am familiar with and know some of these people involved. I mean, I was a young person, I should say. But I think I know how some of these people's attitudes worked, and I imagine that, post Kincaid, it wasn't fun anymore for some of these people.

Well, it was really hard, especially if you were in the broadcast division. Like I said, Hart kind of put me in the driver's seat, and so I was really hot to trot, to build up the business through acquisitions and whatever, but every time I found just an absolute great deal to grow the company, all of the bankers and the guys around Garvice [the Committee], everybody except Hart, they had no interest, whatsoever. Oh, yeah, "Well, when we get time, we'll come down," and I would tell them, "It's going to be gone in a few weeks, I've got the inside track." "Oh, okay. Yeah, we'll get back to you."

So, I soon sort of saw the writing on the wall, and I said, you know, this is going to go nowhere for broadcasting, and it's certainly not going to go anywhere for me. And so, I had been fortunate to have been offered a job in New York to head up the largest radio association, nationally, representing the industry in sales and marketing, and I said, "Well, I'm out of here. I got to get out of here while the getting's good. So that's when I left in 1983.

Author: Let me ask you this, and you may not remember, but just so I can put it in a financial perspective, for my own understanding. If you would have brought them a radio station to buy, how much? How much money would they have been spending?

Well, in that period of time, that was before the big [radio station] boom and the FCC rule changes. So, probably Birmingham was one of my big disappointments, and I think I had it lined up for two and a half million dollars, which, you know, for the guys that bought it, it was another WHOO story later on down the road. They sold it for about 18 million. So, you know, probably the things we were looking at were in the 2 to 3 million range. Yeah. Not a lot of money at the time.

Author: I will tell you one thing that was going on in the late 1970s that I personally witnessed from the investment side of the business. This is after they started building the home office building. I think it cost $22 million, not counting the garage they later put in across the street from it. That building was all financed out of internal cash flow. After I joined the company full-time in January 1981, and they had moved into the building in 1980, and my old boss told me about this, because they had been funding everything out of cash flow. This was because interest rates were so high, and they didn't want to borrow money. So, all the cash flow of the company was going into building Kincaid Towers. [We talked about those years, and he tells me the following story.]

This is one of my favorite Kincaid stories of all time that I'll never forget, and it involves Kentucky Central Life. If you've heard it, tell me and I won't go through with it. But anyway, Garvice you know, he had his own way, and you're right, he was gruff. He was sarcastic, but he was fair, and he gave a lot of "opportunity" to a lot of people, and you're talking to one of them, but anyway, Garvice likes things a certain way. And one evening he goes into Kentucky Central; this is when they were down the old building, the Lafayette Hotel or whatever. And he goes and he goes out on one of the floors, I guess where all the salespeople are located and all this stuff. And it's just, you know, one desk after another. And he walks through, and the desks are all just piled high with documents, bric-a-brac, whatever, but the desks are just covered. And so, he picks up the phone the next day, and I don't know who the person was he called [probably David Brain], but he read them the riot act. And he said, "You know, if they're that sloppy with our business and whatever, then maybe we need to take a look at these people" or something sarcastic like he likes to say. And so, I don't know who that call went to, but I know it was high up. Anyway, two days later, in Kincaid fashion, he decides to go over, and take another look at the floor again. Well, not a thing has changed, and Mr. Kincaid went through that entire floor, and with his arms, swept every piece of paper, every picture, anything that was on top of the desk. He just swept it to the floor. The place looked like a bomb had hit it, and he just turned around, walked out.

Author: I told Bill the story about Charlie Thomas's desk and Kincaid's evening visit and his "encouragement" to Charlie.

Well, he loved to do things like that. I remember when I was the young manager at WVLK, and of course Central Bank and all of his businesses were using the radio station to advertise. And at WVLK, it was always a three-way production job for a client. In other words, you had to have a tape, this is the old days, you had to make a tape for the commercials, an AM a tape and an FM tape, and then you had to make a third tape, to go out to the transmitter because the "all-night show" was broadcast from the station at the transmitter. So, if I'm doing a commercial for Central Bank, it's got to be put in three different production jobs.

Well, I'm sound asleep at 3:00 a.m. and the phone rings, and I recognize the voice. But I say, "Yeah." And all I hear is, and realize, now Kincaid has this massive, diverse empire, right. But all I hear is, "The wrong fucking commercial just ran for my bank." I said, "Excuse me." And he says, "Sweetheart, the wrong fucking commercial just ran for my bank." Click! Well, I lay there in bed thinking, what the hell. I get in to the office the next day, of course, I'm going to hop right on it, and he was right. But how in the hell did he know what commercial was supposed to be running for Central Bank, with everything that's on his desk and on his mind, but he was right. They forgot to make one and send it out to the transmitter facility for the all-night show. Kincaid was up listening to the radio, and the commercial comes on, and it's the wrong damn one. So, he calls.

Well, as you said, he was known for his gruffness, but also there was a family nature within the company and whatever. I know I was pleased. Ralph Hacker and I, and I don't know why, but Ralph and I decided we needed to get married, not to each other. Maybe in this day and time, we would have [laughs] . . . but anyway we wanted to build houses, not big or anything, but we just wanted a home. And so, we got our heads together, and we said, because we didn't have any money, and Ralph says, "Let's tell Mr. Kincaid." I said, "He isn't going to care about us getting married, wanting to build a house," but we go over, and he graciously has us come in, sit down and we tell him we're going to get married, and we'd like to build our first homes, but we really don't have the capital and whatever. And, and we're wondering if you would, you know, kind of help us with your people at Central Bank or whatever. He didn't say a word, he just reached over and got on his phone and called downstairs. I forget who the president of Central Bank was at that time [Clyde Maudlin]. Anyway, he simply says, "Hacker and Stakelin want to get married. They want to build a house and start a life. Make it happen." Click! So, you never knew what you were going to get with him, you know.

Author: *[I tell Bill about a very similar experience that Barry Peel (retired WKYT anchor and Frankfort Bureau Chief) had with Kincaid.] Barry was from Lancaster, Kentucky. He graduated from Lancaster High School in 1964 and went to Eastern Kentucky University in Richmond, Kentucky, but transferred to Western Kentucky University. Barry, a Lincoln Scholar, had always been interested in government and politics and in 1965 was elected president of the Garrod County Young Republicans Club. Peel started working in broadcasting in 1966, at radio station WFKY in Frankfort, Kentucky, where his on-air personality was known as Wayne Barry, and by 1967, Barry was renting a place on High Street in Lexington.*

Barry describes those early WKYT days this way when I interviewed him and tells about his Kincaid meeting for a home loan:

In 1970, I was working at a television station in Bowling Green, Kentucky, and I was on vacation, and I had worked for Ray Holbrook, who had been the manager of the radio station in Danville in 1967, when I was there. I had heard that he had been made general manager of Channel 27, so I drove to Lexington, just to visit with him, and he said, "Are you looking for a job?" and I said, "Oh, no, I'm on vacation." Well, Ray said, "We need somebody in news. "And one thing or another. And that's the way life works, and so I went to Channel 27, during the first week of June 1970, to work in the news department as a reporter. That's how I got to Channel 27.

I'm not even sure, but it was maybe a year later or less, I get a call at home from Holbrook or maybe the news director, Haward Riggins, and they tell me they would like me to do the weather that night. They had fired the weatherman, because they had been caught him drinking in the "prop-room." Well, anyway, the guy wasn't very good. Now, that's just my opinion. They knew I had done weather in Bowling Green, and so I did the weather that evening. I guess I did it for about a year or so, but I actually was hired to report the news. In addition, they also had me doing sports on the weekend. I was also anchoring sports on the weekend. Back in those broadcasting days, one did anything that was needed.

As for my quest to get a mortgage, that began because I was tired of paying rent. It was January 1974 and I wanted to purchase a home. I had been married for a few years and had been renting a place. I decided it was time to get something. After looking around, I found a home that belonged to a teacher. She was moving out of state and was in a hurry to sell, so she agreed to sell me the home for $21,100, if we could close quickly [408 Lancelot Lane, Lexington].

I was still young and didn't have much credit history, but I had a job and thought I could swing it. I decided that my best hope of getting a loan was from WKYT's sister organization, Central Bank & Trust, but I wasn't sure they would even give me a loan. So, being young, courageous and a little naive, I decided to contact Mr. Kincaid and made an appointment. By 1974, Garvice knew me from the station. I had anchored the afternoon and evening newscast and had even worked on a couple of stories he was interested in.

Well, I arrive for my appointment, and I am sitting in this row of chairs outside his office. I guess he is on the phone and after a while I hear "next!" called out of his office, and the secretary tells me to go in.

I go in and sit down, and Kincaid looks at me, from behind that big desk he had, and I start explaining to him why I am there. I am trying to make my pitch. I said, "Mr. Kincaid, this woman is selling her house, she's a teacher, she's got a job out of state, and she's moving. She's in a hurry, and, you know, they've cut the price, and I said, I think I can save $2,000 or $3,000, if I can close quickly." You know, $2,000 or $3,000 was like the national debt to me. I was just squeaking by. I had paid my own way through college, so I said, "I can save $2,000 or $3,000 on this house."

Well, Garvice leans across that big desk and says, "Well, you've already wasted that much of my time." Well, you know, it was the last thing I should have said, but I couldn't help it, and I said, "You know, I bet I have." And I started laughing and Mr. Kincaid started chuckling.

Now, if I said, "Oh, Mr. Kincaid, I'm sorry," he probably would have given me a thumbs down as to my request. But I said, "I bet I have," and he started laughing. He enjoyed it. I think he enjoyed the fact that I said that to him.

Now, he starts scribbling on a piece of paper and said, "I am going to loan you [I think it was] $20,000." Can you imagine that? A house in south Lexington for $20,000. "I'm going to loan you $20,000, for 20 years or whatever it was," and he said, "The house payment will be $198 a month." Can you imagine that?

Then he looks at me and said, "Can you afford that?" And I say, "Mr. Kincaid, I'm paying more in rent than that." Now he never said another word, but he picks up the phone and I hear him say, "Get Fred in here." And almost like rubbing a magic lamp, and a genie appeared, there was Fred. Fred appeared almost instantaneously, with a legal pad in his left hand and a pen in his right, ready to write.

This poor soul. I hate to describe Fred to you, and I want to avoid calling him a flunky, but Fred was just Mr. Kincaid's office boy. He knew he was there to serve, and he was ready to write before he ever sat down.

Now to give you another example of Garvice's attitude about things, I know, because I personally witnessed it, Garvice says to Fred, "You recognize Mr. Peel." Can you believe he called me Mr. Peel? "You've seen him on television," and he said it, not with a reverence in his voice, but with a respect in his voice like, you know this guy is a big deal. He's on television. He's, he's good enough to be on television, you know, talented, doing news, weather or whatever. Well of course Fred says, "Of course, right? Oh, yeah, I see you on television every night." You know how people are.

So now Garvice looks at Fred and say, "I'm loaning this man $20,000." I think it was a twenty-year loan, and he taps the pad on his desk, and says, "I want it done Monday." Now this meeting is on a Friday afternoon at 2:30. We are closing the loan on Monday afternoon and so this was Friday afternoon at about 2:30.

I've always said, I guarantee somebody, most likely, had to do the paperwork that weekend. But it was done, and Fred knew it was to be done.

Now this is a true story, "You've already wasted that much of my time." And today, I can see why he appreciated that I understood. He's a financier. He'd rather loan $2 million than $20,000, because of the interest for God's sake. That's what the financier does. If you're in finance, that's what you do.

[Note: Stakelin had never heard this story.]

The other story that I love so much, and then I ran into it again here in Cincinnati, because I did some stuff for Carl Linder [American Financial Group] and whatever, but he always kind of reminded me of Kincaid. Anyway, I thought about the story when Garvice had wanted to join Idle Hour Country Club. They didn't want anything to do with him, so he buys the property across the street from the club and builds his house. So, he gets to sit there and look right into Idle Hour. Well, Carl Linder did the same thing. The country club up there rejected him, because he was buying up the newspaper and all this stuff. They wouldn't accept him, and so he bought all the property around the country club and built this huge mansion and became their neighbor.

Author: [I bring up the WKYT Sunday morning management meetings.]

I know about them, but I was only in his home once for a meeting, and I don't even remember what the subject was. But it was one of his Sunday morning meetings, and I don't even know why I got called to attend. But no, that was above my pay grade.

Author: [We discuss a story that Barry Peel heard about Garvice acquiring WKYT.] Apparently Garvice had tried two or three times to get Taft to sell him the station and they just ignored him. Well, the way Barry heard it, Kincaid was in a plane flying first class and lo and behold, a Taft executive is sitting next to him. And this sounds exactly like Garvice. He was told Kincaid looks over at him and says, "Why don't you sell me that damn station," and the guy tells Kincaid that you couldn't afford it, and Kincaid said, "Just give me a price, and that subject to whoever the powers-to-be at Taft, they verbally negotiated selling him the station on that plane. And, you know, that sounds exactly like Garvice and how he did things.

Yes, absolutely. Absolutely. You know, I think Dudley Taft may have been a little too young for it to have been him, but Dudley was right in the middle of all that. But yes, does sound like Garvice. Everyone knows he is in the radio business, you know, he also owns the whole town of Marathon, in Florida, and the Dania Bank down there. So, he is down there one night; this is short, so I won't bore you, but he was down there one night and this good old boy walks up to him and says, "Garvice, I'm from Eastern Kentucky and I'm homesick as I can be. Now I know you own radio stations and whatever and I own this damn little radio station here in Marathon and I want to go home. Why don't you buy the damn thing?" Garvice says "Okay." I mean, it was small, and it was no money at all, and there was no way to make any money with it either. You know, I'd go down and check the books once a year and this trip used up all its profit.

Author: Were you ever at the Fontainebleau?

Oh, yeah. I would go down to do stuff in Florida, mostly down in Marathon and the Keys or whatever. And one time he said, "Well, why don't you just stay at my place at the Fontainebleau?" I'm still fairly young, and I'm standing there like, "Are you kidding me?" you know. Well, I show up at the Fontainebleau and God you would have thought I was the King of Siam. And I go into this beautiful suite, refrigerators are stocked full of food. So yeah, I had one trip in and out of there.

Author: How about Duck Key?

Yeah, well, Duck Key was Marathon, right? That was? Yeah, I would go down there, now and again. I usually only made that trip once a year. FM hadn't even come to the Keys. There were no FMs or anything, and so it just wasn't worth going there. So, but I went down and the only thing I remember is two things. I couldn't keep a manager in the radio station down there because every one of them would become a drunk, because there was absolutely nothing to do in Marathon, Florida. So, they would take care of whatever business they were going to do in the morning, and then they all had their own barstools at this very popular bar, and they sat there and would drink all day. And yet it was a sight to see, you know. I kept thinking, how are you supposed to make this work? I don't think I ever figured it out.

Well, you know what I've told several people, and of course that's in the past, but you know, most of us, especially in business, never get a chance to witness genius. Let alone stand beside or work for a genius, and Garvice was absolutely an Eastern Kentucky hillbilly genius and there's no taking that away from him.

Author: Bill, how would you like to see Mr. Kincaid remembered?

Few of us have the opportunity in life to witness true genius. Having been given that opportunity I will always remember Garvice Kincaid as the person that I learned so much from. Being able to have this opportunity set the stage for a young man from very simple beginnings to succeed not only in a business I loved, but in life. I am forever in his debt. Thanks again, Mr. Kincaid.

After Bill Stakelin transferred to Orlando, Ralph Hacker took over as station manager, with oversight from Hart Hagan and Bill Stakelin. Stakelin, though he was in Florida, remained president of the radio group until he left in 1983. Ralph Hacker would be the last and most influential person at WVLK during Garvice's final years, and certainly after his death.

Top left, right, & bottom left: EKU pictures -1931 to 1933
Bottom right: UK Law School picture - 1937

Kincaid's Richmond Road Home

Eva Nell "Nellie" Wilson Kincaid – Transylvania University photo - 1936

Kincaid, his wife, Nelle, and their twin daughters, Joan and Jane - 1960

Showing off his newspaper-throwing ability after being inducted into the National
Newspaperboy Hall of Fame at ceremonies in 1965 in Richmond, Ky

Kincaid's Duck Key Resort, Indies Inn and Marina - 1967

Kincaid's famous Fontainebleau Hotel - 1983

Donald Horton – WVLK's first station manager - Circa 1950

Hart Hagan managed Bluegrass Broadcasting, while Ralph Gabbard was in charge of WKYT. - 1981

WVLK and Blue Grass Broadcasting – Kincaid's communication machine!

Mrs. Kincaid proudly displays his Horatio Alger Award in the presence of daughters
Jane and Joan following presentation ceremonies in New York - 1960

Garvice Kincaid, in a photographic portrait by Warren Bruner, shortly before
Kincaid's death in 1975

The Kincaid family plot in the Lexington Cemetery; Bud Burnett's grave is about 150 feet away

Pallbearers Place Casket Of Garvice Kincaid In Hearse After Yesterday's Services

Kincaid's Committee & business lieutenants - November 1975

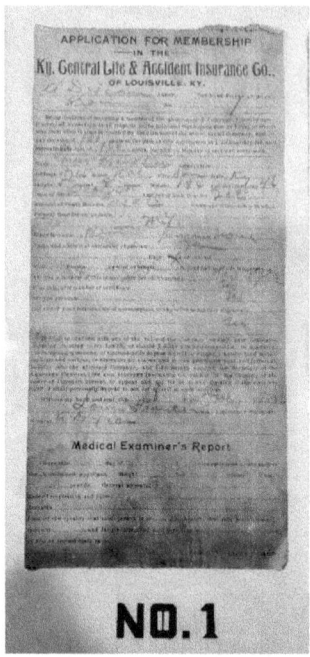
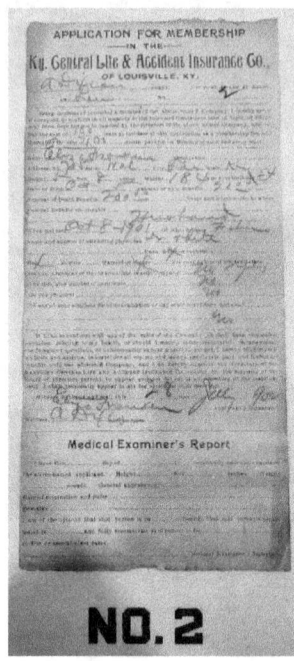

Kentucky Central Life's first and second insurance policy, written in July of 1902

Thomas O. West - 1924

Frank J. Walker - circa late 1920s

Top: KCL's Anchorage Office - 1941 Office staff going to the races

Central Exchange Bank Building, 1941. In 1945, Kincaid purchases the building and, in a year, changes the name to "Central Bank & Trust."

This picture was taken following a dinner for Kentucky Finance veterans in the early Sixties. From left: John Puchala, Ed Mays, Stanley Wilson, Kincaid, Kenneth Davis, Bob Curtin and Al Smith.

Kincaid is shown with the late President Lyndon Johnson in 1961, when Johnson was Vice President, and group of past Kentucky governors

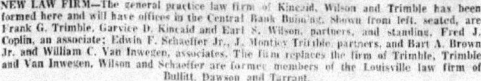

NEW LAW FIRM—The general practice law firm of Kincaid, Wilson and Trimble has been formed here and will have offices in the Central Bank Building. Shown from left, seated, are Frank G. Trimble, Garvice D. Kincaid and Earl S. Wilson, partners, and standing, Fred J. Coplin, an associate; Edwin F. Schaeffer Jr., J. Montjoy Trimble, partners, and Bart A. Brown Jr. and William C. Van Inwegen, associates. The firm replaces the firm of Trimble, Trimble and Van Inwegen, Wilson and Schaeffer are former members of the Louisville law firm of Bullitt, Dawson and Tarrant.

Kincaid formed his law firm in 1963. Earl Wilson and Edwin Schaeffer came over from Louisville. Earl went to law school with Garvice. Frank Trimble would become known as Kincaid's "loan man." (Portrait to the right) Bart Brown prepared Mr. Kincaid's will and estate plan in 1964.

Kincaid talks with a group of local high school seniors to whom he has just presented Kincaid Foundation college scholarships

In 1942, Garvice purchased Lexington's Joyland Amusement Park for $54,000, and following the rezoning in 1965, transformed the twenty-five-acre park into a lucrative residential and mixed-use development valued at over $5 million.

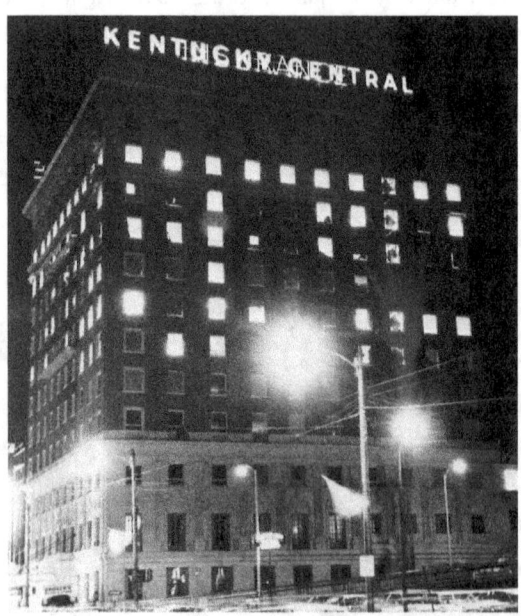

Lights burned until late on October 5, 1963 when Kentucky Central moved its national headquarters from Louisville to Lexington and occupied the former Hotel Lafayette which had been converted into a modern office building at a cost of several million dollars.

Kincaid Towers, the corporate headquarters that Kincaid had always wanted, on the location he purchased the month of his death. His Committee completed it in the fall of 1980, and this began the company's journey to disaster.

KCL Picture: Wally Franklin, Kincaid, and David Brain. Getting right into the spirit of the "Coonskin Hootenanny" of the Executive Sales Division, January, 1965.

Celebrating $1 Billion of Inforce - Billion-Era Jubilee, November 1966

Signal-callers for college team plan for new year!

The University Key teams are raring to go in 1969! Regional Managers were in Lexington Dec 19-21 to meet with Home Office officials on ideas for the new year.

Celebrating $1 Billion of Inforce - Billion-Era Jubilee, November 1966

Saturday Shirt-Sleeve Session, 1970. B.N. Joyner, vice president actuary, Garvice D. Kincaid, president, W.E. Burnett, Jr. secretary-treasurer, David L. Brain, CLU, executive vice president, and E. Wilson Yates, vice president-counsel.

With Kentucky Central officers and then Kentucky Governor Wendell H. Ford at the Lexington Zone 3 meeting of the National Association of Insurance Commissioners in 1972. Kincaid was respected by politicians. They knew he could help them, and he knew he needed them. NOTE: No W.E. "Bud" Burnett in this picture!

Gunn, Forbush and Rampulla

My old boss and dear friend, Cliff Forbush (center). Also, John Rampulla. In the late 1980's John would tell people that KCL's (Bud's) mortgage loan policy was for "friends, relatives, and politicians and not necessary in that order". Wendell Gunn, Burnett's, after the fact, cleanup guy.

Mrs. Kincaid with Craig Browne

In 1972, Mrs. Kincaid attended a KCL agent sales conference in London, England. The attendee list also included their daughters, Jane and Joan, but Garvice apparently did not attend. In January 1972, Clyde Maudlin, who was listed as a primary committee member and was also the president of Central Bank, resigned. Immediately, Kincaid had to quickly update his estate plan and begin a new search for the next president of Central Bank.

MRS. GARVICE Kincaid, third from left, presents the first ONE Card to Al Florence of the Kentucky Group Banks during a meeting Monday at Lexington's Hilton Inn. From left are Gene Worthington, chairman of the board of the Bank of Danville, and Howard Sallee, president of the local bank. (See story on Page 5).

Nelle Kincaid was always active and helping Garvice in his business affairs. Above, Al Florence using her to promote the Kentucky Group Banks in 1976, after his death.

Above, regional manager Robert Lovel and vice president of College Sales, Swede Hanson - 1968

The University Key Division & College Sales was brought to Kentucky Central by Texan, Rudolph "Swede" Hanson. Swede's tenure with the company was only a few years, but the marketing professionals that he initially brought to the company created the backbone of the company's most significant marketing division in the 1980s - Executive Marketing.

Kentucky Central achieved a major milestone in 1971 by surpassing $2 billion of life insurance in force. Insurance Commissioner for Kentucky, Harold B. McGuffey visited the Home Office to help commemorate.

Kentucky Central Life Insurance Company's three top executives (from left): David L. Brain, CLU, executive vice president, Garvice D. Kincaid, president, and W. E. Burnett Jr., secretary-treasurer - 1973

Mr. Kincaid was elected president of Kentucky Central in 1959. Also prominent in law, banking and real estate for more than 30 years, he is a graduate of the University of Kentucky and its College of Law and has received numerous national, state and local awards for civic and humanitarian services.

Mr. Brain was elected executive vice president of the company in 1964 and has more than 25 years of experience in all phases of personal sales and home office management. He is a Chartered Life Underwriter, a magna cum laude graduate of Baldwin-Wallace College and holds a master's degree from the Harvard School of Business Administration.

This is from the 1974 Kentucky Central Life Annual Report which was printed in April 1975, four months before, in January 1975, Kincaid appointed Dave Brain the president of KCL. Ten months before his death, Garvice had made his decision about who should lead the company going forward - Dave Brain!

the keynoter

UK FIESTA!

Kincaid promoting the KCL Fall Sales Conference in Mexico City - 1974

DIRECTORS AND OFFICERS

WILSON

BURNETT

HAGAN

HEMBREE

KINCAID

SCHAEFFER

YATES

Directors

EARL S. WILSON, SR.
Chairman of the Board

W. E. BURNETT, JR.
President

H. HART HAGAN, JR.
President
General Management
Associates, Inc.
Lexington, Kentucky

CHARLES R. HEMBREE
Kincaid, Wilson, Schaeffer
& Hembree
Lexington, Kentucky

MRS. NELLE W. KINCAID
Lexington, Kentucky

EDWIN F. SCHAEFFER, JR.
Kincaid, Wilson, Schaeffer
& Hembree
Lexington, Kentucky

E. WILSON YATES, JR.
Vice President-Counsel

Following Kincaid's passing in November 1975, Nelle Kincaid joined the Board of Kentucky Central Life. She stepped down during her second year after initiating lawsuits against the Committee alongside her daughters.

Around 1979, Bud Burnett moved his son, John, from KCL's supply department to Florida to run the company's orange grove operation. The subsidiary lost money two out of every three years, but Bud didn't care. (left) Bud's other son, Bruce, started out in Kincaid's Lexington Insurance agency, but was soon encouraged to leave. His schemes and KCL loans cost the company millions. He went to prison for 4 years. His deals also destroyed a large portion of his father's wealth.

March 1976. Kentucky Central Life's three top executives (from left): David L. Brain, CLU, president; Earl S. Wilson, Sr., chairman of the board; and W. E. Burnett, Jr., executive vice president and secretary. In five months, David Brain would be forced out of the company, and Bud Burnett would be appointed its president.

Nelle Kincaid and Earl Wilson unveil Kincaid Towers plaque - 1980

The committee that advises the Kincaid Trust consists of (from left) Edwin F. Schaeffer, Jr., Kincaid, Wilson, Schaeffer & Hembree, PSC; W. E. Burnett, Jr., president of KCL; and H. Hart Hagan, Jr., president of General Management Associates - 1980.

1981

Members of the board of directors of
Kentucky Central with key executives of
subsidiary companies, from left:
Robert D. Preston, a vice president of the
property and casualty insurance firms;
Robert E. Curtin, secretary-treasurer of
Kentucky Finance Co., Inc.;
E. Wilson Yates, Jr., board member;
Edwin F. Schaeffer, Jr., board member;
H. Hart Hagan, Jr., board member and
president of Bluegrass Broadcasting Co.,
Inc.; Earl S. Wilson, Sr., chairman of the
board; W. E. Burnett, Jr., board member;
R. M. Bartella, executive vice president of
Kentucky Finance Co., Inc;
Charles R. Hembree, board member;
Ralph W. Gabbard, executive vice presi-
dent of WKYT-TV (Channel 27), Lexington;
and Ralph E. Hacker, executive vice presi-
dent of Radio Station WVLK, Lexington.

Kentucky Central Life Insurance Company's officers - 1970

GUNN   TOZER   REHFUSS

SCHOENFELD   FOLTZ   GORDON

JACKSON   GOHEAN   ROBINSON

HOWE   STEWART   MULLINS

McINTOSH   NEIHEISEL   SNODGRASS

Kentucky Central Life Insurance Company's officers - 1970

CASHER SAMMARTIN FRANKLIN

FORBUSH PRESTON BAKER

HARRIS RAMPULLA THOMAS

ROBERTS ROSS MATTSCHECK

MOSS WELSH COLE

1984 picture of Burnett and Wilson after Wilson's retirement. Bud Burnett is now in full control and so the Committee put in place long-term employment contracts, with each with member having a specified salary and bonus.

Members of the Kentucky Central Life Board of Directors are from left, E. Wilson Yates, Jr,; Wendell L. Gunn; Edwin F. Schaeffer, Jr.; W.E Burnett, Jr., Chairman; Lawrence J. Sammartin; Robert D. Preston; and Charles R. Hembree.

Kentucky Central Life's 1992 Board of Directors. Larry Sammartin would die before the end of the year.

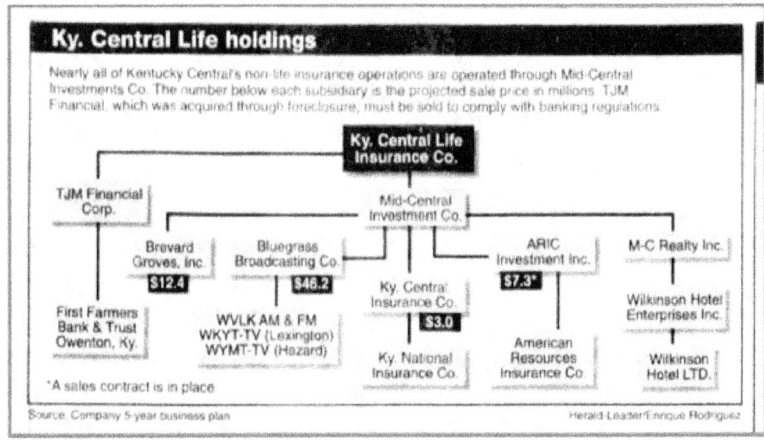

Kentucky Central Life's organizational chart - February 1992

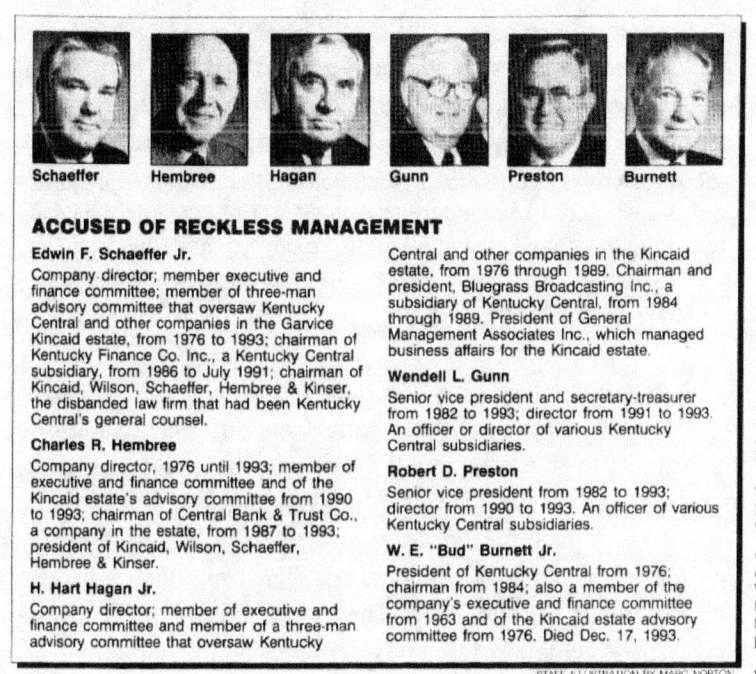

The individuals held accountable by regulators for the collapse of Kentucky Central Life. The Courier-Journal, Saturday, January 8, 1994.

Ralph Hacker—Adapting to Change

Ralph Hacker was born in 1944 in Richmond, Kentucky, which was also the childhood home of Garvice Kincaid in the early 1900s. Garvice developed many important relationships over the years with people who were from the Richmond, Kentucky, area. In fact, people would one day talk about Bluegrass Broadcasting and the "two Ralphs" who both came from Richmond, Kentucky.

Ralph became interested in getting into radio in his teens. He also enjoyed watching sports and would practice his play-by-play skills while watching games. By the time he was 15, he was working part-time at the Richmond radio station WEKY. Ralph said the general manager, Cavin Barnette, gave him his first job covering Eastern ballgames. Cavin Barnette was also a former WVLK sales representative. John Sullivan, program director at the time, remembers asking Ralph, "What kind of experience do you have?" Ralph replying, "I'm fifteen years old," and himself saying, "Oh yeah, I forgot."

In 1962, Ralph Hacker entered Eastern Kentucky University in Richmond. After three years, he left to join WBLG radio in Bowling Green, Kentucky. He says, "I left college after three years to join WBLG for more salary than I could make as a teacher after ten years of teaching and also obtaining a master's degree in education. I always knew what I wanted to do: be in radio and report U.K. sports." He explained,

> It's a big responsibility to not only give factual information about the progress of the ball game but to offer value judgment as well. I just think I have a duty to be honest. I'm prepared for what I'm going to say by going to all of the practices. I have the privilege of knowing the players and the coaches. I know more about what's going on than most fans. [Sportswriters] make their judgments after the game.

Working in radio was exciting to Ralph. While at WEKY, he traveled with the team and worked all the Maroons' games, and in December 1965 he even got the opportunity to take a trip out of the country. The Maroons were playing in the Motor City Classic in Detroit, Michigan, and Ralph and some friends were soon crossing over the border into Canada. When a reporter for the *Lexington Herald-Leader* asked them about their trip, they replied, "Doesn't look much different than America." They were amused by the government inspections of their vehicle before and after crossing the border.

In 1966, Ralph was ready to move to Lexington's number-one-rated radio station, WVLK. George Webb and Ted Grizzard get the credit for hiring Ralph. Claude Sullivan had left for Cincinnati to become the "voice of the Reds," Jim Host was in the process of leaving for a job with Procter & Gamble, and

Earl Boardman was working toward joining WKYT-TV's sports department. In addition, Ted Grizzard began cutting back his hours in 1966, doing only his "Man on the Street" and "Fans in the Stands" programs. This meant that Ralph would quickly be taking on more responsibility and must adapt to these changes.

Hacker joined WVLK after the era of Don Horton, but he does recall when he first met him. "Don had a drinking problem. And when I first ran across Don Horton, it was in 1963, 1964, or 1965. I was just a young pup over in Richmond and I walked into the radio station one day—they had called us all in—and here is this big, tall, skinny guy sitting there, and he says, "Are you, staying or are you going?" and as you can guess, I was a smart aleck, probably only seventeen or eighteen years old, and so my answer is, "Who the heck are you?" He tells me, "I'm Don Horton," and I say, "Big Deal." And he says, "You staying or are you going?" and I say "I'll see you," and I just walk off.

> O. C. Halyard, the general manager, chases me downstairs, and he says, "That's Don Horton," and I say, "I don't give a damn who Don Horton is." You see, Horton had already been let go by Mr. Kincaid and he was trying to take charge of the radio stations that Mr. Kincaid had financially acquired but did not control in his own name. Don had struck some kind of deal with Mr. Kincaid where he could somehow take control of the Winchester station, but he was trying to take charge of all of the stations that Mr. Kincaid owned but weren't in his name. For instance, WEKY, was supposedly owned by Jake Frank Fox, out of Harlan, Kentucky. Winchester may have been in Don's name, but there were others like Danville and Frankfort, that Mr. Kincaid had financed and acquired, but they weren't in his name and Don was trying to control them. I just know that Horton came in there with Jake Frank Fox out of Harlan. This is WEKY and you know, he was, you know, when he was there, he was a total pronk [jackass]. I'll tell you I never had a lot of respect for him.

In speaking with me about those days, Ralph explained that "you could see the love/hate relationship between Mr. Kincaid and the old guard of Lexington. Mr. Kincaid loved Lexington and wanted to see it grow and prosper, and he had the financial resources to help make it happen, but the old guard hated him." He also acknowledged that Mr. Kincaid was a powerful force in politics due to his wealth and his willingness to contribute to those running for office. This also created friction with Lexington's old guard.

Ralph began his career at WVLK as an advertising salesman, but was soon announcing UK freshmen games. According to an interview he gave in

1995 to *Views* magazine, in 1971, the then football coach, John Ray, wanted someone to handle the color part of game announcing; someone who would come to team practices and have an understanding of the football program. It wasn't long, though, until, in 1973, he was announcing color for UK basketball games, which began his long association with Cawood Ledford, the "voice of the Wildcats."

Ralph says his involvement with Garvice was limited, but always memorable. "I worked for him, but not with him. There were meetings, and certainly the annual holiday parties, but I only recall going to his house once, and that was for business." After Ralph joined WVLK in 1966, and in conjunction with the FCC licensing issue that year, Garvice made Hart Hagan the head of Bluegrass Broadcasting and put him in charge of the station's oversight. Kincaid was still actively monitoring WVLK, but Hagan added a layer of management oversight that had been missing. At the end of 1967, Hagan recruited WVLK veteran Ray Holbrook back to the station. The FCC advertising and licensing issue was not going away, and Ray was considered a solid, respected, industry leader whom the FCC could trust to correct this problem.

Ralph Hacker was there during this trying time and explained that the issue was bigger than just WVLK; if it wasn't properly resolved it would affect WKYT's license also. Ralph explained how the licensing issue happened this way:

> The station's general manager, George Webb, had created the problem by how he handled the station's advertising commitments. The problem was described as double billing, but that wasn't really true. Because if he sold you advertising, and let's say he sold fifty spots, but he also sold me fifty spots. George would kind of look at it and say, well, Ralph needs that advertising this week more than you do. He would maybe only put twenty-five on there for you and put my fifty in there, but next week, he may give you seventy-five or he may give you a hundred. You know, you didn't get the advertising you bought because he would look at it and say well, you know their business is doing better than Ralph's. Oh, we're going to run Ralph's this week, because we would be sold out all the time, but we'll double up next week on him at no charge. You know.

> Back in those days they used a handwritten log to keep track of everything we were doing, and this became a huge paperwork failure. They couldn't document what they had done. It was during this time that Bill Stakelin, as program director, moved the station into installing a computer with punch cards to keep track of everything. He was into that kind of stuff.

Ralph Hacker is very humble in describing his interaction with Garvice. He always refers to him as Mr. Kincaid. Garvice apparently liked and appreciated Ralph Hacker's talents. At one point, when Orlando's WHOO station was struggling in 1974 and they needed to send someone there to manage the station, Ray Holbrook had nominated Ralph to go, but things soon changed and he and Ralph Gabbard both became station managers that year. Ray had become president of Bluegrass Broadcasting and was now in charge of Mr. Kincaid's radio and broadcasting properties, with the oversight of Hart Hagan. Ralph explains the story this way:

> I don't know why I became WVLK's station manager. I've heard different stories about it. At the time, they were preparing to send me to Orlando. My wife and I had just gone to Orlando, and they were going to make me WHOO's sales manager. Bill Stakelin was here and the manager at WVLK. We had gone to Orlando to find a house, and when we got back, I get a phone call from Mr. Hagan and he wants me to come to his office, and he says, "We're not going to send you to Orlando." And he says it's because of this reason, but later on, I heard—it was never said to me by him—but I heard that Mr. Kincaid had said, "I don't want him going to Orlando." He'll do us more good by doing the University of Kentucky ballgames," and that was that.
>
> *Author: Well, it was certainly, I hate to call it a niche, but it was certainly an important niche for you in the sense of your career.*
>
> Yeah, well for me it was of great importance, but as I've said, Mr. Kincaid never told me that. He never said anything to me about it; you know, it was just all of a sudden, I was general manager of WVLK.

Ralph's elevation to station manager in October 1974 is important for another reason, in thirteen months, Garvice Kincaid would die, and the Committee would be in charge. One additional interesting detail about the WHOO saga is that although Bill Stakelin and Ralph were close personal friends, he had never heard Stakelin's version of how he ended up at WHOO that year. Apparently, everything happened so quickly that the two men never discussed it. One can imagine that Garvice's meetings with Stakelin and others happened while Ralph and his wife were in Orlando looking for a house, and by the time they got back and he got the news that he wasn't going to Orlando, Bill had already left.

Ralph's relationship with Garvice was built over time. His position in the organization wasn't one that would make him destined to be one of Kincaid's lieutenants, and Ralph says that he, like Ted Grizzard, was occasionally teased by Garvice; he never felt the wrath of Garvice's temper. In fact, both Ralphs—Hacker and Gabbard—appear to have been special to Kincaid. They were childhood friends and had grown up together in Richmond. Hacker had helped Gabbard get his first job, and Gabbard had helped Hacker obtain his job with WVLK. Ralph tells this Kincaid story that helps show Kincaid's feelings about the two Ralphs:

> I learned this at Mr. Kincaid's Christmas party. It was the year [1974] that Ralph Gabbard and I were named general managers. Ralph and I grew up together. We went to grade school together and he went to Berea High School and I went to Madison Central. We stayed friends all of our lives. I helped Ralph get his first job. He recommended me to WVLK when I was working over at WBLB. They hired me at WVLK because Ralph had recommended me. And in the end, I hear they are looking for a sales manager over at channel 27 [WKYT] and I recommended him. By this time, he was over in Richmond at WEKY and had an idea he might buy it. Fred Hensley, who was an old bookkeeper for Hart Hagan, had the station in his name, and things weren't working out.

> So, we're standing at the bar, at the Christmas party, where everybody was expected to be in attendance, and all of a sudden there were hands around each of our necks. And he looked big, but we were much bigger than Mr. Kincaid in height. Well, we look at him, and he says in this southern drawl, "Boys, you know why you all will be running my radio and television station?" Neither one of us said anything. Mr. Kincaid says, "It's because you all are best buddies. Best friends. You've grown up together. You've worked together all your life. Now these other people I've got running my businesses don't get along with each other. You all get along." He says to me, "Now, Blondie, if you've got any time left unsold at WVLK, okay, I want you to run commercials for WKYT. And Mr. Gabbard, if you've got any time available on channel 27, you run some commercials for WVLK." He says, "I want all my companies to work together."

> And that's the way Ralph Gabbard and I worked. Just exactly like that until the day he died. That's the way Ralph and I worked. But I kept that in my mind, that one meeting or conversation with Mr. Kincaid, all my life, I guess, and I tried to always do it that way. I took it to heart, and even after I bought the company [WVLK] in 1993, I went to Central Bank to borrow the money, but Luther Deaton said, "Ralph, we can't handle a loan that size," so I went to several other banks and even with to Louisville, but the terms there were too controlling. The Bank of Lexington recommended I go to Vine Street Trust, and they said they could handle it, but I

was honest with the people there and told them that when I get to the point that Central Bank can handle the loan, my loyalty will be to Central Bank. They actually put me on their board at Vine Street Trust.

So, when the loan size was reduced enough, I called Luther Deaton at Central Bank and asked if he could handle it now. I had discussed it with him before and had an idea about when to contact him. So, I call him and say, "Can you handle this now?" and he says yes. I had always maintained our employee banking and other stuff at Central. I never changed that. We would transfer money from Vine Street Trust to it to cover all of those expenses. And when Central Bank could handle the loan, I moved the entire thing over to Central. And I also made sure I did all the insurance business with Mr. Kincaid's Lexington Insurance Agency, you know, and we did other stuff with Kentucky Central Insurance, Mr. Kincaid's old P&C companies. Whatever I could do. Hey, it was one of Mr. Kincaid's companies and I wanted our company to run just as if it were his, without him being there, even to the point when the Kincaid Wilson law firm disbanded, I went up there one day, and they were on the fifth floor next door to Mr. Hagan's office. I walked in there and this portrait of Mr. Kincaid was lying on the floor, and I looked at that and I said, "What's this?" and Hart said, "They didn't want it." And it's hard to believe today, but nobody wanted it, and I said, "Well, can I have it?" They didn't want it, and I took it down to my office and our conference room. It hung in our conference room until the day I left, and Luther Deaton comes up and says, "You're not going to be needing this," and asks if he can have it, and that's the portrait that hangs in Central Bank's lobby, that was lying on the floor. And that's how I felt about him then and that's how I feel about him now. You know, I just felt like he's never gotten what he deserved in this community; that we would not have a community if it were not for him.

Well, you know, and again, I'm not trying to prove myself or portray myself as something I wasn't, he called me and said, "Blondie, I want you to come over here and see something." And so I went over there to his office. And he says, "We have a council meeting tonight, and I am going to present this." And it was it was a scale model thing of Vine Street to Jefferson Street. Mr. Kincaid says,

> I'm going to propose to them that this is what Lexington ought to look like and I propose to them, these are the capital [major] buildings. This is the design that we should have, and that if they'll condemn them, the people who own them now have first right of refusal to buy them

and fix them up, and if they don't want to do that, I'll buy them at the condemnation price and fix them up.

And I remember saying, "You know, that's a hell of a good idea." I mean, it's just a hell of an idea he had there. . . . And he says, "Now, what I want out of this," he says, "cable television is going to someday be big." I didn't even fully understand what cable television was. He says, "I want the cable television rights. A guarantee for the cable television rights. That's all I want, and I'll pay for putting it in."

Well, he took it to the council that night, and it got voted down. Harry Miller, of Barney Miller's, spoke out against it, because, and I didn't know at the time, Harry already had cable in downtown Lexington. Harry was supplying limited cable television to downtown Lexington. And of course, the council voted Kincaid's offer down. They were controlled by the old guard at what is now First Security Bank. Kincaid's proposal just got dropped.

Garvice had been pushing for Lexington to have a strong urban renewal plan and map since at least 1963. His was also one of the first significant voices to push for a downtown convention center with an arena attached to it. Ralph Hacker's story talks about something that took place in July 1974 in front of the Urban Renewal Agency, which was made up of both council members and private sector leaders. Kincaid had become much more vocal several months earlier about the need to condemn buildings to allow development, but the proposal he personally presented at the July meeting of the agency was certainly his most forceful, detailed discussion of his vision. His scale model and drawings of his plan were on public display and his remarks were blunt, calling various buildings "pieces of junk." The only thing that wasn't mentioned during his presentation was his desire for cable television rights, which one can assume was a private behind-closed-doors discussion.

In April 1974, a new six-story glass and aluminum building had been approved for the corner of Vine and Main Streets. This redevelopment project would require significant infrastructure improvements to the area, and Harry Miller had received approval to install cable, for a future cable television system, in the fire alarm conduit at his expense. Lexington didn't have cable television, but he was trying to get an early foothold. Kincaid publicly challenged him on this, and in the end the city decided to seek bids for laying cable. Kincaid postulated that Miller wanted to control the future of cable television by investing $700 in coaxial cable. Miller probably had the last word, though, when he explained to the city that the FCC was adopting rules for cities to follow when granting cable TV franchises, and those rules prohibit anyone who owns or controls a television station from having a cable TV franchise in the same area. All of this drama was reported in the *Lexington Herald-Leader* for all of Lexington to follow.

Though the Urban Renewal Agency rejected Kincaid's condemnation recommendation, in December 1974, Garvice was unanimously elected chairman of a new Urban Development Committee, which the council had authorized in November. This was twelve months before Kincaid's death.

Another story Ralph tells demonstrates a different side of Garvice, one that shows he appreciated a direct, honest opinion.

> Well, I don't want to ever play up that I was anything bigger than I was with Mr. Kincaid, because I wasn't. You recall that in Louis Grizzard's book, he writes about the Central Bank ads and Mr. Kincaid's phone call about the wrong ads running the previous evening.
>
> In early 1975, WVLK-FM had gotten permission to raise its power to 100,000 watts. So, we put WVLK-FM's antenna on WKYT's 1,000-foot television tower. The new antenna was 982 feet high. The increase in power and the additional height would allow WVLK-FM to reach a larger geographic portion of central Kentucky.
>
> In June of that year, after the installation was complete, we had created some print ads to promote the increased broadcasting strength of the station, and Mr. Kincaid wanted to review these ads. I remember we had one ad where we had a gorilla climbing up the tower, like King Kong climbing up the Empire State Building.
>
> Mr. Kincaid calls Hart Hagan and me in, and I remember I took the brunt of his remarks, and Hart Hagan just sat there. And Mr. Kincaid says in a syrupy southern voice, "Now what's this? What's this thing?" This was probably the closest I ever got to being chewed out by him.
>
> So, I get up and walk around to Mr. Kincaid's side of the desk, and I say,
>
>> Mr. Kincaid, we are not a bank. We don't pay interest. We don't take deposits. We're not an insurance company. We don't sell policies. We're an advertising business. We're in radio broadcasting. We're in show business. We are in show business, Mr. Kincaid, and that's what this is. It's a show business ad; that's what this is.
>
> Well, I'll never forget it, he lays the sheet of paper with the proposed ad down, and by this time I had moved to the front side of his desk. He lays it down and just looks at me, and you know

I sometimes wonder if he ever knew my name, because he says, "Well, Blondie, what makes you so damned independent?" and I say,

> Mr. Kincaid, you've paid me well, and I've got two weeks' pay in the bank and I figure if you fire me, I'll have two more weeks of severance pay coming, and sure as hell somebody wants to work as much as I do will be able to find a job in a month.

> Well, he had picked up the ad again by then, and all of a sudden, he just throws the ad down and says, "Blondie, I wish everybody in my company felt just like you do. Do what you want to do," and just like that, he waves me way, and that was the last word that was ever said about it.

Ralph says Mr. Kincaid was very proud of his broadcasting companies. WVLK was the dominant leader in local radio, and WKYT-TV was a close second to WLEX-TV, having become affiliated with CBS, the number one network in the nation. WKYT-TV would soon become the number one television station in Lexington, shortly after Kincaid's death. Before Garvice died in November of 1975, he decided he needed to move WVLK out of the Phoenix Hotel. The 177-year-old hotel, which Garvice first acquired in November 1959, had been sold to Northwestern Mutual Life Insurance Company in 1967. In 1974, through a series of transactions involving R. W. Crabtree at the end, Kincaid reacquired control of the hotel, and it was soon announced that the hotel would be closed. The *Lexington Herald-Leader* wrote a full-page story on the history of the hotel in May 1974 listing many of the famous celebrities, like Marilyn Monroe and Danny Thomas, and politicians like John F. Kennedy and Dwight D. Eisenhower, who stayed there, and important conventions that were held there. The Phoenix Hotel was the place to be seen, and yet even though it experienced many remodels and refurbishments, its time had come to an end, and it would be a casualty to Lexington's needed urban renewal.

Kincaid understood it was time for the "grand old lady" to go away and make way for new downtown Lexington landmarks. He wanted to get started building his downtown corporate headquarters, which would house all his businesses except for WKYT-TV, but the city's embrace of his urban renewal plan was going too slow, so he was pressed into doing something else.

In 1959, when Kincaid first acquired the Phoenix Hotel, he purchased it from the estate of a wealthy Chicago real estate developer, Sanford S. Ruttenberg. The Ruttenberg family were an old retailing family from Madison, Wisconsin. Their parents, Morris (Meir) and Bessie, were originally from

Russia and had relocated to the United States in 1894. They briefly settled in New York City but soon moved to Chicago in 1910 and then relocated to Madison in the 1920s after the birth of their last child, a daughter, in 1919. Sanford, their oldest child, was born in 1894 in New York, and his brother, Jerome, was born in Chicago in 1909. Morris and Bessie had a total of six sons and three daughters. In the 1940s, Sanford Ruttenberg, a graduate of the University of Wisconsin, and two of his brothers moved to Chicago and organized a real estate development business.

During the 1920s and 1930s, the Morris Ruttenberg family owned and operated a group of Midwest retail clothing stores named Wonder Stores. In 1924, Morris opened his eleventh store in Madison on the corner of Carroll and State Streets on what's referred to as the Capitol Square. In Kentucky, the Dawahare family originated a similar retail clothing store chain in 1907, and its chain of stores grew to nearly thirty stores in Kentucky and a few adjacent states and was managed by four generations of the family. Both family retail chains survived two world wars and the Great Depression, but neither survived competition from the large department store chains and local malls. Nevertheless, both families accumulated a significant amount of wealth from the real estate underlying the buildings that housed their stores. In the 1940s, Sanford and his two brothers, Joseph and Sal, closed their family retail business and proceeded to Chicago to set up their real estate business. The Dawahare family expanded its footprint of stores to nearly thirty stores in 1979 but then began a long retrenchment cycle that saw the chain enter into bankruptcy in 2008 and close its remaining twenty-two stores.

In the mid-1940s, when Sanford acquired the Phoenix Hotel, he soon brought in his brother, Jerome J. Ruttenberg, to supervise the extensive rehabilitation of the iconic property in 1947. After its completion, in 1948, Jerome was put in charge of operating the Phoenix Hotel. Over the next thirty years, Jerome would be involved in the development of many of Lexington's best-known neighborhoods and significant real estate developments, including Lexington's first mall, Turfland Mall. One can easily understand how Garvice and Jerome became associated and why it was natural for Kincaid to acquire the Phoenix Hotel and Madison, Wisconsin, properties from Sanford S. Ruttenberg's estate in 1959.

The Phoenix Hotel had been home to WVLK radio since Garvice acquired it in 1951, and by 1974, Garvice needed to find a new home for his prized radio station. His relationship with Jerome Ruttenberg had been a successful one. When Ruttenberg decided to build Turfland Mall on Harrodsburg Road, Kincaid was also there developing adjacent parcels of apartments. In fact,

Garvice controlled several parcels of land near Turfland Mall, and in 1974, when he knew he needed to find a new home for WVLK, he decided he would use one of those parcels of land for a new six-story glass and concrete office building.

In August 1975, Garvice announced that he was building a six-story office building on Harrodsburg Road near Turfland Mall. The building would have 54,000 square feet and house the operations and corporate offices of WVLK and Kentucky Finance Company. In the drawing provided to the *Lexington Herald-Leader*, the building was called the "WVLK Radio Tower," was estimated to cost $1.25 million, and was expected to be completed in eight months. Ralph Hacker recalled Kincaid's WVLK Radio Tower office building this way:

> Let me tell you a story about that. It's Sunday morning in October 1975, and I get a phone call from Ray Holbrook, and he says, "The boss wants to see us this morning." And I say, "Mr. Hagan?" and he says, "No, Mr. Kincaid." Now, I'm thirty years old, and I say, "Okay, I'll be downtown," and Holbrook says, "No, it's at his house." So, I go up to his house at 96 Chinoe Road, and I pull into the driveway, and I can see Holbrook circling the block, one more time, around the Shriners Hospital and all the stuff around that.
>
> So, he pulls in and we both go in, and we see Bob Curtin, Robert Bartella, and Ken Davis. We are escorted into the dining room and Mr. Kincaid comes in and sits down. He places a big napkin up here on his chest and his big belly is down below it and they bring him in a big plate of country ham and eggs, coffee, and biscuits. They don't offer us a glass of water.
>
> So, Mr. Kincaid says, "Boys, we are here to discuss this building out on Harrodsburg Road." Now, he had been down to the radio station about a month earlier and I would have bet he hadn't been there in years, and while he is there, Mr. Kincaid says, "This place is a dump," and he looked at Mr. Wilson and said, "Earl, we've got to get these people out of here."
>
> So, we are all at his house, sitting in the dining room, and he says in a syrupy southern drawl, "Now, Blondie, tell me what floor you want in this building," and I say, "Well, I figure the top floor, Mr. Kincaid." Now, we are talking about the building out by Turfland Mall. You know, that bank, or whatever it is now.
>
> Well, Mr. Kincaid says, "Why?" and I started explaining to him why and all of a sudden, all three of those guys from Kentucky Finance just started screaming and saying "You can't have the top floor. He can't do this, and you can't do that."
>
> Mr. Kincaid just sits there eating his food and then just looks

over at them, after hearing them argue. I had just shut up and Ray Holbrook hadn't said a word.

Mr. Kincaid says, "Well, here's what's going happen," and he says,

> Mr. Davis, I'm going give you all the top floor. You three take that floor. You take it and decorate it like that brothel which you've got now and run all your whores through there. Mr. Bartella, you take another corner over there and you go ahead and build your bar and stay drunk like you have for the last 25 years. And Mr. Curtin, you go ahead and take the rest of the floor and have your people there because you've been running the place all these years anyway.

And he says, "You take all your staff and put them down on the third floor however you want and divide it up as you want."

Now Mr. Kincaid looks at me and says,

> Now Blondie, you go ahead and figure out a way to get your conduit from the top of the building where your three antennas and all that stuff will sit. You'll have all the second floor of the building for your radio station, and out there on top of the building we'll have, sitting at the top of the building, a sign calling it the WVLK 590 building.

Well, the Kentucky Finance guys start going nuts and saying, "You can't do that, it has to be called the Kentucky Finance Building, it has to be named after Kentucky Finance." And Mr. Kincaid says, "It's the WVLK 590 building located at 590 Harrodsburg Road," and one of them says, "That's not the address," and Mr. Kincaid looks over at them and parts his hands and says, "It will be," and the meeting is over, just like that.

You know the building, it's just beyond Turfland Mall. It reminds you of the Central Bank Branch offices, but is maybe four stories taller. I think a bank moved into it. We never got to move there. Mr. Kincaid died within two weeks of that meeting. Okay. He died within two weeks.

Okay. So that's also when they announced that they had purchased the parcel where Kincaid Towers is now. It was a hotel building foundation that had gone bankrupt [Hotel Lexington]. The Committee bought it and made it Kincaid Towers office building.

Author: *Garvice had struck a deal to acquire it a week before he died.*

Yeah, the Committee made the announcement, and they

eventually came to me and said, "We're going to give you the third floor." They didn't ask me what I wanted. They said "You're going to take the third floor over here. You can do with it what you want; just put your radio stations over there," and that's what we did.

Author: And Paul Dunbar moved you in!

Paul Dunbar, my man, moved us in.

You know Paul Dunbar didn't say much, but he was the funniest sucker. Well one time, we were at a National Association of Broadcasters convention in Las Vegas, and Ralph Gabbard found this restaurant. It was an oriental restaurant. Well, we had this long table that was full of us, and we started making toasts. Everybody is making a toast. Well, right next to us is a very big table full of Japanese, and Paul Dunbar, after taking toast after toast down the table, stands up, and now, Dunbar had been in the Navy. Well, he stands up and says, "Here is to Admiral Yamamoto . . ." The Japanese look up at us, and Paul says, "commander of the Japanese fleet at the Battle of Midway. Too bad yomi." ["Yomi" is a Japanese term meaning "Knowing the mind of the opponent."]

Author: Ralph, you were at the station during the period when Ron Nickell was there. What can you tell me about him, and how did his relationship with Jane develop? I also recently found out that Ron was the cousin of Jim Jordan.

Yes, I knew that; I believe they were first cousins. Ron Nickell was a nighttime DJ, a mobile unit reporter, and all-around announcer. In short, Ron thought he had the world by the tail but could not control the animal within. He was a disc jockey at WVLK when he and Jane started dating, and they were married by the time I arrived at the station. I was told that Jane would sometimes visit him in the evening when he was doing his shift after they started dating.

I think Mr. Kincaid caught him having a lot of extra marital affairs and just flat-out fired him. After he left, I recall he ended up working somewhere for a jingle company. Eventually, he ended up in Dallas, Texas, and he shot through a door and killed a deputy sheriff. He apparently thought some people were after him. Anyway, he spent time in the Huntsville prison down in Texas and after that he went to Virginia Beach. I had seen him in Dallas, at a broadcast convention, after he started working for a production company.

Author: Did you know that he and Jane actually got married in Corydon, Indiana, in February 1963? They get married there and in March, Mr. and Mrs. Kincaid announce the engagement of Jane to Ron in the Lexington Herald. *This wouldn't be so odd, but then in July the couple apply for a Fayette County marriage license. This is reported in the newspaper, and then on August 3 they have a large wedding at Central Christian Church.*

Ron and Jane's wedding was a big deal in Lexington, and the Lexington Herald-Leader reported that before the wedding, various local wealthy families held "prenuptial parties" for the couple, at both the Idle Hour and Lexington Country Clubs, at the Phoenix Hotel, at Spindletop, and at their homes. There were at least thirteen events listed in the paper about a week before their wedding.

It's obvious the Kincaid family didn't want Jane's Indiana civil marriage service to be known, and getting a local marriage license provided the necessary smokescreen to limit questions. Jane wasn't pregnant at the time of their Indiana marriage, because Brett wasn't born until February 1964.

Jane and Ron divorced in May 1970, and their divorce records indicate they separated in March of 1969. It also confirms the fact that they were married in Indiana in February 1963.

Robert, I can't tell you how much I appreciate you writing this book on Mr. Kincaid. I mean that with all my heart, and I hope that Joan [Kincaid] and the rest of Mr. Kincaid's family read it and understand that many people loved him, and while he may have been a tyrant to many, he was still a great man.

I believe Ted Grizzard said it best in this autobiography when he wrote, and I paraphrase, "A lot of people in this town became very important and influential because of Garvice Kincaid's money." I would only add, I hope while enjoying the advantage of that statement, I hope I was never seen as having taken advantage him or his organization but used what he created to help make this a better community and state in which to work, live, and raise a family.

One only needs to look around Lexington to see the legacy of Garvice D. Kincaid; while his name appears on none of it, his presence is there, from the development of Lexington Center and Rupp Arena to including nearly every change in the look of downtown Lexington from Woodland Avenue to Georgetown Road. You can travel around the community and see his influence in the shopping centers and office buildings that have provided all kinds of economic opportunities for this city. Look around and count the major buildings constructed prior to the collapse of Kentucky Central Life, and then count those projects completed since. His influence in life and in death is nearly unmeasurable.

Ralph Hacker joined WVLK as what he calls "a boy." He remained with the station for thirty-three years and adapted to the many changes. In 1982, Ralph made the bold decision to switch WVLK, an easy-listening station, to a country format. He had observed the changes taking place around the country and knew that WVLK needed to adapt to them. Publicly, the station's management was criticized, but within a few short months, it was more than obvious to everyone that Hacker's bold decision was a grand slam home run for the company. He was right, but in February 1993, he probably experienced his biggest change yet, but also his biggest opportunity.

The Kentucky Insurance Department had taken over control of Kentucky Central Life, and the broadcasting properties were being put up for sale. Anyone interested needed to put together their bids quickly. Both the Ralphs hastily put together a consortium of investors to acquire their respective companies; Hacker, WVLK radio, and Gabbard, WKYT television. Ralph Hacker was successful; Ralph Gabbard failed but was paid a significant compliment when the buyer, Gray Communications, relocated its corporate offices to Lexington for Gabbard to manage all its broadcasting properties.

In the spring of 1993, Ralph Hacker and his investors acquired WVLK for $11 million. His entity to control the company was HMH Broadcasting Inc., which he and his wife, Marilyn, named after their daughter, Heather Marie Hacker. Ralph controlled 40 percent of the organization. The other investors were not your normal Lexington elite but folks who had built a relationship with Ralph and the station over its fifty-year history: Jack Kain, Ted Hahn, Patty Clines, Dr. Billy Forbess, George Salem Trust, Heather Marie Hacker, and twelve employees. The station never missed a beat, and in the years that followed continued to be the number one radio station in Lexington, but the competition was changing, and large multistate broadcasting entities were entering the market.

In 1999, Ralph and his investors decided they needed either to acquire more radio stations or negotiate the sale of the radio station to one of the national media giants. After thirty-three years with WVLK, and at the age of fifty-four, Ralph and his investors agreed to sell HMH Broadcasting to Cumulus Broadcasting for $44.5 million. Hacker's 40 percent share of the proceeds before paying off the acquisition debt, which had been significantly reduced over the last five years, was almost $18 million. The HMH entity had sixty-five employees and consisted of five radio stations. It was bittersweet for Ralph, and with tears in his eyes, he told the media, "I will probably always be part of WVLK, because I have been part of it since I was a boy."

In 1949, when Garvice acquired the station from Happy Chandler, the purchase price was never disclosed, but it was reported that Chandler built the station for $100,000 the year before. The station had been struggling financially, so one can probably assume that Kincaid paid about $100,000 to acquire it in 1949. His investment had increased in value to $11 million in 1993, when the Insurance Department sold it, and to over $44 million by

1999. WVLK was just another example of Garvice Kincaid investing in a good business, and good people, and watching it grow.

Ralph Hacker recalled another story that provides some insight into the future problems that would ultimately lead to the financial collapse of Kentucky Central Life Insurance and the loss of most of Mr. Kincaid's empire. It's important because it happened in late 1977, about two years after Kincaid's death. Ralph hadn't realized the importance of it until we discussed it.

The Kentucky Club

By late 1977, Bud Burnett had already begun cementing his control of Kincaid's Advisory Committee, which controlled his estate. Earl Wilson had aged off the Committee when he reached age 70 in March of that year and been replaced by Ed Schaeffer in April. In October, Burnett and Schaeffer were in the process of negotiating Al Florence's resignation from the Committee. Hart Hagan would replace Florence. In less than eighteen months after Garvice's death, Bud Burnett had become chairman of Kincaid's Committee. In addition, he had Ed Schaeffer, who would become his enabler and the needed second vote against any objections to his plans. When necessary, it would always be two votes against one. Bud Burnett had taken charge, but he was personally insecure and knew that he wasn't viewed as having the power and gravitas of Garvice.

Bud Burnett had been with Garvice since 1959 and had lived in Lexington since 1963 but was still relatively unknown. Kincaid never involved him with Central Bank or any of his banks, where Earl Wilson had worked hand-in-glove with Garvice on almost all his business interests. Burnett was Kincaid's insurance accountant, and Garvice limited his involvement to things concerning Kentucky Central Life Insurance Company. Kincaid's law firm handled his mortgage loans, real estate deals, and various legal needs, and his banks and finance companies were his personal passion and had their own accounting personnel. Bud Burnett was also not active in Kincaid's charitable works or political activities, and he had little to no visible presence in the Lexington newspapers until after Kincaid's death. Yet in the span of a little over a year, this Louisville accountant, who had worked at two failed property and casualty insurance companies before getting hired by Garvice, was now chairman of his Advisory Committee. Hart Hagan had a much more visible presence in the Lexington community than Bud Burnett and probably knew more about Kincaid's various business interests than Burnett. Like Earl Wilson, Hagan had been directly involved in the ownership and oversight of many of Kincaid's businesses and investments.

Kentucky Central Life Insurance was a publicly traded company, and just as Hart Hagan was important in maintaining the broadcasting companies' compliance with FCC regulations, Bud Burnett, Kentucky Central Life's chief financial officer, had an important role in maintaining the company's compliance with the SEC's rules and regulations. Kentucky Central Life was its own stock transfer agent during a time when everyone dealt with physical share certificates. As the transfer agent, the company was responsible for recording transactions, canceling and issuing shareholder certificates, processing investor mailings, and handling a host of other investor problems, including reissuing lost or stolen certificates. This department also worked to ensure that investors received their dividend payments in a timely manner and oversaw the mailing of quarterly reports and other shareholder-related mailings.

In addition, Kentucky Central Life had both voting and nonvoting shares, and while Kincaid controlled about 80% of the voting shares, the company still had to maintain SEC compliance for both classes of stock. This was an important function, and one Bud Burnett was responsible for. In fact, ironically, in March 1975, Burnett married his second wife, who worked in the stock transfer department. Bud Burnett was important to Garvice because of his knowledge of insurance accounting and SEC rules and regulations, not because of his ability to run a life insurance company. David Brain was the president of Kentucky Central Life and oversaw the company's insurance marketing and administration operations. Brain was hired by Kincaid in 1961 and was his expert on the marketing and administrative operations of the company. He also had a stronger educational and professional background than Burnett, and these traits were important to Garvice. He was a graduate of Harvard University with a master's degree in business administration and had been a marketing officer at the much larger Monumental Life Insurance Company in Baltimore, Maryland.

I will always believe Kincaid never intended for Bud Burnett to run the day-to-day business operations of Kentucky Central Life Insurance. It wasn't the roll that he was best suited for or how Kincaid was using him before his death. David Brain was president and responsible for running the company.

In August 1976, Burnett, with the help of either Earl Wilson or Al Florence, or both, pushed Brain out of the company and assumed control of it. Earl Wilson was chairman of the board, but Burnett was the president in charge of the day-to-day running of the company. This was the first milestone change that led to the failure of the Kincaid empire. Bud Burnett was now running Kentucky Central Life Insurance but had arrived at that point through manipulation, versus reputation, and would spend the next few years striving to garner the respect that Kincaid had.

My old boss, Cliff Forbush, described Burnett as insecure and said that before Garvice died, he would go around and try to find out what people were doing for Kincaid or David Brain, and after Garvice died, he labored to be considered the man at the top of Kincaid's empire.

In other words, by November 1977, Burnett wanted to be respected and known as a person of power and influence and not just an administrator of Kincaid's estate. This desire for power, with the help of Ed Schaeffer and the financial resources of Garvice's estate, enabled him to go down a path of bad business decisions and unbridled lending that would destroy Kentucky Central Life Insurance Company and most of Kincaid's empire over the next fifteen years.

Everyone makes mistakes, but it's the fool and the incompetent person who doesn't temper their actions and their egos based on the knowledge of negative experiences. I was taught many years ago that an investment person needs to have a strong conviction about an investment, but no matter how convinced they are about the probable outcome, they must always maintain some small fraction of doubt. This fraction of doubt is what enables an investment professional to recognize their mistakes before they drive the investment bus off a cliff. Another way of saying it is that you should never completely believe your own BS. The adage that we learn more from our mistakes than from our successes has been proven true my whole investment career. Mistakes are humbling experiences but also important learning opportunities.

Working on this book, I asked many of my former colleagues whether they remember anyone commenting on Burnett being smart or intelligent, and no one could. In fact, the conversations usually ended with, "Burnett was respected," but the respect people had for him was more out of fear of losing their job than anything else. While Burnett understood insurance accounting, he lacked the analytical capacity to appreciate the impact of what he was doing. Finally, his desire for respect and admiration clouded his ability to view business opportunities with Kincaid's business acumen. Garvice was always investing and risking his own money, but Burnett treated Kincaid's wealth like casino chips and, like most poor gamblers, doubled down in the hope of recovering his losses.

Ralph Hacker's story about the Kentucky Club is probably the first indication of Burnett's desire to be considered a man of influence and power. It's interesting because it demonstrates Burnett's lack of concern about financial risk and his fiduciary responsibility to the Kincaid estate. Ralph Hacker's recollection of the Kentucky Club:

Do you know the story about the Kentucky Club in Florida?

Author: I don't think so.

There's a building down there called the Kentucky Club (1536 South Ocean Drive, Vero Beach, Florida 32963). We lived four complexes away from it. I think I can name most of the people initially involved with it: Don and Dudley Webb; South Creek Properties Partners' Harold Mullis, Ted Hahn, and J. Pat Williams; and also James H. (Mike) Molloy (a Democratic Party heavyweight); Don Wallace; and Dr. Edwin J. Nighbert. These people were all important players in the development of Lexington and Kentucky politics. In addition, there was Dr. David Price, who was a well-known emergency room doctor and also a private pilot.

Well, in 1977, Dudley Webb and some of these other guys fly to Naples, Florida. They are looking for a place they can buy that they can vacation in. They were friends and thought it would be nice to have a place close to each other. In addition, some of the owners would rent their units out at various times. So, they started looking for a fixer-upper in Florida.

Well, they couldn't find anything in Naples, and someone said they should look over in Vero Beach because they thought there was a complex over there for sale. It was on the ocean, and they heard they might be able to buy it.

Author: My research shows that Winter Beach Land Development Company originally began the project in 1973. It was a three-story, nineteen-unit project then and called Ocean View Condominiums. The developers got the thing going but by 1976 were in trouble. One should recall that in 1975, the United States was experiencing a gas shortage, inflation, and high interest rates. A bank called The Beach Bank of Vero Beach ended up with the property in 1977, and it is the entity that sold the units to the original participants of the Kentucky Club. It appears that two units were previously sold, since I found that only seventeen units were sold in 1978.

In 1980, Dudley and the Webb Company began phase II of the project and built a five-story, twenty-six-unit building to complete the complex. There are forty-five units in total at the Kentucky Club. Dudley Webb initially had a unit in phase I and then moved to the new building after completing the 1980 building.

Below are the original owners of the Kentucky Club. Nearly all the property transfers were recorded in March and April of 1978. They are in order by their recording date:

Dr. David Price	(Price Aviation) - ER doctor & pilot	Unit 307	$37,000
Ted & Julia Hahn	South Creek Properties	Unit 305	$37,000
Henry E. Cravens	Lexington	Unit 303	$37,000
Dr. M. Cary Blaydes & Nancy C. Blades		Unit 304	$35,500
Dr. James E. Russell & Sue. T. Russell		Unit 302	$35,500
Robert J. Bell & Karen Bell		Unit 103	$34,000
Mr. & Mrs. Wendell T. Setzer and Mrs. Kenneth Hizon		Unit 104	$34,000
Dr. Len W. Morrow		Unit 205	$45,000
Harold H. Mullis & Will Mullis		Unit 306	$37,000
Pat & Bettye Williams		Unit 304	$37,000
Edwin J. & Sharon Nighbert		Unit 302	$37,000
Webb Properties		Unit 207	$35,000
Judith J. Clancy	Somerset, Kentucky	Unit 203	$35,000
Mr. & Mrs. James Clifton and Mr. & Mrs. John Dicken		Unit 201	$35,000
Thomas & Carolyn Preston		Unit 102	$34,000
Mr. & Mrs. James Clifton and Mr. & Mrs. John Dicken		Unit 101	$34,500
Brilliant Corp. (aka Mike Molloy)		Unit 206	$35,500
Robert J. Bell & Karen Bell	September 1980	Unit 106-B	$45,000

Well, the guys fly over to Vero Beach. Now understand, this is Don Webb telling me this story within thirty to forty-five days of Don dying. We were in Florida, and this was the second time that he had told me this story. Don and Julie are at our house having dinner, and I am just relaying to you what Don Webb told me.

Don was at a board meeting at First Security Bank, and he comes out and Will Rouse's secretary tells him he got a phone call from Dudley and Dudley needs him to call him back.

Don says he returns the call and Dudley says, "I'm in Vero Beach and we found a building for $250,000, and I just wrote him a check for $25,000 for down payment."

Don says to Dudley, "You can't do that. We don't have $25,000. And Don says, "We can't cover it," and Dudley says, "Well, Willie Rouse will cover it," and so Don goes right into Willie Rouse's office, the president of First Security Bank, and tells him what Dudley's done, and Willie says, "I can't cover it. I can't help you out; that's in Florida."

So, Don gets back on the phone with Dudley and tells him Willie can't cover it because it's in Florida. "He won't cover it." Well, Dudley says, "They are going to deposit the check tomorrow!" There's a pause in the conversation and Dudley says, "Call John Rampulla." [Kentucky Central Life Insurance Company's vice president of mortgage loans.]

So, Don says he calls John Rampulla and lays it all out, what Dudley's done down in Florida. John tells him to hold on, and so he waits on the phone three or four minutes and Bud Burnett comes on the line and says, "What you need?" and so Don explains it all to Bud.

Well Bud says, "Okay, so we'll cover your $25,000 down payment" and then says, "We'll also cover the rest of the $250,000 for the purchase of the building." And then says, "How much do you think it's going to cost you to fix it up?" Well Don hasn't seen the property and says, "I don't know for sure" and then gives Bud Burnett a ballpark figure.

Well Burnett tells him, "Well, we'll cover that, and make a loan to you for it," but then he says, "I have one stipulation. I want you to sell the units to people in Lexington, Kentucky, or at least the state of Kentucky, and we'll guarantee that if they're qualified, we'll give them 100% financing!" The condos were around $35,000 at that time. And Bud says again, "That's what I want to do, and that's my stipulation."

Well, Dudley calls Don back, and Don tells Dudley, "You aren't going to believe this shit," and tells him just what Bud had just agreed to do.

Don says that he didn't know why Burnett wanted to do this for about two weeks, but was eventually told that a week before he called, the Florida Department of Insurance had just sent Kentucky Central Life a letter saying they had sold all this insurance in Florida and didn't have enough mortgage loans in the state of Florida to cover the insurance.

That's how they got the Kentucky Club down there in Vero Beach, according to Don Webb, and I think Dudley would back this story up.

Ralph and I discussed this for several minutes, and I explained that I have never heard of an insurance department doing something quite like that. Florida was one of Kentucky Central Life's largest new business states, and so I can see where they may get contacted by the Insurance Department, but I rather doubt that any department would ever put in writing a specific request for a certain type of investment; e.g., mortgage loans.

In my forty-year career I have never seen the state of Florida do anything like that, and during my fifteen-year career in the investment department at Kentucky Central Life, I never witnessed it, and I've never seen any regulations that would imply this. The state of California is the most activist state in the nation in relation to insurance regulation, and it will, from time to time, contact a company to encourage "more investment in their state" or try to get companies to invest in more green energy initiates, but even then, it doesn't have regulations to require it. California's insurance commissioner is elected to office, whereas Florida's insurance commissioner, as in the majority of states, is appointed by the governor. Finally, Kentucky Central Life's investment department had multiple investments related to Florida companies, Florida municipalities, and other state government entities. I have no doubt that Don was told about a letter, but I think there were other reasons.

In April 1977, Burnett, with Earl Wilson, was pictured in a full-page article announcing the construction of the company's new home office building, Kincaid Towers, but he isn't quoted. Earl Wilson provided all the details about the new structure and discussed the other Kincaid companies that would be moving there. Earl was the one in charge.

In September 1977, Burnett was in the Lexington paper, along with Earl Wilson and Governor Jullian Carroll, celebrating the company's seventy-fifth anniversary. In the page-and-a-half article, Burnett discussed the history of the company and what Garvice was able to do with it, but in the article he comes off more as a historian than a "man of strength and power."

By November 1977, Bud Burnett was on a mission to become more of a player in the Lexington community and the state. He had probably been looking for a way to improve his image in the community, and Don Webb's telephone call provided him with the opportunity he was looking for to make a statement, and he knew the Webbs would use it for his benefit. Why not?—

100% financing to qualified buyers during a period of economic problems and high interest rates. I don't know what interest rate the Kentucky Club loans were made at in March 1978, but I suspect they were probably around 10 percent in a 12 percent interest rate environment. Friends of Bud (FOB) always received better terms or deals than the normal market. For instance, a 100% mortgage loan is outside the norms of lending, but not for FOBs.

The Kentucky Club members and borrowers were fortunate that Bud Burnett was looking to become more of a player in the Lexington community, but I suspect that some of the people who purchased their units provided their own funds or financing.

One interesting point to this story is that in 1979 to 1980, the economy was in the grips of a terrible recession due to the energy crisis. It was a period when most commercial projects were not being built, and yet Dudley Webb was able to construct phase II of the Kentucky Club and add twenty-six more units, in a six-story building, to the complex. In September 1980, Webb Brothers Construction recorded twenty-eight transactions for those units in the new building. Many of the units went to new members, including Joe B. Hall, Robert L. Pollard, Cap Hershey, Dr. John D. Cronin, and The Collins Bowling Lanes Inc. (Patrick F. Collins–Lexington). Several were purchased by the original members of the Kentucky Club. Some members purchased better units, while others purchased an additional unit. Today, the two-building Kentucky Club's forty-five units are still sought after by Kentuckians looking for a warmer climate—in a place with a Kentucky accent.

In working on this book, I asked John Rampulla about the Kentucky Club. John said he remembered when it got started and that he knew Burnett was involved in helping the Webbs get it going, but he didn't recall Kentucky Central Life ever making a loan on it. In fact, he was very sure that the company hadn't, but then I suggested that maybe Burnett used the Dania Bank down in Florida to do the financing. Kentucky Central Life controlled this Florida bank in a downstream subsidiary, and by 1977, Burnett and the Committee were already at war with Kincaid's wife and daughters. Dania Bank was an isolated entity, and using it would have more easily hidden this special lending relationship from their prying eyes. John agreed that this is probably where the loans were originated, because in those early years, after Kincaid's death, Burnett and the Committee didn't approve many new mortgage loans. In addition, by April 1978, the Committee had sold this bank to outside investors. I asked John about the financing for the phase II addition in 1980 and whether the company had been involved in that, and he didn't recall it but also said that didn't mean the company didn't finance it because he knew the Committee did some transactions in the company's downstream subsidiary, Mid-Central Investments, that he wasn't involved in.

Garvice TV—"And That's the Way It Is."

Beginning in the 1950s, Garvice went on a mission to acquire a Lexington television station. He spent a great deal of effort and resources applying for licenses and entering into deals that fell through. Garvice had been in a public battle to buy WLEX-TV and had failed. In addition, he also had developed a hostile relationship with the owners of radio station WLAP stemming from his fight for a television license. He was frustrated but persistent.

In 1953, the owners of WLAP, The Community Broadcast System, were given a license to build channel 27 (WKXP-TV) television in Lexington. The owners delayed building the station, but eventually began broadcasting in September 1957. By 1958, the owners decided to sell the station. Garvice was in the running to acquire it for $275,000 until he stipulated that he also wanted to acquire radio station WLAP for a total of $650,000. Negotiations were soon dropped and Hubert Taft, who had broadcasting properties in Cincinnati, soon stepped in and acquired the station. Taft changed the station call letters to WKYT and changed its network affiliation from CBS to ABC. This further increased his clout with ABC, where he already had an affiliate. Taft was building his broadcasting network and soon created the umbrella organization, Taft Broadcasting.

In 1966, Taft Broadcasting broadened the scope of its business and acquired the Hanna-Barbera Company for $12 million in stock. Hanna-Barbera was the creator and owner of the Flintstones, Yogi Bear, and other cartoon characters. It also held the licensing rights to toys related to those characters. By 1967, the company owned a total of seven television stations, which was the FCC limit. This restriction forced the company to evaluate its whole portfolio of stations. Channel 27 operated in the smallest market of any of its stations and, it felt it had the least growth potential, when compared to alternative stations they might like to acquire. In the end, this review steered them to the decision to sell WKYT-TV.

Garvice had expressed an interest in acquiring the station many times over the last several years, with little feedback from the Taft company. Kincaid never publicly explained how the two entities got together, and some believe it was a happenstance meeting on a flight with a Taft executive that did it, but a deal was struck and in June 1967, and Kincaid acquired channel 27 for $2.5 million. This was almost ten times the price he could have acquired it for nine years earlier.

In Francis M. Nash's 1995 *Towers Over Kentucky*, he described Kincaid's acquisitions and the station history of ownership this way[17]:

> In January of [1966], the strategy changed [to get into television] and Kincaid called on Taft Broadcasting of Cincinnati in an attempt to purchase WKYT-TV. A deal was completed with a price tag of almost ten times what he had reportedly offered to pay nine years earlier. Kincaid then petitioned the Commission for dismissal of his application for Channel 62 and instead applied for transfer of ownership of WKYT-27.
>
> WBLG received a construction permit for TV 62 in September 1967, and the switch was thrown to begin transmissions May 28, 1968, from its studio and transmitting facilities on Bryant Road, on the eastern edge of the city, with a 998-foot tower, just below the FAA maximum allowed height. Barbara White, the owner's daughter, and Mayor Charles Wylie participated in the ceremony. The station began regular programming on June 2.
>
> Meanwhile, under Kincaid's guidance, WKYT improved its equipment, enlarged the staff, switched affiliation back to CBS and constructed a new $5 million colonial-style building to house the station on Winchester Road, across from WBLG. The new structure and its state-of-the art studios were occupied in October 1969. The two competitors had considered erecting a common tower for their antennas and then operat[ing] them from separate buildings on the property below, but WKYT decided it would hinder its individual identity and elected instead to settle nearby.
>
> . . .
>
> WKYT had several management changes during the Taft ownership years and struggled financially and in the ratings. In 1970, Ralph Gabbard moved from Richmond radio to become sales manager of WKYT-TV. Two years later he was promoted to general manager and continued to successfully lead the station for the next two decades, turning the station around in profits and audience.
>
> Bluegrass Broadcasting, a division of Kentucky Central Insurance, the owner of WKYT-TV and WVLK radio in Lexington, expanded [its] Kentucky TV holdings in 1985, when it purchased the license of WKYH Channel 57 in Hazard and built a new station, going on the air with WYMT (Your Mountain Television).
>
> But trouble in the empire of the late Garvice Kincaid in 1993, mainly the insurance company, would startle the Lexington

---

17   Francis M. Nash, *Towers over Kentucky* (Host Communications 1995).

community and cause the break-up of the broadcast properties. The state insurance commission takeover of Kentucky Central eventually led to the sale of the assets of the Lexington insurer. The liquidation meant WKYT and WYMT would go to the highest bidder. A Georgia firm, Gray Communications, with president John T. Williams, outbid Ralph Gabbard for the television stations by a small margin. A request by Gabbard to the state that would allow him to increase his bid was rejected and the sale was declared completed. The $38 million transaction was approved by the FCC and Gray took over operations in September 1994.

Gray, which owned stations in Georgia, Florida and Louisiana and two newspapers as well, made Gabbard the president of their television holdings. Wayne Martin became general manager of WKYT and the basic staff of both Lexington and Hazard remained intact. Gabbard said the new owner wanted the "best television possible"—the same philosophy he had followed in the past. Gray moved its headquarters to Lexington and Gabbard took on the task of building and expanding the company's television interests, a job he called "exciting."

. . .

WLEX had the strong advantage in news ratings since its beginning until overtaken by WKYT in the survey of November 1975. That number one position has been held by Channel 27 news since then, with the exception of one brief period in 1983. Ken Kurtz had joined the station in April 1975 as news director and soon began to make changes. Kurtz said, "We began to stress packages, editing and news content, and make more professional news decisions." Both 18 and 27 had been doing half-hour local evening news since the late 1960s, as well as late night and noon reports. Kurtz cancelled the noon, to concentrate on the evening and brought in new people. WKYT hired the city's first black female reporter, Lauretta Harris, who became weekend anchor then moved on to Louisville.

By 1995, according to published reports, there were three men and seven minority women on Lexington TV news staffs, with Valeria Cummings of Channel 27 having the most seniority with eleven years.

Stations began converting their news departments from film to videotape in the mid-1970s and WTVQ first went with the new 1/2-inch tape Akai format, while WLEX and WKYT opted to wait and invest in the better quality 3/4-inch equipment.

WKYT's race to the top was also fueled by money poured into equipment, innovations and larger staff, from nine people to handle all news in 1975 to more than 40 by the early 1990s. Kentucky Central TV's Garvice Kincaid, who had long dreamed of having the best, died, however before seeing his station make it to number one.

A trio anchored by John Lindgren with Denny Trease on sports, then later Rob Bromley, and Brad James doing weather kept Channel 27 first in the news ratings for years, often with double the audience of the other two. Lindgren had come to Lexington from Louisville TV, a reversal of the usual trend. When Lindgren departed to Nashville, Sam Dick took over in 1987 and joined Barbara Bailey as main anchors.

Susan White, for 14 years the *Herald-Leader* TV critic, in an article in 1993, cited more local news, strong reporting, large staff including veteran reporters like Jerry Sander and Barry Peel and good anchor teams as part of the reason WKYT kept the stranglehold on first place.

Competition among the three stations has been keen, with staffs creating expensive promotion campaigns, buying new equipment, polling viewers, modernizing and changing set designs, all in an effort to win over the audience. And there was the usual shifting of reporters and anchors between stations, a practice that seemed common through the years.

Shortly after Garvice acquired Channel 27, he announced plans to build a state-of-the-art, thirty-eight-thousand-square-foot headquarters for the station on Winchester Road at a cost of $1.5 million. In addition, he immediately began negotiations to affiliate with the CBS network, which was the number one national television network. The new location would also have a one-thousand-foot tower and transmit with 2,300,000 watts of power. This was effectively ten times the power of its previous home off New Circle Road.

Ted Grizzard, in his book, *#1 is Chicken*, provided some more information about the transaction and those early days of ownership:

> And now "the man on the street" is approaching the television stuff. I don't like throwing in the business part of my radio time, but I do it to show that the "street" part was not all the picture. I didn't mind arguing with Garvice about radio matters—especially programs, because I felt I knew more about that phase than he. But I never forgot the important thing—he owned the station—and had I owned it I would have run it as I pleased. I always thought he was fairly reasonable, for an owner.

> About television. I doubt that Garvice paid too much attention to my urging that he buy Channel 27 instead of filing an application for Channel 62 and building a station there.

> The Taft Company owned several television and radio stations and at one time were CBS people. They had fallen out with CBS and gone ABC in Cincinnati and elsewhere, which meant Channel 27 in Lexington was ABC since it was owned by Taft.

Channel 18 was an NBC affiliate, but they did take some CBS [programming] and neither NBC nor CBS liked this arrangement and I or anyone else, would know that a new owner at "27" or a new station on "62," would latch on to CBS full-time. CBS was then the number one television network. At least Channel 18 would not have both networks.

Even if Garvice got a station, at Channel 62 we would wind up to hell and gone (way) up the dial with ABC—then the #3 network and have a stinking job trying to get people up [the dial] that far to watch practically nothing [little popular programming]. I kept after Garvice to forget that 62 crap and buy "27," but I am just "The Man on the Street." So, what do I know?

I don't know how much more, if any, it would cost to buy "27" from Taft, than to scramble for and build "62," but it had to be worth the difference. Garvice never admitted to me that he heard a word I said, or that my reasons were sound, or influenced him in any way, but one morning I was having breakfast as usual, in the Phoenix [Hotel] coffee shop, when Garvice came in and sat next to me.

After he ordered his breakfast, he wrote something on a scrap of paper and handed it to me. The note said, "2-7 that's us." I was delighted. Maybe thrilled is a better word. I knew he had figured it would be a better deal. Not because I thought so. Because at some meeting a long time after that he said, in one of his infrequent and half-kidding digs at me, "Ted is a fine radio man, but not a very good business man." I can go along with that with no fuss. Not the "fine" part, make it "good."

The main thing was, he had bought Channel 27 instead of trying to get and build "62."

I never got used to spending money, but I did become accustomed to seeing and hearing big amounts. I happened to be in Garvice's offices the day he gave the Taft representative a check for $2,400,000.00. The balance due on WKYT. He had already paid one hundred thousand.

The Taft man took the check and stood up to leave and Garvice said, "What's your hurry?" The man said, "Mr. Kincaid, I've got to get back to Cincinnati to get this in the bank today. I know you realize that this much money must start earning interest for Taft tomorrow morning." I hadn't thought of that. Garvice was right. I'm not a good business man, but had it been my millions I believe I would have thought of it.

On another occasion we were in Kincaid's office looking at architects' drawings for a (new) building for the television station. His secretary came in with three checks. One was for one million dollars and two for five hundred thousand each. Garvice pushed the

$1,000,000 check over to me and said, "Ted, you sign that one while I sign the other two." I didn't even reach for a pen.

I would have liked to, though just to see "Ted Grizzard" on a check for a million bucks. And I didn't ask what the money was for. If I had he likely would have said it was none of my business. He would kid about things like that, but I had learned, don't ask questions. I learned not much, but a little.

The drawings we saw were, I thought, not just bad, but awful. They looked like concrete block houses and this time, without waiting for Kincaid, I said so. The others who were there, looking, liked them. Garvice and I didn't. And almost at the same time we said we wanted something with white columns on the front. I'm glad I wanted white columns because Garvice wanted them and the Channel "27" building has white columns. If he had wanted pink or polka dot that's what they would have had and if I owned it that's the way I'd have done it too!

In front of that beautiful "27" building there is a gentle rise or slope almost from the highway up to the front entrance and the white columns. I wanted WKYT-TV in letters in hedges on that slope. There still is no identification out there. Garvice never would agree to the idea. He said, of all things, maintenance on the hedges would be too much! I think we would have had the hedge letters if he had thought of it first. They still would be appropriate and beautiful.

When Garvice bought "27" it still was ABC and, naturally, the ABC people came down and put the sales pitch on him to keep that affiliation. I've got a few pages on that but again I'll cut it down. CBS was then the number one television network and I felt sure we could get CBS. The ABC people took us to lunch, but when they found out, as I told them, I was for CBS, boy, they gave me the brush (off) real fast. That was good because there was no use my kidding them, and even though they're number one now, with their programs for third grade pupils, I'd still choose CBS.

The prestige of full time CBS affiliation was what we needed. I'm sure Garvice knew it too, but he didn't want me to think I was the only intelligent one around. Then he said for me to go to New York and talk to CBS-TV. I went. I phoned first and made an appointment with the man in charge of affiliate contracts.

And when I got there, instead of pretending to know all about television contracts and affiliate rates, I told the gentleman I'd never made a trip or a call where I knew so little about what I was doing, but I was a CBS believer inner and would depend on him for the best CBS-affiliate contract for a station in a market the size of Lexington. I have an idea the man liked the approach, and while I can never be sure I think WKYT got a fairly good CBS contract.

We didn't wrap it up then because I wanted Garvice to see and sign any contract. When I got back to Lexington Garvice was busy and couldn't get to New York. I phoned the man at CBS and asked whether he'd ever been to Lexington. He had not. I persuaded him to leave New York for a couple of days and come to see the horse country, meet Garvice and let's close the deal. To my surprise, he liked the idea.

Of course, Garvice told me I was a sucker because of the approach I had taken, but when the man came down, Garvice liked him and signed the contract we had talked about in New York, so I guess that made it a good deal. Maybe the "Man on the Street" guessed right about people now and then. On the other hand, it might have been the worst TV contract in history.

I never knew anything about the history of Channel "27," whether Taft was the first owner or not, but it was obvious that Taft had a minimum interest in the property. It was a mess. "None" is an excellent estimate of my technical knowledge, but all I saw and was told indicated the equipment was pretty bad. A fellow named Remington was left in charge until the FCC approved Kincaid's ownership. I think "Remington" was his name. I always thought of him, damn it, as "Winchester" because the firearms company names confused me.

L. C. Redmon was sales manager at "27" and I think he had picked up a little television know-how. We had nobody who knew anything about television. The deal was that during the interim until the FCC said OK, Taft could spend no money without Kincaid's okay, and Garvice told them whatever they spent they would have to ask Grizzard—old Teddy boy—first.

If Remington wanted to buy some tubes for his junky equipment, or some old movies, he had to get my okay. I forget what the maximum was that he could spend without my approval, but it was pretty low. He was a real nice guy and I know he spent very little during the time we worked together. Taft must have told him not to do anything to louse up a good deal.

I never had to ask Garvice for help in okaying a few thousand bucks for things obviously necessary. We would have liked to have kept Remington, but Taft wanted him for their Kansas City station, so he left. Now this is all executive stuff "the Man on the Street" is going through so I'll cut it short.

These were important things so, of course, I've forgotten them. I wound up as President of the company about this time and everybody was much impressed to beat hell. That is, everybody except Garvice and me. I was President, and "Man on the Street," doing commercials on high school sports, special events and the usual stuff, and that President stuff, a bunch of radio stations too, so watch it, buster!

But we didn't have a television station manager. I liked L. C. Redmon. I never knew why, but Garvice didn't seem to like him, and I don't think Garvice knew why or he sure as hell would have stated the reasons.

Redmon knew some television, knew the market and the station, and I asked Garvice to let me hire him as manager. At the moment he had no better idea to offer, so he okayed it. You know, today I have no idea what I offered L. C. as a salary. I think it was around $35,000 plus a percentage of the profits. He was glad to get the job. When I told Garvice what I had done, he told me I was nuts, naturally. I can remember him saying, "Do you know you just gave him the best job he has ever had?" and I said, "Yes, sir and I wanted him to realize it too. Maybe he'll appreciate it enough to make us a hell of a good manager."

He might have too if Garvice had left him alone. But right from the start Redmon was selected as one of those for Garvice's needling. I've seen others who could go with it, but Redmon was not one of them and it finally got him. I stayed with him. Took his side, because I felt he was a good man and I think he was aware of my feelings.

Eventually, Garvice brought in a guy named Windsor. Windsor was supposed to be in charge of television, as well as radio. And it was about Windsor that Garvice permitted me to give him some of my finest arguments. We needed Windsor about like we need a trampoline act in the control room.

I was and am in favor of letting the station managers run their stations. If they can't do it, find somebody who can. But don't have some "supervisor" going in every week or so and bugging them about things of which he knows little or nothing. After one outstanding session, on the subject of Windsor, in which I finally gave up and said, "Well, they're your stations, if they were mine, I'd do what I wanted to do with them, so go on and hire the SOB."

Garvice said, "Naw, I'm not going to hire him." I said, "Why?" And then, so help me, he said, "Because you've said I'd be stupid!" I was afraid to answer that and of course, afraid to laugh. He sounded like a kid. I just said, "Okay, it's up to you." Hell, he hired Windsor. When Windsor turned out to be a complete loss, Garvice and I were talking one day and he said, in reference to Windsor and Redmon, "Well, we're even, you hired one and I hired one." I said, "Aw now, mine's okay, if you'll just lay off of him. Yours is the terrible one."

He just grinned. About ten days later I heard he had let Windsor go. Redmon was a real sick man during much of this time, and away from "27" for many weeks. About the time Redmon came back to work, Garvice hired a fellow—in Windsor's job, named Evans (I think).

The new TV genius brought his own program director, a guy named Butts. The two of them were double trouble. I don't know how long they lasted but Garvice gave up on them. Sometime during this stretch the needling and the illness must have become too much for Redmon and he gave up too and resigned.

Then began the Hagan and Holbrook era and except for one more station manager, things began to settle down and shape up. Now I'll go back just a bit. One day, shortly after I'd hired Redmon, I was about to start the street program and this real pretty woman passes and stops just long enough to say, "Mr. Kincaid wants you and me to do a television show together." I said, "That's fine." And forgot it.

That afternoon Garvice phoned me and asked me to meet him and the lady at "27," the next morning at 10:00, to tape a few minutes of a possible talk show. The next morning, we sat beside a table and talked about a lot of nothing and kidded and they taped it in color.

Then Garvice, the lady (June Rollings) and I go in to see the tape. June had had some television experience somewhere. I had never been on camera. For some reason, I can't explain, I didn't then nor at any time in the future ever give a thought to a camera being there. Oh, on commercials, sure because you work right into a camera. But on any show, I just forgot about "somebody taking my picture."

We had a good time that morning and even Garvice liked what we had done. In kidding about it, I remember telling Garvice that the sample was much too good for a local program, we should send it to New York right then! That TV audition, by the way, was only my second time in a television studio. There were lots of meetings, discussions and plans and from it all came "Town Talk," 9 to 9:30 a.m., Mondays through Fridays and I'm pretty sure it started on Monday, Labor Day, in 1967.

Kincaid had done it. He owned the most advanced television station in the region and was aligned with the nation's number one television network. Now he just needed to make sure his station became the number-one-rated station in Lexington. To do this, he installed three television sets in his office and three television sets, stacked in a pyramid, in the bedroom of his home. Barry Peel and Ken Kurts both recalled that he would watch all three stations at once, and if he saw what he considered an important story on one that he didn't see on Channel 27, he would call the station manager or whoever was in charge then and ask them why. In addition, if he saw an ad on a competitor's station that he hadn't seen running on WKYT, he would call and ask why. He was very involved and constantly quizzing the station manager and others about what was happening.

Garvice often did things that were insensitive or poorly considered. According to Barry Peel, Mrs. Kincaid came to the station one afternoon and asked the news director, Howard "Buzz" Riggins, if she could borrow a television set. She said, "Garvice has taken all three television sets in the house and put them in a pyramid shape in his bedroom." Barry said Howard told her, "Borrow?" Mrs. Kincaid, take whatever you want; they are all yours!"

According to news anchors John McGarvey and Barry Peel, during that time, after the new building on Winchester Road was built, Kincaid would visit the studio sometimes in the evening. According to McGarvey when I interviewed him,

> It wasn't unusual for him to come out from time to time. I was still quite young, but I recall we had the control room and it had windows into two studios. We had Studio A, which was the larger studio, and Studio B, where the news set was permanently set up. And he would come and just sit there and watch. There was a raised bench behind the technical director, and he would just sit behind it and watch us do the news. He didn't do this frequently, but it wasn't unusual.

Barry Peel recalls a similar story about something that happened around 1971, but for a different reason. In the early 1970s, the local television stations were dominated by men, and the FCC and other organizations had started to exert pressure on WKYT to increase the diversity of its on-air staff. This pressure increased in 1971, just after Bluegrass Broadcasting had concluded WVLK's FCC advertising problem. To comply, Ray Holbrook brought in a new face to anchor the afternoon news with Barry Peel—a young anchorwoman named Rita Channon. Here is Barry Peels's story about a visit from Garvice at the station:

> Get this picture. In those days, we had slides and film, which was Conestoga wagon (a horse-drawn, double-domed canvas wagon) technology. After the noon news, we had a room called studio control, where the director and the audio person sat, as opposed to the master control room. For a newscast, the director and the audio person were in the smaller room called the studio control, and in there was an elevated bench-like seat, where one could sit behind them. After the noon newscast, we would go in there and pick up our slides and film and take them back to the newsroom to be used later or filed.

Rita and I did the noon news. One day we finish our broadcast and go into the studio control room to get our slides and film. And my God, there's that Garvice "Buddha" Kincaid, in the back on the elevated bench. I always described him as "Buddha-like." Well, Rita and I had no idea he was there. He had watched us do the noon news. Robert, again, whatever I tell you, it's the best of my memory, I am not making anything up. I'm not trying to slip anything in or put the wrong emphasis on anything, but I was there, and this happened. I witnessed it.

We walk in and, you know, first of all, we are in shock. Oh God, I didn't know he was here. You know, there he sat. I wasn't afraid of him, but I didn't know he was there. Now, Rita was part Cherokee Indian. She had a slightly darker complexion. Not dark, but darker, because she was part Indian. And she had these very high cheekbones and the like. She really was a gorgeous lady. I'm telling you, she could have been Miss America. Garvice looks at her and says, "Get out in the sunlight, do you?" And Rita, thinking it's a compliment, which is all she ever got about her looks, says "Yes. As often as I can," and Garvice says "Well, God dammit, DON'T!"

I would swear to this under oath, and at the peril of perjury. "God dammit, DON'T!"

Oh, she was gorgeous, with a personality to match. "Well, God dammit, DON'T."

Now, you could imply from that whatever you want. I can't say, because I don't know if Garvice was racist or prejudiced. But I do know we didn't have any black people on the staff. I was there when they did hire the first person. It was a woman from Louisville. Of course, I've forgotten her name [Loretta Harris]. Of course, sometimes, at my age, I can't remember what I had for breakfast, for God's sake.

Again, I would say she was hired under enormous pressure. Probably from the local civil rights groups. I think they may have mentioned this to Garvice. I think the station was under intense local civil rights pressure, and maybe even from the FCC, or the government or whatever, but she was hired.

Now why would Garvice care about the depth of complexion on a beautiful woman like Rita Channon. He didn't want her to be any darker. So, you can imply from that your own supposition and imply what you will. I can't say he was racist. I can't say he was racially motivated. I don't know, but that fact is that is what he said to her.

Rita Paulette McIntosh grew up in Mayfield, Kentucky. She was born in 1942 and had an interesting early career. In 1956, her older brother, Larry

McIntosh, got a job as a sports announcer and disc jockey for the local radio station WNGO. Still a student himself, Larry worked part-time, and Rita, who was four years younger, would accompany him to the station on weekends to practice taping her voice and help him pick out records. Rita, experienced with a microphone and also a local model, was also the first teenage hostess for *Dance Party*. She was on the show, co-hosting with Bob Swicher, from 1960 to 1961. Larry said Rita was very prepared for a career in broadcasting. "She had been ad-libbing commercials since she was twelve. She was fascinated with media, and she had poise as a teenager."

After graduating from Mayfield High School in 1961, she went to the University of Kentucky until, at the age of nineteen, she met and married her husband, James Channon, during her first year of college. Her husband's army career soon had them traveling the world from Japan to Germany. In Germany she also worked for a production company. They returned to Lexington in the early 1970s and Rita went back to the University of Kentucky, where she earned a bachelor's degree in journalism. When she was close to graduation, she was offered a job with WKYT. She was the first woman in news at the station.

Rita was ready to prove herself. She said, "Early on I was discouraged by my university professors. They said women in TV news weren't credible. I didn't believe them then and now we've proved them wrong." Also coming from the small town of Mayfield didn't hurt her. She says, "People use to make fun of the way I talked, but I've lost my accent." Rita began working on her accent after someone at WPSD-TV, in Paducah, told her she had three syllables in the word "hand." She laughed when they said it but also made a decision to improve herself.

The word "beauty" is often mentioned when Rita's name comes up. She competed in various beauty queen competitions from 1958 to 1962 and was crowned Miss Paducah in 1961. She twice tried to win the Miss Kentucky pageant and in all the pageants was usually in the top five. In the 1961 contest, she was in the top three going into the finals. Rita and another top-three competitor, Pamela Farris Brown, the sister of the future governor of Kentucky, were surprised when they both lost in the finals.

Rita's beauty was continually written about during her broadcasting career. In June 1982, in a Paducah Sun article, it was said of her, "She knows TV anchor women are typically young, perhaps younger than she is (age forty). There still is a lot of cosmetic value attached to it and that's unfortunate. The anchor who has learned more and is more experienced is the older one." Rita said she hopes her days as an anchor aren't numbered, just because of her birthdays. "I still clean up well," she joked.

Rita Channon left WKYT in 1973, after just two years, when her husband was transferred to Kansas, and within a year, Rita had a job doing the weather at WDAF-TV in Leavenworth. Within a year, she was anchoring, writing, and producing the midday noon news broadcast. Within two years, she was anchoring the ten o'clock evening news. Kansas is a top-five television market, and Rita's star was recognized. In August 1977, Rita sat down to interview the *Today Show*'s host, Jane Pauley, in Chicago, about women in the news, and Rita, smooth, articulate, and also five years older than Pauley, was the more relaxed participant in the interview.

In Kansas remarks about her looks continued, and so did the progression of her career. In addition to anchoring the news, Rita wanted to continue to do special reports because she felt it was an important part of the job. Asked if she was worried people would consider her doing special reports as a step down from anchoring, Rita had this to say in an August 28, 1977, *Kansas City Star* article:

> "I don't care what they think. A lot of anchor people fall into the rut of being faces—personalities. I want to be trusted and I have to earn that trust by reporting, not by being isolated in a newsroom."
>
> Reminded that her face isn't exactly that of a wicked witch and that the telegenic qualities of newscasters does seem to be important, Rita recalled a letter she received from a farmer who made it a practice to come in from his chores at lunch to watch her Midday show.
>
> "He said, 'I have been watching you for some time. I don't much cotton to the idea of women doing news, but you speak good, you give a lot of news and I enjoy you. P.S. It don't hurt none that you look good.'"

In June 1979, Rita announced she was leaving Kansas for San Francisco, where she would co-anchor the evening news at KRON-TV. This was another huge jump in Rita's career, and she remained at KRON for over ten years as an anchor. In 1989, forty-seven-year-old Rita was removed from anchoring the news and put in charge of a new KRON news magazine program. Rita remained with KRON for the next several years and retired to the San Francisco Bay area in the mid-1990s, focusing her time on helping charities, by doing voiceovers and advertisements. Rita is another successful person whose career began with a Kincaid business entity.

When Rita left WKYT in 1972, the station had lost its first and only woman newscaster. In addition, the station had done nothing to increase its racial diversity. All of that would change in January 1973, when Lauretta Harris began working at the station. Lauretta was an African American who grew up in Louisville and was an Eastern Kentucky University graduate in textiles and design. Lauretta had a brief stint in merchandising but soon followed up on a job lead she heard about in Lexington—in the news department of WKYT-TV. She said she was interested and felt she had nothing to lose and so she applied. News director Howard Riggins gets the credit for recognizing Harris's talent. She interviewed with Riggins and was immediately hired. The former Miss Black Richmond–1972 began her broadcasting career at the station on January 8, 1973.

Lauretta Harris is someone who will forever be known for breaking down the barriers that had previously prevented those in the same struggle from achieving a position of power. Lauretta Harris played a significant role in the struggle for gender and race equality. She is recognized as the first African American to work full time in Lexington televised news broadcasting and also the first African American to become an anchor of a news station in Kentucky (Louisville).

Lauretta began her WKYT-TV career delivering the weather. The *Lexington Herald-Leader*'s Sue George described Harris in February 1974: "She is beautiful but superseding that is the fact that she is smart; she is sharp and she is serious about what she is doing." In the same article, Lauretta was quoted as saying,

> I'd like to think that I have this job because I am qualified for it and because I do it well. I work hard—very hard—to present solid weather coverage to Lexington listeners. Weather is a rather complicated subject, but I am absorbing and learning more about the field every day. Brad James, our night weatherman has been a big help. He really knows the ropes when it comes to the weather.
>
> Lauretta is a faithful fan of her competition at Channels 18 and 62. What better way to learn the dos and don'ts of a job, than by watching the other teams? It's like scouting. And it's a good opportunity to watch local television—and that's something a person doesn't get a chance to do very often when he or she is working at a local TV station. It's one of those paradoxes.
>
> In the beginning my delivery and presentation were pretty stilted. I was really terrified I'd make a colossal mistake. Of late, however, I feel more and more comfortable on the camera. Most people are really only interested in the local weather, and I have good information at my disposal. Still, I try to throw in figures from the nation's warm areas and cold areas by way of contrast, as a frame of reference.

> I try to keep the language plain and simple for
> everyone's easy comprehension. And for that matter, I
> really don't make the rain or snow. I just talk about them.
> But I do get the feeling that I am more popular with my
> audience if I am saying, "Sunny and warmer."

> Lauretta is a private kind of person, poised and thoughtful,
> serious about herself and her job. Not too serious, however, to have
> sacrificed humor and warmth.

Lauretta left WKYT in the fall of 1975, just before Garvice's death. She initially moved to WSMV in Nashville, where she was a news reporter, but soon moved to Raleigh, North Carolina, where she became a weekend anchor at WRAL-TV. She remained in Raleigh until June 1979, when she returned to her hometown of Louisville for a weekend anchor position with WAVE-3 television. Lauretta remained with WAVE-3 for a little over ten years. In early 1990, she made her last broadcasting change and took a position with WDRB-TV, a station that had recently recruited a significant amount of veteran area broadcasting talent. Lauretta was the co-anchor of WDRB-TV's 10 p.m. newscast, a position she retained until October 2001, when her contract wasn't renewed.

In the fall of 2001, fifty-two-year-old Harris decided to leave broadcasting and became a minister for the Jesus Christ of Nazareth church in March 2005. During the years of her broadcasting career and after, Lauretta Harris was an influential voice. In January 1973, the twenty-two-year-old young lady probably didn't fully appreciate how important her groundbreaking journey in broadcasting would be to other members of minorities in broadcasting.

In 1968, Sue Wylie became the first female newscaster in Lexington, working at WLEX Channel 18. Wylie is a member of the Kentucky Journalism Hall of Fame and the Kentucky Broadcasters Association Hall of Fame. She is known for setting the standard in local Lexington newscasts. While working in Miami for WCKT-TV, she became the first female reporter for the midday news. Initially she was relegated to women's features, but her big break came when she reported on an abandoned baby. Her news director was so impressed that he promoted Sue to cover hard news. She was one of the first female television news reporters in the country.

Sue came to Lexington in 1968 from Miami, and her thirty-year tenure at WLEX-TV remains unsurpassed. She created and anchored Lexington's first midday television news program, *Noon Today*, which continues to thrive. She also originated several public affairs shows, including *One to One*, *In Touch*, and *Your Government*, which featured notable local, state, and regional newsmakers along with national guests such as Ronald Reagan, Ted Kennedy, Jimmy Carter, and Jesse Jackson. Those she interviewed were subjected to her tough but fair analysis, and many of them also became some of her greatest friends.

While Sue Wylie broke the glass ceiling for women newscasters in Lexington, it would take WKYT until 1971 to bring Rita Channon into its news department and another two years to bring on an African American female on the staff to do the weather.

Lauretta Harris left WKYT a couple of months before Kincaid's death. While she admits she didn't have many dealings with him, she recalls the following when I interviewed her:

> My impression of Mr. Kincaid was that he was very opinionated. Now I had only ran into him like maybe two or three times, but I remember this one weird conversation I had with him. I was in the process of leaving the station and ran into him in the hall. You know, I had run into him two or three times before, but never ever, ever had any conversation with him, at all. Beyond passing him in the hall, and you know, nodding just to acknowledge that he was there. That was it.
>
> Well, what I remember is that I am walking down the hall, and he is walking toward me, and he slows and says, "You get good and then you decide to leave." That was it. I thought that was so funny and I remember telling that story to a number of people afterwords, when I was leaving. I'm just the kind of person who will remember stuff like that. I even remember what I was wearing, and I just thought, *that was so weird.* I don't even remember what my response was, probably to smile and, you know, get the heck out of there.
>
> There were other things which I thought seemed a little odd about working there. All employees that worked at the station had to have an account at Central Bank. If you didn't have an account, they would open one up for you. I remember I had a checking account someplace else and so I thought to myself, well, I have to have a checking account there [at Central Bank], but I don't have to leave any money in it. So, each pay day, I would deposit money from that Central Bank account into my existing bank account by writing a check.
>
> When I worked there, I did the weather, and it was a very difficult time for me. I wanted to get experience, and I wanted to go ahead and do what I knew I was always good at and that was interviewing people and getting information on people. So, I was pretty focused on improving myself so I could do more than the weather.

Author: Did you feel like you were treated like a colleague by management and the other staff?

Actually, most of the people I worked with have always been very, very nice. And I mean that sincerely. And over time, over years and stuff, in the business. I've worked with people who haven't been so nice, but I have no complaints about any of the people that I've worked with at WKYT. While I was there, I was treated like a regular person. I always watched other people and watched how they conducted themselves, and I tried to conduct myself accordingly.

Author: Did you have any interaction with June Rollings? Maybe talk with her when you got a cup of coffee or anything?

Well, I certainly knew who she was, but I didn't know her well. They [WKYT] had various setups and stuff for the various shows, and they [*Town Talk*] had their own show, their own setup. I never really ran into her. It's funny to hear all these names, because I hadn't heard all those names in years. Is she still alive?

Author: No, she died in 2021. I think she was ninety-six.

The fact that Lauretta Harris was the first African American woman in Lexington history to appear on television and deliver the news to the local population goes to show that she was a pioneer not only for equality for women but for the African American population as well. Lauretta likely knew, going into her interview with Howard Riggins and hoping to one day be the next anchor to bring Lexington the news, that she would be breaking new ground, but chances are, she probably never realized just how much of a difference she would actually make in Kentucky broadcasting.

Another person who arrived at the station shortly before Kincaid died was Ken Kurtz. Kenneth R. Kurtz was formerly a reporter at Channel 3 TV, WSAZ, in Charleston, West Virginia, and the news director at WANE-15 TV in Fort Wayne, Indiana, before accepting the news director position at WKYT-TV in April 1975. He was hired by WKYT's general manager, Ralph Gabbard, who had received a letter from Kurtz's old WANE boss, Chuck Whitehurst. Ken had been replaced at the station, and Whitehurst thought so much of him he sent out twenty letters of introduction to other stations recommending him, writing, "We are losing a good man."

Ralph Gabbard joined WKYT in 1970 as a sales manager. According to Ralph Hacker, Gabbard was working in Richmond as the general manager of radio station WEKY when the sales manager job became available. Ralph said that as soon as he heard about the position, he recommended Gabbard to Ray Holbrook. In November 1974, Ray Holbrook replaced general manager Jim

Pennock with Gabbard. Ken Kurtz was Gabbard's first significant hire since his promotion. Garvice was on a mission to make WKYT the number one station in Lexington, and Gabbard's mission was to make it happen. Ken said that he and Gabbard were simpatico from the moment they first met. They had similar philosophies about how the news department should be run, and both recognized that the news programming needed to be changed and refreshed.

Ken Kurtz—"We're Number One!"

When Kurtz arrived at WKYT, the news department had a nine-person budget but only seven employees, and two of them were leaving in a couple of weeks. This was back in the days of film, and the station didn't have a processor and had to deliver its film to the other side of town for processing at Royal Film. So, five people weren't just writing and producing the news, they were also transporting the station's film footage back and forth. Gabbard and Ken both understood that changes needed to be made quickly.

Ken Kurtz was born in West Virginia and graduated from Pennsylvania's Swarthmore College in 1951. Before coming to Lexington, Ken had a twenty-year television news career working in West Virginia, Indiana, and South Carolina. Ken was respected and in 1988, just before his retirement from WKYT in 1989, became the director of long-range planning for WKYT and the station's sister station in Hazard, WYMT. During his long career, Kurtz served as president of the Associated Press Broadcasters of Kentucky and was on the board of directors of the Radio and Television News Directors' Association. Gabbard's and Ken's positive contributions to making WKYT Lexington's number one station cannot be overstated.

While Ken worked with Kincaid only during the last seven months of his life, he was quickly indoctrinated into how Garvice did things. Ken recalled his first meeting with Kincaid this way when I interviewed him:

> I want to tell you, Robert, that if Mr. Kincaid had not died, I was going to leave the station. I had absolutely no respect for the man whatsoever. I did not want to work for him. I would have worked for Ralph Gabbard until the end of time, but not Mr. Kincaid. He was extremely difficult to work with, and while I had not 100 percent made up my mind to leave, it was only because I didn't have any place else to go at that time.
>
> I had a wife and three daughters and a mortgage, but I had pretty well decided that I was not going to stay on much longer because Mr. Kincaid was not the type of person I wanted to work for.
>
> Let me tell you about my first Sunday after starting at WKYT. I'm at home in my little neighborhood there, which wasn't all that far

from where Kincaid lived. You know where the house was opposite the golf course [Idle Hour Country Club] on Richmond Road.

Yeah, Richmond Road, opposite the golf course. Well, I got a call that morning. I don't remember if it was Holbrook, but somebody called, and he said, "Why aren't you at the meeting?" And I said, "What meeting?" and they said, "the Sunday morning meeting with Mr. Kincaid." "Well," I said, "because nobody told me about it." They said, "Well, you need to get down here right away." And I don't remember whether I shaved or not, but I put on a coat and tie.

Anyway, we had a meeting at his house every Sunday morning. This was pretty much a weekly thing. Mrs. Kincaid was off to church and Mr. Kincaid was there, at the house, by himself. I think they usually started at 11:00.

I get down to the meeting, and to the very best of my knowledge, that's the first time I met Mr. Kincaid. Now, Ralph Gabbard or Al Taylor may have taken me by the law firm or something and introduced me. You know, "Here's our new news director," but I don't remember that. I believe the first time I met Mr. Kincaid was that Sunday morning meeting, and he was not a nice man. He was an arrogant son of a bitch, and he was running down his top staff. Now I know that Ray Holbrook, Ralph Gabbard, and Al Taylor (operations/program director), were there for sure, and I think Jerry Kuykendall, who had succeeded Ralph as the general sales manager, was also there.

Now Mr. Kincaid would review each of their departments and make his comments. The only thing I remember about the news department, and again, I'm sure there were more, but the only thing I remember is that we had mispronounced the name of a prominent Lexington family, George Swinebroad. We called it something like "Swinebrade." We didn't pronounce it correctly and you know, we didn't know any better? No, Mr. Kincaid, I have not been here that long.

Now, I was maybe only forty and Ralph Gabbard was even younger, and Al Taylor was just a little older, but my recollection is that I somewhat turned it [the issue] back on Mr. Kincaid. I'd spent a year in Greensboro, North Carolina, and nine years in Fort Wayne, which has a lot of German heritage in it. There were a lot of German families with unusual names. One very prominent attorney was named Peter Beter. So, I put out a notice that he will never be referred to on the air without his middle initial, so we always referred to him as Peter D. Beter.

There were lots of names like that. He wasn't the only one. Fort Wayne has lots of German families with unusual names. So, mispronunciation was this type of problem. So, I had dealt before with the pronunciation thing, and I told Mr. Kincaid this and I said, "I have ordered a pronunciation guide for Kentucky counties and cities from the Associated Press, and I'm going to have one for everybody on the staff. If you would like to designate somebody in your law firm or Kentucky Central that we can call if we hit a problematic name because there's nobody on the staff currently from Lexington or Kentucky, I will guarantee you we will check with them before using the name on the air." This answer seemed to satisfy him.

I am sure he had a lot of other things for the other departments, and he picked on me a little bit, which made me very unhappy. The other people were not exactly lying to Mr. Kincaid, but let's say they were shading the truth. I picked my words as carefully as I could. When we got out of the meeting, everybody got together in the parking lot ready to get in their cars and go. Ray Holbrook paid me one of the best compliments I've ever been paid. He said, "Well, we have learned something today," and someone said, "What's that?" and Ray said, "Ken can't lie. That's good, and for a news director, it's even better."

These meetings went on almost every Sunday. I don't remember them being every Sunday, but you had to be there. I don't remember Howard Schumacher (tech-engineering) being there, but everybody else was there.

Author: What was Kincaid's demeanor like at the meeting? Was he "Oh, hello, Ken, how are you doing? Sit down, have a doughnut?" Or was he right to the point? How would you describe him? I'm just curious.

You are our news director. How could you possibly mispronounce the name of a prominent Lexington family like that? You're supposed to be the news director. You're supposed to know these things. He was running everybody down.

Author: Was he in a suit, or coat and tie?

Yes, everybody was, and I think he was, or maybe he had just got back from church.

Author: Ken, I am just amazed; he was the richest man in the state of Kentucky and people basically have just forgotten about him.

My guess is that they probably wanted to, because he was—if you had asked me how I would describe Garvice in one word, I would say "arrogant!" He wanted to be considered one of the richest men in the country and probably was, and he wanted people to know it. He wanted to own the best radio station, the best television station, and forgive me if this sounds like self-promotion, but when

I came in May we were a solid number two. We were rated twice in those years, in April or May and then November. We didn't have a July book at that time.

Well, we were being rated in November during the period that Mr. Kincaid died, and when we got the rating books in early December, I get a call from Ralph, down in carpet land. He was at one end of the building, and the news department was at the other end of the building. Well, Ralph said, "I've got the rating books, and you've got to see them." I said, "Ok, I'm coming down." I leave my office and start down the corridor and here comes Ralph out of his office, coming down the corridor toward me with, what my wife would describe as a shit-eating grin. So help me, as I watched him, his footsteps seemed to be about a foot off the floor. By God, I kid you not, I believe his footsteps seemed to be a foot off the floor. We sort of meet at the lobby, and he says, "We're number one in the November book."

So, forgive me, but I had taken the station in one book [ratings cycle] from two to one, and I kept it there for fifteen years, with the exception of one book, which everybody, including Barfield at WLEX, agreed was a mistake. Nobody believed the math. We were either tied or slightly behind WLEX in this one book, and bless Harry Barfield's soul, nobody advertised off of that book; they just dropped it. Most of that time, our ratings were equal to the other two stations combined. There were a couple of periods where our ratings were double the other two stations. We also had two years where our 11:00 news was in the top ten nationally. Now that's not based on the total number of viewers, because obviously, you have places like New York and LA, but on a per capita basis. Here's the number of television sets in your viewing area, here is the percentage you have, and so twice during my fifteen years, we were in the top ten.

I find that kind of interesting, because WSAZ was often in the top ten, and so much of what I learned and put into effect at Channel 27 I learned at WSAZ. So, it was kind of good to be able to tell my old boss that I had learned what he had taught me and applied it here.

Author: Did Kincaid ever go over Ralph's head and go straight to you with a phone call or message or a letter? I'm just curious how his leadership worked.

I don't remember any, and my guess is that he knew that when we finished talking I would have picked up the phone and called Ralph. I suspect that he [Kincaid] respected the line of authority. He might have called Holbrook, okay, certainly if Ralph was not available.

Author: Did you think Ralph earned his money by fending off Mr. Kincaid most of the time? Did you feel any pressure from Kincaid that came down, to be number one; was that something that you ever heard—Kincaid wants us to be number one?

No, I never got a bit of that from Ralph. They [the Committee/ Hagan] left me alone, particularly after I delivered a number one in one book; right. I was sort of the fair-haired boy for a while, and Ralph didn't turn me down very often. I can think of two major things, in fifteen years, that I went to Ralph on that I got turned down. But really, we—as I said, we were simpatico. We were a similar type of broadcaster, and Channel 27 made its reputation as the number-one station on three things: CBS nationally—and during this time, CBS was the dominant national network—Kentucky [UK] sports, and local news. After Kincaid died, Ralph was able to wrestle control of UK sports away from WLEX. He did that as fast as he could, and we held on to them for a long time.

You know Ralph was king, and after Garvice's death, that put him in an even stronger position. He was a visionary broadcaster and simply ran an excellent station, and we deserved whatever ratings we got because of the way he ran it. I never referred to him as Ralph. It was always Mr. Gabbard. We had that kind of respect.

Author: When the station was sold in 1993, I thought the biggest compliment Gray Communications could have paid to Ralph Gabbard was when they moved their corporate headquarters here, to Lexington, and made him the head of all of their properties. I also thought it was so sad when he died, at age fifty, in September 1996.

Ralph Gabbard—Programmed for Success

Ralph Gabbard got into broadcasting as a teenager in 1963, but it was "totally by accident." A high school teacher assigned students topics for speeches, and Gabbard, who claimed he was "a very average student," got the topic that was left over: radio.

He drove from Berea to a small Richmond radio station to ask for an Associated Press release he could use to practice his on-air reading. A young disc jockey named Ralph Hacker was working that night, and he also was from Berea. Hacker told him, "Why don't you come back tomorrow? We're looking for an announcer or two. Come back and apply for a job." Ralph came back, but when he made an audition tape, his style was so poor that the station's manager told him, "You're pretty bad." The manager though, was desperate for announcers, so he hired him anyway.

Ralph almost didn't go into broadcasting. After high school, he enrolled at Eastern Kentucky University to get a pharmacy degree, but by the end of his freshman year, he was making so much money selling ads that he quit school.

Gabbard's career with Bluegrass Broadcasting was an off-and-on relationship. He was first recruited to WVLK in 1966, by Ralph Hacker, to be a disk jockey and sales manager, but left in 1968 to run WEKY radio in Richmond. That lasted until 1970, when he was recruited, at the suggestion of Ralph Hacker, to be the sales manager for WKYT. In late 1974, he was promoted to vice president and general manager of WKYT-TV, and according to the Television Advertising Bureau, this established him as the youngest person ever to attain that position at a network affiliate station.

In 1985, Gabbard opened WKYT's sister station, WYMT-TV in Hazard, and in 1986 he was elected president of the Kentucky Broadcasters Association. This was on top of being named an "Outstanding Young Man of America" in 1979.

Ralph Hacker refers to his friend as "one of the great innovators," and Kincaid Committee member Hart Hagan said, "He comes up with the ideas and puts them into operation." Harry Barfield, the former president of WLEX-TV and past president of the Broadcasters Association, said, "Ralph is a leader in the industry and the state and Ralph has held every position of responsibility in the association."

Success came quickly for Gabbard after Kincaid's death. He soon obtained the rights to broadcast UK basketball games, and he held on to those rights for the rest of his career. In ratings, he obtained Kincaid's number one market share rating within six-months of Kincaid's death. According to Hart Hagan and Ralph Hacker, the station was struggling when Gabbard arrived in late 1974, and his reaction was to develop creative sales packages and market them aggressively. They said he revolutionized the Lexington television market in the 1970s. He used promotions for television, something others thought could not be done successfully. He would package certain sales deals, especially sports promotions, something that no one had thought to try before.

Hacker said that Gabbard further changed the market by bringing in first-rate newscasters and reporters and by hiring executives from outside the television industry. News was emphasized because Ralph believed that "your news broadcast was the image of the station" and "will make you successful." WKYT's share of the news audience grew steadily, and once WKYT cemented its strength in Lexington, Gabbard turned his attention toward the mountains of Eastern Kentucky.

Hart Hagan and the Committee believed in Gabbard so much that in 1985, they allowed him to spend several million dollars and open WYMT-TV in Hazard, a satellite station of WKYT. Gabbard said, "The purpose of WYMT-TV was to capture Eastern Kentucky audiences, which were, previously, only reached by television stations in West Virginia and other states."

Barry Peel says, "Ralph Gabbard defined and dominated our television market for a quarter of a century. All you had to do with Ralph was convince him that something was needed to be number one, and it was done." Barry said that Gabbard was instrumental in WKYT's decision to outbid WLEX-TV (Channel 18) for the University of Kentucky coaches' shows and the right to broadcast replays of UK games. "Some thought he was nuts because the high bid initially lost money for the station, but in the end, Channel 27's identity with UK sports has been a key to its dominance." To be identified with UK sports is a major component of that image, and let's face it, we're in the image business, and he knew that in time he would be proven right." Barry also likes to facetiously say, "Anybody that knows anything about Kentucky knows UK sports is the state religion. I mean, there can be no question of that. It's like a contract for fighter planes with the Defense Department. It's a big deal, and they did get the contract and were now able to advertise themselves as the UK station. It's very lucrative, and Ralph Gabbard understood that."

One can imagine that Kincaid's Sunday WKYT management meetings introduced him to Gabbard's intellect and drive. He was the station's sales manager, working under Ray Holbrook and station manager Jim Pennock, but those Sunday meetings created the opportunity for Kincaid to evaluate Gabbard's strengths and leadership style. In 1974, when the decision was made that Pennock had to go, Gabbard had impressed Garvice with his knowledge and passion. Promoting Ralph Gabbard to vice president and general manager of WKYT was one of Kincaid's last significant personnel decisions, and history has shown it was a good one.

In 1976, about six months after Kincaid's death, Ray Holbrook left Bluegrass Broadcasting. Garvice was gone, the Committee was in charge, and he could probably see that the broadcasting division wouldn't get the attention that Kincaid gave it. As Bill Stakelin remarked, "The organization was now being run by attorneys and accountants, and you could see that their interest was in the insurance and finance arms of the organization." Stakelin, Ralph Hacker, and others indicated that Hart Hagan was interested and supported them, but Burnett and Schaeffer had little time for them.

Ken Kurtz recalled a story that provides some indication of Schaeffer's power and Hart Hagan's understanding of it:

Now, I don't know how Rusty Hembree and Hart Hagan could put up with Mr. Kincaid, but in my opinion, the real power at the law firm was Ed Schaeffer. I remember we had a meeting, some years after Kincaid's death. It was about Kentucky Utilities challenging a series of stories we had done. And I will admit they were not well done by our Frankfort bureau chief at that time. I did not know this until KU started telling us, in a meeting, what was wrong with them. Well, Hart Hagan and Ed Schaeffer were in the meeting with KU and their attorneys. It was a very frustrating meeting, because I could not draw KU out to any extent, but in the middle, I decided we were going to pull the rest of the series. This was like a five-part series, from Monday through Friday, and they had objected to what we aired on Monday. We had this meeting on Tuesday, and it was apparent to me that the Frankfort bureau guy was a bad hire. I can't remember his name.

In the fifteen or so years that I was at WKYT, there were probably three or four hiring mistakes, which I made, and the Frankfort guy certainly was a bad hire.

So, I went to the meeting and simply said, "We do not think the series is up to our standards," which it wasn't. "If we can make it so, we'll continue, but if it's not, it's over." In that meeting, Schaeffer would say statements to Hart. I remember him saying, "He's on point. Do you hear me, Mr. Hagan?" in a jocular way. But what Schaeffer meant was, "Do you hear me?" And Hagan said, "Mr. Schaeffer, I hear you." So, in my opinion, Schaeffer was calling the shots, if he was in a meeting somewhere, and Garvice or Earl Wilson weren't there. He was the guy. I am just telling you this from my limited experience.

Author: I asked Ken and Ralph Hacker what they recalled about Kincaid's death and how the station's staff was told. Did they have an all WKYT/WVLK employee meeting where Hagan or Wilson spoke to them, or was there a memo, or was there a special meeting for the officers? The answer from both was, "No! Employees pretty much learned what they learned from the media outlets."

Ken Kurtz had one story about Kincaid's death that probably puts some context around the subject of his death during this time.

Let me tell you about that, because that's one thing I can tell you about. We're about halfway through the month of November, I am doing the 6:00 news, and one of the cameramen says, "We have a major story coming down. They're writing it now, and they're going to bring it down to you," or something like that. The door of the studio opens, and somebody comes in with a sheet of paper and puts it down in front of me. The red light goes on and I am literally reading ahead a few words as I am speaking it in front of the live camera. It's Garvice Kincaid's death. It's a very short story, something like, "Garvice Kincaid, well-known Lexington banker, philanthropist, owner of WKYT, has died suddenly of an apparent heart attack on a business trip to Elizabethtown. That's all we have at this point; funeral arrangements are incomplete." That's it.

I don't remember them doing anything for the staff, but Ray Holbrook did one of his very few, and maybe only, on-the-air commentaries, which he had called "The Old Man," and a copy of it may be in the archives somewhere. But Ray, to the best of my knowledge, wrote it, and he delivered it on the air. It was a eulogy to Mr. Kincaid, who he called "The Old Man." And in it, Ray expressed a lot of appreciation for Kincaid.

Later I found out that Mrs. Kincaid is watching. She already knows about it. It's not her first time learning about it. She's been told, but she is watching the announcement. In fact, I assume that there was somebody from the law firm, or Kentucky Central, or from the family, that had called the station with the information. And that's the answer to your question about how people found out about it. We told them, and later I heard Mrs. Kincaid turned to someone after the broadcast and said, "Garvice would have liked that; it was short and sweet." It was an odd feeling to find out later that your owner's wife is listening while I am, yes, reading a couple words ahead, as I reported it, but that was how people first heard about how Garvice had died.

Reporters Barry Peel and Bob Hensley both respected what Garvice Kincaid had built and agree that Lexington and the state of Kentucky are a better place because of his efforts and contributions, but both men also agree that he was a difficult person to work for. These were their closing thoughts about Garvice Kincaid.

[Peel] Garvice reminds me of the poet's verdict: The thirst that comes when the well is full is the thirst that's never quenched. At some point it couldn't be money. He had more than enough. Money was the chips you played with to keep score in business battles. Garvice was about winning and controlling. Sadly, his methods and personality prevented him from acquiring the respectability he expected winning to bring him. So, he died thirsty.

[Hensley] When I was hired as a news reporter in late 1971, Kincaid was in the process of pouring significant resources into the News and Sports Departments at WKYT-TV. The size of the staff was expanded to accommodate the additional daily newscasts. The new hires included some talented people who went on to lengthy and successful careers in broadcasting, among them Barry Peel, Frank Ranicky, Rita Channon, and sportscaster Denny Trease.

Kincaid also invested heavily in equipment such as field cameras and sound-on film, the latter the lifeblood of television news in those days. His investments in news and sports returned robust dividends, as WKYT soon became the dominant station in the Lexington market and remained so for decades.

Lexington's Need for Urban Renewal

Garvice Kincaid was interested in improving Lexington's building infrastructure from the early 1960s on. In 1963, he was quoted in the Lexington paper about the need to build a downtown civic auditorium—what we refer to today as the Convention Center. Others were interviewed, but Garvice was the only one who suggested that the city needed to be bold and build a "citadel-style convention center," someplace that can "host convention business and serve our municipality needs."[18]

By 1970, most of Garvice's businesses didn't require as much oversight as they had ten and twenty years earlier. His finance companies, banks, life insurance company, and radio stations had strong, seasoned management in place, and while he was still unhappy with WKYT's position in the market, he seemed satisfied with Hart Hagan's and Ray Holbrook's oversight. He now wanted to devote time and effort to changing the face of downtown Lexington, which in his opinion had become a collection of trashy buildings. He also wanted to construct what he hoped would be a significant, iconic, high-rise commercial office building, which would house all his businesses. It would be the corporate headquarters for his empire.

In December 1971, he did have an important issue develop when Clyde Mauldin suddenly resigned as president of Central Bank. He had respected Mauldin, and in February 1967 had added him as a primary (versus alternate) Advisory Committee member to oversee his estate in the event of his death. Mauldin's departure required him to quickly update his trust and estate plan for the third and final time. He had always intended to have the president of Central Bank on the Committee, but he couldn't afford to install any new guy. Kincaid knew that the backbone of the Advisory Committee needed to come from members of his law firm, and while the insurance, finance, and broadcasting companies were important, he had good management teams running those organizations.

---

18   *Lexington Herald-Leader*, September 20, 1963.

He had to make a quick decision, one that he knew he could change in the future, so in this update to his estate plan, he listed Earl Wilson, as usual, but with a clause that required Ed Schaeffer to replace Wilson if he left the Committee for any reason. He next included Al Florence, whom he had never included in his estate plan or in management at Central Bank. Kincaid probably wasn't happy about including Florence. Florence didn't work well with others, and while he understood a bank's operations, he didn't have the professional, charismatic image of a banker. But Kincaid knew he could change this list in the future. His final addition to the primary three was Bud Burnett. Burnett had been with Kincaid since 1959 and was a known commodity, but he wasn't running Kentucky Central Life Insurance. David Brain had that job and was successful at it.

Bud Burnett was listed as an alternate on the Committee in February 1967, along with Hart Hagan and Robert Curtin (Kentucky Finance). Burnett was a good foot soldier and someone who understood the details around many of Kincaid's businesses and real estate investments. He could work with people and wasn't the bully that Florence could be. Burnett would be able to work with Earl Wilson or Schaeffer after him, plus, again, Kincaid knew he could change this in the future. This is important because in January 1975, Kincaid appointed David Brain the president of Kentucky Central Life and left Burnett as its secretary/treasurer and chief accounting officer.

According to David Brain's daughters, Nancy and Diane, this is what their father relayed to them about his promotion to president in 1975: David Brain appreciated the promotion, but he also understood how Garvice's Committee would oversee things. He knew that if he wasn't on the Committee, his position as president would have no authority, and by 1975, Kentucky Central Life Insurance had become Kincaid's largest asset. Brain told Kincaid that he would accept the promotion only if Garvice put him on the Committee, and he told his daughters that Garvice agreed. Brain was a strong leader, a well-educated professional, and Kincaid respected his frankness. Brain had done a good job and had moved his insurance company, his sleeping giant, from a small regional insurance company to a national insurance company. Garvice had also witnessed the animosity between the two men, and he knew that Brain was the right person to lead the company and that Burnett should be an alternate and work on other issues important to him, such as Lexington's urban renewal.

In 1970, David Brain had been executive vice president of Kentucky Central Life for several years. He was the guy running the company, and beginning in 1970, the company's publications began showing Kincaid pictured with Brain in its annual report, Kincaid the company's president alongside his executive vice president, David Brain. In 1973 and 1974, the annual report pictured Kincaid, Brain, and Burnett, with Garvice and David sitting and Burnett standing.

Garvice had been changing the ownership structure of his holdings over the last few years. He was transferring Kentucky Finance and the broadcasting properties to a downstream subsidiary of Kentucky Central Life. Kentucky Central Life was a publicly traded company, and it had a market value in excess of $50 million. Kincaid was proud of this, but he also believed adding these other businesses to the company would make it have a larger market value. In January 1971, the fifty-nine-year-old Kincaid considered that time was on his side, so adding Burnett as a primary Committee member was as much a placeholder as anything. He knew he could use Burnett in his urban renewal efforts, and in the company's 1973 annual report, there is even a photo of Burnett, outside at a construction project, with a caption that said he was reviewing one of the company's mortgage-loan projects.

In the fall of 1969, Kentucky Central Life began producing an internal company magazine. Its primary purpose was to communicate to its agents in the field, but it also served as a place to celebrate employee promotions, anniversaries, retirements, and significant family events. Kincaid and Brain pepper the pages of these publications, but Bud Burnett is not. Garvice looked at everything affecting his companies, and if he had wanted Burnett to be more visible in these publications, he would have made it happen. Each issue contained an introduction from him, and if the company hosted a convention or meeting for its agents, Garvice was there, along with David Brain—but apparently not Bud Burnett.

In addition, Bud Burnett was seldom listed or mentioned in these pre-1976 publications, while many of Kentucky Central's other department heads were. Most of these department heads were people that Kincaid and Brain had recruited to Kentucky Central Life over the last ten years. Bud Burnett handled the financial stuff, while David Brain was the chief operating officer of Kentucky Central Life. When my old boss, Cliff Forbush, was hired by Garvice, it was Burnett who assisted Kincaid during his interview. Kincaid considered insurance company investments in fixed-income securities and common and preferred stocks as financial business. Also, according to John Rampulla, vice president of mortgage loans for Kentucky Central Life, when he was hired by Garvice in 1971, Bud Burnett had not been involved in the company's mortgage loans, and during his career working with Kincaid, Burnett didn't attend any of his meetings with Garvice. John says, "Burnett was around, but I just never had any dealings with him while Mr. Kincaid was alive."

In 1970, Garvice was considering how to proceed with his urban renewal efforts, but other community leaders were working on a revolutionary way of making local government more efficient. Preliminary discussions were taking place about possibly merging the city and county governments into one body. The state general assembly had recently passed legislation to provide for this option, and both Lexington and Louisville were interested in pursuing it. Bipartisan committees were formed with representatives from both the county and the city. Many decisions had to be made about how to integrate both workforces and governmental structures into one body.

On January 1, 1974, the city of Lexington and Fayette County became the first Kentucky communities to consolidate city and county governments into a single system. The process took three years, and in the end, Foster Pettit was elected the first mayor of the newly merged entity. What's interesting is that Garvice remained silent on the subject. This either didn't interest him or he was focused on other things. Opinions and comments from him are absent from the local newspapers. His time was being devoted to his business and developing a plan for what Lexington might look like in the future—a plan that he presented to the city in July 1974.

Garvice Kincaid was never known to be subtle when providing his opinions or objections about things. In 1970, when he started pushing the city leaders to be more aggressive in its dealing with blighted properties, he expressed his great displeasure about the look of several downtown properties and said the city should require their owners to improve them or force them to sell them to others who could. This criticism wasn't received well by the property owners, who claimed Kincaid was trying to serve his own interests.

The issue was frustrating Garvice and delaying his effort to build a twenty-three-story office building that would serve as the corporate headquarters for all of his businesses. In April 1974, Kincaid approached the city with a significant financial proposal to encourage them to take action and develop and implement a revitalization plan for downtown Lexington. He was focused on (1) the downtown block bounded by Main Street, Broadway, Short Street, and Mill Street (aka the Purcell block); (2) the downtown block to the north bounded by Short Street, Broadway, Church Street, and Mill Street, and (3) the property situated between urban renewal land (adjacent to Sleepy-Head House) and the

Fayette County Courthouse Annex in the block bounded by Main Street, Mill Street, Vine Street, and Broadway. He explained that he would competitively bid for one of the blocks and build a three-hundred-thousand-foot office tower at a cost of $15 million. The city responded to his offer in a letter:

> You stated that you were willing to pay the urban renewal agency a purchase price for the land equal to its total expenditure for assemblage which price would include but not be limited to the cost of the appraisal and legal services, acquisition, demolition, and administration.
>
> Though the need for relocation payments to displaces was discussed, inclusion of that expense was not resolved. The offer also extended at least $10 million to redevelopers of other land in those areas named above.
>
> In your comments to the agency, you emphasized the public spirit of the offer for the betterment of downtown Lexington Center and the to-be-restored Opera House. You made it very clear that your firm would be competing with all other prospective redevelopers for the award of a redevelopment site or sites on the basis of the selective criteria currently in use. It was further made clear that you would look only to the proceeds from the sale of the cleared land for the repayment of the loan.
>
> It was an unusual and generous offer and has been very carefully considered by the members of the urban renewal agency. It was however, concluded by the agency that your officer be declined for several reasons including, it is the opinion of this agency that the proposal would constitute an improper use of eminent domain (condemnation of property) authority and would not be in the best public interest.

As this redevelopment story played out, various members of the Lexington Center Corporation, the governing body of Rupp Arena and the Opera House, along with local developers, approached the urban renewal agency also expressing the need for the redevelopment of various blocks that could provide the additional parking needed for the Center as well as more pedestrian traffic for its tenants. One significant conflict was that Garvice had proposed a three-hundred-thousand-square-foot, twenty-three-story office building, and the local developer groups were proposing building only two- or three-story office structures. From Kincaid's perspective, nothing was going to change because Lexington's leadership was ineffective and lacked the necessary backbone to get things done.

Jewel in a Pigsty

In July, Garvice took a different tack and went to the television airways to push this bolder up its hill. In a July 29, 1974, article, the *Courier Journal* reported,

> Kincaid recently put his big stick into the controversy for another vigorous stir. WKYT Television, a subsidiary of his insurance company, ran two special reports on the subject, at Kincaid's direction. One episode about the condition of the downtown area, referred to the new civic center as a "Jewel in a pigsty" and the other took a swat at the urban renewal's progress in a residential project south of downtown.

WKYT's reporter and Frankfort Bureau Chief Barry Peel was involved in the production of the reports and describes a meeting with Garvice and Ray Holbrook where this project was discussed.

> I'm in my house that Garvice gave me a mortgage for. It's in south Lexington. It's a Saturday morning, and I get a phone call from Ray Holbrook. "Peel, Mr. Kincaid and I are down at the Flap Jack Platter." It was at the Continental Inn and was only open for about a year or so. This all happened in July 1974 and the restaurant was closed by January 1976, shortly after Kincaid died.

> Holbrook says, "He wants to talk to you," and I'm thinking, *it's Saturday morning and Garvice Kincaid wants to talk to me*, and I am wondering, *about what?*

> So, I go down there, and the scene is, they are at a table with Garvice sitting Buddha-like, and Holbrook is sitting to his right, and so I sit across from him. Well, I smoked in those days, and so I lit one up.

> Now picture this, there's an enormous—and when I say enormous, it's outsized; it's a very large plate. Not a normal plate that you would have in your house; this was a platter, and it was full of pancakes with syrup, just drizzling all over this huge stack.

> Garvice says, "Well, you want something to eat?" and I say, "No, I just ate breakfast." But I'm smoking and ask the waitress to bring me a cup of coffee. So, I'm drinking coffee and smoking.

> Well, Garvice says, "I want to do a series of stories on the decline of downtown Lexington," and I'll never forget this, he says, "I want you to be my Dan Rather." Well, I knew what that meant; he wanted me to be his bulldog. He wanted me to, you know, put the worst face I could put on the decline of downtown Lexington and show how desperately a revival is needed.

> He said "I want you to be my Dan Rather" again, and I looked

at him and said, "I can do that. I can do that." In other words, I'm trying to sell myself, you know, which was true; I would have done it and could have done it.

Well, in the course of this, Garvice probably excuses himself at least twice, maybe three times. "I got to go to the bathroom." Ray Holbrook told me that he was taking diuretics, and you know, he had already had a heart attack, I think, and oh my God, he probably weighed four hundred pounds, and again, he's got this story he wants done.

Well, anyway, we go through all the issues he wanted in the story, and I agree to do it. Now it's time to leave, and all of a sudden, Garvice is sitting, with these leftover pancakes in front of him. He had probably eaten three, or four or something like that, right? And he suddenly he takes his hand and pushes the platter away from him on the table and leans back and goes, "Well, Holbrook, that's all I can do; finish these" and pushes that platter over to Holbrook. Well Ray picked up that fork and dived in like a Busby Berkeley–choreographed dance.

That's when I said I thought to myself right there, *he has done this for several reasons.* Garvice wanted me to know he was in control. He wanted to be sure I knew he was in control, and if we do these certain stories correctly, I'll be in control. You'll just be my office boy, and you'll do what I say. The second thing was, see, he's your boss and you have got to follow him. But he's going to finish my pancakes.

Robert, I've told you this before, and I always add it when I tell this story, because I think it needs added, but I probably committed libel for him. But if he had put those pancakes in front of me, I guarantee you, I would not have touched them.

I thought to myself, I have a lot of respect for Ray Holbrook, because we had worked together in Danville, and we'd have had lots of political conversations. I always thought Ray liked me, and I think he respected me. He hired me for God's sake, at the television station, WKYT. But I thought to myself, if I ever need to get or keep a job badly enough to finish another man's pancakes, take me up and shoot me and let God and the governor pardon whoever does it. I would not have touched those pancakes, but Holbrook, my friend, picked up that fork up and dived in just like it was a faithful command, but again, Garvice had him and he knew it. Kincaid knew how to use his wealth and position to keep people loyal to him.

After WKYT ran the two-part series, it had the effect Kincaid was looking for. It created a stir at city hall, in the local press, and among business leaders. It was reported that Kincaid was responsible for the views reflected in the series but that Charlie Thomas, Kentucky Central's head of public relations, was its principal author.

The story had the impact that Kincaid was looking for. City leaders were forced to discuss the problem, and the business community began pushing for help from the city, similar to what Garvice had proposed, so they could acquire parcels for redevelopment. In fact, Kincaid's request that the city use its powers of eminent domain became a focal point of the discussion. The Kentucky General Assembly also contributed to this movement when state senator Joe Graves proposed the Local Development Authority Act, which would authorize the creation of the Lexington-Fayette County Development Authority. This local Authority would also have the power to engage in the use of eminent domain, which would allow it to force property owners to sell their properties to it at market prices. In addition, the Authority would have the capacity to borrow money to build the new convention center and arena and also the necessary parking facilities.

The vision Garvice presented to the city in 1970 finally would become a reality in late 1974. It wouldn't be the coordinated vision that he had proposed, but it was a pivotal change for the future of downtown Lexington and one that helped Kincaid acquire many of the parcels necessary to build his corporate headquarters. The unhappy fact is that he would die in November 1975 and not get to really enjoy the outcomes of his work.

Garvice: Both the Producer and the Director

According to Barry Peel, Garvice Kincaid liked to let you know he was watching. He paid attention, and he wanted you to know he was in control.

> Garvice was in control, and as I've said before, he understood information is power. We all know that. We're in an information age, social media, computers and twenty-four-hour news. You know, as someone said, we're the most-informed and the worst-informed people in history, through social media and all this other crap that you know, but anyway, Garvice knew information is power. Garvice would go to Florida, and I swear he would get the [Lexington] newspaper before we did here in Lexington. I'm sure he must have had somebody here, when the first edition rolled off, and they called and told him all the headlines. He'd called us up and say, "What are you doing about this story in the *Herald* on page three?" We haven't even got the paper yet! Information is power and Garvice always knew that. But again, he also knew what he didn't know, and he never tried to act as if he did.

I know from personal experience—I know that he had great respect and admiration, a strong respect, for those of us who were on the air. I did the news and weather and whatever, and that wasn't his background, and I think he respected us for what he called "a quick story."

This is probably in 1974, and I did the 11:00 news for a short period before I left the job that year. In those days, the anchor, which I did, had to write the script. I had to even edit the film. I mean, you know, talk about a one-man band. I mean, you did it all. You put the newscast together, you put the stories in sequence, you know, you decided what was the lead and so on.

Well, one night, Garvice called me. I'm at the anchor desk. I'm writing the script and the phone rings. It's Garvice. Well, the first thing you did when he called was that you came to attention." You are like, *Garvice is on the phone. Right.* All your senses are focused on this moment, and he says—and I'm convinced that Garvice missed his calling, and he should have been a defense attorney or a prosecutor. He was a trained lawyer, but I don't think he ever really practiced. But I think he would have made a great lawyer in court, because he knew just how to get through to you.

Anyway, I answered the phone and he said—and my life was just stretching out before me. I am thinking the hammer is about to fall and I'm thinking *oh, God, what have I done? What have I written?* You know that he didn't pay you to screw up. I say, yes sir, and he starts to speak, "I just want to tell you," and he would pause. He did it deliberately. I'm telling you, he could have been F. Lee Bailey. But he continues, "I just want to tell you, you did a really nice, tight, newscast tonight." Then silence, and I say, "Well, thank you," and he just hangs up.

Barry Peel further explained that Garvice's influence on what was reported at WKYT generally involved making sure they were covering stories that he thought were important, but he also would suggest important angles for the staff to consider. For instance, in 1973/1974, as the city and county created a merged government, a new mayor had to be elected. Garvice was for Judge James Amato, and old-money Lexington was for H. Foster Pettit, who was the current mayor. According to Peel, Amato was considered a "guy on the move" and someone whose wealth was considered "newly rich," like Garvice.

During the race, Garvice was on the phone a lot about the election, making sure we covered Amato. The election was extremely close and supposedly Amato had won. Well, Pam Miller noticed that one large precinct went to Amato. Miller, who was later mayor, was plugged in enough politically to know the lay of the land and that this couldn't have happened. She said there was no way in the world that Amato won this precinct and that the voting machines needed to be checked. Long story short, Peel was there when this happened. They checked the machine, and sure enough, they found out that there was a flaw in this machine. Apparently, the paper labels on the front listing the candidates had become switched, and whenever someone voted for Pettit, it registered as a vote for Amato, and vice versa. There was a flaw in the machine—not mechanical, but the equivalent of having the wrong price on a menu item.

Now, Garvice thought his guy had won, but the election wasn't resolved until Circuit Judge James Park Jr. ruled that "we know what the voters intended, and they intended to vote for Foster Pettit" when they pulled the lever. In the end, Foster Pettit won by twenty-seven votes and became the merged government's first mayor. When his term was up, James Amato was elected as its second mayor. As for Garvice, he wasn't happy; some wondered if he had something to do with the switched labels, but nothing was ever investigated.

Barry recalled one more story about Kincaid that happened early in his career. Garvice had been a significant benefactor of and financial savior to the Appalachian Regional Hospital System (ARH), which provided healthcare to Eastern Kentucky. In the early 1960s, the ARH had grown by acquiring five hospitals in the region. The concept was to improve costs by having a more efficient organization. The plan made strategic sense but was executed poorly, plus ARH overpaid for the facilities it acquired. By 1964, its debt load was crippling the organization. It had financed the acquisitions with short-term debt and needed help. In May 1964, Kincaid came to the rescue with a $750,000 loan from Kentucky Central Life and was made chairman of the board for the next two years. His financial resources and involvement saved the organization. Garvice had Bert T. Combs, the former governor of Kentucky, appointed to replace him, but he remained on the board.

In 1983, Lewis E. Weeks published a series, "Hospital Administration Oral History Collection," In it, Dr. Karl S. Klicka, ARH's administrator, provided a firsthand account of Garvice's early involvement in saving ARH.

> One day when I was in my most desperate straits, a man who had come to work for me as my communications director made a suggestion. I have been grateful to him, Ed Easterly, ever since. Ed was a wonderful, wonderful fellow. He had been the press secretary for a series of governors of Kentucky. Bert Combs was one, and previous to him, Happy Chandler. Everybody held Ed in high regard. He knew that area like the back of his hand. He said he wanted to introduce me to a man named Garvice Kincaid.

Ed said, "You tell Garvice your story. He just might be able to help you. He was born and raised in Pineville, a community in the mountain area. He put himself through law school. He is now a very wealthy man. He is in finance, he's in banking, he's in the insurance business."

I did talk with Mr. Kincaid. He was a man of my age, very overweight. Easterly told me he had had a heart attack within the past year.

After a brief introduction he said, "Come back and see me next week. I'll have a little more time. We can talk for fifteen or twenty minutes."

I went back the following week. The twenty minutes extended into two hours. I went over the whole story. When we were finished, he said, "Dr. Klicka, I've never heard of a situation quite as poor as the one your hospitals present. I know you have been to the banks in Lexington, and they have given you a short-term loan of $500,000."

I said, "That's right, and it's due next week."

"I know you have been to Louisville, and you have talked to the major bankers in Louisville that carry deposits for the state. Certainly, Governor Ned Breathitt thought they could help you, but they have turned you down as a poor risk, something that they as bankers cannot assist."

I said, "That's right."

"So here you are, the worst possible risk. You are losing your short-term loan at the National Bank in Lexington. The bankers in Louisville won't help you. You have come to me. I'll tell you what I'll do. I will give you a mortgage of $750,000 on those ten hospitals. Believe me, Doctor, they are not worth a dime, but I think you can pull this off. Let's go from here."

I asked, "How soon can I have the money?"

He said, "Next week. This will be a loan from the Kentucky Central Life Insurance Company, of which I am the chairman. I only ask you one thing: I want to be a member of the board of directors."

I said, "I'll tell you what. I have the responsibility of forming this board, and I will not only recommend to those now on the board that you be a member of the board, but I want you as chairman of the board."

He said, "I'll take it."

That was a big step forward. It was essential for me to have working capital, and once I had it, things began to fall my way.

I think one of the interesting facets of the early formation of ARH that helped in the ultimate success of the organization was a concept that I had wherein the membership of the board included two representatives from each of the communities where the hospitals were located. That would total twenty, and then with four members at large, we would have twenty-four board members. Supporting this, we would form little organizations in each community we would call hospital advisory councils. These two people on the board from each community would come from those advisory councils. The councils would be made up of eighteen people representing cross sections of the people living in the communities. They would have no authority beyond advisory authority.

In 1972, according to Peel, Kincaid was angry with Jay Coberly, who was vice president of administration at ARH. He joined the organization in 1963 after ARH acquired the Miners Memorial Hospital, where he was its administrator. His nickname throughout his life was "Smiley," as he was known for his pleasant demeanor. When Kincaid stepped in to help ARH, the system's employees were on strike, and Garvice blamed much of its problems on Coberly. Irrespective of Coberly's nickname, Garvice described Coberly as a "mean son of a bitch."

Barry Peel said that Garvice really disliked Coberly and asked him to embarrass him. He said,

> It was the most reprehensible thing I have ever done. I wrote a semi-level story about Coberly for him but purposely slanted it to embarrass the guy. He liked the story, and so we ran it for like two days. As I said, it was the most reprehensible thing I ever did. There's no excuse for it. It was a moral lapse, but here I am. I'm in college. I'm working my way through college. I was married at the time. I had rent to pay and a car payment. And you know, again, I call it the velvet trap, but he had me trapped also [as he did others]. It's like, what else am I going to do? He calls up. This is what he wants. It's his candy store. There's no excuse. So, I'm not offering one; it's just an explanation. Garvice was in control, and so I did it.

The Making of June Rollings

June Segal was born in Battle Creek, Michigan in 1928. Her father was Leonard Segal, an event promoter, and her mother was from the famous Kellogg Cereal family of Battle Creek. Her mother was taken away to a hospital when she was five years old and died two years later. She never saw her after she was taken to the hospital.

According to Rollings, she was raised by her father, educated by tutors on the road, and lived in hotels and railroad cars as her father traveled to promote football and basketball games and boxing matches. She says she never learned anything about cooking or baking and was always more comfortable around men than women. She was bright and obtained a high-school-equivalency certificate at the age of fifteen. She was also strikingly beautiful.

In 1944, at age sixteen, Rollings changed her birth certificate to show she was eighteen and enlisted in the Marine Corps. She was a camp police officer, which freed up a man to go overseas and fight the battles of World War II. In 1945, June was at Camp LeJeune when she met her future husband, Parnell Rollings, a Louisville doctor who had enlisted in the Navy. They married and moved to Louisville and were part of Louisville's social life. The couple had three children, two girls and a boy, but the marriage was over by 1960, and so June packed up the kids and decided to move to Lexington, where she got involved in amateur theater at the Carriage House. She fell in love with Lexington and appreciated the city, with its small-town feel.

Rollings made a comfortable life in Lexington and soon enrolled the kids in a Maine summer camp. After taking them to the Maine camp, June decided to visit New York City for some shopping and to see a play. While she was having lunch at P.J. Clarke's during the trip, comedian Alan King noticed her when she ordered steak tartare covered in chili. He told her to come back the next day, and when she did, she and some others were driven to New Jersey, where they had her do a Pall Mall cigarette commercial. She didn't even smoke and became a little sick from it. Rollings even had a line in the commercial: "I know what I like, and I like Pall Mall." The commercial was a national hit and soon caught the attention of Garvice Kincaid. June's only other television experience involved a commercial for a local sausage company, but apparently she was considered a natural. Garvice immediately liked something about June Rollings and soon made a phone call that brought her to WKYT to co-host a new morning talk show with Louis Grizzard.

According to several people, Garvice never discussed the show with anyone before he made the call to June in 1966. Louise Grizzard indicated that he didn't know anything about it until Garvice called him and had him show up at the WKYT studio to make a test tape of the show. According to Ted Grizzard, Kincaid phoned him one afternoon to explain the show, and the test tape was made the next day. That was his first meeting June Rollings. Ted said he could see Rollings had some television experience. He said they both were relaxed and laughed a lot, and later, after it was done, he told Garvice the audition tape was so good that he should take the show national.

Town Talk was a success and ran in the mornings from 9:00 to 9:30, Monday through Friday. The show's format was for Ted and June to chitchat and interview local and national celebrities, authors, entertainers, and politicians and provide some light entertainment. A third member of the show was Dave Perry, who was a local celebrity musician who played the piano and organ. The show's popularity was good, and the chemistry between June and Ted was wonderful. National celebrities such as Billy Graham, Ralph Edwards, Art Linkletter, Telly Savalas, Jay Silverheels, Lucille Ball, Ken Curtis, Tony Curtis, Sammy Davis Jr., Danny Thomas, Sophia Loren, John Wayne, Hugh O'Brian, Rory Calhoun, and Forrest Tucker and important politicians such as presidents, governors, and members of Congress were guests. According to Ted Grizzard, Garvice watched the show almost every day.

Town Talk and its successor, *The June Rollings Show*, were staples in Lexington homes. The show was launched in Lexington on Labor Day in 1967 as a one-hour show but was soon changed to a thirty-minute format. *Town Talk* was on the air for eleven years until it was abruptly canceled in September 1978. After Ted Grizzard left the show in 1971, June struggled to keep the audience. She had loyal viewers, but the competition from national shows such as Phil Donahue's was a problem. In addition, after Garvice died in 1975, she lost her biggest champion. After Rollings came to WKYT, she soon became a close friend and companion of Garvice, and this relationship frustrated many at the television station. After Kincaid died, Ralph Gabbard didn't react immediately and get rid of Rollings, but he didn't coddle her anymore either. According to Gabbard's close friend, Ralph Hacker, before Kincaid's death, Rollings had tried to influence station policies using Garvice as her leverage. With Kincaid dead and Hart Hagan, the primary Committee oversight person, Ralph felt more comfortable handling June, and he did, and eventually canceled the fifty-year-old host's talk show, in September 1978. Ralph just got tired of reminding June that she was host of a "talk show," not a "religious show."

Something else happened in 1975. In October, one month before Kincaid's death, June's daughter, Pamella Rollings, contracted herpes encephalitis from a mosquito bite and was in a coma for more than a year, hooked up to a ventilator and a feeding tube. In fact, June was told three times by medical professionals that her daughter wouldn't live, and it was recommended that life support be discontinued. June prayed and held firm, and Pamella eventually regained consciousness. Pamella was left with significant mobility issues from the disease and was in Cardinal Hill Hospital for three years before being transferred to June's home in 1978. When she finally came home in 1978, she found three years of her life gone from her memory and that her husband had divorced her. Her car was gone, her clothes were gone, her house was sold, and even her beloved dog was gone, but she was not! Pamella continued to improve with June's help but would always be physically handicapped from the disease. Over the years, she volunteered at the Veterans Administration Hospital of Lexington, God's Pantry Food Bank, the Gospel Outreach Center, and Habitat for Humanity. She was also involved with the local Democratic Party and worked in election precincts. Pamella died in 2016. Her body had continued to be weakened from the illness, and eventually she succumbed to advanced atrial fibrillation and pneumonia. June Rollings lived another five years and died in 2021.

June Rollings was a popular local celebrity and hosted many benefits and telethons during her life. With Garvice's support, she started the Kentucky Big Sisters organization of Lexington. She saw Big Brothers and wondered why there wasn't a Big Sisters too. Big Brothers was an organization important to Garvice, so when June suggested there should be a Big Sisters organization, Kincaid immediately worked with her to make it happen. June also hosted annual telethons for Cardinal Hill Hospital, Easter Seals, and cerebral palsy and was the master of ceremonies at many of Lexington's major fundraising events.

Rollings had her critics, though. June tended to be "gushy" and emotional on television and quite often displayed the religious aspect of her life on the air. In fact, after leaving WKYT, she eventually ended up with a show on a religious television network. That show didn't last long, and June eventually used her connections to start Encore Galleries gift shop and later an Omnistaff employment agency, but most of her time and energy were always devoted to caring for Pamella.

According to Bob Hensley, June Rollings didn't appreciate some of the changes that were taking place at the station in the 1970s. For instance, when Rita Channon was hired, according to Bob, "June Rollins was the queen bee at WKYT, and while she understood why the changes were being made, she wasn't happy. Rita was young and attractive, and then the station hired a black minority." Hensley said he tried to talk with her one day because he could see she was unhappy. He was trying to be kind to her, but the changes were just too difficult for her to accept.

Another story Bob recalled was about something that happened during an episode of *Town Talk*. The show's producer had arranged for a local woman author to come in and be interviewed on the show. The lady shows up, and she is an African American, and June hadn't realized this. He said June didn't refuse to do the interview, but she worked with Ted to make sure when they went on the air that they kept their monologue segment so long that they basically ran over and didn't have time to do the interview. That was how she avoided doing the interview.

Societal attitudes were starting to change in the 1960s, but this change was slow. The struggle for equality was emotional, and many times the civil rights movement created cultural turmoil. One might speculate that Garvice had some strong opinions about these forced changes. If he did, his views were never mentioned in the press. One should recognize, though, that much of Kincaid's empire was created by providing loans, life insurance, and banking services to the lower- and middle-class public, and he recognized that as these segments of the population economically improved, so would his business interests. I can imagine that if he had any strong racial bias, it was limited to how these changes might affect the public's view of his television station.

The *Lexington Herald-Leader*, on June 2, 2002, did a long interview with June Rollings about her career, her retirement, and her relationship with Garvice Kincaid. Rollings had lived in Lexington forty-two years by then, and even though Kincaid had been dead twenty-seven years, June recognized that she would always be connected to his memory. Almost as soon as she began working at WKYT, there was gossip about a relationship between Kincaid and Rollings.

> The show was enormously popular. Soon there was gossip about Rollings and Kincaid. "It's because we were seen in public at dinner constantly. Garvice never ate dinner at home. He went out to dinner every night at the Coach House, the Imperial House, wherever. He had three male buddies and me that he dined with."
>
> "Gossip about us was inevitable, but laughable. Nell [*sic*] (his wife) and my children knew the truth. He was strictly business; the coldest, most unemotional man I've ever known. And one of the smartest. He knew everything about everybody in Lexington; where they came from, how much money they had, and all their secrets."
>
> She remembers the last time she saw him.
>
> "Ralph Edwards, who had the *This Is Your Life* show, and I were eating at the Campbell House, and Garvice wanted to meet him. He always liked meeting the celebrities."
>
> "I was worried about my daughter in the hospital, and Ralph was worried about a hospitalized relative of his." And Garvice said: "Nobody's worried about me. Hell, I'll die before either one of them."
>
> "And he did," she says. "He died the very next day of a heart attack." Kincaid was sixty-three years of age.

In another part of the article, she discussed how her *Town Talk* days went and provided a little more information about Kincaid:

> I don't see how Barbara Bailey does it all. I went in each

morning, did my show, answered telephone calls for half an hour and then went home for the rest of the day—and out to dinner every night.

The room [they are sitting in at her house for the interview] is full of elephant statues. A large, gold one is named Garvice in honor of the late Kincaid. "It cost about $30 at the old McAlpin's," she says. "That's like $150 now. It was the only gift he gave me. . . . I started working at WKYT at $125 a week."

"I think I reminded Garvice of a daughter, and I was drawn to him because he reminded me of my father; blunt, brilliant, and ruthless but nearly always right. Garvice took credit for creating me as a TV personality and he was right."

If one lived in or around Lexington during the late 1960s and early 1970s, it was hard not to hear the rumors about Kincaid and Rollings. I was a youth in Paris, Kentucky, and I recall my parents talking about them, and after I joined Kentucky Central Life, I remember various people discussing it. Part of the reason is that it was well known that Kincaid hired June Rollings and created *Town Talk* for her to be a co-host with Ted Grizzard. In addition, as June discusses in the interview, they were often seen dining together. Finally, many people heard that Garvice kept a hotel suite at the Campbell House, and this just added to the gossip.

My personal view is that June Rollings was merely Garvice Kincaid's companion. In 1967, June was a strikingly beautiful, forty-two-year-old woman and Kincaid was a fifty-five-year-old man, obese and recently recovered from his second heart attack three years earlier. Kincaid was on heart and blood pressure medication and diuretics. I suspect his room at the Campbell House Hotel was just a place for him to rest during the day or evening and maybe take a shower and change his shirt. In 1967 and the years that followed, everyone knew he wasn't in good health. In addition, this was before the age of Viagra, and most of the medications he was on probably suppressed his libido.

I am not implying that Garvice didn't appreciate a beautiful woman, but he probably more enjoyed having people think he was more virile than he actually was. A friend from the Rotary Club of Lexington told me that when he was a youth, he worked at the Starlight Kentucky Fried Chicken in Lexington, and Garvice gave him the biggest tip he ever received back then. Starlight had a carhop, and Kincaid's Cadillac pulled into it one evening and he waited on Garvice. The car had a driver, and Garvice and June were in the back seat, kind of cuddled together. When Garvice paid the bill, he gave him a $20 tip. I think June knew how to play Kincaid's game and also didn't mind the extra attention he was giving her or the implied power at WKYT it gave her. Also, remember that Rollings provided Kincaid with another set of eyes and ears at the television station—and just how much he liked keeping tabs on everyone.

In a *Lexington Herald-Leader* article on September 23, 1989, June was quoted discussing the rumors:

> Rollings' fame also forced her to cope with criticism. When people complained about her "gushy style," she learned to shrug it off. "They say a cloud will go by and June will cry. I don't mean to, but I just have a real empathy for people."
>
> She even learned to cope with the gossip about her relationship with Garvice Kincaid, the late Lexington financier. Kincaid, who owned WKYT (Channel 27), hired Rollins and Ted Grizzard as hosts of "Town Talk," which became "The June Rollings Show" when Grizzard retired. Kincaid ate dinner with Rollings at least once a week.
>
> "People have said a lot of unkind things about my relationship with Mr. Kincaid, but the waiters and the restaurant owners and the waitresses and the bellboys knew better," said Rollings, who had divorced her husband in 1960. "He [Garvice] ate out every night, except weekends. He loved his wife. Nelle Kincaid was a beautiful human being."

I feel June Rollings is naïve when she says she reminded Garvice of a daughter. By 1967, Kincaid appears to have detached himself from Nelle and his daughters. He was still interested in his family, but it appears that his passion for his business empire and the power it provided was consuming most of his attention. June's arrival at WKYT and the success of the show, which was his creation, also stroked his ego. In addition, the show brought him in contact with many celebrities, which he always had a thirst for, going back to his days of owning Joyland Park. Finally, June Rollings played a different role in Kincaid's broadcasting empire. She wasn't a dealmaker or business manager. Rollings was an entertainer, a socialite, and a community liaison. While I am sure he enjoyed her company, he also could depend on her to not gossip about him. I think June Rollings was also caught in what Barry Peel called "Kincaid's velvet trap." She had an easy job, decent money, community status, and implied power due to her relationship with Garvice, and she recognized that Kincaid was undoubtedly one of the most powerful people in Kentucky.

I have asked many of the people I interviewed for this book about this relationship, and most acknowledged the rumors, but no one felt they knew anything for sure. People who worked at WKYT were certainly aware that she was Garvice's companion, so that was enough to give her implied power. I also think the people she worked with at WKYT were relieved to see her move on when her show was canceled. It's not that they disliked her as much as June was always someone who was not quite part of the WKYT family. Former employees can't recall any small talk with her around the coffeepot or other informal ways people catch up with each other in an office. I am sure it wasn't all due to June. The WKYT staff also had to be concerned about saying something inappropriate that might get back to Kincaid. It just wasn't a healthy situation for either June or the WKYT staff.

Chapter Six: Kentucky Central Life Insurance Company

"Everything you do today will impact your tomorrow."
– Frank Sonnenberg, *The Path to a Meaningful Life*

Author's Note

The journey to create this book began with my desire to document the history of Kentucky Central Life Insurance. Along with my wife and many of our friends, I had worked there for years, and the isolation caused by the pandemic provided the perfect reason to begin such a project. The company's history was just something I thought I would find interesting and something I felt many of our friends might enjoy having.

I began working on it in late 2020 and by early 2021 had completed what I thought was an interesting resume of the significant facts around this place we'd all spent many years associated with. This history wasn't in book form but rather was a collection of stories and articles about the company going back to its beginning in Anchorage, Kentucky, in 1902. I documented how it was formed, who its significant leaders were, and how Garvice Kincaid became involved. I also recorded how Garvice changed the company over time.

Garvice Kincaid's purchase of the insurance company was the single largest investment he made during his lifetime. This investment not only had him investing in a new industry but also put him in charge of a publicly traded, stockholder-owned company. While initially the company's stock traded on a limited basis, in a short time it was quoted and traded on a daily basis. This gave Garvice a new currency to make acquisitions with and allowed him to see how other investors measured the value of this part of his business empire.

The friends I shared these stories and articles with enjoyed learning some new things about the company. These stories also caused them to remember things from those early years after Kincaid acquired the company. Eventually these conversations among friends led to their suggesting that a book should be written about Kincaid and his accomplishments. While I agreed, and I knew I had the ability to research something like this, I questioned my ability to write a book. It just happened that I had recently read Ann Hagedorn Auerbach's book *Wild Ride*. *Wild Ride* is the story of the rise and fall of the Calumet racing dynasty of the Wrights, one of Lexington's most famous thoroughbred racing families.

Warren Wright tried to preserve his family's empire through a multigenerational trust, similar to what Kincaid did. I found it very ironic that two wealthy individuals from Lexington both tried to protect and control their empires, around the same time, through these complex trusts, and both these men's plans failed. Their plans failed because neither man could predict how people responsible for the administration of their estate would so grossly fail in their responsibilities. *Wild Ride* became my inspiration and encouragement for this attempt to write Mr. Kincaid's history.

Garvice Kincaid's Most Consequential Investment: The Beginning

Kentucky Central Life Insurance Company (Kentucky Central Life) began business as a mutual assessment insurance company, meaning that it was owned by its policyholders, similar to a mutual insurance company, but with the provision that in the event it was unable to pay its claims, it had the contractual right, included within its policies, to assess its membership for additional monies.

In addition, over the years, many have wondered if the company was named after a train when it was formed. In 1984, the company's Public Relations Department decided to get to the bottom of the question. It researched the issue, and even included a picture of the Kentucky Central Railroad steam engine in its analysis, but concluded it could find no reference to the railroad in the company's archives. The railroad was founded in 1854 but was in receivership by 1886, so its history wasn't the best. Parts of the company were sold off, and in 1891, its remaining assets were sold to the L&N Railroad, and eleven years later in 1902, Kentucky Central Life's founders created its namesake.

The company's PR Department ended its report by stating that traveling by train was the primary means of transportation during the period in question and it had no doubt that the founders traveled on the KCRR line. It wondered if the founders had fond memories of the railroad and just decided to resurrect the name, like a phoenix. Personally, I think "Kentucky Central" described the focus of the company's business territory in the beginning and that was a description the founders wanted to project to their prospective policy owners.

A Brief History of Insurance

The insurance industry is one of the world's oldest industries, dating back to bottomry insurance contracts in Babylon as early as 4000–3000 BC. A bottomry contract provided loans to merchants with the provision that if the insured shipment was lost at sea, the loan didn't have to be repaid. The interest on the loan covered the cost of the insurance risk. Roman law also recognized bottomry contracts. Marine insurance became extremely popular in the fifteenth century as international commerce expanded geographically.

The concept of fire insurance didn't exist until the Great Fire of London in 1666. Shortly after this tragedy, many insurance companies were started in England. By 1711, though, many of them failed because they were fraudulent, get-rich-quick schemes concerned mainly with selling their securities to the public. Nevertheless, two important and successful English insurance companies were formed during this period—the London Assurance Corporation and the Royal Exchange Assurance Corporation. Their operation marked the beginning of modern property and liability insurance.

No discussion of the early development of insurance in Europe would be complete without referencing Lloyd's of London, which established the international insurance market. Lloyd's began in the seventeenth century as a coffeehouse patronized by merchants, bankers, and insurance underwriters and gradually became recognized as the most likely place to find underwriters for marine insurance. Edward Lloyd supplied his customers with shipping information gathered from the docks and other sources; this eventually grew into the publication *Lloyd's List*, which is still in existence. In 1769, Lloyd's was reorganized as a formal group of insurance underwriters accepting marine risks. The word "underwriter" is derived from the practice of having the risk taker write his name under the total amount of risk he was willing to accept at a specified premium. With the growth of British trade, Lloyd's became the dominant insurer of marine risks, which later included fire and other property risks.

The first American property and casualty (P&C) insurance company was organized by Benjamin Franklin in 1752 as the Philadelphia Contributionship. The first American life insurance company was organized in 1759 as the Presbyterian Ministers' Fund. By 1820, there were seventeen stock life insurance companies in New York State alone. There was a problem, though, because many of the early P&C companies failed due to their speculative investments, poor management, and fraud. In addition, many failed after the 1871 Great Chicago Fire and the 1906 San Francisco earthquake and fire. The industry was still developing, so there was little effective regulation and no sound industry data to aid companies in accepting and pricing risk. Many problems also affected the life insurance industry. After the US Civil War, many managements declared dividends that had not been earned, under-reserved for their risks, exaggerated their contractual promises, and built large office buildings that sometimes cost more than the company's total assets. Historical records show that thirty-three life insurance companies failed between 1870 and 1872, and another 48 failed between 1873 and 1877. The industry needed to change.

After 1910, the US life insurance industry enjoyed a period of steady growth. Its growth rate was steady over the next eighty years. The P&C insurance industry also experienced strong, but not as much, growth. By 1989, the United States had 3,800 P&C companies and 2,270 life insurance companies. The companies were employing nearly two million workers.

Since about 1850, the insurance industry has always almost exclusively been regulated by state governments. The first state insurance commissioner was appointed in New Hampshire in 1851, and a state-based insurance regulatory system quickly developed as the insurance industry grew. Before this period, insurance was primarily regulated by their corporate charters, state statutory law, and de facto regulation by courts through their judicial decisions.

As the various state governments developed their own insurance regulations, insurance companies with multistate business became frustrated by the differing rules and regulatory requirements across states. A policy that could be sold in one state might be unavailable to customers ten miles away in a neighboring state, even though the agent was licensed in both.

By the mid-1850s, the insurance industry and its various stakeholders joined together and pushed for some type of coordinated state-based regulation. In 1871, the National Association of Insurance Commissioners (NAIC) was created to coordinate and propose model laws that could be adopted by its member states.

The NAIC acts as a forum for the creation of model laws and regulations. Each state decides whether to pass each NAIC model law or regulation, and each state may make changes during the enactment process, but the models are widely, albeit somewhat irregularly, adopted. The NAIC also acts to advance laws and policies supported by state insurance regulators and coordinates regulatory actions and exams.

The NAIC's mandate is to benefit state regulators and insurance consumers by promoting uniform laws and regulations. By promoting uniformity of regulation among the states, this coordination also makes it easier for insurance companies to comply with the laws and regulations in all states in which they do business.

Finally, the NAIC is also responsible for creating the statutory accounting principles (SAP) upon which insurance accounting is based. SAP is often contrasted with Generally Accepted Accounting Principles (GAAP) and is considered more conservative than GAAP accounting. NAIC SAP accounting rules are incorporated into each company's NAIC annual financial statement, and these statements must be filed with the department of insurance in each state in which an insurance company writes business.

The NAIC's members are the insurance commissioners, who are the chief insurance regulators of each US state and six territories. In addition, the NAIC is a nongovernmental organization that concerns itself with coordinating insurance regulatory matters. It does not actually regulate, though. States greatly value their regulatory control and have not delegated their regulatory authority to the NAIC.

The creation of the NAIC in 1871 ultimately led to the creation of the insurance industry's version of the banking industry's FDIC. For decades the insurance industry was loosely regulated and subject to much fraud and mismanagement and many poor investment decisions and company failures. Most life insurance company failures were very detrimental to individual policyholders, causing them to lose their coverage and policy values or, in the event their insurance company was a mutual assessment insurance company, potentially creating a legal assessment that they must pay. The insurance industry does provide valuable, necessary benefits to its customers, but because these contracts are very long term by their nature (twenty to eighty years, potentially), the financial condition of the company might become impaired, and it might fail.

The insurance industry has never responded to change quickly. The complexities of state regulation have always been one reason. Getting the majority of states to agree on something is similar to Washington politics. For many years, most state insurance departments saw the need for some form of guarantee fund to help cover consumer losses. The membership of the NAIC knew that company failures and their effect on their state's consumers was a problem, but each state had differing views on how to solve it. To respond to insurer insolvencies, many states sought to independently create some form of state guarantee, but most did not do so.

In 1969, Congress fortunately stepped in and passed a statute that mandated that states create a state guaranty fund. State guarantee funds are nonprofit systems operating in all fifty states, Washington, D.C., Puerto Rico, and the Virgin Islands. Premium taxes and insurance company assessments provide the funds used for the guarantee.

Initially, states maintained a single fund to cover one line of business, such as workers' compensation or personal auto insurance. At the time, many insurance companies were relatively small and wrote only one line of business in a single state. If the insurer went bankrupt, only a limited number of policyholders in that one state would be affected.

In 1983, the NAIC sponsored the founding of the National Organization of Life and Health Insurance Guaranty Associations (NOLHGA). Since many insurance companies were now operating on a national basis, NOLHGA became a mechanism for states to coordinate their efforts to provide protection to policyholders when a life or health insurance company insolvency affected people in multiple states. NOLHGA is a voluntary association made up of the life and health insurance guaranty associations in all fifty states and the District of Columbia. Addressing individual insurance company failures became a national issue and moved beyond the doors of the state regulator.

State guaranty associations provide coverage to resident policyholders, up to the limits spelled out by state law. NOLHGA assists its member associations by providing coverage to policyholders in the event of a multistate life or health insurer insolvency. When an insurer licensed in multiple states is declared insolvent, NOLHGA, on behalf of affected member state guaranty associations, assembles a task force of guaranty association officials. This task force analyzes the company's commitments to its policyholders, ensures that covered claims are paid, and, where appropriate, arranges for covered policies to be transferred to a healthy insurer.

The task force may also support the efforts of the receiver to dispose of the company's assets in a way that maximizes their value. When there's a shortfall in the company's assets needed to pay the claims or policy values of the covered policyholders, the guaranty associations assess the licensed insurers in their states a proportional share of the funds needed to address the shortfall. The larger a company's premium market share in a state is, the higher its assessment.

Since its creation in 1983, NOLHGA has assisted its member guaranty associations in guaranteeing more than $25.6 billion in coverage benefits for policyholders and annuitants of insolvent companies. In that time, the associations have provided protection for more than 2.6 million policyholders and worked on more than 100 multistate insolvencies.

A Rocky Start

Kentucky Central Life Insurance incorporated and filed to be a mutual assessment company with the Kentucky state Insurance Department in August 1902. The company sold weekly premium life and disability insurance to industrial workers. The company claimed it had one thousand applications for insurance with a face value of $200,000 and had raised $4,000 of contributed capital, which was the amount required by statute. Kentucky Central Life's incorporators had a problem, though: the Kentucky insurance commissioner did not want to issue the company a license (certificate of authority) for doing insurance in the state. That same month, Kentucky Central Life's incorporators sued the insurance commissioner to compel him to issue the license. In September, the management won in court and the insurance commissioner granted its license, but the state Insurance Department publicly acknowledged the financial troubles that many mutual assessment organizations around the country were having. The company was initially capitalized with $4,200 and required to hold 2% of all premiums in an emergency fund.

In 1902, Kentucky law stated: "Any number of persons, not less than 13, may own the stock or mutual plan to furnish life or personal accident insurance. Insure against loss or damage by fire, lighting, or storm, or to write marine, livestock, plate glass, fidelity, surety, burglary, or theft insurance."

That year, Kentucky had thirty-four life companies and three P&C and surety companies licensed to do business in the state. The insurance industry was very fragmented and poorly regulated in the early 1900s, the majority of the companies were quite small and undercapitalized, and their officers were appointed as trustees of their company's assets.

In 1902, John N. McEachern was president of a mutual assessment company in Georgia, The Old Reliable Life and Health Insurance Company. He had started this one state company in 1901; it specialized in providing sick-pay insurance to (people who were then referred to as) Negroes. This type of insurance cost the policyholder 5 cents per week and would pay a $1-a-week sick benefit, for up to twenty weeks. If no claim was ever made on the policy, then it would have a cash surrender value of $10 at the end of ten years. In 1909, McEachern and his vice president were charged with cheating and swindling for saying the policies presented for claims were invalid and for reaching settlements with policyholders for far less than what was contracted for. Fortunately for McEachern, he was able to convince the court that some rogue agents, whom he had terminated, had created the issue, and he was allowed time to work through the problem.

In 1902, Charles S. Drake was an insurance agent in Georgia. He knew McEachern understood what was necessary to start a mutual assessment company. Drake also recognized he had the Kentucky connections needed to get the initial required policies sold. In the summer of 1902, McEachern and Drake formed an alliance that created Kentucky Central Life. After Kentucky Central Life began operating, Charles Drake was its "superintendent"; that is, its president. He and his brothers James M. and Cooper Drake were largely responsible for Kentucky Central Life's operations until late 1906, when Cooper Drake drowned. In 1907, the Drakes left the company, moved to Indiana, and started the Empire Health and Accident Insurance Company. Empire was a stock company owned by the Drakes and probably some other investors; its profits benefited its shareholders. Kentucky Central was still a mutual assessment company with its profits going to the benefit of its policyholders.

Charles Drake was progressive in his thinking, and he recognized that most of the policies being sold were being purchased by Black people. In November 1904, the *Courier Journal* reported that R. A. Saulsberry, a collection agent, for Kentucky Central Life, was "the only negro employed by any insurance company of this city" and that "[t]he company is doing a most excellent business among colored people."

Since this was a Kentucky-based mutual assessment company, the listed incorporators needed to be Kentucky residents, so John McEachern's contribution to the founding of Kentucky Central Life stopped shortly after the company's first year in business.

Kentucky Central's Primary Executives

Frank J. Walker – president
Thomas O. West – secretary & treasurer
Ernest H. Speckman (1910) – office boy to president

Kentucky Central Life was originally incorporated in 1902 by eighteen individuals, and after the Drakes left and during its next first four or five years, it had three primary officers who were critical to its future success. It was originally located in a modestly furnished, five-hundred-square-foot, two-room office in what had been a residential building on 5th & Market Streets in Louisville. In that small office, Frank Walker and his partner Thomas West, who had joined the company in 1903, worked at night issuing the policies from the applications they had obtained during the day. As its business grew, it soon relocated to suite 411 of the Paul Jones Building. The Paul Jones Building (now Marion E. Taylor Building) is on the southwest corner of Fourth Street and Jefferson Street in Louisville. Kentucky Central Life's agents were considered employees, and by the end of 1904, the company had twelve employees, eight of whom were agents.

Kentucky Central's Original Incorporators

Humphrey Marshall – Kentucky senator
George M. Glover – old Louisville family

George M. Milburn – Louisville grocer
William H. Pipes – Unknown
Frank A. Lenz – Louisville attorney
Charles S. Drake – Kentucky Central Life superintendent
Garfield P. Drake – Kentucky Central Life sales rep
J. Frank Trisler – Kentucky Central Life sales manager
John Burks – school superintendent
John O. Dixon – surgeon
J. A. Dixon – bank president
Henry Diel – local tailor
W. L. McDougall – Louisville architect
H. H. Duke – surgeon
Herman Thielman – real estate sales
George R. Merhoff – post office
Jacob Reinhardt – tinsmith
F. M. Milburn – unknown

Kentucky Central sold its first and second policies on July 28, 1902. They were written on a husband and wife, Louis and Ella Franklin. Each policy provided a $200 death benefit and a $2.00-a-week "accident and sickness" benefit for up to twenty weeks. The cost was 10 cents a week for each policy. The agent was A. D. Fion, and he was expected to go to the Franklins' home each week and collect the payment of 20 cents for the policies.

Robert Harold West, the half-brother of Thomas O. West, joined the company in 1920. He explained how its early policies worked in a 1977 interview:

> We sold just one policy, a weekly premium health and accident policy. The smallest premium we could write was five cents a week. But mostly it was 35 cents a week on women and 40 cents a week on men. If the policyowner was unable to work, he got a dollar benefit for every nickel of weekly premium, so a 40-cent per week policyowner got $8 per week for up to 20 weeks. There also was a small death benefit: Up to $112, as I recall.[1]

Frank T. West, Robert's nephew and the former assistant vice president of underwriting, in the same interview explained how the policies evolved in the 1920s and 1930s:

> A series of new policies was introduced in the late 1920s and early 1930s, created primarily by Mr. Walker, who had a keen sense of what the public needed and wanted. The original policy was known as the "A" and it was followed by the E, X, XX and W. They were weekly premium policies, which provided disability income, plus a natural and accidental death benefit. The company got into

---

[1]   Kentucky Central Life *Keynoter* publication celebrating the company's seventy-fifth anniversary.

the "Regular Ordinary" market in 1940 and "Weekly Premium" life shortly thereafter.

Ordinary life insurance policies normally have larger face value amounts, usually for more than $1,000, and include a variety of structures and benefits. Industrial life policies are simpler policies, with benefits of $1,000 or less (but may be more). In addition, premiums were usually collected at the insured's home, on a weekly or monthly basis.

While these amounts seem small, in those days, 30 cents an hour was the average wage for an industrial worker, and a person could buy a dinner at a good restaurant for about 20 cents. It was a time when the automobile was in its infancy. At the beginning of the century, there were fewer than ten thousand automobiles in the country. The company's agents sold the insurance policies and collected premiums by walking or riding in electric trolley cars or using a horse and buggy. In rural areas, some of the company's representatives had to walk as many as ten miles a day to collect premiums, pay claims, and provide other services to the policyowners, but the men who were willing to work hard could make a good living as a Kentucky Central Life agent.

Robert H. West, in the same interview, explained it this way:

> We were selling to working class people and I had to get out and ramble through the countryside to find new customers. Most people only had $12 to $15 a week to live on, so spending 40 cents a week for insurance was a sacrifice. The 1920's may have been a prosperous period in some sections of the country, but not in my area.
>
> I had policyowners in several towns besides Elizabethtown. I used to walk 12 miles once a week to collect in Hodgenville. Some of the men used a horse and buggy. It was some time before I could afford a car. The manager had quite a bit of authority. We didn't use the telephone very much so contact with the Home Office was infrequent. Managers were sent out into Kentucky, Ohio, and other states to start from scratch and if they were successful, they were left alone. They would pay virtually all expenses (from the premiums they collected) and send the balance to the Home Office.

Frank added:

> I went on a Debit in 1935 and the country was in a Depression. Money was tight but we still made the increase. Today, most people have a minimum amount of insurance, and they buy more to expand their coverage. When I delivered a $5 or $10 (weekly benefit) to a home, it put food on the table. This was before Social Security, workman's compensation, retirement plans, or anything else.

> When I was hired, I asked Mr. Walker, the President of Kentucky Central, what he would pay me. He said we'll pay you what you're worth. I said jokingly that I couldn't work for that. I started at $15 per week.

Margaret Simpson, who started working for the company in 1929, officially retired in 1975, and then went straight back to work as a part-time employee until 1989, when she finally left the company after sixty years of service, described those early days in a company publication in 1987 this way:

> The company was in Anchorage, 12 miles from Louisville, when I started to work in the actuarial department on August 12, 1929. My salary was $10 a week and bread was 10 cents a loaf in those days, but everything was not so cheap.
>
> I remember the first dressy dress that I bought to wear to work, it cost $15—that was a week-and-a-half's salary.
>
> When I joined the company, it had 11 employees, and everybody knew everybody. Now the company has a sales force of 12,000.
>
> Ten weeks after I took the job, the stock market crashed, and the Great Depression began. When banks closed in 1933, the company managed to get enough money to pay the employees, but a lot of it was in coins.
>
> During the four years of World War II, I never had a vacation.
>
> Mr. Kincaid bought the company in 1959 and moved it to Lexington in 1963. Mr. Kincaid was a thing apart. We didn't exactly know how to take him. Once I dialed what I thought was the maintenance department and a gruff voice answered the telephone. I said, "Is this maintenance department?" and "No!" growled the voice. "This is Kincaid—in bed!" I had dialed the direct line that went from the home office to Kincaid's home.
>
> I went to the comptroller and said, "Well, this is my last day." But it wasn't.

Robert H. West shared these thoughts about Kincaid:

> I thought a lot of everybody and would hesitate to single anyone out. One rule I had was that I never got hard-boiled and chewed out an employee. I treated them like I wanted to be treated.
>
> A lot of people have asked me what I thought of Garvice Kincaid. I tell them that he was a mighty wonderful man and as fine a person as anyone would want to know. Some people resent a person achieving the level of success which Garvice did, but I didn't feel that way. He was always very fair and honest with me. I was named Chairman of the Board after he was elected President in 1959. I had an office at the Home Office in Anchorage, and he spent

> a lot of his time in Lexington. He would call me and say, "What's
> going on, Bob" and I would kid him and say, "Garvice, come on
> over and see for yourself."

Thomas West and Ernest Speckman and others probably did feel like the home office employees were like family, because many of the employees were related to each other. I don't know when the company started to do this, but in 1941, there is a picture of the Anchorage home office staff in front of the building, getting ready to board a chartered bus for a day at Churchill Downs racetrack. Management had closed the office for a "company day at the races."

As for how much compensation agents could receive, during the divorce proceedings for one company agent in the late 1920s, he said he was paid 75% of the first year's annual premium and the Home Office received the remaining 25%. After the first year, the numbers were reversed, and the agent kept 25% and the Home Office received 75%, as long as premiums were paid. The agent was still traveling and collecting the premium and was incentivized to keep the policy in force while also finding new customers. The agents were also company employees and had a base salary, similar to Frank West's $15 per week. The salary was subtracted from their commissions, so, they could earn more if they sold more. Also, according to L. J. Logan, the company's Cleveland District manager, "there were always weekly and monthly promotions where agents could win additional nominal cash awards for selling more insurance." In addition, "[i]n the old days, life insurance was the only benefit available when people died or could not work. There was no substitute, so people needed the help, and they were interested in what we had."[2]

The Franklins' two policies are important, because Kentucky Central Life wasn't officially licensed to do business in July. Their applications, and others, were part of the initial required one thousand applications for insurance—a state statute requirement before a company could obtain its license. In addition, the company had collected $200,000 in premiums and established a capital trust fund of $4,000. The state insurance regulation mandated that the managers/trustees of the company first obtain one thousand applications for insurance before the Insurance Commissioner would consider issuing a license. These applications indicate that the company was originally named Kentucky Central Life & Accident Insurance Co. of Louisville. In 1963, Garvice Kincaid shortened the company's name to Kentucky Central Life Insurance Company.

According to W. E. "Bud" Burnett, during the company's seventy-fifth anniversary celebration in 1977, "selling weekly premium life and disability insurance to industrial workers was a relatively new concept, so many

---

2   Kentucky Central Life *Keynoter* (May 1977).

people were cautious, or even skeptical."[3] The company did have a motto or tagline that seemed to reassure folks, though: "Always a Square Deal." Teddy Roosevelt's administration was calling its own safety-net program "A Square Deal." The company founders had gotten their tagline from that. The management of Commonwealth Life Insurance Company of Louisville (owned by Capital Holding) must have been impressed by Kentucky Central Life's success, because by 1905, they were using the tagline "A Square Deal for Every Policy-Holder."

This little startup company was successful, and by 1912, the company had offices in ten Kentucky communities, 156 field personnel (agents), and a home office staff of twelve. According to Burnett, "the founders knew that fair and speedy payment of policy benefits would spread the company's reputation and popularize the concept of personal and family security provided through the medium of [its] small, weekly insurance premiums."[4]

Thomas O. West, Kentucky Central Life's secretary and treasurer and an important participant in this southern saga, almost didn't make it to the company's ten-year anniversary in 1912. On June 7, 1911, he attended the races at Churchill Downs. He won $100 that afternoon and decided to take a joy ride to Shelbyville. He invited several of his friends, who he had been drinking mint juleps with him at the track. The inebriated party left Churchill Downs after the last race and proceeded to Shelbyville in West's automobile with some vague intention of going to Lexington. After reaching Shelbyville and dropping off one of their party, E. K. Pennebaker, West and W. H. Hettermann stopped by a local saloon for more drinks. West also carried a bottle of whisky with him, which he enjoyed on the ride.

It was after ten o'clock when West and Hettermann decided they needed to head back to Louisville. During the trip back is when things became quite crazy. They passed a man and a woman in a buggy, and the 37-year-old West ordered the car stopped. He jumped out and told his Black chauffeur to give him a monkey wrench, as if someone was after him. The chauffeur gave him a pistol instead, and West took off running after the buggy. Upon reaching the buggy, West ordered it stopped, pistol-whipped the man, and attempted to drag the woman out of the buggy, yelling at her, "Give back my ring." She jerked free of his hold, and he shot her, hitting her in the abdomen, above the right hip, and perforating her bladder. She was able to stagger away and fell to the road. The man who was with her picked her up and transported her to her relative's home, where she was sent to Louisville's Jewish Hospital by an "interurban car." Her condition was listed as critical.

---

3   *Lexington Herald Leader*, September 18, 1977.
4   Ibid.

After the shot, West left the woman lying on the ground and returned to the car. When questioned by Hettermann about the shots, he told him he had fired the gun in the air. Also, just before shooting the woman, West had fired upon the automobile belonging to Charles R. Long but didn't hit anyone. The men returned to Louisville, and West went to the Crescent Bath House, where he was arrested at 2:45 that morning.

Neither the woman, Miss Hattie Wetherby, nor her male escort, Mr. Lee Hibbs, knew Thomas West, and it soon turned out that he shot the Middletown schoolteacher due to mistaken identity. West had been keeping company with a woman named Miss Lucille Gwathmey and had given her a ring, signifying their love. When he thought he saw her with another man, he assumed she was stepping out on him.

West was charged with malicious shooting and wounding and was arraigned and initially released on a $5,000 bond that was soon increased to $20,000. Upon being questioned by the police, West said he couldn't recall anything much after leaving Churchill Downs.

West was considered one of Louisville's prominent businessmen, having moved there from Newberry, South Carolina, to help manage the affairs of Kentucky Central Life. The shooting was Louisville news and well covered during the next several months. The press interviewed anyone connected to the story, but neither they nor the police could locate West's chauffeur. Within a few days after the shooting, Miss Wetherby's condition improved to stable, and in a week's time she and her father, who helped operate on her, were giving interviews to the press.

West's only defense was that he shot her due to mistaken identity and was crazed on drink, and he never seemed to remember anything about that evening. The case went to the grand jury and his trial was scheduled for October. By September, the press was reporting that Miss. Wetherby had agreed to accept $10,000 from West for her suffering. In addition, it was suggested that due to West's wealth and social class, he would be charged only with a misdemeanor and fined $500. Assistant Prosecuting Attorney Mix was incensed by the report and declared, "Any settlement made will in no way stop the enforcement of the law."[5]

West's trial took place in October. Various witnesses testified to what happened that night, and West's physician testified that West suffered from alcohol-related "delirium tremens," which included the symptoms of visual hallucinations and auditory hallucinations, vomiting, diaphoresis, and

---

5   "Deny West's Case Has Been Compromised," *Louisville Courier Journal*, September 14, 1911.

hypertension. West testified that "friends before this trouble had advised him of irrational acts he had committed while under the influence of liquor." F. J. Walker, who had known the defendant for sixteen years, said West was a "jolly good fellow" and that night he had stayed with him because "he was afraid he would do himself harm." West's attorneys were endeavoring to show that West had been a slave to "the drink habit" and had temporarily lost his reason that night. During this part of the trial, a "drunk" wandered into the courtroom, fell over a bench, and had to be ejected by a deputy sheriff.

During the trial, another odd thing happened. Miss Wetherby sat next to Thomas West, and they carried on conversations, smiled at each other, and even laughed. Miss Wetherby testified that she doubted West's intent to do her harm and that she held no anger toward him. The trial lasted only a day, beginning at 10:30 in the morning and then breaking for lunch around noon and reconvening at 2:00 in the afternoon. The jury was given the case around 3:00. Their deliberations lasted only nine minutes, and they returned to the courtroom and acquitted Thomas West of the charges. The next day the headline read, "FREE ON PLEA OF DRINK CRAZE – West Acquitted of Maliciously Wounding Girl."

Thomas West would continue his leadership role at Kentucky Central Life for the next twenty-six years, at the end of which he would die from complications from a stroke he'd experienced three days earlier. Thomas West was sixty-four years old when he died on November 26, 1937. He had been with the company thirty-four years and is largely credited with the vision and knowledge that made the company great. His obituary used the phrase "largely because of his own energy and ability to lead a southern industrial insurance company."

In April 1914, the company changed its headquarters from the Paul Jones Building to the eleventh floor of the newly constructed Stark Building, which was located on Fourth & Walnut Streets in Louisville. In addition, sometime during 1914, Kentucky Central Life's management started the process of converting the company from an assessment insurance company controlled by its policyholders/members to a stockholder-controlled insurance company. On July 26 of the same year, the company made its first strategic acquisition of the business of another insurance company. In June the company's superintendent of the Bowling Green office, P. J. Noel, told the *Bowling Green Register* that the Georgia Insurance Department requested that the company reinsure the Kentucky portion of the "combination Life and Health and Accident Business"[6] of the Standard Life Insurance Company of Atlanta. Standard Life

---

6   Bowling Green Messenger Sun, July 26, 1914.

was licensed to do business in Georgia, Kentucky, Missouri, and Tennessee, and the Insurance Department was not happy with how the company was administering this portion of their business, versus its regular life business.

This would be the first of many acquisitions over the next seventy-five years. Also reported in the press that July was the fact that Kentucky Central Life's president, Frank Walker, was appointed to Governor McCreary's staff as an aide de camp.[7]

In November of that same year, an attorney representing a policyholder named John J. Shelton filed a lawsuit against the company and F. J. Walker and T. O. West alleging mismanagement of the company, excessive salaries, and soliciting perpetual proxies in a manner that perpetuated management and provided them a means of awarding themselves high and exorbitant salaries and commissions.

It appears that this lawsuit was the brainchild of attorney J. S. Lusher. Lusher evidently was using management's decision to convert the company to a stock company as a means of pressuring management to pay some money to his client and himself. A few days after the lawsuit was filed against the company, management published an extract from its October 28, 1914, Insurance Department examination. The full-page disclosure included a glowing letter from the insurance commissioner, Matt C. Clay, dated November 2, 1914. The report covered the quality of its assets and its excess reserve funds, officer compensation, and liberal benefit policy of using its excess profits to increase the value of its policyholders' benefits, which apparently no other similar company was doing in the state. One probably should assume that this mid-year examination was done in anticipation of management's decision to convert to a stock company.

The published report caused the policyholder, John Shelton, to file an affidavit in which he asked that the case be dismissed and stated that he wasn't dissatisfied with the company and knew nothing about the charges that were made in his name. He said he consented to allow attorney Lusher to use his name "because Lusher told him he could make some money out of the case." The case was dismissed. As for management's salaries, the suit alleged that Walker and West together earned salary and commissions totaling $25,000 annually. In 1914, a senior-level manufacturing manager was earning between $8,000 and $10,000. Walker's and West's salaries were voted on and approved by Kentucky Central Life's board of directors. Walker and West certainly controlled the board, but their salaries were limited by state statute to the company's excess profits, after the payment of all benefits and expenses, plus

---

7 Louisville Courier Journal, July 23, 1914.

a 2% emergency contingency fund. In other words, excess profits were the key to any payments. What's interesting is that the company had $78,000 of "net-ledger assets," of which $74,000 was its emergency fund. Their two salaries, totaling $25,000, equaled one third of the company's assets and emergency fund.

The report also showed that after being in business twelve years, the company had 86,953 policyholders and during the first nine months of 1914 had collected $432,693 in premium income and paid "sick and accident" and death claims of $200,000, which left about $232,000 to cover expenses and its required reserves. Finally, the report showed that since September 1902, Kentucky Central Life Insurance Company had paid over $1,034,710 in "sick and accident" claims and $296,135 in death claims, for a total of 1,327,846 in benefits paid to its policyholders. This company, by its nature, had been started with only about $4,000 in capital and had been profitable enough to pay out $1.3 million in benefits to its policyholders during its twelve years of existence. Converting to a stock company now was possible since Kentucky Central Life had accumulated excess capital, aka surplus, of $74,000.

If one uses the September 30, 1914, numbers and factors in some assumptions about policyholders who paid premiums that year but also died and policyholders receiving "sick and accident" benefits, one can estimate that the average Kentucky Central Life policyholder in 1914 was paying about $6.60 annually for their insurance, or about 12 cents a week. In addition, it's important to recognize that the collected premium of $432,693 was essentially all collected in cash. Each business day, company agents collected and sent or delivered thousands of dollars of cash to the company's office along with their receipt book, which recorded the policyholder's payments and any agent expenses. Each day, a large portion of the company's home-office staff was involved in the manual counting and recording of the thousands of the small cash payments it received daily from its agents. In addition, these payments were subject to theft, as reported by the *Lexington Herald-Leader* on April 27, 1912:

Boy Arrested

Earl Thompson Charged at Mt. Sterling with Opening a Post Office Lock Box

. . . For some time past, the local agents of Kentucky Central Life Insurance Company have been missing money from their mail, the sums range from ten to fifty cents in unregistered letters. They informed Postmaster Lockridge of the occurrence, and Mr.

> Lockridge notified the post office inspectors at Cincinnati. The inspectors arrived here Thursday, went to the post office, placed several marked coins in the Kentucky Central Life Insurance box and waited. A short while after the box was opened the inspectors peered through the window and saw the young man take the envelope from the box and go out of the post office. The inspectors followed him to Sewell & Williams confectionery where he spent part of the marked money. Making sure of these facts the inspectors placed young Thompson under arrest.

Not much is reported about the company's intent when it reorganized into a stockholder-owned company or about the associated lawsuits. One can only assume that the litigation may have slowed the process down or that maybe the process took more time than management might have normally assumed. Kentucky Central's management was required to get approval for the conversion from two-thirds of its members, and most of the members may have been slow in responding. In addition, the company would have needed to increase its capital to at least $100,000, and this may have taken longer than expected. All we know for sure is that the process was not completed for almost two years and that the attorney J. S. Lusher sought out other Kentucky Central Life policyholders to continue the lawsuit.

We also know that when March of 1917 arrived, Kentucky Central Life's management did little to publicly acknowledge this significant corporate change. That said, all the company's agents were reportedly brought together in a special meeting about the change and the company's future goals.

An assessment insurance company is a single state–based insurance company, which implies it is limited to operating in one state. In 1914, it appears that Kentucky Central Life's management, after operating in Kentucky for twelve years, wanted to expand and grow the business in other geographic regions of the country. If Kentucky Central remained an assessment insurance company, that would not be possible. In addition, the company had demonstrated its ability to sell and grow profitably. Kentucky Central Life began business in 1902 with just over $4,000 of capital and by 1914 its required capital account had grown to over $77,000. Management needed to change the company's corporate structure if they were going to take the company to the next level and make it even more successful.

Taking Kentucky Central Life to the Next Level

The West family was extremely important to the history of Kentucky Central Life. They were predominantly from the Graniteville and Newberry areas of South Carolina and had relocated to Louisville in the early 1900s. By the time Robert H. West retired from the company in June 1962, a total of twelve family members had worked for the company for a total of 212 years.

James Appleton West: 1845–1915
Charles M. West: 1865–1925
James Henry West: 1872–1940
Thomas O West: 1873–1937
Otis Edward West: 1877–1932
Robert H. West: 1897–1979
Samuel A. West: 1875–1924 (died in war)
William Herman West: 1899–1901
Plus four sisters: Mary Peral, Allis L., Tillie, and Carrie Bell

The following article appeared in the *Lexington Herald* on July 26, 1916. It was a reprint from an insurance trade publication a year earlier. It was reprinted several times, in various state newspapers over the next six months. Something was changing at Kentucky Central Life!

PHENOMENAL GROWTH OF COMPANY THAT OPERATES IN SINGLE STATE

Kentucky Central Life and Accident Has Policy of Fairness That Inspires Continued Confidence

It must be a great incentive for those just beginning in the industrial life, and health business to review the history of the Kentucky Central Life and Accident Insurance Company, of Louisville, KY., which has had a remarkable career which credit is due President F. J. Walker and Secretary-Treasurer T.O. West.

The company was organized in September 1902 and has a perpetual charter. Beginning with little aside from self-confidence in their ability to successfully direct an institution of this character, Messrs. Walker and West now find themselves at the head of a company which is writing probably the largest business of its kind in a single state. It is needless to say that had they not dealt with unusual fairness with policyholders they could not have inspired so much confidence nor could the company have continued growing in such a phenomenal way.

The Kentucky Central Life and Accident is mutual in spirit as well as in fact, and the officers feel it their duty to treat the members liberally and to pay claims with the utmost dispatch. Despite the policy, its loss ratio is not abnormal. In 1914 the premium income in Kentucky, in which state it operates exclusively was $576,721.60

and during that year the company paid over 59,000 weekly "sick and accident" and 1,322 death claims.

So effective is its policy that instead of having to seek agents, the Kentucky Central Life and Accident has more applications than it can care for. Its men [agents] are prosperous and are largely of that clean, young, aggressive type which is a characteristic of the officers themselves.

Although the company operates in a restricted territory, Messrs. Walker and West were among the first to appreciate the public education in insurance and immediately took advantage of the opportunity offered to participate in the Collective Insurance and Universal Safety Exhibit at the Panama-Pacific International Exposition.

In making report of an examination of the Kentucky Central Life and Accident, Commissioner Clay, of Kentucky in one of the most searching of examinations, said in part:

> An investigation of the complaints filed by policyholders with the management show that the company gives special and prompt attention to same, forwarding them at once to the superintendents for investigation with instruction to settle same immediately if found meritorious.
>
> The death claims are principally settled in the field by the superintendents, but the policy premium receipt book proof of death and receipt of payments are turned into the home office for the files.
>
> Your examiners are glad to say in their belief that the company's treatment of policyholders is beyond criticism.
>
> We have found the books in an excellent condition and must commend the bookkeeper for accuracy and neatness.
>
> We found the management exceptionally strong, and commend the president, F.J. Walker, and secretary, T.O. West for their earnest and constant attention to the company's business.
>
> The Company is economically managed, and its officers have the respect and confidence of those with whom they have dealings.[8]

In March 1917, fifteen years after Kentucky Central Life was started as a mutual assessment insurance company, management completed the reorganization and conversion of the company into a stockholder-owned

---

8   Extract from *The Daily Field*, San Francisco, Cal., of July 15, 1915, the only daily insurance newspaper in the world.

company. Nothing was reported in the press except for a couple of minor indications that something had changed. The *Louisville Courier Journal* reported that the company's Articles of Incorporation were amended, and the company held an "All-Agent Meeting" that May with the theme "From Acorns to Oaks."

Kentucky Central Life's reorganization involved segmenting the surplus of the "assessment policyholders" and holding it for their behalf. In addition, the Kentucky Department of Insurance had to examine the company to confirm that the company met the four main regulatory requirements:

- The reorganization must be with the consent of three-fourths of Kentucky Central Life directors. Kentucky Central Life had unanimous director consent.

- There must be the affirmative vote or written consent of two-thirds of Kentucky Central Life's members. Ninety-two percent of Kentucky Central Life's assessment members approved of the conversion.

- There must be paid-in capital of not less than $100,000. Kentucky Central Life's paid-in capital was $102,550, with a contributed surplus of $41,020.

- The surplus accumulated by the old company must be segregated and used only for the reserves and benefits of the assessment policyholders. Kentucky Central Life had accumulated assets of $114,599, a required reserve of $48,942, and other liabilities of $28,199, leaving a surplus of $37,457 for the old assessment policyholders.

In 1917 and 1918, the Spanish flu epidemic depleted all the company's accumulated capital that it had segregated for its assessment policyholders. The company lost over $50,000, and by 1920, it needed to increase its paid-in capital to $200,000 as it continued to grow its business. This additional capital was obtained through a 60% stock dividend. This action converted a portion of the company's paid-up capital to paid-in capital. The 60% stock dividend was an accounting maneuver that transferred money from retained earnings to the company's paid-in capital account. In addition, management purchased 3,592 shares of stock at $30,00 per share, raising $107,760. Walker and West are believed to have purchased the majority of the 3,592 shares along with some of the other management employees (the Drakes, Speckman, and the Fords). In advertisements, the company reported that it was owned exclusively by its officers and employees.

Another significant event happened in 1917: the company relocated its headquarters to 11405 Park Road in Anchorage, Kentucky, a suburb of Louisville. The building had been built in 1911 and was to be the home office for the Citizens National Life Insurance Company. Citizens abandoned the building in 1916 after it merged with the Inter-Southern Life Insurance Company of Louisville. It was an ornate, tile-roofed building embellished with marble corridors and dark wood paneled executive offices. It was designed by Louisville architect William J. Dodd to meet the requirements of an insurance company and cost $146,972 when it was constructed. The site also contained a separate building listed as the power plant.

Thomas West purchased the thirty-thousand-square-foot building on 7.7 acres of land for $100,000 from Inter-Southern and contributed it to Kentucky Central Life for shares of the company's stock. This transaction made West easily the largest shareholder of the company. The 1914 building had been appraised by the Kentucky Insurance Department for $125,000, and in 1917 it was carried on Kentucky Central Life's books at $100,000. By 1926, the value of the property had increased to $220,000.

When a company issues a stock dividend, it rewards shareholders with additional shares of stock for each share they already own. Many companies that pay out stock dividends do so when they don't have enough cash reserves to reward their investors with cash dividends. The number of shares an investor receives depends on the number of shares they already own.

For instance, if an investor who owns one hundred shares receives a total of sixty additional shares, the company is making a 60 percent stock dividend. When a company issues a stock dividend, an amount equivalent to the value of the issued shares is deducted from retained earnings and reallocated to the company's paid-in capital account. The common stock and additional paid-in capital accounts are increased just as they would be if new shares had been issued, except the increase is funded by the company's own retained earnings rather than by investors. The purpose of additional paid-in capital is to provide a source of funding for a company's growth and expansion.

At the end of 1922, Kentucky Central had expanded its state licensing and was now able to do business in Kentucky, Ohio, Indiana, and West Virginia. Additional paid-in capital was needed to support the growth of the company. The company was now paying $100,000 in weekly claims, versus the $700,000 in total claims it had paid in 1921. At the end of 1921, the company had a surplus (retained earnings) account of $150,000.

At the end of 1922, the company had paid-in capital of $200,000, but its surplus had increased to $207,442. In 1923 the company again issued a stock dividend; this time it was a 50 percent dividend, which increased its paid-in capital account to $300,000.

Not much was written about the wealth Frank Walker and Thomas West amassed, but we know from West's 1911 lawsuit and some articles that he employed a chauffeur named Moses and owned a large automobile back then. In addition, by 1925, he owned a large Pierce-Arrow automobile, and his chauffeur, Moses, drove him from Louisville to St. Louis and Newberry, South Carolina, quite often to visit a sister company (the Missouri Insurance Company) and his family. Some other articles and government records also provide a glimpse into some luxury possessions that Frank Walker possessed.

- In 1910 Walker and his family rented a modern five-room apartment (#7), in the Breckinridge Apartment building. According to a listing ad, their rent was $100 a month, which would be over $1,800 in today's dollars.

- In addition, in 1912, Walker purchased an electric roadster for around $1,750. This was very expensive, considering that a gasoline car sold for about $650. By 1935, electric vehicles had all but disappeared.

- In Walker's divorce proceeding in 1915, one report said he had an estimated income of $50,000 a year.

- In May 1923, Walker and his family were attending the races at Churchill Downs when their apartment at 841 South Second Street was broken into. Shortly after the 1917 conversion to a stock company, Walker had acquired a luxury Derby box at Churchill Downs racetrack.

- The police report about the robbery indicates jewels valued at $5,000 were stolen and that the robbers overlooked an additional $2,000 worth of jewelry. Seven thousand dollars' worth of jewelry in 1923 would cost over $125,000 in 2025 dollars. Among the items stolen were a Tiffany gold watch, a platinum ring set with diamonds, a diamond-studded gold bracelet, a diamond ring, a box of antique jewelry, a platinum lava lavaliere, a pair of pearl earrings, and a pair of platinum cuff buttons.

- In 1927, Frank Walker purchased a $350,000 apartment in The Dartmouth, located on Willow Avenue, at Cherokee Park in Louisville. This was a new twenty-two-unit, luxury, high-rise apartment complex with underground parking. The apartment had three master bedrooms, three baths, one small bedroom, a breakfast room, dining room, and a luxury kitchen with a large Frigidaire refrigerator.

By 1927, the company had obtained a license to do business in Pennsylvania (approved in 1925). It now was doing business in five states. In a 1927 examination, the Kentucky Department of Insurance described its business as follows:

> The company confines itself to writing three kinds of Industrial Health and Accident Policies.
>
> It's been writing its so-called "Class A" policy since its organization. This policy is a combination of health and Accident Insurance and is written on the entire family for a weekly premium of 5 cents to 45 cents between the ages of 1 month and 54 years next birthday. This policy pays a weekly indemnity for either sickness or accident and a small Death Benefit according to age of the insured. About three-fourths of the company's business is under this policy.
>
> The Company issues a Special Accident Policy, premium 35 cents, paying weekly indemnity for accidental injuries, a Natural Death Benefit of $100 and Accidental Death Benefit of $1000. This policy is written principally on male risks from age 18 to 50 years.
>
> The Company also writes a combination policy, premium 75 cents, which it issues only on preferred select mail risks between the ages of 18 and 50 years. This policy pays weekly indemnity of either sickness or accident, 100 dollars fatal illness, or $1,000 accidental death.
>
> All of the above policies contain additional features paying an indemnity for Dismemberment, Loss of Sight, Total and Permanent Disability, Etc.
>
> Several years ago, it issued a so-called Monthly Policy, but discontinued this department over four years ago and there is only a small amount of this business now in force as most of this business was rewritten under the Special Accident Policy.[9]

In 1927, ten years after Kentucky Central Life's conversion to a stock company, two policyholders challenged the conversion process in court. They asked for a receiver to investigate the company and accused the management of the following[10]:

1. Fraudulent representations to the Secretary of the State of Kentucky. They claimed the company could not have had two-thirds of the members approval because:

---

9   *Lexington Leader*, March 27, 1927.
10   *Lexington Herald*, March 20, 1927.

    a. Fewer than 10,000 of the company's 69,609 policyholders agreed to the plan.

    b. It is alleged that 12,000 to 15,000 of the signatures were forged by the company's officers, employees, agents, and "minions."

    c. 90 percent of the policyholders were Black, illiterate and incapable of protecting their interests.

2. The appropriation of the company's assets to the private owners of the stock

3. The refusal of payment of premium on certain policies so those policies to lapse and not be counted in the total:

    a. To make the required number of approvals smaller, the company cut off many policyholders who were in arrears when they applied for the amendment.

    b. The company had a reserve trust fund of $124,813, all of which was a reserve or trust fund for the purpose of helping policyholders, and the officers were only trustees of the fund, but this fund was converted to the private uses of the new corporation.

4. When the new corporation was formed, stock was issued in the amount of $105,000. T. J. Walker, the president, and T. O. West, the secretary of the company sold a building in Anchorage to the company for $100,000 for capital stock of the company.

    a. The building is believed to be worth less than the transactional value of $105,000.

5. The corporation issued policies in the new company, substituting them for the old Assessment Policies, thus causing the policyholders to lose their interest in the reserve.

6. The directors, T. West, F. Walker, W. Bennett, E. Taul, F. Matthews, W. Fahey, E. Speckman, W. Beecher, G. Ford, J. Ford, R. Ford, R. West, E. West, S. Manly, and P. Nole, did not possess the average business of businessmen and were without any special talent or qualifications for the transaction of insurance business.

The court required the Insurance Department to respond to the allegations, and the department provided its 1926 examination of the company and included its finding at the time of the transaction in 1917, ten years before the complaint was filed. The company placed a copy of this response as a full-page ad in the local newspapers. The case appears to have been dropped after that.

Most, if not all, of Kentucky Central Life's business in 1917 was industrial life & health weekly premium-paying business. In those days, agents went to people's homes each week and collected their premium payments in cash.

The agents also maintained a book they called their premium register and provided the policyholder with a receipt. When Kentucky Central Life sought policyholder approval for the transaction, one can assume it used its agents who were visiting these policyholders weekly and collecting their premiums to also help get the necessary policyholder approval for the transaction. Yes, some signatures may have been X's or even agent-assisted, but the process worked.

In addition, many mutual companies during this period also addressed their annual membership voting needs by having a proxy vote section as part of the insurance application process. In the early 1900s, communication by mail took time and much of the population was made up of short-term renters or living in very rural areas. Mutual companies require annual member meetings with a quorum of the membership present. The reality, even today, is that many if not most policyholders just ignore sending in their proxy vote. For much of the 1900s, many mutual-type companies added a proxy vote section to their applications. It allowed the applicant to choose management to represent them in corporate matters until they revoked it in writing. One may think this sounds self-serving or unethical, but in truth it was more a matter of just trying to comply with the law. It certainly wasn't illegal at the time, and many of the nation's largest mutual companies adopted this practice for a long time. Mutual insurance companies were dealing with customers who were often hard to reach, had no telephone, and had little to no interest in the corporate affairs of the insurance company.

One shouldn't assume that in 1917, the company was trying to hide the reorganization of the company. The United States had just declared war on Germany on April 2, 1917, entering the First World War. Immediately, our country's focus was on the war and what we had to do to win it. Buying U.S. savings bonds and promoting women's efforts to help keep the country going were more important, and the news of the day was focused on how the war was going. When the war finally ended on November 11, 1918, more than 2 million American soldiers had served on the battlefields of Western Europe, and some 50 thousand of them had lost their lives. Americans would be paying for this war and the next war for decades to come.

Thomas West was a smart guy. At the end of 1914, Kentucky Central Life Insurance had a reported surplus of around $77,683. By the end of 1916, just before its conversion to a stock company, it appears the company's surplus was about $37,400. This reserve was then segregated for the benefit of the association policyholders, and West's contribution of the home office building for $100,000 effectively gave him control of the newly converted stock company. It appears that Frank Walker's minority ownership of Kentucky Central began in 1920, when the company raised $71,740 by selling additional stock to management. This capital was needed to offset the $50,000 in losses the company experienced due to the 1917–1918 Spanish flu pandemic.

In addition to the losses from the flu, one can imagine that the cost to relocate the company to its new Anchorage home office building would have been several thousands of dollars in 1917. When the home office building stock transaction was accounted for in March, the company had a surplus of about $103,000, which meant that West owned and controlled 100 percent of Kentucky Central Life's stock. In later years, we also see that other family members and employees owned shares, so West did issue stock to others after 1917. Also, Kentucky Central Life was becoming very profitable, as demonstrated by the 60 percent and 50 percent stock dividends management declared in 1920 and 1923. This moved about $170,000 from retained earnings to its paid-in capital account. In 1926, with the company earning over $50,000 annually, Thomas West's initial $100,000 investment was worth probably close to $280,000, based upon the company's 1926 examination. This also assumes his ownership interest had been reduced to 75 percent after Frank Walker and other management acquired their shares.

In 1922, when the company marked its twenty-year anniversary, it had 240 field agents, up from 156 agents in 1912. A lot had changed over those ten years, and the foundation for more growth had been laid, but World Wars I & II, along with the Great Depression, would repress its potential. For instance, Kentucky Central Life's new business fell off substantially during the early 1930s, but on the bright side, the company continued in business, as did the overwhelming majority of those in the insurance industry. Many other financial institutions and businesses failed during this period. During the 1930s, the company enjoyed moderate growth. It opened new offices in Philadelphia and Maysville, Kentucky, and focused its investments on U.S. war bonds to support our war efforts.

In July of 1932, another significant event happened. Otis West (the younger brother of Thomas West), who had been with the company almost twenty years, died of peritonitis from a burst appendix. Otis was a regional sales manager for the Central Kentucky area, primarily Lexington and its surrounding counties. His official title was vice president in charge of agent management. He was fifty-four years old. He had worked closely with his brother Thomas, arriving at the company a few years after it had been converted into a stock company. He died shortly before the company would celebrate its diamond (thirtieth) anniversary that September.

Frank James Walker

Frank Walker left the company in 1936 after thirty-four years. He had started with Thomas West in 1902, processing applications so the company could obtain its insurance license. He was given the title of president after Charles Drake left in 1907.

In the 1922 Southern Biographical Association's reference work, Frank Walker is credited with the development of the insurance field, "assisting the people of the country to solve an economical problem in its most satisfactory way." Frank J. Walker was born in Fort Wayne, Indiana, on December 10, 1873, and "received the usual education of the child of those times":

> He started in the insurance business 25 years ago [in 1897] and represented various companies until the year 1902 when he organized the Kentucky Central Life & Accident Insurance Company, of which he was elected president and of which he is still president. By his thorough knowledge of the science of insurance, steady application to the business, personal integrity, and recognized probity of character, he has developed one of the most prosperous insurance businesses in Kentucky, Indiana, Ohio and West Virginia and in 1920 the premiums were increased over a half million dollars.

> Frank J. Walker is a member of the Audubon Club and of the Board of Trade and is an optimist in all things for the good of his community, his State, and his country. He was also a believer in doing everything to assist his country in winning the late war with Germany and her allies and his company went to the limit of its maximum investment and donating capacity in the purchase of Liberty Bonds, War Savings Stamps, and donation to all patriotic movements. His home place of residence and business is Anchorage, Kentucky.

Frank Walker married his first wife, Clarice Burdick, on December 2, 1902, in Macon County Georgia, the same year Kentucky Central Life was formed. Waker was twenty-nine and Clarice was nineteen. The couple moved to Louisville, where they established their family of three boys: Frank J. Walker Jr. (1906), Joseph E. Walker (1909), and Thomas West Walker (1911). In 1913, after their last child was born, their marriage fell on difficult times. Clarice decided she had had enough of forty-year-old Frank's antics and locked him out of his house. The *Louisville Courier Journal*, on December 5, 1913, reported the situation this way:

SAYS HOME WAS CLOSED TO HIM

Because Frank J. Walker, president of Kentucky Central Life Insurance Company, said he had not been allowed to enter his own home for three weeks to see his children and as he charged his wife, Clarice B. Walker, had threatened to dispose of household effects and an automobile and leave the jurisdiction of the Jefferson County courts, a restraining order was issued against Mrs. Walker yesterday afternoon by Judge James Quarles.

The plea for the restraining order was accompanied by the filing of a petition of absolute divorce by Walker. The order of Judge Quarles was given to a deputy sheriff who hurried to the Walker home, 2807 Virginia avenue, one of the most attractive residences in Parkland.

Upon being asked for a reply to the charges of her husband, Mrs. Walker last night stated she could make no statement as she was ignorant of the action taken by him. With reference to the charge that she intended leaving the city, Mrs. Walker declared her husband knew she had no such attention as she had told him so.

Without Funds, She Says.

"Besides I couldn't leave if I wanted to as I have not the money to do so," she said. The wife engaged an attorney and declared she will make answer in a few days.

Allegations of a sensational character are contained in the petition filed by Mr. Walker. He charges improper conduct by his wife and further stated he was driven from the home three weeks ago and not permitted to re-enter or see his three children.

It is also charged that the wife threatened to sell the furniture and the electric automobile and remove from the city with the children. The husband stated he has borne much ill treatment from Mrs. Walker for the sake of their children. He says he furnished a ten-room house for the proper sheltering of his family.

An absolute divorce is asked with custody of the children, Frank J. Walker Jr., seven years old, Joseph Edward Walker, 4 years old, and Thomas W. Walker, 3 years old. Walker also asks for the possession of the household furnishings and the house.

The couple were married in Macon, Georgia, December 2, 1902.

After the judge issued the order, the husband and wife attempted reconciliation, and the judge's order was dismissed without prejudice several weeks later. On December 31, 1914, everything came to a head and Frank Walker was again back in court requesting a divorce. In March 1915, their divorce was granted, and Walker signed a settlement contract agreeing to financially support his ex-wife and their children. In the fall of 1916, Frank and Clarice began reconciling again, and in December, Frank made a trip to

Macon, Georgia, to have Christmas with his children. This reunion culminated with the couple getting remarried that month. This reunion marriage didn't last long, though, and by 1920 the couple had legally separated again, and Frank eventually filed for divorce. The records are confusing, however, because the 1940 U.S. Census indicates that Clarice had moved to Florida and listed her status as "widow (Frank)."

On September 22, 1936, Kentucky Central Life celebrated thirty-four years in business. We don't know exactly what happened to sixty-two-year-old Frank Walker, but in 1935, E. H. Speckman, Kentucky Central Life's auditor and vice president, became president of the company. In January 1935, Frank Walker is still listed as Kentucky Central Life's president, but research indicates that he soon became a defendant in multiple lawsuits. One lawsuit even involved his wife, Clairice Walker, suing him over a contract dispute (probably related to their divorce). The 1929 stock market crash, which began in September, contributed to the Great Depression of the 1930s, and one can imagine that a successful life insurance company executive like Frank Walker probably had significant personal investments, including borrowings for real estate. Frank was a member of the Chicago Board of Trade, which implies he did some level of investment speculation.

By 1935, Frank West was probably bankrupt and trying to avoid his creditors. The 1929 crash was exacerbated by financial leverage, and this leverage led to massive personal defaults and bank closures. One can probably assume, because of Frank's quick exit from the company, that he had used his holdings in Kentucky Central Life as collateral for personal loans and by then had lost his ownership in the company. In 1930, Frank married Martha Jane Koch of Louisville, and by 1940, they were renting an apartment in Los Angeles and his career was listed as "salesman—general insurance." Frank West died in 1949, at age 75, and he is buried in the Forest Lawn Cemetery in Los Angeles. An interesting fact: In the 1940 U.S. Census, Frank indicated his highest level of education was eighth grade.

While Frank Walker had the title of president, his primary responsibility was recruiting and building the company's field force. Before coming to the company, he had been an insurance agent in Indiana, so he was familiar with how the sales process worked. By 1930, Thomas West was described as a quiet, conservative man who played a little golf and did some "city farming." Frank Walker, on the other hand, was considered flamboyant and was reported to take many vacations and to be living a life of luxury. His home on 28th Street and Virginia Avenue, in Louisville was considered "one of the show places of Parkland."[11] Thomas West was the investor and saver, and his wealth was vested in his 40 percent interest in Kentucky Central Life. Frank Walker, on the other hand, was the life of the party, a spender who assumed the money he received from Kentucky Central Life would never stop.

Thomas Oliver West

Thomas O. West was born May 30, 1873, in Aiken County, South Carolina. He was the son of a confectioner, James Appleton West, and his wife Mary Anne Lucreatia Smith. Thomas was the fourth oldest of six brothers. His parents were married in 1863 at the young age of eighteen. Thomas's mother died in 1882, and James soon married Mary Elizabeth Head, in 1883. Mary Elizabeth was twenty-one and James was thirty-eight. The couple went on to have seven children: five daughters and two sons. Thomas O. West was from a large family made up of six brothers and seven step-siblings. In the late 1950s, the size of his family would become an important factor in the sale of Kentucky Central Life to Garvice Kincaid.

Not much is known about how Thomas West ended up at Kentucky Central Life. We know that he was educated at Newberry College; he is listed in its records as "Intermediate Class" in 1890-1891, and in 1903, he came to Louisville to work for the company. Thomas Walker was the quiet man who managed the company's finances and dealt with any regulatory matters. Walker was the dapper dresser who enjoyed recruiting agents and creating their loyalty to the company. West apparently became pretty comfortable in his position, because beginning around 1922, he and his wife began taking many long-extended vacations.

After 1935, there is no question that Thomas O. West was the driving force behind the success of the company. In fact, in 1924 and 1930 profiles about the company, West was characterized as the "man behind the desk" and the "important anchor to the success of the company."

Missouri Life and Accident Insurance Company

In 1906, a thirty-seven-year-old Tennessean, Walter A. Johnson, had been working for a few years with Thomas West at Kentucky Central Life. Johnson got his start in insurance in Chattanooga and wanted to do what West and Walker had done and create a mutual assessment company to do business. Joseph A. Walker, a relative of Frank James Walker, also worked at the company and expressed interest in a partnership similar to what Thomas West

---

11   "Frank Walker and Wife Remarry in Georgia," *The Atlanta Constitution*, December 27, 2016.

and Frank Walker had created. Neither man had significant capital for the new endeavor and understood they needed Thomas West's help and expertise if they were going to succeed. They also recruited an old Johnson contact, James C. Jones, as general counsel. Johnson had worked with Jones in Tennessee at the National Life and Accident Company.

West agreed to help and suggested they create the entity in Missouri, where some of his and Walker's family lived. They initially had resistance from the Missouri insurance commissioner, who had pressed the state legislature to do away with "association insurance companies" or at least increase their required capital amounts significantly, which the legislature did. West contributed most of the initial capital the company needed to get started, and on January 1, 1907, Missouri Life and Accident Insurance Company (Missouri Life) opened for business in St. Louis. Its slogan was taken from what Kentucky Central Life was known for: "The Prompt Paying Company." Missouri Life was the first industrial accident company started in the state, and it initially sold policies identical to what the Anchorage company was selling.

Missouri Life grew slowly and, sometime around 1920, was converted to a stock life insurance company. Walter Johnson was its president, Joseph Walker its secretary and treasurer, and James Jones its general counsel. At the time of the conversion, it appears that Walter Johnson owned about 40 percent of the company, Joseph Walker owned 12 percent, and Thomas West, 25 percent. James Jones and others owned the remaining 23 percent. Thomas West was listed as vice president and a director of the company and would spend time in St. Louis reviewing its affairs. West's two nephews, James C. West and Charles C. West were officers and managers of the Missouri company.

The company never did business outside the state of Missouri, and in January 1924, Walter Johnson passed away after being hospitalized. After his death, it was alleged that his widow, Pearl Tinsley Johnson, was not mentally well and that she was addicted to prescription medication. Her brother Claud, at one point went to court to petition for guardianship, but Pearl hired an attorney to fight the allegation. Walter Johnson owned nine hundred shares of Missouri Life's stock, out of its two thousand shares issued, and Pearl and her attorney alleged those shares were worth over 1 million dollars.

Shortly after Johnson died, Pearl asked her brother Claude Tinsley to help her settle her husband's estate. Claude knew Thomas West and Joseph Walker, and he reached an agreement for West to purchase the estate's Missouri Life stock for $283,000 "in a check and a promissory note." Pearl initially agreed and accepted the payment and then decided her brother and West were trying to commit fraud against her. She sued to rescind the sale, and after a week of back-and-forth, she returned to court to say she was wrong and request that her case be dismissed. Thomas West now owned about 75 percent of Missouri Life, and Joseph Walker was appointed its president.

The company continued to grow slowly over the next several years, and then the 1929 crash and the Great Depression slowed its progress even further. By late 1937, Thomas West realized that Joseph Walker was having significant personal troubles and that a change was needed. In November 1937, before any changes could be made, sixty-four-year-old Thomas O. West was stricken with a stroke and died three days later. His long tenor as a founding leader of Kentucky Central Life was over, and a new era would begin for the company. In December, Robert Harold West, Thomas's forty-year-old stepbrother from his father's second marriage, was appointed the secretary and treasurer of Kentucky Central Life. Robert had been a vice president with the company since 1919, serving as an agency manager for its important Kentucky region.

While Thomas West directed the company from his secretary and treasurer position, going forward, Ernest Herman Speckman Sr., the company's forty-four-year-old president, would be its next driving force. Speckman had joined the company as an office boy in 1910 , eight years after it was founded. He advanced through various minor positions to auditor and then became a vice president. Ernest Speckman was the right balance and combination of Thomas West's conservatism and Frank Walker's promotional strength. Over the next twenty-four years, Speckman would provide the leadership to take the company much further, creating substantial value for Thomas West's heirs.

One of the early changes Ernest Speckman made was to negotiate the sale of Missouri Life to a consortium of St. Louis businessmen headed up by H. G. Zelle. Speckman recognized that this entity was a distraction and that Joseph Walker also needed to go. In February 1939, Walker resigned, and J. C. West was made president. The Missouri company had just over $1 million in total assets, and the purchase price was reported to be $525,000.

Joseph Walker had already separated from his wife when the company was sold, and his share of the sale was only $64,000. He had worked for the company fifteen years and earned between $18,000 to $20,000 annually, but in 1941, at the time of his divorce, he had only $20 in the bank. He claimed he had used $34,000 of the sale proceeds to settle bank debt and the rest to support himself and his sister, with about $5,000 going to his soon-to-be-ex-wife. Just like his relation, Frank J. Walker, Joseph Walker allowed personal problems to take over his life.

Thomas Oliver West's Estate

When Thomas O. West died in 1937, he had never married and had no
children. In the end, Kentucky Central Life had been his mistress and, excluding
his thirteen siblings, the focus of his life. We know family relationships were
important to him because he traveled to Newberry, South Carolina, often to
visit family. He also provided jobs at Kentucky Central Life and Missouri
Life for most of them. When he died, his estate was estimated to be $1 million
was divided into twenty-two equal shares for his brothers and sisters and their
children.

Thomas West's will was executed eight years before his death, in 1929,
when he was age fifty-six, and it provided for the following bequests:[12]

- Niece, Miss Lillian West (Colorado Springs, Colorado):
  $90 a month through a trust fund for her benefit, plus a
  share of the residuary estate

- Mr. Lucille Gwathmey Beehler: $5,000

- Corbelia Scharf: $2,500

- Halliebel Scharf: $2,500

One share of the residuary estate:

- Widow and children of deceased brother, Charlie M. West

- Children of deceased brother, O. E. West

- B. W. West (Newberry, South Carolina/Terre Haute,
  Indiana)

- James H. West (Newberry)

- Stepmother, Mrs. Mary E. West (Newberry)

- Half stepsister, Mary P. West (Newberry)

- Half stepsister, Alice L. West Yates (Newberry)

- Half stepsister, Tilla L. West (Newberry)

- Half stepsister, Carrie Bell West Youmans (Newberry)

- Half-sister, Carabella West (Newberry)

- Half stepbrother, Robert H. West (Louisville)

- Nephew, Charles West Jr. (Newberry)

---

12   *Louisville Courier Journal*, December 3, 1937.

Friends who will share

- Frank J. Walker (St. Louis): one share of the residual estate plus one share of the residual estate divided with J.A. Walker

- Edward L Coakley (Chicago): one share of the residual estate

- T.H. Mathews, William B. Fahey, and the children of Hugh Rose: divide one share of the residual estate

- Judge Arthur Peter, general counsel for Kentucky Central Life (Louisville): one share of the residual estate

- Harry W. Maples (Louisville): one share of the residual estate

- Richard Bean (Louisville): one share of the residual estate

- E. H. Speckman (Louisville): one share of the residual estate

- Mary Jane Pemberton (Louisville): one share of the residual estate

- Edward Wohlwender (Columbus, Georgia): one share of the residual estate

It appears that Thomas West tried to remember everyone who was important to him. Even financially broken Frank Walker, who had moved to Los Angelas, and his relation Joseph Walker were remembered. Ernest H. Speckman and Thomas West must have had an enduring relationship, because in 1927, Ernest named a son, Thomas West Speckman, after his friend.

The West estate comprised two main holdings, his shares of Kentucky Central Life Company, and his shares of Missouri Insurance Company and was valued at $1 million. West owned about 40 percent of Kentucky Central Life and about 75 percent of Missouri Insurance Company. He probably controlled more than 40 percent of Kentucky Central Life, given how much of his family also worked for the company. At the time of West's death in 1937, Kentucky Central Life had over $1.4 million in assets and, according to company records, employed between eighty to ninety employees and was approaching having 500 field agents.

In addition to the above, since the company's conversion to a stock company in 1917, West's sound guidance had permitted the company to pay a total of $1.7 million in shareholder cash dividends and $262,000 in stock dividends—a remarkable amount of money given that it had to navigate the

Spanish flu epidemic, the 1929 stock market crash, and the Great Depression of the 1930s. In later years, under the control of W. E. "Bud" Burnett, Burnett would use this history to justify why the company would be able to withstand its current financial problems. One significant difference, though, was that in 1934, mortgage loans and real estate represented only 13% of the company's assets, and it had capital and surplus of 44 percent. In 1989 and 1990, Burnett's company had 30 percent of its assets invested in mortgage loans and real estate, and his bad decisions had reduced the company's capital and surplus to about 3.5 percent. Thomas West died after running a bulletproof company during the Great Depression, while Bud Burnett's decisions had significantly damaged the company's balance sheet and capital position.

Though Thomas West was dead, his impact on the company would continue through the efforts of his friends and relatives over the next fifty years. For instance, in 1917, his stepsister, Alice Lillian West, married Eugene Wilson Yates from Charleston, South Carolina. The couple soon moved to Winnsboro, South Carolina, where Yates taught school at the Mount Zion Institute. He later took a position as cashier at the Winnsboro Bank, and following that he worked at the U.S. Post Office. Winnsboro is about thirty miles from Newberry, where most of the West family lived.

In the early 1920s, the couple had two children, Mary Elizabeth Anne Yates, born in 1921, and Eugene Wilson Yates Jr., born in 1923. Both children had successful lives, with Mary Elizabeth marrying an Atlanta psychiatrist and Eugene Wilson graduating from the Citadel and the University of Virginia Law School. In June 1948, Wilson married the love of his life, Isabel Elliott McCants of Winnsboro. Isabel graduated from the University of South Carolina and had a master of arts degree in English from the University of Ohio. Thirty-two-year-old Wilson Yates briefly worked in private practice in Newberry but moved to Louisville in 1955 to work at the company. Four years later, Garvice Kincaid would gain control of the company and begin relocating it to Lexington in 1963. Kincaid, in an acknowledgement to the accomplishments of the West family, retained Yates as the company's general counsel and also installed him on the company's board of directors.

E. Wilson Yates, as he was known at the company, remained an important member of the company's management staff. He was a quiet-talking southern gentleman who chose his words and evaluated policyholder, employee, and agent issues both legally and fairly. While Kincaid's law firm always handled complicated mortgage loan, real estate, and corporate issues, Wilson and his staff attorneys worked on the policyholder-, regulatory-, and employment-law-related issues. Wilson was extremely respected by Kentucky Central

Life's employees and became a great sounding board for many of its staff over the years. Wilson and Isabell moved to Lexington in 1963 and soon became important, respected members of the community. In 1989, Wilson retired from the company at the age of sixty-six after thirty-one years of service. He died in 1997 at the age of seventy-four, just four years after the ninety-one-year-old company that his family founded was taken over by the state. He was the last member of the West family to work for the company.

The 1940s: A Decade of Expansion and Change

The 1937 death of Thomas West created a significant change for the company. With the death of the founder, his estate had to be valued and distributed. His estate was valued at $800,000 and, adjusted for inflation, would be worth about $16 million in today's dollars. His death and the settlement of his estate also meant that the shares of Kentucky Central Life, which had been considered closely held since 1917, would now be distributed to multiple heirs. Before 1944, the company's stock was traded only privately, meaning that buyers and sellers had to find each other. In January 1944, small brokerage firms started to trade Kentucky Central Life's stock over the counter, meaning these firms would match buyers and sellers together for a commission.

Over the next fifteen years, as more of the original stockholders retired and/or died, providing shareholders better access to the value of their shares became more important. In the late 1940s and early 1950s, Kentucky Central's stock was quoted at $80 per share, up from the $20 a share of just five years earlier. The company's founders and management had created millionaires, and in the future, they would want access to their money.

In 1938, the company didn't pay a regular annual dividend but rather just an occasional special dividend. That changed in 1939, when the company announced an annual dividend of 50 cents per share, which over the next three years raised to a stated dividend to $3 per share in 1944. In addition, management established 10 percent stock regular dividends, which had the effect of giving shareholders more shares. In 1950, Kentucky Central Life's management instituted a 33-1/3 percent stock dividend, which reduce the company's share price by one third. Before the dividend, the company's stock was quoted at over $100 per share, and after the dividend was paid, it was trading at $71. If someone wanted to buy 100 shares, they would need over $7,000 dollars.

Kentucky Central experienced significant changes during the decades of the 1950s and 1960s. Not only would the company be fifty years old shortly, but age would also begin to affect its management. In addition, technology would soon be introduced in the insurance industry that would revolutionize how the industry operated and help the company expand and grow its business more efficiently.

The insurance industry has historically been a paper-intensive industry. Insurance companies are required to use different state-approved policy forms, customer service forms, and other regulatorily required disclosure forms. They bill their customers monthly and printed and mailed thousands of checks daily. It required death certificates, physician statements, and multiple other types of documents, depending on the type of insurance involved. Finally, it was required to keep this voluminous documentation for decades, since many policy contracts may be active for ten, twenty, or even 100 years. In 1924, Kentucky Central Life had over 200,000 policyholders and was issuing 25,000 new policies annually, and by 1950, the company had grown sevenfold and had over 1 million policyholders. The company was producing and managing a significant amount of paper.

Around 1946, Kentucky Central Life's management took a big step forward and purchased an IBM Tabulator Computer. The insurance industry had slowly been incorporating these large machines during the last ten years, but less than 25 percent of the industry—only the largest companies—was using them. That same year, the Anchorage management hired a thirty-seven-year-old Louisville native, John Phillip Pulliam, to manage its new bulky computer. Various industries were exploring using this new technology, but the U.S. Government and many state governments were the largest early adopters. They also became the early training ground for many private-sector employees.

John began his professional career as a bookkeeper at the St. Mathews and Lincoln Banks and obtained his tabulator computer experience at the Kentucky Unemployment Cooperation Commission in Frankfort. He had worked there for over six years when he joined the company. After joining the company, John's initial responsibility was to advertise for an IBM Tabulating Machine operator, "18 months' minimum experience and some general accounting experience preferred." This or a similar ad would be a regular, recurring ad in the *Louisville Courier Journal* for the next ten years. John moved with the company to Lexington in 1963 and remained a valuable, loyal employee till he retired in 1982.

The early tabulator machines were crude by today's standards. They could create periodic premium bills for mailing and support some of the accounting and actuarial reserving needs of the company, but it was clunky to use. By 1950, the life insurance industry had become one of the largest adopters of computer technology, and little Kentucky Central Life was there. The processing of data was not an ancillary function for the industry because policyholder information was the industry's only product. Managing this information was the equivalent of a manufacturing company's production line.

West Virginia native Ed Winiarczyk started working for the company in 1961 at the age of twenty-three. Ed lived in Louisville and was hired to work in the Anchorage office, helping with the additional business Kincaid and Carr were bringing into the company. Ed was young and eager to learn and did whatever was needed, including working with John Pulliam and the IBM Tabulator. Ed explained that the Anchorage computer was programmed by connecting different input digits to outputs or functions via physical cables; that is, he changed what the machine did by changing the wiring. An IBM article stated the computer could process 150 keypunch cards per minute and print its output on a built-in printer.[13]

Technology would continue to be an important investment for Kentucky Central Life over the next several decades. In 1961, shortly after Garvice Kincaid acquired the company in 1959, the company upgraded its systems again and installed an IBM 1401 computer system. This system married the punch card interface with magnetic tapes so that data could be more efficiently processed and backed up. These were machines that electronically stored programs and required a Data Processing Division to load and maintain data and to develop and run programs and then distribute the output to the various departments in the company. Finally, in 1971, Mr. Kincaid reported in the company's 1970 annual report that the company had just installed a 360 IBM System Model 40 "in further interest of economy and efficiency." This was the first computer with its own integrated keyboard. Garvice never hesitated to spend money on technology if he thought it would make the business more efficient or provide better customer service.

Not every significant industry innovation involved computers, though. In 1961, IBM created the IBM Selectric typewriter. It was made at the IBM plant in Lexington, Kentucky. The Selectric was revolutionary in the way it worked, and it worked very well! IBM replaced type bars and moving carriages with a printing element, a sphere no larger than a golf ball, which bore all alphabet characters, numbers, and punctuation symbols. The element moved along a slender metal rod, tilting and rocking at very high speed as it selected the

---

13   1947 IBM ad, in Frank da Cruz, "Columbia University Computing History: A Chronology of Computing at Columbia University," Columbia (updated May 22, 2024, 12:31:55), https://www.columbia.edu/cu/computinghistory/.

desired character. These machines significantly increased office productivity and were quickly adopted by the insurance industry.

In 1964, IBM added a magnetic tape system for storing characters. The Magnetic Tape Selectric Typewriter became the country's first word-processor-type device. In July 1964, Paul Carr and Kentucky Central Life purchased the first IBM Magnetic Tape Selectric Typewriter ever manufactured. It was such an important announcement that the *Lexington Herald-Leader* published a story about the purchase and included a photograph of Paul Carr and the IBM plant manager signing the contract. By 1978, IBM had a 94 percent share of the typewriter market. IBM's innovation of the electric typewriter was revolutionary and significantly improved the productivity of office workers. Garvice loved innovation and quickly started introducing both versions of IBM's Selectric throughout his business empire.

In 1944 the company had over $4.3 million of admitted assets, $48.0 million of insurance in force, and capital and surplus of $1.3 million and was writing $24 million of new business and earning over $1.2 million annually. By 1954 the company had grown significantly and had over $16.5 million of admitted assets, $135 million of insurance in force, and capital and surplus of $3.4 million and was writing $58 million of new business annually and earning just over $900,000. The company was now paying $2.7 million in commissions versus $485,000 ten years earlier. It had more than doubled its new business written but was paying more than five times as much in commissions, and this had a negative impact on the company's profitability. This change was also occurring at a time when several founding-family stockholder heirs were interested in accessing the value of their Kentucky Central Life shares. E. H. Speckman Sr. was now receiving calls almost daily about selling the company. In May 1958, after working for the company for forty-eight years, Speckman retired. Then, the sixty-two-year-old president, Robert West, began receiving frequent enquiries from family members about selling the company.

In April 1959, the number of family members interested in finding a buyer for the company further increased after the death of forty-two-year-old Edward L. West. He had been with the company for twenty-four years and was the nephew of Robert West. In 1958, Paul Carr had recently worked with Kincaid on gaining control of Cardinal Life Insurance Company and had heard about the family unrest and their desire to see the company sold. He suggested to Garvice that the company could be purchased and helped Kincaid come up with a value for the company. Garvice was interested, but only if he could control at least 51 percent of the company.

Garvice Takes Control—"All Hail the Chief"

On May 28, 1959, Kincaid announced a deal: he would pay $115 per share for between 51% and 100% of the company's stock. Eight of the company's directors had already agreed to sell their shares to him. The company had 100,000 shares outstanding, and Kincaid's offer would require him to spend between $5.9 million and $11.5 million to acquire the company. This would be the largest investment of his career. On July 1, it was announced that Kincaid had received offers to sell him 82,000 shares at $115 per share. He had won. During the month of June, Quaker State Life in Pennsylvania tried to upset the deal by offering to buy 51% of the company for $116.50 per share. Kincaid's offer was considered superior because he was willing to buy 100% of the company. The purchase closed in November, and Garvice spent almost $10 million dollars acquiring control of the company.

When Garvice acquired the company, it had over $24.8 million of admitted assets, $163.7 million of insurance in force, and capital and surplus of $4.8 million, and it was writing $48.0 million of new business and earning over $1.7 million annually. In three short years, the Anchorage employees wouldn't recognize their old company.

By February 1960, Garvice had already begun formalizing the roles of his management team. He maintained the foundation of the old Kentucky Central Life by combining some of its existing management personnel with a spattering of new people. In addition, the company was now considered a multiline insurer with the addition of Kincaid's other new 1959 acquisition, Kentucky Central Insurance Company, a property and casualty insurer.

Mr. Kincaid's most consequential management addition was announced in May 1959, when William Earl "Bud" Burnett joined the company. Bud Burnett came to Kentucky Central Life with little insurance experience. He had served in World War II and had graduated from the University of Louisville in 1949, at the age of twenty-two, with a degree in accounting. Burnett's first job out of college was working for an insurance agency in Louisville, Kentucky, but he soon joined the small Louisville Fire & Marine Company (LFM) in 1952 or 1953. In 1955, LFM became insolvent due to hurricane losses. That same year, Burnett moved to Inland Empire Insurance in Louisville when it acquired the business of LFM. That company was also struggling, and by February 1956, Inland Empire had failed and was under the control of the Kentucky Insurance Department. Both Inland Empire's and LFM's business were now in runoff, and Burnett stayed on and worked with the Insurance Department to wind up the company's affairs. Earl Wilson's law firm had represented Inland Empire when it acquired LFM's business, and he and his protégée, Ed Schaeffer, had come to rely on Burnett for Inland Empire's financial information.

In the 1950s, Kincaid was very involved in the political landscape, and he knew the former insurance commissioner, Syl Goebel, from his investment in Cardinal Life. Syl Goebel had helped start Cardinal Life in 1955, just before leaving the Department. As insurance commissioner, Goebel had been put in charge of managing Inland Empire's runoff of its business, and he had also relied on Burnett's efforts. Kincaid had decided to invest in Louisville's Cardinal Life Insurance Company in December 1958. Cardinal was a small, struggling life insurance company, and Kincaid thought it just needed more capital to grow, but the company continued to struggle financially, so Garvice negotiated to get rid of the other shareholders and purchased the entire company.

Burnett joined Garvice in March 1959 at Cardinal Life Insurance Company. Cardinal was still struggling, but Burnett and its consulting actuary Paul Carr worked to stabilize it. In 1959, after Mr. Kincaid acquired Kentucky Central Life, he installed Burnett, age 32, as its secretary and treasurer. While Paul Carr, its executive vice president, handled Kincaid's insurance acquisitions, Bud Burnett managed the integration of the acquired business. Paul Carr and Burnett worked to complete six acquisitions over the next four years. Burnett was an insurance accountant, and he understood the regulatory accounting rules; Paul Carr understood how to run an insurance company. Garvice knew little about running an insurance company or its regulatory hurdles, but he had the capital to maintain and grow one. He also had two men to locate, negotiate, and integrate any of his new acquisitions, plus an operating company in Anchorage to house everything in.

History shows that before the purchase of Kentucky Central Life, Garvice had never owned and controlled a publicly traded company. He had controlling interests in banks and other investments where he had partners, but they weren't traded on an exchange, and in various interviews, he said he liked having control so he could make decisions quickly. When he acquired 85% of Kentucky Central Life, it had 100,000 shares outstanding, and while its stock was considered publicly traded, it was considered illiquid and traded only on a very limited basis.

In December of 1959, six months after acquiring the company, Garvice dramatically changed its capital structure by instituting a ten-for-one stock split. Overnight, he increased the shares outstanding from 100,000 to 1 million, and this translated into reducing the par value of the company's stock to $1 per share from $10. This change also reduced the market price per share and increased the number of shares available for trading, which should have made the stock more attractive to investors. The most important change he made, though, was that the newly issued 900,000 shares were a new class of nonvoting stock. Since Mr. Kincaid owned 85% of the voting shares of the company, he could maintain control of the company without much interference from others and use his nonvoting shares as currency for future acquisitions.

Dual classes of common stock date back to at least 1923. Many banks back then were started by wealthy individuals, and these founders wanted to have publicly traded companies but also wanted to maintain control of their organizations. Thus, nonvoting stock was created. Since Mr. Kincaid had a strong knowledge of banking, he understood how to use this concept to his advantage. This also meant that in the future, anyone responsible for his estate would have this same unbridled control of Kentucky Central Life.

Kincaid had big plans for the company, and he understood he needed its employees and agents to know that he couldn't succeed without their help. In February 1960, Garvice did something that most companies wouldn't consider doing until the late 1990s: he made all his employees and agents owners of Kentucky Central Life by giving each of its seven hundred home office staff and agent employees one share of the company's stock. The stock was then valued at $12 per share.

By the end of 1960, Paul Carr could see that the Anchorage staff were not adjusting well to the changes and he needed to recruit a strong professional to manage the daily operations of the company and its growing agency force. Paul was too busy looking for deals and frankly didn't enjoy the administrative side of the work.

In April 1961, Kincaid and Carr recruited Dave Brain to Kentucky Central Life. Brain had worked for the Monumental Life and Fire Insurance Company in Baltimore, Maryland. Kincaid and Carr believed a multiline division would provide agents with the opportunity to cross-sell life insurance when families inquired about insurance coverage for their homes and automobiles. David Brain was appointed the company's vice president and chief operating officer. Brain would develop the marketing and administrative infrastructure the company needed to expand and grow.

Many things were changing in those early years of Kincaid's ownership. The company was working to expand geographically, so it needed to obtain more licenses from more states. When Kincaid acquired the company, Kentucky Central Life was doing business in only eight states, and Garvice wanted to operate nationally. In addition, he wanted to grow the business quickly, and as he suggested on the day he acquired Kentucky Central in June 1959, he wanted to do acquisitions—and he did. Over the next four years, Garvice would make six acquisitions of other insurance companies or just their in-force business. The company was quickly building the necessary policyholder base and creating the annual premium income needed to support a much larger and more sophisticated operation.

Not everyone was happy, though, with the new Kentucky Central Life, and some of the old guard began to leave, with the most significant change happening in June 1962 when Robert H. West, one of the original founding members of Kentucky Central Life, retired as chairman of the board at age 65, after forty-two years with the company.

In January 1962, another major change was announced: Garvice would be relocating Kentucky Central to Lexington. Mr. Kincaid had purchased the Lafayette Hotel in 1960 for $1.2 million, and he planned on converting it to office space. The estimated cost to remodel the hotel was $750,000, and the move was expected to take place in late 1963 and early 1964. A big, new employer was coming to downtown Lexington, Kentucky!

Moving to Lexington

Relocating a life insurance company to new offices is a major undertaking, but relocating a company to a new city an hour and half away is a major challenge. Either change is going to disrupt operations, which will disrupt its policyholder/customers, its agents, and its employees. This next chapter in Kentucky Central's history would take much planning and an understanding that most of the company's existing workforce would not relocate to Lexington. Paul Carr and David Brain understood that the move needed to be prepared for with military precision. Moving a company to another city is an expensive operation, and having trained staff in Lexington was going to require a period of overstaffing and training. An insurance company's two most important business functions are managing its huge amount of data and providing the agent and policyholder services of billing, making claim payments, and processing new business and paying commissions. According to Paul Carr, the Anchorage office had about eighty-eight employees when Mr. Kincaid acquired the company. To relocate the company to Lexington and also handle the increased business from Mr. Kincaid's recent acquisitions, staffing would need to be more than doubled from 1960 to 1964. Fortunately, Lexington was home to the University of Kentucky, Transylvania University, IBM, Trane, Square D Electric, and other organizations whose employee base and their families would complement the operations of the company.

A University of Kentucky website article described Lexington's workforce in the '50s and '60 s as follows:

Once the war was over, women continued to work where they could do so and the population of women in the workforce continued to grow as it has done so to this very day. Employment between 1947 and 1967 increased from 5.5 million to 11.6 million, and about 85 percent of that growth came from jobs offered at the state and local level by privately owned businesses. Business owners as well as local and state governments needed more workers than were available in the traditional job pools, so many of those jobs were offered to Blacks and to women workers in numbers never seen before in peace times. Typically, the women's jobs were found in teaching, nursing, clerical work, and domestic service, but in Lexington, Kentucky this was all about to change.

New industries made their way to Lexington in 1958. IBM, Trane and Square D Electric were slated to locate in an industrial park located on the north-western side of Lexington. The plan for the industrial park expanded Lexington's boundaries and proposed thousands of new jobs to the area, not only for factory work but also in housing construction. New subdivisions were proposed to be built nearby, and from 1950–1970, the population of Fayette County rose from 100.9 thousand to 174 thousand people.

The insurance industry for decades has been known to provide a large number of entry-level jobs to the American workforce. Many of the industry's jobs in the '60s and '70s were designed around a limited scope of work. In other words, many of these jobs required a person only to learn a certain process or procedure. This made training simpler and more efficient. Many of these task-oriented jobs tended to be boring, and job advancement tended to be slow. Women in the workforce were particularly important to the insurance industry. They tended to appreciate the work, and many companies in the '60s began to offer benefits tailored to their needs. For instance, many insurance company home offices closed by 12:00 or 1:00 on Fridays so their staffs could address personal or family needs. In addition, many large insurers maintained a nurse on staff to handle minor health issues and created rest lounges in the women's restrooms.

One Women Leadership Researcher (melindasleadership.com) wrote the following:

WOMEN IN LIFE INSURANCE DURING THE 1960S

The number of women in the U.S. workforce continued to grow throughout the decade much as it had over the last several years. By 1964, the number reached 22 million women workers, and by 1969, had reached 27 million. In 1963, white-collared women outnumbered white-collared men. These women largely filled clerical and lower paid jobs, but slowly but surely, they were rising in the ranks. Already in 1960, the Census Bureau classified just over one million women as "managers, officials, and proprietors," up from 450,000 in 1940. Also, Harvard Business School opened its MBA program to women for the first time in 1963 to help train women for the higher-ranking positions.

In the 1960s, the life insurance industry employed approximately 500,000 people, 1/3 of which were women. These women primarily filled clerical roles within the home offices. In 1963, 25 of the 1,325 fellows of the Society of Actuaries were women. By 1966, this number had only risen to 26.

Leadership and management were still largely a man's world. Many times, women were held back by the fear that they would soon leave the workforce to raise a family. Other times, it seems that women held themselves back, lacking the full confidence to deal with the struggles of getting ahead.

Women reported having to work harder than men to get ahead and had to be better than men to retain the same rank. Some women clearly believed that to become an executive, a woman had to dedicate herself fully to her career, foregoing a husband and children. A *Wall Street Journal* article from 1963 quoted a female executive saying, "Men doing the same sort of work advanced more rapidly. They would climb two rungs up the ladder while I climbed one." A Harvard Business School survey from 1965 found that 41% of businessmen "viewed female executives with undisguised misgivings" (Newsweek 1966) ["Women at the Top," *Newsweek*, June 27, 1966, pg. 70–73].

While jobs in the insurance industry have evolved as the industry's products have become more complicated, a study by Liberty Mutual and Safeco made this point:

> Women make up 96% of customer service representatives (CSRs) and 68% of producer/agents but only 31% of agency principals/managers. Women are overrepresented in entry-level and service positions but still underrepresented in leadership positions. More than 1 in 3 female agency principals/managers say they are often the only woman in the room.

Not much is known about those early years after Mr. Kincaid acquired KCL, but we do know how most of Paul Carr's, David Brain's, and Bud Burnett's time was spent getting to know Kentucky Central's management and employees and understanding how the company operated; negotiating and merging Mr. Kincaid's other insurance acquisitions (a total of six); planning for the move to Lexington, which meant significantly remodeling the old Lafayette Hotel to be the company's new home office space; and hiring and training Kentucky Central Life's new Lexington staff, which was an extraordinarily large and important undertaking since most of the eighty-eight Anchorage employees were unwilling to relocate to Lexington.

The city of Anchorage is located about seventy-five miles from Lexington. Kentucky Central Life's management needed to train its new Lexington employees at Kentucky Central Life's home office in Anchorage, and to do this, it needed to transport them there. In January 1963, construction of Interstate 64 had only just begun in Kentucky and wouldn't be completed until the mid-1970s. The initial solution was to take a train from downtown Lexington, with a stop in Frankfort, which would arrive in Louisville. From Louisville, the staff would take a bus to the home office in Anchorage. Kentucky Central Life's director of personnel, Mary Ann Miller (Zeidler), discussed this in a 1983 issue of *Horizons*[14]: "The train was not a great solution, and employees were spending as much time traveling as they were in the office. After several months, management chartered a bus that would greatly improve their daily trip." For almost a year, more than a hundred people boarded charter buses and traveled to Anchorage to learn tasks they would assume after the company was relocated to Lexington.

Ed Winiarczyk, who was with the company for over 30 years, told this story about those early years in Anchorage. Ed was working at the original company in Anchorage, Kentucky and also partially responsible for moving the company from Anchorage to Lexington (to the Lafayette Hotel). The story Ed told me involved Kincaid's various trips to Kentucky Central's Anchorage office, prior to the move. This was the largest investment Garvice had ever made and he wanted to understand the operations and the people who were managing it for him, so he traveled to Anchorage quite often.

Wayne Tipton was one of the new Lexington-based employees and he had been assigned to drive him to Anchorage and bring him back to Lexington. As it was explained to me, on this particular day Kincaid had something he wanted to get back to in Lexington and he wanted Wayne to drive faster on the trip back. He had something he wanted to do. Well Wayne, being a young guy, just did what he was told, and put his foot on the gas. As one can expect the next thing Wayne knew, a State Trooper was pulling him over. Wayne was sure he was in trouble because he was traveling more than 20 miles over the speed limit.

---

14   "Successful K-C Executive," Kentucky Central Life, *Horizons*, December 1983, pg. 1-2.

Wayne pulls the car over to the side of the road and a funny thing happens as the State Trooper approaches the car, Mr. Kincaid, who was sitting in the back of the car, rolls his window down. Mr. Kincaid then asks the trooper as he is walking by his window, "Do you know who I am" and then suggests that before the trooper starts writing any tickets that maybe he should get on his radio and call the station house. Wayne said the trooper was surprised and just looked at Mr. Kincaid and glanced at the car and then after hesitating for a second walks back to his vehicle and radios the station. The next thing Wayne knows, the trooper comes back to their car and says, "You can go, but SLOW DOWN". Wayne said the trooper never actually spoke to him or looked at his license, he just kind of spoke to the car. This story was relayed to several employees by Wayne and relayed to me at a former employee lunch in recent years. I have always wondered what the other end of the trooper's radio told him and how big a smile Garvice must have had as they pulled away.

One needs to appreciate that the company's management was introducing these new employees to an industry they knew little about. In addition, the company was growing through acquisitions, which added new customer records, policy forms, and agents to the Anchorage office. It was a very busy period; new employees were traveling to Kentucky Central Life's Anchorage office to be trained by the Anchorage staff, many of whom would not be moving to Lexington. In addition, the books and records from Kincaid's acquisitions were being delivered and merged with the Anchorage office's records. Finally, everyone was working to integrate the business Garvice and Carr had acquired and trying to fit into the company's operations.

Garvice had another important recruitment in 1962—one that helped Kincaid grow and promote the company and that is near and dear to me: Emmett Robbins Crump Jr. Emmett was born and raised in Paris, Kentucky, and in 1942, at the age of 17, he enlisted in the U.S. Navy and served on the USS Albert Grant. The USS Grant was torpedoed by the Japanese in 1944, killing thirty-eight of his shipmates and injuring 50 percent of its crew. Luckily, Emmett and the ship were able to limp back to port. After arriving, Emmett and two other men were responsible for retrieving the bodies of the dead from inside the ship. It was an experience that he said he would never forget.

Emmett was a person full of life and someone committed to the life insurance industry. During his long career, he was active in various leadership roles in local, state, and national industry associations. Emmett was also active in the Lexington community. He was highly respected and a strong influencer for the insurance industry. Emmett had begun his career in insurance with Kentucky Central Life in 1950 but moved to Nationwide Life Insurance

Company a few years later. At Nationwide, he found more and better products to sell, as well as better advancement opportunities.

Kincaid became interested in hiring Emmett as early as 1960. Emmett was a young, energetic insurance agent who had grown up in Paris, Kentucky, and was one of Nationwide Insurance Company's top agents and district managers. Every week, when Kincaid opened his morning paper, he would be subjected to another Nationwide ad promoting Emmett and his Southland Drive office, and if it wasn't an advertisement, it was another story about Crump doing something with the local or state underwriters association. Emmett had two sayings that he lived by: (1) if you don't promote yourself, nobody else will, and (2) when you quit learning, you quit earning. He practiced both mottoes religiously, all during his career. Kincaid now wanted Emmett's help in managing some of the new agency groups he had acquired.

In August 1962, Kincaid finally persuaded Emmett to come to work for him at Kentucky Central Life as a district manager in Bowling Green, Kentucky. Garvice felt so strongly about recruiting Emmett that he allowed him to continue to represent Nationwide Insurance on products not available from Kentucky Central Life. This accommodation was to last for about a year, when Garvice promised that Kentucky Central Life would have replacement products for him to sell. Another reason Crump came to Kentucky Central Life was David Brain. Emmett felt a connection with Brain, whom he saw as a kindred spirit. David Brain was a solid insurance professional and had progressive ideas for growing the company, and Emmett liked that.

After Kincaid recruited Emmett to run the Bowling Green district office, he paid to relocate him and his wife Nonie to Bowling Green and promised to bring him back to Lexington in about a year. Emmett's Bowling Green office did well, but by August 1963 Garvice decided he needed Emmett to go to Charlotte, North Carolina. Kincaid had just acquired a Charlotte-based life insurance company, and he needed Emmett to go there to work with its agents. Emmett became the Charlotte district manager, responsible for recruiting, training agents, and expanding Kentucky Central Life's geographic footprint. Emmett and his wife Nonie were in Charlotte until late in 1964, when Mr. Kincaid decided Emmett could come back home to Lexington and continue where he had left off.

Over the next thirty years, Emmett would be responsible for Kentucky Central's top district career agency office (district #5, as it was known), and Emmett "Boss" Crump" would become known in Lexington as "Mr. Kentucky Central." He loved the company and worked hard to be recognized for his knowledge of insurance and his professionalism. He promoted industry professionalism and the need for education and was elected to senior officer positions in all the local, regional, and national life insurance underwriter associations.

Emmett and Bob Casher both began working for Kentucky Central Life in the early 1950s. While Emmett left to work for Nationwide, Casher continued representing Kentucky Central Life, and in 1964 he was promoted to manage the Career Agency Division. This was the same year that Kincaid brought Emmett back to Lexington from Charlotte. This made Bob Casher Emmett's boss. Bob Casher and Emmett never had a great working relationship. Casher was considered a bully; he was known for intimidating people and chewing them out, and this wasn't Emmett's style. In addition, Emmett always had the respect of Garvice and David Brain, so Casher knew Emmett was considered "protected." After Garvice's death in 1975, and David Brain's resignation in 1976, Casher and Emmett's relationship quickly deteriorated.

Emmett tolerated Casher's harsh personality until he retired from management in the early 1980s, but after he retired, he immediately signed up with the company's Executive Marketing Division and in his first year earned over $100,000 in commissions and bonus. After he received the commission check, he immediately walked into Casher's office and showed it to him and said, "Maybe I'm not as incompetent as you think." Emmett said Casher just looked at him with disgust, so he just turned around and walked out of his office, whistling. He came to my office that day, with the check and the story. After he told me the story, he added, "You know, when they were discussing building this building, before Mr. Kincaid died, I had been promised an office in it, but after he died, everything just changed."

Emmett Crump was just the type of person that Garvice wanted to represent Kentucky Central Life, both in the community and in the industry. Emmett was a motivator, and in the late 1970s, because of his strong belief in education, he and Kentucky Central Life created the Eastern Kentucky University School of Insurance. Garvice Kincaid's alma mater now had the state's only school of insurance.

In October 1963, more than forty van loads of furniture, equipment and records were transported to the company's new headquarters at 200 East Main Street. The city of Lexington was thrilled, and the *Lexington Herald-Leader* was filled with big advertisements from businesses, both large and small, welcoming the company to town. The editorial page also contained many positive letters, and Lexington's mayor, Richard J. Colbert, couldn't believe his good fortune.

One thing that Kincaid, Carr, and Brain did before the move was invest in a new computer system, an IBM 360 computer tape system. The Anchorage computer was already out of date, and the trio believed its system should be upgraded and tested before the move. They hired John Belcher to head the company's newly created data processing department. Belcher had been with Prudential Insurance Company's Jacksonville, Florida office, and he would oversee the installation of the new equipment. The new system was reported to cost $1 million and weigh three quarters of a ton; it was housed on the newly reinforced seventh floor of the Kentucky Central Life building. The vans began the move on Thursday, October 3. Carr and Brain had designed the move to be completed during the weekend, so when the employees showed up for work on Monday, everything would be ready for them to get to work.

The month of October was also filled with tours of the building and speeches from various dignitaries. Kincaid started the month off by announcing the promotion of Paul Carr to president of the company, and the *Lexington Herald-Leader* quickly conducted an in-depth interview with the new president and his family; Carr also had also delivered newspapers as a boy. Newspaper articles discussed the company's "youthful" leadership: "Among the company's top 16 officials, the average has had four years of college, a number of [them] with graduate degrees, and can claim a background of more than 15 years in the insurance industry," and "the average age of an officer is 42.5, with the range in age extending from 52 to 31 years old."[15]

Various state newspapers carried articles about Kincaid and the history of the company and listed many of its officers. The company was initially expected to have a workforce of two hundred, but it significantly exceeded that number by the end of 1964, with a home office staff of three hundred. Only about sixty of its now one hundred twenty-five Anchorage staff made the move to Lexington, so the sixty-one-year-old company was now almost a completely new company. By the time the company moved to its new home, Kincaid had grown it substantially: it had over $101 million of admitted assets, $776 million of insurance in force, and capital and surplus of $22.3 million, and it was writing $281 million of annual new business and earning just over $2.6 million. In addition, it was now licensed in thirty-four states and the District of Columbia and had 1,200 agent representatives. What Garvice had achieved in a span of three years was considered amazing. Kincaid had awakened his "sleeping giant."

In addition to changing the internal dynamics of the company, Kincaid had also changed the composition of its shareholders. In 1959, the company had eight hundred shareholders, and by the end of 1964 the company reported

---

15   "Company Old, Officers Are Youthful," *Lexington Herald*, September 30, 1964.

that it had thirty thousand shareholders spread across all fifty states and a few foreign countries. The Anchorage founders had employed a bank to manage its shareholder stock transfer needs, but in 1963, with the larger base of shareholders, management created an internal stock transfer department to save money. The person who provided oversight of the department was the company's secretary and treasurer, W.E. "Bud" Burnett. Burnett would now be the person responsible for not only handling the company's financial statements and Insurance Department regulatory filings but also keeping the company compliant with the Securities and Exchange Commission.

Garvice's first experience with dealing with a government regulator occurred in the early 1960s with the IRS. It was a long, painful experience and the reason he recruited Bart Brown from Louisville was to help him handle it. Brown was also the attorney responsible for drafting Kincaid's first estate plan, of course under Garvice's direction. His next experience involved dealing with the FCC and the potential loss of WVLK's radio license, which also would have created an issue with WKYT's television license. Kincaid appointed Hart Hagan and Ray Holbrook to address this issue, and after some strategic negotiations and the introduction of an ad-tracking computer system, it was eventually resolved.

Now Garvice owned a publicly traded life insurance company regulated by thirty-four states. The company was required to operate under statutory financial accounting rules, and IRS tax rules and regulations, and it soon would be required to create GAAP financial statements, since it was a publicly traded company. In effect, the company was required to maintain three different sets of financial statements. In addition, the company had to remain compliant with the SEC's rules and regulations for publicly traded companies. Garvice recognized he needed someone like Bud Burnett to oversee this quagmire of rules and regulations. Burnett wasn't a brilliant or overly talented employee, but he was well suited to this role. He was the company's chief financial officer and pseudo regulatory compliance officer and did a thorough, good job keeping the company compliant.

Bud Burnett was neither charismatic nor outgoing and preferred corporate solitude, in contrast to the optimistic and outgoing attitude of David Brain. Burnett had never worked at a successful insurance company before coming to work for Garvice Kincaid. His insurance career involved working for two bankrupt property and casualty insurance companies, and these companies operated under a different set of statutory accounting rules. Brain had the education, knowledge, and experience to manage a life insurance company. He understood life insurance products, how the agency force worked and the necessary home office infrastructure, and the policyholder service, new business, claims, agent licensing, etc., that a large company needed to have. This is why Kincaid and Carr recruited him to the company and why he was executive vice president of the company and Burnett was just the secretary and treasurer.

Kincaid loved bringing the company to Lexington. Overnight the company had become one of the city's largest employers, a position it would hold for the next thirty years. In addition, in May 1964, Garvice embraced some new technology, and the company installed one of the state's first WATTS lines at its office and later in Kincaid's and David Brain's homes. This new technology allowed for direct dialing of long-distance calls and had been commercially available only since 1962. Garvice's bedroom and downtown office would now each have three telephones.

Garvice was also excited about the company's new computer system and wanted to find ways to use it more fully. Carr and Brain had assured him the company would need it to support his growth plans, but he wanted to do more with it now, and he did. In November 1964, he had WVLK use it in a promotion to predict election-day results, and in 1965, Kentucky Central Life started a promotion where the public could send in their personal details and the company's computer system would produce a personalized "Electro-Vision Report" detailing what financial risks they should be concerned about. These risks involved the company selling the family life insurance, disability insurance, and annuities and property and casualty insurance. The ad said, "You will find it a most useful guide in planning for the future."

In December 1964, something unexpected happened: Paul Carr resigned, and David Brain was elevated to the post of executive vice president, Carr's title. Kincaid was unhappy to see Carr leave, but the announcement noted that Carr would remain a company consultant. After Carr resigned, he and his family moved back to Louisville and he set up a national actuarial consulting practice. Carr wasn't interested in managing a life insurance company; he enjoyed doing M&A deals and working on projects with different companies. In addition, his family was homesick and wanted to move back to Louisville, where they had friends and family. Garvice understood Carr's issue, and it does appear Carr departed on good terms because in 1966 and 1968, Carr worked with the company on two additional acquisitions.

It's important to note that Kincaid could have elevated Burnett to executive vice president or even president, but he didn't. Kincaid added the title of president to his chairman's title and made Dave Brain executive vice president. Burnett remained the company's secretary and treasurer. This is important because in January 1975, Garvice again could have made Burnett the company's president but instead chose David Brain. One should assume that in January 1975, Garvice had made the decision that David Brain should be the person running the company, not Bud Burnett. According to David Brain's daughters, Nancy and Diane, David Brain even told Kincaid he would take the promotion to president under one condition: he required Garvice to commit to adding him to his estate's Advisory Committee, and Kincaid assured him he would.

In 1975, Garvice had to know there was animosity between these two professionals, Brain and Burnett, and he also had to understand that making David Brain president would make it impossible for Burnett to be a primary Committee member. I believe that if Kincaid had lived a few more months, he would have created a fourth amendment to his estate plan and added Brain as a primary Committee member and probably listed Burnett as an alternate. Kentucky Central Life was the largest business enterprise in Kincaid's empire and just as with Central Bank, Garvice would have wanted to have its president as a primary Committee member. The problem that developed was that Kincaid's sudden death in November prevented him from making this change in January 1976.

In 1965, David Brain assumed control of an incomplete organization. It was a mixture of the old Anchorage organization and a collection of the acquired business and its general agencies, with a lot of new, inexperienced employees. Brain understood he quickly needed to create more structure to the organization and bring in other experienced professionals, from other larger insurance companies, to help him manage and grow the business and the company's three hundred home office employees.

Garvice had awakened his "sleeping giant" and he now wanted it to become a formidable marketing organization. Kincaid had a passion for marketing and for growing his businesses, and now Brain needed to focus on building the organizational infrastructure that could take the company to the next level. Kincaid's acquisitions, the upgraded computer system, and the new corporate headquarters were a great foundation, but now the company needed people who could help move the ball forward. David Brain would have to simultaneously redesign and develop the marketing and administrative sides of the business. The evolution of the company's management team would begin in 1966 and continue through 1975.

In 1966, excluding Kincaid, Brain, and Burnett, the company had eighteen officers, mostly focused on the financial and marketing sides of the company. By November 1975, the month Garvice died, excluding Earl Wilson, Brain, and Burnett, the company had twenty-seven officers spread among the departments of new business underwriting, policyholder service, administrative services, systems, investments, mortgage loans, tax, finance and accounting, and various marketing divisions, plus its property and casualty insurance company personnel. Kincaid and David Brain had created a top-notch management team. The company was still considered small by industry standards, but it possessed the internal talent necessary to compete with larger companies. Most of the new management staff had been recruited from larger insurance companies because Garvice preferred to purchase experienced talent than spend time trying to develop it internally. After Kincaid's death, Bud Burnett would disregard this important Kincaid principle.

Kentucky Central Life's Sales Divisions

1. Home Service – Employee Agents

    a. Career Agency Division (1902–1991): Industrial / Ordinary Life/ Annuities / disability

    b. Combination Division (1964): Multi-line Agents—MDO life/ disability & P&C

2. Consumer Savings (1973) – State of Kentucky policyowners insured under the state employee and teacher group life insurance contract

3. Executive Marketing Division (1983) – Managing general agents and personal producing general agents (PPGAs)

    a. Professional Marketing Division (1979)

        i. University Key Division (1968)

        ii. College Sales (1968): Kentucky Central provided loans for first-year premium

    b. Executive Sales (1973): Ordinary life & annuities, large case policies, estate planning, endowments, pensions, salary savings

4. Diversified Sales (1972): Institutional sales relationships/Kentucky Central Life sales managers

    a. Group

    b. Credit

    c. Bank Sales

History of Kentucky Central Life's Sales Division

Before Kincaid, Kentucky Central Life sold industrial and ordinary life insurance policies, and its agents were assigned to the company's Career

Agency Division. After Kincaid acquired the company, management rapidly expanded through acquisitions, and these acquisitions brought new agent groups, new products, and new marketing opportunities to the company.

In addition, before 1960, Kentucky Central Life's in-force business was managed by its debit agents. The acquisitions significantly changed this, since monthly billing was now required. Much of the acquired business was billed directly to the customer, and in some cases "family billed" to funeral homes, which collected the premium from the policyholder. Beginning in 1960, the company's home office began playing a greater role in the life of the policyholder.

In June 1959, Kentucky Central Life entered a new chapter in its history. Kentucky financier Garvice Kincaid acquired 85 percent of the company's stock for about $9.75 million, giving the company a total value of $11.5 million. At the time of the transaction, Kentucky Central Life had about $4.5 million of capital and surplus. Kincaid had paid almost two times the company's stated book value to acquire controlling interest in the company. In his remarks about his acquisition, he stated that he had big plans for what he called "a sleeping giant!"[16]

Kincaid got involved with Kentucky Central Life because of Paul Carr. Carr had done actuarial work for R. H. West, and West had discussed his shareholder problem with him. Kincaid had worked with Carr when he acquired Cardinal Life Insurance Company. Carr convinced Kincaid that he should acquire control of the much larger company and merge Cardinal Life Insurance into it. When the company was sold, West and the founding family members were responsible for a company with assets approaching $24.8 million, not bad for a company that had been started with only $4,000 in 1902.

Garvice liked Paul Carr and thought he was a smart professional and that he could help him manage and grow Kentucky Central Life. Carr was a native of Louisville and had worked in the industry for twenty years, which meant he had many contacts around the country. Using those contacts, Carr soon helped Garvice locate other insurance companies to acquire. Carr's job was to do due diligence on the companies and negotiate a price. If Kincaid agreed with his analysis, a deal was struck. Bud Burnett was then responsible for getting the acquired business to Kentucky.

Initially the acquisitions were sent to Anchorage, but acquisitions after 1962 continued to be administered by the selling company until the new Lexington office could administer them. The Anchorage office was already too crowded and unable to handle the extra workload. After acquiring Kentucky Central Life, Kincaid was appointed its president and chief executive officer,

---

16   *Lexington Herald Leader*, September 18, 1977.

Paul Carr was installed as its executive vice president, and Bud Burnett was appointed its secretary and treasurer. Burnett held this position until Kincaid's death. By 1961, Kincaid was so pleased with the work Paul Carr had done that he appointed Carr president of the company.

In three short years, Kincaid acquired six other insurance companies and reinsured various blocks of other insurers' in-force business. Most of these acquisitions had the additional benefit of bringing in new agents working in new geographic areas of the country:

- 1959: Cardinal Life Insurance Company, Louisville, Kentucky (reinsurance)

- 1961: The Skyline Life Division of Guaranty Savings Life Insurance Company, Charlotte, North Carolina (reinsurance of a four-state division)

- 1960: Muscle Shoals Life Insurance Company, Florence, Alabama (merger)

- 1960: Life Insurance Company of the South, Charlotte, North Carolina (merger)

- 1961: Domestic Life & Accident Insurance Company, Louisville, Kentucky (merger)

- 1962: Gulf States Life Insurance Company, Birmingham, Alabama (merger)

- 1962: Gulf States Life Insurance Company, Atlanta, Georgia (merger)

- 1963: Professional and Business Men's Insurance Company, Houston, Texas (merger)

- 1966: Trans-Continental Life Insurance Company, Chicago, Illinois (reinsurance), which included two Chicago district offices

- 1968: Rio Grande National Life Insurance Company Dallas, Texas (merger)

In 1961, when Kincaid acquired the North Carolina division, Skyline Life, the acquisition brought Dick Gordon to the company and the Skyline Agents, who were writing monthly debit ordinary and monthly billed ordinary and doing funeral home sales (family billing). In 1963, when Kincaid acquired the Texas company Professional and Business Men's Insurance Company, this acquisition brought in more new agents. These agents were writing monthly ordinary business.

David Brain created the Combination Division in 1964 and put Bob Casher, who had been with Kentucky Central Life since 1954, in charge of it. Bob was from Decatur, Pennsylvania, and lived in Cleveland and started selling life insurance in 1950 after getting out of the U.S. Navy. His father had moved the family there in the 1940s.

During 1960, Kincaid and Paul Carr also created a property and casualty company, Kentucky Central Insurance Company, and this company inspired the creation of the Combination Division. This division would provide some of the company's career agents with the opportunity to become multiline agents selling life insurance, homeowners, and automobile coverage. Bob Casher and Dick Gordon, who had also been put in charge of managing the different types of business the Skyline agents and the other new agency groups were selling, would now transition some of these agency groups into multiline agencies.

It wasn't a perfect solution, but the company's agency force had increased from seven hundred to twelve hundred and now comprised career agents, multiline agents, and personal producing general agents (independent agents/ PPGAs) operating in new regions of the country. Agent management needed more structure and resources, and David Brain began working to create a formalized structure to manage it.

These acquisitions represented a period of exceptional growth for the company, but they also strained the company's Anchorage staff and created many internal problems. In just three years, Kincaid, Paul Carr, and David Brain had completely changed the nature of the company's quiet little Anchorage operation. In addition, almost overnight the company's staff had many new products to understand and follow, and it also had to incorporate the acquired customer records and billing processes into its existing simple debit business model. In 1962, to address these problems and plan for future acquisitions, David Brain created the company's first Policyowners Service Department. Before this, the company mainly relied on its debit agents to handle customer service, but with the inclusion of the monthly billed business and the new personal producing general agents, the home office was expected to do this type of work. Robert H. Speckman, in a company interview[17] about the Anchorage office, said,

---

17   Kentucky Central Life, *The Keynoter April* (1977), p. 16.

The Home Office wasn't subdivided like it is today, simply because we weren't very big, and didn't have many people. It was more of a family atmosphere. Most of us had worked together for years and were friends as well as business associates. The Home office was first divided into departments with the introduction of Regular Ordinary in 1940. The decentralization progressed in the early 1940s as Weekly Premium Life was introduced, and record-keeping was transferred from hand operations to machines. . . . We all did a little bit of everything.

University Key Division & College Sales

In 1968, the University Key Division was started with the creation of the College Sales Division. Before this, in 1966, the company introduced a new home office and field magazine. This collaborative publication was put together with input from Kentucky Central Life's forty field offices and the company's publication relations department. This important publication was called *The Keynoter* in acknowledgement of the term "keynote speaker." An earlier, less sophisticated publication had been called the *Eagle*. Each monthly issue of *The Keynoter* celebrated the successes of various field personnel and field offices as well as the lives of Kentucky Central Life's home office employees. In 1980, *The Keynoter* was updated with a more modern name, *Horizons*. These publications soon became important communication tools for the company and, from my perspective, an important historical archive of information about the history of Kentucky Central Life and Mr. Kincaid's empire.

In January 1962, one other major change was announced: Garvice Kincaid would be relocating Kentucky Central Life to Lexington. Mr. Kincaid had purchased the Lafayette Hotel in 1960 for $1.2 million and planned on converting it to office space. He and Paul Carr estimated the cost to remodel the hotel at $750,000, not including a new computer system and new office equipment. The move was expected to take place in late 1963 and early 1964. The *Lexington Herald-Leader* announced, "A big new employer is coming to downtown Lexington, Kentucky!"

In October 1963 the Anchorage office began moving into Kincaid's recently renovated Lafayette Hotel, now known as the Kentucky Central Life Insurance Building. The move was completed in 1964. This move also provided the company with a new, more sophisticated computer system to address its data-processing and billing needs, as well as the addition of a full-time Public Relations Department and in-house print shop. In January 1961, shortly after Kincaid acquired the company, Charlie Thomas joined the Anchorage office as the head of public relations. By 1964, Thomas was winning national awards for Garvice and the company in the categories of shareholder, policyholder, and direct mail communications. In Anchorage, when Charlie created communication materials, he didn't have any staff or an in-house print shop. These wouldn't be added until the company relocated to Lexington.

By 1964, the company had a lot of field agent communications that needed to be produced and distributed. Fortuitously, Kincaid's recruitment of David Brain had brought someone to Kentucky Central Life who understood how much communication and what types of communications were needed, and Charlie Thomas had the knowledge and artistic flair necessary to get it created and produced. Having an internal print shop allowed these communications to be produced quickly by the standards of printing presses in the 1960s and 1970s.

The importance of Kincaid's acquisitions was on display in 1966 when the company celebrated reaching $1 billion of insurance in force. That November, the company held a huge celebration at the Phoenix Hotel that included all the district managers and company management. It was called the Billion-Era Jubilee. By the end of 1964, Kincaid had increased the size of the company fourfold. Its assets had increased to over $100 million from $24 million and its premium income had increased to $30 million from $10 million. The company also had sold its first $2 million policy in 1966, to a Texas oilman, and was now operating in thirty-four states, versus nine states at the end of 1959.

In 1968, David Brain established the University Key Division. It was the company's initial attempt to segregate its personal producing general agents from its Career Division. By 1968, the company was a collection of legacy career agencies, newly acquired career agents, and a large collection of acquired PPGA agencies. The College Sales Division was the first sales division to be placed under this umbrella. The division's name came from its leader, Swede Hanson. The general idea was to add other sales divisions under the umbrella of the University Key Division. Things changed, though, in June 1970, when Swede Hanson departed the company and Larry Sammartin was promoted to vice president of the College Sales Division. Larry, a native of Pennsylvania, had risen through the ranks of the College Sales Division and was responsible for the Northeast Region. By 1975, Larry was selected to lead the entire University Key Division.

R. A. "Swede" Hanson and Larry Sammartin

In 1970, Swede Hanson left Kentucky Central Life to be the president of Continental Life Insurance Company in Fort Worth, Texas. At Continental Life, Swede intended to use his knowledge of the college market and have this company specialize in marketing insurance to college students. Hanson's marketing program at Kentucky Central Life had been to recruit young college students and graduates and then teach them how to sell insurance to other college graduates and young families. His method was unusual at best, because under his innovative approach, a person could buy insurance without any money. The company would pay the customer's first year's premium and have them sign a five-year note. The note required the policyowner to pay off the note on a fixed schedule. The foundation for the idea was that a young college graduate would soon earn more money and this would allow them to pay off the note. Many life insurance companies at this time were focused on the potential of the college market, but few, if any, were using Hanson's unique model.

From Kentucky Central's 1969 Annual Report:

> The Great strides made by our new college-market division, which specializes in life insurance plans designed especially for college seniors and graduate students, was a major development in 1969. With this new division, not only are we tapping a new market of great potential, but we are building a strong manpower base for the future since many of the division's young salesmen can be expected to "graduate" (migrate) in coming years to more diversified markets, such as pensions, estate planning and other phases of advanced underwriting.
>
> ***
>
> The sales highlight of the year was Kentucky Central is now one of the nation's major writers in the college-student life insurance market. This increasingly affluent group doubled in size in the 1960–1970 decade and is expected to total 12.5 million young adults by 1980.
>
> ***
>
> The sales highlight of the year was the rapid expansion of the company's new college student life insurance marketing program division, which was established in the fall of 1968. In this period of time, Kentucky Central has emerged as one of the nation's top writers of college life insurance, with 90 general agencies and some 300 sales personnel having been placed under contract in 29 states.
>
> ***
>
> In addition to selling special plans for college seniors and graduate students, this sales force is producing a steadily increasing volume of other types of ordinary life insurance.

Swede Hanson's marketing program was marketing success but a financial failure for Kentucky Central Life. The truth was that the program forced Kentucky Central Life's legal department to become a hybrid collection agency trying to enforce the terms of the policy owners' notes. In addition, a large portion of the insurance sold failed to remain in force. Of course, the agents sold a lot of business, and a lot of commissions were paid, so from their perspective the program was a great success. In the 2000s, other insurance industry marketing groups would again take a bite of this same promotional apple and partner with credit card companies to promote a similar concept, many times without the insurance carrier understanding what they were doing, until the policies started lapsing for nonpayment of premiums. Yet again, the agents earned a nice commission so the program was considered a success from their perspective, while the companies lost money.

Hanson was raised on a farm in San Angelo, Texas, and spent eleven years as a vocational agriculture teacher in Ballenger and Winters, Texas. In 1959, he started his insurance career working in a Fidelity Union Life's San Angelo, Texas, agency. Swede was a successful marketer and soon became an agency manager for Commercial & Industrial Life Insurance Company (C&I) of Houston, Texas. C&I was a one-state life insurance company created by Houston's Jesse H. Jones, a multimillionaire industrialist and banker. Jones established C&I to provide insurance for his employees. He had started the company in the 1940s, and in 1964, after his death, Jones's Houston Endowment sold the company to American General Life Insurance Company in Dallas.

After American General acquired C&I, Hanson went to work in the marking department of Dallas-based Reserve Life Insurance Company. Reserve Life was owned by Charles A. Sammons, who had also acquired the South Dakota–based Midland National Life Insurance Company in 1958. Sammons owned a total of ten life insurance companies and had been active in the insurance business for over forty years. These companies had made him quite wealthy, and by 1968, his business success had allowed him to acquire control of or have substantial stock ownership interests in several other industries. These businesses included hotels, travel-related companies, equipment companies, industrial and energy distribution companies, cable television, and bottled water, real estate, and manufacturing enterprises. Sammons had acquired Midland National in 1958 because he admired its rapid growth. In a period of five years the company doubled its life insurance in force, increasing the company's insurance in force from $275 million to almost $1 billion. Charles Sammons was the kind of businessperson Kincaid would have read about in financial news publications, and he probably admired and respected his success.

In 1961, Midland National brought in William A. Rigsbee as its president. Rigsbee was from Franklin Life Insurance Company, and he immediately began converting the company's agency force into a personal producing general agent (PPGA) model. This would be Midland Life's primary marketing system for distributing its products to consumers. Charles Sammons liked it and soon adopted this marketing approach in his other insurance companies, including Reserve Life in Dallas.

In 1964, Swede Hanson joined Reserve Life's marketing department in Dallas. Swede had always had a passion for young people, and even after getting out of teaching had remained active with the Texas Future Farmers of America, coaching and judging teams at various state livestock shows. Working in the marketing department of Reserve Life provided Swede with the opportunity to combine his interest in college youth with a career in insurance. Reserve Life was a progressive company, and its management was attracted to new, innovative ways of marketing insurance. When Hanson contacted the company about a plan to recruit young agents to sell insurance to college graduates and young families, the head of marketing saw the potential benefits and brought Swede in to develop the program.

Swede Hanson's program soon showed success. There are thousands of colleges and universities in the United States, and Reserve Life was licensed to do business in forty-five states, so Hanson was able to immediately launch his program nationally.

As told by Larry Sammartin in 1982, in a company commentary for *Horizons*:

In 1964, the young, twenty-five-year-old Lawrence J. Sammartin from Clairton, Pennsylvania, was just completing his student teaching degree at California State University in Pennsylvania. Larry had been married about two years, and the young couple had a child on the way. Larry was excited; he had already lined up a job to teach and coach basketball at a high school in Pittsburgh and would earn an annual salary of $5,000. He had bought a life insurance policy about a year earlier and been approached by the salesman's general agent about selling insurance as a career. Larry dismissed the opportunity. He was concerned about selling life insurance. It seemed so uncertain; he might fail and not have another job to fall back on.

The general agent was persistent and made several attempts to recruit Larry. Finally, one day, sitting on the couch in Larry's apartment with a big recruiting manual open on the coffee table, the man became so frustrated by Larry's decision that all of a sudden, he slammed this big book shut, so hard that the windows shook. He said, "Look you dummy, don't you think you're worth more than $5,000 a year?" With that, he got up and left without saying another word.

Larry said he had finally gotten through to him and gotten him to rethink the offer. He called the general agent a couple of days later and said, "Sign me up." Larry never did any teaching or coaching. In later years, Larry said he had found, as the general agent said, that "most people are not aware of their potential, and they resist things they are unfamiliar with and are apprehensive." He said he had been like that, but he was glad he accepted the challenge and knew things had turned out much better than he ever expected.

In 1964, Larry became an insurance agent working for Reserve Life Insurance Company in Dallas, Texas, and working with the company's College Sales division under the leadership of Rudolph Andrew "Swede" Hanson. His story was the model that Swede's division used to recruit young, new agents. Hanson found it beneficial to the division to recruit people who had played college sports. He knew they would be competitive and appreciate sales goals and could be motivated to win!

After a few years, Swede and his division were being courted to come to Kentucky Central Life. It was a big step for Swede; he would be moving to Lexington, Kentucky, and be depending on his College Sales agents to follow him to the new carrier. At Reserve Life, in four short years, Swede had established College Sales as a national distributor, with agent representatives segregated in eight separate regions of the country. Larry's region was called the Northeast Region. Switching to a new insurance carrier was risky and would initially be disruptive to his operation. In 1968, Kentucky Central Life was licensed to do business in only thirty-six states, so Hanson would immediately lose a portion of his agency force since Reserve Life was licensed in forty-five states. In addition, the product would need to be approved in every state, and this was a long process usually taking six to eighteen months. David Brain and Kincaid understood this and provided transitioning compensation to Swede and his regional managers and also promised to provide them with better compensation and products than they had at Reserve Life. In the fall of 1968, Swede and his regional managers made the move.

Kincaid released a significant press release about the new division in the *Lexington Herald-Leader* on September 15, 1968:

A new nationwide merchandising division specializing in sales to the rapidly growing college-student market has been established by Kentucky Central Life Insurance Company, it was announced this week by the firm's president, Garvice D. Kincaid.

The new unit—the University Key Division—will offer a special plan of life insurance to college seniors, graduate students, and recent college graduates.

"There are several reasons why Kentucky Central has formed a new division to specialize in the college market," Kincaid said.

"It has always been our basic belief that college students need a good life insurance program just as much as anybody else. But because they are students and not regularly employed, the problem has been financing. The University Key Division has developed a new plan of life insurance which has virtually eliminated this problem.

"From a business point of view," Kincaid added, "the new division will give Kentucky Central a competitive advantage in one of the nation's fastest growing life insurance markets."

Delayed Premium

The unique feature of the University Key Plan is that Kentucky Central does not require payment of the first-year premium until five years later.

At that time, the policyowner may pay his premium with his own funds, or a special provision in the plan will automatically pay it for him.

"We feel it is realistic to defer the first-year premium for this class of policyowner because of the excellent job opportunities that exist today for persons who have college education," Kincaid stated.

The University Key Plan will be offered throughout Kentucky Central's 36-state operating area.

Heading the University Key Division for Kentucky Central with the title of vice president is R. A. Hanson.

Hanson joined Kentucky Central in August and is currently developing the division national sales organization. "We have applied for approval of the University Key Plan to the insurance departments in all states in which Kentucky Central is licensed to operate," Hanson said. "Kentucky approved the plan the week of August 26th and we expect approval in the rest of Kentucky Central's 36-state operating area very shortly."

Hanson said when the division is fully developed, it will operate through eight regional headquarters with a general agency plan of merchandising.

New Executives

The division has been working closely with Kentucky Central's Marketing Division, which has the responsibility to develop new sales plans and techniques. The division is managed by Edward D.

Brown. Hanson has been in the life insurance industry for nine years and has specialized in college sales for the last four.

He was raised in Brady, Texas, and has been making his home in Dallas with his wife, Betty, and their two daughters. He holds bachelor's and master's degrees from Texas A&M and taught school for 11 years prior to entering the insurance field.

Kincaid said that two other men have been named to executive positions. W. H. Frey is national sales director for the new division and William R. Carman is director of service.

Frey has been specializing in college sales during his 11 years in the insurance business. A native of Austin, Frey received a Bachelor of Science degree from Southwestern University, Georgetown, Texas. Frey played four years of football at Southwestern and was a high school coach for five years after graduation.

Carman also has extensive experience in both the sales and administrative phase of life insurance plans for college students.

Carman holds a degree in business administration from Sul Ross College in Alpine, Texas. At Sul Ross, Carman graduated in the top 10-percent of his class and was elected to Alpha Chi scholastic honorary society. He spent two and half years in the Marine Corps and is a Korean veteran.

General Agent

"We feel that the University Key Division is on solid ground with these three men," Kincaid said. "They are all college graduates, former teachers and have vast experience in dealing with the life insurance problems of the college student."

Hanson also announced the appointment of the division's first general agent. He is Emmett O'Donnell, who will be based in Lexington, home of Kentucky Central's national headquarters. O'Donnell will be responsible for establishing a sales organization in Lexington and the Eastern Kentucky area.

A native of Sweeney, Texas, O'Donnell is a 1963 graduate of Sul Ross College. While in college, O'Donnell played three years of varsity basketball, was editor of the school newspaper and selected for Who's Who Among College and University Students and had worked for a year in television before starting his insurance career in 1964.

Jim Howe was one of Kentucky Central Life's original College Sales general agents and worked for Swede Hanson at Reserve Life. According to Jim, Larry Sammartin was a very successful agent and became one of Swede's best agents and elite recruiters. Swede liked and respected Larry, and after moving to Kentucky Central Life, Swede made Larry a regional manager responsible for Pennsylvania, West Virginia, Kentucky, Ohio, Maryland, and Washington, D.C.

Building the Foundation for Growth

The year before Swede Hanson joined Kentucky Central in August 1967, David Brain had recruited Edward Brown to the company. Brown's role was to establish and direct the company's new marketing support division. Brown was a twenty-year insurance industry veteran and a native of Louisville, where he had worked for the Mutual Life Insurance Co. of New York for the last thirteen years. His primary job involved market research, the development of new products, and modification of the company's existing products. Brain was formalizing the company's product development and market research process, and it was this approach the company would continue to use for years to come. Brain recognized that Kincaid's acquisitions had brought a different type of agent to the company, one that needed more and better products and a higher level of agent support and training.

In addition, in September 1966 Brain had recruited Bill Joyner to the company as its chief actuary. Thirty-four-year-old Joyner had been practicing actuarial science for eleven years. He was a Tennessee native and had spent the last one-and-a-half years working for Girard Life Insurance Company in Dallas, Texas. Girard Life was about four times the asset size of Kentucky Central Life and operated in forty-two states and the Districts of Columbia and Puerto Rico and had operations in Germany and Spain. More importantly, the company offered a comprehensive line of life and health insurance products. Joyner and Brown were expected to bring more industry knowledge and experience to the marketing and development of insurance products. Bill Joyner is another example of how Kincaid and David Brain appreciated a person's academic qualifications. Joyner, like David Brain, was a Harvard graduate, having received a full scholarship to the university at age 16 and having graduated in only three years in 1952. Upon graduation, Bill was commissioned as an officer in the U.S. Navy and served his country during the Korean Conflict. He was honorably discharged in 1956, having achieved the rank of lieutenant.

In 1971, with the establishment of the College Sales Division and the addition of the acquired agency groups, the company was now receiving three times the number of new business applications it had received just five years earlier. In addition, its field force was now approaching two thousand agents, and it was receiving new business on multiple types of products and from areas of the country operating in different time zones. The legacy Anchorage company had never dealt with these types of issues. To complicate matters, most of the Anchorage staff hadn't moved to Lexington, so most of the company's employees were from Lexington and the surrounding areas and relatively new to the life insurance industry. There was an advantage in this, though, because this meant that its employee base lacked the Anchorage staff's preconceptions about how things should be done and were more willing to adjust to all the changes taking place.

For instance, in 1971, David Brain recruited Harry J. Bradlaw to manage the company's New Business Department. Bradlaw had spent twenty-three years in the industry and had been with Gulf Life Insurance Company in Jacksonville, Florida, since 1955. He had a degree in accounting and economics from the University of Manitoba and was a Fellow in the Life Management Institute and a chartered life underwriter. Bradlaw was tasked with the responsibility of reorganizing the company's New Business Department to reduce errors and make it more efficient. Bradlaw's first major challenge was to train the company's employees on the various existing and future new products it would be selling.

As an example, each product had its own specific policy forms. In addition, many policies had state variations of those forms or special consumer disclosures requirements. Bradlaw's job was to organize the flow of work so that mistakes were avoided and help the employees understand the unique differences that they had to work with. Kentucky Central Life had become more complicated, and its employees needed to adjust to how its business was changing. The appropriate underwriting of risk was still very important, but the product platforms for these risks had changed, requiring the company to adopt a better approach to processing its new business applications.

The Executive Sales Division was created in 1973 as a stand-alone division. It appears to have been a direct consequence of the 1963 acquisition of Professional and Business Men's Life Insurance Company and the 1968 acquisition of Rio Grande. The company was now operating in forty-three states, Washington, D.C., and the Commonwealth of Puerto Rico and had agencies selling life insurance, personal health insurance, annuities, business insurance, automobile and homeowners insurance, group insurance, and credit insurance. Douglas R. Schoenfeld, a Princeton University graduate who had worked in agency management for fifteen years at the larger Western Reserve Life Insurance Company and The Life Insurance Company of North America Company, was recruited to run the division.

Many of the company's top agencies were now in Texas, Florida, Ohio, and California, and the products sold were larger and more sophisticated. In addition, the Kentucky Central Life agency force had become dominated by personal producing general agents versus its original career agents. Finally, after seven years, the company took the knowledge it had gained and formally created the more structured agent hierarchy that was necessary to manage its growing general agency force. The company was now measuring its agent force in the thousands versus the seven hundred agents it had when Kincaid acquired it in 1959.

In 1972, Kentucky Central Life formalized its scattered approach to its institutional and wholesale marketing and created the Diversified Sales Division. The division formally leveraged relationships with banks, credit unions, finance companies, and other organizations to sell products downstream to their customers. Kentucky Finance Company and Kincaid banks were already important relationships, but now the company would strategically build programs targeted at these and other groups.

In 1973, the company created the Consumer Savings Division. This division would service the tens of thousands of "State of Kentucky employees and teachers" who were covered under the state's group life contract. This was considered an important contract for the company. It not only increased its life insurance and annuity business but provided direct access to those employees for the marketing of other products.

The Professional Marketing Division was started in 1979. This division replaced the University Key Division, where the focus had moved past the college market. The young college agents recruited in the late 1960s were now young professionals with professional contacts. These agents needed a brand that matched their identity and the more sophisticated products they sold and the lifestyle the higher commissions on these products earned them. Professional Marketing was less about a change of direction and more about the evolution of this group's agency force and the market they were serving.

From Now on the Clouds Have Company

The years 1979 and 1980 were pivotal for the company. On Friday afternoon, November 2, 1979, the company began moving some of its employees into its new corporate headquarters at the intersection of Broadway and Vine Street. It was a $24 million, twenty-two-story building consisting of 421,000 square feet of office space. It was initially projected to cost $20 million, but at its dedication in September 1980, its cost was listed at $24 million. The initial move in November involved six hundred of the company's seven hundred employees. A significant portion of the building was still under construction, so everyone could not move into Kincaid Towers at the same time. Kentucky Finance and Kincaid's law firm also moved in during this time, while Central Bank, with its two hundred thirty employees, and WVLK radio, with its thirty-five employees, had to wait till April 1980, when their space was completed. The building was dedicated in September 1980 in a well-attended and well-publicized event. Nelle Kincaid attended, and she and Earl Wilson unveiled a large plaque dedicating the building to Garvice Kincaid. Nelle had been estranged from the Committee since 1977, but she honored the memory of her husband that day. Kincaid's dream of a building where all his businesses could be located was now a reality. Over a thousand of his empire's employees were now located at Kincaid Towers, and in ten years that number would reach almost fifteen hundred.

Garvice had been dead five years, and Burnett and the Committee had just completed Kincaid Towers. It was a new era for the company. During the next ten years, the insurance company's employee count would increase to over one thousand. Every Kincaid business was now housed under one roof, except for WKYT, which needed its television broadcasting facilities on Winchester Road. In later years, many former employees believed moving into Kincaid Towers changed the personality of the company and that this new important structure required the company to live up to a new, more modern image. Certainly 1980 was a pivotal year, one that set the stage for rocket-type growth followed by a fall into an ocean of disaster.

In Kentucky Central Life's old Kentucky Central Life Building (the Lafayette Hotel), the company had already begun to burst at its seams. Every inch of the building was used, including most of the lobby. Employees had learned to adjust and manage to work in the space allocated to them. Things were efficient, though, and internal communication was easy, even though we still used a company switchboard located in the basement of the building. One pretty much saw everyone sometime during the day, and the old second-floor cafeteria, which operated as an automat-style vending restaurant, was a place you ran into most of the company's employees during the week. If an all an-employee meeting needed to take place, like the one Earl Wilson and Burnett held in 1977 when American General wanted to acquire the company, everyone gathered in the main lobby and around its upstairs balconies and on its marble staircase. The building was old, but it served its purpose.

The new Kincaid Towers was beautiful, and its twenty-second floor contained an onsite agent and employee training center and reception area.

Its executive offices were spacious and spread out on the twenty-first floor, with two large corner offices across from each other for Bud Burnett and Earl Wilson. Departments were now more isolated, though, with each floor serving a specific purpose. Policyowner service was on one floor, with new business, marketing and sales, and accounting each on three other floors. The fourteenth floor was home to the corporate service–related departments of legal, investments, mortgage loans, tax, personnel, and conservation. It also housed the company's public relations department for many years, until personnel needed more space. Then it was relegated to the lobby of the building, in the old space formerly occupied by Wallace Wilkinson's corporate office, Wilkinson Enterprises. Agency management (agent licensing) and word processing and central files were on another floor, with the supply and mailroom departments spread somewhere else. Finally, the property and casualty companies had their own floor. The *Lexington Herald-Leader* did a front-page story, after the company moved in, with a picture of Ed Winiarczyk looking out the window at Lexington from the twenty-second floor on a cloudy day. The headline was "From Now on the Clouds have Company."

Kincaid Towers was the tallest building in Lexington for about two years, and then the Webb Company built the Financial Center, affectionately known as "Big Blue." Wendell Gunn said Earl Wilson wasn't happy about that and let his opinion be known. Gunn said Wilson claimed the two brothers had broken their promise that it wouldn't be visually taller than Kincaid Towers. Apparently, Burnett knew something but hadn't told Wilson. The Financial Center's land sat lower than Kincaid Towers, so they expected it would have more stories than Kincaid Towers's twenty-two stories, but thirty-three stories was a surprise.

In total, the life insurance company occupied ten floors of the new building, and as for our old gathering spot, the cafeteria, it was now located on the second floor of the building and managed by Morrison's Cafeteria, with every Kincaid company employee receiving a 25 percent discount on their meal—even in the evening, for Rupp Arena events. Burnett and the Committee had just provided the equivalent of a new-car experience for everyone. In fact, in the beginning, the official rule was no eating at your desk because each floor also contained a large employee lounge with vending machines, coffeemakers, and tables and chairs, and they could easily seat thirty people. I am told the rule lasted a little over a year, and while it was never officially changed, word began spreading that it was okay to eat at your desk.

There was nothing wrong with our new home, but in later years, people realized that we all knew less about what was going on in the company. You

saw and spoke to colleagues as you rode on one of five elevators or passed
them in the garage or lobby, but it wasn't the same. In the old building,
information flowed more easily because long-time personal relationships and
casual conversations were valuable communication tools. After moving into
Kincaid Towers, the number of new employees and new faces grew quickly,
and because we were more segmented, personal relationships developed more
slowly and informal conversations between different areas of the company
happened less frequently. Nothing ever really stays the same, but it's regrettable
that this cultural shift occurred on the cusp of the other significant changes in
the 1980s.

One observation that means more to me today than when I was working at
the company in the 1980s, and that supports the perception of an atmosphere
of restricted communication, was the competitive nature of some of the
senior officers. Walter Rehfuss joined the company in 1974 as the head of
administration, overseeing systems, policyholder service, new business, agency
services, personnel, mail/supply, and building operations. Rehfuss's span of
control was quite large. Walter Rehfuss was smart and a senior vice president
and considered a close Burnett confident on things related to the operations of
the company. Kentucky Central Life didn't have a chief operating officer, but
if it had, Walter Rehfuss probably would have held that title.

Wendell Gunn joined the company in 1966 as its controller, overseeing
the day-to-cash and accounting operations of the company. In December
1976, after Burnett assumed the role of president, Gunn was promoted to
Burnett's former position as secretary and treasurer of the company and as
its chief financial officer. Gunn oversaw all the accounting functions and the
production of the company's financial statements, regulatory filings, and stock
transfer activities. After the company's chief actuary, Bill Tozer, retired, Marty
Uhl stepped into the role as chief actuary, but was a vice president and, as I
understand it, on paper reported to Burnett but also had a strong line pointing
to Gunn. In other words, from a professional perspective, the chief actuary
was reporting to Burnett, the president of the company, but from a day-to-day
function perspective, Wendell Gunn was his primary contact. This made some
sense given that actuarial reserving has such a large impact on a company's
financial statements. So, Gunn's span of control was also quite large.

As the company was growing rapidly in the 1980s, there was a little bit of a
power struggle between Rehfuss and Gunn. Both men wanted to be considered
as essential to the success of the company and, more importantly, Burnett. If
one of them found out something was disturbing in the other person's division,
they would sneak over to Burnett's office like a ferret to relay what they had

learned. In fact, their lieutenants soon became informally known as "Gunn's Gunners" and "Rehfuss's Raiders." By no means were these two senior officers at war with each other, but they both recognized that the company didn't have a successor to Burnett. Both men were five to six years younger than Burnett and probably assumed that he might consider them as his successor to run the company. Burnett would turn 65 in 1991. Burnett could remain chairman, and they could handle the day-to-day operations, just as Wilson and Burnett had shared their positions.

Their competition for Burnett's recognition was recognized by many employees, and over time, it was generally known that it was wise to limit what one might say about anything to someone from either of their departments. The wrong casual statement might be used as ammunition in their quest for power.

A New Decade and a New Direction

In 1980, with the introduction of universal life and the continued growth of the company's general agency force, one final significant change was made, which recognized that the two largest sales divisions were focused on similar target markets. In 1983 the company created the Executive Marketing Division as an umbrella for the Executive Sales Division and the Professional Marketing Division. The general intent was to streamline and improve the agent management process and support work and reduce costs through the consolidation of regional oversight. The projected efficiency was never realized because in early 1984 the company set an aggressive in-force growth goal and soon began growing its field force from around two thousand five hundred agents to what was eventually over fifteen thousand agents in 1990. This growth led to many internal problems, but from an agent management perspective, it was a pure catastrophe. The company had grown its field force so fast that it couldn't get rid of its bad agents fast enough. By 1991, the company was adding and terminating over one thousand agents a month. The company had achieved its goal of $50 billion of insurance in force by 1990, but it had also destroyed much of what made the company so special after Kincaid acquired it.

Another problem with the combined sales divisions was their different cultures. The Executive Sales Division had older agents who had been selling insurance longer, and the average age of the Professional Marketing Division was about ten to fifteen years younger. The Professional Marketing Division was created from scratch, with its roots grounded in Kentucky Central Life's College Life Division. The Executive Sales Division was a collection of experienced agents and agencies accumulated over time through acquisitions and normal agent recruitment. These agents had more work experience and had worked with more than one insurance company, while many of the Professional Marking Division's agents and managers had only worked for Kentucky Central Life and/or Reserve Life. Another issue that never was totally resolved was that Swede Hanson and Larry Sammartin had provided some Professional Marketing agencies with more generous contracts, and as Executive Sales agents learned about these differences, this also created some internal conflicts.

I don't want to take away from the work and effort that the sales managers and staff of these marketing divisions did or imply that they were doing anything wrong. Far to the contrary, they were like soldiers given a mission and the resources necessary to complete it, and they did. One could even say they were more successful than anyone expected. In retrospect, though, one can see that the company lacked the strategic knowledge and management strength to cope with this type of agent growth. Also, it wasn't just the marketing division that was involved in this new initiative. The actuarial, finance, accounting, administration, policyholder service, systems, investments, and other departments were involved in the planning to accomplish this goal. By the end of 1983, Burnett's $50 billion in-force goal had taken on a life of its own and would be announced in 1984.

In the early 1980s, as the company began developing its first universal-life product, another important change swept through the life insurance industry. In 1981, the first reported case of AIDs appeared, and this "death sentence" virus really spooked the life insurance industry. Though HIV arrived in the United States around 1970, it didn't come to the public's attention until the early 1980s.

In 1981, the Centers for Disease Control and Prevention (CDC) published a report about five previously healthy homosexual men becoming infected with pneumocystis pneumonia, which is caused by what is considered a harmless fungus. This type of pneumonia, the CDC noted, almost never affects people with uncompromised immune systems. The following year, the *New York Times* published an alarming article about the new immune system disorder, which, by that time, had affected 335 people, killing 136 of them. Because the disease appeared to affect mostly homosexual men, officials initially called it a gay-related immune deficiency, or GRID.

By 1983, the CDC had discovered all the major ways the virus was transmitted, including that heterosexual relations with female partners of AIDS-positive men could lead to infection, but the public still considered AIDS a gay disease. It was even called the "gay plague" for many years. In

September 1982, the CDC used the term "AIDS" to describe the disease for the first time. By the end of the year, AIDS cases were being reported in Europe.

It wasn't until 1984 that the industry's paranoia began to cautiously fade. Researchers had finally identified the cause of AIDS—the HIV virus—and the Food and Drug Administration (FDA) licensed the first commercial blood test for HIV in 1985. By the end of 1985, there were more than twenty thousand reported cases of AIDS, with at least one case in every region of the world, but the virus hadn't been the devastating crisis that the insurance industry had thought possible.

Something else important happened at the beginning of 1984. Earl Wilson had retired as chairman of the board at the end of 1983, and Burnett now held the title chairman and president. In addition, he also held the position of lead member of Kincaid's Advisory Committee. With Wilson gone, the Committee put in place multiyear employment contracts for themselves, with salaries and bonuses defined. This had not been done before 1984. Now, each Committee member had their own Kincaid business to oversee, and that business would pay them compensation and bonuses. Burnett's was tied to Kentucky Central Life, Ed Schaeffer's was tied to Kentucky Finance, and Hart Hagan's was tied to Bluegrass Broadcasting. These payments were in addition to Schaeffer's compensation from Kincaid's law firm and Hagan's salary from General Management Associates, the accounting and management firm that did work for various Kincaid enterprises. In addition, Rusty Hembree would now receive a salary and bonus from Central Bank and Trust in addition to his compensation from the Kincaid law firm.

On February 9, 1993, Burnett announced that there would not be a $100 million deal with Whitman and that the company would look at disposing of various noncore assets to replenish its capital. That evening, the company's stock closed at $6.75. On Thursday, February 11, the states of California and Florida banned the company from selling insurance in their states, and on Friday, February 12, the company was taken over by the State of Kentucky Insurance Department and Burnett and Kincaid's Committee were banned from the company's offices. Of course, the stock collapsed on the news, and the stock closed at $3 per share on February 19 after trading at a new low of $1.75.

On Tuesday, February 23, Garvice Kincaid's daughters agreed to an out-of-court settlement with Burnett, Schaeffer, and Hembree. The settlement ended the daughters' eight-year court battle to wrest control of the company and the Kincaid estate's other assets from the Committee. All Committee members resigned from the Committee and from any positions they held at Kincaid companies. Their war was over, but now they had to fight the State of Kentucky's Insurance Department to try to save the company from liquidation.

In the early years after Kincaid died and David Brain was gone, I was told by John Lang that Burnett would attend some of the American Council of Life Insurance Company meetings. This is an association whose members include many of the senior management personnel in the life insurance industry. They hold national meetings on topics involving the financial, investment, legal, administrative, and regulatory functions of life insurance companies. One of the main benefits of these meetings is the opportunity to network with other insurance company executives and learn what issues they're dealing with. Apparently, according to Lang, in the late 1970s, Burnett attended one or two these meetings annually, but then in the 1980s reduced his attendance to maybe one per year until 1984, when he quit attending altogether. Lang initially thought Burnett was too busy and figured his other senior leaders could attend these meetings and report relevant information to him.

In later years, John Lang reconsidered this thought and decided that Burnett wasn't comfortable in meetings where he would be asked questions and expected to discuss specifics about the company and industry. He said he developed this opinion in February 1987, after Burnett announced that the company would seek to offer 3 million additional shares to the public. Burnett had recruited Lang, who was at Merrill Lynch then, to complete the transaction. Merrill Lynch scheduled a week of investor meetings on the east and west coasts with several prospective institutional purchasers, and John traveled with Burnett to the meetings. Lang said Burnett was terrible; "he didn't want to answer their questions" or seemed "irritated that they were asking him certain questions." John said that after the second investor meeting, he decided Burnett was doing more harm than good and they canceled the rest of the investor meetings. When the day came to sell the stock, Merrill Lynch was able to sell only 1.1 million of the proposed 3 million shares offered at $15 per share. John said those two investor meetings confirmed to him why Burnett stopped attending industry conferences: "He didn't like having to answer questions and being put in the spotlight. He wasn't in charge there." Lang said he had never seen Burnett so uncomfortable.

In 1983, when Executive Marketing was formed, Larry Sammartin was made vice president in charge of the division, and in 1991, after reaching the $50 billion goal, Larry was promoted to senior vice president over the division and put on the company's board of directors. In November 1992, after a dozen years of his being on the road working to build, grow, and manage Kentucky Central Life's large agency force, the banquet circuit had caught up to him. In November 1992, with the company's life on the line, its fifteen thousand agents wanted to know if the company would survive. That November, Larry died of a massive heart attack at his home in Lexington at the age of 53. Larry had started working for the company in 1968 at the age of 29 when the company was just moving into other markets. His career had begun with the formation of College Sales, where he started as an agent and soon was promoted to the northeast regional manager's position and later vice president.

After Kincaid died in 1975 and David Brain was pushed out of the company in 1976, Bud Burnett was fully in charge of the Kentucky Central Life Insurance Company. Burnett was an accountant, and now the new, insecure leader oversaw the largest entity in Garvice Kincaid's empire. In the late 1970s, Burnett was concerned that others in the company might compare him to David Brain, who was both a stronger leader and someone more knowledgeable about the workings of the insurance industry. Outside the company, he was concerned about being compared to Garvice Kincaid. Burnett had a simple strategy in those early years of his reign. He wanted to garner loyalty from whomever he could in the company. He was suspicious of folks who were loyal to David Brain, like Dick Gordon, so he arranged to shuffle them over to jobs where they would be more isolated. In addition, whereas Kincaid and Brain opted to bring in experienced management talent from larger companies, Burnett took a different approach. He promoted younger, less experienced internal people into new management roles. He knew these employees would be indebted to him for their success and demonstrate their loyalty by being less critical and direct in their responses to him.

Many leaders enjoy having people smarter than themselves on their staff, but Burnett didn't. He was always concerned about being criticized and worried that people thought he was only leading the company because of the boardroom coup he had orchestrated with Earl Wilson. In January 1975, Kincaid had promoted David Brain, the more knowledgeable industry professional, to the position of president of the company, not Bud Burnett. Kincaid had made his choice of leader of the company after him less than a year before his death, and Burnett and Wilson had overruled it.

The king had died, and the community was now placing bets on the success of his handpicked Committee. Burnett knew they were judging the head of the life insurance company in particular. In fact, several newspaper accounts suggested Burnett had been Kincaid's right-hand man; one said, "His rise has been gradual but steady, and he is known as a man who knows how to invest money, the secret of running a life insurance business." This quote was included in the February 29, 1976, *Courier Journal* multipage magazine article about the Committee and was not attributed to anyone. My guess is that Earl Wilson or Ed Schaeffer made it during the interview to confirm the reason Burnett was in charge of the life insurance company. This John Pearce article was published three months after Kincaid's death, and it was essentially introducing the Committee's resume.

In 1983 when Executive Marketing was being created from the merger of the two sales divisions, the majority of the agent management leadership came from the Professional Marketing Division, formerly known as College Sales. These individuals were loyal to both Larry Sammartin and Bud Burnett. They had started their insurance careers with Kentucky Central Life and were loyal and eager to do both men's bidding. These guys (they were all men) were like a small fraternity, where each brother competed with other brothers but easily joined together to celebrate the collective success of their brotherhood. The problem this created was twofold: (1) they were all friends who had been working together for the last ten years, so their objectivity was less reliable, and (2) these people were more agent recruiters versus agent managers. Most of their early careers had been devoted to recruiting young college graduates to sell insurance for Kentucky Central Life, not to the management of a complicated agent distribution system.

The newly merged Executive Marketing Division in 1983 began with a field force of fifteen hundred agents and the was led by Vice President Larry Sammartin. Doug Schoenfeld was moved to a support unit called the Financial Service Center to provide advanced underwriting and field support. The primary field managers, known as regional directors in the merged entity, were the following:

Jim Howe, CLU – Professional Marketing
Bob Gibbons – Executive Sales
Tom Parker – Professional Marketing
Allen Salmon, CLU – Executive Sales
Bob Lovell – Professional Marketing
Joe More – Executive Sales
Jim Mader – Professional Marketing
Don Boozer – Professional Marketing
Wayne Hudgens – Professional Marketing
George Surmick – recruited to the role by Sammartin

All the field managers from Professional Marketing were given regional director positions, and the remaining Executive Sales field managers were given managing general agency contracts. No one was terminated or lost compensation due to the reorganization, and in fact history would show that Burnett's huge 1984 growth goal would create a compensation windfall for these regional directors. Of course, the regional directors were unable to manage and control their field forces. With the company increasing its field force from twenty-five hundred agents to over fifteen thousand in six years, enormous problems were created for the company and its employees. Kentucky Central was indeed bigger and spending a lot of money, but the company, like the old king, wasn't wearing any clothes. Burnett's big plan was ridiculous both in concept and in practice, and while Burnett was aware of most of the issues, he didn't become concerned about the problems this growth caused until 1991, when the field force began turning against him due to the financial problems the company was experiencing. Bud's famous answer, "no problem," wasn't working anymore.

As for Executive Marketing's regional directors, some of their excesses slowly surfaced by 1991 as the company was trying to control costs and expenses. One simple example was that the regional directors were going to lunch together a lot, and each time a different regional director would pick up the group's tab and turn it in on his expense account. These were two-hour, martini-style lunches at places like the Coach House or the Hyatt Regency in Lexington. Larry Sammartin would sign off on the expense account and, given his travel schedule, probably without even reviewing it. The expense report was sent to accounting, and the regional director was then reimbursed. This practice went on for a long time, but finally one day someone from accounting brought it up to Wendle Gunn. Burnett had issued a cost reduction edict, and the person in accounting wondered why the company was still allowing this. According to the company grapevine, Gunn went to Burnett and explained what they were doing and Burnett raised hell and called Sammartin to his office. After that closed-door meeting, the regional directors were responsible for their own lunches and Larry Sammartin started reviewing the expense accounts more thoroughly.

Life Insurance Industry Changes in the 1980s

To understand all the changes that were taking place in the early 1980s, one needs to understand the economic environment. Inflation had been rampant in the late 1970s, and the Federal Reserve was raising interest rates to never-before-seen levels. By the end of 1980, the Federal Funds rate was at 19%. In the late 1970s, the money market mutual fund had been developed. This product offered the consumer a higher-interest-rate alternative for their short-term cash. After the Federal Reserve raised rates in 1980, these high-quality products were providing yields of 12% to 15%.

The life insurance industry was also on the cusp of an evolutionary change in 1980. Old whole-life insurance policies provide low returns but had a valuable consumer feature that allowed the policyholder to borrow their cash value from their policy at interest rates of 5% to 8%. With money market rates so high, consumers could now perform an arbitrage and borrow money from their old policies, deposit it in their money-market account, and earn and additional 6% to 9% risk free. The life insurance industry was hit hard with policy loans as hundreds of millions of dollars of policy loans were requested by their customers. This happened at a time when their investment portfolios were underwater due to where interest rates were. In other words, they couldn't sell assets to raise money easily, so they were forced to borrow money from the banking industry. This had never happened before in the history of the industry, and managements were shocked.

Another major development happened in 1982 when Congress passed the Tax Equity and Fiscal Responsibility Act. This law took away various tax deductions but established the opportunity for life insurance to become an investment product. Before this, life insurance had been purchased for protection purposes. The life insurance industry lobbied Congress for this change because it believed money market mutual funds and new brokerage products were a threat to its existence. This act was the foundational building block that allowed for the creation of universal-life insurance. Universal life was the 1980s product that revolutionized the life insurance industry. This complicated product combined insurance protection with an investment component, via which the cash value of the policy could earn an attractive interest rate on a tax-deferred basis.

The product was very complicated, and to sell it, multiple policy illustrations needed to be produced. The illustrations also had to be flexible and provide for alternative assumptions about interest rates, costs of insurance, and changing deposit amounts. Initially, companies considered using their mainframe computers to prepare these illustrations, but this was time consuming and would significantly slow the sales process and the agent's production.

In 1982, the age of the personal computer was just beginning, and companies were still trying to figure out where it was going. As mentioned, universal life required the insurance industry to provide illustrations for its agents to use to sell these new policies, and the Panasonic Company initially came to the rescue with its Panasonic HHC handheld computer, which had a built-in mini printer. The Panasonic HHC was like a large rectangular calculator with a built-in paper roll printer. Insurance companies would pay Panasonic to program the specifications of their products into the device, and the device could then provide the agents with the capability to print off illustrations for their prospects. The Panasonic HHC had great success with life insurance companies thanks to its custom, built-in, insurance calculation application. Insurance agents could provide insurance quotations on the fly and print them anywhere, anytime. In addition, these devices made the agents appear more sophisticated and knowledgeable about universal life. These devices weren't cheap, though, and required hardware updates as companies developed new products.

The life insurance industry was very interested in offering universal-life products, but most companies hadn't considered their downside. Universal life was the perfect product for replacing their existing very profitable whole-life insurance policies. The policies usually had cash value, and when replaced with a UL policy the customer would earn a higher return on this value. Therefore, many agents in the 1980s spent much of their time finding customers with existing whole-life policies and replacing them with UL. The agents benefited from their commissions and the customers benefited by getting a higher return, but the carriers saw a large percentage of their most profitable business replaced, sometimes by their own agents.

By 1982, insurance distribution had been evolving. Many companies were not growing their more expensive career agent divisions but were developing large general agency field forces. A career agent system has a significant amount of fixed costs associated with it (offices, benefits, training, and recruiting) versus the general agency system, in which it's up to agency owners to manage and pay for these costs from the commission they earn. In the early 1980s, the commission difference earned for selling a UL policy might be 50% more to a general agent as compared to what the same product might pay a career agent.

Kentucky Central Enters the Universal-Life Market

In September 1983, Kentucky Central Life introduced its first universal-life insurance product: VIP Life. The company had begun development of the product and the systems and tools necessary to sell it over the last two years. It even had created a unit, Financial Service Center, staffed with Richard Loy and an IBM PC to provide illustrations for its agents and held agent training sessions at the company headquarters. Its largest investment was providing Panasonic HHC computers to interested agents. The company would purchase the calculator-type device for $1,500 and sell it to agents for $1,200, taking a note back from the agent for the purchase price. This worked until about 1986, when the agents started purchasing their own personal computers and didn't want to use the Panasonics any longer. There is always a lot of agent turnover, and over a thousand of these units were returned to the company, with many of the loans left unpaid. At one point, Kentucky Central's legal department felt like a collection agency chasing down agents for nonpayment of their notes. The HHCs had become the 1980s version of the 1970s 8-track tape player; they weren't wanted anymore.

$50 Billion Life Insurance In-force Goal

Another thing happened in the spring of 1983: Larry Sammartin attended a Life Insurance Marketing & Research Association (LIMRA) conference. LIMRA is the professional association for home-office life insurance management. The LIMRA provides a lot of information to the industry about demographic and consumer trends and works with companies on specific projects. At this spring conference, one of the presentations was about the changing dynamics of the industry and the fact the larger companies were just getting larger while smaller companies were finding it more and more difficult to compete. According to Senior Vice President Wendle Gunn, Larry came back and told Burnett and the other senior officers at their next morning coffee meeting that the LIMRA predicted that to survive, a company would need to have $50 billion of insurance in force by 1990.

Evidently, Burnett took the prophecy to heart and said, "Then if we need to get to $50 billion, let's do it." According to Gunn, there wasn't much discussion or analysis of what they'd just heard. Burnett's statement was taken as a general directive and the next thing he knew, marketing was developing plans around a strategy to do it.

In 1984, Burnett announced the enormous sales goal of $50 billion of in-force insurance by 1990 to the employees in an all-company meeting, to the agents in printed flyers, and to the public through press releases. At the time of the announcement, the company had $11.8 billion of in-force insurance. The path to reaching the goal would be to offer the most competitive products with the most competitive commissions and to quadruple the number of agents representing the company. VIP Life and its future versions would be the product, and Executive Marketing became a marketing division on steroids.

The Great Oz

In an insurance company, the chief actuary is considered the regulator or mediator of the company. The finance departments are usually the conservative areas of the company working to comply with rules and regulations and to maintain adequate capital. The marketing department is the creative area of the company looking at new products to sell and new ways to sell them. The actuarial department and the chief actuary are trained to understand the issues related to the needs of both these areas and usually work with the investment department and other departments to understand and evaluate the issues and provide strategic input. For instance, how much expense will need to be priced into the new product? How much capital will it use? How important are investment returns to its success? What is the expected return on the capital used, and how many years will it take to achieve the expected return? Finally, how will it affect the rest of the company's business?

During the Bud Burnett era, there were few strategic discussions about these types of issues. Departments operated in their own little silos. Burnett did hold regular coffee sessions with a group of his senior officers on Monday and Friday mornings, but these sessions were more tactical in nature than strategic. His senior officer group mainly reported on issues and problems related to the daily operations of the company. In the 1980s, most of these significant issues were resolved by adding more personnel or new equipment.

In most insurance companies, the chief executive officer remains in close contact with the investment department. At Kentucky Central Life, Burnett never invited Cliff Forbush, its chief investment officer and my old boss and friend, to any of his coffee sessions, nor did he have regular meetings with him. Mr. Forbush had been recruited to Kentucky Central Life in January 1973 by Mr. Kincaid, through a headhunter, and was considered by many to be one of the most knowledgeable insurance people in the company. He had worked at the much larger Connecticut Mutual Life Insurance Company and in earlier days had been a naval intelligence offer. Cliff was a strong investment professional, and people respected his knowledge about the markets and investments.

Cliff Forbush's Introduction to Garvice and Kentucky Central Life

Mr. Forbush was working for Connecticut Mutual in 1972 and was frustrated with his job. His boss had gotten pigeonholed in his career, so the only way for Forbush to move up in the company was to do a lateral move out of the private placement department and into another area of investments. Nothing interesting was available, so he had contacted a headhunter to see what he might find. One day he got a call about this little company in Kentucky. He looked up the company and told the guy that this company was too small. The headhunter told him he didn't understand the whole situation. He told him about Mr. Kincaid and what he knew of his holdings and that Mr. Kincaid had some real plans to grow the life insurance company and his empire. The recruiter said, "Cliff, this guy will keep you very busy, and you might just have some fun." The headhunter also thought a move to Lexington might offer his family a more enjoyable place to live and a much better work commute. Mr. Forbush considered the situation and, with a push from the headhunter, came to Lexington for an interview with Mr. Kincaid.

Bud Burnett, the company's executive vice president, met Mr. Forbush at the airport and drove him to Mr. Kincaid's office. Cliff said the men exchanged pleasantries and Mr. Kincaid explained that he had some major growth plans for the company and needed someone to manage its investment portfolios and help him with some of his other investment endeavors. Mr. Kincaid then proceeded to ask Mr. Forbush various questions about Connecticut Mutual—its mix of business, portfolio composition, and the various types of assets it held. Garvice wanted Mr. Forbush to demonstrate his knowledge of the company, a company he'd worked for over ten years. After about ten minutes, Mr. Kincaid looked up and says, "Bud, Cliff has worked for this company for over ten years and doesn't know a damn thing about it." Cliff said he could see Mr. Kincaid had an A.M. Best book open in his lap and that he was using it to ask his questions. He also thought he was looking at Connecticut General and not Connecticut Mutual. After Mr. Kincaid made that comment, Mr. Forbush told him, "You know, Mr. Kincaid, I work for Connecticut Mutual, not Connecticut General." He said Mr. Kincaid snuffed and slammed the A.M. Best book closed and said, "Well, I guess you are right." And that was the end of the formal interview.

Mr. Forbush said the three men went to lunch at the Coach House, and Mr. Kincaid wanted to know when he could start. Cliff said he couldn't take a job without discussing it with his wife and letting her see the place, and they had a vacation planned for the next week. Mr. Kincaid said, "Bud, we can't really hold it against a man for taking a family vacation" and looked at Mr. Forbush and told him that he owned a suite at the Fontainebleau Hotel, in Miami, and that Cliff should take his family there and use his personal suite. He also suggested that after his return, he should bring his wife to Lexington and spend the weekend. I'm not sure what Mr. Forbush's original vacation plans were, but the next week he flew his family to Miami and stayed in Mr. Kincaid's personal suite. I believe the next weekend he and Rita flew to Lexington, and the rest is history. I've always thought that Garvice appreciated Mr. Forbush's direct answer about Connecticut General and decided then and there that he'd found a person who would tell him the truth. Mr. Forbush joined the company in January 1973 as vice president, investments. John Rampulla had already joined KCL in August 1971 as vice president of mortgage loans. John had been a reserve quarterback for UK and had grown up in Miami, Florida.

When Mr. Forbush showed up at the home office, he was met by Mr. Burnett and escorted to his office. This was in the old building, and apparently the office had only a simple manager's desk. When Mr. Kincaid called him later to see how he was getting along, Cliff said he told Mr. Kincaid that he needed some office furniture. Mr. Kincaid called someone and told them to see about getting Mr. Forbush some furniture. I guess someone brought Mr. Forbush a catalogue or an office supply vendor came over and discussed it, and Cliff ordered his full "Executive Office Suite." A couple of days later he got a call from Mr. Burnett (who was also secretary and treasurer) about the order. Burnett told him he had this requisition for his office furniture. He said the company had never spent anywhere near that amount of money on office furniture. Mr. Burnett wanted to know if he really needed everything, and Mr. Forbush told him, "Well, yes. I need a place for all of my investment books and investment records, and I certainly need a place for guests to sit." Cliff said he never heard any more about it and the furniture just showed up a couple of weeks later. Side note: When KCL was being liquidated, I purchased all of Mr. Forbush's office furniture and moved it to Wisconsin, where I used it for the next twenty-five years. I would tell Cliff when we spoke on the phone sometimes that I was sitting at his desk and that only an investment professional had ever used his prized office furniture.

Bad Loan, Good Cause: 1973–1974

Cliff explained that he learned early on that Mr. Kincaid made much of his money from owning and lending against real estate. In those early years, Cliff said, he worked pretty independently of Mr. Kincaid, but occasionally Mr. Kincaid would summon him over to his office, which was in the "old" Central Bank building a few blocks away, to discuss a particular investment. From the way he explained it, Mr. Kincaid was essentially Kentucky Central Life's commercial loan operation.

Cliff said many times that Mr. Kincaid always said he didn't like making a loan on a property he couldn't drive to. Garvice liked to monitor the progress of his investments himself.

One loan he told me about sounded like classic Kincaid. The Sisters of Charity of Nazareth had contacted Mr. Kincaid wanting to borrow money to build another building on its campus. Mr. Forbush said he got a call from Garvice and was to come to his office. They discussed the loan, and Mr. Kincaid was thinking about it, and he finally just said, "bad loan, good cause"—so the company made the loan. Cliff said that Garvice had already decided what he wanted to do and just wanted Cliff to appreciate that he wasn't all about the numbers. There were other reasons to make investments. The loan was done as a private placement and held in the company's investment portfolio. Cliff was responsible for getting it completed and listed on the company's books. Cliff also made a point of telling me that Bud Burnett was not involved.

Garvice Wanted to Be on the Board of Kentucky Utilities

Cliff explained to me many times how Garvice felt the power structure of Lexington was against him. He said Kincaid felt that Kentucky Utilities, First Security Bank, and the local papers were the most influential entities in Lexington. Garvice could not be on the board of the First Security Bank because he owned Central Bank and other banks, and the newspapers were privately owned, so he decided that if he owned a big slug of KU stock, he could persuade KU to add him to its board.

So, in spring 1974, without discussing it with anyone, Garvice called up three local brokerage firms in Lexington (Merrill Lynch, Hillard Lyons, and E.F. Hutton) and put in three large orders to buy KU stock. Cliff said Garvice liked competition for his business and thought that having the three firms involved would get him the best price. Of course, this was a mistake, because having the three firms all trying to buy him stock at the same time caused the price to spike. This stodgy old utility saw its stock price run up 5 or 6 percent in just a few days.

Well, John Irvin over at Merrill Lynch had friends at these other firms and found out what Garvice was doing and called Cliff. After Cliff heard about it, he told Irvin that "the damn fool doesn't know what he is doing" and he would get ahold of Mr. Kincaid. Cliff called Mr. Kincaid's office and asked if he could come and discuss something with him. He said he worried about what he was going to say to him all the way over to his office but knew he had to say something.

Cliff said he went into Kincaid's office and explained that he had had gotten a call from John Irvin and asked Mr. Kincaid why he was buying KU stock. Kincaid explained what he was up to, and Mr. Forbush asked him why he was using three firms. "To get the best price," Kincaid said. Mr. Forbush said it doesn't work like that and what you're doing is causing the stock price to increase because you're bidding against yourself by using three firms. He said Kincaid just stared at him like he didn't know what to say, or maybe he was considering what Mr. Forbush had just told him. Cliff said he told Mr. Kincaid that he would be glad to help him if he'd let him and that he would be glad to purchase the stock for him. Kincaid agreed. Mr. Forbush said he would cancel any orders Mr. Kincaid had outstanding and give the stock a week to cool off. The stock fell about 4 percent over the next week or so. He then started buying the stock for Mr. Kincaid through Merrill Lynch, since it was the primary market-maker for the stock.

Cliff also said that Mr. Kincaid's strategy to use this position as a springboard to get on KU's board would never have worked because in the end Mr. Kincaid would own less than 5 percent of the company's shares. Garvice's plan didn't work, and while I don't know what happened to all the shares of KU stock they purchased, when I arrived at Kentucky Central to work for Mr. Forbush in 1981, we still had a large position of Kentucky Utility stock in Kentucky Central Life's portfolio. These were the shares that Cliff had purchased for Mr. Kincaid. KU paid a nice dividend in those days and also had a history of regularly increasing it, so Cliff said he decided to just hold on to it as an investment for the company. When interest rates started declining in the mid-1980s, we realized some substantial profits from those shares. Garvice may not have gotten on KU's board, but he made a lot of money off investing in them.

Cliff and Bud's Relationship

I think it would be fair to say that Cliff's relationship with Bud Burnett lacked the comradery that one hopes to find in their work circumstances. Bud tended to stay out of the investment area unless he needed something and really didn't use us as a professional resource. Bud seemed to understand that Cliff knew what he was doing, and after several years under Bud's leadership, Cliff just accepted that if Burnett wanted something, he would ask. Things did happen from time to time that created friction between the two men, but in the end, Burnett tended to leave Cliff alone.

One thing that happened around 1989 or 1990 involved both Kentucky Central Life and Central Bank. The company kept a large safety deposit box at Central Bank to hold all our investment securities, private placements, mortgage loan original documents, and other important documents. Investment securities were held via physical certificates back then, so Cliff was always going to the vault safety deposit box to deposit or pull out certificates. Accessing the box required two officers, and usually he took Tom Robinson, Kentucky Central Life's vice president of our tax division, or Wendell Gunn. In addition, our outside auditors would audit the box once a year to verify it held everything we said it did.

Well, one afternoon, Cliff needed to go to the vault, and he called Tom Robinson to go to the vault with him. They met at the vault and signed in, and it was a little before 4:00 and the bank's lobby closed at 4:00 and the vault was locked. About 4:10 we got a call in our department, and one of the bank's lobby officers wanted to know if Mr. Forbush was up there. We checked and he wasn't, and Tom Robinson wasn't back either. They called back five minutes later and asked if he was back yet, and we said no. Later the truth came out.

Apparently after Cliff pulled out what he needed from the vault, he and Tom Robinson just left. They closed the door to the box and took the company's key, and no one saw them. We learned later that Cliff had walked over to his wife's decorating shop on Short Street, and I guess Tom Robinson just went home. Evidently, they left, and the vault person never saw them leave, and their card was still out. The problem was that the vault door had been closed and locked since 4:00 and it was on a time lock. Remember, back then few people had cell phones.

Now the bank's people were becoming convinced that they'd locked them in the vault and the door was on a time lock. They called Wayne Smith, and he started calling around to see if Mr. Forbush was in the Trust Department. "No, he isn't here." A little after 4:30, Forbush came walking around the corner to our department, and we explained what was going on. He called them "damn fools" and got on the phone to the vault area to tell them that he and Robinson weren't in the vault. The bank was literally in the process of getting approval from the Committee to force the bank vault door open.

Another funny story about Mr. Forbush and locked doors involved an incident in about 1988. Kentucky Central experienced tremendous growth in the 1980s. The company made Universal Life its flagship product and was rapidly growing its independent distribution network of agents, Executive Marketing. A huge growth in sales meant the home office staff was struggling to keep up. I think Walter Rehfuss came up with the idea, and Burnett agreed, that the company needed an efficiency expert to come in and evaluate our operations and staff and make suggested changes to improve things. These types of consultants usually demand 100% support from the company's senior management and these consultants were no different. I guess they spent more than a year at Kentucky Central and not only looked at policyholder service departments but also stuck their face in every other department, including investments.

To begin the project, Burnett as CEO sent out a memo telling the whole company how important this project was and that attendance at all meetings was mandatory. In addition, we should be very cooperative with the consultants when they were in our departments. The company set up a series of meetings on the twenty-second floor where the consultants would educate people on their process and start listening to our departmental areas of concern. Again, attendance was mandatory! I don't recall why Mr. Forbush and I got scheduled in the same meeting, but we did. There had already been several meetings that week, and the word was out that the consultants locked the door, and if you arrived after the meeting had started, you wouldn't be allowed in. Someone forgot to tell Mr. Forbush, though.

I remember this moment like it was yesterday. We went into the room and took our seats. Two or three people from the consulting group were at the front of the room. Our meeting was an afternoon meeting, and I think it began at two o'clock. One consultant got up and closed the door, and I was scanning the room. No Mr. Forbush. The guy began discussing the importance of the project and how all of top management was behind the process. He was fully into his own B.S. It was about fifteen minutes into the meeting when we heard the doorknob rattle, and of course the door was locked. I think about half of us in the room knew that Mr. Forbush was on the other side of that door. The doorknob rattled again, and then knocking on the door started and people began to giggle. After a few minutes the guy finally gave up and went to the door and opened it.

Mr. Forbush: "SOME DAMN FOOL LOCKED THE DOOR."

Consultant: "You're late. People need to be on time or not come at all. That's why I locked the door."

Mr. Forbush: "YOU MEAN YOU ARE THE DAMN FOOL THAT LOCKED THE DOOR?"

The consultant started to open his mouth again and Mr. Forbush just shut him down.

Mr. Forbush: "WELL, I AM SORRY I AM LATE, BUT I WAS DOWNSTAIRS MAKING THIS COMPANY MONEY TO PAY YOUR BILL. I RUN A PROFIT CENTER AND WE HAVE A VERY SKINNY STAFF. WE ARE ALREADY EFFICENT; JUST ASK ANYONE ON WALL STREET."

The guy just looked at him and quietly said, "Well, you're here now; that's all that counts."

The only other thing I remember about this exchange is that Mr. Forbush got a call from Burnett the next day—I think it was courtesy of Rehfuss. Burnett told Mr. Forbush what he had heard, and I heard Mr. Forbush say, "The damn fool locked the door. . . . BUD, YOU KNOW WE RUN A PROFIT CENTER DOWN HERE,

AND WE DO A LOT WITH A VERY SMALL STAFF. RESULTS
ARE WHAT MATTER AND I WOULD PUT OURS UP AGAINST
ANYONE ELSE IN THE INSURANCE INDUSTRY."

The only time the consultants from this group stepped into our area was to talk to JoAnn about her accounting entry work. When they saw that we had to cut and paste info onto large annual statement sheets/pages to make the large required annual statement blue books, they thought we were nuts. Mr. Forbush heard them discussing this and walked out of his office.

Mr. Forbush: "CAN I HELP YOU?"

Consultant: "I see you do all of this cutting and pasting of pages, and I am thinking we can help you with this."

Mr. Forbush: "OH REALLY? WELL, THAT WOULD BE WONDERFUL, SINCE EVERY INSURANCE COMPANY IN THE COUNTRY HAS TO DO IT THE SAME WAY."

Mr. Forbush walked back to my office bookshelf and got the NAIC books that we used to price our securities. We would pour over these books for two days each February, finding our securities and getting the NAIC prices, and if a security wasn't priced in the book, we had to contact the NAIC to see if we could get them to provide one.

Mr. Forbush showed the guy the books.

Mr. Forbush: "SEE THIS. YOU MIGHT WANT TO START WITH THIS FIRST. WE GET THIS IN THE MAIL, LIKE EVERY OTHER INSURANCE COMPANY IN THE UNITED STATES, AND MANUALLY GO THROUGH THEM TO FIND OUR SECURITIES. IT TAKES ME AND MY ASSOCIATE TWO DAYS TO FIND THEM ALL AND TO FOLLOW UP WITH THE NAIC ON MISSING INFO.

MY SUGGESTION IS THAT IF YOU ARE GOING TO START MAKING CHANGES, YOU SHOULD PROBABLY CONTACT THE NAIC FIRST AND DISCUSS IT WITH THEM. THEIR NUMBER IS IN THIS BOOK!"

The guy looked at the book, JoAnn, and then Mr. Forbush, and just left. I never saw them again in our area, and as Paul Harvey said, "And now you know the rest of the story."

The consultants were at the company for well over a year, and many of the changes they made were undone shortly after they left, after various departments decided that making things more efficient doesn't always make the results better. One thing that they instituted before they left was a management training program. The consultants were concerned that the company had promoted a lot of employees into leadership roles, and they had no management training.

The company had a lot of talented employees who could get the work done but lacked the management training necessary to manage our large employee base. In other words, the company's rapid growth had created a workforce that needed to be less autocratic and adopt the professional management principles that most successful businesses were using in the 1980s.

This next story is about something that happened in fall of 1991, and it was probably the only time I saw Cliff humbled by Burnett. In fairness to Cliff, 1991 had been a traumatic year for everyone at the company. It was a period when people both inside and outside the company were beginning to recognize that Burnett's mortgage loan and real estate deals were sinking faster than the Titanic. The company was involved in a special state audit of these investments and had raised capital by selling both Kentucky Finance and the Career Division. In addition, the company's chief actuary had suddenly taken early retirement at age 56 at the end of 1990. My point is that Cliff's lapse of judgment should be considered in relation to everything that was happening. Emotions were raw, and there was general unspoken uncertainty.

Well, on this fall day back in 1991, Cliff needed to pull a security out of the vault. We had sold something and needed to ship it to an investment banking house for settlement. In those days, transactions settled in five business days. I recall it was a late Thursday afternoon and Cliff called Wendell Gunn to meet him at the vault, and he went on down. Gunn was running about fifteen or twenty minutes late, so Cliff became frustrated and bullied his way into the vault and our box. They knew him and were a little intimidated by him. He told them Gunn would be along any minute and he would go ahead and get the security out. The young lady let him in, and he retrieved the security from our box and then left. Wendell Gunn then came along and asked where Mr. Forbush was, and the young lady told him he'd gotten what he needed and left. Gunn knew Forbush had screwed up and didn't want to be complicit, so he called Burnett.

Burnett went down to the vault and talked with the young lady and then called Forbush down. I don't think Forbush realized how much trouble he was in. Burnett was mad, and Forbush knew it. He said we needed to have the vault box audited immediately and called Tom Freeman, head of Audit Services, to come down and audit the box. Freeman contacted Jo Ann Conner, who handled our investment accounting, to get a listing was what should be in the vault. Burnett then had Forbush and Gunn sit in one of the bank's customer conference rooms for the next two hours or so while Tom Freeman conducted his audit of the box. Of course, everything was in order, and Freeman called Burnett and told him so, but now the bank wanted to know who would sign the second signature on the vault card. Burnett said he would sign it and came down and signed it under Forbush's name. I don't think I ever saw Cliff intimidated by Mr. Burnett until that day. As someone later said, he got his wings clipped that day.

Of course, it was all over the building by the next morning, Wendell Gunn made sure of that. I remember Cliff coming in my office that afternoon at about 6 p.m. and telling me what had just happened. He said he was stupid, but then proceeded to blame Wendell Gunn for not coming down sooner. Cliff still had a decent relationship with Burnett, though, but maybe he was a little less intimidating for a few weeks. As I said, I think the stress of the company's situation caused this lapse in judgement more than anything else.

After Kincaid's death, Burnett seemed to have confidence that Cliff would just come to him with any problems and recognized that he would invest the company's assets prudently in bonds, preferred stocks, and common stocks. Burnett, like Kincaid, would handle all the company's mortgage loan and real estate investments, which he did to the company's detriment.

According to Cliff, he initially tried writing white papers on different subjects and sending them to Burnett. For instance, he might go to an investment conference and hear of something pertaining to investment law changes, or how the economic outlook was changing, or something other insurance companies were doing. Cliff would author a report and interoffice it to Burnett. He said he did this for about three years after Kincaid died, and never once did he receive any feedback from Burnett. I know this bothered him, and I think on some level he felt snubbed, but he was professional and just continued doing his job. After a couple of years of not sending Burnett any white papers, Cliff said he decided he should just do his job, and if Burnett had an issue or a question, he could come to him. The problem was that this was the way many of Kentucky Central Life's senior management staff were working with Burnett.

An example of how Burnett dealt with the officers can be seen in how he handled their annual performance reviews. There were none! He would just stop by the officer's office, go in, close the door, and be out in less than five minutes. The whole purpose of his visit was to inform Cliff and others what their raise was going to be for the coming year. I imagine this is probably similar to how Garvice did it.

In 1980, five years after Kincaid's death and four years after the eviction of David Brain, Burnett had done nothing to develop any kind of internal strategic planning process, and he was still managing the company in his autocratic way. The difference from Kincaid, though, was that under Garvice, one knew he made the final decision on things but that he also liked hearing input, while Burnett avoided it. In 1983, as the $50 billion in-force goal planning was moving forward, no one inside the company questioned its rationale, did sensitivity modeling of the company's financials to see how it would impact them, or more importantly asked where the company would earn 11% on its investments to support the initial proposed interest rate on the company's first UL product, VIP Life. In most insurance companies, this would be a function that the chief actuary would perform.

In 1972, William T. Tozer was recruited to Kentucky Central as its chief actuary. The thirty-eight-year-old Tozer grew up in Illinois and graduated with an actuarial degree from the University of Illinois in 1957. He moved to Cedar Rapids, Iowa, in 1960 and worked for American Republic Life Insurance Company in its actuarial department. American Republic was licensed in forty-six states and had double the premium and investment income of Kentucky Central Life. In 1963, Bill was promoted to vice president in charge of both the data processing and actuarial departments. Bill enjoyed actuarial science but had a passion for what computers could do. Actuarial work involved the dry crunching of numbers and statistics, while the world of computerization was evolving and expanding the pace and scope of work.

In 1966, Tozer was made responsible for the installation of IBM's new next-generation computer system in American Republic's new corporate headquarters. This work brought him accolades from IBM, and the computer manufacturer even flew him to Amsterdam to speak at an international conference on computerization in the life insurance industry. In 1967, American Republic began the development of its first variable-annuity product. Variable-annuity products were relatively new to the industry and complicated to create and administer. Tozer may not have enjoyed the new direction the company was taking, because by 1971 he'd moved back to Chicago to work for United Insurance Company of America, where he was just a staff actuary. United sold only traditional life and health products. In August 1972, when Tozer joined Kentucky Central Life as its chief actuary, the press release reported that his primary responsibilities would be product development and cost analysis.

Throughout Tozer's career, he was active in the Society of Actuaries and the American Academy of Actuaries, and he participated in many their working-group panels over the years. Many of the studies involved proposed changes to reserving and the valuation of business and how they would affect companies. In 1983, he certainly had the knowledge and the industry contacts to evaluate a new product like universal life and how Burnett's $50 billion in force goal would affect the company, but he didn't. When Kentucky Central's universal-life product was being developed in 1983, I recall one brief discussion between Cliff Forbush and Tozer about what investment returns we could obtain. The rate for ten-year fixed -income securities were approximately 11 to 13 percent in 1983 but by 1984 had drifted lower to about 10 to 12 percent and by 1986 had dropped another 1 percent to 9 to 11 percent.

While universal life was new to America, it had been available in Canada since about 1970. In fact, the president of the Canadian Institute of Actuaries, in a speech at its annual meeting in 1971, discussed the positives and negatives of the product and demonstrated them through a fictious story about a company called Cannibal Life. The main theme of his presentation was that universal life addressed the changing needs of society so well that companies had to accept the fact that a large portion of their existing in-force ordinary whole-life business would be cannibalized by either competitor agents or their own agents.

This is exactly the effect Kentucky Central Life's VIP Life had on its existing block of ordinary whole-life business. The company's new business department was inundated with what are known as 1035 (tax-free) exchanges. Much of the company's new business, from 1983 to about 1986, involved replacing whole-life policies with VIP Life. The company's agents were replacing Kentucky Central Life's whole-life policies and other companies' whole-life policies, due to the competitive nature of the product. What seems strange now, after reading about what happened in Canada several years before this, is how frustrated Kentucky Central Life's management and employees were about this. They should have expected it, based on Canada's experience. But if it was expected, Burnett, Tozer, and others did a very poor job of communicating it.

I personally believe that it was never discussed or anticipated until it actually started happening and that Burnett and Tozer thought they could control the number of internal replacements. In his speech about Cannibal Life, the association's president addressed this specific issue and suggested that if a company didn't provide for internal replacements, then competitor agents would replace the business. His point was that a large percentage of whole-life customers would naturally want the better economics of the policy. A significant point he never addressed, though, was how poorly universal-life policies perform in a low-interest-rate environment. Agents were replacing many whole-life policies that had cash value and illustrating how the higher crediting rates would pay for their annual cost of insurance. A problem developed when crediting rates dropped to the 6 to 7 percent range. The illustrations failed, and policyholders were then forced to make premium payments or lose their insurance. In addition, as the policyholder grew older, their cost of insurance increased.

The insurance industry generally categorizes whole-life and universal-life insurance as "permanent" life insurance. A permanent policy is designed to provide coverage for the insured's entire life if sufficient premiums are paid. This is unlike term life insurance, which provides coverage at a set rate for a set amount of time (for example, twenty years). Whole-life insurance policies have level premiums and a set death benefit, meaning you pay the same amount every year for a set amount of coverage. Universal-life insurance offers flexibility, meaning you may be able to adjust your premiums and coverage amounts. Both forms of permanent insurance have the potential to accumulate cash value over time.

The main expense of a universal-life policy is the cost-of-insurance charge. The cost-of-insurance charge is the amount you must pay to fund the policy's death benefit. As a person ages, the rate of the cost-of-insurance charge increases. Policyholders may have some options that provide for level premiums or allow the policy to be paid in full by a certain age. However, due to changes in the charges and crediting rates, the consumer needs to continuously monitor and manage the policy to assure that coverage will last as long as intended.

Many consumers purchased their policies expecting a period of level premium payments based on the policy assumptions at the time of sale. These assumptions include the cost-of-insurance rates and interest rates (or investment returns). If the cost-of-insurance charge increases or interest rates decrease, their cash value may not be sufficient to cover the costs of the contract over time, and additional premiums may be required to keep the contract in force. This is what happened by the late 1990s and 2000s with most of the universal-life policies sold in the 1980s.

When Kentucky Central introduced VIP Life in September 1983, its initial non-guaranteed rate was 11 percent. This rate would remain unchanged for the next six years, through December 1990. On January 1, 1991, the company dropped the rate to 10 percent and held it there through July 31, 1991, when it was reduced to 9.5 percent through December 31, 1991. On January 1, 1992, it was again reduced to 9 percent; on March 1, 1992, it went to 8 percent, where it remained until the Insurance Department took over the company in February 1993. By 1990, the failure of Burnett's emperor's-new-clothes investment strategy of high-interest-rate mortgage loans was on display for everyone to see.

When VIP Life was introduced, the product was the equivalent of an ordinary whole-life insurance policy on steroids. The product offered a better return to the consumer, and the agent was able to earn a higher commission due to the complexity of the sale and the larger policy amounts. The product was created with a tremendous amount of what is known as "front-end load" (commissions, bonuses, and expenses), such that heavy sales of it would quickly use up a lot of the company's surplus. Kentucky Central Life's product was one of the most competitive, which also means one of the most expensive. A typical whole-life policy might pay 40 percent of the first year's premium in commissions, while VIP Life carried a 70 percent commission rate. In addition to the commission, the managing general agent and the selling agent could earn production bonuses for volume and quality and of course wonderful trips to places like Hawaii, England, and Las Vegas.

VIP Life was also more expensive to underwrite because the individual policy amounts were larger. With large cases, the insurance company might order "MIBs" (a person's medical history from the Medical Information Bureau), order a physical inspection, or request a person's actual medical record. If the case was large enough, a physical examination might be requested. These tests and reports are expensive, and combined with VIP Life's commission schedule and other sales incentives, it probably cost the company between 110 and 120 percent of a policy's first-year premium to put it on the books.

The profitability profile of many life insurance products requires an up-front expense that is capitalized as an investment. This is called "deferred acquisition cost" (DAC), and it's carried in the company's financial statements as an asset and gets amortized over five to ten years, depending on the product. If a significant number of policies lapse, exceeding what was projected, then DAC is amortized quicker. The intent of DAC is to spread the costs associated with selling a policy against the future profits it should produce.

Regulatory or statutory accounting immediately expenses these costs through the income statement, so they're a reduction to a company's balance sheet. It's the most conservative method, and it's used by regulators to evaluate a company's capital position. The reason for this is that DAC isn't an asset that can be liquidated for monetary value. You can't pay for anything with it, just as accumulated depreciation can't be used to pay for anything. This became important at Kentucky Central Life because by 1991, the company had a DAC position of 27.5 percent of its assets, which meant that it showed GAAP equity of 16 percent. Most life insurance companies have a DAC position of 2 to 5 percent of their GAAP assets. Kentucky Central Life's DAC had ballooned due to all the new business sold to reach Burnett's in-force goal. Over the last seven years, the company had written enough new business to increase its in-force to over $55 billion from $11 billion at the end of 1983. This fivefold increase in new business had increased the company's DAC to $513 million from $101 million. As a comparison, in 1980, the company's DAC was 16.4 percent, and at the beginning of 1984 it was 15 percent, but it had ballooned to 27.5 percent by 1991.

In 1991, during the Insurance Department examination, on a regulatory or statutory basis, the company had about 2.5 percent of statutory equity. This was why the Insurance Department was so concerned. Statutory accounting focuses directly on the solvency of a company, while GAAP accounting strives to capture the long-term economic value of an enterprise by capitalizing certain expenses as investments and amortizing them against future profits. Statutory accounting is concerned with making sure a company can pay its liabilities today, not how much it might earn in the future. It's a better measure of the possible risk of failure.

Burnett always discussed the company's percentage of mortgage loans and real estate as a percentage of the company's GAAP assets, which included over $513 million of DAC. It was a ridiculous and inappropriate comparison. During 1991, Bud would argue that the company had only 23.7 percent of the its assets invested in commercial mortgage loans and real estate, using GAAP total assets as the divisor, but if one excluded DAC, the actual number was 33 percent and the company's statutory equity was only $88 million, or 2.5 percent of total assets. A 10 percent impairment in the value of the company's $440 million of commercial mortgage loans and real estate would have reduced the company's capital by 50 percent. In 1991, the Insurance Department could see the company had a major solvency issue.

Burnett would also say that Garvice had always invested 30 percent to 40 percent of the company's assets in mortgage loans and real estate. This was technically true but avoided a few relevant facts.

When Garvice Kincaid was making commercial mortgage loans for the company, he was realistically risking his own money. In fact, in various interviews, he suggested this was one of his strengths. Any mistakes were his. Yes, Kentucky Central Life had outside shareholders, but Garvice had the wherewithal to move problem loans or assets to his personal estate.

Garvice never overconcentrated his risks. He was a prudent investor and would never have concentrated 40 percent of the company's mortgage loans and real estate investments with entities under the control of one person or group. Kincaid had a history of not destroying problem borrowers. He would work with a problem borrower and give him an opportunity to restructure the deal or bring in another partner. Generally, these restructurings weren't very successful and he would end up owning the property, but he would never do business with the person again. As my old boss, Cliff Forbush, would say, Kincaid would "cut them off at the knees; they were blackballed." What he didn't do was cut their throats. Garvice was well known for saying "things didn't work out like I thought; I was wrong." Kincaid expected people to be honest with him, and if they were, he would take back the property and decide how to deal with it. After Kincaid acquired Kentucky Central Life, he maintained a capital ratio of 11 percent to 13 percent. When he made life insurance acquisitions, the company's capital ratio might fall to the low end of this range, but it was never below 10 percent. He always maintained a strong balance sheet and a diversified portfolio of investments, which protected the company. Bud Burnett was reckless; he drove the company's capital ratio below 5 percent and refinanced other lenders' problem loans with Kentucky Central Life's assets. He didn't manage the company like it was his money. Garvice didn't invest in geographic areas of the country he wasn't familiar with or invest in projects when he didn't fully understand the business risks. Cliff Forbush told me on more than one occasion that Kincaid would say he preferred to invest in areas he could drive to. Garvice wasn't provincial and certainly didn't have a problem with flying, but he liked to easily follow the progress of his investments.

Burnett was borderline stupid and/or incompetent, and his need for approval made him easily influenced by fawning people giving him respect and admiration. He invested in areas of the country he and his staff knew nothing about—Colorado, San Franscisco, New Mexico, Michigan, and Texas. I discussed this with John Rampulla and Cliff Forbush, and they agreed with me that Burnett had no mortgage-loan strategy and Dudley Webb had become his unofficial real estate expert. Burnett also differed from Kincaid in how he looked at real estate projects. Where Kincaid evaluated financial projections, business risks, and the financial strength of the borrower or partner, Burnett appears to have relied more on gut instinct. According to reports, borrowers claimed he made loans without reviewing and questioning the financial forecasts. Garvice would never enter a partnership where he was the only one with any money unless he had an ulterior motive. Also, after he made his Joyland Park investment, he preferred partnerships where he retained voting control. By 1989, the company's problems were becoming more apparent, and there was no way Burnett could turn anything over to anyone. Rehfuss and Gunn may have wanted to run the company, but it would never happen. The pressures from the company's rapid growth and the developing financial problems from Burnett's failed investment strategy soon took their toll on

Rehfuss, and he died in June of 1990 at the young age of fifty-three. The company had achieved its $50 billion in-force goal in March, but at a high cost. There was little time to celebrate because the company's problems were mounting. Larry Sammartin, who had worked so hard to achieve this sales goal, would be dead by November 1992, while Bill Tozer, the company's chief actuary, had quietly retired from the company in early 1990 at the age of fifty-six. Bill Tozer leaving the company surprised some people, like my boss Cliff Forbush, who in later years suspected that Tozer understood just how fragile the financial foundation of the company had been but never said anything. Cliff always felt that Gunn and Tozer betrayed him and the rest of the company by not speaking up about what they knew.

I hadn't spoken to Wendell Gunn in over ten years when, in 2005, I discovered him in Deston, Florida. We discussed the company's last years, and he insisted that Burnett kept everything so close to the vest that what little he did know was nothing compared to what came out after the state took the company over. While Gunn never paid a fine, in August 1995, the SEC took him to task in an official SEC auditing and enforcement action. After investigating Kentucky Central Life in conjunction with the State of Kentucky Insurance Department, they found Gunn had materially misstated the company financial statements from 1989 to1992.

Gunn was criticized for knowing about the restructured mortgage loans and the uncollectable capitalized interest income; for not disclosing the company's full relationship with the company's largest creditor/developer, Dudley Webb, including that it had $143 million of loans related to him, it had modified the terms on $71 million of these loans, and it was committed to lend an additional $18 million to him; and finally for the company having created, with a third-party lender, a $16 million contingent liability to cover a loan that Webb received from a third-party bank.

In addition, SEC investigators were extremely critical of Gunn's involvement in the 1991 (Deloitte) analysis of the company's mortgage loans; they said he failed to disclose that instead of using an appraisal, he and the company had used unrealistic eight-year cash flow projections provided by the developer. These projections assumed the properties would be 100 percent leased in twelve months and in some cases that the vacant space would be leased at a rate higher than current rates, with no estimation of the costs and leasing commissions needed to get the properties leased. Gunn and others at the company took these projections and used them as a starting point and then modeled the properties over a thirty-year time, discounted at 8 to 10 percent to develop a "modeled value" for the property.

Two of the properties, even using the most favorable discount rate of 8 percent, could not recover their value, but the company ignored this and still carried them at $3.7 million more than their projection. If the company had just used the current appraisals it had, the appraised values for the $78 million properties supporting the restructured credit agreement would have been $26 million, or 33 percent less than what the company recorded. The SEC wrote that Gunn and the management should have concluded that all the properties backing the credit agreement were "in-substance foreclosures."

The SEC's final criticism summary violation was the harshest:

> From at least 1989 and continuing until 1992 Kentucky Central Life had virtually no system of internal accounting controls, to monitor losses inherent in its mortgage loan portfolio and evaluate the adequacy of its allowance for loan losses. Gunn knew that Kentucky Central's system of internal counting controls related to mortgage loans was inadequate.

Gunn's Violations:

> Gunn, as Kentucky Central Life's principal financial and accounting officer, was responsible for preparing Kentucky Central Life's filings with the Commission at all relevant times. He also reviewed and signed the 1990 Form 10-K and the quarterly reports prior to Kentucky Central Life filing them with the Commission. As described above, Kentucky Central Life materially understated its allowance and provision for mortgage loan losses, overstated its net income, and made materially false and misleading statements in the 1990 Form 10-K and the quarterly reports for the quarters ended June 30 and September 30, 1990, and March 31 and June 30, 1991. As described above, Gunn knew, or was reckless in not knowing, that the allowance for mortgage loan losses and the related provision were materially understated and that Kentucky Central Life's earnings were materially overstated. He also knew that material facts concerning Kentucky Central Life's financial exposure to its largest borrower were not disclosed. With respect to the quarterly reports for the quarters ended March 31 and June 30, 1992, Gunn knew that Kentucky Central Life was improperly recognizing a material amount of interest income that could not be collected on loans for which it previously had established an allowance.

Gunn and his wife Roberta had retired to Florida by the time this SEC final enforcement order came out. From what I understand, after the Insurance Department took over the company, he had quickly put all his assets in either a trust or Roberta's name to protect them. He wasn't fined by the SEC, but he was ordered "to cease and desist from committing or causing violations and any future violations of Sections l0(b), 13(a) and 13(b)(2)(B) of the Exchange Act and Rules l0b-5, 13a-l, 13a-13 and 12b-20 thereunder." These statutes all pertain to financial statement misrepresentation.

I think part of the reason the SEC was lenient with Gunn was that he was the first person to quickly step up and try to help the state of Kentucky, the SEC, and others try to figure out what happened. In addition, his complicity happened near the end, after things had snowballed so badly for Burnett. At one point, in early 1994, I heard from someone helping to manage the company for the state that Gunn had said he was "happy to testify for anyone that needed him."

In addition, Gunn's compensation wasn't exorbitant. Here's what he made during his last five years of employment: 1988: $125,694; 1989: $153,193; 1990: $131,286; 1991: $143,593, and 1992: $151,851. It's a nice salary, but not the kind of money a person would knowingly commit fraud over. I think Gunn was banking on John Lang and ultimately the WHR deal to bail out the company in 1992. He spent as much time as anyone putting together everything, with and for John Lang. It doesn't explain why he did what he did in 1990 and 1991, but I doubt he even understood everything Burnett had done. He had worked closely with Burnett for over twenty years, and he thought he probably knew or at least understood the man, but nobody really understood everything Bud Burnett was doing, so by 1991, he probably felt trapped by his loyalty to Burnett.

Bud Burnett had made all the loans and negotiated all the restructuring agreements, so he was the person most responsible, but he died in December 1993 and you can't put a dead man in jail. Burnett's grave, in the Lexington Cemetery, is less than 150 feet from Kincaid's grave, and many of my Kentucky Central Life colleagues and I hope that Garvice is visiting Burnett on a regular basis.

Something else happened in May 1991. The rating agency Standard & Poor's downgraded the company from A to A- and maintained its negative outlook. The rating agency A.M. Best would follow suit in July and downgrade the company from A to A-. Two years earlier, A.M. Best had given the company a rating of A+. The downgrade created a mountain of agent- and policyowner-related concerns, with many agents counseling their policyowners to switch their policy to a new carrier. The red flags also made it to Frankfort, Kentucky, where the state of Kentucky had $190 million of its employees' deferred compensation plan invested with the company. The state quickly renegotiated its contract and began a series of scheduled withdrawals. It withdrew $33 million in 1991 and another $105 million in 1992 and early 1993, leaving a balance of $85 million to be concerned with after the state takeover. This money belonged to twenty-seven thousand state and local government employees.

Just before the Kentucky State Retirement System negotiated the withdrawal of its money, the Kentucky Department of Insurance was inside the company conducting a financial examination. The state said it wasn't a special examination, just the company's normal examination done every four years. I was there, and this was no ordinary Insurance Department examination. The examination required that Kentucky Central Life pay Deloitte and Touche, the company's auditor, to do a special examination of the company's mortgage loan and real estate investments. Deloitte had a team of about ten people pouring over Burnett's investments, trying to understand what they were and what their valuation should be. It was a challenging project due to how many loans had been restructured multiple times and/or converted to real estate partnerships. Plus, the company had done a poor job of obtaining the financials for many of the projects.

The examination began in late 1990 and wasn't completed until the fall of 1991, and by June 1991, Deloitte was already sharing its findings with the state. This is around the same time the Retirement System began withdrawing its money. Deloitte's report indicated that the company should take a $75.8 million impairment on these investments. In addition to Kentucky, the states of Ohio and Nevada also participated in the examination but were not allowed to review Deloitte's work or its report. In the end, the company set up only a $30 million reserve for losses, and when the Kentucky legislature's bank and finance committee wanted to question former Insurance Commissioner Elizabeth Wright, she refused their request.

In the end, an attorney for the Insurance Department, Patrick Watts, indicated in a letter that he recalled Burnett resisting the $75.8 million number and that he believed the final number was negotiated between the department (the commissioner) and the company. He also implied that the examiners were willing to temper their comments because of the $30 million reserve. Remember that in April 1991, Burnett sold the company's profitable career sales division and those policies to Liberty Life for $39 million and then in May 1991 agreed to sell Kentucky Finance to Ford Motor Credit for about $145 million, which was a $65 million premium over the equity invested in the division. Burnett knew he would be realizing more losses but was trying to delay taking them.

When the 1990 annual report was released in April 1991, the company had set up a $30 million reserve. When the financial adjustments were finalized for the year, the company's statutory surplus had dropped $20 million to

$62.86 million. This was just 4.8 percent of the company's statutory assets, a range that provided little cushion for future problems. Behind the scenes, the examiners had determined that the company's surplus was overstated due to the number of loans not producing income and required this to be corrected. Now, if the company's asset values declined by just 5 percent, the company would be insolvent. I believe one of the reasons the Insurance Department agreed to a $30 million reserve, versus the $75.8 million that Deloitte's work had suggested, was that the larger reserve would have reduced the company's surplus to $17 million, which would have required the state to take over the company, which they were trying to avoid.

From 1987 to 1990, fixed-income investment rates had stayed in a range of 8.5 percent to 9.5 percent, and yet Burnett continued to hold our universal-life crediting rate at 11 percent and didn't reduce this rate until he was pressured by the concerns of the rating agencies and state insurance departments. They were concerned about the company's excessive exposure to mortgage loans and real estate. In addition, over the prior three years, he had sold off profitable radio stations, completed a sale lease-back of the company's home office building, accomplished a partially failed secondary offering of Kentucky Central Life's common stock, and finally in 1991 was forced to sell the company's profitable career agency block of in-force business and its agencies and then its crown jewel, Kentucky Finance. By selling these two operations, he had removed over $25 million (71 percent) of the company's annual earnings. In 1989 and 1990 (before write-offs) the company had reported $35 million in annual earnings.

In 1984 and subsequent years, Burnett began making 100 percent leveraged, 12 percent interest rate commercial mortgage loans. The loans provided the company with the necessary 1 percent spread to cover the 11 percent crediting rate on VIP Life, irrespective of whether this investment strategy was a responsible strategy. One of the initial problems with the loans was the fact that they were speculative construction and development loans, and in areas of the country that Burnett knew little about. A second issue was an overconcentration of lending to three or four borrowing groups.

I doubt that Bud Burnett planned to do the amount of mortgage lending he did. Many of Burnett's actions tended to be responses to what was happening in the moment. From his perspective, he wasn't gambling with the company's assets, just doing what was necessary to maintain the company's competitive position in the universal-life market. He probably assumed things would get rebalanced over time, just like a gambler will assume his luck has to change. Whatever Burnett's logic was, he never recognized that as long as he prolonged this strategy, he was actually doubling down on his gambling bets. As various mortgage loans failed, he needed to restructure and repackage the problem loan or asset into another loan to keep his Ponzi-like lending scheme going. He was literally capitalizing the interest Kentucky Central Life never received into new loans to support his 11 percent crediting rate strategy. This capitalized interest was initially classified as interest income on the company's financial statements but was eventually written off during the early 1990s.

In addition, consider that two years of capitalized interest on an initial 100 percent leveraged loan means that the property is now 124 percent leveraged. What Bud Burnett was doing could be classified as accounting fraud because he was recognizing income that realistically would never be recovered. Finally, many of the restructured loans never had one mortgage payment made or were turned into "cash flow loans" and little, if any, cash flow was ever received by the company. Of course, when a restructured loan didn't magically improve, Burnett would either convert it into a joint-venture partnership with the current borrower or another unrelated third party or, as a last resort, take the property back from the borrower as real estate owned. The main thing was to avoid writing down its value on Kentucky Central Life's financial statements.

I can't take credit for the following comparison; someone else said it to me years after the company was gone, but it thoroughly describes the company's situation in the late 1980s and early 1990s. Bud Burnett was the "man behind the curtain" in The Wizard of Oz.

> Do you presume to criticize the Great Oz? You ungrateful creatures think yourselves lucky that I'm giving you audience tomorrow instead of 20 years from Now. The Great Oz has spoken! Oh, oh, pay no attention to the man behind the curtain.[18]

In April 1991, Burnett sold the cornerstone of the company's business, its Career Agent Division, to Liberty Life Insurance in South Carolina for $39 million. The sales proceeds were used to replenish Kentucky Central Life's capital that had been lost through his aggressive real estate lending. To further add insult to this transaction, in February 1991, the company's home office and field publication, Horizons, did a full-page story, with a large picture of Bob Casher and Tom Stinnett, announcing that the division would be adding personnel and field agents in 1991. In addition, it recognized the better quality and persistence of the division's life business. The old adage that the left hand doesn't know what the right hand is doing was never more on display. Bob Casher retired shortly after April, and in July 1991, Tom Stinnett and some of his staff were transferred to a new unit in Executive Marketing called

---

18   The Wizard of Oz, 1939 (movie).

"Quality Control." Casher had devoted thirty-seven years to the company, and specifically the Career Agency Division, only to see it sold off like a valuable family heirloom to pay for Burnett's mistakes.

David Brain had created a strong marketing organization, one that produced substantial profits for the organization over the years. Brain had also instilled a tremendous amount of employee and agent devotion to both the company and himself. Tom Stinnett's devotion to the company was a product of the loyalty that Brain had created. In addition, as I did, Tom met his future bride, Barb, at the company, and in 1972 they were married.

People's relationships and loyalty to the company cannot be understated, and in talking with Tom about those years, he told me a story that demonstrates how people went the extra mile.

A Picture Worth a Thousand Words or at Least a Good Flood

Tom Stinnett joined the company in 1970, and he spent much of his career working with Bob Casher in the company's career division. In the early 1970s the company held an agent awards conference in New Orleans. David Brain and his wife were there, along with others from the company. What made this conference so memorable was that the city was experiencing its worst flooding since 1927. It was reported that more than two dozen people died, and the damage was estimated at $427 million. But the levees held and prevented a much greater catastrophe. For the first time in the city's history, a major flood had been successfully diverted to the sea.

The company's meetings began just before the storm's arrival, but before the meetings were over several of the streets around the French Quarter had begun to flood. Well, twenty-six-year-old Tom was also at the conference, and he'd never experienced anything like this, but the locals didn't seem to have a problem with streets beginning to flood and he knew the conference was ending the next day. Well, Tom got a call from David Brain that evening because he and his wife, Frances, needed to leave the next morning. Apparently, that morning they'd been walking around the French Quarter and found a shop that had a painting they liked, so David wanted Tom to go there the next morning and buy it for him. The problem was that Brain and his wife couldn't recall the name of the shop or who the artist who created the painting was, but David told Tom the street the shop was on and the name of some business that was nearby.

I guess Brain really wanted the painting, because the next morning Tom got a call from him reminding him to buy this painting for him. Tom assured him he would head there first thing that morning, but he was concerned because he wasn't quite sure about the actual shop or the painting. All he had is a vague description of the painting.

Tom said, "You have to understand the streets were flooded," and so he walked around the flooding street of the French Quarter with his pants rolled up as he waded through the water. He said he found the shop without too much of a problem and the owner remembered David and Frances from the previous morning, which made him feel better. Tom said he told him David's vague description of the painting and the guy said, "This is it" and showed it to him. Tom was a little worried but purchased what the guy showed him. He then took it back to the hotel and started looking for a place that could package it for him so he could take it on the plane.

He said when he finally got back to Lexington and he went to the office, he left the painting in his car but soon got a call from David asking if he had it. He told him he did and it was in his car. He guessed David wasn't in the office then, because he arranged for someone else to come to Tom's car and collect the painting and take it to his office.

When Tom found out that I'd been interviewing David Brain's daughters, Nancy and Diane, he said, "I have thought about that painting many times over the years and wondered what happened to it. I didn't know if it was for David's office or what, but if you talk to them again, please asked them if they recall the painting and what happened to it."

After speaking with Tom, I contacted them and told them Tom's story and received this update from Nancy:

> We know the painting and remember when my parents acquired it. They hung it over the bed in our former bedroom. Mom was very proud of it. She said it reminded her of us. When she returned to the hotel, she asked Dad if she could buy it. Of course, Dad said yes. She asked for very little, but Dad gave her all that she wanted and more.

In Nancy's opinion the painting was ordinary and conventional, but she thought the story behind it was both revealing and meaningful. The story was meaningful because she never knew the lengths their dad went to to buy this painting for her mother, and she also doubted that her father asked his employees to do personal errands for him very often, but she assumed this painting had been important to their mother and thus became important to him. She said, "It is yet another insight into the complexities of our lives."

I like this story because it demonstrates how Kentucky Central Life employees all worked for the good of the company and each other.

The 1991 divestures of the Career Agency Division and its business and Kentucky Finance did help calm the waters a little. The transactions increased the company's surplus to $95 million, which was a 7.25 percent surplus position. This was still considered low, but it was a reasonable amount of equity for many life insurance companies. The problem was that Kentucky Central Life was not a normal company. Burnett's high-risk mortgage loans and bad loans converted into real estate partnerships were still overvalued by over $100 million. Kentucky Central Life wasn't a normal company, and the man leading it was in denial. In 1991, he was drowning in a pool of garbage mortgage loan and real estate investments and blaming the company's problems on real estate tax law changes, rumors by short sellers, libelous attacks by competitor agents, and anything else he could come up with.

The Insurance Department knew the company's problems weren't behind it and ordered the company to provide quarterly financial and cash flow statements to it and to hire consultants to advise on its problem real estate investments. During the audit, it had found that the company's loan files for problem and restructured loans were a mess. Loans converted to cash-flow basis loans were not being followed and documented, and partnerships where the only partner with any money was Kentucky Central Life were not being accounted for correctly. These problems were not documented in the department's examination but were discussed, and the Department ordered these problems be resolved during the reserve negotiations.

By the end of 1991, as things continued to deteriorate, the department ordered the company to bring in some outside expertise to help it come up with a restructuring plan and potentially raise additional capital. In addition, by the beginning of 1992, the company was ordered not to make any more investments in real estate or mortgage loans without the department's approval.

Access to Capital and WHR

In December 1991, Burnett brought in John Lang from Lang Capital, and for the next twelve months the company worked with Lang and his associate Frank Dinucci on a plan. It was a secret project and probably involved only about ten company employees. John and Frank poured over the company's mortgage loans, reviewed each of the company's downstream subsidiaries, and began reviewing the company's options with Burnett, Schaeffer, and Wendell Gunn. The problem was that while Lang felt he could liquidate some of the company's mortgage loan and real estate investments, further losses would be realized. Lang offered Burnett three options.

- Option one: Allow him to quietly contact some investors about bringing in some outside capital. He explained that they would want seats on the board of directors and that there would be a significant change in how the company would be managed going forward.

- Option two: Look at selling Bluegrass Broadcasting's television and radio properties, Brevard Groves, the P&C companies, and any other non-core assets and creating pools of mortgage loans and non-performing real estate that could be auctioned off.

- Option three: Sell the whole company to either another insurance company or a third-party investor with the capital to help the company navigate out of its problems.

In the end, Burnett wasn't happy with any of the options but decided to try option one. In October, Lang brought in the vulture investor Marty Whitman, who was a pioneer deep-value investor and the originator of the Third Avenue Fund. Whitman was a legendary investor and someone Lang had worked with at Merrill Lynch. Whitman and his partner Kirk Rein Jr. quickly began reviewing the company's information that had been assembled in the board of directors' meeting room. Burnett and Lang had turned the room into a war room soon after the project started.

Marty Whitman had been working with his partners James Heffernan and Kirk Rein Jr. (WHR) for several years, and they were known to represent the interests of many pension funds, endowments, foundations, and institutional investors, who invested with them. Their analysis continued for about a week, and eventually the private investors and Burnett came to an agreement after one final meeting where Whitman looked Burnett in the eye and asked, "If anything happened to you, who would run the company?" Lang said Burnett immediately looked over at Schaeffer and pointed and said, "He would." Lang said Whitman just quietly sat there and nodded, and he and Rein regrouped and phoned their partner, James Heffernan, back in New York.

On Monday, December 7, 1992, Whitman and Burnett signed a letter of intent stating that Whitman's Heffernan & Rein Workout Fund II and IIA, limited partnerships, would provide Kentucky Central Life with up to $100 million of capital in exchange for three new board of directors seats.

The letter of intent indicated that WHR would purchase units consisting of (a) 3,661,327 shares of newly issued Class A nonvoting common stock and (b) convertible mezzanine securities with a par value of approximately $96,338,673 and a floating-rate coupon that would produce an interest rate lower than Kentucky Central's return on assets. The investment would be redeemable by WHR after ten years and would be callable at any time by Kentucky Central Life.

The letter of intent also provided that Kentucky Central Life would annually elect two board members nominated by the holders of the mezzanine securities. In addition, one independent board member would be designated mutually by the mezzanine securities holders and Kentucky Central Life. The transaction was subject to completion of further due diligence, the execution of a definitive agreement, and the necessary regulatory approvals. In addition, the mezzanine securities could be converted into 8,399,187 shares of Class A nonvoting stock.

In short, if WHR's due-diligence staff found the information they were shown to be sound and the parties reached an agreement on the final terms that would form the legal agreement, WHR would provide the company with $100 million of capital. The investors were receiving 3,661,327 shares of the company's class A nonvoting stock for $1.00 per share and a $96,338,673 note. If the agreement was consummated and WHR converted the mezzanine securities, WHR would own 52 percent of the company's Class A nonvoting stock and have a role in picking three of the company's ten directors.

The WHR deal came at a high cost, but by then the company had few other options—but Burnett and the Committee had another problem. For the last seven years, the Kincaid daughters, Jane and Joan, had been fighting the Committee over allegations of mismanagement and personal enrichment at the expense of the beneficiaries. The announcement of the WHR transaction could provide the daughters with the ammunition they needed to hold the members of the Committee personally libel for the very actions they were accused of. Fayette County Circuit Court Judge James E. Keller had been overseeing this case for years. His inability to get the parties to reach a settlement or to make a final ruling had led him to one last ditch-effort in December. On Wednesday, December 16, 1992, just days after the WHR deal was announced, Judge Keller oversaw a mock trial where both sides presented their case to a jury made up of three attorneys he had appointed. Their verdict wasn't legally binding, but it would provide a venue for both sides to hear the weaknesses of their case.

There is no doubt that the WHR agreement impacted the results of the mock trial. Bringing in a vulture investor to get $100 million of capital demonstrated just how desperate the financial situation was for the company. Burnett had already sold assets and completed transactions that brought in close to $200 million over the last few years, and now this. The only argument the Committee seemed to be able to make was that it was not their fault; it was tax law changes and a bad economy. In fact, on February 23, 1993, the day the Committee members resigned from their company positions and Kincaid's Committee, Ed Schaeffer said this to a reporter for the *Lexington Herald-Leader*:

> The Advisory Committee was not to blame for the estate's financial problems. Central Bank had its finest year ever last year. But the real estate market developed problems. Look at First Security Bank. We now find them merged and they were a fine institution. It's the economic times we live in.

The terms of the Kincaid daughters' settlement agreement were not revealed, but an attorney for the estate said no monetary damages were paid. One can only guess that the daughters and their advisors knew time was of the essence. After the state took control of Kentucky Central Life, the Committee had been booted out of the company, and now the daughters had to concern themselves with stabilizing the image of Central Bank and trying to figure out a way to save some portion of Kentucky Central Life and Bluegrass Broadcasting. The Committee took advantage of the state takeover of the company to force the daughters to settle.

In retrospect, one also has to wonder if Judge Keller's mock trial was the straw that broke the camel's back. Consider what the Committee heard that Wednesday and recognize that December 31 came and went with no final agreement and that on Tuesday, February 9, 1993, Burnett issued a press release announcing that negotiations had ended. His new plan was to sell noncore assets and reduce costs and downsize the company.

I remember that day as though it were yesterday. I had been involved in providing some of the due-diligence work and had become friends with John Lang and Frank Dinucci. In fact, while John Lang and Cliff Forbush didn't know one another from their days in Hartford, they knew many of the same people from Connecticut Mutual and Merrill Lynch, so there was a friendly relationship between them, which I benefited from. That Tuesday, the employees of the company were shocked, and everyone was trying to understand what this meant. Frank Dinucci didn't have any immediate details about what happened because John Lang hadn't told him what had happened, but several weeks later, Frank told me in a phone call that John Lang had said that Whitman was willing to do the deal under one condition: Burnett had to go. He and his staff had reviewed enough information and interviewed enough people to realize that Bud Burnett was the problem and that he had to go. Whittman wanted a clean, unsoiled, seasoned insurance professional to lead the company. Burnett had to go, meaning he couldn't remain associated with the company. He could still be a director due to his role on the Advisory

Committee, but his days being involved in the management of the company were over.

This must have been a shock to Burnett, Schaeffer, and Hembree. Burnett knew where all the skeletons were buried, and their ship was tied to his anchor. With independent management controlling the company, many of those skeletons could surface. In fact, it would now be easier for the Kincaid daughters to get the information they were after for their lawsuit against them. They had just had the results of the mock trial, and without the cover of being on the Committee, they all might end up facing some large monetary penalties and, in some cases, potentially criminal charges. The details of Burnett's deals related to politics, such as the purchase of Wallace Wilkinson's Frankfort hotel and transactions with the Webbs, Teddy Mims, and others, along with what he'd been doing for his son Bruce, might all come out and get them removed from the Committee.

In the end, the trio decided they couldn't do the WHR deal. Of course, they probably never considered that they might have only a few days remaining to be in charge of the company. After the February 9 announcement that the WHR deal was dead, on Thursday, February 11, both the California and Florida insurance departments pulled the company's insurance license to "protect the interests of the insurance buying public." Burnett was now blaming the state insurance departments for overreacting and for not understanding the value of the company's mortgage loan and real estate investments. It didn't matter anymore, though, because those two states' actions were the final nail in the coffin, and according to what we learned later, Burnett, Schaeffer, Hembree, and Gunn all drove to Frankfort that Friday and asked Insurance Commissioner Don Stephens to put the company into statutory rehabilitation.

In December 1991, Brereton Jones had been elected governor of Kentucky, so Burnett's perceived political protector, Wallace Wilkinson, was gone. Jones had been Wilkinson's lieutenant governor but had had a poor relationship with him throughout their four-year term. When Jones announced his candidacy for governor, Wilkinson ran his wife, Martha, against him in the Democratic primary. Burnett had been a supporter and financial backer of Wallace Wilkinson and now had to deal with his nemesis.

A very politically connected attorney joined the company in 1990. He (his name is withheld on request) had been Lt. Governor Wendell Ford's campaign treasurer and his legal counsel and legislative assistant after he was elected. He had been recruited to the company to help the property and casualty insurance companies improve their claims procedures. He was a native of

Richmond, Kentucky, and remained active in Democratic politics throughout his professional career. He was a wonderful friend and someone who provided me with a lot of emotional support after the state takeover.

This attorney had a large Rolodex of political contacts, and he told me the following story about something that happened during the company's final weeks. After the 1991 election, and as the company's financial situation was worsening, Burnett would call him from time to time to discuss what he was hearing. After Jones was elected in December 1990, Burnett had to deal with Jones's aide, Jack Hall. Hall had been with Jones since his term as lieutenant governor and was believed to be working behind the scenes to raise money to help Jones retire about $2 million of campaign debt, some of it left over from his lieutenant governor campaign.

My friend explained that during 1992, Burnett was talking with Hall about his issues with the Insurance Department, and Hall had apparently been telling Burnett that everything was under control. The problem was that this politically connected attorney wasn't hearing the same message from his Frankfort contacts. Sometime in late 1992, after another conversation with one of his contacts, he went up to Burnett's office to tell him that he thought Jack Hall was lying to him and that Frankfort wasn't as supportive of him as he thought. He said Burnett disagreed, so my attorney friend just politely left his office.

An additional back story he told me was that Garvice Kincaid had turned Brereton Jones down for a loan years ago, and his understanding was that Jones still held that against the company. The Kentucky political landscape has always been messy. You have a state with 120 counties, and each county has its own political power structure. In addition, the economic prosperity gap between counties is quite large and magnifies any differences of opinion. So, hearing my friend say that Jones held a grudge against Kincaid over being turned down for a loan wasn't surprising, especially when you consider Burnett's support of Wilkinson. The reason this history is important is that after the company was taken over, Governor Jones ignored the Kincaid daughters' request that he meet with them. At one point in December 1993, the governor held a Saturday afternoon "open door" meeting with the public, and the daughters stood in line that day to get their ten minutes alone with him. Their number in line was twenty-five. He saw eighty-two people that day. Can you imagine what Kincaid would have said?

I think in December 1993 the company was too much of a political grenade for anything positive to happen. Every week there were more stories about what Burnett had been doing, more investigations into possible corruption, and more litigation. Being involved with Kentucky Central Life was now the equivalent of walking into quicksand—you sink. I suspect the governor had decided that it was better to remain silent and be criticized than to speak and potentially fall into a sinkhole. I am confident that the state's politically connected attorney, Steve Beshear, discouraged the governor from being involved. In addition, by June of 1993, the state had already selected its partner to rescue the policyholders.

~ The Day the Music Died ~

"American Pie"
by John McLean

A long, long time ago
I can still remember how that music used to make me smile
And I knew if I had my chance
That I could make those people dance
And maybe they'd be happy for a while

But February made me shiver
With every paper I'd deliver
Bad news on the doorstep
I couldn't take one more step

I can't remember if I cried
When I read about his widowed bride
But something touched me deep inside
The day the music died

By that fateful Friday, the Insurance Department had already made its decision, so the Committee's trip to Frankfort was merely its attempt to continue to be involved with the company. The employees learned about the company being placed in rehabilitation around 10:30 that Friday morning, February 12, 1993. A brief statement had been issued, and the Insurance Department had selected an internal group to manage the company through the process. The group would work with Wendell Clark, the department's director of financial examinations. The internal group would be made up of three people from the property and casualty companies, since those companies were excluded from the rehabilitation order. The internal group would also include the company's general counsel, Joseph Hudson, who had once been a young attorney at the Insurance Department, and the Kentucky Central Life's executive vice president, Robert D. Preston, who had been the insurance commissioner before Kincaid's death.

That morning, the management group quickly walked around to each floor where the company had operations and instructed everyone to stop working and go home. We were to return at eight o'clock on Monday morning. Data processing was allowed time to run the system's backup procedures under the watchful eyes of someone from the department. People in our area (investments and mortgage loans) were instructed to leave our desks and all filing cabinets unlocked and leave immediately. I recall there was some mention that this was just a temporary measure to stop the financial drain from policyowners trying to cash in, and there was some mention that Burnett would be involved in the process.

My wife, Jan, also worked at the company, and we usually rode to work together. That morning, after being instructed to leave, we were numb with shock. We, like most of the company's employees, had invested our lives in the company and had never considered working anywhere else. The company was like our family, and now a major disaster had struck it. *What would happen and what did this mean?* was all we could think of. Cliff Forbush, my old boss, initially tried to get some answers. He explained that we had money to manage and that we couldn't just leave; we had responsibilities. Wendell Clark knew Cliff, and he tried to ease the sting of what was happening by going into his office and discussing it with him. Clark knew that Cliff and I had done a good job for the company, and he wanted to assure Cliff that he understood him and ask him to just give them the weekend to figure things out.

By eleven o'clock, we had all left our desks and exited the building. By then it was all over the local news, and that evening and many other days for the next two-and-a-half years, the headline story was about the company and what happened. Exiting the company's garage, Jan and I didn't know what to do. Go home? Just drive? We started driving toward home but knew we needed to go somewhere else, just to clear our heads. The golden arches answered the question. We seldom ate at McDonald's, but that Friday afternoon it answered the question of where to go. For the next several Fridays, we ate lunch there and then headed to our home off Clays Mill Road and, once there, watched the news and read the newspaper to learn what was happening to the company.

In 1991, cell phones were still clunky devices usually installed in people's automobiles. They were a luxury and few people had them, so it wasn't until we arrived home that we started getting calls from people who knew we worked there. Of course, the first call was from Jan's parents, and then we had a call from an older couple who treated us like their kids. Everyone wanted to know what this meant for us, and all we could say was we didn't know.

My uncle, Emmett Crump, was in Florida by this time, and he called that evening. He had been associated with the company for forty years, and the news hit him hard. Our phone had been ringing busy, so he'd been on the phone to several other people trying to find out whatever he could. There was nothing to learn, though. Emmett was crushed but optimistic. He couldn't believe the state wouldn't do whatever it could to save the company. Yes, Burnett had screwed up, but you don't replace a thousand jobs easily, and given everything that Kincaid had done for Lexington and Kentucky, something would be done. It was a song sung by many over the next several months, but it was out of tune with reality.

Things quickly started changing after we arrived at work on Monday. Each area was told what they could and could not do and that the Insurance Department was putting together a plan. The internal management group changed. Robert Preston was forced to retire after the property and casualty companies' controller, Bob Mattscheck, informed the insurance commissioner about Preston's involvement with Bud's son, Bruce Burnett. Bruce had been writing performance bonds and collecting the premiums but then submitting the applications only if a claim was later received. Apparently, Bud knew about it, and Preston, as the senior officer overseeing the property and casualty companies, had been covering it up.

The property and casualty companies had never been consistently profitable. The fact was that they were too small to compete with the national players. Their automobile premiums were higher, and their limited size meant that a bad regional storm could easily push them into losses for the year. Burnett accepted their limited profitability and occasional loss years and basically ignored them. Bruce used them, so they served a purpose, and as Bruce's schemes collapsed, he began stealing from these entities by writing business and keeping the premiums. Preston wasn't getting anything out of this; he was just helping his old friend and Kincaid lieutenant, Bud. Besides, Bud ran everything; who was he going to complain to?

On Monday, when my department arrived at work, we could see that someone had been through our files. Our desk drawers and our investment files had been opened and searched. Some of the drawers were left open and some items were caught up in the file drawers. We never figured out what they were looking for, but in later months, it became obvious that the state thought there was a secret set of files somewhere in the company. I know I was asked the question twice, once in a casual interview and the second time after the state had hired a forensic investigator to come in and look at things. I don't remember the guy's name, but he looked and acted like a 1950s television detective who just knew you were dirty and was sure he'd get you to crack under pressure. Later I heard from someone in the management group that the Insurance Department was paranoid that Burnett had a secret set of J. Egar Hoover–type files.

By the time the company was placed into rehabilitation by the Insurance Department, Brereton Jones had become governor. Jones had succeeded Burnett's political confederate, Wallace Wilkinson, as governor, and in 1991, the FBI's operation BOPTROT had already implicated several politicians. Operation BOPTROT was an undercover sting operation that began in September 1990. BOP refers to the legislature's Business, Occupations and Professions Committee (which was responsible for state law governing horse racing), and TROT refers to harness racing. The operation netted twelve Kentucky legislators, including then Speaker of the House Don Blandford, and others, including then Governor Wallace Wilkinson's nephew Bruce, his appointment secretary, all of whom accepted bribes "and other inducements" for influencing horse-racing legislation.

By 1993, many Frankfort politicians were concerned about getting a call from the FBI, so it wasn't much of a stretch to figure out that they were also concerned about having their name in some political Burnett file. Bud had followed Kincaid's footsteps and always kept close relationships with Frankfort's leadership, and none was greedier regarding his patronage than Wallace Wilkinson. Wilkinson's Frankfort hotel sale to Kentucky Central life the day before his inauguration was under investigation. So, we assumed that our invaded files and records were just part of Frankfort's paranoia.

By the following Monday, Bud Burnett wasn't allowed back in the company, so he parked himself up in Kincaid's law firm. Cliff and I, along with others, were instructed not to have any contact with him and to report any contact. By ten o'clock that morning, Cliff Forbush and I had both received calls from him and had to explain to him that we'd been instructed not to talk to him. You could tell Burnett was shocked. Burnett actually thought this was going to be a friendly state control. Apparently during the weekend, the Insurance Department had been informed about Bruce Burnett's shenanigans and had decided that both Bud Burnett and former insurance commissioner Bob Preston had to go.

On Tuesday, there was an episode that got around the building in about fifteen minutes. Cliff was in the building's lobby heading to meet his wife for lunch when he ran into Burnett. Burnett, instead of being embarrassed by the company's financial mess, came over and put his hand out to Cliff. Cliff, always willing to call a spade a spade, just looked at him and suddenly said loudly, "Burnett, you ass, you have ruined my retirement." I was told that Burnett just stared at him in shock and then dropped his head down, turned around and walked off to the low-rise elevators.

I guess there must have been about a dozen or so employees in the lobby at that time who heard and saw their exchange, because we heard about it in our area before Cliff returned. I know Ed Winiarczyk witnessed it. Ed brought it up recently during a former-employees lunch. He was proud of Cliff, as were a lot of the folks in the building at the time. Before the state stepped in, Burnett had no one to be accountable to, and now, after being kicked to the curb, he was truly the naked king standing in the street in his invisible clothes. His hubris and thirst for power and admiration had destroyed almost everything that Garvice Kincaid had dedicated his life to building, and Cliff's public humiliation of him had struck him like a stake in his heart.

Cliff had met Burnett twenty years earlier in Kincaid's office during his interview, and after Garvice's death had tried to be supportive of the self-appointed leader, but he never understood the man. Burnett didn't want his help or input, and he didn't try to learn about what changes were taking place in the industry. In Cliff's eyes, all Burnett wanted was to garner the respect and admiration of others any way he could get it. Cliff told me years ago that he thought Burnett was paranoid and insecure. So, I guess when you combine those traits with absolute power, you end up with a corporate type of monarchy. Many people have asked me why Burnett did what he did, and while there are multiple suggested answers, I think the short answer is that William Earl Burnett, Jr. had a king complex. He thought it was his duty, as a superior person, to lead and take care of everything, irrespective of how he did it and who it hurt. How else can one explain why he used money from the property and casualty companies to pay off a third-party bank loan that his son, Bruce, had defaulted on?

My Uncle Emmett Crump told me a story shortly after the events it refers to happened in the early 1980s.

Emmett was visiting Kincaid Towers on business, and as he did quite often, he stopped by our department to say hello. He came back to my office, sat down, and proceeded to ask me how things were going. Emmett was the person who introduced me to Louis Rukeyser's "Wall Street Week," which aired on KET in the mid-1970s, and he always liked talking about the markets. Well, on this day something else was on his mind, and suddenly, he said, "You be careful around here; these walls have ears." I looked at him like he was nuts, and he then began to elaborate. Apparently, a couple of weeks before he'd been over in Frankfort and decided to stop by the Insurance Department.

Emmett always knew everybody and never met a stranger. In fact, he was good friends with Wendell Clark, and everyone at the Insurance Department knew he'd been president of the National Association of Life Underwriters and was still a director.

On this trip, he decided he would stop by the records area and look at Kentucky Central Life's compensation schedule for its highest-paid officers. While Burnett had always been protective of what he and others were making, the company had to prepare this schedule and file it with the department. It was considered public information and available to anyone upon request. Anyway, he requested the company's most recent year's annual filing, which included the compensation schedule, and reviewed it in a conference room. He took a few notes and gave the receptionist back the folder. I think he was curious about what Burnett, Larry Sammartin, and Bob Casher were making. Anyway, he drove back to Lexington and the next morning headed into his office and got a phone call from Bud Burnett at 8:30. He explained that Burnett said, "I hear you were at the Insurance Department yesterday and pulled our annual filing. Anything wrong?" Emmett told him he just wanted to see how the company was doing. Burnett told him, "We're doing great and next time you want to know, just come see me."

I asked Emmett, "How did he know you went to the Insurance Department, and more importantly how did he know you pulled the company's annual filing?" Emmett looked at me and said, "Burnett must have eyes inside the department," and then proceeded to tell me, "You should remember that whenever you are talking to people about the company." Even today, after all these years, I find this story a little creepy. Emmett said he thought Burnett wanted to make sure Emmett knew just how powerful he was.

Emmett told me that in the 1950s he would sometimes offer to include Garvice's daughters, with his young son Ricky, on trips to the Kentucky State Fair or maybe the Bluegrass Fair or the Junior League Horse Show. It was something he casually mentioned to me before I worked at the company. He must have had a good relationship with the family, because I was told that after Garvice died, Earl Wilson asked him to pick up Nelle Kincaid and escort her to Kentucky Central Life's board meetings. The Committee had made her a director after his death. In retrospect, and knowing about the animosity and lawsuits between the daughters and the Committee in the 1980s, I wonder if Burnett was concerned about Emmett's relationship with them. It was more likely his perceived relationship, because I don't recall Emmett ever mentioning seeing or talking to either Jane or Joan after I joined the company.

I think Emmett's call-from-Burnett story supports the suggestion that Bud

Burnett was paranoid. It also demonstrates that Burnett had a close relationship with various people in Frankfort.

I believe Burnett was probably shocked, upset, and angry after Garvice appointed David Brain as president of the company in January 1975. It was a signal to Burnett about his own importance. David Brain had managed the company and was instrumental in its growth, and Kincaid had rewarded him. Burnett had to accept that Kincaid's estate plans were changing.

In a long interview with the Committee members on February 29, 1976, in the *Louisville Courier Journal*'s magazine, Al Florence commented about how informed Garvice kept his successors. He said they had regular meetings to review his will and trust and he would update them if necessary. Florence said, "We must have met 100, maybe 150 times."

I don't believe that. Kincaid's estate plan was created in 1964 and updated in 1967 and 1972, and the only time Florence was on the Committee was 1972. The man died in November 1975, so if they even met every three months, that would only be about sixteen meetings. Also, I don't see Garvice reviewing his plan with people who were not attorneys. I interviewed the attorney who created the first document in 1964, Bart Brown, and he told me that no other attorney or person was involved in a meeting about it with Garvice and himself. I suspect Garvice did keep Earl Wilson informed of his thoughts and potentially Wilson might have shared those thoughts with Ed Schaeffer, and Ed might have informed Burnett. Earl Wilson was a primary Committee member in all three versions of Garvice' estate plan.

Cliff Forbush and Dick Gordon both told me that in the early 1970s, Burnett was running around always trying to find out what Brain was up to. If Kincaid kept the Committee members so informed, why would he need to do that?

I believe the Committee offered to do the *Courier Journal* interview to stop outsiders from questioning their solidarity and ability to succeed. The article quoted some people as saying, "They'll be cutting each other's throats in a week." "There is too much money at stake." "Nobody but Garvice could run it." "He never let anybody else know what was going on." In the article, Burnett was called "something of a surprise to the public," and then an unnamed Lexington attorney familiar with the firm said it was because "he is bright, he knows insurance, and Garvice trusted him." Of course, the problem with this statement is that Kincaid had already selected David Brain to run Kentucky Central Life.

After the state took over, the department's insurance examiner, Wendell Clark, stayed actively involved with the company for about a month. During that period, the management group worked with him and the Insurance Department's general counsel to get things more settled and to understand the rules and limits of their role. After a deputy rehabilitator was appointed, he assumed Clark's duties. The first week had been very stressful for everyone, but this was just the beginning of a two-and-a-half-year fight about what to do with the company. The emotional stress for all the employees made coming to the office every day difficult, so difficult that many of us started to refer to this place we'd all once loved as "Hellhole."

Initially Commissioner Stephens publicly said the correct things, but many of us knew he was out of his depth. Don Stephens was a politically appointed insurance commissioner and had been selected by Governor Brereton Jones. According to others at the company, Stephens had briefly worked for Kentucky Central Life many years ago, and in 1978, he defaulted on a $10,000 loan from the company. Stephens began a career in insurance as an agent for Metropolitan Life Insurance Company. He did that for two years in the mid-1960s and then ran for the state legislature. He was active in the Democratic Party, and his legislative resume said he owned a food mart and was a farmer. Stephens didn't have the business resume necessary to handle a problem as large as Kentucky Central Life, but with the help of Steve Beshear and a lot of outside advice, he was the man in charge, and every significant action he took had to be approved by the Franklin Circuit Court.

In those early days, Commissioner Stephens publicly acknowledged how big the problem was and said his intent was to work through the issues to get the company back up and running, but his first responsibility was to Kentucky Central Life's five hundred thousand policyholders. Stephens's first official act was to prevent a run on the bank by stopping policyholder surrenders, and his second official act was to terminate Kentucky Central Life's public relations department. Brent Clay and his staff were quietly terminated the last week of February, along with Bob Preston. Stephens said his department would handle all public communications.

Stephens's third significant action happened in March, when he appointed Michael Cuscaden as his deputy rehabilitator. Cuscaden had been president of Raleigh-based Durham Life Insurance Company, which had been acquired by Louisville-based Capital Holding in 1991. Cuscaden had been retained by Capital Holding to manage the acquisition and had been recommended to Stephens by the company's president, Irving Bailey. Stephens needed a person who could represent him and make decisions about the day-to-day operations of the company, and Cuscaden had the resume to do it. Of course, one of the first things Cuscaden did was adopt a no-smoking policy in the building. If things weren't stressful enough, we now had a large percentage of employees suffering nicotine withdrawal. I know several employees thought it was the state's attempt to get more people to leave.

During the first thirty days, Stephens sounded cautiously optimistic about saving the company. Most of the management understood that if the company could be saved, it would be a totally different entity and possibly be owned by someone else, but it probably would still employ at least five hundred people. The biggest issue the state's attorneys and consultants faced was trying to understand Burnett's spaghetti mess of deals. They discovered early on that the appraisals were questionable and that many of the cash-flow converted loan projects were losing money. This concerned everyone, and the question soon became just how much additional capital the rehabilitated company would need.

Early on, Stephens made a smart move and started working with John Lang reviewing his plan. Lang had negotiated the $100 million WHR deal that fell apart, and Stephens wanted to understand more about it. The problem was that WHR had only been interested in investing in an operating company, before any state takeover. The principals at WHR knew it would be years, not months, before the company could operate normally again, and during that hiatus key employees and the marketing organization would leave.

John Lang said he reviewed the plan with the commissioner and his advisors, and they got excited about the prospect of selling the broadcasting entities. The money they would bring in was material and would give the department a big win. The department was being criticized in the press for not acting sooner, and the member states of NOLHGA were on the phone daily to the department wanting updates and offering their expertise in situations like this. Stephens understood that if they directly participated, his department would lose control of the situation, and that was unacceptable.

From February 1993 through probably the middle of 1994, the local and state television, radio, and print news outlets reported on the company's situation almost daily and certainly weekly. The organizations, especially the *Lexington Herald-Leader* and *Louisville Courier Journal*, provided some of the best investigative journalism the state had ever seen. The reporters and editors spent weeks covering the history of Garvice Kincaid and the creation of his empire and then delved into the histories of the various Committee members, the company's major borrowers, and many of the failed projects Burnett provided money for. They also focused their attention on the Insurance Department and its efforts and, some would say, non-efforts to save the company. These news outlets spent hundreds of hours covering all the court litigation and forced the Insurance Department to answer many difficult questions. Thanks to their dogged work, the employees were able to gain some understanding of what happened to the company and what was happening to the company in the present. I personally want to thank them for their remarkable efforts and persistence.

The commissioner needed help, and by the beginning of March he had brought in the accounting firm Ernst & Young to help him with the actuarial analysis of the situation. In addition, he needed experts on real estate to manage Burnett's mortgage loan and real estate mess, so he brought in New York–based Bankers Trust Company and Creamer Realty & Associates as asset managers. Their job would be to investigate each deal and recommend what actions the company should take. By the end of 2005, Ernst & Young had billed the state over $7.8 million in consulting fees and his asset managers had collected $11.3 million from the estate of Kentucky Central Life.

By March, the employees in the new business and marketing areas of the company knew their jobs were in jeopardy. Areas of the company that had been vibrant and active were now quiet and almost zombie-like. No new business was coming in, and most of the work dealing with agents had to do with taking their phone calls and updating them with the same story every day: nothing new to report, but they're still talking about rehabilitating the company.

The marketing organization that David Brain had developed, which focused on agent relationships and customer service, had also instilled in its people a sense of loyalty to the organization. Kentucky Central Life was a marketing machine, and even after the state takeover, much of the agency force demonstrated a level of loyalty to and concern for the home office employees that was just remarkable. The company may have been in a major car crash, but they wanted their home office friends to know they would be there for them.

During March, Michael Cuscaden and the internal management team started to work on downsizing the company. There were just too many staff, especially in the area tied to new business, so a plan was developed. The commissioner was responsible for the conservation of the company's assets, so a large layoff was planned for the end of March. Something else was also taking place in Frankfort: the commissioner's office started receiving unsolicited calls from parties interested in working with him. They knew the company had been a strong competitor and had a valuable block of business, so they wanted to get their name listed as a potential investor or acquirer.

On April 6, 1993, the first wave of terminations hit, with 218 employees terminated, mostly in the new-business and systems areas. Total expected savings, $5 million. Cuscaden said the employees were terminated and not laid off because he "didn't want them to think that three months from now, we are going to be calling them back."[19] In addition, he reported that the department had received about a half dozen expressions of interest in bidding for the fallen insurer. Cuscaden said, "The 218 jobs that were eliminated will make the company more attractive to potential buyers and more financially secure for its 460,000 policyholders."[20]

The layoffs were bad enough to see happen, but his remarks about potential buyers were the first of many conflicting statements coming from the rehabilitator's confederates. For most of March, I, along with most of the officers, were hearing that the department wanted to rehabilitate the company. We all understood that state insurance departments usually look for an in-state buyer when a small insurance company gets in trouble, but Kentucky Central Life was not considered small. In addition, there had been two recent rehabilitation cases that had suggested that a slow and methodical approach would be better. Certainly, a portfolio of real estate would not recover its value quickly, but it would recover when the national real estate storm subsided. In fact, John Rampulla returned from a National Mortgage Bankers Conference in 1992 and reported that the major theme of the conference was "stay alive till '95." Most of us believed that prudence dictated a slower, more planned approach.

In July 1991, the New Jersey–based Mutual Benefit Life Insurance Company was taken into receivership for rehabilitation by the New Jersey Department of Banking and Insurance. It also experienced substantial losses due to the real estate market, as its ratings had been reduced, triggering a run by its policyholders. At the time of its collapse, it was considered the largest insurer to ever be taken over. The Insurance Department managed it in rehabilitation until 1998, when it was finally sold to Sun America Life Insurance Company.

Mutual Benefit was reported to be the United States' eighteenth-largest insurer, with over $13 billion in assets. Its management had invested about 40 percent of its assets in commercial mortgage loans. New Jersey decided to manage this problem insurer to avoid the fire sale of its commercial mortgage loan portfolio and to also avoid losing its fourteen hundred home office jobs. The company would become smaller, but it would do it over time, which would allow the commercial real estate markets to recover. The remaining Kentucky Central officers and managers didn't understand why the Insurance Department wouldn't take a similar approach. Both management and the state

19   *Lexington Herald*-Leader, April 7, 1993.
20   Ibid.

understood that any policyholder plan would require a multiyear moratorium, of some type, on policyholder withdrawals.

In addition to Mutual Benefit Life, in April 1991, First Executive Life Insurance Company of California and its sister company in New York were placed into rehabilitation by their respective state insurance departments. First Executive's chief executive officer, Fred Carr, saw himself as a great investor and put 66 percent of its $15 billion in assets into high-yield junk bonds sold by Michael Milken at Drexel Burnham Lambert. Drexel and Milken are credited with the creation in the 1980s of the modern-day high-yield bond market. Drexel had also championed the era of leveraged buyouts using his high-cost debt. Drexel's culture was aggressive, and Milken eventually got involved with insider trading, which forced the firm into bankruptcy in 1990. After Drexel fell, the junk-bond market collapsed, and with it, so did First Executive Life.

In April 1991, with one quarter of its bond portfolio already in default and the high-yield bond market in disarray, and just weeks after becoming California's first elected insurance commissioner, John Garamendi seized Executive Life, contending that its junk-bond portfolio was too risky to support payments to more than three hundred thousand retirees and annuitants.

A few months later, Garamendi sold the junk bonds to Leon Black and his investors for $3.25 billion, but the bonds soon turned out to be worth billions more, which netted Black personally somewhere between $500 million and $1 billion, and his investors turned out to be fronts for Credit Lyonnais, a bank controlled by the French government. A significant element of the Garamendi deal was that the offer included $300 million in new capital for the insurance operations of Executive Life and $3.2 billion for the bond portfolio. The $300 million, in what was later described as a roundabout way, put the French government in control of the company, although federal law barred a foreign government from owning a U.S. insurer.

Garamendi faced sharp criticism in the financial media and from policyholders whose checks had been reduced. "Smart buyer, dumb seller" was the headline in a 1994 *Forbes* magazine critique concluding that Black had exploited Garamendi's desire for a big political splash.

By the end of February, the Kentucky Insurance Department had been inundated with people and companies interested in the company's parts. Some entities were looking at bidding on the whole entity, some were interested in just the insurance company, some were interested in just the television station, and some were interested only in the radio stations. The Insurance Department had lost control of the process. Stephens salivated at the prospect of someone else putting in a bunch of capital and then handing them the keys, yet he was also supposed to try to get the best deal for everyone, if possible. In addition, he failed to fully comprehend that until his experts unraveled the details of Burnett's mortgage loan and real estate mess, no one would know how much money would be enough. The answers to this analysis would take months to determine, not weeks.

By early March the Insurance Department began doing its due diligence on the perspective purchasers for the insurance company, and by the end of the month had selected eight companies that it would invite in to look at everything.

On Tuesday, April 13, the Insurance Department entertained the first interested potential buyer, Jefferson-Pilot (JP) from Greensboro, North Carolina. In 1987, Jefferson Standard and Pilot Life insurance companies combined and formed JP. After a few years, some of the founding family members were upset with the poor performance of the combined companies. The company had a large amount of unused surplus, and the family wanted either to see it used for growth, which would impact its stock price, or to make special dividend payments.

In 1992, fifty-one-year-old David Stonecipher, a high-profile insurance executive from Life of Georgia in Atlanta, was brought in to run JP. The charismatic Stonecipher had a strong track record, and he was also the first non-insider chosen to lead the company. Stonecipher's mission was clear: transform a solid but sleepy regional insurance company into a national heavyweight that rewards its shareholders handsomely.

In February 1993, Stonecipher wasted no time courting the Kentucky Insurance Commissioner. The two men didn't know each other, but the North Carolina Insurance Department had made the introductions. Stephens had a mess on his hands, and Stonecipher offered to help him clean it up and promised to take care of his policyholders. I don't want to imply that there was an early deal or anything, but Stonecipher's approach and sympathetic attitude were certainly appreciated.

So, in retrospect, it isn't surprising that Stonecipher and his insurance team were first in the door on April 13. I believe they were on site from Tuesday through Friday, working in what Stephens called the "confidentiality room," which I still think sounds like *Get Smart*'s Cone of Silence. The state's attorney, Stites and Harbison, and its accounting firm, Ernst and Young, provided background to the JP team on what they found, and then they were allowed to go to various departments and look at records, systems, etc., as well as interview key management personnel. I remember when they came down to investments to review our information. Cliff knew the senior investment person, John Ingram, from the ACLI Chief Investment Officers Conferences. John and the JP team loved our investment portfolios and complimented us on being able to get in some private placement deals they had never seen. In fact, everyone who looked at the company and reviewed our information told the Insurance Department the same thing: those guys have done a great job. Some even said it was a shame that Burnett hadn't given our department all the company's investable cash flow to invest.

Martin Uhle joined the company in January 1987, about one year before Bill Tozer was scheduled to leave. Marty was a smart, experienced, no-nonsense actuary and was slated to be the company's chief actuary after Tozer departed. Marty and I hit it off immediately. A new regulation called "cash-flow testing" was forcing all life insurance companies to upgrade their investment management and actuarial systems for calendar year 1991. Life insurance products had become more interest sensitive in the 1980s, and the Society of Actuaries made cash-flow testing and asset adequacy a requirement. I oversaw providing the actuarial department with our investment portfolio's projected cash flows under seven mandated interest-rate scenarios as well as other scenarios. The actuarial industry was concerned with a run-on-the-bank scenario in response to a rapid change in interest rates, and these tests were designed to demonstrate how interest-rate changes would affect a company's capital ratios.

One of the first red flags that surfaced after the state took charge happened in early May 1993. Insurance products that pay a contractual interest rate subject to change also have what the industry refers to as a "minimum guaranteed rate." This interest rate represents the lowest rate the product may pay the policyholder and is meant to be the floor interest rate for the product. During April, after Michael Cuscaden joined the company as deputy rehabilitator, Marty had been pressing Cuscaden to allow him to drop all our products' interest rates to their minimum guaranteed rate. One problem with Cuscaden was that he didn't like making decisions, so that suggestion lingered, with Marty continuing to press the issue. Marty wrote a one-page memo and called the move prudent given the financial situation of the company. He explained that it made little sense to provide a crediting rate that was not being earned by the company.

Marty hand delivered the memo to Cuscaden and again made his case. According to Marty, Cuscaden contacted Commissioner Stephens and explained what Marty was recommending, and the commissioner agreed.

Cuscaden wrote "ok to implement" and signed and dated the bottom of the memo. For a company to make a change like this requires a significant amount of systems programming, so Marty and his staff began working to implement the change. The red flag happened a few days later when Marty got a call from Cuscaden. Apparently, the commissioner had mentioned the change that was being implemented to JP's David Stonecipher and JP told them not to do it because it might cause more policies to lapse or be canceled. From Marty's perspective, JP was already making decisions for the company, so in his mind, there would be no rehab of the company; we were going to be sold to JP.

When Marty came to my office in early May to tell me, it was about three weeks after Jefferson-Pilot impacted the interest-rate change. Marty wanted me to know about it and brought me a copy of the memo, which I eventually shared with one of the Kincaid daughters' representatives, Michael Foley. They were fighting what turned out to be a two-and-a-half-year legal war trying to stop the sale to Jefferson-Pilot, and occasionally I would pass along information to them that I thought might help them. When Marty came to see me, he had just turned in his resignation and met with his staff. I had been more vocal than some about trying to save the company, and he wanted me to know about the memo and how much of an impact JP was already having.

I was shocked. Marty's area was a key participant in creating any rehabilitation plan, and he had assumed the state would not want to keep promising an unrealistic interest rate. Our interest rates weren't guaranteed, so the consumer was always subject to changes. Marty had been contacted by a recruiter shortly after the state took over but thought it was too early to jump ship, but after Cuscaden contacted him, that made the decision for him. He told his staff the same thing he told me, and after that most of his staff soon left the company for other actuarial jobs. I don't blame Marty for leaving. He had a family and in retrospect made the correct decision, and frankly no one trusted Michael Cuscaden, apparently for good reason. A few months later, it came out that David Stonecipher had promised him a job running the office for eighteen months and then a position back in North Carolina, where he was from.

This information soon made its way to the Kincaid daughters, and everyone was back in court. It apparently happened during the bidding process, and the daughters' attorneys accused JP of "chilling the bidding process."[21] Stonecipher was smart, though. He wrote a memo in August 1993 to the commissioner and told him he had offered Cuscaden a job. This helped remove the smell of the whole ordeal. I learned about Stonecipher's job offer from Bob Matscheck, who

---

21   Neil Roland, *The News & Observer*, May 4, 1994.

was on the internal management committee. I didn't know about Stonecipher's memo until the court was reviewing the issue. This would just become another red flag suggesting that the company wouldn't be saved.

Insurance Commissioner Don Stephens knew most of the management team just from being around the insurance industry. Kentucky Central Life wasn't the state's largest life insurance company, but I would argue it was the state's most well-known insurance company. Garvice had spent fifteen years aggressively promoting the company, and after his death, Earl Wilson and the company's public relations department did a good job continuing his mission. By mid-1993, Stephens had already told the management team that he would find a friendly buyer for the P&C companies; all they had to do was toe the line, which most of them did. Bob Matscheck was the only financial person in their group, and he also wanted a fair and honest process. He understood a state-managed rehabilitation might not work, but he expected it to be considered. He found out about Cuscaden's job offer from Cuscaden himself, who was trying to reassure this group that they would all be taken care of.

I always appreciated Bob's attitude during that time. He supported the Insurance Department, but he also drove the process that created an internal rehabilitation plan that the Franklin Circuit Court had to evaluate. It was a ten-year plan, with five-year policyholder limits and constraints similar to those the JP purchase agreement contained. It assumed that it would take ten years for the company to start writing new business but suggested that fresh capital could be brought in after five years. The main difference was that JP was a capital-rich company, so there was practically no risk of failure for the policyholders. This fact, along with the recommendation of the insurance commissioner and the national guaranty association, drove the court's decision. The Kincaid daughters' attorneys and consultants fought hard and did a good job showing the public how biased the process was but finally lost the battle in 1995. By the end of June, the company's business was transferred to JP. Jefferson Pilot was obligated to keep a 150-person customer service office in Kincaid Towers for five years.

The bidding process was supposed to involve six or seven entities looking at the company. JP was in the door first; then GE Capital came through second, followed by Leucadia National Corporation (a diversified investment company that specializes in takeovers and managing acquisitions) and finally Americo Life, Inc., which was controlled by the Merriman family. All the interested parties were professional and considerate of what the employees were going through until it came to the Americo Life group. They created so many employee complaints that the insurance commission asked them to leave early. After Americo left, we found out that the commissioner had decided enough groups had been through and stopped the review process.

In the first round, bidders were permitted to bid on either Kentucky Central Life or its insurance business. According to the commissioner, no bidders were interested in Kentucky Central Life itself, but several bidders did bid on Kentucky Central Life's in-force business. By August 1993, JP emerged as the leading bidder after the first round of bidding and proceeded to negotiate a "definitive" reinsurance agreement with Kentucky Central Life's rehabilitator. The final agreement had JP receiving $850 million of assets, the guaranty association putting in $110 million, and JP contributing $250 million. JP took only cash and securities.

As the interested parties were coming through, I think many employees were rooting for GE Capital. Of course, GE Capital had the money and also had another insurance company, Genworth Financial, and everyone agreed its people seemed to understand the company and its due diligence team was the most professional. In addition, they didn't seem scared off by Burnett's real estate mess. Their team spent a lot of time looking at those records. At the end of GE Capital's week, John Rampulla saw the team having breakfast at the Radison Hotel, and he stopped over to see how things were going. He told me they said, "We're sorry, but our bid was rejected." According to John, they had agreed to put in $200 million in new capital and take over the company. What they needed in return was for the guaranty association to put in another $100 million, which they would pay back over five years, with policyholder restrictions similar to those JP had requested. Apparently, GE Capital also had a five-year plan.

In 1993, the troubled real estate markets were predicted to recover by 1995 or 1996: "stay alive to '95." I assume GE Capital was predicting the same thing our internal plan did: slowly dispose of the problem assets. In retrospect, I think the department's issue with the GE proposal was losing control of the company's corpus, which included all investigations and litigation. The department was under enormous pressure to explain its role, and that of others, in the company's collapse. Members of the state legislature were calling for an investigation, and the state's newspapers appeared to be reporting new information on a weekly basis. I think the reports about the department's 1990 examination of the company was the most toxic news. They were on site, had an accounting firm brought in, and had allowed the company to post a reserve much lower than what it appeared their examination staff wanted. I think the department and its attorneys knew they could not afford to lose control of the corporate entity.

JP's plan was designed for the Insurance Department to liquidate the real estate and mortgage loan assets and to also clean up all the various corporate lawsuits. As illiquid assets were converted to cash, the department would distribute the cash first to JP to reduce its purchase price to about $110 million, and then the excess cash flow would be distributed to the guaranty association to repay its $110 million payment. The department's experts hadn't projected the guaranty association would be being paid back, but it was. By 2007, the insurance department had paid back the guaranty association, made an extra contingent payment to JP, cleaned up the agent's non-qualified pension plan, redeemed the company's preferred shareholders stock, which was held by the Kincaid Trust, and finalized and closed out the court-ordered liquidation. Kentucky Central Life's final chapter had been written, 105 years after it began.

The guaranty association was so proud of the rehabilitation that in 2000, it wrote up a special report summarizing its success. "Not only has the Kentucky Central plan been a financial success, it has done so without controversy from the policyholders." As a former employee of the company, the one thing that bothered me the most about their self-applause was that they failed to appreciate that the company's internal rehabilitation plan had projected a similar outcome. Our plan had projected that the policyholders would be made whole in five years, which is what happened, and while I appreciate the organization's enthusiasm for its own plan's success, it failed to appreciate that much of what it accomplished could have been done under a self-rehabilitation process.

Clyde Honaker and I discussed the guaranty association's report, and we independently came to the same conclusion. There will always be differences of opinions about how the company's problems were resolved, but we both felt politics had influenced the situation too much. Judge Keller had avoided acting, the department had hoped the problem would go away, and in the end, after the first thirty days, self-rehabilitation was never given much consideration. Michael Cuscaden certainly made his position known quickly, and after JP emerged as the leading bidder, its influence was too obvious. The JP transaction would have closed in early 1994 if the Kincaid daughters hadn't fought so hard. I don't believe the Insurance Department expected to encounter so much opposition to its plan. The daughter's legal fight, as directors of the company, went all the way to the state's supreme court. After the final court decision was announced, Jefferson-Pilot's transition team was on site two days later. It was over, and my job lasted until mid-July 1995, when I stepped on the fourteenth-floor elevator for one last trip down.

About sixty-days before the transaction closed, Stonecipher was on site.

He was meeting with various people that his staff thought might be helpful with the transition. In addition, anyone transferred to Greensboro, North Carolina, reduced their Lexington job commitment requirement. About a week before he came, he scheduled a meeting with me, and of course the meetings were held on the twenty-first floor, in the company's boardroom, whose walls were lined with pictures of every Kentucky Central Life president before Burnett. While all the pictures were hung normally, Garvice's stood out about four inches away from the wall like a statement. His picture was hung in front of the room's thermostat.

Jan and I had discussed my upcoming meeting at length and made our decision, and when Stonecipher presented me with my offer, I politely thanked him and declined. We had decided we would figure out the next chapter of our lives on our own. He was surprised and wondered if I had something lined up, which I didn't. I had looked on and off since early 1993, and Cliff Forbush had been calling his contacts for me, but the investment industry had been experiencing its own recession that was tied to the collapse of Drexel and Burnham and the commercial real estate markets. I didn't know what I would eventually find, but after two-and-a-half years of "Hellhole," we agreed that moving to North Carolina would just be a continuation. The last thing Stonecipher said was, "Are you sure?" and "All right," and the meeting was over.

Things did quickly work out. Jan and I were terminated, received our severance packages, and, for the first and only time in our lives, signed up for unemployment. Two weeks later, though, my life's frequent lucky streak continued and a friend of mine learned about a situation in Madison, Wisconsin. They weren't looking for anyone, but he felt it might be worth contacting them, since their treasurer had unexpectedly resigned—that day! He sent me what he had on them, and I went to the downtown Lexington library and was able to gather some more information on the company and its president. It was a small mutual life insurance company started in 1910, and it had been run by a father and now his son since the 1940s. It was just a nice little regional life insurance company, with about $625 million in assets. My call to the president intrigued him since the person had resigned only the day before and here I was calling him from Lexington, Kentucky. He knew Lexington from being in the National Guard, and of course the Kentucky Central Life story had been well publicized. We spoke and I sent him my resume and some references and a recommendation letter from the insurance commissioner's current deputy rehabilitator, Richard Wright, who also had worked with Cuscaden at Durham Life.

The president soon hired me after an interview, and we became great friends. We each had been raised as only children with a strong work ethic. He liked my blunt honesty; it frustrated him sometimes, but he understood my opinion was usually worth considering. Over the next twenty-five years we completely changed the direction of the company and increased its asset size to over $5 billion. He promoted me to executive vice president and treasurer. I was its chief investment officer and had Human Resources, Legal, and Building and Grounds reporting to me and also headed the administration of qualified pension and retirement plans. I retired after twenty-five years with the company, and Jan and I moved back to Lexington on January 4, 2020.

One final side story about Jefferson-Pilot. After Jefferson-Pilot acquired Kentucky Central Life Insurance Company, it went on to quickly acquire Alexander Hamilton Life Insurance Company (October 1995), Chubb Life Insurance Company (February 1997), and Guarantee Life Insurance Company (September 1999). By 1995 it was the second-fastest-growing insurance company and the fifteenth-largest life insurer in the United States. In January 1998, the company adopted Jefferson-Pilot Financial as its brand name to reflect its position as a "national company with financial savvy." By 2002 Jefferson-Pilot had 3,770 employees, and its companies had more than $210 billion of life insurance in force. One of its best-known subsidiaries, Jefferson-Pilot Communications Company, owned three television stations and eighteen radio stations in the Southeast.

David Stonecipher's Pac-Man–type acquisitions had done what the Pilot family had wanted, and he had used the company's excess capital and significantly grown the company. Some of my old Kentucky Central Life friends moved to Greensboro and later told me that by 2010, it was generally known within the company that the Kentucky Central Life acquisition was the most profitable block of business in the organization. In 2005, David Stonecipher did one last deal, though; he merged the company with Lincoln Financial and a large consolidation of operations took place. Greensboro, which had benefited from Stonecipher's previous deals, now felt the raw consequences of a major corporate restructuring and downsizing.

Lusby Brown worked at JP and was on its Kentucky Central Life team reviewing and taking over the investment area. In 2007, I saw him at a conference, and he told me how lucky I was that I hadn't taken the job in Greensboro. He said the company he had loved so much started changing shortly after the Kentucky Central Life deal, and in 2005, after the Lincoln Financial deal was announced, all the company's investment assets were quickly transferred to Lincoln's Pittsburg office and the Greensboro employees, including himself, were all terminated. Lusby had spent twenty years at the company. He said everyone had to relocate to other places and many were still looking. I told him my reasoning for not going and said, "It also always bothered me that JP was assuming me, versus recruiting me. Their offer was just merely fulfilling an M&A contract requirement and not a real need."

Several of Kentucky Central Life's employees ended up with long-term Greensboro jobs, but there were also employees sent to North Carolina who were terminated within twelve months. Jefferson-Pilot just needed their historical knowledge and/or marketing relationships during the transition. As for the Lexington office, Clyde Honaker was appointed its manager, and he ran it for five years and then worked in Greensboro for another five. Clyde said the Lexington office really never averaged more than about 100 employees, and by year three, fewer than that. Heck, who was left to care by then.

There are lots of other little stories about those "Hellhole" years, but frankly, they are irrelevant in the grand scheme of things. Burnett and his partners and enablers, both inside and outside the company, destroyed it and destroyed most of the value of Mr. Kincaid's estate. The long-term employees wanted justice, or at least an understanding of "why it happened," but in the end, that never came. The Insurance Department spent over $79 million on attorneys, accountants, consultants, and asset managers, and multiple investigations were performed and depositions taken, but in the end, the only definite answer was Bud Burnett's failed strategies, with many dotted lines to various other people. I guess it's like a wife who believes her husband is having an affair but is unable to know beyond a reasonable doubt. Parents intuitively know when their kids are lying and usually can get them to confess, but adults are different; their willingness to lie usually is stronger the more detrimental the potential penalty is. So, in the end, all one can do is be one's own detective, analyze the evidence, consider people's motivations, and respect the unbridled opportunities various parties had. Remember, "two votes to one," a thirst for respect and power, and drug dealers and users need each other.

As the End Approaches

Red sky at night, sailors' delight. Red sky in the morning, sailors take warning.
– by Unknown

I joined the investment department of Kentucky Central Life Insurance and also began my career in investments on January 5, 1981. I had worked part-time for the company since the summer of 1977, in various positions:

mailroom, supply department, front desk security, and special projects. In December 1980, an interview had been arranged for me with Cliff Forbush. That afternoon established my career in investments. I was to be there for a 1:00 p.m. meeting with him, but he was running late. I knew the building closed at 1:00 on Friday and most of the staff would be leaving, but personnel knew me and just had me wait in his reception area. It was after 1:30 when he came walking around the corner, and when he saw me, he said, "Mr. Mucci, I am glad you waited." That afternoon changed my life and set me on a career path in investments. A path that has been very good to me. Mr. Forbush and I had a three-hour chat that afternoon. "Chat" describes our meeting better than "interview" because he probably spoke more than I did.

Cliff[22] tested my general knowledge about investments and financial statements and discussed his friendship with my uncle, Emmett Crump. He told me that he had checked with several of the folks I'd worked for in the company, and they all praised me and said that as a person I was a good employee, but whether I could be a strong investment professional was up to him to find out. I remember when I left his office it was almost 5:00 p.m., and I didn't have a clue how I'd done. I liked Mr. Forbush and enjoyed listening to him talk about his career and what a career in investments could mean for me, but I suspected he had candidates more qualified than me and was just interviewing me because of his friendship with Emmett.

To my surprise the following Tuesday morning, the phone rang in my Transylvania University dorm room. It was Mr. Forbush:

> Mr. Mucci, Mr. Forbush here. Well, I thought about it over the weekend, and I think I would like to give you a try. I like the fact you are getting a finance degree and a liberal arts education, and I have always respected Transylvania. You told me you graduate at the end of May, but I need you now. If you can start at the beginning of January and work at least twenty hours a week, I will give you a try, and in June after you graduate, if I like you and you still like me, you have a job.

I have always felt blessed or lucky to get to work with Mr. Forbush, and it will always go down as one of the most important events of my life. He mentored me and taught me how to be a strong investment professional. He and his wife Rita became dear friends, and he is someone I never lost touch with after the company was sold. Cliff taught me not only how to ask good questions about investments but also what questions to ask, and he always stressed, "If it sounds too good to be true, it probably is." He also instilled in

---

22   After he retired Cliff always asked me to call him by his first name, but even today I still feel more comfortable calling him "Mr. Forbush" or "Boss."

me a passion for investment history and learning about the lives and careers of some of the great investment professionals: Barnard Baruch, Warren Buffet, Peter Lynch, Benjamin Graham, and many more.

One advantage I always felt I had was learning financial analysis before the advent of personal computers. The personal computer is a wonderful invention, and it has revolutionized the world of investments and every other industry, but in my opinion the greatest computer will always be the human mind. The mind can be trained to do just about anything, and it's always learning. In 2025 we talk about artificial intelligence and its future impact on "everything," but in 1980, we had only green columnar pads to organize our information and the early calculators and adding machines with paper rolls to do our computing. The advantage they offered over computers is that I learned that numbers are not just figures but a flow of information, using assumptions, that create a picture, and if just one assumption is changed, then the picture might completely change.

I know one can perform sensitivity analysis with a computer, but working with the raw numbers from the beginning provides a better understanding of the picture you create. Mr. Forbush taught me that "figures don't lie, but liars figure" and that "lies, damned lies, and statistics" is a phrase describing the persuasive power of statistics to bolster weak arguments. During my forty-year investment career, I learned to value my knowledge of the details and knew it made me a stronger investment professional than some others in the profession. I will always give Mr. Forbush 100 percent credit for this element of my education.

In the mid-1980s, during the time I was undertaking the work necessary to be awarded the proud designation of Chartered Financial Analyst®, I was interviewed by a University of Kentucky graduate student. She had been given my name by someone at the Lexington Merrill Lynch office and wanted to discuss my role as a financial analyst. She wanted to know how I got my job and what I did, but her best question was, "What is the difference between a financial analyst and an accountant?" Now, I was still young and naïve, and I doubt that I gave her the best answer, but the question has always remained with me, and during my career I've used it to explain the problems with financial numbers and the output of spreadsheets, which can be garbage in equals garbage out.

The answer to the question is simple. An accountant uses accounting rules, assumptions, and hopefully ethics to prepare the journal entries that eventually roll into the creation of financial statements. A financial analyst studies those statements for validity and consistency and uses the information and footnotes to project a future outcome based upon various assumptions. The financial analyst is evaluating the integrity of the data and working to understand how changes in various individual items might impact future results. A financial analyst understands that company A may apply accounting rules differently than company B. This happens because some companies legally use more aggressive accounting techniques than others or interpret the regulations differently. What is the useful life of new manufacturing equipment; when and how should an installment sale be accounted for? Accounting, like investment management, is as much an art as it is a science. For instance, when a significant accounting rule change is announced and a company has three years to implement it, when does the company decide to implement it? The "art" part of accounting is the interpretation of the rules and the creation of the assumptions around those rules. It's the financial analyst's job to understand the implications of it.

In the 1980s, Bud Burnett and his chief accounting officer, Wendell Gunn, regularly interpreted the rules and regulations to put Kentucky Central Life in the best light. That was fine, but in today's world, after the failures of companies like Enron and Executive Life Insurance Company, it would be considered not only aggressive but at times fraudulent. Their actions and decisions not only suppressed the truth but, more importantly, enabled Bud Burnett's unbridled lending. In the end, Bud Burnett was not responsible to anyone. Ed Schaeffer was Burnett's chief enabler, always providing the valuable two votes to one vote on Kincaid's Committee, and Wendell Gunn fell into the role of the cleanup guy. He was always being forced to push the interpretation of accounting standards and statutory regulations to the extreme.

Burnett's strength was his knowledge of statutory accounting, but his weakness was his knowledge of GAAP accounting. Burnett had been the company's chief accountant when Kentucky updated its investment statutes in the 1970s, and according to Cliff Forbush, he had been on the working group that created those Kentucky statutes. He knew the statutory accounting rules and how to interpret the rules to his advantage extremely well, but in my opinion, he never respected the differences of GAAP accounting or recognized that one could not use the two sets of financial statements interchangeably. Because of this, Burnett in later years would report the percentage of mortgage loans and real estate as a percentage of total GAAP assets, which included over $500 million of deferred acquisition cost (DAC) as an asset.

DAC isn't a real asset but a calculation that amortizes the money the company paid to put an insurance policy on the books. The company has spent the money, so it's gone, and whereas statutory accounting removes those expenses from the company's balance sheet, GAAP accumulates them as an asset that gets amortized over time. GAAP accounting does it to better match a company's expenses against future profits. Statutory accounting limits a growing company's profitability in early growth years, while GAAP enhances it then but reduces it over time as DAC is amortized off or sales growth slows. By the late1980s, DAC was 25 percent of Kentucky Central's GAAP assets, so including it greatly distorted the perception of the company. Now, financial analysts and regulators understood the difference, but the average Kentucky Central Life employee did not.

Life insurance GAAP accounting rules were announced around 1970, Kentucky Central Life adopted them in 1973, and the impact of DAC was insignificant until the early 1980s, when the company introduced its universal life policy and Burnett announced his $50 billion in-force goal. As the company's sales exploded, so did its GAAP assets, and its growth made the company appear healthier to the average employee or shareholder. The company was growing and profits were robust in the early 1980s, but Burnett was also growing the company's exposure to his cancerous mortgage loans.

By 1990, many employees, agents, and others wondered why more people didn't appreciate what Burnett was doing. The answer was that Burnett controlled what information people had. He probably couldn't get away with it today with the internet and technology providing so much more access to information and education, but in the 1980s and early 1990s, information was more inaccessible. You couldn't read a San Francisco newspaper online, and the SEC didn't have a portal for investors to get publicly traded company information. In addition, Kentucky Central Life was just a small publicly traded company with very little analyst coverage. In fact, what reported coverage there was tended to be from Wall Street bucket shops and other lesser known investment houses. The boutique brokerage house H. J. Meyers put out a report in January 1992, when the stock was trading around $7.50, and Burnett secretly had John Lang in our offices trying to raise capital. The report was titled *Kentucky Central Life—Finger Lickin' Good ??!* It had sent a copy to Burnett, who immediately had it copied and distributed to the officers. The report looked more like a racetrack tout sheet than a research report, but Burnett liked it. The H. J. Meyers company shut its doors and filed for bankruptcy protection in 1998.

Probably Mark Boyar, of Boyar Asset Management, was one of the more-often-quoted individuals recommending the company's stock. Cliff and I had never heard of Boyer until he was interviewed by *Barron's* magazine in the mid-

1980s and was recommending Kentucky Central Life's stock. We didn't have the internet then so we couldn't find any information on him, but I remember that Wendell Gunn said that after the *Barron's* articles, Burnett would always take a call from him. Boyar first showed up in the press discussing the company in December 1984, when the company's stock was trading around $33 per share, up from $18 in April.

Boyar was a self-described "most patient investor in the world"[23] and projected the company's actual intrinsic value was "in excess of $53 per share" in 1984. By May 1988, in another *Barron's* article, with the stock at $13 per share, he was talking about the value of the consumer finance company being "very profitable" and said the stock could triple to $30 a share.[24] Boyar believed the booster for the increase in price of the stock would be the Kincaid heirs, who were "tired of seeing their stock not do anything."[25] He was forecasting a breakup of the company. By March 1990, in a *Lexington Herald-Leader* article, Boyar claimed his investment management firm owned 3% of the company's nonvoting shares and that he was banking on Kincaid's daughter's 1985 lawsuit against the Committee to prompt a change of control.[26] The stock was trading at $14 per share, down from a fifty-two-week high of $21 per share.

Philo Smith and his company, Philo Smith & Co. Inc., also began following the company in the mid-1980s. He personally visited the company early on and interviewed Cliff Forbush and other senior officers. Smith's company wrote the *Insurance and Financial Review* and managed funds that invested in insurance and financial service company stocks. He wrote a quarterly report on the industry and irregular reports on various companies. In July 1991, he also wrote about the company. It was after Burnett had sold the career divisions and Kentucky Finance Company. His focus was always on the insurance business, and in this report, he liked that the company was becoming more focused. He also failed to be concerned about the company's exposure to mortgage loans and real estate and assumed the capital raised from the recent sales would be enough to weather any further market decline.

Philo was a smart investment analyst and understood the insurance industry, but he didn't understand what Burnett had been doing. Philo was

---

23   Brendan Boyd, *News*, December 3, 1989 (quoting *Barron's* magazine).

24   Vartanig G. Vartan, *Roanoke Times and World* News, December 30, 1984 (quoting *Barron's* magazine).

25   Jim Thompson, *Courier Journal*, May 9, 1988 (quoting *Barron's* magazine).

26   Jim Jordan, *Lexington Herald-Leader*, March 5, 1990.

assuming the company had a normally underwritten commercial mortgage loan portfolio, when in fact much of the mortgage loan portfolio was probably 125 percent loan to value, with a significant amount not paying normal interest. In addition, because "figures don't lie, but liars figure," Philo was unaware of the concentration risk associated with Webb entities and others.

In for a penny, in for a pound!

In November 1988, the Webbs' San Francisco Partnership investment was off the table, and Burnett was doing a $50 million construction loan with no third-party permanent financing commitment in place. Kentucky Central would have to be the permanent financing, and the San Francisco tower only had one tenant commitment for 47 percent of the space: First Nationwide Bank.

If you read the articles about this building or talk with John Rampulla, you find that Dudley Webb referenced the involvement of a wealthy Libyan real estate investor, a Canadian insurance company, or a pension fund as takeout entities for Kentucky Central's $50 million loan. All of which failed to close. The Libyan investor was a former minister of Libya when Khadafi overthrew the government. He had just happened to get his wealth out of the country. Here is a guy with laundered petrol dollars who became a Saudi national. How the heck would Kentucky Central Life ever be able to sue him if everything were to fall apart? Think about it: the property is in foreclosure, Kentucky Central Life is up to its eyeballs in mortgage loans and specifically Webb entity–related loans, which are pretty much all in trouble, and an $8 million partnership investment request becomes a $50 million loan.

After the $8 million partnership investment was proposed, John Rampulla testified[27], he went out of town on business for two days, and when he returned, he ran into Dudley on the street an asked him, "Well, are we partners? But he [Dudley] said, "No we're not going to be partners. You're going to make a $50 million construction loan." He said he nearly fell over and thought he might get run over crossing the street.

> I was completely bewildered because the proposal I had sent up had not mentioned a construction loan at all. We had never made a loan over $20 million, and I was shocked. And I said, 'Well, fine.' And I crossed the street, and I went up to my office and there was the approval on my desk for a $50 million construction loan. I was told to close it as soon as possible, and I did.

Burnett was known to usually discuss loan terms with borrowers and

---

27   Kit Wagar and Jamie Lucke, *Lexington Herald-Leader*, May 9, 1993.

then provide John Rampulla with the terms of the proposed loan. John would write them down and have his staff prepare a mortgage loan term sheet. The sheet would be hand delivered by his staff, usually Carolyn Haulter, to get the appropriate signatures. After it was returned, Rampulla and his team would work with the Kincaid Wilson law firm to create the loan documents and fund the loan.

Theoretically the Executive and Finance Committee had met and voted on the proposed loan, and this document would bear their three signatures. In all probability, though, the trio probably discussed it over lunch in the company's cafeteria and Burnett would just sign the term sheet and then have his secretary, Shirley McCullough, take it around to the offices of Schaeffer, Hagan, and later Hembree for their signatures.

In addition, before getting their signatures, Shirley would also prepare minutes of the Executive and Finance Committee meeting approving the loan and bring them along with the term sheet and have each member sign them at the same time. At the end of year, Kentucky Central Life's auditors, Deloitte Touch, would review the mortgage loan term sheets and compare them to the actual terms of the funded loans and then review the company's board of directors and committee meeting minutes to verify the approval. It was more a documented show than substance.

After the Insurance Department took over the company, it discovered that during the last few years, Burnett had exerted so much control that many of the reported Executive and Finance meetings never actually took place and were not documented. The details were vague, but they implied that in later years, many of the restructured loans and real estate partnerships were just processed under the direction of Burnett. The defaulted loans had already been funded in prior years, and now Burnett, working with Schaeffer and his staff at the law firm, would prepare the legal documentation restructuring the loan or turning it into a partnership. Apparently, things became so chaotic that in 1989 and 1990 there was a rush to create committee minutes approving the restructured loans for meetings that had never happened. I imagine this was one of the reasons Hart Hagan resigned from the Committee at the end of 1989: Burnett and Schaeffer were doing things and he was being asked to approve them after the fact.

Kentucky Central Life gambled nearly 4 percent of its assets on one single building investment without consulting its professional staff. This 1988 decision was the most extreme example of Burnett's ridiculous lending practices and how much he did to help and protect Dudley Webb and his interests. Around 1985, John Rampulla started saying that "Kentucky Central Life's lending criteria was friends, relatives, and politicians, and not necessarily in that order." Burnett again used Kentucky Central Life's money to pay off a third-party lender (GATX) and provided a loan to finance the construction of the San Francisco Tower. The building opened in 1990 but never had enough tenants to service its debt. Kentucky Central foreclosed on the building in March 1992. It was sold in June 1993 for $25.3 million to a founder of Oracle Software. Kentucky Central's loss from this crazy transaction: $19 million.

Consider this: In 1988, Dudley Webb had only about $2 million invested in the San Francisco project when he went to Burnett with the $8 million partnership proposal. Considering the magnitude of the company's existing problem real estate loans and partnership investments with Webb entities, why in God's name did Burnett do it? I suspect that Dudley had guaranteed the GATX loan, using the equity security in other projects as collateral, and the failure of the GATX loan might start a snowball of foreclosures. If this isn't the reason, and considering that the building was only 47 percent leased, why would Burnett add to the commercial loan and real estate problems the company was already dealing with?

In June 1992, just eight months before the state took over Kentucky Central Life, Burnett did one final transaction for the Webbs. Dudley Webb had borrowed $15.5 million from the Bank of Louisville and pledged the Webbs' partnership interest in the Lexington Financial Center. When the loan came due, Dudley didn't have the ability to repay it and the bank wouldn't renew the loan. In 1991, the Kentucky Department of Insurance had ordered the company to not make any further mortgage loans or real estate investments, and Dudley needed Bud's help again.

In an action that I believe was deceptive and prohibited, Burnett pledged $15 million of Kentucky Central Life's AAA-rated GNMA bond securities to a trust controlled by the bank to guarantee Webb's loan. Dudley wanted Burnett to have the company guarantee the loan, but that was prohibited, so Dudley came up with a scheme to create a hybrid guarantee.

The whole problem began in 1988, when the Bank of Boston, which had funded the construction of the Lexington Financial Center (aka "Big Blue"), wanted its money back. The building had a lot of vacancies and negative cash flow. Dudley persuaded the bank to give him a little more time, and he started giving out sweetheart leases and eventually got most of the space leased. This enabled him to get a $38 million loan from Aetna Life to pay off the Bank of Boston, but the total cost of the building had been $15 million more than what Aetna was lending. He got Burnett to enter into a three-way agreement where he would put up his equity interest in the Merrill Lynch building and the Vine

Center complex as security and the Bank of Louisville would give him a $13.5 million loan. The Bank of Louisville agreed to take those equity interests as security because Kentucky Central Life agreed to be a financial backstop. If Webb defaulted and his equity interests in the two properties didn't cover the loan, Kentucky Central Life would be on the hook for the remaining amount. If Webb defaulted, Kentucky Central Life could purchase his two-thirds interest in the Financial Center for $35 million. He said it had been appraised for $39 million.

The loan came due in June 1992 but was extended for two years, with Kentucky Central Life continuing as a party to the deal. The problem was that the Bank of Louisville was concerned that both the Webbs and Kentucky Central could be unable to pay, so it had Kentucky Central Life put up the $15 million of GNMA collateral. Dudley Webb said Burnett did it because Kentucky Central Life would get a good deal on his equity interests in the Financial Center. Given that the Kentucky Insurance Department had Burnett on a leash, I don't believe his reason is an acceptable answer.

What Dudley proposed and Burnett executed was an agreement to purchase his interest in the three properties two years in the future, and the Bank of Louisville accepted this contract as collateral. The properties were the Merrill Lynch building, the Vine Center complex, and parcels tied to Lexington Green. Kentucky Central Life already owned a 50 percent interest in the Merrill Lynch Building and the Vine Center complex. The agreement was later amended to substitute the equity interest in the Financial Center for Lexington Green. The trigger for the $15 million of GNMA collateral was that if Kentucky Central didn't purchase the three equity-interest parcels in two years, the Bank of Louisville could take the securities to pay off its loan.

According to court records, in February 1989 Dudley was at an impasse in finding a bank that would provide him the $13.5 million (later increased to $15 million). He had been trying to obtain a loan from Citizens Fidelity Bank and wrote Burnett:

> In any event, to expeditiously resolve this impasse, and allow me to retain what we have worked so hard to build, I am reiterating my request for Kentucky Central Life Insurance to enhance the Ten Million ($10,000,000) dollar "real estate" portion of the line by offering to Citizen's your "standby" loan commitment whereby you would agree to take them out of their loan by March 1, 1992, unless I had sooner prepaid same.

After about a month of negotiations with Citizens, Citizens wrote Dudley Webb and called the "sales agreement" from Kentucky Central Life a "take-out." After further negotiations and some research by Citizens Bank, it informed Dudley that it "believe[d] Kentucky Central is at their limit" on certain types of loans and this is why they needed the purchase agreement two years out. After expressing further uneasiness with the proposed loan structure, Citizens encouraged Dudley to look elsewhere, and on May 24, 1989, Dudley contacted Merchants Bank of Indianapolis with the proposal. After not getting positive news, on June 30, 1989, he contacted the Bank of Louisville with the same proposal. On September 15, 1989, the Bank of Louisville entered into the proposed loan agreement and Kentucky Central Life entered into the tri-party agreement on the properties for the original $13.5 million.

On February 25, 1991, the agreement was amended to substitute the interest in the Lexington Financial Center for the Lexington Green property. The reason for the property substitution was that the Webb entity that controlled the Lexington Green property had a separate commercial loan that had gone into default and the Bank of Louisville needed the substitution.

In June 1992, the Bank of Louisville was concerned that Kentucky Central Life would not be able to acquire the properties if Dudley was unable to pay off its loan. In addition, Webb needed more money, so the loan was increased to $15.5 million and Burnett was required to secure the purchase agreement. This required him to deposit Kentucky Central Life's GNMA securities in a Bank of Louisville trust account. The company could monitor the account and collect the principal and interest payments the securities paid, but it did not control the account, and if the market value fell below $15.5 million, it had to add more securities.

This whole transaction was kept secret from everyone. Burnett came down to Cliff Forbush's office one morning with a page of instructions for electronically delivering the securities to the bank. According to Cliff, Burnett said it was somehow tied to Wilkinson's Frankfort Hotel and was needed because Kentucky Central Life's credit rating had dropped. Also, according to Cliff, Burnett said we needed to put up the additional collateral or be forced to pay off the bonds. By this time, Cliff had had enough of Burnett's crazy antics. I think the $50 million San Francisco tower was the straw that broke the proverbial camel's back, and he wasn't happy and Burnett knew it.

One needs to appreciate the way Bud Burnett operated. Burnett provided the employees, whether they were senior officers or important departments, with only enough information to do their jobs. Over the years, after the company was gone, many of us discussed this and agreed that no one ever received the full story. We doubted that Committee members Hagan and Hembree ever knew the whole story (though the other Committee member, Schaeffer, did). It was the way he operated, and Dudley Webb's scheme to bypass the legal restrictions the company was operating under is probably the best example of this.

I referred to this transaction as deceptive or prohibited, and the Kentucky Department of Insurance tried to pursue a charge of fraud against Dudley. The problem was that neither the Bank of Louisville nor Dudley Webb did anything fraudulent. Both entities knowingly entered into the tri-party agreement or performance contract. Neither person or entity held a fiduciary responsibility to the shareholders or policyholders of Kentucky Central Life.

Every day, many companies receive proposals for opportunities that they can choose to either ignore or proceed with. All Dudley did was make a proposal to Burnett and plead with him to consider helping him given his precarious financial circumstances. From an ethical perspective, he never should have made the request—it was obviously a sham and all three parties to the tri-party agreement knew it—but in the end all Dudley did was enter into a contract. The Bank of Louisville also knew this was a problematic transaction, but again it was legally just a credit agreement. The fraud that was committed was by Burnett as an officer and director of the company and probably by Ed Schaeffer and Wendell Gunn as an officer and a director. Ed Schaeffer had been an active participant in getting the legal work done for the transaction. Wendell Gunn wasn't involved in creating the accounting for the transaction but knew about it after the fact. As the chief accounting officer for the company, secretary and treasurer of the company, and a director, he had a fiduciary responsibility to the policyholders and shareholders.

This agreement existed in 1990, when the Insurance Department was doing its exhausting examination and the record shows that the examiner requested information about the agreement from Wendell Gunn. The examiners had found out about the transaction when they did their review of the Investment Department's state deposits and found we had $16 million of GNMA securities in a restricted account at the Bank of Louisville. I recall the examiner asking our investment accounting administrator, Joann Conner, about it. The only thing she knew was that "Mr. Forbush had been instructed to do it by Mr. Burnett." When they asked Cliff about it, he told them what he thought was the truth: that it had to do with Wilkinson's Frankfort Hotel and our credit rating. The examiner went back to the examiners' conference room and five minutes later Wendle Gunn was in the room and providing them with a copy of the agreement.

In my opinion, the state Insurance Department and its attorneys wasted a lot of money suing Dudley Webb for fraud. Burnett and other company insiders committed the fraud against the company, and while Dudley was a willing participant, he had no fiduciary responsibility to the company. At worst he knew the agreement was a wink, wink sham transaction meant to avoid immediately triggering a regulatory reprisal from the Insurance Department, but he wasn't Kentucky Central Life's legal counsel. The court came to the same conclusion and after several years of litigation found in favor of Dudley Webb and the Bank of Louisville. The Bank of Louisville still had to deal with its Kentucky banking regulator, though, who I understand (but don't know for sure) imposed several regulatory fines against it. The bank's trust department's management had a duty of care to avoid conflicts of interest and to act prudently as a reasonable person would, and they didn't.

If this all of this sounds a little crazy by now, it gets crazier. After the Insurance Department took charge of the company, Stites and Harbison became the department's primary outside counsel and legal advisor. Politically connected Steve Beshear was the partner in charge of the account. In the early 1970s, Steve Beshear and the insurance commissioner, Don Stephens, had both represented Fayette County in the state legislature. Everyone knew the state takeover of Kentucky Central Life was going to be complicated and the Insurance Department wasn't staffed for handling a problem this large and complex. Beshear immediately became tethered to the insurance commissioner, and while the Insurance Department had to hire other law firms to advise and litigate the quagmire of problems it had inherited, Beshear and Stites carried out the greatest magnitude of the legal work.

After our department returned to work the following Monday, February 15, the Insurance Department came to our area to explain how we should handle our investment duties. Basically, things were fairly normal, except now we had to work with the property and casualty management team and Joe Hudson on issues. Cliff Forbush immediately told them about our GNMA securities, "which were being held hostage at the Bank of Louisville." Apparently, the insurance commissioner, Don Stephens, who was relatively new to the job, hadn't heard anything about this issue.

After Kentucky Central was taken over by the state in February 1993, the following June, the Bank of Louisville liquidated our bonds. I was the one who found out about it when I called the bank's trust department to find out where our July GNMA payments were. (We hadn't received our July interest and principal payments.) This moment became my fifteen minutes of fame, as the saying goes, because my deposition was taken (several times) and parts of it were printed in various Kentucky newspapers. The lawsuits about the $15 million of GNMA securities that were backing the unrelated Webb loan and a sham purchase agreement went on for fourteen years.

I remember it like it was yesterday. There was a trust officer at the bank named Eva Shiley, and I contacted her about our payments. The value of the account had been dropping each month due to the monthly payments they were sending us, so the bank had contacted its attorney about what its options were. It had been evaluating the situation since May, and in July had sold all our securities to get its money. Shiley told me on the phone, "Mr. Mucci, I am not supposed to tell you this, but we sold your securities." I said, "What? Who told you to do that?" and Shiley said, "Our attorneys, Stites & Harbison." I immediately contacted one of the Management Committee members and told him what happened, and they couldn't understand why Stites would tell the bank to do this.

Apparently, Stites and Harbison had represented the Bank of Louisville in the 1989 transaction and, it was later discovered, in the 1991 and 1992 amendments. Stites's lead attorney for the Insurance Department, Janet Craig, wrote the commissioner a letter in March 1993 acknowledging the conflict and said the firm would represent neither the department nor the bank in any matter regarding the transaction. With the help of Stites, Commissioner Stephens brought in a Cincinnati law firm to work on the matter. From the department's perspective, the issue was resolved, but Craig's communication apparently never made it to the Louisville office, and when the bank contacted its Stites attorney, it was told it could liquidate the securities.

Stites and Harbison is a large, reputable law firm, and what's hard to understand is this: The state takeover of Kentucky Central Life was all over the news, and Steve Beshear's role as the partner in charge for the Insurance Department was well known. So how does a partner in Stites's Louisville office not consider that there might be a conflict? The state legislature had the same question, and a long investigation was conducted. Beshear and Stites, while criticized, were never found libel for anything. After this mess, the insurance commissioner brought in Frost and Jacobs and built a Chinese wall between the two firms in relation to the Bank of Louisville litigation. By the time the Kentucky Central Life estate was wound up in 2007, Stites and Harbison had billed the company more than $21 million in fees for its work. As for the Bank of Louisville, in 2002, its successor bank, MidAmerica Bancorp, paid the estate of Kentucky Central Life $27 million to settle the matter. The law firm Frost and Jacobs didn't do too badly either; by 2006, the firm had charged the estate of Kentucky Central Life over $11 million for its work on various matters.

"The Old Girl"—gone but never forgotten!

Most of the employees who worked for the company for any length of time appreciated it. Some department was always celebrating someone's birthday or wedding or having a baby shower, and the opportunity to get Fridays off for personal things was attractive to many folks with kids. We were a family, and in the end, we never really got to say goodbye. After the state took us over, there was a series of layoffs, and people were slowly leaving as they found other jobs. The fun times were gone, and we still had our memories, but everyone's feelings were raw. Many couldn't talk about it, and most just wanted to try to forget how bad the end was. After moving to Wisconsin, I tried to keep in touch with folks, but it was almost five years before some of the internet tools we have today came into being, and it wasn't like we had everyone's telephone number. So, in the end, most of us just went our own way and stayed in touch with a few of our closest colleagues.

People reading this should appreciate that I was pretty attached to "this old girl." I worked there after high school; during college, it was the beginning of my investment career; and I met my wife, Jan, there. Oh, and my uncle Emmett introduced me to the company and Mr. Kincaid during my childhood and then helped me be part of the Kentucky Central Life family. Given all the above, I had one last thing I wanted to do for the old girl.

In early 2016, I created a private Facebook group called "Former Employees of Kentucky Central Life." We have 298 members today. I started with fifteen names and in six months had about 100 members. People really liked reconnecting with people after twenty years. They liked it so much that by the next year I had over 200 members. I scanned some old Kentucky Central Life monthly magazines, annual reports, and other things and then started posting historical things about departments, people, and events. The first time I posted a bunch of old pictures from our Christmas parties, the comments went wild. It's been a nice way to let everyone reconnect and relive some stories and to let folks know about their friends—illnesses, deaths, new grandbabies, and birthdays. The Facebook group page did better than I ever expected, and by late 2016 and early 2017, the members were asking if we could have a party somewhere, and I guess, since I started the page, I was supposed to be the one to figure out if we could.

After much cajoling, I agreed to see what I could do. I didn't know how many people would come, where we could do it, or how much we could charge, but I figured it out. I charged $25 a person (cash bar) and had heavy hors d'oeuvres, and we had it at the Round Barn at the Red Mile in September 2017. It ultimately cost me about $2,800, but that was cheap joy' given that we had over 200 people show up. It was a September evening of tears, hugs, smiles, and laughs. Isabell Yates (Wilson Yates's wife and the former vice mayor of Lexington, who was in her early 90s at the time) even came. We had tables of old Kentucky Central Life items, and people didn't want to leave. I believe "the old girl" would have been proud, and I know my Uncle Emmett would have been!

John Rampulla, III—Vice President, Mortgage Loans

Before 1988, the investment department didn't interact very often with the actuarial department. We might occasionally answer a question about interest rates, but generally it was understood that Bud Burnett was instructing them on the interest rate they should use in their product work. Burnett had created an environment of departmental silos, and this limited what information people had and allowed him more control. The investment department handled the company's fixed income, common stock, and preferred stock portfolios, while Wendell Gunn's financial statement area provided the actuarial department with the projected cash flows from the company's mortgage loan and real estate portfolios. The mortgage loan department used a mainframe accounting program to track mortgage payments, but it didn't have a personal computer or anyone with strong analytical skills. The mortgage loan department was still operating the way it had under Kincaid. The department processed new loans, tracked late and delinquent mortgage loan payments, and notified Burnett when a loan developed problems or the borrower wanted something.

According to John Rampulla, Garvice met with the borrowers and he did his own financial analysis. If he wanted to make a loan, he would provide Rampulla's mortgage loan department with the information. John would then work with Kincaid's law firm to create the loan documentation and with Wendell Gunn's area on funding the loan.

Kentucky's main newspapers did an excellent job reporting on Kincaid's activities beginning in the late 1950s. Before that, he was frequently reported on, but beginning in the late 1950s, he began issuing more press releases and began sitting for more interviews. Garvice had become a respected and powerful business leader, but he wasn't finished. The press releases and interviews provide a very detailed record of his activities and also an indication of the people who assisted him. After Kincaid acquired Kentucky Central Life and brought in Charlie Thomas to handle his public relations work, he employed press releases to announce significant staff changes and other important business-related activities. These articles seemed to support the supposition that Garvice preferred to make his own lending and investing decisions. Frank

Trimble was still Kincaid's loan man, but by the late 1960s, Trimble's personal issues had diminished his importance.

Before he acquired Kentucky Central Life, Kincaid's lending and investing activities were primarily restricted to the geographic areas where he owned banks, mainly Kentucky and Florida. After acquiring the life insurance company, Garvice could now expand into other areas of the country. This appears to be when he created the position of vice president, mortgage loans at Kentucky Central Life. His first attempt at adding this position occurred in August 1965, when he brought in John W. Polk, Jr., a local mortgage loan broker. That same month, Kincaid also brought in William R. Engle to manage the company's growing investment portfolio. Cliff Forbush would eventually take over this position after Engle left.

Polk worked with Kincaid until around 1968. When he left the Kincaid organization, he went to work for Hilliard Lyons as an investment broker. In December 1967, Kincaid acquired the Rio Grande National Life Insurance Company in Dallas, Texas, from its founder Robert W. Baxter. This acquisition increased Kentucky Central Life's assets by 36 percent, to $161 million. Baxter was an active real estate investor, and his company had a sizable mortgage loan portfolio. When Kincaid acquired the company, he moved the insurance operations to Lexington but appointed Rio Grande's James A. Banowsky Kentucky Central's vice president, mortgage loans. Banowsky remained in Dallas, though. It appears that Banowsky's primary job was to help Kincaid understand and monitor the Rio Grande loans and to also manage and dispose of the large amount of real estate that came with the deal. The acquisition had included the company's nine-story office tower and the land around it. By January 1969, the real estate had been sold and Banowsky was no longer with the company.

In1970, Kincaid appointed Donald L. Smith vice president in charge of Kentucky Central Life's mortgage loan department. Smith had work in the mortgage loan department at General American Life Insurance Company in St. Louis. Smith was a strong lending professional. In addition to St. Louis, he had worked in Dallas, Cleveland, and San Franscisco. Kentucky Central's mortgage loan portfolio had increased to over $90 million in size, and Garvice realized he needed some professional help. The company now controlled assets of $186 million, 48.6 percent of it in commercial mortgage loans. Smith's tenure with Kincaid appears to have been the shortest, not lasting even a year. Kincaid had filled the position, three times in five years, with experienced lending professionals, and none of them had worked out. It is important to note that Garvice apparently never considered Bud Burnett for this role, which was the idea that members of his Committee promoted in the 1976 *Courier Journal* article.

John F. Rampulla was born February 5, 1940, in Queens, New York. Shortly after his birth, his family moved to Miami, Florida. In 1958, he was recruited to play football at the University of Kentucky, where he was a reserve quarterback. John graduated from UK with a commerce degree in 1963 and was accepted into UK's law school. He graduated and passed the bar in 1965 and then did a 13-month tour in Korea, where he was a captain in the army. After John's tour of service, he returned to Lexington, where he joined Keller & Hughes law firm in February 1969. "Keller" was the same James Keller who, in the future, would be the judge presiding over the Kincaid daughters' 1985 lawsuit against the Committee.

John said he enjoyed practicing criminal and family law, but in those years the profession didn't allow advertising and the only way to obtain new clients was through referrals from other attorneys and friends. Building a practice was a slow process, and after a couple of years, in 1969, James Keller left the practice to serve as the master commissioner of the Fayette County Circuit Court, and shortly after that, Henry Hughes began pursuing other interests. The law firm never officially disbanded, but it became obvious to Rampulla that he needed to evaluate his options.

After struggling to pay his bills for a couple of years, John ran into his law school classmate Steve Wilson and told him he was interested in being a corporate attorney. Steve was already working with his father (Earl) and brother (Phil) at the Kincaid, Wilson law firm and told John that he knew Mr. Kincaid was looking for someone to help him with Kentucky Central Life's mortgage loans. John said he knew who Mr. Kincaid was and assumed this was a position connected to the company's law department.

In the summer of 1971, Steve introduced thirty-year-old Rampulla to Garvice during one of Kincaid's summer pool parties at his house. Steve told him, "The job is in the mortgage loan department basically servicing loans, reporting to Mr. Kincaid, and preparing reports for him." That was basically it, John told me, but the main job was the collection of delinquent loans. His most vivid memory of that day is of Garvice saying, "So you want to work in the mortgage department" and then abruptly turning and just walking off, with John's hand still extended. John said he was a little shocked and thought, "What have I gotten myself into." Garvice brought John into the company as the assistant vice president, mortgage loans. John didn't have any mortgage loan experience, but he was an attorney, and Kincaid would be handling all the lending.

John said his work consisted of meeting with Mr. Kincaid on an irregular basis and getting his marching orders regarding whatever Mr. Kincaid wanted him to follow up on. Early on, John learned that Mr. Kincaid had acquired a bunch of mortgage loans on properties in Texas and that the company maintained a small, two-person mortgage loan servicing office in Dallas. One of John's early responsibilities was to travel to Dallas about every two weeks and review what was going on and coordinate with local attorneys on dealing with problem loans, of which there were many. John learned later that these loans were acquired as part of the Rio Grande Life acquisition that Garvice had made a few years before he joined the company. John said these trips continued for about three years, but by 1975, they had closed the Dallas office and were servicing everything from Lexington.

John said he learned early on that Mr. Kincaid did all the lending and John's department's main responsibility was to process the loans and work with Mr. Kincaid's law firm to create the initial loan documents. He said one of his main jobs was to put together a monthly report on delinquent loans and send it to Mr. Kincaid. The department processed the payment information on the company's mainframe computer system, but the tracking details about the loans were all manual. John said after about three or four months he got a call from Garvice, who was mad and wanted to know why he (John) hadn't instigated foreclosure on somebody's loan. John thought he had screwed up and asked Mr. Kincaid if he could call him back. He researched the loan and told Mr. Kincaid that the loan had a six-month grace period and that legally it was too early to file foreclosure. Kincaid then told him he was wrong and just abruptly hung up.

John was worried now and decided to go through every loan and do a report, including all the terms for each loan, including their grace periods. He guessed there were probably two hundred loans. What he found disturbed him, because the grace periods were all over the place, with some being over a year. He called Mr. Kincaid and told him he needed to see him, and Garvice told him to come to his barber shop in thirty minutes. Yes, John went to his barber shop and there Kincaid was in the barber chair. He explained to Mr. Kincaid that he had put together a report on all the loans and the grace periods were all over the place. Garvice grabbed the report and looked at it, grunting from time to time, and then told John, "Thank you; I'll handle it." A day or two later, John got a call from Steve Wilson, and Steve wanted to know what the heck he had done. Apparently, Kincaid had just been over to the law firm and read the riot act to the law partners that worked on his mortgage loan deals. Apparently they were giving what one might call friends and family terms to some of Kincaid's borrowers. John never heard if they were getting kickbacks or anything for doing this, but it never happened again.

John said he never met with potential borrowers about loans. They all went through either Garvice or Frank Trimble. He also said he never knew of an occasion when Burnett was involved with Kincaid on any mortgage loans. In his opinion, Kincaid decided what he wanted to do and did it and probably didn't care what Burnett or anyone else thought, and to his knowledge, no loans ever were sourced to Kincaid by Burnett. From John's perspective, Burnett was the company's chief accountant and regulatory person, and that was it.

Wendell Gunn had been brought into the company as its controller in 1966 to assist Burnett in running the accounting department. He was also from Florida and had worked at a couple of insurance companies as well as the Florida Department of Insurance. Burnett was now consumed with getting the company licensed in all states, excluding New York, which was a slow, time-consuming process, many times requiring a trip to the state insurance department and setting up a special state securities deposit at an in-state bank. By the end of 1968, the company was licensed in thirty-seven states and the District of Columbia. Each individual state insurance department had its own set of rules and regulations, and in the 1960s and 1970s many of their staff enjoyed the power they had over companies. It was always their choice whether to fast-track or slow-walk a company's request, and they sometimes required a company to bring in a certain favored local law firm to help expedite their requests.

John had fond memories of working for Mr. Kincaid, which is what he always called him, even after he died. In fact, he said he cried after he died, not so much because of any special treatment he had, but because Mr. Kincaid was such a force:

> In the short period of time I was acquainted with him, this is how he impressed me. He knew and understood how to play the game of life. He was an enigma to people. He kept people thinking and guessing. He could run them through the gamut of emotions quickly and exhaust them. He could size up any person very quickly. He hated incompetence and wastefulness.
>
> He played insecure people off and against each other and he could be a domineering manipulator when appropriate but very shrewd and accommodating when necessary.
>
> He is the most impressive person I met during my lifetime, and I have met a couple of US presidents, and a lot of prominent people. He lived his life to the maximum of his efforts, and he was

a dedicated family man and protected his family.

Mr. Kincaid knew the answer to the questions he asked, and the best way to get along with him was to be straightforward and honest with him. Loyalty and commitment were very important to him. He set a standard of performance for employees, and they were expected to live up to it.

If he asked a person a question and got an inappropriate answer, his reply would be "my ass."

He had a wonderful sense of humor as long as he wasn't the joke. There was nothing fake about him. He had a good heart, in every sense of the word, and he was sensitive and kind and cared about the common person, children, and young people, regardless of their race. You can see that in all his charitable donations and things he did that never made it into the papers.

He loved the telephone, and he probably would have had three cell phones if they had been around back then.

Mr. Kincaid was a very accomplished, successful person and very much misunderstood and underappreciated for his good efforts. He deeply cared about Lexington, Fayette County, and Central Kentucky and worked hard to improve them. He received little, if little appreciation for his efforts.

If he had wanted to be, he could have been

- A great football coach,
- An appreciated politician,
- An outstanding military leader (a General Patton type),
- A commanding preacher, or
- A great trial lawyer, etc. etc.

He died too young!"

John's memories of Kincaid capture what I have described as a "complicated man." He was a man with a low tolerance for incompetence, and he rewarded people for hard work. He demanded loyalty and expected his employees to live up to the standards he set. If he wanted to call you at midnight to discuss something, that was the price one paid for being in his universe. If there was a problem developing in one of his businesses, he expected the person to bring it to his attention quickly because nine out of ten times, he would find out about it.

John Rampulla enjoyed working for Garvice but wanted more from his job. John told me that when Mr. Kincaid offered him the job, he thought he was going to be part of the general counsel's office, working in the law department. He started getting frustrated that his job was mainly to get the mortgage loans processed and closed, which Mr. Kincaid had negotiated without his involvement. He said one day his frustration got the better of him and he told Mr. Kincaid that he felt pigeonholed and wanted to be involved in more of the company's legal work (thinking about a path to becoming general counsel). He said Mr. Kincaid looked at him and said, "Well, we could do that," but that he would have to take a pay cut and that he should "realize that all the real legal work was done by his law firm." He said Mr. Kincaid asked him if he didn't see that all the action in the company was on the lending side of things. Rampulla quickly said thank you and that they didn't need to discuss it any further.

Garvice Kincaid was already a respected and feared businessman when John Rampulla came to work for him in 1971. John didn't have anything to do with Central Bank, and so what loans Kincaid was doing through the bank was something he was unfamiliar with. In 1972, Central Bank had assets of $125 million and capital of $6.4 million. Most of its assets were invested in government-related securities, and it had only $47 million in commercial loans. A large commercial loan for the bank would have been $500,000, and these would have been few and far between. Cliff Forbush told me that Kincaid liked to keep his bank's balance sheets clean. They were regulated entities, and he didn't want problems. If a larger loan had a problem, many times he would purchase the loan from the bank. Insurance company investment regulations were more to Garvice's liking. He could invest across state lines, invest in larger loans, and be less concerned with holding real estate foreclosed on. In 1972, Kentucky Central Life was Kincaid's primary lending machine and Central Bank was his high-quality small bank.

From 1972 to 1975, John worked as Garvice's mortgage loan processer and manager. His department kept track of all of Kincaid's loans and let him know when borrowers were having problems. John agreed with Cliff Forbush that when Garvice had a problem with a borrower, he generally accepted the mistake and moved on but never loaned money to the person again, unless it was something he wanted to personally be involved in like the Fontainebleau or the Duck Key Resort. According to both men, Garvice didn't let problems linger. He would initially work with a borrower to correct a situation, but his experience taught him that resolving problems quickly and moving on was the best approach. In addition, my research shows that Kincaid had a knack for bringing new partners into problem situations. He could restructure the old borrower out of the problem loan and bring in someone stronger to take over the property. During the 1980s, Burnett did the exact opposite by restructuring loans over and over with the same participants and even doing more deals with failed entities.

After Kincaid's death in 1975, things quickly changed for John. He continued his normal reports on the mortgage loan portfolio but had few if any conversations with Burnett or Earl Wilson. According to Cliff Forbush and Dick Gordon, no one knew what to expect from the newly created Kincaid Committee and people tried to keep their head down and just do their job. Everyone also wondered how this would affect David Brain and remembered Burnett's suspicion of him. Everyone expected changes, and the first significant change was the resignation of David Brain and then the resignation of Al Florence from the Committee at the end of 1976. By the middle of 1977, after the Committee announced the construction of Kincaid Towers, things were getting a little more settled internally, but the nation's inflation rate was running rampant and would eventually reach almost 15% on an annual basis and require Federal Reserve Chairman Paul Volker to raise the federal reserve rate to 20 percent, driving the economy into a deep recession.

During this time, Cliff Forbush and John Rampulla said, they had little to do. Most of the company's cash flow was going into the construction of Kincaid Towers, no commercial mortgage loan projects were being proposed, and policyholders were now borrowing cheap money from their old whole-life policies and investing it in AAA-rated money market funds at a ridiculous spread difference. Kentucky Central Life, like many life insurance companies, was eventually forced to borrow money from one of the major banks to fill in its negative cash flow. After I joined Cliff in 1981, I learned that the company had borrowed $2 million from the banks during this time. While Cliff didn't have a lot of new investable cash to invest, he used this period to sell and buy securities to improve the company's future cash flow. The yield curve was inverted, so short maturity bonds had higher yields than longer-term securities, so he had opportunities to do swaps and potentially upgrade the portfolio's credit quality or just improve its internal investment yield.

John's job was quieter. He would monitor problem loans and send his mortgage loan reports to Burnett, from whom he never received any feedback, and just sit around waiting for the phone to ring. By 1980, he was so frustrated with his job that he decided he needed to discuss it with Burnett. The company had just moved into Kincaid towers, and Burnett's office was on the twenty-first floor. Rampulla called Burnett's secretary and made an appointment for the afternoon. When he arrived, Burnett assumed there was an issue with a borrower, and after John explained his frustration, he just stared at his desk and then told him he understood and for him to consider coming into the office in the mornings and taking off at lunch. Burnett told him this malaise should be ending soon and John could take advantage of this quiet period and still get his day-to-day work done.

This one action by Burnett stigmatized John for the rest of his career because people inside the company didn't understand what had happened. John would come in during the morning and leave at noon. If Keeneland was in session, he could run to the track for the afternoon, and if the Cincinnati Reds were playing a game, he might drive up and catch it. From his perspective, he was doing what his boss said he could do given the circumstances, but from an outsider's perspective, it just didn't look good. The company's vice president of mortgage loans was at Keeneland most afternoons! Internally, the other officers didn't understand it either, and they began to talk, the way people normally gossip. Instead of suggesting that John offer to do some legal work for the company's legal department, Burnett just told him to take the afternoons off. It was just another bad Bud Burnett decision.

John's friendship with me evolved over time. Initially I was this young guy working for Mr. Forbush, and yes, John usually called him Mr. Forbush. It wasn't until about 1986 or 1987 that John started spending more time in my office. It may have started with the 1987 stock market crash, or it may have been because of his growing frustration with Burnett, but around that time, we would have more conversations about things. By this period, he had been flying all over the country handling Burnett's loans. He and Charlie Curtis of Mason Hanger (engineering) were constantly on planes, looking at commercial properties being developed by Burnett's loans. Burnett was doing speculative construction and development loans, and the company was not equipped to perform this type of lending. John and Charlie needed to visit the properties, confirm what work had been completed, and then compare it to the borrower's construction draw request. At one point, Delta airlines told John he had more frequent flier points than anyone else in the state of Kentucky.

John never signed up to be a corporate road warrior, and as Burnett's loans started turning sour in the mid-1980s, his enthusiasm for what he was doing also began to sour. He was watching Burnett lend money on projects already in default or ones that soon would be in default. He couldn't explain it, and by the time Burnett agreed to do the $50 million San Francisco Office Tower loan, he was saying that Burnett has lost his mind. John usually attended the annual national conference for commercial loan brokers, and by 1988 he had been hearing about the growing problems in the commercial real estate markets. In a February 23, 1998, deposition, he described Burnett's fatal error this way: "Basically, they converted an insurance company into a savings and loan. The company just changed completely. It just got out of control and when the real estate market tanked in the recession of the early 1990s, Kentucky Central did too."

Another thing John couldn't understand was the lending relationships Burnett was funding. For instance, Teddy Mims was an inexperienced high school football coach who went to high school with Burnett's son Bruce, and over five or six years Burnett had allowed him to borrow close to $80 million in loans. Then you had Bud Burnett's former Louisville friend up in Michigan, Walter Walden, whom he lent money to and then turned around and purchased some commercial loans from his Michigan insurance company. As for the Webb-entity loans and partnerships, by 1985 things were starting to fail, yet he continued to fund new and bigger projects and take out other third-party Webb-entity lenders. Burnett wasn't just an unbridled lender with too much money to invest, he was acting like a gambler doubling down on the next hand.

To this day, John Rampulla wishes there had been something more he could have done. As I've been working on this book, we've had many conversations, and I've tried to explain to him that Burnett held all the cards. He and Schaeffer controlled the Committee, Burnett appears to have had the Insurance Department in his pocket via the governor's mansion, Judge Keller appears to have had more than enough information to have ruled in favor of the Kincaid daughters but failed to act, and finally, if he had gone to the newspapers, all it would have done is force Burnett to sue him in court. Kincaid's fail-safe had been having three trusted people on his committee, but he never anticipated the unbridled power that two members working together would have. Ed Schaeffer might disagree with being called Burnett's enabler, but what did he try to do to stop him? When Burnett participated in the Bank of Louisville transaction for the benefit of Dudley Webb, Ed Schaeffer appears to have been actively overseeing the legal work.

One of the primary problems with what happened to Kentucky Central Life is that various people who played significant roles in its destruction failed to ever take responsibility for what happened. Whether they were on the Committee or were significant borrowers, they participated in the collapse of a large, wonderful company and in doing so destroyed much of Garvice Kincaid's empire. John and I discussed that one of our biggest disappointments was that no one ever took responsibility for what happened. It wouldn't have brought anything back, but there was never a postmortem on the failure of one of Kentucky's largest companies.

After Kentucky Central Life's business was transferred to Jefferson Pilot and Jan and I moved to Wisconsin, I occasionally spoke with John. Shortly after the company was taken over, John tried to leave his past association with the company behind, but he soon found out this was an impossibility. The attorneys representing all sorts of litigants were interested in interviewing and deposing the "vice president of mortgage loans." In addition, the SEC was investigating the collapse and wanted his time.

John Rampulla willingly provided whatever information he could, but he couldn't explain why Burnett invested so much of the company's money in projects that failed. I think the only loans that Rampulla ever recommended to Burnett were loans for a handful of employees or agents. If someone contacted him about potentially doing a large loan, his instructions were to take their information and send it up to Burnett's office. John's primary responsibilities included processing the approved loans, monitoring the portfolio for problems, and reporting any problems to Burnett. One of the challenges he faced was dealing with problem loans tied to Burnett's friends, relatives, and political friends. For instance, how does one tell the chairman and president of the company, and your boss, that his son is a delinquent borrower?

By 1994, John accepted that his reputation as a mortgage loan professional was beyond repair and decided to put his UK law degree back to work. Initially two or three local attorneys provided him with office space, and he began getting work from the Fayette County Public Defender's office, but John hadn't practiced law in over twenty years and these relationships began to fall apart. John's life had become another victim of Bud Burnett's mess. Eventually an old friend, Kilbern Cormney, came to his rescue and provided John an office in a commercial building he owned along with lodging at the Campbell House Suites, which he also owned. In addition, he started using him for some of his own legal work.

John to this day credits Mr. Cormney with getting him back on his feet. Kentucky Central Life's downfall affected many lives. Older employees had their retirement plans wrecked, and other employees saw their savings dramatically reduced. People who had invested ten, twenty, and thirty years with the company were now being forced to start over, and while some made it OK, others found that the stress of the situation drove them into an emotional crisis. Clyde Honaker and I have discussed this many times, and we agree that for many people it took about twenty years before the scab of the situation finally healed over. The whole thing had been like a long-term marriage falling apart, followed by the pain of the actual separation and divorce proceeding. Bud Burnett and the other members of Kincaid's Committee didn't just destroy Garvice Kincaid's estate, they destroyed many lives. So, when I talk about never getting an answer to the "why?" and recognizing that no one ever accepted responsibility for what happened, one should appreciate why it took so long for the emotional scab of this failure to heal over.

Burnett: Empire Building, One Deal at a Time

The point is, ladies and gentlemen, that greed—for lack of a better word—is good.

Greed is right. Greed works.

Greed clarifies, cuts through, and captures the essence of the evolutionary spirit.

Greed, in all of its forms—greed for life, for money, for love, knowledge—has marked the upward surge of mankind.

– Gordon Gekko in the Movie *Wall Street* (1987)

Garvice Kincaid's relationships with various politicians and his ability to work the system have been well documented. Kincaid lived and operated during a time when political relationships were the business standard in Kentucky and the nation. Some might say not much has changed, but certainly twenty-four-hour news, the internet, social media, and stricter oversight regulations have limited their impact.

In his early years, Garvice used his political influence to get a seat at the table. His interest in politics dates all the way back to his college days, and he remained active in various Democratic groups throughout his life. He adored A. B. (Happy) Chandler and purchased the WVLK radio station from him. He helped Frank Trimble become a city commissioner, a position he held for many years, and one that benefited Kincaid by helping move along the approvals for his Lexington real estate projects.

Garvice understood that politics played an important role in his life. His banks and finance companies had to deal with the changing consumer regulatory environment, and getting approvals to buy radio and television stations required managing the rules and regulations of the Federal Communications Commission. After acquiring Kentucky Central Life, he then had to deal with Kentucky's Insurance Department, the insurance departments of other states, and, because Kentucky Central was a publicly traded company, the Securities and Exchange Commission. Kincaid understood that he needed to have relationships with people who would be making decisions that involved his enterprises. There wasn't anything nefarious about it; he needed to be able to make his case about subjects that might affect him and wanted to have an interested ear to listen to it.

Kincaid was quite open about his political interests and his political relationships. He was a strong Democrat and was open to supporting Democratic causes, and the politicians he built relationships with appreciated his support until the relationship became a problem for them. At one point, even Ed Hahn, who was running for Fayette County Judge Executive in 1965, had to say publicly several times, "Garvice Kincaid doesn't own me."[28] The opposition was calling him Kincaid's puppet. Garvice was popular, though, and governors came to his birthday celebrations and legislators attended his post–football game parties at the Campbell House Inn. When Garvice needed assistance, he or one of his lieutenants could call a political friend and see if they could help. Kincaid wasn't demanding their help, but he was demanding that they listen to his issue or problem and try to help him find a solution.

In 1976, when Burnett became president of Kentucky Central Life, he didn't have the political relationships Garvice had. In fact, he didn't have the name recognition that one might have expected since he'd been working at Kentucky Central Life for sixteen years. Kincaid had used Bud Burnett more as a loyal foot soldier than as one of his powerful lieutenants. Other than Kincaid, David Brain was the face of the company. His face was displayed in *Keynoter* articles, and his picture was attached to local charitable events. In addition, and maybe more importantly, his name was the one the field force associated with the operations of the company.

Bud Burnett was an accountant, and his 1976 board room coup was the reason he was running things. Burnett could have done what Garvice did— allow Brain to run the insurance company and provide Committee oversight— but he didn't. He was an empty vessel wanting the power and stature of Garvice, but he wasn't Garvice, and he wasn't a known commodity. I will always believe that if Kincaid had lived to January or February of 1976, he would have amended his estate plan again and put David Brain on the Committee. According to Brain's daughters, their father told them that Garvice said he would put him on the Committee when he promoted him to president of Kentucky Central Life in January 1975. Kincaid also knew Earl Wilson would soon age off the Committee in April of 1977, so updating his estate plan in early 1976 would have made sense.

One might ask why Kincaid hadn't put Brain on the Committee when

---

28   *Lexington Herald-Leader*, March 10, 1965.

he last updated his trust agreement in January 1972, and I think the reason is that he hadn't planned on updating it then. He was happy with the February 1967 amendment that had Wilson, Schaeffer, and Clyde Mauldin running things. Burnett was just an alternate back then, a placeholder, but Mauldin had surprised Kincaid and resigned at the beginning of January and Garvice was forced to quickly remove him. Kincaid didn't like sloppy legal work, so he didn't just attach an addendum removing him. The document provided for an orderly succession and he didn't want it challenged, so he decided to revise the whole list.

I think Garvice had a problem, though; he had always intended for the president of Central Bank to be on the Committee and had never included Al Florence even as an alternate. Florence wasn't polished, and his management style was rough. Where Kincaid would use a carrot and a stick, Florence just used a stick. Al was a good bagman or henchman because he carried out orders well, but he wasn't a leader. After Mauldin resigned, Garvice took over the position of president at Central Bank and promoted Robert Powers to executive vice president. This action alone seems to indicate his view of Al Florence. It wasn't until May 1975 that he brought in Harold A. Yates to be Central Bank's president. This new lieutenant was still unproven, but he had the right resume and would probably be considered in the next update. Recall that Kincaid brought Clyde Maulding up from one of his Florida banks in 1965, and by February 1967 he was listed as a primary Committee member.

I believe in January 1972, Garvice's faith in Earl Wilson gave him comfort, so he included Florence on the Committee until he could find a new president for Central Bank. As for Burnett, Garvice had a problem. Burnett and Schaeffer were friends, and Burnett had been a loyal lieutenant since 1959, when Garvice acquired the Cardinal Life Insurance Company. Burnett handled Kentucky Central Life's accounting and regulatory issues, including dealing with outside shareholder issues and the SEC. Garvice trusted Burnett, so having him on the Committee as an alternate in 1967, along with Hart Hagan (broadcasting) and Robert Curtin (finance company), was logical. When he rushed to update his estate plan in January 1972, Burnett, like Al Florence, was just a placeholder. In January 1975, Kincaid made his decision about who should be in charge of running Kentucky Central Life when he made David Brain its president.

I strongly believe that Kincaid's long-term intent was to have the presidents of Kentucky Central Life and Central Bank, along with the senior partner of his law firm, as the primary Committee members. The alternates would have then been their backups: Schaeffer (law firm), Burnett (insurance), and possibly Al Florence (banks) but more likely Robert Epling (Dania Bank) or Central

Bank's Wayne Smith.

After Kincaid died, Earl Wilson brought Robert Epling up from Florida to run Central Bank. Kincaid knew and respected him, and I think Wilson's decision to do this was an acknowledgment of Kincaid's thoughts. Earl Wilson was Garvice's closest confidant and friend, and he knew more about how Kincaid thought than any of the other Committee members. Garvice brought Wilson over from Louisville to start his law firm, and he had always been involved in Kincaid's banking and real estate efforts. Wilson's two sons also now worked at the law firm, and Steve Wilson had introduced John Rampulla to Garvice.

After Kincaid died in November 1975 and the Committee was activated, Earl Wilson was its senior leader. According to early reports, all six of its members usually met to discuss things, even though only three of the members had the power to vote, but after Florence resigned and Wilson aged off the Committee, Burnett, Schaeffer, and Hagan ran everything, with only casual input from Rusty Hembree. Burnett was now the senior member of the Committee, and he and Schaeffer always had the majority vote on all decisions. Kincaid's intention of always having three independent votes was eliminated by the Burnett-Schaeffer alliance, which also led to Burnett's strategic blunders.

It appears that Earl Wilson initially maintained Kincaid's political relationships. Wilson was a well-known and respected attorney in Lexington and the state and probably Garvice's most trusted and loyal friend. He had been involved in all aspects of building Kincaid's empire, and he knew how Garvice worked the political circuit. Kincaid understood that politicians were transactional creatures and their value lasted only as long as their time in office. He also knew that a heavy hand with them could backfire on him in the future. Earl Wilson also knew who he could call upon when he needed help. For instance, in 1978, when American General was trying to acquire the company, Wilson was the person who contacted Governor Julian Carroll, who then encouraged the Insurance Department to fight it. In the end, Carroll's appointed insurance commissioner, Harold McGuffy, signed an order barring the transaction.

By 1980, Burnett had lost his training wheels. Kincaid Towers was completed and everyone had moved into the new corporate headquarters. Earl Wilson, who was seventy-four years old, had been slowly stepping back from his duties and was on the cusp of a full retirement. He had been the senior member of Kincaid's Advisory Committee until he aged off at seventy, and Ed Schaeffer and Hart Hagan were comfortably overseeing their respective areas of Kincaid's organization. Democrat John Y. Brown Jr. was governor in 1980, and James Amato was the second mayor of the new Lexington-Fayette merged government, and his relationship with Don and Dudley Webb had grown since their Florida Kentucky Club endeavor.

In 1979, the Committee agreed to sell to the Webbs and Wallace Wilkinson Kincaid's valuable Purcell block. On this full city block parcel, the developers proposed building a hotel and office center. It would be the largest project in the city's history and the largest project the Webbs had ever attempted.

Wallace Wilkinson was a Casey County farm boy who had moved to Lexington in 1962. He made his fortune through his ownership interests in a chain of college bookstores. Wilkinson had a checkered past for most of his business career. For instance, in the 1960s, Wilkinson refused to pay Kentucky sales tax on his used-book transactions; he and Joe Kennedy, the owner of Kennedy Book Store, both claimed that paying the sales tax would put them at a competitive disadvantage with the university-owned book store, which did not pay state taxes because it was operated by the state institution, a tax-exempt entity.

With the success of his chain of bookstores, Wilkinson pursued other business ventures in the fields of real estate development, farming, transportation, banking, coal, and construction. He was flamboyant and even purchased several private aircraft to help him manage his diverse interests. In 1977, after Rupp Arena opened, he purchased a one-third interest in a Purcell-block building on Lexington's Vine Street, and this purchase led to the proposed joint venture between him and the Webbs.

After Kincaid's death, the Committee, through Kentucky Central Life, purchased the bankrupt and uncompleted Hotel Lexington project across from the new Hyatt Regency on Broadway. Kincaid had publicly agreed to purchase this hole in the ground just before his death. Garvice said this would be the location for his new corporate headquarters. After this change, the Committee needed to figure out what to do with the Purcell block. In those early years after Kincaid's death, the Committee had a lot on its plate. It had to address the administration of Mr. Kincaid's estate and develop a method for managing each of his business interests and his other properties. It also had to deal with his family, Nelle, Jane, and Joan, who were not pleased with how the patriarch had arranged things.

In 1978, the Webbs were very anxious to get their hands on this large block of downtown Lexington. They had spoken to the Committee about it several times, but every conversation led back to Kentucky Central financing their scheme. The company had already invested $24 million in building

Kincaid Towers from the company's internal cash flow. In addition, in 1980, Kentucky Central Life had $437 million in assets and just under $50 million of statutory equity and had always followed Kincaid's philosophy of limiting a single investment to about 1.5 to 2.0 percent of company assets. The amount of financing the Webbs needed was considered an abnormal risk. In addition, the company didn't usually do speculative construction and development lending except for Garvice-directed projects. Finally, Earl Wilson could see that the two brothers didn't have the 20 percent equity ($12 million) that was required by the insurance statutes. Wilson told them to find a partner with some financial resources.

In 1979, the Webbs had their partner, Wallace Wilkinson, and in October, the trio made a major announcement about building the Vine Center Hotel and Office Complex across the street from Kincaid Towers. The Webbs had never done a project this large, and in 1980 commercial mortgage loan borrowing rates were around 14 percent. The developers' projected construction cost soon expanded from $40 million to $60 million in 1980.

It was a significant and important transaction for the Committee to sell them Mr. Kincaid's Purcell block, and as we found out later at Kentucky Central Life, the Webbs and Wilkinson didn't have the financial resources and wherewithal to pull off a project of this magnitude. So the Committee, with the aid of Kentucky Central Life's financials, came to the aid of the partnership. By the end of 1980, Wilkinson was out and Kentucky Central Life had stepped in as a 50 percent joint venture partner with the Webbs. With Kentucky Central Life's corporate guarantee, the project was now able to get a $34 million construction loan from Metropolitan Life. In 1981, Metropolitan Life would finance the project only if the partnership had a deep-pocket partner like Kentucky Central Life. So, Wallace Wilkinson went away and Bud Burnett and Kentucky Central become the Webb Company's brand-new best friends. In addition, after Kentucky Central Life became involved, and with the help of Governor John Y. Brown and Mayor Jim Amato, the project received $5.5 million in state-sponsored financing for its 493-space parking garage. Kentucky Central's political connections came through again.

Burnett hadn't had much interaction with the Webbs before Kincaid's death. I suspect that negotiations tied to selling the Purcell block began Burnett's relationship with the Webbs and created the opportunity for them to become closer with Burnett. Certainly the 1980 partnership between Kentucky Central Life and the Webbs brought them formally into a close working relationship.

Wilson knew Kincaid's opinion of the Webbs, and that probably set the tone for the partnership. He didn't intend to be the only partner with deep pockets, and he expected the Webbs to share in the risk by contributing cash equity. Kincaid had even discussed the Webbs in a September 7, 1975, *Courier Journal* article about the future of downtown Lexington. This article was written was just before his death. The article included the following:

> The Webb boys as Garvice and almost everybody calls them, are like a two-man latter day version of Garvice—as they and almost everybody calls Kincaid.
>
> The Webb boys came to town from Whitesburg a few years ago. They also went to law school and bought some houses. Now they own the restaurant, two warehouse developments, 10 duplexes, and electric supply house, and two hamburger outlets, and they have an interest in three bars.
>
> "What we've done," Dudley Webb said last week, "is make good use of what we have." He indicated they don't see the downtown area, which does have a few mattress stores and slum bars . . . and which has 21 empty store fronts on Main Street alone—as an exception.
>
> Webb said he thinks his restaurant is part of the wave of the future—one of the many entertainment establishments that will serve the downtown area when the civic center begins operation. And he said he thinks it can "make it on the lunch crowds" until late next year when the center is open.
>
> Their projects are to be somewhat more modest than Kincaid would like to see, but the Webbs aren't worried about them foundering in a sea of dog-eared buildings.
>
> "Our experience has been if you have something valuable, people will come to it no matter where it is," Dudley Webb said.
>
> Kincaid also snorted at the operations of the Webb boys. "They sat right in here last Friday and laughed" about the urban renewal agency approving their office project "when they don't have a nickel to build it," Kincaid said.
>
> He (Kincaid) does not disagree with others that entertainment and specialty shops will figure in the new scheme of things, but he thinks the big buildings with their office workers are needed to create the market.
>
> "The Webb boys would sell in a minute" if somebody would offer to clear the blocks, Kincaid said, and he suggested, and the job should be done by the urban renewal agency. "I think the urban renewal agency has the authority if they just would put some people in there with a little vision instead of those idiots," he said.

The article is important because it begins to show, in Kincaid's own words, his lack of interest in what the Webbs were doing. After he died, Dudley, over a period of years, provided conflicting accounts of the Webbs' relationship with Garvice.

In an October 31, 1976, *Lexington Herald-Leader* article, Dudley described their early years:

> At first, of course, financing was difficult, he said. It since has become much easier. "When I started, I faced that dilemma (of getting financing) every day. They'd look at me like I was nuts," Dudley said.
>
> "But I think what we were able to do was to sell individuals more than institutions, getting people to help us by carrying second mortgage-type loans."
>
> The Webbs received special financing a few years ago from the late Garvice Kincaid, Dudley said. It involved a long-time dream that Kincaid had of developing an entire block in downtown Lexington.
>
> By happenstance, the Webbs purchased a couple of pieces of property in the dream block and then agreed not to develop them on condition that Kincaid would finance some other downtown property for them.
>
> That led to the purchase of half a city block and the construction of a restaurant, a night club and an office building on the site.
>
> In fact, Dudley said the project sort of got out of hand.
>
> "When we started, we planned to develop a downtown businessmen's luncheon sort of place. It was going to be a $40,000 investment, but suddenly it mushroomed into a $300,000 development.

For a June 27, 1993, *Courier Journal* article, Dudley elaborated further on those early days:

> The Webbs' first real estate ventures were small residential and warehouse projects, but in the mid-1970s they moved on to larger commercial developments. In November 1975, they obtained their first loan from Kentucky Central Life Insurance Company, $90,500, on six tracts of land on Lexington's West Main Street.

From a May 17, 1978, *Herald-Leader* article:

> A comment heard frequently around downtown Lexington is Dudley Webb wanting to be "the new Garvice Kincaid." The Webbs and the late Lexington financier shared a similar dream and the Webbs had financial dealings with Kincaid.
>
> But Webb laughs off the comparison and says if Kincaid were alive, he would laugh it off also. I'm more of a developer. I don't think anybody can stereotype us like anybody else.

In a *Lexington Herald-Leader*, May 16, 1993, open-letter full-page advertisement, Dudley commented on the Kentucky Central situation:

> In many of our projects, Kentucky Central has been our lender. Without them, Lexington's skyline would be vastly different: there would be no Kincaid Towers, Vine Center, Victorian Square, Festival Market, Financial Center, Park Plaza Apartments, The Woodlands, and so forth. We dared to share a vision for and of Lexington, including its downtown with the late Garvice D. Kincaid who enticed us into the redevelopment of the heart of the city. In accordance with his commitment that Kentucky Central would lead the effort, his successor had the courage and the faith to help us make it happen, yet today, much of that has been forgotten. Instead, both Kentucky Central and we are being analyzed and dissected in 20-20 hindsight by certain members of the press and others. Fortunately, we recognize that the history, and the citizens of the Bluegrass area, and not the press, will ultimately judge our intent, and our efforts. To that end, thank you for investing the time to read this article.
>
> Q. Exactly who borrowed the monies for a variety of real estate loans from Kentucky Central?
>
> A. All loans were to various legal entities (corporations, partnerships, etc.) of which I (and very rarely Don) were and/ or are investors. The Webb Companies, the Lexington-based real estate management and servicing entity, has never been a Kentucky Central borrower.
>
> Q. Why did Kentucky Central get so deep into real estate with more than 40% of its assets in real estate-related investments?
>
> A. Obviously, I cannot speak for Kentucky Central, and I have no knowledge of why, to what extent, or in what Kentucky Central has invested.
>
> I can only speculate that Kentucky Central's officers recognized the tremendous returns that most other real estate lenders and institutional investors had consistently realized during the twenty years prior to this period, and that they wanted to capitalize on similar investment opportunities for their policyholders and shareholders. I would also assume that the 40% figure includes their accrued but uncollected interest which they have never written off. This probably increased and distorted that percentage of actual dollars invested.
>
> Q. That virtually all large loans went bad. Of 23 larger than $2 million that Kentucky Central had on its books last September, all but five were in default or had been renegotiated so no payments were required unless the project made money.
>
> A. Certain Webb related entity loans were reduced from prior

higher interest rates (up to 13 1/2%) to lower minimum rates, plus 100% cash flow until real market rates could be realized and paid. Documentably, most other major lenders in today's troubled marketplace have had to adopt similar strategies or programs to allow the commercial real estate industry to survive until the economy recovers.

Q. Did Kentucky Central charge higher interest rates than many other lenders?

A. Yes. However, in spite of that fact, *we chose to continue to do business* with them, and to pay the premium because they were local, they had an appreciation of our effort, and of the ongoing commitment to deliver quality projects. Their Company had tremendous amounts of money to invest, and they needed good projects in promising locations in which to invest it. Our projects were well-sponsored, and properly processed and administered in exactly the same fashion as that required by every other major life insurance company lender with whom we dealt. Kentucky Central chose to charge higher rates instead of other complex formulas for lending. *We chose to do business with them* because "what you saw was what you got . . . straight-up, higher interest rates." Also, we were keeping business in our own community, any profits realized would remain here in Central Kentucky, and last but not least, Kentucky Central did not pursue personal guarantees, unless you violated their trust. These far *outweighed the disadvantages of doing business with distant competitors at somewhat lower rates but in a much more complicated fashion.*

Q. Since John Rampulla had no lending authority, who made the decisions on whether Kentucky Central would make a loan?

A. I had no direct knowledge of their in-house loan approval process. I can speculate that the approval process for our loans involved our supplying our application packages to the Mortgage Loan Department which forwarded them to the Executive Committee for their scrutiny, and from there the packages went to the Board for their approval or rejection.

Q. About what percentage of the Webb Companies borrowings was from Kentucky Central?

A. Again, a reminder that Webb Companies was not a borrower—various other investor entities were. Regardless, I assume that all of the partnerships in which I invested with others were, when considered collectively, probably their largest borrower; but they were one of the smaller lenders to *some of these entities*. Together these partnerships and *their participants* have borrowed and *repaid billions of dollars* to lenders all over American, including Kentucky Central, and *made those lenders millions in profits*. That is that bottom line of our business: we borrow money, use it, and pay it back, with interest. *I believe Kentucky Central chose to lend to and invest with these partnerships because our projects were well conceived, of superior quality, in diverse markets, and of the type (office, retail, apartments, industrial) that investors wanted.* Kentucky Central was never the only option for financing—other institutional investors were available on virtually every project *to make proposals* to either acquire or finance. Regardless, if Kentucky Central had instead invested in the portfolios of other real estate borrowers, it would still be experiencing the same challenges and frustrating problems. The biggest difference is that I'm still here . . . just across the street, working harder than ever, sticking with the rehabilitator, employing hundreds of local people in the process, and fighting our way through this mess. Our people will, if given time, work to restore Kentucky Central's portfolio of Webb related investments to profitability . . . assuming reason and good judgment prevail.[29]

There is an old adage, "figures don't lie, but liars still figure," and much of what Dudley wrote, while technically true, skirted the actual facts. Including the words "proposals" and "participants" in his answers watered down the truth to the point that his answer had little value or meaning. For instance, "repaid billions" is an interesting concept, when one considers that over half of the $140 million of loans and investments in Webb-related entities were made to refinance other lenders out of the failed projects. The magic of his words can also be seen from the following sequence of events. An entity borrowed $50 million from a bank for a construction of a project and then refinanced it with an unrelated life insurance company, and then the project developed problems and Burnett and Kentucky Central refinanced it. Then a Webb entity has repaid $100 million of loans, even if Kentucky Central Life's loan goes into default, and this is what happened with many of their entity-related loans.

In 1986 and early 1987, Kentucky Central had made loans totally $22.7 million on the Webb-entity projects in McAllen, Texas; Baton Rouge, Louisiana; and Colorado Springs, Colorado. The projects included a hotel, various office buildings and retail/shopping centers, and a cinema. In addition, the projects contained large amounts of speculative raw land. The Webb entities went to other lenders for most of the money they needed for the construction these projects, but by 1987, the projects were struggling and already in default or foreclosure. So, Kentucky Central refinanced its loan and the other lenders' loans into a thirteen-loan package totaling $66.3 million. By mid-1990, the projects' problems continued, and the loans were all in default to Kentucky

---

29   Emphasis added.

Central Life, so the company took back the undeveloped raw land parcels on four of the loans and refinanced the remaining nine loans for $68.9 million.

Burnett and the other Committee members refused to comment to the *Courier Journal* when asked about these loans, but John Rampulla testified[30] that he was told by Burnett that a pension fund was supposed to refinance Kentucky Central Life's loan, but after the stock market crashed in 1987, the pension fund deal fell through. John also testified that he didn't even go visit the McAllen, Texas, property until after the loan monies had been disbursed. I asked John if he had ever reviewed a letter or any documentation from a specific pension fund, and he said he hadn't. He agreed that normally Burnett would have forwarded a document like that down to him. In retrospect, he doubted Burnett ever had anything in writing that evidenced that the pension fund refinancing was real. One can probably correctly assume that Burnett just trusted what he was told by Dudley, or he used the idea of the pension fund refinancing to justify to Schaeffer and Hagan doing a $68.7 million loan. Webb says he got involved with the McAllen property after Texas Commerce Bank foreclosed, but the original partners involved in the project dispute this. Webb does agree he was involved with the property when Kentucky Central Life lent the partnership $17.4 million.

It impossible to follow, in the depositions and newspaper reports, the financial impact of all the Webb-entity properties being taken over, but here's one example: "In 1995, Kentucky Central took back the McAllen, Texas retail center that had a $17.4 million loan. The state managed it and made repairs for the next 3 years and sold it in 1998 for $7.4 million."

By 1988, one can see, many of the Webb-entity projects were starting to gasp for air like a fish washed up on dry land, but that didn't stop them from coming to Burnett for more help. In 1985, Dudley Webb reportedly got involved in what became known as the $50 million San Francisco office tower. In 1982, a large Canadian developer, Daon Corporation, the Bay Area's leading developer, had fallen on hard times and exited the market. Part of its local management team formed Norland Properties and took over this parcel in the financial district. In 1985, the Libyan development group struggled with the project and brought in Dudley Webb to help them. Webb invested $2 million, and Norland invested $8 million to move the project forward.

In March 1986, Webb got temporary construction financing from GATX and started building the foundation. In December 1987 the foundation was completed but work stopped because of a lack of further construction financing.

---

30   David Heath and David McGinty, "Big Loans to Webbs Imperil Insurer," *Courier Journal*, June 27, 1993.

In February of 1988, the Norland/Webb partnership filed for bankruptcy protection to stop its lender, GATX, from foreclosing.

Dudley Webb contacted Burnett and, according to John Rampulla, in the fall of 1988 he got a call from Burnett telling him that Kentucky Central Life was going to invest $8 million in the partnership. It was reported that Norland had invested $8 million in the partnership, so one can assume that Dudley was trying to get Kentucky Central Life to take over Norland's position. Remember, this project was still two years from completion, with the bulk of construction spending yet to be done.

The *Lexington Herald-Leader* reported on his situation in September 19, 1998:

> In court, the brothers testified that until they met Kincaid, they had been doing some small scale residential real estate investing along with their law practice. Dudley Webb testified he met Kincaid in the early 70s.
>
> As a member of the Urban Renewal Commission, Kincaid had a vision for downtown Lexington—which he called a pigsty—but had alienated other commissioners. Kincaid was determined to build his vision. But, because of the "bad blood," some people wouldn't sell to him. So, a relationship evolved in which the Webbs fronted for Kincaid, making deals then deeding properties to him.
>
> Dudley said they did not make money on these transactions for Kincaid. But clearly, they did benefit from the relationship.
>
> "Everybody knew . . . that suddenly we were in favor of Mr. Kincaid, and he would loan us anything we wanted," Donald testified. "We became the fair-haired boys. The fellow who was president of the (Central) bank (said) why don't you come bank with us. Mr. Kincaid said whatever you all wanted . . . [I'll] loan it to you.
>
> So, the brothers were in business, with ready access to capital they needed to move out of the piecemeal residential market into larger commercial projects.
>
> The special relationship continued even after Kincaid's death, when the late W. E. "Bud" Burnett Jr. became chairman of Kentucky Central.
>
> "There was no formal procedure" for proposals, Dudley said. They presented them to Burnett, and he decided the terms. "As far as I know they never even looked at a financial statement," Donald said.
>
> Kentucky Central did not provide all of the Webbs financing but was often the critical first lender with the temporary financing to get a project off the ground.
>
> Despite the public image of a stable company with boundless

horizons, by the late 80's things were not going well. Dudley sold his interest in 11 New England properties in 1988 as the real estate market there unraveled.

Dudley testified that, in 1988 when The Webb Companies was named business of the year by the Lexington Chamber of Commerce, some of the brothers' projects were not producing enough revenue to meet loan payments.

By 1990, according to court documents, Webb wrote a letter to Burnett saying he was struggling to make payroll and turning back properties to lenders.

"A dismal story, sad but true, and, to put it bluntly, my alternatives are reorganization or straight bankruptcy," he wrote.

Kentucky Central converted some of the loans to cash flow basis, Dudley testified, meaning the lender got any cash produced over and above expenses rather than a guaranteed payment.

"At extraordinarily high interest rates," Webb said. "That was another problem, we just couldn't keep up with the interest rates that they had to have.

The Deal according to the Webbs:

While Kentucky Central's rates may have been a touch high, its demands on the Webbs were not so hard.

Early on, both brothers testified, Kincaid made a deal with them. The deal, Donald explained, was "If you cooperate with us in these deals, you don't steal from us, you don't rob us, you cooperate and do what you're supposed to do, we're not going after your deficiencies.

Oddly, that seemed to mean that, in a business that rewards risk-taking, the Webbs had a financing partner who was taking the risk instead of them. When Burnett took over at Kentucky Central, he continued the policy.

Dudley described Burnett's philosophy. "If there was upside, we should keep them (the projects) and he would work with us to work through them. And if there was not upside, he would go ahead and take title to the projects and release us from the guarantees."

The personal guarantees were one thing Kincaid and Burnett required to make this arrangement work, according to the Webbs. Those written guarantees of personal liability were there to assure cooperation.

In this the brothers did not act as one. Dudley testified that he signed the personal guarantees from the earliest days. But Donald, with his wife and young child, was more cautious about putting his resources on the line.

After years of litigation about the guarantees, in 1998, the court released the Webbs from their personal guarantees on loans with Kentucky Central Life. The judge ruled that since Kentucky Central had never enforced a guarantee against either Webb, he agreed with Donald and Dudley that they should not be required to pay now.

I personally struggle with many of the Webbs' statements about Garvice:

1. Donald and Dudley Webb formed their law firm in September of 1971, and based upon Dudley's own words, "The Webbs' first real estate ventures were small residential and warehouse projects, but in the mid-1970s they moved on to larger commercial developments. In November of 1975 they obtained their first loan from Kentucky Central Life Insurance Co.: $90,500, on six tracts of land on Lexington's West Main Street. This is supported by the October 1976 article say that they, by "happenstance," owned two parcels of land tied to Kincaid's Purcell block. In addition, Garvice died on Friday, November 21, 1975, so it's reasonable to assume that their first loan was established in the month that he died. In addition, John Rampulla said he never knew Kincaid to have any dealings with them, and it was only a couple of years after Kincaid died that Burnett's relationship took off, beginning with the Kentucky Club in Florida.

2. Dudley talked about meeting Kincaid in the early 1970s, which seems reasonable. They were both very active in the Democratic Party. In addition, Kincaid said, in his own words, that he was always open to meeting with someone and listening to what someone had to say, so it's reasonable to assume that he met with the brothers several times after 1972. But recall how he described "the Webb boys." He discussed the Webbs' proposed Professional and Legal Arts Building, which was supposed to cost $4 million. Kincaid snorted at the "operations of the Webb boys" and said, "They sat right in here last Friday and laughed" about the urban renewal agency approving their office project "when they don't have a nickel to build it." In fact, Garvice said, "The Webb boys would sell in a minute if someone would offer to clear the block." This was referencing the location for their proposed project on Vine and Main. The existing buildings would need to be demolished before even one footing could be installed. To me, this doesn't sound like a man enamored with the young developers.

3. As for whether the Webbs actually "fronted for Kincaid," I think it's debatable. On Friday, August 30, 1974, the Lexington Urban Renewal and Community Development Agency held what was described as an unprecedented "special meeting" about the site of the Webb's Legal and Arts project. Apparently, Vice Mayor Scotty Baesler had called the meeting. At the

last meeting, the agency had approved the Webb project, subject to getting a financial stability statement. The Webbs had submitted a letter from American Fletcher Mortgage Co. to show they had their financing lined up. The company would provide 80 percent financing, subject to the Webbs providing 20 percent ($800,000) in equity.

The original project was supposed to be a fifteen-story tower and was projected to cost over $5.5 million. The 20 equity would be $1.1 million. This was a lot of money for the young developers to come up with, so they reimagined the project as two five-story towers, with a connecting courtyard. They would build and fund one building at a time to make financing the project easier. The Lexington agency had proposed this project in 1972 and had received just a few proposals.

By 1974, nothing had been agreed to and Kincaid was pushing hard to build his corporate headquarters on the entire Purcell block. In August 1974, before the meeting, Kincaid formally asked the agency to delay the sale of land to the Webbs for the project because it "might foul up redevelopment of the entire block." By February 1975, the Webbs were again reimagining the project and said there could be further delays due to the economic environment. They blamed the level of interest rates, now around 9 percent versus 8 percent in 1973, for the expiration of their construction contract and the need to renegotiate it and, finally, the increase in the cost of materials and labor. The project was so significantly changed, with the initial phase now costing only $1.5 million, that the agency considered reopening the entire bidding process. In the end, the agency accepted the design to avoid the further stigma of failure. The agency members were not happy, but they needed a win for the agency. The Downtown Development Commission was very upset with the agency and the changes the Webbs made. The project had been reduced in size, and there was nothing that required the second phase of the project to be built by the developers.

Councilwoman Pam Miller was extremely angry with the agency and, as a member of the Downtown Development Commission, stated that the Commission would be taking over its role on June 30, 1975, and that the agency needed to start listening to the wishes of the Commission. A significant additional issue the Commission had with the agency was that it was breaking up large parcels of downtown land for smaller developments. In July 1975, the Urban Renewal and Development Agency transferred the parcels to the Webbs' Lexington Arts Co. for $67,818. I believe this may have been when Kincaid made the deal that required the Webbs to not develop the parcels and in return he would finance something else for them, and thus the Kentucky

Central Life loan for $90,500 was made.

While all this drama was taking place, in August 1975, Webb Properties got a permit to build a $250,000 warehouse at 333 West Vine Street. This parcel was on the same block as the Purcell building, but in January 1976, it was sold to Kentucky Central Life for $240,495.

I never found any property transfers reflecting that the Webbs could have been fronting for Kincaid. In fact, until 1975, Kincaid was correct when he said that "they are more interested in putting in bars and restaurants and small buildings." According to the *Lexington Herald-Leader*'s September 7, 1975, article, "Now they own the restaurant [Postelwaite's Tavern], two warehouse developments, 10 duplexes, an electric supply house, and two hamburger outlets and they have interest in three bars." Garvice Kincaid did sometimes bring in partners or use associates to accomplish a strategy, but generally these were people he had known and worked with for several years and were also people he could control. It seems out of character for him to use a couple of guys new to Lexington to do his bidding. If he did, then in my opinion it was out of character. In addition, no one I knew at Kentucky Central Life ever heard anything about it except what the Webbs said that was reported in the paper.

In addition, in a few news stories and depositions, the Webbs said that they "owned some parcels that 'they' hoped to develop and if they were unable to, they had hoped Garvice Kincaid would have considered developing it with them." After reading this, I wondered if their statement about "fronting" wasn't merely referencing a hoped-for partnership with Garvice. John Rampulla began working for Kincaid in 1971, and he said that Kentucky Central Life wasn't involved with them, and while it's possible that Garvice was doing something with them using his personal assets, this seems less likely considering that in 1973 he began cleaning up his estate and moving much of it into Kentucky Central Life. This is documented in the company's annual reports, and he discussed it in his management letter to shareholders.

I found one transaction that I think supports my view of a hoped-for partnership. It involved Jack Hagler, who owned the Sleepy-Head House property at 358 West Main Street. On November 10, 1977, Hagler gave Dudley Webb a 120-day option to acquire this property. Dudley eventually assigned the option over to Kentucky Central Life, and it exercised its option to acquire the property on the last day of the option agreement (March 10, 1978). This purchase made Kentucky Central Life the owner of the entire block bounded by Main, Broadway, Vine, and Mill, also known as Kincaid's Purcell block. Kentucky Central paid $1,495,000 for the property.

What I find interesting is that it wasn't until the last day of the agreement that the transaction was accomplished. This was a transaction for real property and required a title search and the preparation of a deed. If it had been a planned transaction, I don't believe the company would have waited until the last possible day to execute the purchase. Kentucky Central Life had the money to complete the transaction anytime it wanted, and its management wouldn't have wanted to risk losing this opportunity. In my opinion, this sounds like more of a reactionary purchase than a planned one. Also remember that it wasn't until 1979 that the Webbs and Wallace Wilkinson announced their partnership to develop the block.

4. The other part of the story that sounds more like a dream than reality is the statement by Don Webb that "everybody knew . . . that suddenly we were in the favor of Mr. Kincaid, and he would loan us anything we wanted." "We became the fair-haired boys. The fellow who was president of the (Central) bank (said) why don't you come bank with us. Mr. Kincaid said whatever you all wanted . . . [I'll] loan it to you."

This statement sounds more like a line from "Alice in Wonderland", than a statement made by Garvice Kincaid. Kincaid was a serious man, and he didn't share his power and influence with anyone. In addition, he liked people to grovel and be beholden to him. If this did take place, the statement reminds me more of something Bud Burnett might have said. In my opinion, the relationship that the Webbs built with Burnett made them "the fair-hair boys" in town. Burnett wanted respect and power and the Webbs promoted his greatness, which benefited him.

5. In Dudley Webb's May 16, 1993, Ad responding to questions from the Lexington Herald-Leaders, he wrote, "I have no direct knowledge of their in-house loan approval process. I can speculate that the approval process for our loans involved our supplying our application packages to the Mortgage Loan Department which forwarded them to the Executive Committee for their scrutiny, and from there the packages went to the Board for their approval or rejection."

In their sworn testimony, the brothers stated, "There was no formal procedure," for proposals, Dudley said. They presented them to Burnett, and he decided the terms. "As far as I know they never even looked at a financial statement," Donald said.

While both statements could be true depending on the situation and the years, I suspect the sworn statement reflects the truth of what happened in the 1980s. The Webbs, especially Dudley, had a special relationship with Bud Burnett. One that professionally and logically doesn't make sense. On one hand Don Webb states that Burnett didn't even look at financials and on the other hand Dudley says they presented their proposals directly to Burnett.

I think the $15 million Bank of Louisville credit scheme probably describes Dudley's and Burnett's relationship the best. Burnett went out of his way to try to protect Dudley by agreeing to the tri-party agreement. Dudley Webb's own words showed that he was on the verge of losing everything, including his interest in the Financial Center and so Burnett agreed to a scheme to secure his loan with the Bank of Louisville. This arrangement, more than any other, makes me wonder if Burnett financially benefited from his lender relationships. Burnett was around when Kincaid's law partner Frank Trimble was receiving kickbacks from Central Bank borrowers and in 1977, after becoming president of the Kentucky Central, his total compensation for the year was just $120,000. Not a bad salary, and it was comparable to many other executives in state, but he probably knew it was less than what the other Committee members were receiving.

The following is a sample list of Kentucky corporations' executive compensation for 1977:

Citizens Fidelity Bank	David Grissom	$119,500
Citizens Fidelity Bank	Daniel Ulmer	$79,500
Bank of Louisville	Samuel Klein	$110,000
Capital Holding Corp.	Robert Yoder	$143,000
Brown Forman Distillers	Roger Coleman	$164,057
Brown Forman Distillers	W.L Lyons	$189,314
Humana	Wendell Cherry	$224,893
Humana	David Jones	$286,333
Ashland Oil	John Hall	$321,028
Ashland Oil	Robert McCowan	$279,935

When the Advisory Committee became activated, Burnett quickly realized that he was its least wealthy member. Earl Wilson had financially benefited from his position at the law firm and also by participating in the ownership of some of Kincaid's banks and early business ventures. Al Florence was well compensated for the services his bank management company provided to Kincaid's banks and he also personally held stakes in some of Kincaid's banks. Garvice treated Burnett differently though. He was paid a salary and given some stock options, but his net worth had not benefited as much as the others from his years with Kincaid.

Garvice always provided his leaders with a reasonable salary and the ability to earn a bonus based upon performance. Generally, the better one of his companies did, the better your bonus would be. Things were a little different at Kentucky Central Life, because it was a publicly traded company. Beginning around 1965, Kincaid began granting stock options to what he called "key employees." Not a lot is known about these options, but it appears that each year he would grant a limited group officers stock options on a total of 8,000 to 13,000 shares of stock. I am guessing, but I believe the group was primarily possibly Kincaid, David Brain, Bud Burnett, Wilson Yates (General Counsel) and Bill Joyner (Chief Actuary). Brain, Burnett, and Joyner were primarily responsible for the financial performance of the company and Wilson Yates controlled some of his family's voting shares of the company's stock.

Based upon footnotes in the company's financial statements the options appeared to be valid for five years and had an exercise price that was 10% or 15%, out-of-the-money. The problem was that the Kentucky's Central Life's stock price traded in a narrow range and my review of the company's financial statement show most of these options expired worthless and if any were exercised, they provided little additional compensation to the holder. So, consider your Kincaid and you keep granting David Brain or Bud Burnett these options, and they keep expiring worthless, what do you do? I think this is also part of the reason that Garvice decided he needed to make the company bigger, and why he moved Kentucky Finance and some of his banks into a downstream subsidiary.

Garvice had tried share buybacks and they had very little impact on the company's stock price and so now his plan was to increase the company's earnings potential. In Kincaid's mind, the stock price was a reflection of him, and having it languish bothered him. By 1970, he had done many things to "awaken his sleeping giant", but the stock price wasn't reflecting what he believed was the company's huge potential.

After Kincaid died, it appears that the Committee began winding down the option program. In 1976, only a 1,000-share grant was made, and I am sure it was for Bud Burnett, and it probably indicates what the size of his prior option awards were.

In 1984, when the Committee put in place employment agreements for themselves, they also did something else. According to Cliff Forbush, in 1984 he received his first stock options from the company. It was a ten-year option appreciation agreement, and it vested after one or two years, and the exercise price was 15-18% out of the money. Burnett had provided all the company vice presidents and above officers with an option agreement. The number of shares covered under each agreement varied by the person. A total of 248,250 shares were granted in 1984 with a strike price range of $17.75-$18.64. Stock appreciation rights had an advantage over standard option agreements in that the holder didn't have to purchase the stock when exercised but could just collect the difference in the option price and the closing price of the stock from the company.

By 1991, the company's stock had fallen below $10 a share and so everyone's option agreements were 100% out of the money. In order to improve morale, Burnett offered every option agreement holder an opportunity to cancel their old agreement and obtain a new agreement at a lower strike price, with a new vesting period and 10-year term. Option agreements covering 296,383 shares were cancelled by mutual agreement and new agreements totaling 310,410 shares were issued at strike a price of $7.88. In addition, agreements totaling 211,446 shares expired worthless in 1991. At the end of 1991, the company had a total of 854,059 shares covered under option agreements. In 1990, Burnett had also issued option agreements covering 380,758 shares at a strike price of $10.63. These options remained outstanding at the end of 1991.

The 1990 options apparently were a reward to Burnett and some of the officer group for achieving the $50 billion in-force goal. They were also probably another attempt by Burnett to continue to buy loyalty from the group. If the other Committee members, who were also on Kentucky Central's Board, ever received stock options, it wasn't reflected in any of the materials I have reviewed. Of course, none of the option agreements issued in 1990 and 1991 ever had any value and by the end of 1992, the company's stock was trading around $8.75 per share. Burnett's early December announcement of a capital injection of $100 million into the company from the vulture investor Marty Whitman and his Third Avenue Fund had provided encouragement to investors and many assumed the worst was behind the company.

I don't know if Burnett had any financial "agreements among friend's arrangements", but from my perspective, an arrangement like this would begin to answer the question of "why" he might have done some of the loans that he did. A commercial mortgage loan broker arranges loans for borrowers from unrelated financial companies. They typically charge a fee of 3% to 5% of the loan amount, for this service. I can see where Burnett might feel comfortable getting something for providing financing to some of his friendly borrowers. In many cases he provided 100% financing for the projects and supported, what most investment professionals would agree, were speculative developments. A borrower might consider it a bargain to provide Burnett, say 5% equity participation in the funded project. All they would need is a private, one-page, side letter between the two friendly parties. In addition, an agreement like this would be difficult for the Kincaid daughters, any regulators, or even the other Committee members to discover. Finally, if the project fails or Kentucky Central Life is taken over by the state, the office shredder could easily dispose of the evidence. It would be just another example of "heads, Burnett wins, and tails Kentucky Central Life loses'.

Earl Wilson, Ed Schaeffer, and Rusty Hembree were making a lot of money from all the legal work Kentucky Central Life and the other Kincaid businesses produced. In addition, each borrower paid the law firm for its work on their loans. Hart Hagan had been making money from managing Blue Grass Broadcasting for years and his accounting firm made money from its work for other Kincaid entities. Bud Burnett had never been offered a seat at the Kincaid money table and he probably felt entitled. The stock options Kincaid had given him had been a failure and so he had never benefited like the other Committee members.

In the days after the insurance department took the company over, many people sought an answer as to why Burnett did the deals he did. Some people suggested the $50 billion in-force goal pushed him into these transactions. Many other employees and I never believed this was a reasonable answer. If you're cooking dinner and your stove catches fire, you stop cooking and try to put the fire out. What happened at Kentucky Central Life didn't happen overnight. Burnett not only caught the stove on fire but then increased the velocity of fire's destruction by pouring more grease on it.

Considering that by 1987, when Burnett began repossessing, the former high school physical education teacher/football coach, Teddy Mims's $80 million of properties, it was obvious that Bud's mortgage loan decisions had failed. He had announced the $50 billion in-force goal in early 1984 and many of the projects he had financed since then were already failing. In addition, it wasn't a surprise that the commercial real estate markets were in a decline. A July 1985 article in the Lexington Herald-Leader was titled "Office Space: How much is too much" and reported:

> Experts such as Cushman and Wakefield and local developers such as Joe Graves described the office space market as "soft." Graves said, "I would say that if the owners of a really good building have to offer free rent to get a tenant, then that means it (the market) is overbuilt. He went on to say he was aware of instances in which developers had offered as much as a year's free rent to prospective tenants, but he refused to name the developers, or the projects involved. Of course, Donald Webb, had a different view, "What does soft mean?" I would say it's not as hot as it once was. If we didn't feel like the market was good, then we wouldn't continue to build."

The article also mentioned the cities of Dallas and Houston, that had experienced rapid growth in the last decade, now had many office buildings standing vacant.[31]

If 1985 was described as soft, by 1987 and 1988, a person had to be blind not to realize that the commercial real estate markets were in a major decline. For instance, in 1985, when a Houston developer of a 50,000 square foot office building in Lexington, at the corner of Richmond Road and Man O' War failed, the building's rusty steel skeleton sat abandoned for three years. The building had been financed by Liberty National Bank in Louisville and the bank had repossessed it. In 1988, Liberty Bank finally sold the property to the partnership of Mims, Graves and Turner. The bank financed their purchase and also provided the funds necessary for the completion of the building with a $5.5 million loan. By 1993, the Bank again repossessed the building, taking it back in lieu of foreclosure. It was eventually sold it for $3.5 million in 1996.

6. Finally, the concept of "heads I win, tails you lose" that Don and Dudley describe when they described Kincaid's and Burnett's "philosophy" is hard to imagine:

Dudley described Burnett's philosophy. "If there was upside, we should keep them (the projects) and he would work with us to work through them. And if there was not upside, he would go ahead and take title to the projects and release us from the guarantees."

Both Kincaid and Burnett are dead and so we can't ask them, but this description doesn't reflect the Garvice Kincaid I have researched. This depiction sounds more like the remarks of a partner than it does of a lender. Garvice did have a history of not destroying borrowers who failed, but he never gave them a second chance, unless they were doing something that was supposed to benefit him. If Bud Burnett applied this philosophy, then one must ask, "why?". How would Kentucky Central benefit from this agreement. We know that in many of the partnerships Burnett formed with Webb entities, ended up with Kentucky Central Life funding their losses. Lexington's Festival Market is an example:

From the Feburary 20, 2017, *Lexington Herald-Leader:*

> The $16 million, three-story mall opened in 1986 as Lexington Festival Market, designed as an upscale center with dozens of shops and restaurants. While children rode the merry-go-round on the top floor, a jazz pianist played at lunchtimes in the courtyard below. However, the mall, which was expected to have as many as 70 businesses, never found its niche, and it lost money each year since

---

31   Sheila M. Poole, *Lexington Herald-Leader*, July 8, 1985.

it opened. At the time of the auction, it was being converted from an upscale center to a factory outlet mall. It was developed by the Webb Cos. in partnership with Kentucky Central Life Insurance Co., but when the insurance company failed in 1993, the mall was placed in receivership. The estimated debt of the mall was more than $13 million, according to court records. The Webbs had managed the mall since it opened but gave up, citing frustration over efforts to revitalize it. A judge's order dissolved the partnership between The Webb Cos. and Kentucky Central, and the building went to auction, where it sold for $600,000.

The rest of the story on Festival Market is the following. In 1984, the state had set aside urban renewal development money for Wallace Wilkinson's "World Coal Center. The project was to be done in conjunction with the Webbs, who had attached a Galleria project to it. The project was cancelled, but the states urban renewal money for Lexington still remained outstanding. The Webbs soon looked to use a portion of it to build Festival Market. The Collin's administration reallocated $7.5 million of this money to the Lexington Project. Festival Market was to be modeled after Toledo's Portside Festival Market, which had opened nine months earlier. It had opened with a burst of traffic, but traffic had soon declined. The Webbs even hired Toledo's Portside Festival Market manager, Jim Blew, to be operations manager for the Lexington project.

In 1985, Kentucky Central Life's name became connected with the project, when it was announced that they were a 50% partner with the Webbs in the development of Festival Market. Kincaid had acquired the property as part of his urban renewal efforts, but it had never been developed. Burnett contributed the land to the Festival Market partnership for $1.5 million, but no money changed hands. Instead, the Webbs swapped a 50% interest in the Merrill Lynch building to Kentucky Central Life for the land. This is the same building that Dudley used as security for the Bank of Louisville transaction. Festival Market has been described as a "build it and they will come" project. It was fashioned after similar projects in cities which had harbors and riverwalks as their primary public draw. Downtown Lexington had neither. In a postmortem article in 2019, Portside Festival Market is remembered this way:

> When Portside Festival Market opened in 1984 along the Maumee River, the Rouse Company's Portside Festival Marketplace was supposed to revitalize Toledo's downtown. However, what worked for Rouse in Baltimore (Harborplace) and Boston (Fanueil Hall) had no impact on the continued decline of this rust belt city. During its first year, the $14.5 million, 100,000-square-foot festival marketplace attracted 4.5 million visitors. Yet, two years later it was

attracting half as many and in 1990, it closed for good.[32]

I recall when Lexington's Festival Market was announced, listening to John Rampulla explain to me why this was a mistake. He explicitly talked about San Antonio's Riverwalk and Boston's Harbor and said to do what the Webbs want to do, you need a natural draw, and downtown Lexington has neither, except for Rupp Arena during UK basketball games and concerts. John predicted this would be a "white elephant" and he was right. In July 1984, shortly after Webb announced the project, the *Lexington Herald-Leader* editorial page editor wrote an op-ed also questioning the logic of project stating, "Without such attractions, it is difficult to see how a festival marketplace can succeed. The [July] fireworks show brought people downtown. So do concerts and basketball games, but you can't have the Fourth of July and UK basketball year-round."[33]

By January 1985, Dudley Webb may have also had some similar concerns about both the Festival Market and Victoria Square downtown projects, because he spoke to the Rotary Club of Lexington and proposed the city build an 11-acrea "Lake Lexington" near the downtown convention center. He said it would cost $5 million dollars and could be developed with the help of government funding. I am not sure where the funding might come from, but after Governor Collins provided $7.5 million for Festival Market, that left an unused $7.5 million that was to be used for the World Coal Center.

When Festival Market was sold at auction in July 1994, the bondholders lost $9.9 million, and the city of Lexington lost $2.1 million. Both creditor groups then became unsecured creditors of the Kentucky Central Life estate which the insurance department was responsible for. In Augus 2006, after settling a claim with the company's auditors, Deloitte and Touche, for $22 million, the Commissioner made a distribution to creditors, which made both the city of Lexington and the project's bondholders whole, excluding their loss of interest. In all, the Commissioner distributed $40 million. These distributions also made-whole the National Organization of Life and Health Insurance Guaranty Associations (NOLHGA), Festival Market's creditors, and 50 more unsecured creditors. The state even sent additional monies to Jefferson-Pilot for the policyholders transferred to them and withheld $22 million for a final settlement of all claims.

---

32   *Lexington Herald-Leader*, July 26, 1994, quoting Ennis Davis, *The Jaxon magazine*, February 27, 2019.

33   David Holwerk, "Festival Market," *Lexington Herald-Leader*, July 15, 1984.

By the time Festival Market was sold in 1994, Kentucky Central had been responsible for all the project's operating losses. In other words, the company kept sending money to the partnership. Each of these payments increased Kentucky Central's ownership interest of the partnership and by the time the project was auctioned off in 1994, the Webb's interest had been reduced to 5% and Kentucky Central's had increased to 95%. The 50/50 partnership was in name only, because Kentucky Central Life was making up for 100% of the partnership's losses. I don't believe Garvice Kincaid ever participated in such a lopsided investment as this. Consider the initial partnership where Webb Properties Inc.'s equity for the partnership, was their half interest in the Merrill Lynch Plaza building and not cash. In addition, when the bonds backing Festival Market went into default, consider which partner, twelve years later, was responsible for their payment: the estate of Kentucky Central Life.

Bud Burnett was more than dishonest; he was also a fool. He squandered Mr. Kincaid's assets and did it to promote himself as the man with the keys to the city. Burnett provided the company's money to developers like a drug dealer providing a fix to a user. Neither party cares about the other, but they both need each other. Remember Don Webb's reaction to Burnetts offer for the Kentucky Club, "Don tells Dudley, "You aren't going to believe this shit", and tells him what Bud had just agreed to do. So, when Burnett and Kentucky Central Life buys Wallace Wilkinson's failing Frankfort Hotel for $12.6 million, in what many agree was a sweetheart deal, Wilkinson then puts Bud Burnett on the University of Kentucky' Board of Trustees. It's been estimated that Kentucky Central Life paid twice what the hotel was actually worth.

Wilkinson constructed the hotel in 1983 after receiving $12.6 million from various state-sponsored lending authorities. The hotel had been a money pit from day one, and in 1987, Wallace had already pumped in at least another $3.2 million to keep it afloat; at the time of the sale, it was running a $1.5 million deficit. Burnett paid Wilkinson $3.8 million for the project, and of course Kentucky Central assumed the debt. In addition, Burnett agreed to pay Wilkinson a consulting fee of $120,000 annually for five years. The project was held in a downstream subsidiary, M-C Realty Co. Neither Wilkinson nor Kentucky Central ever disclosed the price or terms, and Wilkinson assured the public that he took a loss on the transaction. He had initially put in $1.1 million in equity, and with the additional $3.2 million operating contribution his projected investment would be $4.3 million, so on paper he did experience a loss. In addition to the purchase price, the project had sixteen condominium units on its top three floors, and Kentucky Central was required to lease the unsold units for $77,000 a year. The problem with the purchase price is that this hotel had consistently posted losses since it opened at the end of 1983, so in most people's eyes, the $3.8 million payment to Wilkinson was some type of payoff, especially after the governor appointed Burnett to the University of Kentucky Board of Trustees twelve months later.

Garvice Kincaid wasn't a perfect lender, but with any mistakes he made, he was always risking his own money. Kincaid also admitted his mistakes and tried never to repeat them. Bud Burnett kept committing the same mistakes over and over. Dudley Webb indicated that Kentucky Central's underwriting was in-line with other institutions. I disagree.[34] Life insurance companies

- Typically limit their financing to 80% loan-to-value of the property,

- Typically require the borrowers to have cash equity in the deal,

- Typically require a minimum level of signed lease agreements, and

- Typically limit how much they will lend to any one borrowing group.

Bud Burnett failed to follow all four of these normal lending tenants. Why did Bud Burnett do the deals he did? You as the reader will have to decide. I have my opinion, but it is just an opinion. What's yours?

After the state took over the company, the state's attorneys, accountants, and consultants struggled for years to understand what Bud Burnett had been up to. Everyone could see that normal business practices had not been followed, but all the people who participated in Burnett's deals declined to provide any answers, with most only pointing the finger at the dead man.

Bud Burnett was not an honest man, and he certainly didn't operate as Kincaid had. Burnett, with the help of Bob Preston covered up at least $2 million of stolen premium payments on unauthorized underwritten surety bond policies, involving his son, Bruce. Bruce was convicted of the crimes and went to prison and if Bud Burnett hadn't died, he might have shared a cell with him for aiding and abetting in his fraudulent scheme. So, when one

---

34   One can see that Metropolitan Life wouldn't lend to the Webb/Wilkinson partnership to build the Vine Center project (Radisson Hotel and office) until Kentucky Central replaced Wilkinson in the partnership. This large institutional lender required cash equity and someone with deep pockets before it would commit to financing for the project.

considers "the why?" Bud Burnett did what he did, remember, while his death prevented his trial, the state documented that many of his deals were either illegal, or unethical, or both, and that many of his loan transactions were not done for the benefit of Kentucky Central Life's policyholders or shareholders and that they did not conform to Kentucky's regulatory rules or the norms of the insurance industry. Inflated "friendly" appraisals were used to justify loan amounts, as appraiser Michael Dolan Jr. testified in 1992, "we sort of know what they want, and we give them what they want."[35]

Today we communicate using email, texts and even have video calls, but in the 1980s and early 1990s, the telephone, the fax machine and Federal Express were Burnett's primary communication tools. People still used the post office to send important correspondence and documents, but communications were slower and paper/digital trails were a fraction of what is generated today. After the state took control of the company, its army of attorneys, accountants and advisors investigated and litigated, looking for the answer, but in the end, the answers were always without substance or proof.

Kincaid's Committee members and other officers just pointed their fingers at Burnett. Hart Hagan said, Burnett copied Kincaid's style and habit of making all the decisions, "He asked no one for any opinion. His was the rule.", Hagan said. John Rampulla, Kentucky Central's vice president of mortgage loans testified that like Kincaid, Burnett lent money through an old-boy network. He personally screened each loan, "each file, each piece of paper." Where Kincaid discussed deals with Rampulla, Burnett gave him no power, "He dealt only with people he knew." Wendell Gunn, a 27-year-employee and secretary treasurer of the company, said that when it came to mortgage loans and real estate, "it was handled by Mr. Burnett exclusively."

I believe the only people who could shed light on what Burnett was doing were some of the company's larger borrowers, Bud's son Bruce Burnett, and Ed Schaeffer, Bud Burnett's enabler and fellow Committee member. Just like the famous reporters did in the book *All the President's Men*, following the money probably held most of the answers. The problem was that this path always led to more people pointing their finger at Bud Burnett. "Silence is golden" and "taking it to their graves" never had more meaning.

---

35   "Festival Market," *Lexington Herald-Leader*, July 15, 1984.

PART III: The Difference Between Success and Failure

Two things define you: Your patience when you have nothing and your attitude when you have everything.

– Imam Ali

Chapter Seven: Celebrating 90 Years in Business

In September 1992, Kentucky Central Life celebrated 90 years in business. While it was a celebration, most of the employees were tired and concerned about the company's future. The public relations department produced some pieces about our long history and the local paper applauded our birthday but questioned our recent history. It was like a family celebrating Christmas knowing that come January 1st, the parents were going to file for divorce.

In addition, in August of 1992, the company held a large sales conference in England and Scottland. This was probably one of the most expensive conferences the company had ever put on. These conferences are for the company's top producers and a select group of home office employees usually management level employees who worked with the agents and a handful of senior officers. This conference was different though in that most of the company's directors, senior vice presidents and vice presidents were invited. My old boss, Cliff Forbush and his wife even got to attend (Cliff had to pay the tax on Rita's cost to attend).

The size and cost of the trip were remarkable, but it had been planned and partially paid for in 1990, when the company reached $50 billion of life insurance in force. I understand more home office officers were invited because the company couldn't qualify enough agents because (1.) they were now rolling their Kentucky Central Life customer's policies to other carriers and (2.) because of the loss of agents in May 1991, when the Committee was forced to sell Kentucky Central's Career agency division to Liberty Life Insurance Company because it needed to strengthen its capital position.

While Burnett and Larry Sammartin tried to make this a celebration, we later learned that the event evolved into a sort of wake by the time it ended. Cocktail hour talk was dark, and agents were discussing what they were going to do if the company didn't make it. At the end, when people were leaving for the airport, the good byes were longer and people's moods were even darker. The attendance at the conference was as much a statement about who wasn't there as who was. Some regional agents and their producers, who had been coming to these events for many years, were absent and I guess some of the questions people were asking were not getting suitable answers. In the end, it was more a swan song trip than anything else. A last hurrah to a place pretty much everyone had never been. In six months, the company would be controlled by the state, Burnett and his enablers would be gone, and the agents attending the conference would be signing contracts to sell for another carrier, if they hadn't already done so.

Happy 90th Anniversary KC!

W.E. "Bud" Burnett, Chairman of the Board and President, welcomes home office employees to the celebration.

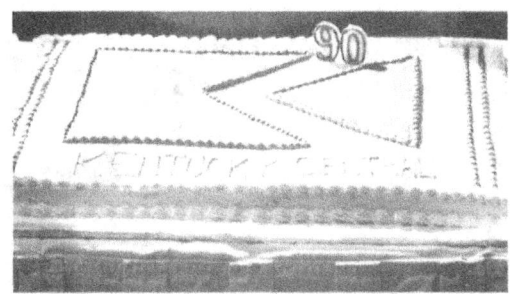

One of five cakes along with punch enjoyed by KC employees.

Vice President Wally Franklin, Consumer Savings, "tux" his shirt in for the party.

Participants gather for a group shot at Festival Market, a nearby shopping center where the event was held.

Sue Cooper, Michele Crawford and Rita Pierce, all of P&C Administration, added sparkle to the fireworks on KCs commemorative T-shirts given to the home office employees.

Joanne Hall, assistant division manager, Personnel, presents Teresa Brookins-Jones, Policyowners Service, with a portfolio, one of the many door prizes won during the event.

HORIZONS

September, 1992

The Great British Adventure

The Cover

In this issue we take a look at the Great British Adventure. Our cover shows Chairman of the Board and President W. E. Burnett, Jr. greeting guests at Hopetoun House along with views of Picadilly Circus, Edinburgh Castle, the Changing of the Guards and the stained glass windows of York Minster.

HORIZONS

Many Kentucky Central agents and their spouses traveled across the Atlantic to participate in the Great British Adventure.

Beauty and excitement awaited them in Scotland and England. On the following pages we recreate the fun and festivities for everyone to enjoy!

Above: Vice President Larry Sammartin and his wife, Shirley. *Below:* Jan and Steve Lewis of Rapid River, Mich. at Stirling Castle in Scotland.

Left: Loretta Williams, Consumer Savings, of Louisville, Ky. at Trossachs. *Right:* A street in York.

Left: (L to r) Diane Kyle of Baltimore, Md., Mary and Mark Darrell of Baltimore, Md., Ed and Judy Gray of Fairfax, Va. and Keith and Flo Casper of Gaithersburg, Md. *Above:* Darla Howe of Lexington, Ky. at Holyrood House, the official residence of the Royal Family in Scotland.

Right: Hopetoun House. *Below:* KC players practice before teeing off at St. Andrews.

Right: Bertha and Jamie Delgado of Laredo, Texas at Trossachs in Scotland. *Far right:* Bobby Clayton of Dallas, Texas with his wife, Sharon, and their daughters.

The Edinburgh closing reception at Hopetoun House was charming with the sound of bagpipes in the air and Mr. Burnett and the Executive Marketing vice presidents in kilts it was a true Scottish celebration.

At right Senior Vice President Wendell Gunn and his wife take the floor at the banquet.

Above: **Chris and Patricia Thompson of Kinston, N. C. and Jim and Dee Campbell of Lexington, Ky. enjoy the grounds of Hopetoun House.** Right: **(l to r) Bobby Clayton of Dallas, Texas, Jean Preston of Lexington, Ky., Vice President Paul Sewell, and Bill Wooley, Bank Sales.** Below: **KCers follow "the pipes" across the grounds.** Below right: **(clockwise from front left) Susan Shapiro of Tallahassee, Fla., Pam and Barry Eisen of Harrisburg, Pa., Bill Pickering of Orlando, Fla., Assistant Vice President Tom Stinnet, Barbe Stinnet and Howard Shapiro.**

The second part of the Great British Adventure took our travelers to London, England where they were treated like royalty at the elegant Grosvenor House and Hilton International hotels.

The convention-goers stepped back in time as they traveled the streets of the centuries-old city.

Double-decker buses travel the streets of London.

Above: Jane and Chris Wismer of Nazreth, Pa. with Madaline and Ray Partlow of Columbus, Ohio relax at a resturant in Petlow, England, a small town outside London. *Right:* Susan and Howard Shapiro of Tallahassee, Fla. at Stratford-upon-Avon. *Below:* Vice President Dick Epps along with Judy and Jim Gerren of Lincoln, Ill. leaving for the tour of London's West End.

Big Ben

Rita and Vice President Cliff Forbush , representatives of the Home Office at Blenheim Castle.

The Streets of London

Consumer Savings Vice President Wally Franklin, his wife Deanna, and son, Chap, celebrated Deanna's birthday.

Above: Tim Wylie, Consumer Savings, and his wife, Paula, of Frankfort, Ky. Below: Board Member Wilson Yates (right) with Mariann and Jim Johnston of Austin, Texas.

Bill Bovinette of Blue Springs, Mo. met his son Bill in England who is attending the University of Grenoble in France.

A British "Bobby"

On November 30, 1992, two months after returning from the trip, Larry Sammartin died and just over twelve months later Bud Burnett would be dead from brain cancer.

Senior Vice President Larry Sammartin

Company mourns the loss of Senior Vice President Larry Sammartin

Services were held Nov. 30 for Senior Vice President Larry Sammartin. The company suffered a tragic loss with the sudden death of one of our most outstanding officers on Thanksgiving morning.

Larry was born in Clairton, Pa., south of Pittsburgh. He graduated from California University in Pennsylvania. Larry's wife, Shirley, is also a native of Pennsylvania. Their two daughters, MarciLynn and Kelly, graduated from the University of Kentucky.

Both daughters are married and reside in Lexington. Kelly is in a marketing development program for a local department store and MarciLynn is a Kentucky Central sales representative.

Larry will be remembered as a very valuable person to Kentucky Central. He began his career in insurance in 1963, and came to Kentucky Central in 1968 as a regional manager in the newly-created University Key Divi-

Larry and Shirley stand between Executive Sales Vice President Paul Sewell and his wife Becky, Peg Burnett and Chairman of the Board and President W.E. Burnett, Jr.

sion, which catered to college students. He was promoted to vice president in 1970.

Under Larry's leadership, the division grew and the name was changed to Professional Marketing. Later the Professional Marketing Division merged with the Executive Sales Division to form the Executive Marketing Division. Executive Marketing is KC's largest sales division. It operates through a nationwide general agency system with thousands of representatives. Larry became head of the combined operation in 1983.

In 1990 Larry was elected to a three-year term as a director of the Life Insurance Marketing and Research Association, one of the major industry trade organizations. He worked with LIMRA throughout his career. Larry was also a member of the Marketing Vice Presidents Association, an 18-company national study group.

Larry was named Senior Vice President and was elected to the Kentucky Central Board of Directors in 1991.

" Larry Sammartin possesed a characteristic that strong leaders must possess — vision. Larry's vision provided the path for all of us to follow. For those of us in both the home office and the field, continuing to build the Executive Marketing Division as Larry envisioned it will be our greatest challenge." said Vice President Dick Epps.

As a youth Larry excelled in football and developed his lifelong love for teamwork and team spirit. One of his favorite quotes was from legendary football coach Vince Lombardi: "The quality of a man's life is in direct proportion to his commitment to excellence."

This commitment to excellence was a recurring theme in many of Larry's talks. He set high goals and helped his division and the company meet these goals.

Larry had a mission, and his mission lives on through those who will carry out his plans for the division. He will be missed, but his legacy will remain with us in our own "Commitment to Excellence."

" He was a 'people person' and this special gift enabled him to work well with people in all walks of life. He was truly an inspiration to everyone in the Executive Marketing Division. Larry was able to bring out the best in people."

W. E. "Bud" Burnett, Jr.

Larry, right, with guest speaker Dr. Robert H. Schuller, center, and an associate at the 1986 convention in California.

Chapter Eight: Garvice Kincaid—The Family Man

Like most people, Kincaid's life was impacted by the environment he grew up in. He came from a family where his father had a strong work ethic, and it appears he instilled that drive into his son. His mother also seems to have been well organized and had a head for business, and Garvice certainly shared these traits. When Garvice marries Nelle in 1940, she had been working in another attorney's office and Kincaid quickly involves her in his real estate transactions. In his early years, business transactions were almost like a game to him, with his successes recorded as demonstrable wins. Garvice Kincaid had an intense focus on things that were important to him, and he would spend an enormous amount of each day on his business affairs and expected others to keep up with his pace of work. Most people in Garvice's orbit had never seen this type of passion and commitment to work and many just couldn't understand it.

Garvice liked having a plan or a short-term goal and his history seems to suggest that his personal frustrations were more obvious when something disrupted them, and as he grew his business empire, his impatience with people also grew. He needed them to implement his business strategies, but many times they never quite lived up to his high expectations. I think this characteristic also impacted his family life. He loved his family but expected them to appreciate his passion for his work, and one can assume this probably impacted how Nelle and his daughters related to him. He could give his family the world financially, but he probably always struggled to provide them with the emotional support they might want.

John Rampulla stated the Mr. Kincaid loved and protected his family and Nancy and Diane Brain also made similar remarks about the Kincaid household. Several people I interviewed described seeing Garvice and Nelle at events and stated how happy they appeared. Former University of Kentucky vice president, Ray Hornback recalled a U.K. football event in the president's suit and just how much of a couple Garvice and Nelle were. He called Nelle a warm and gracious lady and said she socialized with many of the other ladies in the room. John Rampulla said all Garvice's family attended the company's annual Christmas parties at the Phoenix Hotel. He said Garvice and Nelle would greet people coming in and later Garvice would circulate the room saying hello to the non-company guests he had invited. John said while Kincaid was doing this, "Nelle would stay huddled with the girls, making sure they were comfortable."

Bart Brown, who prepared Kincaid's will and trust agreement, described Mrs. Kincaid as a lovely lady and never heard Kincaid say anything negative about his family. WKYT's Ken Kurtz also thought Nelle was a wonderful person who cared a great deal about Garvice and their daughters. Only WVLK's Bill Stakelin observed Kincaid's anger involving his family, and then it had been directed at Jane's husband, Ron. Finally, June Rollings talked about how much Garvice "loved his wife and that Nelle Kincaid was a beautiful human being," but then bluntly said this about Kincaid: "He was strictly business; the coldest, most unemotional man I've ever known. And one of the smartest. He knew everything about everybody in Lexington; where they came from, how much money they had, and all their secrets."

Not a lot is written about Kincaid and his family in the 1950s. There were early articles about his daughters at various school and social club functions and a picture of the family boating on the on the Kentucky River in 1959, and we know they had family vacations in Miami, but after Kincaid's second heart attack in 1964 things appear to begin changing. Certainly, his business interests were taking up more of his time. He now had Kentucky Central Life and in 1967 had acquired WKYT-TV. In addition, he had invested in the Fontainebleau Hotel and the Duck Key Resort after selling his Miami Mansion in 1956, and he had started acquiring his Florida banks.

In 1964, Garvice created his original estate plan, in this version he had his wife and twin daughters on the Committee. They also shared Committee responsibilities with four non-family members: T. C. Quisenberry, Frank G. Trimble, Earl S. Wilson Sr., and Ralph G. Worster. The Committee was made up of a total of seven voting members and this version also included his sister, Beulah K. Norris, as a family alternate and four non-family alternates: Bart A. Brown, Edward F. Schaeffer Jr., Robert E. Layman, and Kenneth C. Davis. In 1964, Kincaid had already experienced his first heart attack (1953), and he would experience his second attack while in Florida during 1964.

In 1967, when he updated his estate plan again, he excluded any family member participation and reduced the Committee's size to three voting members—Earl S. Wilson, Sr., Clyde W. Mauldin, and Edward F. Schaeffer Jr.—and three alternates: W. E. Burnett Jr., H. Hart Hagan Jr., and Robert E. Curtin. In fall 1967, Garvice also made his last insurance company acquisition, Rio Grande National Life Insurance Company. Negotiations for the transaction began in early 1966 but were complicated due to the company's risky military risk. This acquisition introduced Kincaid to Robert W. Baxter, the company's founder. After the acquisition, Garvice added Baxter to Kentucky Central Life's board of directors. It may be that Garvice's exposure to Baxter's experiences running his company as a family business affected his estate plan update.

Kincaid liked the eighty-two-year-old Baxter. Baxter was an Arkansas native, who had moved to Dallas in 1922. He began his career by selling door-to-door and was considered a "super" salesman. His first selling experience came during his summer vacations from Hinemon University in Monticello, Ark., where he graduated in 1909. He walked from house to house, selling photograph enlargements. Garvice could relate to Baxter's life, both men were self-made, both men were attorneys, both men had a passion for real estate, and both men cared deeply about their communities. Baxter and his father had entered business together in 1917, selling lumber. Their lumber yards also handled general merchandise and by 1922, Baxter was managing five of their lumber yards and operating a brokerage business specializing in the buying and selling of sawmill plants.

Baxter got into insurance almost by accident. He had made a made a substantial loan to the Rio Grande Mutual Life Insurance Co. This was in the fall of 1928 and a few days after the loan was made, he found that he was not only an interested party but had also inherited the responsibility for the company. Many of his new friends advised him to sell out—that only an experienced life insurance man could possibly hope to succeed, especially in a territory such as the Rio Grande Valley, under the poor social economic conditions that existed in the valley at that time.

Baxter, however, did not intend to see his "loan" evaporate and ignored the advice of his friends. He applied for a charter for the Rio Grande National Life Insurance Co. The charter was granted on December 18, 1928, and Robert Baxter was elected president. Baxter and the company never looked back on those desperate times. The company had limited territory and so in 1930, during the Great Depression, Baxter moved the Rio Grande National Life to Dallas. The company never stopped growing and at the beginning of its 21st year, it had more than $65 million of life insurance in force, along with a large base of hospitalization and accident insurance premium income.

Robert W. Baxter was a force and in additional to his duties as president of the company, he was agency director, personnel manager, and general sales director. In 1960, at the age of 75, he was still actively involved with the company, meeting his various district managers and their agents, and actively looking for new policy ideas. Baxter retired from Kentucky Central Life's board of directors at the end of 1968 and died in February 1984 at the age of 98.

When Baxter sold Kincaid Rio Grande National Life in the fall of 1967, its 82-year-old founder had turned over the day-to-day operations of the company to his sons. Baxter and his wife had four sons and three of them, Bob, Turner, and Bill, had executive positions with the company and the fourth son, Murphy, was in the oil business in Midland, Texas, but retained a financial interest in Rio Grande National. Robert Patrick "Bob" Baxter Sr. was president of the company when Garvice acquired it, Bill Baxter was vice president and headed the mortgage loan department. A position he had held for seventeen years.

Rio Grand National was a nice regional life insurance company, but it had begun selling insurance on military bases in 1964. The policies had a larger death benefit of up to $25,000 and did not include the normal "war exclusion" just as the country was increasing its efforts in the Vietnam War. The Department of Defense had created an accreditation program where insurance carriers could be approved to sell insurance to military personnel, on the military bases. By 1964, more than 90 carriers had received approval, most of them small regional companies. In three years, Rio Grande National's insurance in force increased by more than 30%.

In 1964, Lyndon Johnson ran as the "peace" candidate against conservative Barry Goldwater, who wanted to escalate the military offensive against North Vietnam and the Viet Cong guerillas. In October, at a campaign appearance in Ohio, Johnson promised that "we are not about to send American boys 9 or 10,000 miles away from home to do what Asian boys ought to be doing for themselves."[1] But in the months after the Gulf of Tonkin Resolution, Johnson rapidly increased the U.S. military presence in the defense of South Vietnam, with 184,000 troops stationed there by the end of 1965.

In July 1965, at the beginning of this steady escalation, President Johnson attempted to explain the need for increased military intervention in Vietnam in a press conference announcing that draft inductions would increase from 17,000 to 35,000 per month. He explained, "America had no choice, because North Vietnam and Communist China sought to "conquer the South, to defeat American power, and to extend the Asiatic dominion of communism. . . . An Asia so threatened by Communist domination would certainly imperil the security of the United States itself."[2]

---

1   Lyndon B. Johnson, "Remarks in Memorial Hall, Akron University," October 21, 1964, Public Papers of the Presidents of the United States, 1964, Book II, pp. 1391–1393, quoted in *Resistance and Revolution: The Anti-Vietnam War Movement at the University of Michigan, 1965-1972.*

2   Ibid.

By 1967, Robert Baxter knew his company had a problem. Between 1964 and the end of 1967, about one million men had been drafted into military service, equal to the total amount of men drafted during the previous ten years. The company was seeing a rapid increase in claims this was impacting the company's financials and Baxter was smart enough to see that his son's entry into this market was a disaster. Kincaid, David Brain, and Kentucky Central's chief actuary, Bill Joyner, discussed the situation and agreed that everything outside of the military business was great; just traditional weekly and monthly debit business and a small mixture of college life insurance.

Garvice decided he just couldn't risk buying the military business and told Baxter he would acquire his whole company in a stock swap, but Baxter would need to get rid of the military business first. Baxter agreed and eventually was able to sell the military business to Illinois based Bankers Life & Casualty Insurance Company, on November 6, 1967. Clyde Honaker and I believe Baxter had to pay Bankers Life money to take over the policies due to the losses they produced. One week later, Kincaid and Baxter announce that Kentucky Central Life Insurance Company would acquire Rio Grande National Life in a stock swap valued at $11 million. Kentucky Central Life would give Rio Grande shareholders (primarily Robert Baxter), 14.5 shares of Kentucky Central Life's non-voting stock for each of its 100,000 shares. Kentucky Central was trading at $7.625 when the deal closed.

This acquisition was completed on January 1, 1968, and Rio Grande's operations were transferred to Lexington over the next six months. Bob Baxter, the president of Rio Grande soon moved to Scottsdale, Arizona. He and his wife didn't return to Dallas until 1990. Kincaid also added Robert Baxter to Kentucky Central Life's board, and Baxter helped transition the operations to Lexington. The Rio Grande was licensed to operate in 36 states, but the majority of its business was in Texas, New Mexico, Arizona, Arkansas, Utah, and Wyoming. After the merger, Kentucky Central Life now had 150 branch offices and 2,000 employees and sales personnel. During this time, Clyde Honaker had several conversations with Robert Baxter, and he said, Baxter said he wasn't happy with the price Kincaid paid him, but admitted it was probably the best offer he was going to get.

Prior to 1965, Baxter's company had been on track to earn over $600,000 annually, but beginning in 1965, the company lost over $200,000. This implies the military business was already losing about $800,000 annually due to claims.

Rio Grande stopped including its financial statements in ads in 1967 and so we don't know what its actual surplus level was on December 31, 1967, but my guess is that it was probably less than $4.0 million. If Baxter paid $5 million to

Bankers Life to take over the military business, this meant Baxter only netted about $6 million on the sale to Kincaid. Since Garvice only purchased the "good business", and it was earning around $600,0000 annually, the implies Kincaid paid around 18 times its annual earnings. In reality, Kincaid paid a much smaller multiple, because he and David Brain eliminated most of the company's administrative expenses and corporate overhead when they moved the business to Lexington. In addition, the company significantly expanded its marketing and sales division overnight. During the 1970s, the former Rio Grande agents were important contributors to the growth of the company.

I don't know if Baxter's experience impacted Garvice, but I suspected it did. Baxter had trusted his sons with the management of the company, and they had made a significant strategic mistake. Baxter himself may have been involved in the decision but he was 79 years old in 1964 and his son had been running the company since 1961.

In addition, not only had his sons got into the military market in a big way, but they had also put over $25 million or 60% of the company's assets in commercial mortgage loans and had another $4.5 million tied up in the company's home office real estate. The company had over $39 million in assets, but $30 million of it was illiquid. Baxter's sons had also taken on more risk than Robert Baxter had ever done. When Patrick Baxter became president, the company had $14.5 million in mortgage loans and $28.4 million in total assets and in 1967, the military business was forcing the company to liquidate assets to pay claims.

What seems apparent today is that Garvice changed in the 1960s, becoming more detached from his family and more driven by his desire to grow his business. His twin daughters, now in their mid-twenties, were no longer kids and were more independent, and his businesses were all prospering. Kincaid was enjoying his wealth and his expansion into television and the addition of his Florida banks and stayed up late into the night talking on the phone. He had each of his business lieutenants in place and now was expanding his empire further into Florida.

In 1964, Kincaid experienced his second heart attack while in Florida, at the age of fifty-two and according to reported interviews, his doctors told him he probably wouldn't survive the next one. In my opinion, his attitude toward life just changed after that. His wife Nelle probably had finally given up trying to get him to slow down and decided to just let him be and he had never included his now grown daughters in the running of his business. Garvice was a man of the 1950s and according to John Rampulla, wouldn't miss an episode of "Green Acres", which began airing in 1965 and ran for six seasons.

Attitudes about domestic roles were evolving in the1960s, but still primitive when compared to today. The Khan Academy described it this way:

> The 1950s is often viewed as a period of conformity, when both men and women observed strict gender roles and complied with society's expectations. After the devastation of the Great Depression and World War II, many Americans sought to build a peaceful and prosperous society. However, even though certain gender roles and norms were socially enforced, the 1950s was not as conformist as is sometimes portrayed, and discontent with the status quo bubbled just beneath the surface of the placid peacetime society. Although women were expected to identify primarily as wives and mothers and to eschew work outside of the home, women continued to make up a significant proportion of the postwar labor force. Moreover, the 1950s witnessed significant changes in patterns of sexual behavior, which would ultimately lead to the "sexual revolution" of the 1960s.[3]

There are many stories about Garvice dining out in various Lexington restaurants on most evenings. I heard about them from both Cliff Forbush and Charley Thomas, and Mr. Cormney, the owner of the Campbell House also confirmed this to me years ago, "Various restaurants around town would hold his table until he showed up, and then call the other places to let them know the eagle has landed." June Rollings talked about it in an interview, "It's because we were seen in public at dinner constantly. Garvice never ate dinner at home. He went out to dinner every night at the Coach House, the Imperial House, wherever. He had three male buddies and me that he dined with."[4]

It was also common knowledge at Kentucky Central Life that Garvice maintained a suite at the Campbell House. As a young guy hearing this, my mind probably thought the worst, but after researching Mr. Kincaid, I now think the man got tired sometimes and just wanted a place to take a shower and put on a clean shirt. In 1967, when Kincaid did the second update to his estate plan, he was fifty-five years old, recovering from his second heart attack, significantly overweight and probably taking several prescriptions related to his blood pressure and heart. Garvice enjoyed growing and expanding his business empire, but I imagine this physical exertion drained him at times, and he needed a place to recover. Here is man, who has WKYT management meetings at his house on Sunday and who is calling his staff after mid-night to complain about things. He was burning the candle at both ends.

---

3   *Women in the 1950s*, Khan Academy, https://www.khanacademy.org/ humanities/us-history/postwarera/1950s-america/a/women-in-the-1950s.

4   Don Edwards, "June Rollings Career," *Lexington Herald-Leader*, June 2, 2002.

In the Lexington Herald-Leader on November 11, 1973, David Holwerk published a long interview with Garvice. It's probably the most telling writing about the man that I found. It was written two years before he died, and one year after he last updated his estate plan, and provides first-person insight about the man:

Garvice Kincaid . . . a Builder, a Toiler, a Legend

"Kincaid here," the voice on the telephone said in a tone that did not encourage discussion. "I find that I'm going to have to have to be in my office all day Sunday. So, I guess we'll have to have our interview here instead of at my home."

. . . For almost 40 years, Kincaid has more often than not spent his Sunday afternoons at work in his office, assembling and managing a financial empire that now exceeds a half-billion dollars. His holdings included insurance companies, loan agencies, real estate investments, and more than a score of banks in Kentucky and other states.

Kincaid inspires both ardent admirers and virulent detractors. He has been hailed both as a major force in the growth of Lexington and decried as a heartless, money-grubbing fanatic. He has been denounced by the leaders of the Lexington business community and has had his share of troubles with the local news media. But through it all, Kincaid has kept working, putting in hours which most people would find intolerable, but which afford him his main pleasure in life.

The office in which he spends so much of his time is perhaps indicative of the man's character. It is paneled in walnut and furnished with handsome chairs and a large executive desk, but Kincaid's big leather swivel seat shows signs of wear and heavy use. Its seat is well-worn, and the green leather of its arms has been rubbed down to a natural brown by the constant friction of Kincaid's shirtsleeves. Two large stacks of magazines and reports lie on a shelf near the desk, and nearby sit five telephones, connected to two nationwide and three statewide network lines.

There are piles of paper on the desk and shelves of lawbooks on one wall. Another wall sports awards and commendations which Kincaid has received, including his membership in the Newsboy's Hall of Fame and his Horatio Alger Award from the American Schools and colleges Association. But the wall on which they hang is poorly lit, and they seem to be there almost as an afterthought. Above all, the office is a place to work.

It is also a place in which Garvice Kincaid is comfortable. Sitting behind his desk on a Sunday afternoon, Kincaid has the ease of a man who is on his own turf. He is a heavy man, but his bulk rest easily in his chair. He talks freely and, at least in an interview, smiles readily and occasionally makes himself the butt of a small joke.

Eight to ten hours a day, six and sometimes seven days a week, Kincaid is in the office on the fourth floor of the Central Bank Building, or in some other office in some other city where he has interests. He works hard not because he has to; no man worth as much as he is needs to work at all. Rather, Kincaid works because he likes to.

"Money doesn't mean that much to me, not as money anyway," he said stretching in his chair. "You don't have to be too smart to know that I have more of it than I can ever use for myself and my family. But money lets me do the things I like to do, make the business deals I like to make. It's all kind of a game, really."

If finance is a game, then Kincaid is the Dick Butkus of the local league. His tactics are often questioned, his character maligned, his motivations sneered at. But he is preeminently successful in his game, and he doesn't mind showing his pride at his success.

…But despite his success, or maybe because of it, Kincaid has long suffered a poor reputation in the Lexington community. His lack of connections in the community didn't help, nor did his early involvement with what many thought, at the time, to be the "unsavory" loan business. Nor did his keenly competitive business practices make him popular.

"Banking is a lazy man's business.", Kincaid said of his profession. "You sit in this chair all day and make decisions about money. But you can work at this lazy man's business, or you can loaf at it. I like to work at it, I like to compete for business, and I think that's what upsets some people. Bankers just aren't used to competing, and if somebody makes them compete, they just figure there's something wrong with him."

By far the most bitter conflict between Kincaid and the other Lexington businessmen occurred over the merger of First National and Security Trust banks in the early 1960's. Kincaid had become a shareholder in First National, and there were fears by some executives of the bank that he was trying to take over the institution. The merger of the two banks was announced shortly after Kincaid asked for the First National stockholders list. The merger was opposed by the Justice Department on antitrust grounds, and local businessmen began falling into pro- and anti-Kincaid camps.

Kincaid now takes great pains to deny that he was behind efforts to block the merger, or that he ever had any conflicts with the Lexington business establishment.

"I never had any conflict with these people here." He said, shaking his head. "Why the First National Bank sold me my first bank in 1945."

"I think they later got scared of me because I competed with them. I never tendered an offer for First National stock. I never tried to take anything that was theirs. All I did was compete with them."

Competition is a key word to Kincaid. He seeks out and thrives on it, and he thinks other businessmen should thrive on it as well. He has a reputation as a man who does not tolerate incompetence and sets high standards for men in his organization.

"We set standards in 17 categories for our banks last year," he said with a little pride in his smile. "All but one of our banks met or exceeded the standards. Now everybody knows they've done a good job, and they have the satisfaction that comes with that. And so", he laughed, "we'll set next year's standards a little higher."

Kincaid is not a social man by nature, and this has not helped his standing in a community in which business and pleasure are often mixed. He and his wife of 33 years, the former Nelle Wilson, live in their nice home on Richmond Road in Lexington. They entertain very little. They belong to the Lexington Country Club, but Kincaid uses it only once or twice a year; he had a yacht in Florida but sold it because he didn't use it.

"I went to the races once." He recalled with a laugh, "and people were pointing at me and acting like I was crazy. It just happened that I had a business associate who wanted to go to the races, so I took him."

The only social events which he attends regularly are UK athletic contests, which he seems to enjoy greatly. He retains an abiding interest in his alma mater, but his actions as a University Trustee show where his heart lies. Shortly after his appointment to the board, Kincaid raised a fuss about the interest UK was receiving on money it had on deposit in local banks. His mind is always on finance, and this makes him an asset to boards of non-profits, and charitable institutions.

In addition to his position on the UK Board, Kincaid also served on the Kentucky Wesleyan College, the Lexington Deaf-Oral School, and other institutions. He has given thousands of dollars to scholarship funds throughout the state, has donated $100,000 for the expansion of the Lexington YMCA, and has helped start the Boys Club and Big Sisters programs in Lexington.

"Some days there are four or five people in here looking for money for one cause or another. It's just part of having money, I guess," he said.

A lot of people call on Garvice Kincaid in the course of a day, and they are often surprised to find that they have little trouble getting in to see him. The door to his office is usually open and telephone calls are transferred to him with few questions asked. He keeps his own appointment book and says that he'll see and talk to anybody.

"Why not?" he said, "It takes a little more time, but I figure that if it's important enough for people to want to come and see me it's worth my time to listen. I guess I waste a little time, but I learned some things to. An anyway, I've got lots of time."

Or, at any rate, he used to have. Time is catching up to Garvice Kincaid just as it does to everyone else. He has had two heart attacks, and his doctors tell him that he has to slow down. But he still keeps his long hours, goes to Florida to see after his holdings there every three or four weeks, and makes frequent trips to New York to deal with the major financial institutions there. He maintains an apartment at Miami's Fontainebleau Hotel, but it is strictly for business, and though he knows he can't keep up the pace forever, he shows few signs of thinking about retirement.

"What would I do if I were retired?" he asked, partially to himself. "I don't know. Besides, I've learned that it's a hell of a lot easier to buy businesses than to get rid of them. Some mornings I get up and don't feel too well and then I think about slowing down a little, but that doesn't happen too often."

"Of course, I try to pace myself now. I used to go at things like a windmill, but now I try to plan a little better. And anyway, I'm having some fun."

"You know, it's a sad thing to see so many young fellows who get married and go to work because they have to work because they have to. They get a job and stick with it even though they don't like it, and they never get to know that there's a lot of enjoyment in working, if you are working at something you like to do. And I think that's too bad, because I think working is the most enjoyable thing in the world."

How much longer can Kincaid keep up his participation in "the most enjoyable thing in the world?" His heart is in pretty bad shape, and the long hours spent in his chair are beginning to tell in his physical condition.

"Who know?" Kincaid said, shaking his head. "I might decide to quit it all tomorrow. But I've got a few ideas cooking right now that look like they'll be pretty interesting. We're going to build a new bank building in one of the towns around here and show them what banking is all about. We're going to knock the other banks' eyes out with service, and then that town will have not one but three good banks. The others will have to improve to keep up with us."

"As for me… Well, they tell me I have to get out of this chair and get some exercise, but I don't seem to do it. I say there's not time, but I know that's not so. I think it's just like everything else. It's just a matter of willpower."

When I began researching Kincaid's history in early 2021, this was one of the first articles I read about him. I think it does an exceptional job showing the human side of Garvice. For me, it's obvious he understood his health was declining, but he wasn't going to let this significant issue distract him. He had things he still wanted to get accomplished, and they were his priorities. He was living for himself and no one else, and if you were in his orbit, you just had to accept it.

While we can't read Garvice's mind, his actions provide some indication of his state of mind. For instance, we know that sometime in 1968, he had heard enough about the philandering of Jane's husband, Ron Nickell, that he paid him to get out of town and agree to a divorce. Their divorce documents indicated they separated in March of 1969, and the divorce was finalized at the end of May in 1970. There is no way of knowing how this changed Jane's relationship with her father, but I imagine it had some effect on it.

We also know that someone Kincaid trusted, Clyde Mauldin, suddenly left him at the end of 1971. Kincaid had brought Mauldin up from one of his Florida banks to run Central Bank. He had been president of the bank for several years and his resignation shocked and probably hurt Garvice. Kincaid had had assigned Mauldin as a primary member of his estate Committee in 1967 and now in January 1972, Garvice had to quickly update his Committee list to exclude him. On January 5, 1972, Kincaid made his last and probably his most consequential update to his estate plan listing his Committee members as: Earl S. Wilson, Al Florence, and W.E. Bud Burnett Jr. and alternates in this order, Edward F. Schaeffer Jr., H. Hart Hagan Jr., and Charles Rusty Hembree. Neither Al Florence nor Rusty Hembree had ever been included in the past updates. In addition, while Bud Burnett had been listed as an alternate in 1967, he was now a primary Committee member. In addition, this amendment is his short and to the point verses this prior two amendments.

In May 1975, Garvice did something a little unusual for him, he recruited Harold Yates, a thirty-year banking professional, from Merchants National Bank in Indianapolis, Indiana. Merchants was a $1.1 billion bank and Yates had been with them for eleven years. At the same time, he also brought Wayne Smith in as the bank's executive vice president. Wayne Smith came from

Union Commerce Bank in Cleveland. Union Commerce was a $1.5 billion bank and Smith had been in banking for 16 years and a senior credit officer overseeing the bank's $125 million commercial loan portfolio.

I say this move was unusual because previously he had brought in people from his larger Florida banks, like Robert Layman and Clyde Mauldin into senior positions at the bank. Now he had jumped outside of his own ecosystem and recruited two experienced people from much larger banks. I believe he did this because he appreciated the importance of Central Bank and knew he needed knowledgeable and experienced professionals leading the bank if it was going to become much larger. Remember that Al Florence hadn't held any position at Central Bank until Garvice made him vice chairman of the board in January 1975. His primary role had always been managing Kincaid's network of small-town banks. In addition, Harold A. Yates had only lasted a few weeks and after he left, Garvice again had reclaimed the title of president for the bank, and not Al Florence.

I believe these strategic hiring decisions were expected to lead to the replacement of Al Florence as a primary Committee member. The vice chairman position is not an officer or management position. I think Garvice knew Florence couldn't lead the bank, he wasn't a polished professional banker and tended to push people around, and that's why he brought in Yates and Smith. In addition, in March of 1975, Kincaid had recruited John Irving to the bank from Merrill Lynch. Irving knew everyone around town and would be able to quickly introduce Yates and Smith to Lexington. Kincaid was putting in place a class-A banking team to move the bank forward.

I think if Kincaid had lived a few more months, he would have updated his estate plan again in early 1976 and added David Brain as a primary Committee member and possibly included Robert L. Epling or Wayne Smith as primary members. When Garvice died, he was still the bank's president and in early 1976, Earl Wilson quickly recruited Epling to be the bank's president. Epling had been president of Kincaid's Dania Bank in Florida, and Kincaid had known him since the early 1960s. The main point is that I believe Garvice was creating a path around Al Florence. Kincaid and Earl Wilson both understood that his estate would have trouble owning his collection of smalltown banks after his death due to the bank holding company laws and this meant Florence's role would be substantially reduced. In addition, Florence had trouble working with people. This was demonstrated by the fact that Florence pressured Richard Epling out of the bank in November 1976. I believe this is one of the reasons Wilson and Burnett negotiated the deal with Florence to get him to resign from the Committee.

We will never know what Kincaid's final solution to his estate plan might have been, but in my opinion neither Burnett nor Al Florence would have been primary members of his estate Committee. The reason I think this is relevant to his personal life is that this just increased the pressure he was under to finalize how he wanted things to work. The first key to his mindset was his appointment of David Brain as the president of Kentucky Central Life in January 1975. The second key was the consolidation of all of Bluegrass Broadcasting and Kentucky Finance into a holding company owned by Kentucky Central Life. The third key was the recruitment of Robert Eppling as president of Central Bank. In addition, in 1975, Garvice understood that Earl Wilson couldn't remain on the Committee after April 1977 and so he needed to amend his estate plan, but the clock just ran out on him.

In June 1994, the *Lane Report* interviewed Jane Kincaid Johnson[5] and Joan Kincaid about their 18 years of litigation against the Committee. Their remarks suggest that Garvice never intended that the members of his estate Committee were to be employed to run his various businesses. In addition, they suggest that the Committee undervalued his business assets held in Fund C and overvalued the assets held in fund A and fund B, in order to move all of Kincaid's businesses to fund C. I appreciate their remarks and frankly believe things would have been better if Garvice had completely removed this conflict of interest, but in 1973, had had already started consolidating his assets under Kentucky Central Life. He even discusses it in Kentucky Central Life's 1973 and 1974 Annual Reports:

> 1973 – We are pleased to report that our diversification program carried on through our subsidiary, Mid-Central Investment Co., Inc., moved solidly forward in 1973. During the year, we completed the acquisition of Kentucky Finance Company, a large regional consumer finance organization, and put into the market place two additional property and casualty insurance companies, providing us with the added capability of writing all classes of automobile and homeowner insurance.

> 1974 – Other elements of our diversification program—which includes banking, consumer finance and television broadcasting— progressed at a satisfactory rate during the year.

In 1973, Kincaid made the decision to move his broadcasting and finance company businesses into a subsidiary of Kentucky Central Life. I believe one reason he did this was to make Kentucky Central a larger publicly traded company and more of a conglomerate. He may have had some other estate

---

5   Jane remarried after her divorce from Ron Nickell.

reasons though, since Mid-Central and the other entities were issuing notes and/or preferred stock to his trust. Upon his death, these debt obligations would be easier to value and provide a steady income stream for his estate's beneficiaries. Garvice began moving these assets as percentages of his shareholding holdings and Kentucky Central Life didn't end up owning 100% of everything until 1976, about six months after his death. In my opinion, his intent was obvious since about 80% had already been transferred to Mid-Central Investments between 1972 and 1975.

In addition, Kincaid's trust agreement indicated that members of the Committee should be employed by or doing work for his business interests. If you were a member of his advisory Committee and you quit working for one of his entities, then you were removed from the Committee. He acknowledged there would be conflicts of interests, with Committee members earning money from his businesses, and his trust agreement indemnified them for everything but fraud, bad judgement and gross negligence.

From the Garvice Kincaid Trust Agreement's Third Amendment:

- A vacancy in the membership of the Advisory Committee shall occur: (1) on the refusal of any appointee to serve; (2) on the attainment of seventy (70) years of age by, or the death of, any member; (3) on the resignation of any member; (4) on the legal incompetency of any member; (5) on the inability of any member to serve because of physical and/or mental illness; or (6) on any member failing to be or remain a member of, or associated with the law firm known as Kincaid, Wilson & Trimble, or any successor thereof or to be retained as general counsel for, or be employed by, or performing services on a regular basis for, any corporation or corporations in which (a) the Grantor's estate, (b) any trust created by this Trust Agreement, (c) any trust created by Grantor, (d) the Grantor's wife, (g) Joan D. Kincaid, (h) any trust created by Joan D. Kincaid, (i) Jane K. Nickell, and/or (j) any trust created by Jane K, Nickell, owns in excess of five percent (5%) of the voting Stock there.

- It is the Grantor's express desire to have as members of this Advisory Committee, persons who are employed by, represent, have financial interests in, or receive compensation from, corporations in which the trusts created by this Trust Agreement have, or are likely to have, financial interests; therefore, any such employment, representation, or financial interests shall not disqualify a person from being, becoming or remaining a member of the Advisory Committee.

- The Grantor realizes that there are certain risks involved in conducting the affairs of the trusts created by this Trust Agreement. The Grantor, therefore, directs that each member of the Advisory Committee shall be indemnified by the trusts created by this Trust Agreement against claims, liabilities, expenses and costs actually and necessarily incurred by him in connection with, or arising out of, any action in which he is made a party by reason of his being, or having been, a member of the Advisory Committee, except in relation to matters as to which he shall be adjudged in such action to be libel for fraud or bad faith or gross negligence.

Garvice's daughters, Joan and Jane, had a series of lawsuits against the Committee beginning in 1977. The 1985 lawsuit went to the heart of "except in relation to matters as to which he shall be adjudged in such action to be libel for fraud or bad faith or gross negligence." They were fighting the Committee in court and their father's estate was paying for it. The judicial system works slowly and as it was explained to me by someone, there was a fight about any information they requested. This was a high-profile case, and any court ruling would be appealed to the highest court. Add to this, Judges always prefer negotiated settlements to bench rulings, and you can imagine how frustrated Kincaid's daughters must have been.

I think Garvice expected that his family would be unhappy with his plan. Bart Brown never met with Nelle Kincaid about it and said he didn't get the feeling that Garvice discussed it with her. He may have, but his bet would have been he hadn't. He said it was him and Kincaid in the room. No Earl Wilson. No Frank Trimble. Just Garvice and him.

During Kincaid's life he did many interviews, and I never found one where a reporter asked Garvice what would happen to his estate after his death. They probably were afraid to ask him, and I am confident his answer would have been something like, "None of your damn business." When I started working on his history, my real-life understanding of the ending always made me wonder why he hadn't included his daughters in his estate plan. They were college educated and while like all of us in our twenties, they were also probably young and naïve but they were certainly responsible enough in their thirties to be involved. At a minimum, even if he hadn't wanted them to be advisory Committee members, he could have required they or their representatives be included as directors on all his companies' boards. Certainly, this would have limited what Burnett was able to do.

I don't have an answer to why his family was not included in the management of his estate and businesses. I think it was a mistake and whatever

Kincaid's concerns were, they certainly couldn't have been as problematic as what actually happened. I really do believe he would have updated his estate plan again if given a few more months to live and believe at least David Brain would have been a member and this may have been enough to change the future direction of things.

After Kincaid's death the Committee's relationship with the Kincaid family quickly soured. Initially there were legal fights about Garvice's option agreements pertaining to some bank stocks Joan held, and another fight about the Lexington Finance Company and finally the largest disagreement involved the valuation of assets used in the distribution of assets to each Kincaid's three trusts. The disputes eventually led to the September 1978 public announcement by American General Life Insurance Company. It wanted to purchase the estates voting shares of Kentucky Central Life for $14 million. According to press reports, a Louisville attorney, Barnard H. Barnett, who represented Nelle Kincaid, had contacted the company to encourage them to make an offer.

The Committee spent almost a year fighting the unsolicited offer. Twelve months earlier the Committee had filed an estate tax return valuing those same shares at just $1 million. American General was offering $17,500 for each of the 800 voting shares held by Kincaid's trust verses the $14.50 price that the non-voting shares were trading for the day before. The voting shares had a par value of $100 and the non-voting shares had a par value of $1.00. This meant the voting shares were being valued at $1,160,00 the day before American General made its offer. The Committee hadn't undervalued the shares in the estate's tax return, it had just used the publicly traded stock's value. Remember Garvice controlled the company by owning 80% of the voting shares, which made up 10% of the company's capitalization. The non-voting shares were 90% of the company's capitalization.[6]

---

6   In reality, the estate's voting share were worth more than the nonvoting shares, and normally if a business is being sold, these shares would be valued differently. Kincaid's estate plan anticipated this and guided the Committee to use its best efforts to reduce any tax liability. The Kincaid family's argument that these shares were undervalued as it relates to the division of assets is a fair argument, but using American General's bid for just the voting shares was just as unfair, in my opinion. Business valuations usually value the whole business first and then back in to a premium for the voting shares. The implication of what they were doing is interesting, but in my opinion, the voting shares lost most of that premium because the Committee controlled Kincaid's trust, so their wish, to not sell those shares and lose control of the company, eliminated most of the implied premium. In other words, their decision to sell or not sell, not the shares themselves, retained the premium.

The conflicts between the Committee and the Kincaid family during the first few years after his death created a fractured relationship between the two groups which should have been working together. It's regrettable that it happened, but I doubt either side ever tried to repair the relationship. After Earl Wilson left the Committee in 1977, Burnett became more powerful by assuming the Committee's leadership role and by 1980, he was wheeling and dealing, trying to become respected and powerful. He would have been the last person wanting to mend any bridges. In fact, after I joined the company and in doing the research for this book, I heard the rumors and stories about employees being warned off from having any contact with Kincaid's family. People who had previously had a personal or business relationship with the Nelle and/or the daughters were warned off. Given Emmett Crump's story concerning Burnett's call to him about his visit to the insurance department I have always assumed Bud Burnett was the hammer (the Committee) delivering the message to the nail (the employees).

In the June 1994 Lane report, "The Fall of Kincaid's Dynasty—An Exclusive Interview," the warnings were explained this way by the Kincaid daughters:

> The Kincaid sisters said during the 18 years subsequent to their father's death, "We were not allowed in Kentucky Central (the building). The only information that we got about Kentucky Central was either street gossip, or one or two people making phone calls. We did not know what exactly they were doing. Employees were told that if they spoke to us on the street, they would lose their job, Joan Kincaid said.
>
> According to court records, Johnson testified that certain employees had been instructed not to speak with her, her mother or her sister, without the penalty of losing their jobs.
>
> For example, Johnson testified that Calvin Hooten, who at the time of the testimony worked for Central Bank, also did yard work for Nelle Kincaid. Johnson said he was told, "He would lose his job if he stepped foot in mother's yard again." Johnson testified that this was relayed to Mrs. Kincaid by Hooten.
>
> Also, Johnson testified that she had lost several friendships. "We had heard that employees of dad's companies were not allowed to speak to us on the street." She testified that a close friend to hers, who worked for Kentucky Central, related that she could no longer be friends with Johnson, but could possibly reconcile after she had retired from the company. Johnson added, "We have led a very isolated, lonely life life for 18 years."
>
> Kincaid said if the family wanted any information about the companies they had to resort to the court system.

People who are paranoid are usually paranoid for a good reason, and Bud Burnett was a paranoid person. According to my old boss, Cliff Forbush, he was always trying to find out what David Brain was up to and after Kincaid's death he was paranoid about people's perception of him. How paranoid was Bud Burnett? Consider this, Calvin Hooten was the "building engineer" (building maintenance) for the Central Bank building. He held that position for many years. What important information could he possibly have that could harm Burnett and the Committee. Calvin Hooten passed away in September 2022 at the age of 95. I am sorry I never had the opportunity to interview him. He probably had some wonderful stories about Mr. Kincaid.

Paranoia is the seed of self-destruction. It causes people to act irrationally, to hide information, and to keep secrets and Bud Burnett's insecurity about people's perception of him, was the seed that led to the destruction of Garvice Kincaid's empire. Other people enabled him and fed his ego, but it all began with his own personal insecurities. Burnett knew he was never a successful insurance company executive in Louisville, and he recognized in January 1975, when Kincaid made David Brain the president of Kentucky Central Life, that Garvice also recognized his limitations. He was an accountant. He was someone who kept the regulators happy. He wasn't active in the community or actively involved in Garvice's real estate investments. Kincaid didn't replace Paul Carr by promoting Burnett after Carr left. Garvice recognized that Burnett didn't have the resume and experience of David Brain, and Brain's promotion in January 1975 reflected his recognition of this. Bud Burnett was just Garvice Kincaid's greatest mistake, and Burnett knew it. That's why he was so paranoid.

Garvice Kincaid's history indicates that he really didn't trust people when it came to money. He knew people could be influenced by money, and Kincaid himself used money to influence people. His idea for a multigenerational trust was a reasonable estate plan, but it was always subject to human desires for something more, especially wealth and power. He made Central Bank the trustee, but the bank couldn't provide independent oversight, because it was controlled by his advisory Committee. His family beneficiaries couldn't do anything because he had created a trust agreement giving almost absolute indemnification to the members of the advisory Committee.

Garvice Kincaid was a man ahead of his time and probably one of the smartest people in Kentucky during his day. He wasn't perfect, and while his mistakes were few and his losses small, his biggest mistake was trusting some of the people he put on his advisory Committee. Kincaid assume each member would have one vote, but in 1977, it always became two votes to one. Just like the television show "Survivor," the contestants formed alliances to get what they wanted. There is a saying, "It's always the quiet ones you have to look out for." It is a common expression that suggests that people who are quiet or reserved may have hidden depths or unexpected qualities, which can sometimes be negative or dangerous. Bud Burnett was a quiet one, and someone Kincaid should have been worried about. He certainly turned out to be dangerous! Jim Parks of the *Courier Journal* wrote this in May of 1978.

> Garvice Kincaid manipulated his investments furtively, keeping friend and foe alike guessing while he relished the intrigue. In the end, he controlled a massive estate with gross assets of more than a half a billion dollars, but its composition belies the image of a roller-coaster investor.

> Kincaid's tidiness is revealed in the two-page, double-spaced list of his holdings. He had one personal checking account in Central Bank. Three other checking accounts were for apartment complexes he owned in Lexington. He had only one other real estate holding, the Richmond Bank building. Five notes cover loans to two business associates and his daughters, and they were generally tied to friendly stock purchase and option agreements. He owned stock interest in 35 enterprises, but these were mainly tied to Kentucky Central Life Insurance Company, Bluegrass Broadcasting Company, Kentucky Finance Company, and Central Bank & Trust. He owned 22 banks located in Kentucky and Florida and eight other entities associated with real estate holdings, a finance company and insurance agency. He had some cash and one share of the Lexington Trots Breeding Association.

> His will was also simple in that we bequeathed his law books to his law firm and his only residence to his wife of 35 years, Mrs. Nelle Kincaid. Everything else mentioned above was left to his trust. Kincaid's will also provided Nelle Kincaid with $450,000 for two years of service with Kentucky Finance Company. The daughters are not mentioned in his will, but they were taken care of through his estate trust, along with Nelle Kincaid.

What happened to Garvice Kincaid's estate wasn't an economic accident or just bad luck. It was the momentum of individuals' greed meeting the wall of reality. While Bud Burnett never had to answer why he did what he did, I am hopeful that today, that Garvice Kincaid regularly discusses it with him.

> *Some people have a difficult time facing truth and reality. They prefer to live in a make-believe world, pretending that certain things aren't happening.*
> – Joyce Meyer

Chapter Nine: Salaries and Special Payments

Bud Burnett took great pains to withhold the compensation details from the public and while the SEC required a compensation disclosure report from publicly traded companies as early as the mid-1970s, these reports were not easily available to the public. The insurance department also required a similar disclosure document, but again it was not easily available to the public. The compensation I have recorded came from newspaper reports of the Kincaid's daughter's lawsuit against the Committee and other documents I found.

In 1984, after Earl Wilson retired from the Board, Burnett, Schaeffer and Hagan created compensation agreements for themselves. The agreements provided individual compensation for each of the Committee members tied to the performance of the individual business entities. Burnett's primary compensation came from Kentucky Central Life Insurance Company, Ed Schaeffer's came from Kentucky Finance Company, and Hart Hagan's came from Bluegrass Broadcasting. Schaeffer was the managing partner at Kincaid's law firm and was receiving his primary compensation from it. Hart Hagan also received compensation from General Management Associates. Rusty Hembree received compensation from Central Bank and compensation from Kincaid's law firm. It appears all of the Committee members, including Rustee Hembree, were receiving various director fees from all of Kincaid's business entities.

While there is nothing to prove the following, I suspect that the Committee's general intent was to for each Committee member to end up with about $500,000 annually from all the combined entities. Without the compensation numbers from Kincaid's law firm and Central Bank it's impossible to know for sure.

When Bud Burnett died, his probate file doesn't reflect this type of wealth. The insurance department's attorney reviewed his financials going back five years prior to his death and found he hadn't hidden or sheltered assets. In speaking with his probate attorney, he suggested he had used his assets to support his son, Bruce Burnett's schemes and businesses. In addition, he had purchased $250,000 of Kentucky Central Life's stock in 1991.

Earl Wilson retired from the Committee at age 75 in 1987. In 1987 he received $22,800 from Kincaid companies, with $7,600 being from director fees from Bluegrass Broadcasting. 1989 was his last year on the Board. Earl Wilson retired in January 1986 and became Chairman Emeritus. He was probably also still receiving some money from his equity in the law firm and payments for director fees from Kentucky Finance Company and Bluegrass Broadcasting. The law firm and Central Bank never reported those payments. When he retired he had been dealing with dementia.

Bud Burnett's base salary was $165,000 annually, adjusted for CPI. Included in these payments were director fee payments from Bluegrass Broadcasting and Kentucky Finance of $15,200 to 14,000. His bonus in 1987 was $205,400; in 1988 ($289,729); in 1989 ($300,557); in 1990 ($246,125); and in 1991 ($152,159). He also received an unknown amount of fees from Central Bank.

In 1985 **Ed Schaeffer** earned $184,241 from his Kentucky Finance Company salary (Chairman) and Director fees from all the Kincaid company boards he served on. He also received $171,800 from the Kincaid law firm. In 1987 he earned $217,834 from Kentucky Finance Company, plus ($15,400 and $7,600) in annual director fees from Bluegrass Broadcasting and Kentucky Finance. Kentucky Finance was sold in July 1991. We don't know his law firm salaries, but one might assume it was at least $250,000. Schaeffer had a Kentucky Finance employment agreement that was to pay him $100,000 annually for the next 2.5 years after it was sold. Part of his Kentucky Finance Company compensation came as bonuses. He also received director fees from Central Bank. His Kentucky Finance Company 10-year contract was established in 1984 to start in 1985 at $70,000 adj. for inflation and some type of incentive bonus (probably tied to Luther Spence Compensation).

In 1985, **Hart Hagan** shows salary from Blue Grass Broadcasting, but no one knows how much he was making from General Management Associates. From 1987-1989 Hagen received $1,364,774 as Chairman of Blue Grass Broadcasting. At the same time, he ran his own company General Management Associates (accounting & management). It did work for several Kincaid companies and while he was on the boards, he was receiving $7,400 to $11,000 in Kentucky Financing director fees annually. He also received director fees from Central Bank. In 1984, the Committee provided him with a, five-year contract for $120,000, adj. for inflation, plus annual incentive compensation tied to Bluegrass Broadcasting's income.

In 1985, **Rusty Hembree** was receiving compensation from the Kincaid Law firm plus a salary from Central Bank and annual director fees and bonuses from Bluegrass Broadcasting and Kentucky Finance Company (1987-1991). Hembree was Chairman of the bank from 1987 - 1993 and there isn't a record of his salary. One would assume it was at least $250,000. He was also President of the Law firm. He also received director fees from Central Bank. Hembree was probably making more than $500,000 annually from all the Kincaid companies.

Luther Spence of President of KFC. Received a $842,000 bonus for Services Rendered in the sale of Kentucky Finance in July 1991, plus $162,100 in salary. From 1987 his salary began at $177,400 and ended in 1990 at $230,700. I estimated 1988 &1989. From 1987 to 1990 he received a total of $318,000 in Kentucky Finance bonuses, which I averaged at $79,500 each.

As of 1992, Kentucky Central Life held personal residential loans for insiders totaling almost $5 million. Bruce Burnett was $3,700,000. The remaining amount were for Burnett, Schaeffer, Sammartin, Spence, Gunn, Forbush, Rampulla and two loans to Robert Preston's sons. Kincaid gave Forbush his loan when he joined the company in 1973 and Rampulla got his around 1988 for a condo in the Vince Center. Kincaid usually provided residential loans to executives he was recruiting to the company.

Chapter Ten: Legal Consequences

One of the regrettable, if diverting, effects of extreme inequality is its tendency to weaken the capacity for impartial judgment. It pads the lives of its beneficiaries with a soft down of consideration, while relieving them of the vulgar necessity of justifying their pretensions, and secures that, if they fall, they fall on cushions.

– R.H. Tawney, British social scientist (1880–1962)

The SEC and the Kentucky Insurance Department both tried to hold various parties accountable for Kentucky's version of Enron. If it was an institutional entity, they were more successful holding the institution accountable. In most cases the clock ran out when it came to the individuals. The SEC sanctioned some, but most had sheltered their assets quickly and generally the SEC allowed the insurance department, as rehabilitator/liquidator, to collect any penalties. Actual monetary penalties were pathetic though:

William Earl "Bud" Burnett's estate. Burnett died in December 1993 of brain cancer. He tried to protect his assets, but his death froze everything. His probate file suggests his support of his son, Bruce, and his other bad investments destroyed the bulk of his wealth. The State of Kentucky's Insurance Department went back 5 years and looked for large asset transfers but found none. I contacted the estate's attorney and he said he was surprised at how little remained. One example he gave me was that Burnett had over $250,000 of Kentucky Central stock that he held to the end and another example I saw was his holdings in Bruce Burnett companies. When all the litigation was finally settled in 1996, the estate had spent $254,000 in legal fees. Burnett's largest listed asset was his Kentucky Central Life qualified pension, which was valued at $718,000, in which his wife, Margaret, was the surviving spouse beneficiary. Margaret's portion of her husband's estate, excluding his monthly pension was approximately $70,000. When the state finally settled everything in 1996, it received thirteen items, of which about one-half were considered worthless. For instance, a $200,000 loan to Bruce Burnett's bankrupt Bond Management was considered worthless or the claims for unpaid compensation from Kentucky Central Life were listed. In the end, in 1996 I estimated that the state collected about $62,000 from Burnett's estate. What was not explained is how much they spent in legal costs getting the $62,000.

Edwin Schaeffer. In 2005, Schaeffer settle with the liquidator for $100,000. Schaeffer is still living. Schaeffer was sanctioned by the SEC in 1995 for similar reasons as Wendell Gunn, mostly reasons tied to knowingly, materially, misrepresenting the company's financial situation.

Charles Hembree. In 2005, Hembree settle with the liquidator for $17,000. He died in 2020 and had an estate valued at $932,000. Hembree had put most of his assets in a trust. Hembree was sanctioned by the SEC in 1995 for similar reasons to Wendell Gunn, mostly reasons tied to knowingly, materially, misrepresenting the company's financial situation.

Hart Hagan. Hagan died in 1997 and his probate file indicates he also had used a trust to protect is assets. His personal assets, outside the trust, were estimated at $500,000. His estate paid no settlements to the Liquidator and there were no SEC sanctions listed.

Wendell Gunn. Gunn was sanctioned by the SEC in 2005 but paid no settlements to the liquidator. I was told in 1993 that he had put all his assets in his wife's name.

Robert Preston. Preston settled with the liquidator for $15,000 in 2004. He was never sanctioned by the SEC. He died in 2008.

Bruce Burnett. Burnett's son, Bruce, was sentenced to one year after he pleaded guilty to some charges and also to three years in prison after he was convicted of stealing $1.5 million in insurance premiums. He was fined $57,000 and $44,000 and ordered to make restitution to various parties for the money he stole. He filed for bankruptcy. After serving his prison sentences, Bruce sold office forms and was involved in a store front shipping store. He died of congestive heart failure on May 28, 2019, at the Lexington Country Place nursing home. He was apparently a Medicaid resident. He had been diagnosed with diabetes, COPD, hypertension and sleep apnea. His body was claimed by his daughter Blair Elizabeth Burnett, and it was donated to the University of Cincinnati College of Medicine. He was 71 years old. Prior to his death, his residence was at the Emerson Center 55+ Senior Apartments in Gardenside. This facility provides government supported subsidized housing assistance for qualified low-income renters and veterans.

Deloitte Touche. In 2023, Deloitte Touche settled with the liquidator for $23 million.

The Bank of Louisville and its successor, Mid-America Bank - In February 2002, after the mediation of the claims between Mid-America, (Bank of Louisville) and the liquidator, the bank paid $27 million in full settlement of all its claims associated with the $16 million of securities.

Donald Webb. In August 2005, the Liquidator entered into a settlement agreement with Donald W. Webb and Julie H. Webb whereby the parties paid $2,850,000 to the Liquidator in exchange for a full and final release of all claims asserted by the Liquidator against them. These parties also released all pending counterclaims and proofs of claims that they had asserted against the Liquidator as a condition of the settlement. The settlement payment of $2,850,000 was paid to Kentucky Central Life in August 2005. Donald Webb died in 2016.

One of the obligations satisfied by the settlement was the repayment of a mortgage loan reflected on the balance sheet as of June 30, 2005, in the amount of $754,400. Pursuant to the settlement agreement with Donald and Julie Webb, the liquidator released his mortgage and security interests in three buildings located in Lexington, Kentucky on West Main Street, known as the "West Main Properties," in exchange for the settlement payment.

Bud Burnett's deathbed affidavit which effectively said their personal guarantees weren't meant to be real guarantees unless they committed fraud helped them win their case. The question I never saw asked was, since this was a legal document for real property, if it had been sold to a third party, wouldn't the purchaser had the right to their guarantee. I recognize that hundreds of thousands of dollars in legal bills were spent litigating this issue, but I and others feel the courts got it wrong. As an investment professional, history demonstrates that the written document rules. The courts depended on Burnett's affidavit and the remaining former Committee members, testimony that the company had not been pursuing personal guarantees. Consider this, if one of the brothers had run over Burnett's wife crossing the street and later defaulted on a loan, what would the rule had been. Donald Webb reduced doing these types of personal guaranteed loans in the mid-1980s due to his concern about the issue.

Dudley Webb. In October 2005, the Liquidator entered into a separate settlement agreement with R. Dudley Webb and numerous Webb business entities whereby these parties paid $1,000,000 to the Liquidator in exchange for a full and final release of all claims asserted by the Liquidator against them. These parties also released all pending counterclaims and proofs of claims that they had asserted against the Liquidator as a condition of the settlement. The settlement payment of $1,000,000 was paid to Kentucky Central in October 2005.

Bud Burnett's deathbed affidavit which effectively said their personal guarantees weren't meant to be real guarantees unless they committed fraud helped them win their case. The question I never saw asked was, since this was a legal document for real property, if it had been sold to a third party, wouldn't the purchaser had the right to their guarantee. I recognize that hundreds of thousands of dollars in legal bills were spent litigating this issue, but I and others feel the courts got it wrong. As an investment professional, history demonstrates that the written document rules. The courts depended on Burnett's affidavit and the remaining former Committee members, testimony that the company had not been pursuing personal guarantees. Consider this, if one of the brothers had run over Burnett's wife crossing the street and later defaulted on a loan, what would the rule had been.

Chapter Eleven: Letters from the Phantom

Beginning around 1990, cracks began to form around people's opinion of Kentucky Central Life and Burnett's management. The company's mortgage loan delinquencies and defaults were rising and while internal information was held close to Burnett's chest, the negative press reports were becoming more frequent. In 1987, the company had already done the sale-leaseback of Kincaid Towers raising $20 million of capital, but clouds were forming, and questions were starting to be asked by rating agencies, investment analysts and others.

One needs to understand that Burnett managed information on a need-to-know basis, so very few people could see the whole picture. For instance, while some of us would hear rumors about the Kincaid daughters' lawsuit against the committee, we didn't know any actual details. Also, while some of us could see the large increase in mortgage loans, specifically to the Webbs, over the last few years, we just didn't know the actual details. Certainly, the 1988 $50 million loan, on the San Francisco building was a red alarm, but the company's auditors, Deloitte Touche hadn't raised any of the normal red flags that one would have expected. All of that said, inside the company management and employees were beginning to discuss their concerns.

By the fall of 1991, things had become more alarming as S&P reduced the company's quality rating to "BBB" from "A-", Forbes (a national business publication) ran a short but scathing article on the company questioning its soundness, and Kentucky Central Life's agents began to question if we were going to follow the path of Executive Life Insurance Company and be taken over by the state. The alarms were going off and yet Burnett didn't waver in his positive communication—"No problem, this too will pass."

I don't know who the Phantom was or if it was the creation of more than one person. Certainly, their knowledge of the company was significant, and they had a critical understanding of our marketing operation and its people. Whoever or whatever the Phantom was, they began communicating directly with Burnett and the rest of the company's management staff in the fall of 1991. I have included some of the Phantom's communications that my Kentucky Central Life colleagues were able to provide me, including the famous "Twas the Night before Christmas" themed piece, that was very well done, and also the Phantom's reflections on "The Plan" that refers to the consultants that Burnett brought in to restructure our operation after we achieved Burnett's "$50 Billion of In-force Goal." He now wanted everyone to cut costs and restructure departments to improve our profitability, by being more efficient. Whoever the Phantom was, I appreciated their efforts to get Burnett to consider how bad things had gotten.

As I reread these pieces and remembered how concerns were growing, I still wonder why Burnett did what he did. His actions remind me of a gambling addict who has lost so much of his wealth that they feel they have no option but to double down. I believe Burnett felt this way and felt trapped by the many bad decisions he had made over the last seven years. Remember Dudley Webb's 1990 letter to Burnett saying he was struggling to make payroll and turning back properties to lenders: "A dismal story, sad but true, and, to put it bluntly, my alternatives are reorganization or straight bankruptcy," he wrote.

Finally, I will personally always believe that Burnett was trying to protect his own financial interests in deals which he had intertwined within the business of the company. As Burnstein and Woodword once wrote, "always follow the money", but in the case of Bud Burnett, he ended up losing it all.

T'was the Night Before Christmas

T'was the night before Christmas
    In Kincaid Towers
Life policies weren't selling,
    especially ours.

The ratings had dropped
    to the floor with a thud
Everyone soon realized,
    the *problem* was Bud.

His mortgages are *crap*
    and his real estate *sucks*,
He would give his stock bonus
    for a few extra bucks.

His reserves are depleted
    his ratings are down,
He has sold his best assets,
    he looks like a *clown*.

The stockholders are pissed
    at decisions he's made,
With the money they've lost,
    they could have all gotten laid.

While out in the street
    there arose such a clatter,
I sprang to the door
    to see what was the matter.

T'was the State of Kentucky
    with a fist full of *duns*,
They don't trust ole Bud
    with their *employees funds*.

Now, what should appear
    outside on the steps,
A bald headed old Fart
    and eight field reps.

More sluggish than snails
   his courses they came,
And he shouted and whistled,
   and called them by name.

Now, George! Now, Wayne!
   Now, Allen and Jim!
On, Lovell! On, Parker!
   On, Mader and Ken!

The leader was smiling,
   so lively and quick.
I knew in a moment,
   It was Epps . . . *the big Dick*.

To the front of the bar
   from the shelf on the wall.
"Now, drink 'em down! Drink 'em down!
   Drink 'em down all!"

The courses they drank
   from bottles and glasses,
their only concern,
   protecting *their* asses.

They had no concern
   for the lowly producer.
They had *all* cast their fates,
   with a *heavyweight loser*.

As I drew in my head,
   and was turning around,
Straight from the elevator
   he came with a bound.

He had hair of silver
   and a big round belly
That shook when he laughed
   like a bowl full of jelly.

He was chubby and plump,
   a right jolly old elf.
And I laughed when I saw him
   In spite of myself.

A bowl full of pasta
  and a fist full of bread
His only concern . . .
  was *just to be fed.*

His briefcase was packed,
  with all he could carry.
He was a portly old gent,
  my goodness, it's Larry.

"We'll beef up our term
  and capture some sales."
The kind of shrewd logic . . .
  you'd expect from a whale.

He spoke not a word
  but went straight to his food
He ate and he ate,
  he was one *heavy* dude.

And putting his finger
  inside of his nose,
With a great deal of help
  he *eventually* rose.

He turned to his helpers
  and said "lets go eat"
They *snapped* to attention
  as they sprang to their feet.

I heard him exclaim.
  as they drove out of sight.
"Piss on 'em all . . .
  lets *get laid* tonight."

*Merry Christmas
THE PHANTOM.*

The Plan

In the beginning was the Plan, and the Plan was without form.
    And with the Plan came Assumptions.
And the Assumptions were without form
    and the Plan was without substance.
And Plan and Assumptions were given unto the Workers.
Then darkness soon came upon the faces of the Workers
    and they spoke amongst themselves, saying:
"The Plan is a crock of shit, and it stinks!"
And the Workers went unto their Managers and sayeth:
"The Plan is a pail of dung and none may abide the odor
    thereof!"
And the Managers went unto their Directors and sayeth unto
    them:
"The Plan is a container of excrement that is very strong, such
    that none may abide with it."
And the Directors went unto their Vice-Presidnets and sayeth:
"The Plan is a vessel of fertilizer and none abide its strength."
And the Vice-Presidents spoke amongst themselves, saying to
    one another,
"The Plan contains that which aids plant growth, but it is very
    strong."
And the Vice-Presidents went unto the Senior Vice-President
    and sayeth unto him,
"The Plan promotes growth and is very powerful."
And the Senior Vice-President went unto the CEO and sayeth:
"This new Plan will actively promote the growth and efficiency
    of this Corporation."
And the CEO looked upon the Plan, and knew that it was good
    And the Plan became policy.
And this, my children, is how shit happens.

KENTUCKY CENTRAL
Trust tomorrow to us.

National Headquarters: Kincaid Towers, Lexington, Kentucky 40507
(606) 253-5111

Postmarked 10-11-91

October 11, 1991

Dear Bud:

Attached is a listing of the attendees at the recent LIMRA Business Skills Seminar held in our home office. As a part of this company I feel compelled to send you this letter with my observations.

I am vitally concerned that the company is heading for more severe times. The obvious impact would be terrible. I've put in many years of hard work with this company. As the industry has seen rating services can ruin a company with even the *hint of financial instability.* As you know in-force business is rapidly coming off the books as competitors replace our policies. The drop of our Best rating has caused great concern with our policyholders. What worries me and others is the impact this is having on our home office staff and field force. The recent meeting had some of the most concerning *"bar talk"* ever by attendees. It's amazing how the attitude in the formal daytime business meeting changed dramatically in the evening bar sessions from 9:30 to midnight. Are you aware most of the attendees are negotiating with other companies about the possbility of making a move if the situation with Kentucky Central worsens?

Bud, the one thing that consistently comes through from the field force is their disbelief in *your* continued support of *all* the regional directors. If you review the attached listing you'll see Executive Marketing has 41 RGA's with eight RD's to "manage" them. This is an average of 5 RGA's per RD to manage. However, in terms of *actual hands on management* it is probably more like 3 RGA's per RD since limited support is given to many. Bud, the obvious questions now become:

With the *close* scrutiny of industry analysts and rating services looking at company "profitability" you need to cut overhead. Can Kentucky Central *really justify* maintaining this *full* layer of management? How do the analysts at Best, Standard & Poor's, Moody's & Duff & Phelps view this unncessary expense?

Reviewing the *total budget* of the RD's salary & bonuses, benefits, support staff salary and benefits, office and travel expenses etc. it averages approximately $500,000 per RD. Much of that figure is made up of *direct compensation to the RD's* in terms of salary & bonuses. Kentucky Central is paying out approximately $4 million per year for a layer of management that is obviously seen as needless and ineffective. *What effect do you think it would have on the rating services, field force, home office personnel and stockholders if you cut that figure by two thirds and put it into profits!? Industry studies show that comparable companies to Kentucky Central do not compensate this level of management so highly.*

Bud, if you *really* believe the money you just spent on this LIMRA Business Skills seminar was a wise decision then this is an area *within our own company* you should correct today. The company can not afford another rate reduction and continued public criticism. Also, the company can not afford to start losing quality RGA's, GA's and Agents. I am asking you to improve the company's fianacial position and morale by *taking action* on behalf of the ones who stand tall beside you and Kentucky Central!

CC:

Earl; Wilson Yates
Clinton H. Forbush Jr.
Richard Gordon
Charles R. Hembree
Robert D. Preston
Edwin F. Schaeffer Jr.
Clyde Honeker Jr.
Theodore Moss
Edward Winiarczyk
Robert G. Mattschek
Buford McIntosh
Enoch G. Roberts
Don Baker
Lee Barbee
Steve Bivens
Richard Brumfield
Bob Clark
Brent Clay
Richard Epps
Robert Guise
Wendell Gunn
Billy Harris
Marianne Hershey
Clyde Honaker
Joe Hudson
Lucian Huguely
Bill Jackson
Patrick Kane
David Kitchen
Sue Lawrence
Tom Laughlin
Richard Loy
Lloyd Moore
Ken Neiheisel
Carla Potter
Ben Reynolds
Brenda Rogers
Larry Sammartin
Paul Sewell
Bobby Turner
Myles Witchey

KENTUCKY CENTRAL
Trust tomorrow to us.

National Headquarters: Kincaid Towers, Lexington, Kentucky 40507
(606) 253-5111

Postmarked 10-25-91

October 24, 1991

Dear Bud:

Planning the 1992 budget is an important task . As somebody concerned with helping our company acheive a more profitable picture I must react to your request for submitted budgets to be lean and conservative. I acknowledge and support your request **100%.** If there is inefficiency and waste it should be eliminated.

Bud, I find it hard to justify cutting back on minor items where .**at best,** limited savings would occur. If commonly accepted management and personnel decisions were made increased profits of hundreds of thousands, **if not millions of dollars,** could be realized. Such prudent actions by the company's senior management would solidify the necessary unity and support of the company's employees.

CC:

Don Baker
Lee Barbeee
Steve Bivens
Richard Brumfield
Bob Clark
Brent Clay
Richard Epps
Robert Guise
Wendell Gunn
Billy Harris
Marianne Hershey
Clyde Honaker
Joe Hudson
Lucian Huguely
Bill Jackson
Patrick Kane
David Kitchen
Sue Lawrence
Tom Loughlin
Richard Loy
Lloyd Moore
Ken Neiheisel
Carla Potter
Ben Reynolds
Brenda Rogers
Larry Sammartin
Paul Sewell
Bobby Turner
Myles Witchey
Earl Wilson Yates Jr.
Richard Gordon
Charles Hembree
Robert D. Preston
Edwin F. Schaeffer Jr.
Theodore Moss
Edward A. Winiarczyk
Clifton H. Forbush Jr.
Robert G. Mattscheck
Buford McIntosh
Enoch G. Roberts

KENTUCKY CENTRAL
Trust tomorrow to us.

National Headquarters: Kincaid Towers, Lexington, Kentucky 40507
(606) 253-5111

Postmarked 12-4-91

December 3, 1991

Dear Bud:

Employee morale is something very important to Kentucky Central. The fine building we work in, the revised employee retirement plan and a solid employee benefit program has made Kentucky Central a great place to work. Even with the depressed economy, constant harassment from the Lexington Herald and dejected agents we are managing to keep a positive attitude. Those of us who care about and have helped build this company know that in time we will weather this storm.

However, once again I have been forced to endure the loftiness of the regional directors. Bud, this company has grown to this level **despite** their **minimal** efforts . Unfortunately they fail to acknowledge and understand that. They parade around the building and town like they are something extraordinary. I can not tell you what that does to the morale of the hard working typically paid staff person.

I can't help but continue to wonder what justification you and the board of directors have for keeping these overpaid, prima donas. The insurance department and rating analysts certainly must have noted this over compensated layer of management when they made their analysis. Kentucky Central has a chance with the start of a new year to show the home office employees, rating analysts, stockholders and agents that we are serious about improving this company.

Bud, in this holiday season there would be no greater gift you could give our people than to make a New Year's resolution to cut a large portion of the waste in the regional directors' area.

I hope you are taking these letters in the spirit of concern, not criticism, with which they are intended.

National Headquarters: Kincaid Towers, Lexington, Kentucky 40507
(606) 253-5111

Postmarked 2-7-92

Dear Bud:

I haven't written to you for several months. Frankly I wanted to see what you would do to help stop the low home office morale, agent defections and bad press. I had hoped some **decisive** action in all three areas would have been taken by now.

My concerns seem to be going unanswered however. Three months later the attitude among the employees is slipping, the agents are leaving and the press is getting more specific in it's charges. In all my years here I have never seen things as bad. Yet all I see coming from your office are fainthearted memos which have done little to give any of us strong hope that you are handling all this with the urgency it demands. People's careers, futures and retirements are at stake here. The average employee, field representative and policyholder does not have the luxury of large holdings in company stock to sell or a comfortable retirement plan to fall back on. All we have is the faith that you, as the head of this company, are looking out for our interests too.

The <u>Forbes</u> article you tried to refute in your December 18th memo hit us very hard. A publication of it's reputation has to have some basis in fact to go on record with such severe charges. While "sensationalism" does seem to be the norm in today's press coverage, I can't help but be concerned because some of their points **are** valid and were skirted by your vague replies. I have written you several times about how unrealistic the compensation levels of the Regional Mangers are. Obviously the people at <u>Forbes</u> saw that and even took it to higher management levels. For you to state that "this is not the case" is ludicrous and incorrect.

Bud, the feeling in the building and from the field who call us is that there must be something the board and company is hiding. I guess that feedback will stop now that our conversations with the field have been curtailed. There is just too much zeroing in on specific indicators of poor management, "sweetheart deals", stacked high upper management compensation levels and the lack of accepted business practices for there not to be some validity. I must admit that even with all my years and my high degree of loyalty and trust that even I am now getting very concerned. In the first letter to you last year I told you I was concerned about long term career and retirement with Kentucky Central. The way the public is starting to **perceive** Kentucky Central is just as important as what **actually** is going on. This is evident by the increased amount of policyholder calls and the declining production.

Many, many years ago we adopted the company slogan "Trust Tomorrow to Us". Obviously those outside in the rating services, press and even state governments aren't buying that any longer. The time has come where it is imperative upon you to take some dramatic action to explain **fully and openly** to the employees, agents and policyholders just what shape this company **really** is in. If in fact we have nothing to hide or to be worried about please let us know **now** . A lot of damage has been done and a lot of trust has been lost, but the Kentucky Central team will stay together if proper financial and management decisions are made.

CAN OR WILL YOU MAKE THOSE DECISIONS <u>NOW?</u>

Kentucky Central Life Insurance Company, Founded 1902

NOTE THE PHANTOM'S INCREASE IN THE LENGTH OF THE DISTRIBUTION LIST:

CC:

Don Baker
Lee Barbeee
Steve Bivens
Richard Brumfield
Bob Clark
Brent Clay
Richard Epps
Robert Guise
Wendell Gunn
Billy Harris
Marianne Hershey
Clyde Honaker
Joe Hudson
Lucian Huguely
Bill Jackson
Patrick Kane
David Kitchen
Sue Lawrence
Tom Loughlin
Richard Loy
Lloyd Moore
Ken Neiheisel
Carla Potter
Ben Reynolds
Brenda Rogers
Larry Sammartin
Paul Sewell
Bobby Turner
- Myles Witchey
Earl Wilson Yates Jr.
Richard Gordon
Charles Hembree
Robert D. Preston
Edwin F. Schaeffer Jr.
Theodore Moss
Edward A. Winiarczyk
Clifton H. Forbush Jr.
Robert G. Mattscheck
Buford McIntosh
Enoch G. Roberts

CC:

Earl; Wilson Yates
Clinton H. Forbush Jr.
Richard Gordon
Charles R. Hembree
Robert D. Preston
Edwin F. Schaeffer Jr.
Clyde Honeker Jr.
Theodore Moss
Edward Winiarczyk
Robert G. Mattschek
Buford McIntosh
Enoch G. Roberts
Don Baker
Lee Barbee
Steve Bivens
Richard Brumfield
Bob Clark
Brent Clay
Richard Epps
Robert Guise
Wendell Gunn
Billy Harris
Marianne Hershey
Clyde Honaker
Joe Hudson
Lucian Huguely
Bill Jackson
Patrick Kane
David Kitchen
Sue Lawrence
Tom Laughlin
Richard Loy
Lloyd Moore
Ken Neiheisel
Carla Potter
Ben Reynolds
Brenda Rogers
Larry Sammartin
Paul Sewell
Bobby Turner
Myles Witchey

"LIMRA BUSINESS SKILLS SEMINAR"
KENTUCKY CENTRAL LIFE INSURANCE COMPANY
SEPTEMBER 30 - OCTOBER 1, 1991

"ATTENDEES"

NAME   CITY / STATE

ROCKY MOUNTAIN REGION

       Wayne Hudgens   -   Regional Director

Bobby Carter	Lubbock, TX
John Coffman, CLU	Dallas, TX
Bobby Clayton	Dallas, TX
Bob Ehlers	Houston, TX
Larry Noyes	Denver, CO
Hedi Slimane	San Antonio, TX

FAR WEST REGION

       George Surmick   -   Regional Director

Paul Burleson, CLU	Phoenix, AZ
Jack Cole	Las Vegas, NV
Bernie Koss	Diamond Bar, CA
Jerry Larkin, CLU, ChFC	San Diego, CA
Craig Madsen	Sacramento, CA
Joe Moore	Cypress, CA
Francis Phillips, CLU, LUTCF	Honolulu, HI

"LIMRA BUSINESS SKILLS SEMINAR"
KENTUCKY CENTRAL LIFE INSURANCE COMPANY
SEPTEMBER 23 - 24, 1991

"ATTENDEES"

NAME	CITY / STATE

NORTHEAST REGION

Jim Howe, CLU, ChFC   -   Regional Director

Martin Browder	Richmond, VA
Dick Follett	Indianapolis, IN
Joe Malizia	Columbus, OH
Bob McClary	Charlotte, NC
Ron Nisbet	Huntington, WV
Ray Partlow	Columbus, OH
Terry Register	Raleigh, NC
Chet Smith, CLU, ChFC	Louisville, KY
Ken Thomas	Lexington, KY

SOUTHEAST REGION

Tom Parker   -   Regional Director

Bob Andrews	Atlanta, GA
Dan Brooks	Cookeville, TN
Glenn Curtis	Mobile, AL
Bill Pickering	Orlando, FL

NEW ENGLAND REGION

Ken Hoover, CLU   -   Regional Director

Wayne Bailey	Billerica, MA
Dennis Libby, CLU	Guilford, CT
Jim Roderick	Farmington, CT
Russ Urffer, CLU, ChFC	Williamsport, PA

NORTHWEST REGION

Bob Lovell   -   Regional Director

Reed Collingwood	Bellevue, WA
Mike Richter	Missoula, MT

Epilogue: The Man Behind the Legend

When Garvice Kincaid died in November of 1975, it was front page news in just about every newspaper in the state. In addition, the New York Times and the Wall Street Journal wrote stories about his life. Garvice Kincaid the man had died, but his financial legacy and legend would continue on.

Kincaid's funeral was attended by 1,200 people and was held at Central Christian Church. It was attended by a who's who of Kentucky Governors and mayors, and of course a large roster of his most faithful friends and business associates. His family was there, but there was little mention of them. It's reported that the service only lasted a half-hour, and two ministers provided his eulogy, but apparently no friends or family spoke. David Brain and his Committee made up most of his pallbearers. He was lauded as a master financier, praised for his support of the community, and described as not being active in church, but as having "church in his heart."

After the service, his casket was transported to the Lexington Cemetery and he was buried in a family plot in section 46, lot 46. Today, his wife Nelle and his daughter Jane are both buried there. In keeping with Kincaid's fondness for "crisp, clean, modern lines, the plot is marked with an eight-foot tall, simple tower-like gravestone labeled with "KINCAID" on its front.

David Brain wrote a letter to the editor of the *Courier Journal* on March 28, 1976. He wrote it in response to an article ("The Kincaid Legacy") that had been published on February 29. I believe if Brain had spoken at his funeral, he would have provided similar remarks:

> To the Magazine:
>
> Having been a close business associate of Garvice Kincaid from 1961 until his death last year, I read John Ed Pearce's February article, "The Kincaid Legacy," with a great deal of interest.
>
> It is unfortunate that Pearce failed to mention Mr. Kincaid's wife, Nelle, and the significant contribution she made to his business and personal life. Nelle Kincaid is a fine loving person, as are the daughters, Joan and Jane.
>
> To me Garvice Kincaid was a man of vision who had the ability to marshal forces, so that his visions became realities. By this I mean Kincaid could see the potential of a business or community situation,

or the potential of an individual better than anyone. Continuing to recognize the potential of a situation or individual will be the real challenge faced by all of those who want to see the Kincaid Legacy continue to grow.

Kincaid admitted on one occasion[1] that his routine did not always please him, He would have liked to have done more reading; he enjoyed music, paintings and flowers, but there just wasn't time. He said as a younger man when he owned Joyland, he used to take an occasional swim in the pool in the late afternoon, and he said he would like to spend some time on the beach and go fishing again. "I went fishing one time down at Pompano and enjoyed it," he once said, "but I just don't get the chance to do things like that."

Garvice Kincaid expected other people to work as hard as he did, and "he may have been considered a taskmaster by those who didn't know him," says one colleague, "but actually it was more than that. He was always trying to challenge those who worked with him to reach their full potential."[2]

"There was a deep sense of loyalty and admiration for Garvice Kincaid throughout all his enterprises. His co-workers soon discovered they were working with a true managerial genius and hoped some of it would rub off on them. He was one in ten million. He had a knack for seeing opportunities others had missed, and the courage to grab those opportunities and develop them for all they were worth.

Even his competitors were awed by his organizational abilities and his bear trap mind. Those who knew him best will tell you though, there was an underlying shyness about the man that sometimes manifested itself in what seemed to be curtness."[3]

"He never found it easy to engage in amenities, even as a college student," says one of his oldest friends. "But once you got to know him, you found a person who was very warm and human, with a lively sense of humor."[4]

UK's vice president, Ray Hornback, said Garvice always walked the tight rope line of saying too harsh a comment or not saying enough. Hornback tells a story that happened in the early 1970s. Garvice and Nelle were attending a big doner event at President Singletary's suit at a University of Kentucky football game. Hornback is at the door greeting people and when Kincaid gets there, he helps Garvice and Nelle out of their coats and stores them. "Kincaid looks at him, without a smile, and says, "You have the most expensive coat-

---

1   Charlie Thomas, *Kincaid Towers Grand Opening Magazine*, 1980.
2   Ibid.
3   Ibid.
4   Ibid.

check job that I have ever seen."[5] After that comment, he never offered to help Garvice with his coat again.

Ray said, Garvice loved Nelle, and she loved him. The UK alumni event wasn't a Kincaid function and so there were many people there that Kincaid probably never associated with. He said Nelle and Garvice pretty much remained together, accept when Nelle spotted some ladies she knew, but for the most part, they were a couple. They kept each other company, and in a way, you could see this helped keep Garvice from being forced to make small talk. Ray said, "Garvice was a bully, but Nelle Kincaid was just a very sweet lady."[6]

Ray Hornback said Robert and Polly Lehman were some of the nicest people he had ever been associated with, and that Robert Lehman had dropped hints that he thought Ray should come and work for Garvice at the bank. He talked about "doubling my salary." Well one time he started down this road and Polly was there and she started shaking her head. Robert looks at her and says, "What are you doing?" and she says, "There is no way I would let you do that to him" and then goes on to tell me why their life was never their own. She said, "Garvice might call at two o'clock in the morning or on a Sunday morning, and you were expected to answer." Ray said they acknowledged the money was nice, but you had to sacrifice a lot to work for him.[7] As I re-read this Ray Hornback story, it made me think of his family, yes, he loved them, but they also probably had to sacrifice a lot, just to be his wife and daughters.

Garvice was inordinately proud of his wife, Nelle, and his twin daughters, Joan and Jane, and it was said that one of the greatest joys in his later years was watching his two grandsons, Brett Delmar and Kevin Reed, play Little League baseball. Mrs. Kincaid said that one of the things they may remember most about their grandfather is that "he liked ice cream cones as much as they do." Kincaid once said that one of the few things he would do differently with his life would be to spend more time with his family.

Various associates, those who knew him longest and best, said they were convinced he was mainly interested in trying to make Lexington a better place in which to work, a place where there were more opportunities for young people, where power would be spread around, a place to be proud of. Apparently, he never forgot his own beginnings and was determined to open doors for others who could not open doors for themselves.

One of the best pieces of evidence about his interest in Lexington was his charity work. It might be argued that he used his gifts as a weapon to goad

5   Interview of Ray Hornback by author.
6   Ibid.
7   Ibid.

other millionaires into sharing, but his philanthropies began too early in his career to be only that. And to this day, many of them are not clearly known, and may never be.

There were many informal gifts, the typewriter that showed up at Christmas, the anonymous deposits into bank accounts (he was fond of simply depositing money into the accounts of employees he thought had earned a bonus, and the account didn't have to be in one of his banks), the spur of the moment things he enjoyed doing for people,

Kincaid invested in his businesses in order to make them the best. He installed new systems and continually updated existing ones, but all the time, making sure his employees knew he was giving them the tools they needed, now it was up to them to get the job done. He also established many "firsts" in Kentucky, such as automobile give aways at his banks and also including being the first bank to pay interest on Christmas Club accounts, the first bank to pay Christmas bonuses to its employees, the first bank to have a woman bank officer (Fern Scott in 1947), and the first bank to offer an employee stock ownership plan.

Kincaid gained national attention in 1960 for winning the Horatio Alger Award. He was the first Kentuckian and the first banker to win the award. Other distinguished persons to have won the award, which was established in 1946, include Herbert Hoover, Bernard Baruch, John Galbreath, Conrad Hilton and Dr. Milton Eisenhower. In presenting the award to Kincaid, the Rev. Dr. Norman Vincent Peale, himself a former recipient, said, "Sir, your life is an inspiration to everyone in these United States and God bless you and give you strength to carry on for many years."

New honors came to Kincaid almost every year thereafter. Service awards from the Boy Scouts, the Lexington Chamber of Commerce, the Kentucky Broadcasters Association, the UK Alumni Association. Outstanding Kentuckian for 1965 by the Kentucky Press Association, Membership in the Senate of the Junior Chamber of Commerce International, the National Newspaperboy Hall of Fame, the UK Alumni Hall of Fame, and Beta Gamma Sigma. The Feagans Award by the Lexington General Agents and Managers Association. An award from the Chamber of Commerce "for dedication and tireless efforts in achieving the construction of the Lexington Civic Center." and various honorary degrees and other awards. But he didn't push them on you, in fact you had to ask about them, sometimes several times. It was almost as if they embarrassed him.

Garvice Kincaid was far more inclined to talk openly about the things he had done for others. One of my favorite stories that I think reflects this compassion and empathy for others involved the dedication of the Kincaid Home for troubled and abandoned children. The facility had burned, and the county was $25,000 short of having funds to replace it. Kincaid learned of the deficiency and before anyone had a chance to try to raise funds, Kincaid called Judge Bart Peak and simply gave the money. During the dedication, he was asked why he had made such a gift. He pointed to the children around the home and said, 'Except for a great deal of good luck I might be any of them."

Another good example is when Kincaid was being inducted into the Shriners. As part of his induction, he was required to tour the Shriners Hospital for Crippled Children in Lexington. He began a conversation with a little girl who told him she wished she could see the clock from her bed. As he was leaving, he asked the nurse if he could buy the little girl a watch and was told that no one was allowed to send a gift to only one child in the hospital. He gruffly asked how many children were hospitalized, and within a week a box of watches arrived - one for each child there—accompanied only by his business card.

The late Rev. Bob Brown, pastor of Trinity Baptist Church, liked to tell about the phone call he made to Kincaid to interest him in serving on the board of directors of the Housing for the Handicapped, a non-sectarian group Brown had organized to assist the aged blind. Kincaid not only agreed but became so involved in the organization that he donated $10,000 and later provided the facilities of WKYT-TV for a series of money-raising telethons.

Perhaps the most dramatic of his charitable ventures was one for which he received unjust criticism. The Appalachian Regional Hospitals, virtually the only major medical facilities in the mountains, were faltering badly due to a financial crisis in 1964. It was the second such crisis, and more severe than the previous one, and no bank would float them a loan. Kincaid arranged a $750,000 loan and agreed to serve on their board and help guide them out of financial trouble. Dr. Karl Klicka, then president of the group, said, "Kincaid saved these hospitals for Kentucky, that's the truth of it."[8] Publicly, however, Kincaid was criticized for securing the loan against future payments from the state—though the exact the same security had been utilized in the previous crisis,

His donations to formal charities are well known. The ones that got the greatest publicity were the Lexington Boys Club and the Kincaid Foundation, most notably the college scholarships for high school seniors, and the annual bequest to a number of charities on the part of his Kentucky banks. The latter was started in 1974, when Kincaid announced he would give $100,000 to

---

8   Charlie Thomas, *Kincaid Towers Grand Opening Magazine*, 1980.

various charities which "will do the greatest good for the greatest number of people." The following year the bequest was raised to $200,000. The college scholarship program he began in 1952 still flourishes today in his memory.

Most people didn't understand Garvice Kincaid. Many thought he was too fixated on money, but he said he wasn't in love with money, and that it just allowed him to do the thing he really enjoyed—doing more business deals. Most Lexingtonians enjoy their success as a means to a social end. For Kincaid, it was simply the excitement of building something that worked and worked well.

One business colleague said this about him in an interview, "He doesn't know how to spend money. He doesn't like to drink or feels he can't afford the time. The doctor told him to take a little whiskey, might be good for his heart. So, every night he swallows half a glass just to get it over with. Women bore him, I think; so do parties, mostly I think because he doesn't know how to make small talk. About the only thing he really likes that costs money is food."[9]

When asked one time about money Kincaid answered, "I don't care for money as money, but if I didn't have it, I couldn't make the business deals that I enjoy and get satisfaction from." When asked why he keeps adding to his empire? Kincaid answered, "Why does a man with a hamburger stand want two?"[10]

Garvice Kincaid had many distinctive personal traits, and he will likely be remembered longer for them, than his long list of accomplishments or honors, which over his lifetime he received many. It is no exaggeration to say that Garvice Kincaid was one of Kentucky's most respected and accomplished businessmen, but also one that demonstrated a passion for helping his community and fellow man. Most people couldn't keep up with his work ethic or follow the quickness of his mind, and those who confronted him, often found themselves drowning in the wake of his actions, because Garvice Kincaid was always "Ahead of the pack!"

---

9   Ibid.
10   John Ed Pearce, "Garvice Kincaid—Lexington's Maverick Millionaire," *Courier-Journal Magazine*, March 24, 1968.

Acknowledgments

It's impossible to thank everyone that helped me make this book possible. Many people that provided assistance did so from works they created years ago, people such as Kentucky Central Life's Charlie Thomas and Brent Clay and the many reporters at the Lexington Herald-Leader and the Louisville Courier Journal. Most are dead now, but their creative works were invaluable in my research into Mr. Kincaid and his many business ventures. I also want to include Ted Grizzard and Jim Host in this group, both men wrote first person accounts of important aspect about Mr. Kincaid and his business interests, and I believe their recorded histories added an important dimension this work.

Special thanks must also be given to the many people who gave me the privilege of interviewing them about their memories of Mr. Kincaid and others in his universe. Their stories, whether first person accounts or providing the recollections from others were invaluable in helping me understand this complicated man and the people he worked with. I specifically want to thank, Ken Kurtz, Barry Peel, Ralph Hacker, Bart Brown, Loretta Harris, Bob Hensley, George Hampton, John Lang, John McGarvey, Shirley Sammartin, Stan Galbraith, Steve Pate, Ray Hornback, William Stakelin, Nancy and Diane Brain and the many former employees of Kentucky Central Life, who provided their stories about Mr. Kincaid and the company, either in the past or in the current day. Specifically, my old boss and friend Cliff Forbush, Dick Gordon, Robert Spurlin, Emmett Crump, Jim Howe, Clyde Honaker, John Rampulla, Ed Winiarczyk, Bob Guise, Tom Stinnett, and the many others I have come to know over the years.

When I decided to try to get started on this book, one of the first conversations I had was with WKYT's Sam Dick. He appreciated my apprehension in considering this large task, but also provided me with some invaluable support to get me started. Sam even helped me setup my first interview and attended it with me, and for that I will always be grateful. This was a new road I was beginning to travel down and both my destination and the path to get there were uncertain.

In addition, I need to thank attorney John Talbot. I have known John for close to forty years and his interest in this project and his perspective on various aspects of things that transpired at the company and the Kincaid law firm were important conversations. We had many lunches over the last few years and discussed various things that transpired during the 1980s and early 1990s and debated different assumptions about the "why this or that happened." John is a good friend and someone who has a different history and perspective about those years than myself, and I believe our conversations were important contributions in the development of various aspects of this work.

Several people declined to be interviewed, and I appreciate their reluctance to dredge up the past. I know that many lives were changed and, in some cases, destroyed by the events that led to the downfall of Kentucky Central Life, and I hope they will let me know if I missed the mark on anything material.

A special note of acknowledgement to my friend and Kentucky Central Life colleague, Clyde Honaker. Clyde has followed the progress of this work from its beginning to the end. At one point I began to answer his many phone calls with, "Yes, boss, I am working on it." He contacted other former employees and other people about allowing me to interview them and suggested different topics for me to research. Clyde began his career at Kentucky Central Life in 1964 and so his perspective about Mr. Kincaid and things that transpired at the company was invaluable. Clyde was an important resource and someone I bounced ideas off. He and Bob Guise even traveled with me to Frankfort to look at various people's old probate files and court records. Thank you, Clyde, for being such a good friend all these years.

I also owe a thank you to the wonderful employees at the Kentucky Department for Libraries and Archives who helped me find and retrieve the various probate and court records from the various litigations surrounding the Kincaid estate. These fine folks along with their counterparts in the various county clerk and probate offices in Kentucky and other states were an invaluable resource in understanding various parts of this southern saga. In addition, thank you Ben Chandler for providing a forward that strives to easily describe the importance of Mr. Kincaid and why the reader may find it of interest.

Of course, this book would not be possible with the support of my publisher, Erin Candler and her partner, Emily Wilhoit and their staff at Rabbit House Press. Erin immediately recognized the importance of this project and took a gamble on an inexperienced author to make it a reality. Also, I need to thank my editor, Liz Seif, who tirelessly worked to improve my writing and make me double check my sources. This is a large book and any mistakes or inaccuracies you discovered are solely mine.

Finally, and most importantly, I want to thank my wonder wife, Jan. You patiently listened to the many stories I discovered and provided me with the support I needed to keep moving forward. Neither one of us knew if I would get this book completed. I didn't know what I was undertaking, and we both knew it would take a long time to do the research and also develop a story that spanned over 100 years. I love you sweet lady and I appreciated your help and observations about what I was finding and writing about.

One other important person to mention is our dog, Diva. Our wonderful, sweet dog never wavered in lying next to my desk each morning as I worked on this project. Diva was always there, providing me with love and support and also telling me when it was time to take a break. Love you little girl!

Index

About the Author

Robert Mucci began his investment career at Kentucky Central Life Insurance Company in 1981 and worked there until it was sold in 1995. In his youth, he was introduced to the Kincaid organization by a relative and worked there during college. Robert has a business degree from Transylvania University and is a Charter Financial Analyst. His extensive knowledge of the company and his long association with many of its former employees provides a remarkable about of personal information about Mr. Kincaid and the various individuals that were important participants in the building of his empire and later in its destruction.

Robert retired as executive vice president of a Midwest life insurance company in 2020 after a forty-year career managing insurance company assets. Robert and his wife live in Lexington, Kentucky.

www.ingramcontent.com/pod-product-compliance
Lightning Source LLC
Chambersburg PA
CBHW070901130626
46555CB00001B/1